International Economic Relations

INTERNATIONAL ECONOMIC RELATIONS

JOHN S. HODGSON
University of South Florida

MARK G. HERANDER
University of South Florida

PRENTICE-HALL, INC., Englewood Cliffs, New Jersey 07632

Library of Congress Cataloging in Publication Data

Hodgson, John S.
   International economic relations.

   Bibliography: p. 425
   Includes index.
   1. International economic relations.   I. Herander,
Mark G.   II. Title.
HF1411.H418   1983   337   82-23147
ISBN 0-13-472753-3

Editorial/production supervision and
interior design: Linda C. Mason
Cover design: Ray Lundgren
Manufacturing buyer: Ed O'Dougherty

Printed in the United States of America

10 9 8 7 6 5 4 3 2 1

ISBN 0-13-472753-3

Prentice-Hall International, Inc., *London*
Prentice-Hall of Australia Pty. Limited, *Sydney*
Editora Prentice-Hall do Brasil, Ltda., *Rio de Janeiro*
Prentice-Hall Canada Inc., *Toronto*
Prentice-Hall of India Private Limited, *New Delhi*
Prentice-Hall of Japan, Inc., *Tokyo*
Prentice-Hall of Southeast Asia Pte. Ltd., *Singapore*
Whitehall Books Limited, *Wellington, New Zealand*

CONTENTS

Part III   INTERNATIONAL CAPITAL FLOWS AND INTERNATIONAL CREDIT MARKETS   167

11   International Capital Movements   169

12   International Credit Markets: Operations and Issues   187

Part IV   INTERNATIONAL COMMERCIAL POLICY: THEORY AND APPLICATION   205

Preface

Interest in international economic relations is expanding rapidly. As domestic firms become more and more involved in international business, international economic conditions and the trade policies of other countries begin to impact more and more on the lives and fortunes of individual home residents. In addition, as the world economy becomes more and more interdependent, monetary policies pursued in one country can have important effects on the performance of other economies and the ability of the home authorities to deal with problems that arise within the home economy. Our objective in writing this book is to provide the tools necessary for analyzing international economic relations and to apply this analysis to some of the more important problems and developments within the world economy.

The text is designed for use in a one-semester, undergraduate course in international economics. It is intended to serve a broad range of students, both majors and non-majors in economics, having an interest in international economic affairs. The focus is on the major current issues confronting the international economic community in general and the United States in particular. A sufficient theoretical framework is developed to permit a rigorous analysis of the issues and associated policy proposals. The level of the analysis is appropriate for those who have completed an introductory course in economics, either principles of economics or one of the more basic introductory courses now being offered in many schools.

This text makes a significant departure from the traditional format, which divides the subject matter into two discrete blocks. Traditionally, trade theory, trade policy and associated topics occupy the first half of the book, while international monetary relations and associated topics occupy the second half. As a result, trade theory and international monetary analysis are seldom applied jointly in discussing a given issue. In this text basic trade theory, the foreign exchange market and balance of payments analysis are treated concisely in the first few chapters of the book. With the analytical framework thus established, the text then proceeds to explore a series of major problems and issues in international economic relations. The analysis of these issues draws on both trade theory and international monetary analysis as appropriate.

The analysis of issues is treated in modular form, with each module devoted to a particular issue or a cluster of closely related issues. The modular form provides some latitude to the instructor in selecting the sequence in which to cover the issue. Each module opens with an introduction that defines the issue and identifies its importance in international economic affairs. The introduction is followed by two to three chapters that explore and analyze the various aspects of the issue in question. Each module is closed with an essay that pulls together the main points of the analysis and draws implications for the present and future state of international economic relations.

Part I, consisting of Chapters 1–8, represents the core chapters of the text, presenting the theoretical foundation of international trade and monetary analysis. In Part 2 special attention is directed toward the international effects of macroeconomic policy, while Part 3 examines international capital markets, capital flows, and the Eurocurrency market. International trade policy (both economic and political) is the subject of Part 4. Part 5 discusses economic integration, Part 6 the problems of less-developed countries, Part 7 the role of multinational enterprises, and Part 8 recent global efforts at reforming the international monetary system. Throughout the text, we attempt to maintain a balance among theory, policy and institutional arrangements.

We would be remiss if we did not mention the clerical efforts of Annette Weiser whose perseverance in the face of seemingly endless revisions and corrections is most appreciated. Also, many thanks are due to the acquisitions and production editors of Prentice-Hall, Dave Hildebrand and Linda Mason.

INTERNATIONAL ECONOMIC RELATIONS

International Economic Relations: 1
A Preview of Some of the Issues

Nations of the world are bound by a complex network of economic, political and social interrelationships. The objective of this book is to focus on the international economic relations among the countries of the world. It will be seen that, although the economic relations among nations are an issue in and of themselves, they cannot be totally separated from international political and social relations.

Economies of the world are deeply linked in a number of ways. First, a tremendous quantity of goods and services produced in one country are purchased by residents of other countries, as when Americans purchase shirts produced in Hong Kong. Second, billions of dollars of financial assets that are issued by one nation are purchased by residents of other nations; this would occur when Americans establish demand deposits in German commercial banks. Third, corporations headquartered in one country often establish subsidiaries in a foreign country as when Ford Motors builds a factory in Spain. Fourth, the domestic economic policies of one nation often affect, either directly or indirectly, the economies of another nation. For example, if the United States were to impose a tight monetary policy, not only would the demand for U.S.-produced products decline, but Americans would likely also reduce their demand for Japanese imports. These links represent only a partial list.

Specific topics of international economics are traditionally divided into two categories; those issues relating to the trade of goods and services, and those relating to the international flow of monetary assets. In fact, however, this dichotomy is not entirely appropriate, as trade and monetary issues cannot be easily separated. After all, when a foreign good is purchased by a resident of another country, that individual must receive credit or make a monetary payment across national boundaries. Thus even though this text addresses the topics of international economic relations by examining, separately, specific trade and monetary issues, we at all times attempt to take into account the interrelationship between the trade and monetary issues. Before proceeding to the body of the text, let us briefly look at some of the most important economic issues affecting the world's economy.

THE IMPORTANCE OF INTERNATIONAL TRADE

International trade of goods, services and assets represents one of the most powerful linkages among the various economies of the world. Many nations are heavily dependent on foreign countries for supplies of important commodities. These commodities range from manufactured products that can be obtained abroad at lower prices than domestic producers can offer, to natural resources, such as petroleum, with which the importing countries are simply not well endowed.

On the export side, home producers often depend on foreign markets for a substantial proportion of their sales. For many producers, the size of their domestic markets, alone, is insufficient to support their operations in a profitable manner. On a national level, exports account for a substantial portion of many countries' gross national product (GNP) and contribute significantly to domestic employment.

While most countries depend heavily on imports and exports, the degree of dependence varies. Among the industrialized nations, the United Kingdom and Canada are especially dependent on imports; imports, in 1978, amounted to 25.4 percent of Canada's and 21.7 percent of the U.K.'s GNP. The economies of Japan and the United States were somewhat less dependent on foreign sources for goods; in 1978, U.S. imports amounted to 8.6 percent of the U.S. GNP, while Japanese imports amounted to 8.1 percent of the Japanese GNP. Even though the dependence of the United States and Japan on imports is not as great as it is for some other countries (as

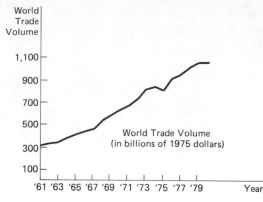

Sources: *International Monetary Fund & ACLI International Inc.*

FIGURE 1-1 Growth in World Trade Volume (1960-1980)
Source: International Monetary Fund and ACLI International, Inc. Reprinted from the *Wall Street Journal*, May 28, 1981, pg. 50.

measured as a fraction of GNP), their import volume still represents a substantial amount of goods and services in absolute terms.

The European countries are among the most heavily dependent on exports. For example, in 1978, exports accounted for 23 percent, 22 percent and 16 percent, respectively, of the GNPs of the United Kingdom, West Germany and France. Again, the economies of the United States and Japan are somewhat less trade oriented, as exports, in 1978, accounted for only 6.6 and 10 percent, respectively, of their GNPs.

It is clear that international trade accounts for a substantial amount of the economic activity within the world economy. And its magnitude has increased dramatically over the past twenty years. Figure 1-1 shows the inflation-adjusted trend in world trade during the 1960s and 1970s. During this twenty-year period, the real volume of international trade increased about 3.5 times, or at an annual compound rate of growth of about 6.5 percent; this growth rate exceeded the growth rate of real world output during the same period. Thus, not only has the absolute size of international trade increased, but so has its relative importance in the world's economic activity.

The Pattern of International Trade

Given the importance of trade in the world economy, it would be interesting to examine its global pattern. Table 1–1 shows the trade flows, in 1980, among four blocs of nations:[1] the industrialized nations, the developing nations, the Organization of Petroleum Exporting Countries (OPEC) and the centrally planned economies. Table 1–1 reflects several important features of international trading relations. Let us review the most important of those features, and examine

[1]See Table 1–1 for descriptions of the country blocs.

TABLE 1-1

The Pattern of International Trade (1980): Volume (millions of dollars) and Percentage of Total World Trade.

Exports to Exports from	Industrial Countries (percent of World Trade)	Developing Countries	OPEC (Organization of Petroleum Exporting Countries)	Centrally Planned Economies	Total Exports
Industrial[a] countries	$847,797 (43%)[b]	$193,601 (10%)	$99,598 (5%)	$61,482 (3%)	$1,202,478 (61%)
Developing countries	151,900 (8%)	118,742 (6%)	22,142 (1%)	15,768 (<1%)	308,552 (16%)
OPEC (Organization of Petroleum Exporting Countries)	217,349 (11%)	65,869 (3%)	4424 (<1%)	4487 (<1%)	292,129 (15%)
Centrally planned economies	57,065 (3%)	25,791 (1%)	6287 (<1%)	85,903 (4%)	175,046 (8%)
Total imports	1,274,111 (65%)	404,003 (20%)	132,451 (7%)	167,640 (8%)	1,978,205
Net balance with rest of world (exports–imports)	−71,633	−95,451	159,678	7406	

Source: United Nations, *Monthly Bulletin of Statistics* (New York: United Nations Publications, July 1981).
[a]Country Bloc Descriptions:
Industrial countries: the United States, Europe, Canada, Japan, South Africa, Australia and New Zealand
OPEC: Algeria, Ecuador, Gabon, Indonesia, Iran, Iraq, Kuwait, Libya, Nigeria, Qatar, Saudi Arabia, United Arab Emirates and Venezuela
Centrally planned economies: USSR, Poland, Romania, Bulgaria, Czechoslovakia, Hungary, East Germany, China, North Korea, Vietnam, Mongolia
Developing countries: All other countries
[b]The figures in parentheses represent the percentage of total world trade accounted for by the bilateral trade between the various blocs of nations.

how they affect international economic relations.

The Features of International Trade and their Effect on International Economic Relations

1. The largest flow of trade occurs among the industrial nations themselves; in 1980, these countries accounted for approximately 43 percent of all world trade. In addition, the industrial nations accounted for 61 percent of the world's total exports. No other bloc of nations was even close to generating this volume of trade.

The industrial nations that dominate world trade account for less than a fifth of the world's population. Thus a small minority of the world's population accounts for a disproportionately large share of world commerce.

2. The developing countries, which account for almost three-quarters of the world's population, account for only about 16 percent of the world's total exports, while intra-developing country trade accounted for only 6 percent of the world's total. The developing countries are also heavily dependent on the industrialized countries as both a source of imports (48 percent of their imports originated from the industrialized countries) and as an export market (49 percent of their exports were sold to the industrialized nations).

These trade patterns make it clear that the developing countries have a secondary role in international economic relations. The limited role of the developing countries in world trade reflects a more general problem plaguing those nations; a low level of economic well-being characterized by income levels much lower than those prevailing in the industrialized countries.

3. From Table 1–1 it is clear that the OPEC nations are incurring huge trade surpluses (the excess of exports over imports) with the rest of the world. In fact, the trade deficit (the excess of imports over exports) of the industrial nations with the rest of the world can be entirely attributed to their bilateral deficit with OPEC.

The huge surplus position of OPEC first occurred during the 1970s, when a group of thirteen oil-exporting nations collectively raised the price of petroleum. Periodic price increases during the 1970s caused the per-barrel price of petroleum to rise from approximately $2.00 to $32 between 1973 and 1980. The oil-price increase, and the resulting OPEC surplus, has placed tremendous strains on international economic relations, and both the international trade and monetary systems have had to make adjustments to accommodate these developments.

4. The role of the centrally planned economies in world trade is much more limited than their overall level of economic activity would suggest. In fact, the volume of trade between these countries and the rest of the world accounts for less than 5 percent of the world's total.

The small degree of participation of these nations in world trade occurs partly by choice (often based on political motives) and partly because of an inability to compete in international markets.

Recent Developments in the Trade Position of the Industrialized Countries: The Case of the United States

Events during the 1970s significantly influenced the trade positions of many countries. It might prove useful to see how these events affected the trade position of the most powerful country in the system, the United States, particularly since the changes in the U.S. trade position are representative of the changes that occurred in the positions of other industrialized countries.

One of the foremost developments of the 1970s was the appearance, in 1971, of the first U.S. trade deficit in decades. Although the U.S. trade balance was periodically in surplus between 1971 and 1975, the United States returned to a deficit position in 1976, and this deficit continued to grow for the remainder of the decade. By 1979, the United States was running an annual trade deficit of about $24.6 billion compared to a surplus of $2.6 billion in 1970.

One of the main reasons for the appearance of the U.S. deficit was mentioned previously: the tremendous increase in the price of petroleum. This is reflected in the worsening trade balance of the United States with the oil-exporting countries; the U.S. position moved from a surplus of $.1 billion in 1970 to a deficit of approximately $30 billion in 1979.

Another important component of the decade-long deterioration of the U.S. trade position was the worsening of the U.S. trade balance with Japan. The U.S. deficit with Japan increased from $1.2 billion in 1970 to over $11 billion in 1980. Why did the deficit increase so dramatically? First, many American exporters argue that Japanese markets are strongly protected by import restrictions. Second, import-competing industries in the United States contend that Japanese producers enjoy certain unfair competitive advantages, including cheap labor and significant subsidization by the Japanese government.

More impartial observers point out that the Japanese have simply become the world's most efficient producers of many products. This proposition is supported by the fact that many U.S. consumers insist on purchasing Japanese-produced consumer goods, such as television sets and automobiles, on the basis that they are the highest quality products available.

A third area of the world in which the U.S. trade account has suffered is with the non-oil-exporting developing countries. The bilateral U.S. trade position with this bloc of nations has moved from consistent surplus positions (as high as $8.7 billion in 1975) to periodic deficit positions (around $2 billion in 1977 and 1978). Although the turnaround in this bilateral trade balance is

not as great as with OPEC and Japan, it is nonetheless significant.

One reason for the shift in this bilateral balance is the significant increase in the exports of manufactured products by the developing countries to the United States. Many of these manufactures are labor intensive and require low levels of technology, and include such products as textiles and electronic components. For example, the U.S. deficit in textile trade with the developing countries increased from $637 million in 1970 to $4.5 billion in 1980.

The changes in the trade position of the United States during the 1970s were similar to those experienced by most industrial nations (the main exceptions being West Germany and Japan). The problems posed by the widening trade deficits are immense and threaten to severely strain international economic relations.

The issue of the U.S.–Japanese trade deficit, for example, is causing a great deal of friction between the two allies. The United States has imposed import restrictions on Japanese-produced automobiles in an effort to protect the ailing U.S. auto industry. Obviously, this action did not please Japanese auto producers. And in 1982, the U.S. Congress was threaten ing to impose further restrictions on Japanese imports, unless the Japanese opened their markets to U.S. products. The U.S.–Japanese situation is just one of many examples of how changes in trade flows can strain international economic relations.

While these developments represent but a handful of recent international economic events that threaten to alter international relations, they do provide insights into the fundamental issues that bear on international trading relations. Those issues include changes in trade patterns brought about by changes in the competitive position of countries over time. For example, just as in the case of the developing countries, trading nations may become more efficient in the production of certain tradeable goods over time, and thus challenge existing producers in world markets and in the process strain relations with those producers. One of the objectives of this text is to analyze the issues that affect international relations.

INTERNATIONAL MONETARY ISSUES

The multinational network of international trade and investments could not exist without elaborate arrangements for making international payments. This requires a highly coordinated international banking system to facilitate the extension of credit and the transfer of funds across national boundaries. It also requires that residents of the various countries be able to make rapid and inexpensive conversions between home and foreign currencies. This means that international currency markets must remain as free as possible from artificial controls and restrictions; it also means that facilities must be available for minimizing the risks of dealing in foreign currencies.

Throughout the course of international relations, nations have attempted, often unsuccessfully, to develop international monetary systems that would meet these conditions and that would also be capable of absorbing the stresses caused by diverging macroeconomic conditions within the various countries. As we shall see, differences in rates of monetary expansion, differences in rates of inflation, differences in cyclical activity and differences in interest-rate movements across countries can create pressures that can cause international monetary arrangements to break down.

Following World War II, the principal trading nations established a highly organized international monetary system in order to provide currency convertibility and to facilitate international payments. These arrangements, which were known as the *Bretton Woods System,* also attempted to establish exchange-rate stability through an elaborate set of exchange-rate pegs which set the values of national currencies vis-à-vis each other. During the 1960s, divergent economic forces within the different countries began to produce strains within the system, and in the early 1970s it collapsed.

The collapse of the Bretton Woods system underscores the fact that international monetary institutions must be sufficiently flexible to accommodate changing economic pressures among and within the countries that make up the system. It also raises important questions about the kinds of monetary arrangements that will be required to cope with contemporary monetary pressures and disruptions. Among the questions that must be addressed in considering various options for reforming the system are: which system can best cope with disruptions of the kind that were brought about by the international oil crisis of the 1970s; which system will best be able to survive divergent macroeconomic pressures across countries; and which systems will contribute to and which systems will help to diminish world inflation. These questions are still largely unresolved and are the subject of ongoing analysis and debate.

After the Bretton Woods System collapsed, it was superseded by a system of managed floating exchange rates in which official exchange-rate pegs were abandoned and countries could let their currencies float on the foreign exchange market. The transition from fixed to floating exchange rates has important implications for international economic relations. To begin with, flexible exchange rates present a different set of problems in making international payments. Governments no longer undertake to assure traders and investors that exchange rates will remain stable, and parties accepting financial obligations that extend across national borders must now take specific steps to estimate and reduce the risks associated with potential exchange-rate movements.

Not only did the transition from fixed to flexible rates affect the operations of international traders and investors, it also altered the set of international economic problems with which governments have to deal. It changed the policy mix required to correct international payments imbalances, and even altered the effectiveness of the standard macroeconomic policies through which governments attempt to resolve *internal* economic problems. In addition, the transition affected the extent to which cyclical fluctuations, inflation and other economic disturbances can be transmitted between countries. Often, in recent periods, the transmission of inflation has severely strained economic relations between countries.

If intelligent policy choices are to be made in attempting to deal with international economic problems (or for that matter in attempting to deal with internal, domestic economic problems), an understanding of international monetary relations and the implications of alternative policy choices is essential. In particular, it is important to know how balance-of-payments policies and domestic macroeconomic policies will be affected by the choice of international monetary arrangements and by different degrees of integration across the economies within the system.

ORGANIZATION OF THE TEXT

To organize our investigation of the issues raised in this chapter, we will first need to know something about the basic structure of international trade and payments. Accordingly, we begin our discussion, in Part I, by describing the primary theoretical relationships within the international economic system. This will serve as the framework for analyzing, in subsequent parts of the text, the major problems facing the system and the countries that it comprises.

In Part II, we explore the monetary interdependencies that exist between countries that are closely linked by trade and investment. We shall examine the channels through which economic disturbances can be transmitted among countries and see how alternative policies can afford different degrees of insulation against foreign economic disturbances. We shall also see, in Part II, how domestic macroeconomic policies are affected by interaction with foreign economies.

In Part III, we examine international capital flows and international financial markets. International capital flows represent the transfer of purchasing power among countries and provide the vehicle for allocating real investment resources throughout the world. Part III will analyze the mechanisms that generate capital flows among countries and will explore the extent to which current credit facilities facilitate these flows and the extent to which they contribute to such problems as world inflation.

Part IV of the text examines the economic effects of international trade policy. As we saw previously, in the case of U.S. imports of Japanese automobiles, importing nations are reluctant to allow foreign-produced products to injure domestic competitors. Often importing nations react to the threat of imports by imposing trade restrictions such as tariffs and quotas. It is the objective of this part not only to analyze the economic effects of such trade measures, but also to look at the problems they create in international relations among trading nations.

In Part V of the text the topic of economic integration is examined. Economic integration involves two or more countries undertaking measures that make their economies more interdependent. Such measures include the mutual reduction of trade barriers, closer coordination of economic policies, and the coordination of banking and monetary systems. As we will see, there exist both benefits and costs to those nations involved in integration. One objective of this part, then, is to delineate those benefits and costs, and to examine whether the actual efforts at economic integration have resulted in a net benefit to those nations.

The economic plight of the less-developed countries is examined in Part VI. We will see in this part that the nations of the world differ significantly in terms of their economic well-being. As a result of this disparity, the international economic relations among the nations of the world do not always take place in an equitable manner. The poorer nations feel as though they are hindered in their efforts to improve their economic well-being by several conditions, including the economic policies of the rich nations. The international economic relations between the rich and poor nations will be emphasized in this part.

In Part VII, the role of the multinational enterprise (MNE) in international economic relations is examined. A multinational enterprise is essentially a corporation that produces in more than one country. The scope of the economic activity of the MNE is large and growing rapidly. Because the operations of a subsidiary of a multinational are controlled by managers outside the country where the subsidiary is located, the multinational can seriously influence international economic relations.

Finally, in Part VIII, we shall examine proposals for reforming the international monetary system. As we shall see, there is an entire spectrum of options, each of which has its advantages and problems. Insight into the pros and cons of the various alternatives will be gained by examining how these different systems have performed in the past. We shall then evaluate the more prominent reform proposals in light of current international economic conditions as well as conditions that are likely to prevail in the foreseeable future.

Let us begin, now, by developing a framework for analyzing these issues.

FRAMEWORK FOR ANALYSIS $\blacksquare$

INTRODUCTION

Our main purpose in studying international economic relations is to develop an understanding of how the international economic system works and to gain insight into the major problems and issues facing the system and the countries it comprises. As you can imagine, some of these relationships are complex, and understanding them would be quite difficult without some logical framework with which to organize our thinking. Before we can analyze problems associated with trade and payments linkages among countries, or evaluate proposals as to how they ought to be changed, we first need to know what these linkages are and how they operate.

Our objective in Part I will be to develop just such an analytical framework. Here, we shall identify the principal economic linkages among countries and describe the mechanisms through which trade and payments adjust to changing economic conditions. Once these basic relationships are established, they will serve as the basis for analyzing the more topical problems and issues.

The first few chapters of Part I focus on the fundamentals of trade in goods and services among countries and are concerned mainly with the incentives for trade and the factors that determine international trade patterns. Chapter 2 develops the rudimentary framework for analyzing trade relations. It illustrates the potential gains that motivate a country to participate in trade and shows the relationship between trade patterns and relative production costs within countries. Chapter 3 develops this theme further by showing *why* production costs differ across countries, and by bringing in the role of demand in determining international trade patterns. In chapters 2 and 3, the analysis is kept at a very simple level by assuming that the countries operate in a static environment under perfect competition. This is done to facilitate an understanding of the fundamental relationships without bringing in undue complications.

In Chapter 4, we extend the analysis into a world of imperfect competition and analyze how the presence of imperfect markets would affect trade incentives and trade patterns. Chapter 4 also shows the role of money prices and exchange rates in transmitting information about comparative demand and cost conditions among countries. Chapter 5 then introduces the dynamic dimension by examining the effects of changes in the determinants of trade over time.

Chapter 6 picks up the discussion of money payments and exchange rates once again. It shows how international payments are made and analyzes forces that determine exchange rate fluctuations; it also shows the interaction between trade patterns and exchange rate movements. Chapters 7 and 8 examine the forces that generate changes in a country's balance of payments and show how these are related to the foreign exchange market itself. These chapters also explore some of the policy options available to countries in trying to deal with balance of payments problems. They also analyze the linkages between monetary conditions within countries and balance-of-payments and exchange-rate movements, showing how changes in monetary conditions can affect the balance of payments and vice versa.

Once the primary relationships and mechanisms have been established in chapters 2 to 8, we will be prepared to investigate some of the specific issues and problems facing the international trade and finance system. Let us begin, now, by seeing how trade patterns develop between countries.

Early Developments in Trade Theory: 2
The Supply-Side Determinants
of International Trade

International trade theory as we know it today has its roots in the eighteenth-century writings of Adam Smith. Prior to Smith, the prevailing view regarding international trade was that of the mercantilist school of thought. Underlying the mercantilists' view of trade was the belief that the total wealth of the world was fixed. Hence, any material gains achieved by one nation were at the expense of another. When this belief was applied to the area of international trade, the conclusion reached by the mercantilists was that unimpeded trade between nations would be detrimental to at least some of those nations. Specifically, they postulated that a nation which imported more goods than it exported abroad would lose gold and silver (measures of wealth) in paying for these goods, and in so doing would lower its stock of wealth. Moreover, the mere fact that a nation would willingly participate in trade with the expectation of material gain, indicated a potential for its trading partner to lose materially, given the world's fixed stock of wealth. Thus the mercantilists argued that the proper trade policy for a nation would be one which discouraged imports and encouraged exports.

Adam Smith's efforts were in part an attempt to refute the mercantilists' arguments for restricting free trade by demonstrating the potential gains from unimpeded trade. In the course of pursuing this objective, Smith presented the first systematic analysis of the causes of international trade. His work became the basis for the so-called *classical analysis* of international trade. As will be seen, the classical analysis emphasized the production processes within the trading nations as the determinants of international trade patterns. Because the classical analysis concentrated solely on supply-side factors, it may seem to be oversimplified and incomplete; yet it was an invaluable contribution to trade theory, as it provided crucial insights into the fundamental reasons of why trade occurs and also served as a basis for future investigations into the causes of trade.

Before presenting the classical analysis, let us note that throughout the ensuing discussions of the causes of international trade, it is assumed that money is not used as a medium of exchange or unit of account. That is, the two countries engage in barter, whereby goods are exchanged for other goods without the use of money. Also, the prices of the various goods are not expressed in terms of monetary units such as dollars and cents, but in terms of other goods. The rationale for assuming barter exchange is to concentrate on the real determinants of trading relations, postponing the monetary determinants until later chapters. Let us now begin our discussion of the classical analysis of international trade by examining the contribution of Adam Smith.

CLASSICAL ANALYSIS

Absolute Advantage

According to Smith, two nations can increase their combined output if each specializes in producing the good(s) in which it is most efficient and then engages in trade with the other nation. Both countries will be better off, in terms of the quantity of goods available for consumption, as they trade and thus divide up the additional output obtained through specialization.

Smith's proposition can be illustrated by way of an example. Suppose there are two islands, Bali and Hai. Before trade opens between the islands, each produces and consumes two commodities, fish and coconuts. Borrowing an assumption from the classical analysis, we shall assume that only one factor of production, labor, is available to both Bali and Hai to produce coconuts and fish. Let us assume then that Bali can either produce 6 coconuts per man hour of labor or 2 fish per man hour of labor, while Hai can produce either 4 coconuts per man hour or 3 fish. Obviously, Bali can produce more coconuts with a man hour of labor than Hai (6 >

4), and conversely, Hai can produce more fish with a man hour of labor than Bali (3 > 2). In this situation, Bali is said to possess an *absolute advantage* in the production of coconuts, since it can produce a larger quantity of coconuts than Hai with a given amount of labor (one man hour). Likewise, Hai will possess an *absolute advantage* in the production of fish since its fish output per man hour exceeds Bali's.

gains from specialization and trade with absolute advantage

Now assume that trade opens between the two islands, and that Bali and Hai each specialize in the production of the good in which they enjoy an absolute advantage; Bali in coconuts, Hai in fish. For each man hour that Bali transfers from fish into coconuts, its coconut production rises by 6 and its fish production falls by 2. For each man hour that Hai transfers from coconuts into fish, its fish production rises by 3 and its coconut production falls by 4. These results, in which each island transfers one man hour into the production of the good in which it has an absolute advantage, are summarized in Table 2–1. For each man hour the islands switch toward the good that each produces more efficiently (that is, possesses an absolute advantage), there will be 2 additional coconuts and 1 additional fish available for consumption. This increase in output would be allocated between the two countries through the process of trade;

TABLE 2-1

Change in World Output Resulting from Specialization According to Absolute Advantage		
	Coconuts	*Fish*
Bali	+6	−2
Hai	−4	+3
Change in World Output	+2	+1

each nation would export to the other the good in which it held an absolute advantage in return for the good in which it held an absolute disadvantage. The gain from specialization and trade, then, is the increase in world output that would arise if each nation specialized according to its absolute advantage, and which is allocated between the two nations by the process of trade.

In demonstrating the potential gains from specialization and trade, Adam Smith was able to refute the mercantilists' support of restricted trade and espouse the virtues of free trade. However, Smith's analysis left many questions unanswered. Foremost among those questions was: What if a nation did not possess an absolute advantage in the production of any commodity? In what manner would such a country engage in trade? This question was addressed by another prominent classical economist, David Ricardo, who demonstrated that a basis for trade existed (as did the potential for gains from that trade), even if one of the trading nations did not possess an absolute advantage in the production of any commodity.

COMPARATIVE ADVANTAGE
AND THE PROCESS OF TRADE

To examine the situation where one trading nation does not possess an absolute advantage in the production of any commodity, the concept of opportunity cost[1] will be employed. *Marginal opportunity costs (MOC)* measure the quantity of one good (say, fish) that has to be given up

[1]Ricardo's analysis did not explicitly make use of opportunity costs, but simply used numerical examples predicated on the labor theory of value. The use of opportunity costs to explain trade was first introduced by the so-called neoclassical economists in the early 1900s. However, opportunity costs verified Ricardo's propositions and are employed here simply for expositional convenience.

to produce an additional unit of another good (say, coconuts). To illustrate the concept of marginal opportunity costs, let us return to our two-country, two-commodity world, maintaining the classical assumption that labor is the only factor of production. Assume that by using one man hour of labor, Bali can produce 10 coconuts, whereas Hai can produce 9; and with one man hour, Bali can produce 10 fish, while Hai can produce 3. This information is summarized in Table 2–2(a). It should be noted that Bali possesses an absolute advantage in both fish and coconut production.

Marginal opportunity costs can be computed on the basis of the above information. In Bali, to produce 10 additional coconuts requires the sacrifice of 10 fish (assuming all resources are fully employed), since one unit of labor will have to be transferred from fish to coconut production in order to produce the additional 10

TABLE 2-2

| | (a) Production per Man Hour | |
	Coconuts	Fish
Bali	10	10
Hai	9	3

| | (b) Marginal Opportunity Costs | |
	MOC of Coconuts	MOC of Fish
Bali	1 fish	1 coconut
Hai	1/3 fish	3 coconuts

| | (c) Change in World Output Resulting from Specialization According to Comparative Advantage | |
	Coconuts	Fish
Bali	−1	+1
Hai	+1	−1/3
	0	+2/3

coconuts. Thus, in Bali, 10 coconuts have an opportunity cost of 10 fish or, equivalently, the marginal opportunity cost of 1 coconut is 1 fish. Likewise, in Bali, if fish production were to increase by 10, coconut production would fall by 10; in other words, the marginal opportunity cost of fish equals 1 coconut. By applying the same reasoning to Hai's situation, it can be shown that the shifting of labor from fish to coconut production in Hai will yield a marginal opportunity cost of coconuts equal to 1/3 fish; while the reverse process of shifting labor from coconut to fish production will yield a marginal opportunity cost of fish production equal to 3 coconuts. These calculations are shown in Table 2–2(b).

In this example, the marginal opportunity cost of coconuts in Hai (1/3) is less than in Bali (1), while the opposite is true with regard to fish production; Bali's marginal opportunity cost (1) is less than Hai's (3). This situation is described as one where Bali has a *comparative advantage* in the production of fish and Hai possesses a *comparative advantage* in the production of coconuts. In more general terms, a country is said to possess a comparative advantage in the production of a commodity if its marginal opportunity cost of producing that commodity is lower than the marginal opportunity cost in other producing nations. It is important to notice that, even though Bali has an absolute advantage in both goods, it has a comparative advantage in only one.

Comparative Advantage and the Gains from Specialization and Trade

Ricardo was the first to recognize the difference between absolute and comparative advantage. He demonstrated that the basis of international trade patterns (as well as its benefits) was not absolute advantage, as suggested by Adam Smith, but comparative advantage. Specifically, Ricardo demonstrated that if each country specialized in the production of the commodity in which it held a comparative advantage, world output would increase.

Applying Ricardo's proposition to our example, let Bali produce 1 more unit of fish, the good in which it has a comparative advantage. This would entail a sacrifice of the production of 1 coconut (refer again to Table 2–2[b]). Similarly, let Hai produce 1 coconut, the good in which it enjoys a comparative advantage. Such a transfer of labor will of course be at the expense of 1/3 fish. Since Hai produces 1 more coconut and Bali 1 less coconut, total coconut production remains unchanged. However, while Bali's fish production increases by 1, Hai's decreases only by 1/3. There is a net increase in world output, since coconut production remains unchanged and fish production increases by 2/3. These results are summarized in Table 2–2(c).

This increased production can then be allocated between Bali and Hai in the process of trade between the two nations. The increased quantity of goods available for consumption represents the gains from specialization and trade.

COMPARATIVE ADVANTAGE: A GRAPHICAL ANALYSIS

It is useful, at this point, to introduce a graphical analysis of the comparative advantage relationships between the two countries. This not only facilitates an understanding of comparative advantage, it also provides a convenient means for discussing its role as a determinant of international trade patterns.

the production possibilities curve

The focus of the graphical analysis is the *production possibilities curve (PPC)*, which shows all possible combinations of the quantities of the goods that a nation could produce if its resources were fully and efficiently employed. Suppose that Bali's and Hai's stock of resources were 10 man hours per day each, and that these 10 man hours could be divided between fish production and coconut production within each country as each country chooses. Maintaining the output-per-man-hour figures used previously, it is possible to construct a PPC for each country.

Bali's production possibilities curve is illustrated graphically in Figure 2–1(a), with coconut production per day measured on the vertical axis and fish production per day measured on the horizontal axis. Using the information provided in Table 2–2(a), two points (commodity combinations) on Bali's PPC are known. If Bali were to devote all of its available man hours (10) to coconut production, it could produce 100 coconuts per day, but no fish (point A). Conversely, if it were to devote all of its man hours to fish production, it could produce 100 fish per day, but no coconuts (point B).

Bali's PPC can now be constructed by joining points A and B by a straight line. All points on line AB represent possible combinations of coconuts and fish that Bali can produce, given its stock of resources. Movement along AB, from one point to another, reflects the transfer of resources from the production of one commodity into the production of the other. Note that the slope of the PPC is equal to the marginal opportunity cost of producing fish. The slope of the PPC is given by the following ratio:

$$\frac{\text{change in coconut production}}{\text{change in fish production}},$$

which in the case of Bali equals 1; this is equal to the value of the MOC of fish production.[2] The equality between the MOC of fish and the slope of the PPC will hold at all points on the PPC.

An additional point concerning the characteristics of the PPC has to do with its linear representation. The fact that the PPC is linear means that its slope is constant, which implies

[2]Actually, the slope will be negative, which of course suggests that as the output of one good increases the other decreases. Also, it should be noted that the reciprocal of slope of the PPC,

$$\frac{\text{change in fish production}}{\text{change in coconut production}},$$

equals the marginal opportunity cost of coconut production (or 1 fish).

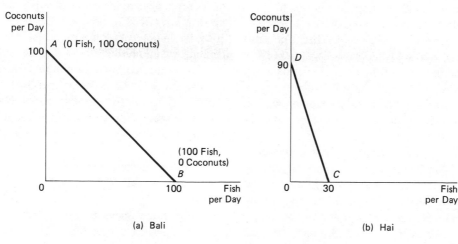

(a) Bali (b) Hai

FIGURE 2-1 Production Possibilities Curves of Bali and Hai

that the MOC of producing fish will also be constant. The constancy of marginal opportunity costs is referred to as the *constant cost assumption,* and it was implicit in the classical analysis. The basis for the assumption of constant costs will be discussed later in the chapter.

The production possibilities curve for Hai can be constructed using the same procedure as was used to construct Bali's PPC. Hai's production possibilities curve is depicted in Figure 2–1(b). As in the case of Bali, the slope of Hai's PPC is assumed constant, and is equal to the marginal opportunity cost of producing fish (that is, 3 coconuts).

If the two countries refrain from trading with one another, their PPCs reflect not only the maximum commodity combinations that may be produced, but also the maximum combinations that may be consumed. Thus, in the absence of international trade, both countries will produce and consume at a point on their PPC.

terms of trade

At this point, let us introduce another important concept: the *terms of trade (TOT).* The terms of trade between two goods are defined as the quantity of each good that must be provided in the market place in order to obtain a unit of the other good; thus it is the rate at which two goods exchange for one another. The terms of trade can also be thought of as the price of one good in terms of the other. For instance, if 2 coconuts must be provided in order to receive 1 fish, the TOT would equal 2 coconuts per fish; or, equivalently, the price of 1 fish would equal 2 coconuts.

Like marginal opportunity costs, the terms of trade can be depicted in graphical form as the slope of a line. If the terms of trade equaled 2 coconuts per fish, it would be shown by the slope of a line joining 1 fish and 2 coconuts, as with line *AB* in Figure 2–2. Similarly, if 1 coconut exchanges for 1 fish, those terms of trade

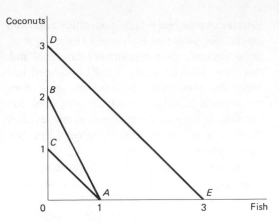

FIGURE 2-2 Graphical Representation of the Terms of Trade

could be represented by the line *AC*. It should be noted that it is the *slope* of the line which indicates the terms of trade, not the position. For instance, line *DE*, joining 3 coconuts and 3 fish, represents the same terms of trade as line *AC*, since their slopes are equal.

It is important to distinguish the meaning of the terms of trade from that of marginal opportunity cost. The terms of trade reveal how much of one good must be sacrificed to obtain more of the other in the process of *exchange* in the marketplace. Marginal opportunity costs, it will be recalled, also indicate how much of one good must be sacrificed to obtain more of the other good, but in *production,* not exchange. The terms of trade thus represent a market price and, like any price, are determined by the interaction of supply and demand, whereas marginal opportunity cost is strictly a supply concept, determined by production technology and the availability of resources.

Pretrade Equilibrium: The Equality of the TOT and MOC

Before trade opens between Bali and Hai, assuming perfect competition, there will be a tendency for the pretrade terms of trade in each country to equal marginal opportunity costs. To verify this proposition, suppose that in Bali, prior to trade, the terms of trade are such that one fish costs 2 coconuts while the marginal opportunity costs of producing one additional fish equals 1 coconut. Note that the divergence between the terms of trade and marginal opportunity costs provides an opportunity for gain, since fish production can be increased by 1 at the cost of only 1 coconut. Yet, according to the terms of trade, the one-unit increase in fish production can be exchanged for 2 coconuts— a gain of 1 coconut. The incentive to increase fish production (at the expense of coconut production) will continue for as long as this divergence persists. However, the increase in the supply of fish relative to the supply of coconuts will lower the price of fish in terms of coconuts, thus causing the TOT to converge with the MOC. When this equality holds there will be no incentive for further shifts in production from one good to the other; this situation is called *pretrade equilibrium*.

Thus, before the opening of trade, both Bali and Hai will be producing and consuming on their PPCs at a point where the terms of trade

are equal to the marginal opportunity costs.[3] Because of this equality, *comparative advantage* can be determined by comparing the TOT, since this will be equivalent to comparing the pretrade MOCs. Thus, a country can be said to have a *comparative advantage* in a commodity if the pretrade terms of trade of that commodity are less than the pretrade terms of trade of the commodity in the other country.

The Process of Specialization and Trade

As just demonstrated, both nations, previous to trade, would be consuming and producing at a point on their respective production possibilities curve. The exact combinations of coconuts and fish consumed and produced in pretrade equilibrium cannot be determined without knowledge of the demand conditions of each country. For now, however, we will simply *as-*

[3]It is possible that in pretrade equilibrium a nation may specialize completely in the production of a commodity—the so-called corner solution. Under such a circumstance, it is possible that the pretrade terms of trade may differ from marginal opportunity costs.

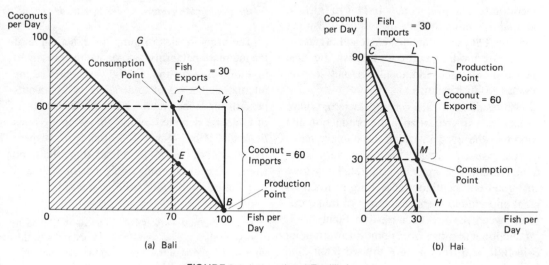

FIGURE 2-3 International Equilibrium

sume pretrade equilibrium positions for both nations and will explicitly introduce demand conditions in the following chapter. As will be seen, most of the effects of the opening of trade between two nations can be demonstrated without explicit demand conditions.

In Figure 2–3 the production possibilities curves of Bali and Hai are reproduced from Figure 2–1. Assume that, prior to trade, Bali is producing and consuming at point E in Figure 2–3(a), while Hai's pretrade position is at point F in Figure 2–3(b). The pretrade terms of trade (and marginal opportunity costs) are represented by the slopes of the production possibilities curves: 1 coconut per fish in Bali and 3 coconuts per fish in Hai.

Now let trade open between Bali and Hai. Upon the opening of trade, residents of Bali observe that, while the marginal opportunity cost of fish is 1 coconut at home, the terms of trade in Hai are 3 coconuts for each fish. Residents of Bali will have an incentive to shift resources from coconut production to fish production, since they calculate that for each additional fish they produce at a sacrifice of 1 coconut, they can obtain 3 coconuts from Hai in trade. At the same time, residents of Hai observe that the marginal opportunity cost of coconuts in Hai is 1/3 fish, but that the terms of trade in Bali are 1 fish per coconut. They calculate that each additional coconut they produce will cost 1/3 fish, but that they can sell each additional coconut so produced to Bali for 1 fish.

The residents of each country, therefore, have an incentive to specialize in the production and export of the good in which the country has a comparative advantage. The incentive to continue shifting resources into the relatively low-cost good will continue for as long as the marginal opportunity costs (and terms of trade) differ between the two countries. In Figure 2–3, production will move from point E toward point B in Bali, and from point F toward point C in Hai.

The opening of trade between the two countries has in effect created a single world market for fish and coconuts. Under free trade, then, a single "international" terms of trade will be established: that is, the rate at which fish exchanges for coconuts will be the same both between and within the countries.

The international terms of trade must lie between the two countries' pretrade terms of trade. To illustrate this proposition, remember that for Bali to have an incentive to specialize in the production and export of fish to Hai, producers of fish in Bali must receive more coconuts for one fish than they could prior to trade. That is, they must be trading at terms of trade which yield more than 1 coconut per fish. Similarly, in Hai, which is exporting coconuts in exchange for fish, purchasers of Bali's fish must be paying a smaller number of coconuts for one fish than they would pay under the pretrade situation (3 coconuts) in order for them to engage in trade. Thus, for two-way trade to occur, the international terms of trade must lie between the pretrade terms of trade of the two countries;[4] that is, between 1 coconut per fish and 3 coconuts per fish.

the production pattern under free trade

The basis for determining the exact value of the international terms of trade will be presented in a following section. For now assume that the international terms of trade settle at 2 coconuts per fish (or 1 coconut = 1/2 fish). These terms of trade are depicted by the slopes of the lines BG and CH in Figures 2–3(a) and (b), respectively, and, of course, both lines share the same slopes. The final production point of Bali will be point B, while Hai's will be at point C. That

---

[4]If one of the nations were a small country, then it is possible that two-way trade could occur, with the international terms of trade equal to the large nation's terms of trade.

is, both countries under free trade will *completely* specialize in the production of the commodity they export (possess a comparative advantage), producing nothing of the commodity that they import.

Complete specialization occurs because of the divergence between marginal opportunity costs and the international terms of trade. Because Bali can receive more coconuts (2) in trade with Hai than it has to sacrifice in production (1), Bali will continue to increase its fish production until its entire stock of resources is devoted to that production. Similarly, Hai will have an incentive to devote all its resources to coconut production as long as the marginal opportunity cost of producing coconuts (1/3 fish) is less than the international terms of trade of coconuts (1/2 fish). To summarize, both trading partners will completely specialize in the production of the commodity in which they hold a comparative advantage if (1) the international terms of trade lie *between* their respective pre-trade terms of trade and (2) the marginal opportunity costs of production remain constant.

consumption under free trade

We have identified the production points of Bali and Hai under free trade as points B and C, respectively, in Figure 2–3. Bali produces 100 fish that are available to export to Hai in exchange for coconuts, while Hai produces 90 coconuts which are available to export to Bali in exchange for fish. Both countries can trade their output with one another at the international terms of trade, 2 coconuts per fish. Bali can trade its fish production to Hai for coconuts along the line BG while Hai can trade its coconut production to Bali for fish along the line CH, since the slopes of these lines represent the international terms of trade. The international terms of trade line originating from the production point of a trading nation is referred to as the *consumption possibilities frontier (CPF)*, be-

cause points on those lines represent the consumption possibilities available to the trading nations under free trade.

Without explicit demand conditions, the particular commodity combinations consumed under free trade cannot be determined. For now, let us suppose that Bali is consuming at point J on its CPF, where point J represents 70 fish and 60 coconuts, and that Hai's consumption combination is represented by point M on its CPF; where point M represents 30 fish and 30 coconuts.

Trade Patterns and the Determination of International Equilibrium

From the information just presented concerning the production and consumption points of Bali and Hai, the exact trading patterns of the two countries can be determined. Bali exports 30 fish (the difference between the production and consumption of fish, 100–70) and imports 60 coconuts, while Hai exports 60 coconuts (90–30) and imports 30 fish. When the quantity of Bali's fish exports equals the quantity of Hai's fish imports and also the quantity of Hai's coconut exports equals the quantity of Bali's coconut imports (as in the above example), *international equilibrium* is said to exist. Under international equilibrium, the world demand for each product equals world supply.[5] Market forces will cause the *international terms of trade* to adjust until it settles at that value which equates the total supply and demand of

---

[5]If imports equal exports for a good, it must be the case that total world demand for the good equals total world supply. For instance, the total world supply of fish in our example equals the 100 units produced by Bali, 70 of which are consumed in Bali and 30 of which are exported to and consumed by Hai. Since Hai's imports of fish equal the 30 fish Bali exported, total world consumption of fish (Bali plus Hai) must equal total supply.

each commodity. If the international price of fish in terms of coconuts were higher than the equilibrium value, Bali would desire to export more fish than Hai would desire to import. This excess supply of fish would result in a decrease in the price of fish toward the equilibrium international terms of trade. The converse would occur if the price of fish in terms of coconuts were less than the equilibrium level.

The trading combinations of the two countries can be depicted graphically by constructing *trade triangles*. In Figure 2–3(a), Bali's trading patterns are represented by the triangle *JKB*, with sides *JK* and *KB* representing the quantity of Bali's exports of fish and imports of coconuts, respectively. The slope of the hypotenuse of the triangle, *JB*, represents the international terms of trade. Hai's trade triangle equals *CLM* in Figure 2–3(b), with its quantity of fish imports and coconut exports being represented by sides *CL* and *LM*, respectively. Again, the slope of the hypotenuse, *CM*, represents the international terms of trade. Under international equilibrium, then, the distance *JK* will equal *CL* (Bali's exports equal Hai's imports) and the distance *KB* will equal *LM* (Bali's imports will equal Hai's exports). In other words, the two trade triangles must be congruent under international equilibrium.

Gains from Trade

In our earlier numerical examples, we described the gains from trade as the increase in world output that resulted from international specialization under free trade. With graphical analysis the discussion of the gains from trade can be extended. Our graphical analysis not only provides a convenient means to demonstrate the increase in world output resulting from specialization, but also to examine the allocation of the gains from trade between the two trading partners.

The gains from free trade can be shown by comparing the consumption points of the trading nations before and after the opening of trade. Since the consumption possibilities frontiers of both Bali and Hai lie outside their production possibilities curves in Figure 2–3, it is clear that the two countries will be able to consume more of each good, if desired, than prior to free trade when they were constrained to their PPCs. In fact, their consumption points under international equilibrium, point *J* for Bali and point *M* for Hai, were unattainable prior to trade. Thus, the gains from trade can be thought of as the ability of trading nations to attain commodity combinations lying outside their PPC.

the magnitude of the gains from trade and its allocation between trading partners

Within the range of possible values of the international terms of trade, certain values will yield greater gains to one country relative to its trading partner. In general, it can be stated that the greater the relative price of the commodity in which a nation has a comparative advantage, the greater are the gains from trade to that nation. In Figure 2–4, several values of the international terms of trade between Bali and Hai are depicted, along with their respective PPCs (*AB* and *CD*, respectively). As the terms of trade of fish, the commodity in which Bali enjoys a comparative advantage, increases, Bali's CPF will move further rightward from its PPC. For example, if the terms of trade equaled 2.5 coconuts per fish, represented by the slope of the line *NB* in Figure 2–4, Bali's consumption possibilities would lie further from its PPC than those represented by the line *GB*, whose slope represents terms of trade equal to 2 coconuts per fish. At the higher terms of trade (2.5) Bali could attain commodity combinations that are unattainable at the lower terms of trade. Thus, the gains from trade to Bali will increase as the price of fish increases in terms of coconuts.

A nation's gains from international trade will

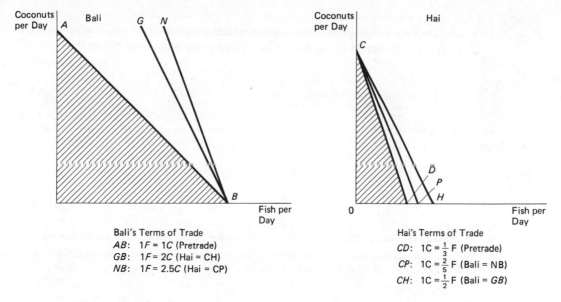

FIGURE 2-4 Consumption Possibilities with Varying International Terms of Trade

Bali's Terms of Trade
AB: 1F = 1C (Pretrade)
GB: 1F = 2C (Hai = CH)
NB: 1F = 2.5C (Hai = CP)

Hai's Terms of Trade
CD: $1C = \frac{1}{3} F$ (Pretrade)
CP: $1C = \frac{2}{5} F$ (Bali = NB)
CH: $1C = \frac{1}{2} F$ (Bali = GB)

thus be greater, the greater the divergence of the international terms of trade from its pretrade terms of trade. This result is not totally unexpected. If a nation can obtain a greater quantity of imports per unit of export production, it follows that the economic well-being of that nation will improve. For the same reasons, the gains from trade accruing to Hai will be greater, the greater the price of coconuts in terms of fish under international trade.

Finally, it should be noted that as the price of one country's export good increases relative to the price of the export good of its trading partner, the gains from trade accruing to the former nation will be the expense of its trading partner. For example, the gains accruing to Bali because of an increase in the price of fish—say, from 2 to 2.5 coconuts—implies that Hai will be worse off since the price of coconuts (its export commodity) will decline from 1/2 to 2/5 fish. Graphically, in Figure 2–4, as Bali's international terms of trade line rotates outward toward NB, Hai's international terms of trade line will simultaneously rotate inward toward

CP. Thus, the further the international terms of trade line (the CPF) lies from the PPC of one nation, the closer it lies to the PPC of its trading partner.

A NONRIGOROUS DISCUSSION OF RECENT CHANGES IN INTERNATIONAL LABOR PRODUCTIVITY AND EXPORT PERFORMANCES

Although the classical model does present a reasonably straightforward explanation of international trade, it may appear to the reader to be unrelated to the real world causes of trade, particularly in light of its restrictive assumptions. Remembering that the classical analysis argues that a country's comparative advantage, and thus its trade patterns, are based on the productivity of its labor (output per worker), it might prove interesting to take a descriptive look at recent changes in the labor productivity of several nations and the relation of those changes to changes

TABLE 2-3

Changes in Labor Productivity and World Export Performance for Selected Countries

Countries	Percentage of World Exports		Absolute Change in Percentage	Average Annual Change in Labor Productivity 1965–1979 (output per man hour)
	1965	1979		
United States	14.6%	11.7%	− 2.9%	2.1%
Canada	4.5	3.6	− .9	3.8
Japan	4.5	6.6	+ 2.1	8.1
France	5.4	6.3	+ .9	5.6
West Germany	9.5	11.1	+ 1.6	5.2
Italy	3.8	4.6	+ .8	5.6
United Kingdom	7.3	5.8	− 1.5	2.7

Source: Calculated from data presented in *Twenty-Fourth Annual Report of the President of the United States on the Trade Agreements Program, 1979.* Office of the U.S. Trade Representative.

in their export performance. Such data are compiled for several industrial nations in Table 2–3, for the years 1965 to 1979. A casual comparison of the productivity changes (changes in output per man hour) and changes in the individual nation's share of world exports lends some support for the classical predictions. For example, the three nations with the lowest gains in labor productivity over this period, the United States, United Kingdom and Canada, suffered losses in their share of world exports. Japan, which experienced the greatest gains in productivity, increased its share of world exports by the greatest percentage. The other nations which experienced relatively high gains in labor productivity, also experienced above-average gains in their share of world exports.

Obviously, many factors other than changes in labor productivity influenced trade patterns during this time period and thus the remarks put forth in this section are meant to be interpreted only as suggestions, not conclusions. It will be the object of the following section and the subsequent chapters to examine the other factors which may influence trade patterns. Let us begin that discussion by continuing to concentrate on

supply-side determinants of trade, but examining international trade patterns when the classical assumption of constant marginal opportunity costs is dropped.

INCREASING MARGINAL OPPORTUNITY COSTS

One of the earliest amendments to the classical trade model was the dropping of the constant cost assumption. As mentioned above, the labor theory of value was a keystone in classical economic analysis and, when combined with an assumption of homogeneous labor units, it implied constant marginal opportunity costs. By the end of the nineteenth century, economic analysis had begun to incorporate more than one factor of production. With this development came the realization that factor combinations most efficient for the production of one good might not be most efficient for the production of another.

Suppose that two commodities—say, coconuts and fish—are produced using two factors of production: labor and capital, where capital is better suited for fish production and labor is better suited for coconut production. That is, more capital relative to labor is used in fish production than in coconut production. If fish production were to increase at the expense of coconut production, more capital relative to labor would initially be transferred from coconut to fish production to meet the relatively greater capital requirements of fish production. But as this process continued, the amount of capital available to be released from coconut production would decline, and a larger proportion of labor (the factor better suited to coconut production) would have to be released from coconut production. As the quantity of labor (relative to capital) released from coconut production increased, the quantity of coconut production sacrificed in order to obtain a given increase in fish production would increase. In other words, as the country specializes increasingly in the production of fish, the marginal opportunity costs of producing fish will increase. In general, then, as a country increases the production of one commodity at the expense of another, where the two goods use factors of production in differing proportions, the marginal opportunity costs of producing more of the commodity will increase.

The presence of increasing marginal opportunity costs implies that a country's production possibilities curve will be concave to the origin as shown in Figure 2–5.[6] In Figure 2–5 the movements along the PPC, from point A to point B and from point B to point C, both entail an increase in fish production equal to 1. However, the corresponding decrease in coconut production necessary to obtain the 1-unit increase in fish production increases from 1 coconut (6 to 5) to 2 coconuts (5 to 3): that is, the MOC of fish increases as fish production increases.

[6]A concave production possibilities curve may also result from decreasing returns to scale in the production of one of the goods, even if the two factors of production are used in the same proportion in producing both goods.

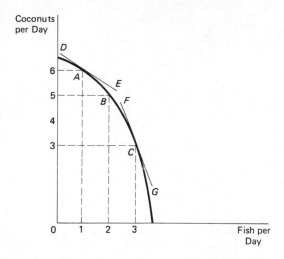

FIGURE 2-5 Production Possibilities Curve with Increasing Marginal Opportunity Costs

Just as in the constant cost case, the MOC of producing fish is equal to the slope of the PPC at the point of production. Therefore, with the increasing marginal opportunity costs of fish, the slope of the PPC will increase as fish production rises. The slope of the PPC at any production point is represented graphically by the slope of a line tangent to that point. For instance, in Figure 2–5 the slope of the PPC at point A is equal to the slope of the line DE which is just tangent to point A. Similarly, the slope at point C is represented by the slope of the tangent line FG. The tangent line DE is flatter than FG, implying that the slope of the PPC at point C exceeds the slope at point A.[7]

Pretrade Equilibrium

From our earlier discussion, we know that, prior to trade, Bali and Hai will both produce and consume at a point on their production pos-

[7]Because the slope of the PPC is negative, we are referring to the absolute values of the slopes of tangent lines DE and FG.

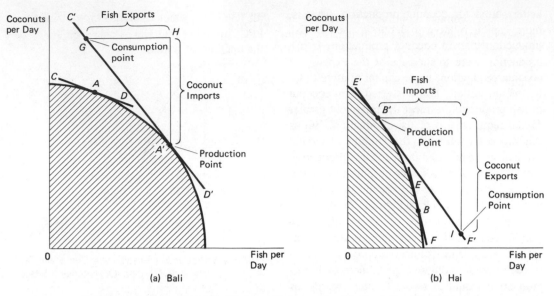

FIGURE 2-6 International Equilibrium with Increasing Marginal Opportunity Costs

sibilities curves. In Figure 2–6 let us assume that Bali and Hai are producing and consuming at points *A* and *B*, respectively, before the opening of trade. Because of the assumption of perfect competition, both the pretrade terms of trade and the marginal opportunity costs of fish production are represented by the slopes of the lines tangent to point *A* in Bali (line *CD*) and point *B* in Hai (line *EF*).

From observation it is clear that the tangent line, *CD*, is flatter than the line *EF*, implying that the marginal opportunity costs (and the price) of fish is lower in Bali than in Hai and, conversely, the marginal opportunity costs (and price) of coconuts will be lower in Hai than in Bali. Bali will thus have a comparative advantage in fish and Hai in coconuts.

The Opening of Trade Under Increasing Costs

Let us examine how the analysis of trade patterns under increasing marginal opportunity costs proceeds. As trade opens, Bali, having a comparative advantage in fish, will begin to

specialize in fish, transferring resources out of the production of coconuts. As in the constant-cost case, Bali's incentive for switching resources into fish production is that the extra fish production can be traded to Hai in exchange for a greater number of coconuts than Bali had to sacrifice in order to achieve the greater fish production. Thus, the combination of fish and coconuts being produced by Bali (its production point) begins to move toward the southeast along its PPC. As this happens, the slope of the PPC at the production point becomes steeper and steeper, reflecting the increasing marginal opportunity costs of producing fish. Competitive forces keep the terms of trade in line with the marginal opportunity costs, so that the price of fish in terms of coconuts becomes greater in Bali. Meanwhile, Hai begins to specialize in coconuts, the good in which it enjoys a comparative advantage. Hai's production point begins to move toward the northwest along its production possibilities curve. As this happens the marginal opportunity cost of coconuts becomes greater and greater in Hai, as does the price of coconuts in terms of fish.

As each country continues to transfer resources into the good in which it has a comparative advantage, the slopes associated with the two production points begin to converge. At the points where the slopes do converge (point A' for Bali and point B' for Hai), the marginal opportunity costs in the two countries will become equal as will the terms of trade in the two countries. At the point where the marginal opportunity costs are equal, neither country will have an incentive to continue shifting resources from one good to another. If trade is balanced at these points, international equilibrium will occur with the international terms of trade equal to the slopes of lines tangent to A' and B'.

Fish and coconuts will be traded between as well as within the countries at the newly established international terms of trade. In Bali the international terms of trade are represented by the slope of the line, $C'D'$, and in Hai by the slope of the line, $E'F'$. It is easy to see that the international terms of trade (the slope at points A' and B') must lie between the initial pretrade terms of trade (the slopes at points A and B in Bali and Hai, respectively).

Starting at point A', the final production point for Bali, Bali can export fish and import coconuts according to the international terms of trade. Under free trade, then, Bali will consume a commodity combination on its consumption possibilities frontier, line $C'D'$. In Figure 2–6, assume that Bali consumes the combination of coconuts and fish represented by point G. Of course, the fact that this commodity combination lies outside the production possibility curve of Bali indicates that Bali, through specialization and trade, has increased its economic well-being.

Hai, on the other hand, will export coconuts to Bali in exchange for fish, at a rate given by the international terms of trade. Hai is thus able to consume a commodity combination indicated by its consumption possibilities frontier, line $E'F'$. Assume that Hai consumes at point I along

the line $E'F'$, which of course lies outside Hai's PPC, implying that Hai is also better off after the opening of trade.

Trade triangles for each country can now be constructed. The quantity of fish exports from Bali is given by the distance GH in Figure 2–6(a), and the quantity of coconut imports is given by $A'H$. Using the consumption possibilities frontier as the hypotenuse, Bali's trade triangle would equal GHA'. Likewise, the quantity of coconut exports from Hai to Bali is given by the distance JI in Figure 2–6(b) and the quantity of Hai's fish imports by the distance JB'; Hai's trade triangle will therefore equal $B'JI$.

International equilibrium, of course, occurs at that value of the international terms of trade at which the quantity of each good that one country desires to export is equal to the quantity the other desires to import. In Figure 2–6, international equilibrium is depicted, since at the terms of trade indicated by the slopes of the tangent lines $C'D'$ and $E'F'$, the distances GH and $A'H$ equal the distances JB' and JI, respectively. In other words, the trade triangles of Bali and Hai in Figure 2–6 are congruent, and thus international equilibrium prevails.

constant costs versus increasing costs

The introduction of increasing marginal opportunity costs does not significantly alter the conclusions reached earlier regarding the determinants of trade patterns. It was shown that countries experiencing increasing marginal opportunity costs will specialize in the production of and export the commodity in which they enjoy a comparative advantage; the same conclusion that was reached in the constant cost case. However, with constant costs, it was demonstrated that each country will specialize completely in the production of the good in which it holds a comparative advantage, while under increasing costs, both countries were shown to partially specialize: that is, both will still produce some of each good under free trade. This incomplete specialization results from the fact that as each country increases the output of the good in which it holds a comparative advantage, the opportunity costs of producing the commodity increase. If opportunity costs increase, so that the MOCs are equalized before complete specialization has occurred, both countries will continue to produce some of both commodities under free trade. In summary, with increasing marginal opportunity costs, both countries will tend to specialize under free trade in the good in which it holds a comparative advantage; however, this specialization need not be complete.

The introduction of increasing costs generalizes the earlier analysis of the constant cost case. While it is difficult to make a clear-cut judgment as to whether or not increasing or constant costs more accurately describe the production processes of trading countries, the introduction of increasing costs into the analysis does allow us to explain the widely observed phenomenon of incomplete specialization; this was a situation which the classical model could not address.

QUESTIONS AND EXERCISES

1. What is the distinction between absolute and comparative advantage? Explain why comparative and not absolute advantage is the basis of international specialization and trade.

2. What is the distinction between the gains from specialization and the gains from exchange? Can there be profitable trade between two countries if neither country is capable of reallocating resources among industries? Explain.

3. Suppose the production possibilities of Bali and Hai are as follows:

	Coconuts	Fish
Bali	8	4
Hai	6	3

Assuming that all of the classical assumptions hold, compute each country's marginal opportunity costs for each good. Present the gains from trade (a) should Bali specialize in fish and Hai in coconuts and (b) should Bali specialize in coconuts and Hai in fish. What does this example demonstrate about the necessary conditions for trade to occur between nations?

4. Evaluate the proposition that it is impossible for a country to have a comparative advantage (or a comparative disadvantage) in all goods.

5. Explain why the international terms of trade that emerge after trade opens between two countries must lie between the domestic terms of trade that existed within the two countries before trade opened.

6. Suppose that after trade opens between two countries, one of the countries becomes completely specialized in the production of its export good while the other country continues to produce some of both goods. Is this situation possible under the classical assumptions? Can you say anything definite about the international terms of trade that would prevail under these circumstances?

7. What would be the implications of assuming increasing marginal opportunity costs as opposed to constant marginal opportunity costs in the classical trade model?

8. Evaluate the statement that the classical trade model with constant marginal opportunity costs implies that comparative advantage is determined entirely by relative production costs. How is this changed if increasing marginal opportunity costs are assumed?

9. Using an appropriate model, illustrate the proposition that, through trade, each country can end up consuming a combination of the imported and exported goods that it could not have attained in the absence of trade.

Further Developments 3 in International Trade Theory

Chapter 2 emphasized the role of international differences in the cost of producing tradeable goods as the primary determinant of international trade patterns. We demonstrated that a trading nation would export that good(s) in which it held a comparative advantage in production, and import that good(s) which could be produced more efficiently elsewhere. However, we avoided the question of *why* a country would be relatively efficient in the production of a particular commodity. We simply assumed that comparative cost differences did exist among nations and then went on to examine the patterns of trade that would emerge.

In addition, scant attention was given to the role of demand patterns in determining trade flows. Although we did allude to the role of demand, our explanation of trade patterns emphasized solely the supply-side differences between trading nations as the basis for two-way trade. The objective of this chapter is to address those omissions and, in so doing, to provide a more complete and satisfactory explanation of international trade.

THE INTRODUCTION OF DEMAND CONDITIONS[1]

Because the previous chapter emphasized only the supply-side (production) determinants of international trade patterns and ignored the influence of demand conditions, we were unable to determine: (1) the pretrade equilibrium points on each country's production possibilities

[1]This section can be omitted without loss of continuity if the instructor wishes to forego the use of indifference curves in explaining the role of demand in international trade.

curve, (2) the equilibrium value of the international terms of trade and (3) the consumption and production points of each country under free trade. To circumvent these limitations, we simply assumed equilibrium production and consumption positions as well as the value of the international terms of trade. By explicitly introducing the demand conditions of each country into our earlier analysis, we will be able to determine the magnitude of these items. We will also be able to examine the role of demand conditions in the determination of trade patterns.

Indifference Curves[2]

Indifference curves (IC) are the geometric devices that will be employed to represent the demand conditions of the trading countries. An indifference curve of an individual consumer represents the various combinations of two goods which provide equal satisfaction or *utility* to the consumer. Thus the consumer will be indifferent in choosing between commodity combinations lying on a single indifference curve. Figure 3–1 depicts an individual consumer's *indifference map,* which consists of a set of indifference curves. In Figure 3–1 the various combinations of coconuts and fish lying on a single indifference curve provide equal utility to the consumer. For instance, IC_1 implies that the consumer is indifferent between commodity combinations A (10 coconuts, 1 fish), B (5 coconuts, 2 fish) or C (3 coconuts, 3 fish).

Two properties of consumer indifference curves should be noted. First, they are downward sloping (negatively sloped) to the right.

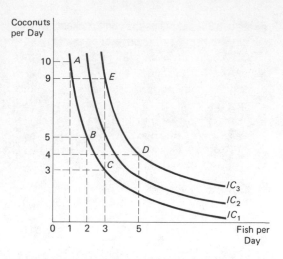

FIGURE 3-1 Indifference Curve Map

This implies that if the consumer sacrifices some of one good, an increase in the quantity of the other good is required to keep the consumer at the same level of utility. For instance, in moving from point A to B on IC_1, the consumer gives up 5 units of coconuts; in order to maintain the same level of utility, the consumer must increase his (her) consumption of fish by 1 unit. Second, as the consumer increases his consumption of one commodity at the expense of the other, the quantity of the second commodity that the consumer is willing to sacrifice to obtain an additional unit of the first, decreases. This can be explained by the *principle of diminishing marginal utility,* which states that the greater the quantity of a good an individual consumes, the lower will be the additional satisfaction obtained from consuming additional units. For this reason, the consumer will sacrifice fewer units of the other good to obtain more of that commodity. Returning to IC_1 in Figure 3–1, we see that the movements from point A to B and from B to C both entail an increase in fish consumption equal to 1 unit. However, the quantity of coconuts the consumer is willing to sacrifice declines from 5 to 2 units. This property of con-

[2]This discussion of indifference curves is not intended to be complete, but merely to provide an understanding sufficient to comprehend the role of demand in determining trade patterns. For a more thorough discussion of indifference curves, see any intermediate microeconomics text.

sumer behavior explains the convex shape (bowed toward the origin) of indifference curves.[3]

The *indifference map* in Figure 3–1 shows several of the consumer's indifference curves. Those indifference curves lying farther from the origin (the "higher" curves) represent greater levels of utility. To illustrate this we can show that for any commodity combination on a particular indifference curve, we can find some point on any higher indifference curve that will contain a greater quantity of *both* goods. For example, we might ask whether the consumer prefers the consumption bundle represented by point D (4 coconuts and 5 fish) which lies on IC_3 or that represented by point B (5 coconuts and 2 fish) on the lower indifference curve, IC_1. This is a reasonable question since point D offers more of one good (fish), but less of the other (coconuts) than does point B. The question can be answered by observing that point E (9 coconuts, 3 fish) lies on the same indifference curve as point D, so that the consumer would be indifferent between bundles D and E. However, point E represents more of both commodities than does point B, so that point E would be preferred to point B. Since points E and D are equally valued by the consumer, and E is preferred to B, it follows that point D (the point on the higher indifference curve) would be preferred to point B (the point on the lower indifference curve). In a similar manner it can be demonstrated that, for any pair of points, a consumer would prefer the one that lies on the higher indifference curve.

Note that our discussion regarding indifference curves has focused on the individual consumer. Our discussion of international trade, however, is concerned with the demand patterns of an entire country. To make the transition from individual consumer preferences to those of a country, it will be assumed that an indifference map, with the properties discussed above, can be specified for a country. The indifference curve of a country as a whole is referred to as a *community indifference curve (CIC).*[4]

Equilibrium with Demand Conditions

In Figure 3–2 the production possibilities curves of Bali and Hai are depicted, assuming increasing marginal opportunity costs. In addition, the community indifference map of each country is introduced. It should be recalled that prior to the opening of trade a country is constrained to be producing and consuming at a point on its production possibilities curve. Thus, before trade, a country will attempt to maximize its utility by consuming on the highest possible CIC, subject to the constraint of its PPC. This means it will produce and consume at the point at which its PPC is tangent to an indifference curve. Thus in Figure 3–2 Bali and Hai, prior to international trade, will produce and consume at points A and B, respectively. Point A is preferred by Bali, since of all the points on its production possibilities curve, it alone will maximize Bali's utility. That is, at point A residents of Bali are consuming on the highest community indifference curve that they can attain (CIC_1^B), while still producing on their PPC. At point A, the PPC is just tangent to the community indif-

---

[3]Actually, the principle of diminishing marginal utility is neither a necessary nor a sufficient condition for the convexity of indifference curves. This is so because the increase in the consumption of one good may itself affect the utility provided by an additional unit of the other good.

[4]Strictly speaking, indifference curves are appropriate only when applied to the preferences of a single individual. It is impossible to add up individual indifference curves to obtain an unambiguous map of indifference curves for a country as a whole unless the indifference maps of all individuals are identical (i.e., all individuals have identical tastes). Community indifference curves are used, despite their conceptual problems, for analytical convenience.

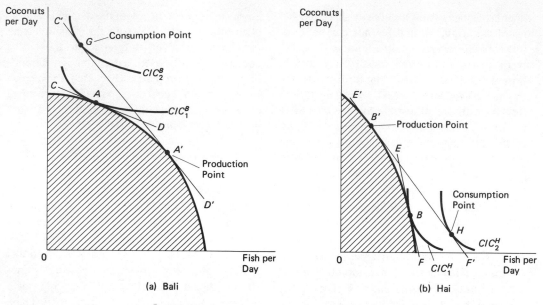

FIGURE 3-2 Equilibrium with Demand Conditions

ference curve, CIC_1^B. For the same reasons, Hai will choose to produce and consume at point B before trade opens.

International Equilibrium

From the previous chapter we know that the slope of the line just tangent to each country's pretrade equilibrium point represents both the marginal opportunity costs and the pretrade terms of trade between fish and coconuts. In Figure 3–2 the slope of line tangent to point A, line CD, is flatter than the line just tangent to point B, line EF, indicating that the pretrade price of fish in terms of coconuts is lower in Bali than in Hai. Thus Bali will enjoy a comparative advantage in fish production and Hai a comparative advantage in coconut production. Upon the opening of trade, then, Bali will increase its production and its export of fish while Hai will increase its production and its export of coconuts. Bali's production point will move to the southeast on its PPC, while Hai's will move to

the northwest on its PPC, until the terms of trade in the two countries converge.

Let us assume that under free trade the terms of trade converge at a value represented by the slopes of line $C'D'$ in Bali and $E'F'$ in Hai. At these new international terms of trade, Bali will be producing at point A' and Hai at point B'. Each country will be consuming at some point (some commodity combination) along its consumption possibilities frontier (CPF); recall that the consumption possibilities frontier is equivalent to the international terms of trade line ($C'D'$ in Bali and $E'F'$ in Hai). The preferred consumption point will be that commodity combination on the consumption possibilities frontier that yields the highest level of utility. In Bali, consumption will occur at point G and in Hai at point H, since those commodity combinations lie on the highest CIC that is attainable while still consuming on the consumption frontier; here the community indifference curve is just tangent to the consumption possibility frontier. Under free trade, then, trading nations will maximize their utility by consuming on the CIC which is just tangent to the consumption possibilities frontier.

Under free trade equilibrium, we know that the international terms of trade must be such that the quantity of fish Bali desires to export is just equal to the quantity Hai demands as imports; likewise, the quantity of coconuts Hai desires to export must just equal Bali's import demand for coconuts. If international equilibrium does not hold, market forces (supply and demand) will cause the international terms of trade to adjust until equilibrium is established.

Finally, note that before trade, CIC_1^B is the highest indifference curve attainable by Bali, and CIC_1^H is the highest indifference curve attainable by Hai. After trade, CIC_2^B and CIC_2^H are the highest curves attainable by Bali and Hai, respectively. Residents of both countries have gained in utility as the result of specialization and trade. The gains from trade can now be described as the gain in utility, as represented by a movement to a higher CIC, achieved by each country, as the result of participating in trade.

Gains from Exchange and Specialization

The gains from trade achieved by a country are made up of two components: (1) the gains from exchange and (2) the gains from specialization in production. With the introduction of indifference curves it is possible, graphically, to isolate the components of the total gains from trade. Figure 3–3 reproduces from Figure 3–2 the effects of free trade upon the consumption and production positions of Bali. Again, Bali's total gains from trade are represented by the movement from CIC_1^B to the higher community indifference curve, CIC_2^B.

This movement can be separated into two distinct components. First, assume that Bali continues to produce at its pretrade position, point A, but trades at the international terms of

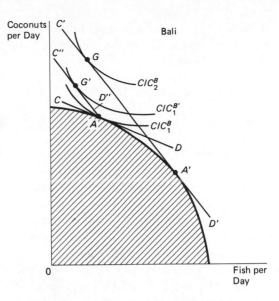

FIGURE 3-3 Gains from Trade: Specialization and Exchange

trade. In Figure 3–3 this implies that Bali can consume along the line $C''D''$, whose slope equals the slope of the line $C'D'$, the international terms of trade. Bali would consume at the point along $C''D''$ which yields the greatest utility, point G', which is tangent to the community indifference curve, $CIC_1^{B'}$. Since the $CIC_1^{B'}$ is higher than CIC_1^B, Bali has achieved a higher level of utility by simply trading at the international terms of trade, yet maintaining its pretrade production pattern. This movement from CIC_1^B to $CIC_1^{B'}$ is referred to as the *gains from exchange*.

If Bali also specializes in the production of fish according to the international terms of trade, and moves from point A to A' on its PPC, residents of Bali can reach CIC_2^B. The movement from $CIC_1^{B'}$ to CIC_2^B is a result of this change in the pattern of production and is referred to as the *gains from specialization*. Thus, the total gains from trade are derived from two sources: (1) specialization in the production of the commodity in which a country holds a comparative advantage and (2) trading the commodity in which it holds a comparative advantage to its trading partner at better terms of trade than were possible in the home market prior to trade.

Importance of Demand Conditions

With increasing costs in production, the determination of the pretrade terms of trade, and thus comparative advantage, is a result of the interaction of supply and demand conditions. By employing indifference curves, it will be possible to demonstrate a case where differences in demand patterns alone will be sufficient to establish a basis for trade, even if the two countries produce the two commodities equally well.

This situation is depicted in Figure 3–4, where it is assumed that Bali and Hai have identical production possibilities curves. This implies that both countries have the same resource base and that each can produce the commodities with equal efficiency. However, suppose that residents of Bali have a strong preference for coconuts and residents of Hai have a strong preference for fish. The difference in demand preferences is depicted by the differing positions of the two countries' community indifference curves; Ba-

li's community indifference curve map is positioned closer to the coconut axis, and Hai's is positioned closer to the fish axis. Pretrade equilibrium occurs at point A in Bali and point B in Hai. The tangent line at point A (CD) is flatter than the tangent line at point B (EF), indicating that the pretrade price of fish in terms of coconuts is less in Bali than in Hai, where coconuts are relatively cheap. Bali, having a comparative advantage in fish, will, upon the opening of trade, increase its production and export of fish. Hai, holding a comparative advantage in coconuts, will increase its production and export of coconuts.

This example demonstrates the importance of preferences in determining the direction of trade. Since both countries produce the two commodities equally well, it is the difference in demand conditions that causes the divergence in pretrade prices and thus determines the direction of trade. In Bali, strong preferences for coconuts drive the price of coconuts up relative to fish; that is, fish are relatively inexpensive. Conversely, in Hai, strong preferences for fish drive its price up relative to coconuts; coconuts are relatively cheap. Because of the differences

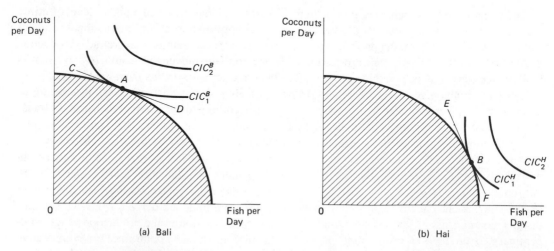

FIGURE 3-4 Trade Patterns with Different Demand Preferences

in demand conditions alone, two-way trade between Bali and Hai will proceed in the manner described above.

TRADE OFFER CURVES

We saw that, with the introduction of indifference curves, it is possible to determine the exact production and consumption positions of each country and the international terms of trade prevailing at international equilibrium. However, this determination can be quite cumbersome graphically, since the terms of trade must be adjusted until a position is reached where the quantities of each good traded is balanced. Around the turn of the century, an alternative concept was developed that permits a more direct determination of the international terms of trade as well as the exact volume of trade that would emerge between two trading nations. This concept, known as reciprocal demand, originated with John Stuart Mill and was formalized by Alfred Marshall as the trade offer curve. The trade offer curve reflects the fact that, in a barter model, the demand for foreign goods (imports) by the home country implicitly embodies an of-fer of home goods (exports) in exchange. It thus reflects both demand and supply conditions within the country in question.

A trade offer curve shows the quantity of imports that a country desires to purchase at various terms of trade and the quantity of exports that the country will have to provide in order to obtain those imports at those prices. Without getting into a formal derivation, an intuitive understanding of the trade offer curve can be easily developed. In offer curve analysis, the terms of trade between two traded goods are represented as the slope of a ray from the origin. In Figure 3–5, for example, rays A, B and C imply that one coconut exchanges for 1, 2 and 3 fish, respectively. In graphical terms, then, the price of coconuts in terms of fish becomes cheaper as the slope of the ray becomes steeper or, equivalently, as the ray rotates upward.

Figure 3–6(a) depicts the trade offer curve of Bali (TOC_B), which is constructed on the basis of the information contained in Table 3–1; it is assumed that Bali is exporting fish and importing coconuts. The horizontal axis measures the quantity of fish exports while the vertical axis measures the quantity of coconut imports. A single point on the offer curve represents the quantity of fish exports that Bali must offer to obtain the quantity of coconut imports desired at the prevailing terms of trade. For instance, TOT_2, the terms of trade line depicting 1 coconut = 4 fish, intersects Bali's offer curve at point B. This indicates that Bali desires to import 9 coconuts at those terms of trade. Because 1 coconut exchanges for 4 fish, Bali will have to offer (export) 36 fish (4 × 9) to its trading partner in order to obtain the 9 coconuts. At point D, where the price of coconuts in terms of fish is lower (1 coconut = 2 fish), Bali will increase its demand for coconuts to 14. Since 1 coconut exchanges for 2 fish, Bali will have to offer 28 fish to obtain the 14 coconuts at those terms of trade. The remaining points on Bali's offer curve can be interpreted similarly.

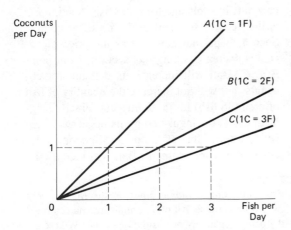

FIGURE 3-5 Terms of Trade as Represented by Slope of Ray from Origin

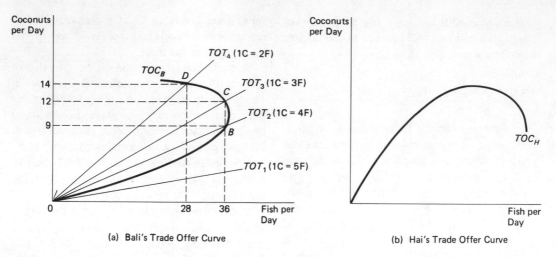

(a) Bali's Trade Offer Curve

(b) Hai's Trade Offer Curve

FIGURE 3-6 Trade Offer Curves of Bali and Hai

Let us examine more closely the characteristics of Bali's offer curve. First, the offer curve passes through the origin (point *A*), implying that at some terms of trade Bali will prefer not to engage in trade. The terms of trade at which Bali would refrain from trade would of course be the pretrade terms of trade; represented by TOT_1 (1 coconut = 5 fish) in Figure 3–6. As the price of coconut imports decreases (the TOT

line rotates upward), Bali will desire to engage in trade since the residents of Bali will be able to obtain coconuts more cheaply abroad than they could domestically.

Second, Bali's offer curve consists of three distinct sections: *AB, BC* and *CD*. Section *AB* is characterized by being positively sloped which implies that, as the price of coconuts in terms of fish declines, Bali will desire to import more coconuts in exchange for more fish. Section *BC* is the vertical segment of Bali's offer curve.[5] Such a shape indicates that as the price of coconuts decreases along this section, from point *B* to *C*, Bali will increase its demand for coconuts, but will not increase the quantity of fish offered (36 fish) for these imports. Finally, segment *CD* is distinguished by its negative slope, which implies that as the price of coconuts declines along this segment, Bali will increase its

TABLE 3-1

	Bali's Trade Preferences		
1	*2*	*3*	*4*
Points on Bali's TOC Figure 3-6(a)	TOT: Fish per Coconut	Quantity of Coconuts Demanded	Fish Offered (2 × 3)
A	5	0	0
B	4	9	36
C	3	12	36
D	2	14	28

[5]Actually, only a *single* point on the *BC* segment would be vertical. All other points are characterized by being negatively or positively sloped. We are referring to the entire *BC* segment as vertical for convenience.

import demand for coconuts, but will offer less fish for the increased quantity of coconuts.[6]

Note that the trade offer curve of Bali bends away from the axis which measures the quantity of fish and toward the axis measuring the quantity of coconuts. In general, a country's offer curve will tend to bend away from the axis that measures the quantity of the country's export good and toward the axis measuring import quantities.

Hai's offer curve can be derived in a similar fashion as Bali's. Since Hai exports coconuts and imports fish, individual points on Hai's offer curve will show the amount of fish that Hai would desire to import at alternative international terms of trade and the quantity of coconut exports it would offer in exchange. Hai's offer curve (TOC_H) is represented in Figure 3–6(b)

---

[6]The different segments of a TOC can also be distinguished by their different price elasticities of demand $\left(\dfrac{\text{percentage change in quantity demanded}}{\text{percentage change in price}}\right)$.
In the case of Bali's TOC, the segments *AB, BC* and *CD* would correspond to a price-elastic demand, a unitary elastic demand and an inelastic demand, respectively.

and would bend away from the coconut axis and toward the fish axis.

international equilibrium

The outcome of the opening of trade between Bali and Hai can be shown by combining Bali's (TOC_B) and Hai's (TOC_H) trade offer curves in the same diagram, as in Figure 3–7. In Figure 3–7, it is apparent that there is but one international terms of trade at which the quantities Bali and Hai want to import and export will be consistent. These are TOT_e, given by the slope of the ray which passes through the intersection of the two trade offer curves (point *A*). At TOT_e, Bali's trade offer curve shows that Bali wishes to import OC_e coconuts and export OF_e fish. Meanwhile, Hai's trade offer curve shows that Hai wishes to export OC_e coconuts and import OF_e fish. Thus, the market for fish and coconuts is in international equilibrium at TOT_e.

It can be shown that at any other terms of trade, the quantities the two countries wish to trade will not be consistent, and that supply and demand forces will push the terms of trade toward the equilibrium terms of trade, TOT_e. For example, suppose the existing terms of trade

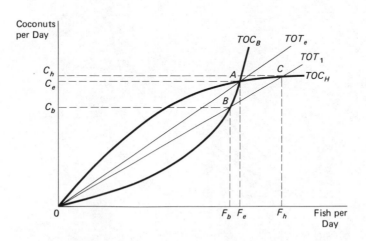

FIGURE 3-7 International Equilibrium with Trade Offer Curves

were as indicated by TOT_1, instead of TOT_e (coconuts are more expensive in terms of fish). Bali's trade offer curve shows that at TOT_1 (point B), Bali would wish to export OF_b fish in exchange for OC_b coconuts. Hai's trade offer curve shows (point C) that it would wish to import OF_h fish in exchange for OC_h coconuts. Since $OF_h > OF_b$, there would be an excess demand for fish in the world market, and since $OC_h > OC_b$, there would also be an excess supply of coconuts. The excess demand for fish and excess supply of coconuts would drive the price of fish upward and the price of coconuts downward until the excess supplies and demands are eliminated. In other words, market pressures would rotate the terms of trade line upward until it is restored to TOT_e, the equilibrium terms of trade.

A similar analysis would show that if the terms of trade happened to lie upward to the left of TOT_e (where coconuts are less expensive in terms of fish), an excess demand for coconuts and an excess supply of fish would prevail. Here, market forces would increase the price of coconuts in terms of fish (rotating the TOT downward) until it equals TOT_e. Thus TOT_e, the slope of the ray which passes through the intersection of the two trade offer curves, is a stable equilibrium toward which the market terms of trade will move.

Changes in the Terms of Trade

Let us now see how trade offer curves can be used to examine how the international terms of trade may change in response to various economic events. We shall consider two examples, one of which involves a change in demand conditions and one of which involves a change in production costs.

First, in Figure 3–8, assume that Bali and Hai's trade preferences are represented initially by the trade offer curves, TOC_B^1 and TOC_H^1, yielding an equilibrium terms of trade of TOT_1 (at point A). At TOT_1 the quantity of fish exported from Bali to Hai equals OF_1 and the quantity of coconuts exported from Hai to Bali equals OC_1. Now suppose that residents of Bali shift their consumption preferences from fish toward coconuts. The increase in the demand for coconuts is depicted graphically by an outward shift in Bali's offer curve—say, to TOC_B^2. Such a shift implies that for any given

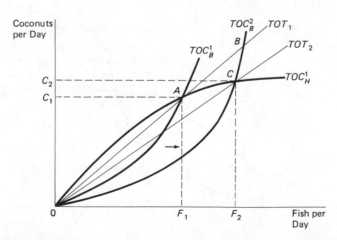

FIGURE 3-8 Change in Terms of Trade Resulting from Increased Demand for Coconuts by Bali

terms of trade, Bali will desire an increased quantity of coconuts. For example, after Bali's shift in demand preferences, residents of Bali will demand the quantity of coconut imports corresponding to point B on TOC_2^B at the original terms of trade, TOT_1. Obviously, that quantity exceeds the quantity demanded at those terms of trade prior to the shift in preferences (the quantity OC_1).

With the outward shift, a new equilibrium point will be established at point C, where Bali's and Hai's offer curves intersect. At the new equilibrium point, the price of fish in terms of coconuts is lowered to TOT_2. Because of the shift in Bali's demand preferences toward its imports, its terms of trade vis-à-vis Hai have deteriorated. Of course, from the perspective of Hai, the results were just the opposite. Because of increased foreign demand for its export good, coconuts, its terms of trade have improved.

Now let us consider an example of how the terms of trade can respond to changing cost conditions. Suppose producers of coconuts in Hai become more cost efficient in producing coconuts due, say, to an improvement in labor force skills. With declining per-unit costs, producers are willing to supply more coconuts at given

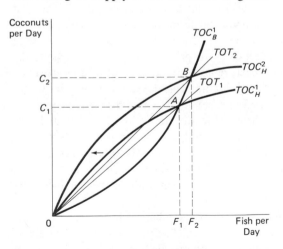

FIGURE 3-9 Change in Terms of Trade Resulting from Increased Supply of Coconuts by Hai

terms of trade. This increase in supply is represented in Figure 3–9 by an outward shift of Hai's offer curve to TOC_H^2, implying that at any terms of trade Hai will be willing to offer more coconuts to Bali. The new equilibrium terms of trade will occur at the intersection of TOC_H^2 and TOC_B^1, point B; where the price of coconuts in terms of fish is lower than its original equilibrium value (TOT_1 to TOT_2). Thus, Hai's terms of trade have deteriorated and Bali's have improved as a result of the increase in the supply of coconuts by Hai.

Does the deterioration of Hai's terms of trade (the fact that each unit of exports now exchanges for fewer units of imports) mean that it is economically worse off? Will it become worse off despite the fact that it can now produce coconuts at lower costs? To answer these questions, we must also consider the effect of the increase in labor productivity on Hai's income and output. First, the lower unit costs will enable Hai to provide a greater quantity of coconuts to its residents for consumption. Second, residents of Hai have a greater quantity of coconuts to exchange for fish. This second effect is reflected in Figure 3–9 where it is seen that both the quantity of Hai's coconut exports and its fish imports have increased, despite the rise in the relative price of fish. To assess the net effect on Hai's economic well-being, then, we would have to weigh the beneficial effects of the increase in coconut production (and the income it generates) against the costs associated with the reduction in the terms of trade.

RECENT DEVELOPMENTS IN THE WORLDWIDE PATTERN OF THE INTERNATIONAL TERMS OF TRADE

From the foregoing discussion, it is evident that the terms of trade of a nation can change as a result of any number of occurrences. In light of that discussion, it may prove interesting to examine recent changes in the terms of trade of several trading nations, and to relate them to recent international economic events.

Table 3–2 depicts the average annual terms of trade for several trading nations for the years 1970–1978. During that period, many significant economic events occurred which may have influenced the terms of trade of these nations. While it is difficult to isolate the impact of individual events, the effect of the enormous rise in petroleum prices is clear. Oil prices increased dramatically during the 1970s as the result of the international cartelization of much of the world's oil production by the Organization of Petroleum Exporting Countries (OPEC). Those nations which depend heavily on petroleum imports, such as the United States and Japan, saw their terms of trade decline over this period while the OPEC nations, which include Iraq and Saudi

Arabia, saw their terms of trade skyrocket. Canada and Mexico, two non–OPEC members who nonetheless produce substantial quantities of petroleum for both domestic use and for export, fared much better than did those nations heavily dependent on petroleum imports.

What are the implications of these developments for the economic well-being of the trading nations that import and export oil? Our discussion in Chapter 2 would suggest that the oil-exporting nations of the world have benefited economically at the expense of those nations whose imports consist heavily of petroleum. In the language of this chapter, nations such as Saudi Arabia have moved to higher community indifference curves, while nations such as Japan and the United States lie on lower community indifference curves than they would otherwise have attained.

More specifically, the United States must offer a greater quantity of its export goods to Saudi Arabia to receive a barrel of petroleum today than was required in 1970; or, equivalently, the United States receives a smaller quantity of petroleum imports for the same amount of exports. Although the bilateral terms of trade between any pair of nations cannot be obtained from Table 3–2, let us assume that the 22 percent decline in the terms of trade of the United States between 1970 and 1978 reflected a 22 percent decline in the price of an American export, say wheat, relative to the price of oil imports from Saudi Arabia. This development implies that if the United States exported the same quantity of wheat to Saudi Arabia in 1978 that it did in 1970, it would receive, in return, 22 percent less petroleum. Obviously, the economic welfare of the United States was lower in 1978 than it would have been without the decline in its terms of trade.

As we can see, changes in the terms of trade have a substantial effect upon the global distribution of economic welfare. We shall have more to say in later chapters on both OPEC pricing

TABLE 3-2

Terms of Trade[a] of Selected Nations (1970–1978)
(1970 = 100)

Year	United States	Canada	Japan	Mexico	Iraq	Saudi Arabia
1970	100	100	100	100	100	100
1971	98	99	99	98	124	122
1972	95	100	104	100	123	120
1973	92	105	101	108	131	126
1974	80	114	75	112	427	400
1975	82	109	72	120	431	407
1976	82	111	69	122	457	435
1977	79	105	71	131	449	422
1978	78	101	81	NA	NA	NA

Sources: International Bank for Reconstruction and Development/World Bank. *World Tables* (1980). International Monetary Fund, *International Financial Statistics Yearbook 1979.*

[a]The terms of trade above are indices, with 1970 as the base year. A particular calculation for year i is equal to:

$P_i Q_{70}$ (exports)
$P_{70} Q_{70}$

$P_i Q_{70}$ (imports)
$P_{70} Q_{70}$

policies and the role of the terms of trade in affecting international economic relations.

UNDERPINNINGS OF COMPARATIVE ADVANTAGE: THE HECKSCHER–OHLIN THEOREM

In the preceding analysis it was shown that the pattern of trade depends on pretrade marginal opportunity costs. The country having the lowest marginal opportunity costs of producing a good would enjoy a comparative advantage in the production of that good and would export the good under free trade. However, we have yet to identify the factors that determine whether a country will have a cost advantage in the production of a particular commodity. During the early part of this century, two Swedish economists, Eli Heckscher and Bertil Ohlin, devised a theory to explain why different countries would have a relative cost advantage in producing different goods. Their theory was based solely on supply-side considerations, with preferences for the two goods considered to be identical in the two countries. Although we have demonstrated that demand conditions are important in any complete theory of comparative advantage, the Heckscher–Ohlin theorem extends our earlier analysis in an essential manner by providing valuable insights into the role that production conditions play in determining comparative advantage and trade patterns.

The Heckscher–Ohlin (H–O) theorem states that if consumption preferences are identical in two countries (and if certain other conditions are met) relative production costs will be determined by the relative factor endowments of the two countries, coupled with the relative intensity with which the factors must be used in producing the goods. The theorem assumes that there are two countries, each producing two goods using two factors of production. It then advances two propositions:

1. The two trading countries have different relative factor endowments.
2. The method of producing the two commodities differs. Specifically, each commodity is produced using the two factors of production in different proportions or intensities.

Given these propositions, the pattern of relative production costs, and thus the pattern of comparative advantage, can be determined. Let us proceed to demonstrate the H–O theorem within our two-country, two-good framework.

Assume that Bali has a relative abundance of capital while Hai has a relative abundance of labor; that is, the ratio of the quantity of capital to the quantity of labor is greater in Bali than in Hai. Assume further that fish production is relatively capital intensive compared to coconut production; that is, fish production requires a greater ratio of capital to labor than does coconut production. These relative factor intensities are assumed to apply identically to both countries. Because capital is relatively abundant in Bali and relatively scarce in Hai, capital will be relatively cheaper in Bali than in Hai. Because labor is relatively abundant in Hai and relatively scarce in Bali, labor will be relatively cheaper in Hai than in Bali.

Since capital is relatively cheap in Bali, Bali will have the cost advantage in the production of fish, the good that requires relatively more capital in its production. Similarly, since labor is relatively cheap in Hai, Hai will have the cost advantage in the production of coconuts, the good that requires relatively more labor in its production. When trade opens, Bali therefore specializes in and exports fish to Hai, while Hai specializes in and exports coconuts to Bali. The conclusion of the Heckscher–Ohlin theorem regarding the pattern of trade can be summarized as follows: In a two-country, two-commodity world, a country will specialize in the production of and will export the commodity which uses the country's abundant factor intensively.

Factor Price Equalization

The adjustment process by which international equilibrium is attained within the Heckscher–Ohlin framework produces an interesting corollary to the Heckscher–Ohlin theorem known as *the factor–price equalization theorem*. This theorem holds that with the opening of trade between the two countries, not only will the terms of trade converge, but the relative factor prices in the two countries will also tend to converge. Thus as trade opens between Bali and Hai, the ratio of the price of labor (wage) to the price of capital (interest) will tend to equalize between the two countries, even though labor and capital cannot migrate between Bali and Hai.

To understand this theorem, it is necessary to examine the adjustment process that occurs within Bali and Hai upon the opening of trade. Bali is increasing its production of fish, the capital-intensive good, at the expense of coconut production, the labor-intensive good. As the production of fish increases, the derived demand for capital (relative to labor) increases. However, the quantity of capital relative to labor being released from coconut production is less than that demanded by fish producers. This implies that initially there would be an excess demand for capital and an excess supply of labor as resources are transferred from coconut to fish production. The result would be an increase in the price of capital relative to the price of labor in Bali.

In Hai, the opposite movement of factor prices will occur during trade. Coconut production, which is labor intensive, will increase at the expense of fish production, which is capital intensive. The quantity of labor relative to capital being released from fish production will not be as great as the quantity of labor relative to capital being demanded by the expanding coconut industry. As a result, the price of labor relative to capital would increase in Hai.

In both countries, a situation exists in which the price of the originally less expensive factor is rising, and the price of the originally more costly factor is falling. This implies that the relative factor prices will tend to converge. It can be shown that, under certain rather strong assumptions, relative factor prices and even absolute factor prices will converge completely. With absolute factor price equalization, the factor prices in the two countries would be such that real wage rates and interest rates would be identical across countries. Of course, there is a simultaneous convergence of commodity prices occurring as the relative price of each country's export good rises while that of its import good falls.[7]

free trade and income distribution

The factor price equalization theorem has significant implications regarding the effect of free trade upon the distribution of income within a country. It demonstrates that under free trade the returns to the factor of production used intensively in the production of the export commodity (the abundant factor) increase, while the returns to the factor used intensively in the importing-competing commodity (the scarce factor) decrease. In our example, the relative price of capital in Bali (its abundant factor) increased while in Hai the relative price of labor (its abundant factor) also increased. Of course, these increases in the returns to the abundant factor came at the expense of each country's scarce factor (labor in Bali and capital in Hai).

Before we can draw any conclusions about the change in the overall well-being of each factor, we must also consider the changes in commodity prices that take place under free trade.

[7]If one country becomes completely specialized in the production of a good, factor price equalization may not occur, although commodity price equalization will.

For instance, payments to labor in Bali declined upon the opening of trade, as did the price of the imported good, coconuts. If laborers have a strong preference for coconuts relative to fish, the decline in the price of coconuts would offset, to a certain degree, the decrease in wage payments. It can be demonstrated, however, that the factor income changes caused by free trade will generally dominate any consumption effects in determining the well-being of a factor of production.

The Heckscher–Ohlin explanation of trade clearly has limitations. Its contribution to trade theory lies in its analysis of the role of production considerations in determining comparative advantage. In the context of our earlier graphical analysis, it can be viewed as a theory about the shapes of the production possibilities curves of the two countries. While other considerations certainly affect trade patterns, relative factor endowments and factor intensities play an important role, and the Heckscher–Ohlin theorem provides insight into why this is so. By the same token, although relative factor prices are not typically identical across countries engaged in trade, there is a *tendency* for them to converge as suggested by the factor–price equalization theorem.

Empirical Tests of the Heckscher–Ohlin Theorem and the Leontief Paradox

The Heckscher–Ohlin theorem served as the keystone of accepted trade theory until the late 1940s, when Wassily Leontief attempted to test the theorem against real world data. Leontief reasoned that the United States was relatively heavily endowed with capital compared with its trading partners, and that the United States should thus be exporting relatively capital-intensive goods and importing relatively labor-intensive goods. He computed the capital/labor ratio for a broad set of U.S. exports and did the same

for U.S. imports.[8] Leontief then compared the capital/labor ratios of U.S. exports and imports. The results were unexpected: U.S. imports were relatively more capital-intensive than U.S. exports.[9] These findings, known as the Leontief paradox, caused considerable consternation among trade theorists, and a number of additional tests of the theory followed. Many of these tests also failed to confirm the theorem.

These subsequent studies did, however, produce several possible explanations of the "paradox." Two explanations in particular provide plausible arguments as to why Leontief obtained his seemingly contradictory results. Economists noted that Leontief ignored natural resources as both a factor of production and as tradeable commodities. Many natural resources and their byproducts (for instance, minerals and forest products) require a large amount of physical capital in their production. The United States happens to be a heavy importer of many of those products, which would help to explain the large capital intensity associated with U.S. imports. Conversely, natural resource-based agricultural products, of which the United States is a large exporter, use labor intensively, and would thus contribute to the large share of labor embodied in U.S. exports. The importance of the role of natural resources in explaining the Leontief paradox is illustrated by the fact that when natural resources are omitted from Leontief's calculations, the paradox is reversed and the U.S. export commodities are more capital intensive than imports.

---

[8]Data on the capital/labor ratio associated with foreign production of U.S. imports were not available, so Leontief used the capital/labor ratio of U.S. import-competing industries.

[9]Leontief found that the ratio of the capital/labor ratios of exports to imports $\left(\dfrac{K/_L \text{ exports}}{K/_L \text{ imports}} \right)$ equaled approximately .77.

A second explanation of the Leontief paradox which has emerged concerns the manner in which labor is treated as a factor of production. Leontief's approach assumed that all labor units were identical. This, of course, is not true. Labor differs by skill level, and some occupations require larger amounts of training and education, or human capital, than others. Differences in human capital requirements across different occupations suggest that labor should be broken down into more than one factor of production, distinguished by the amount of human capital embodied in each type of labor. Subsequent studies have indicated that U.S. export production uses skilled labor relatively intensively when compared to import production. Since the United States is relatively abundant in skilled labor or human capital, this would be consistent with the H–O prediction.

One study which illustrates the intensive use of skilled labor in U.S. export production is that of Donald Keesing. Keesing divided occupations into eight categories, as shown in Table 3–3, with the greatest skill requirements represented in category I and the least in category VIII. The contribution of each category to the total labor required to produce exports is shown (in percentage terms) for several countries. It is evident that the United States uses a greater percentage of highly skilled labor in export production than do the other countries listed.

Keesing's study suggests that the Heck-

TABLE 3-3

Labor Requirements by Skill Class to Produce 1962 Exports of Fourteen Countries, Using 1960 U.S. Skill Combinations, for Forty-Six Manufacturing Industries Including Natural-Resource Processing

Country	Man Years per Billion Dollars of Exports	Percentage Distribution of Labor Requirements by Skill Class							
		I	II	III	IV	V	VI	VII	VIII
U.S.	48,194	5.02	2.89	2.74	4.85	8.38	14.96	15.73	45.42
Canada	34,881	4.17	2.33	2.43	4.76	5.39	16.45	14.70	49.76
U.K.	49,833	3.77	2.29	2.36	4.79	7.20	15.01	14.91	49.68
Austria	52,954	2.76	1.76	1.91	4.15	5.71	15.97	12.87	54.87
Belgium	48,611	2.83	1.71	1.98	3.86	4.67	17.35	12.75	54.85
France	49,381	3.15	1.92	2.15	4.58	5.28	15.55	14.14	53.24
Germany	50,459	3.89	2.48	2.33	4.69	8.44	15.84	14.54	47.79
Italy	52,304	2.75	1.75	1.97	4.33	4.32	12.78	13.24	58.86
Netherlands	44,519	3.62	2.39	2.31	4.65	5.04	15.62	14.50	51.87
Sweden	49,984	3.53	2.34	2.23	4.41	8.92	18.87	13.73	45.96
Switzerland	54,971	3.50	2.39	2.18	5.29	7.76	12.66	15.65	50.56
Japan	57,842	2.48	1.66	1.78	3.96	4.56	15.15	12.04	58.38
Hong Kong	74,304	0.69	0.49	1.13	3.75	1.34	8.48	10.39	73.73
India	66,517	0.71	0.58	1.06	3.47	1.33	11.13	9.62	72.09

Source: Donald B. Keesing, "Labor Skills and Comparative Advantage," *American Economic Review*, 56 (May 1966) 249–58 (Table 1). (Reprinted with permission).
Skill Classes are:

    I. Scientists and Engineers   V. Machinists, Electricians and Tool- and Diemakers
   II. Technicians and Draftsmen   VI. Other Skilled Manual Workers
  III. Other Professionals   VII. Clerical Workers
  IV. Managers   VIII. Unskilled and Semiskilled Workers

scher–Ohlin predictions of trade patterns, based on factor endowments, may prove valid after all if more than two factors of production are considered. Thus, the error underlying the paradox may lie in the Heckscher–Ohlin assumption of only two factors of production and not in the logic of the theorem itself. The role of human capital in determining trade patterns not only helped to explain the Leontief paradox, but also provided the basis for some of the more recent theories of international trade. These theories will be the subject of Chapter 5.

QUESTIONS AND EXERCISES

1. Using appropriate graphical models, demonstrate that if there are increasing marginal opportunity costs and if the production possibilities of two countries are very similar, demand conditions can govern which country has the comparative advantage in each good.

2. Construct a trade offer curve diagram for two countries trading two goods between themselves. Identify the equilibrium terms of trade and the quantity of each good that will be exported and imported by each country. Demonstrate that the international terms of trade will return to the equilibrium level if disturbed, assuming that the trade offer curves remain fixed.

3. Show how the information provided by the trade offer curve analysis is related to the information provided by the production possibilities curve model in Figure 3–1.

4. What is the rationale for the statement that a country will have the comparative advantage in the good that requires relatively intensive inputs of the factor of production in which the country is relatively heavily endowed?

5. Explain how the opening of trade can cause relative factor prices to converge even though there is no change in the relative *supplies* of factors within the countries.

6. How can we say that a country will be better off as a result of the opening of trade if the prices that must be paid by the consumers of the *exported* good increase and if home production of the *imported* good diminishes?

7. Analyze the potential effects of a decrease in the world demand for a product on both importing and exporting nations. Focus, in particular, on the prices of exported goods, the prices of imported goods, the quantities of exported goods and imported goods produced, the price of the factor used intensively in the import industry and the price of the factor used intensively in the export industry. Also, analyze the effects upon the gains from trade.

8. Assume that the world is divided into two blocs of nations: petroleum exporters and petroleum importers. Suppose the petroleum exporters restricted the supply of petroleum to the importing nations. Analyze the effect of such an action on world trade patterns and the volume of trade and prices, using trade offer curves.

9. Do you believe that the Heckscher–Ohlin theorem of trade is adequate to explain real world trade patterns? Why or why not? How would you improve upon the original theorem so that it conformed better to actual trade patterns.

Imperfect Competition and Other 4 Topics in International Trade Theory

Our analysis of the process of specialization and trade presented in chapters 2 and 3 has established some of the fundamental determinants of international trade patterns. However, that analysis was somewhat limited in that it was based on a set of restrictive assumptions. In this chapter we shall see how the pattern of trade is affected when several of these assumptions are removed. First, we shall drop the assumption that traded goods are bartered and introduce money prices and exchange rates. We shall then present a partial equilibrium model of trade, a model that concentrates on the trade patterns of only a single good. This partial equilibrium model will then be used to examine the impact of transportation costs upon the pattern of trade. The final modification will be to drop the assumption of perfect competition. We shall see that monopolistic and oligopolistic market structures, as well as the presence of differentiated products, can produce trade patterns considerably different from those suggested by our earlier models of trade based on perfect competition.

COMPARATIVE ADVANTAGE WITH MONEY PRICES

The analysis, so far, has assumed that the two countries are engaging in barter. Fish and coconuts are traded directly for each other without regard to money prices. It may be instructive, at this point, to show that the barter model is consistent with a world in which money prices are explicitly included.

Let us assume that the pretrade equilibrium conditions for Bali and Hai are characterized by the information contained in Table 4–1(a), where it is assumed that Bali has a comparative advantage in fish and Hai in coconuts. In Bali, 1 coconut will exchange for 3

TABLE 4-1

Pretrade Barter and Money Prices of Fish
and Coconuts

**(a) Marginal Opportunity Costs of Production
and Pretrade Barter Prices**

	MOC—Coconuts	MOC—Fish
Bali	3 fish (F)	$\frac{1}{3}$ coconut (C)
Hai	$\frac{1}{2}$ fish (F)	2 coconuts (C)

Pretrade Barter Prices

Bali	$1C = 3F$ $(1F = \frac{1}{3}C)$
Hai	$1F = 2C$ $(1C = \frac{1}{2}F)$

**(b) Money Prices of Fish and Coconuts in Bali and
Hai (at $1.00 = £2)**

Purchasing Country	Fish Prices		Coconut Prices	
	Source		Source	
	Bali	Hai	Bali	Hai
Bali ($) (1C = 3F)	$1.00	$2.00[a]	$3.00	$1.00
Hai (£) (1F = 2C)	£2[b]	£4	£6	£2

[a]To convert Hai prices (£) to Bali currency units ($), the price of goods in Hai is multiplied by the exchange rate. For example, the $ price to Bali of fish produced in Hai, where the price is £4, is obtained by:

$$£4 \times \frac{\$1.00}{£2} = \$2.00$$

[b]To convert Bali prices ($) to Hai currency units (£), we must divide the $ price by the exchange rate. Thus, the £ price to Hai of fish produced in Bali ($1.00) is obtained in the following manner:

$$\frac{\$1.00}{\$1.00/£2} = £2$$

fish (or 1 fish = 1/3 coconut) prior to free trade. A set of money prices that reflects this rate of exchange would be: the price of 1 fish equal to $1.00, and the price of 1 coconut equal to $3.00. Meanwhile in Hai, prior to trade, 1 fish will exchange for 2 coconuts (or 1 coconut = 1/2 fish). Assuming that the Hai currency unit is the pound sterling (£), a set of money prices that would reflect these terms of trade would be: the price of 1 fish equal to £4, and the price of coconuts equal to £2.

Let us now select a plausible exchange rate between the dollar and the pound, say $1.00 = £2,[1] and assume that this exchange rate remains constant throughout the analysis. Translating foreign prices into home prices for both countries using the $1.00 = £2 exchange rate, the price relationships facing residents in the two countries are those shown in Table 4–1(b).

It is clear that after translating foreign prices into home prices, both countries will find coconuts to be cheaper if purchased from Hai and fish to be cheaper if purchased from Bali. Upon the opening of trade, Bali will specialize in fish production and will import coconuts, while Hai will specialize in coconut production and will import fish. This is consistent with the analysis based on marginal opportunity costs in the barter model.

Let us assume that the international (barter) terms of trade settle at 1 fish for 1 coconut. These are clearly within the limits set by the pretrade terms of trade. A set of money prices within Bali consistent with these terms of trade would be: 1 fish costs $1.50 while 1 coconut costs $1.50. A set of prices in Hai consistent with these terms of trade would be: 1 fish costs

[1]To be "plausible," in this example, the exchange rate must lie between $1.00 = £2/3 and $1.00 = £4. Otherwise, two-way trade between Bali and Hai (and thus international equilibrium) would not exist. As a result, competitive forces would drive the rate back into this range.

£3 while 1 coconut costs £3. It must also be the case that in international equilibrium, the money price of each good, after translating by the exchange rate, will be the same in both countries. For example, the price of fish in Bali ($1.50), translated into Hai's currency at the exchange rate, ($1.00 = £2), will be £3. This is, of course, equal to the price of fish in Hai.

THE EFFECTS OF TRADE: PARTIAL EQUILIBRIUM

Up to this point, the effects of trade have been analyzed within a general equilibrium framework—a framework in which the effects of trade on all goods were analyzed, taking into account their interdependence. Another approach is to examine the effects of trade on an individual commodity, assuming that the impact of trade on other goods has no effect on the good in question. This approach is referred to as *partial equilibrium* analysis.

Figure 4–1 shows the domestic supply and demand conditions for coconuts within Bali and Hai. The supply and demand curves for coconuts in Hai are given in the right-hand panel by *SS* and *DD*, respectively, while the supply and demand curves for coconuts in Bali are given in the left-hand panel by *S'S'* and *D'D'*, respectively.[2] Before trade opens, the price of coconuts in Bali is P_B, and the price in Hai is P_H. Because of the lower price in Hai, residents of Bali will turn to Hai to purchase coconuts and away from producers in Bali upon the opening of trade. As residents in Bali turn toward coconuts produced in Hai and away from coconuts produced in Bali, the price of coconuts in Bali will decline, while in Hai the price will be bid upward until the two prices converge at a single "international price." In Figure 4–1 the international price of coconuts would be equal to P^*, which lies between the pretrade prices. At the

[2]Note that Bali's supply and demand graph has been reversed so that a single price axis can serve for both countries.

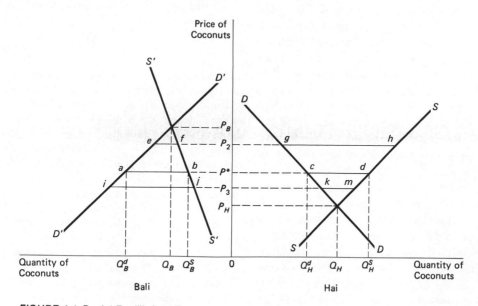

FIGURE 4-1 Partial Equilibrium: Trade Patterns of Coconuts

price, P^*, the quantity of coconuts supplied in Bali will be OQ_B^s, and the quantity demanded OQ_B^d. Meanwhile, the quantity of coconuts supplied in Hai will be OQ_H^s and the quantity demanded will be OQ_H^d. For the international market to clear, the excess demand in Bali, $OQ_B^d - OQ_B^s$, must equal the excess supply in Hai, $OQ_H^s - OQ_H^d$. That is, the quantity of coconuts available for export from Hai *(cd)* must be equal to the coconut imports demanded by Bali *(ab)*.

Unless these conditions are met, the international price, P^*, will continue to adjust until they *are* met. Suppose, for example, that the international price somehow stood at P_2. At this price, the quantity of coconut imports demanded by Bali *(ef)* would be smaller than the quantity Hai would desire to export *(gh)*, creating an excess supply of coconuts in the international market. This would cause the price of coconuts to fall to P^*, where the market would clear. If, on the other hand, the international price lay below P^*—say, at P_3—there would be an excess demand for coconuts in the international market, as the supply of exports by Hai *(km)* fell short of the imports demanded by Bali *(ij)*. The price would be driven upward to P^*, the price at which the market would clear. There is, thus, a unique international price at which the quantity of imports demanded by Bali is equal to the quantity of exports offered by Hai.

With this approach, we can note some important effects of the opening of trade. First, the price of the traded good will rise in the exporting country and fall in the importing country, so as to establish a common international price. This means that consumers in the exporting country will have to pay a higher price for the good than before trade opens, while consumers in the importing country will pay less. Second, because of these price changes, consumers in the exporting country will consume less of the traded good (OQ_H^d is less than OQ_H),

while consumers in the importing country will consume more (OQ_B^d is greater than OQ_B). Third, the quantity of the traded good being produced in the exporting country will increase as trade opens (OQ_H^s is greater than OQ_H), and fall in the importing country (OQ_B^s is smaller than OQ_B).

Within a partial equilibrium framework, a limited discussion of the effects of trade on the economic well-being of the trading nations can also be conducted. To accomplish this, the production and consumption effects of free trade must be compared. For example, consumers of coconuts in Bali have benefited upon the opening of trade, since the quantity of coconuts consumed has increased and they pay a lower price. However, producers of coconuts in Bali have lost since they produce a smaller quantity of coconuts and receive a lower price. To determine the change in Bali's overall well-being, these two effects must be weighed against one another. A similar analysis could be applied to Hai. However, even in a partial equilibrium model, it is possible to demonstrate that free trade will provide overall benefits to both countries.[3]

[3]To make a judgment regarding the gains from trade in a partial equilibrium model, we would need to discuss the concepts of producers' surplus and consumers' surplus. Upon the opening of trade, it can be demonstrated that in Bali consumers' surplus increases by a greater amount than producers' surplus declines, suggesting that overall a country benefits from free trade. In Hai, it can be similarly demonstrated that the increase in producers' surplus exceeds the decrease in consumers' surplus. Consumers' and producers' surplus will be discussed in more detail in Chapter 13.

It should be noted, however, that to obtain a true determination of the effects of free trade, the effects of trade on all traded goods must be considered. That is, a general equilibrium model is needed.

Transportation Costs

The partial equilibrium model can also be used to show the effects of transportation costs on trade, prices, production and consumption, within and between the trading countries. Thus far, transportation costs have been assumed to be zero. With zero transportation costs and perfect competition, a single world price would emerge for a given commodity after trade opens. As was shown above, any intercountry price differences that do exist would be removed, since residents of the countries would have an incentive to buy the good where it is cheaper and sell it where it is more expensive.

The effects of transportation costs can be seen by comparing a situation in which transportation costs are zero with a situation in which they are positive. In Figure 4–2, a partial equilibrium model similar to Figure 4–1 depicts the trade of coconuts between Bali and Hai. Assume, initially, that trade is under way between Bali and Hai, that transportation costs are zero and that

Hai is exporting coconuts to Bali. $P*$ is the common world price for coconuts. At that price, OQ_B^d coconuts are being consumed in Bali, while OQ_B^s are being produced; and OQ_H^d are being consumed in Hai, while Q_H^s are being produced. The quantity of coconuts being exported by Hai, $(Q_H^s - Q_H^d)$, is equal to the quantity being imported by Bali, $(Q_B^d - Q_B^s)$.

Now assume that positive transportation costs are introduced. The effect will be to drive a wedge between the price of coconuts in Bali and the price in Hai, so that a single international price will no longer exist. The inequality between the prices exists because in order for exporters of coconuts in Hai to be willing to sell coconuts to residents of Bali, they must receive a price which covers the costs of transporting the coconuts to Bali. In equilibrium, the difference in coconut prices in the two countries will be just equal to the per-unit transportation costs.

Suppose the transportation costs per unit of coconuts are equal to an amount shown by t in Figure 4–2. This means that in equilibrium the

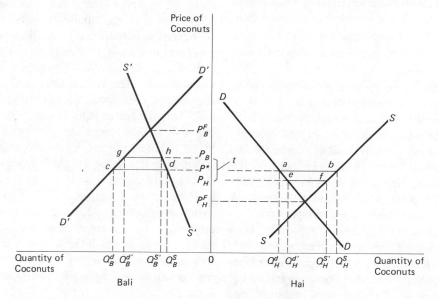

FIGURE 4-2 The Impact of Transportation Costs on Trade

price of coconuts in Bali, the importing country, will stand above the price of coconuts in Hai, the exporting country, by that amount. In other words, if we let P_B represent the price of coconuts in Bali and P_H represent the price in Hai, the difference between P_B and P_H will be equal to t. The reason for the difference is that even though coconut producers in Hai are charging a price equal to P_B to consumers in Bali, a portion of that price must be used by coconut exporters to cover the per-unit transportation costs equal to t. Once those costs have been covered, the price actually received by coconut producers in Hai will be equal to P_H (equal to $P_B - t$). In equilibrium, the quantity of exports from Hai must equal the quantity of imports to Bali, so that *ef* must equal *gh*. If *ef* were not equal to *gh*, the prices would be driven upward or downward until exports become equal to imports.

Note that with positive transportation costs, the quantity of goods traded is lower; imports to Bali have decreased from *cd* to *gh,* and exports from Hai have decreased from *ab* to *ef.* Consumption of coconuts in Bali has fallen from OQ_B^d to $OQ_B^{d'}$, while production has risen from OQ_B^s to $OQ_B^{s'}$. Consumption in Hai has risen from OQ_H^d to $OQ_H^{d'}$, while production has fallen from OQ_H^s to $OQ_H^{s'}$.

The effect of positive transportation costs, as compared to zero transportation costs, is to move the prices and the quantities traded partially back toward the pretrade situation. Indeed, if transportation costs were to equal or exceed the initial, pretrade differences in price between the two countries (if t were equal to greater than $P_B^F - P_H^F$), there would be no trade to begin with. One can think of numerous goods (for example, bricks) that are not typically traded between nations for just this reason. The analysis of trade relationships between countries frequently makes a distinction between traded and nontraded goods. The distinction, of course, rests on transportation costs; nontraded goods are those whose transportation costs makes it unprofitable to trade them between countries. In fact, if there were no transportation costs there would be no nontraded goods.

TRADE UNDER IMPERFECT COMPETITION

So far we have analyzed the process of specialization and trade within a perfectly competitive framework. Although this analysis has been quite useful in establishing some of the fundamental relationships underlying international trade, it has obvious limitations, since most trade takes place in a setting of imperfect competition. In this section, we shall examine conditions that can produce trade patterns considerably different from those suggested by the perfectly competitive models examined previously.

Monopoly in the Domestic Market

In considering imperfect competition in world trade, let us first examine the situation where prior to the opening of trade, the product under consideration is produced in the home country under pure monopoly. Pure monopoly exists when there is a single seller of a given good within a given market. The typical price and quantity decisions of a monopolist are displayed graphically within a partial equilibrium framework in Figure 4–3. The monopolist will maximize profits by producing at the level of output corresponding to the point at which marginal cost *(MC)* equals marginal revenue *(MR);* in Figure 4–3 this occurs at point *C,* which corresponds to the output level Q_1. The monopolist will then refer to the demand curve for its product (*D*) to find the price at which the market will absorb its output level. According to Figure 4–3, the market will be willing to purchase Q_1 at a price equal to P_1.

One further observation regarding the monopolist's price and quantity decision needs to

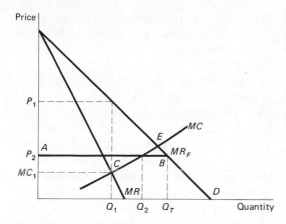

FIGURE 4-3 International Trade with a Domestic Monopolist

be made. The marginal cost curve of the monopolist can be thought of as representing the marginal opportunity cost of producing an extra unit of output. At Q_1, the price set by the monopolist exceeds the marginal costs of producing an additional unit of output ($P_1 > MC_1$). This result is at odds with our conclusions reached earlier, under perfect competition, where the pretrade price of the commodity (i.e., the terms of trade) was shown to be equal to the marginal opportunity costs of producing the commodity. Under a monopoly, however, the producer finds it profitable to restrict the level of output of the commodity and charge a higher price than would prevail under perfect competition.[4]

Now let trade open between the domestic monopolist and a foreign country. Suppose that foreign producers of the commodity are oper-

ating in a perfectly competitive market within their country so that the price they charge will be equal to their marginal opportunity costs. Furthermore, assume that foreign producers have a perfectly elastic export supply curve[5] (as shown by the horizontal line AB in Figure 4–3) and that it occurs at price P_2, which is lower than the pretrade price set by the domestic monopolist. The monopolist will now be unable to set a price higher than P_2, since in that case domestic consumers would simply turn toward imports to satisfy their demand. The effect, then, of introducing the foreign competitors is to change the effective slope of the monopolist's demand curve. It will now be given by the horizontal line AB for quantities less than Q_T, since the monopolist can sell any quantity of output up to Q_T at the price P_2. However, in order to sell levels of output greater than Q_T to the domestic market, the monopolist would have to lower prices according to the original demand curve. When a firm's demand curve is horizontal, it will be identical to the firm's marginal revenue curve. Thus, in Figure 4–3, line AB also represents the marginal revenue curve of the monopolist under free trade (MR_F). Under free trade, then, the monopolist would increase its production from Q_1 to Q_2, where marginal revenue (MR_F) equals marginal cost *(MC)*, and would establish a price equal to P_2. Total domestic demand at P_2 would equal Q_T; the difference between the total quantity demanded and the quantity supplied by the monopolist ($Q_T - Q_2$) of course represents imports.

Two particular results of the opening of trade

[4]Under perfect competition, prior to trade, the domestic industry would produce at point E, where the industry marginal cost curve (or supply curve) intersects the market demand curve. The price associated with point E would equal marginal cost at point E, and is less than the price set by the monopolist, while the quantity produced is greater than that of the monopolist.

[5]The interpretation of a perfectly elastic supply curve and its representation as a horizontal line is that the foreign industry is willing and able to supply an infinite quantity to the home country at the price, P_2. That is, the price does not have to increase in order for the foreign industry to increase the quantity supplied. This implies that the importing country is small relative to the foreign exporting country.

need to be underscored and explained. The first is the pattern of trade that emerges. As mentioned above, the marginal cost of foreign producers is equal to their price, P_2; this is greater than the pretrade marginal cost of the domestic monopolist (MC_1). This suggests that the home country has a comparative advantage in the production of this good. However, in our example, we have demonstrated that the home country might import the commodity if a domestic monopoly prevails. Although this apparent violation of the law of comparative advantage (which is based on marginal opportunity costs) will not *always* occur under monopoly, the pretrade divergence between price and marginal costs makes it a possibility.

The second result is that the monopoly power of the domestic producer has been eroded by the introduction of foreign competition. The domestic monopolist has been forced to increase its output and to sell at a lower price in response to foreign competition. In addition, domestic consumers are "better off" since the total quantity consumed has increased and is being purchased at the lower price.

If the foreign producers, instead, were to establish a price which exceeded both the pretrade price of the monopolist and the monopolist's marginal cost, then the monopolist would enjoy a comparative advantage in terms of both price and marginal costs. Under such a situation, the law of comparative advantage would hold unambiguously; the monopolist would increase the production of the commodity and export it to the foreign country upon the opening of trade.

pricing practices of an exporting monopolist

When a monopolist exports a good, a question arises regarding the monopolist's pricing strategy. The monopolist may simply set a uniform price for both domestic and export sales based on combined foreign and domestic demand. On the other hand, the exporter may find

it possible and profitable to separate the domestic and foreign markets, charging a different price at home and abroad; such a practice is known as *price discrimination*.

Price discrimination at the international level, in which the exporter finds it profitable to charge a lower price in the foreign country than it charges in its home country, is referred to as *dumping*. There are two conditions that must exist for dumping to occur. First, the exporter must be able to separate the two markets. Otherwise, the lower priced exports might be purchased and then resold in the domestic market, thereby undercutting the differential pricing scheme the monopolist is attempting to establish. Second, foreign demand for the product must be more price elastic than domestic demand in order for dumping to be profitable to the exporter.

Dumping is illustrated in Figure 4–4, where it is assumed that a monopolist is selling its output in both the home and foreign markets. The foreign demand curve (D_F), in the left-hand panel, is assumed to be more elastic than the domestic curve (D) in the right-hand panel. For convenience, the quantity axis of the foreign market is reversed, measuring output from right to left. The analysis is further simplified by assuming that the marginal costs (MC) of the firm are constant. Under these conditions, the firm will maximize profits by equating marginal cost and marginal revenue in each market; establishing the price P_F in the foreign market and a higher price, P_D, in the domestic market.

Complaints by import-competing industries against dumping by their foreign competitors are common in most industrialized countries, and have been increasing in recent years. These industries feel that the practice of dumping places them at an unfair competitive disadvantage, and they have reacted by petitioning their governments for protection. While import-competing industries may feel they are placed at a disadvantage by dumping, consumers in the importing country will benefit, since they will face a

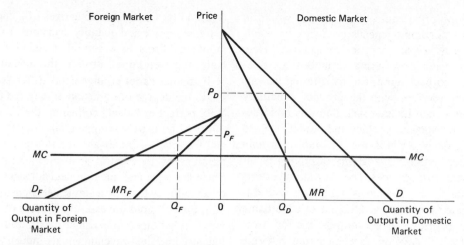

FIGURE 4-4 Dumping by a World Monopolist

lower price for the good than would be the case if the foreign firm set a common price in all markets. There is thus a conflict between the interest of consumers and producers in the importing country with regard to the foreign dumping of imports. We shall have more to say about the reactions of governments to complaints of dumping as well as other important aspects of this problem in Chapter 14.

OTHER WORLD MARKET STRUCTURES

Most markets are characterized by neither pure monopoly nor perfect competition. In fact, most international trade in manufactured goods or in mineral resources takes place under conditions of either oligopoly or monopolistic competition. Oligopoly is a market structure in which there is a small number of sellers. No one seller can completely dominate the market, and the rivalry among the participants can be fierce. Each firm in the industry is very sensitive to its rival's actions, and it must carefully evaluate the potential response by its rivals to any actions of

its own. Under this type of market structure, just as with monopoly, there can be significant differences between commodity prices and their corresponding marginal costs.

Under monopolistic competition, the number of firms in the industry is so large that no one firm can dominate or even strongly influence the overall market. On the other hand, product differentiation is a fundamental characteristic of this type of market structure, and a firm can exercise limited control over the market for its particular differentiated product. Although prices will equal average costs in the long run under monopolistic competition, there will still tend to be some discrepancy between prices and marginal costs.

Product Differentiation and Nonprice Competition

Product differentiation can occur under oligopoly as well as under monopolistic competition, especially in the manufacturing industries. Product differentiation has an important effect on the way in which firms compete for their share of the market. Instead of relying heavily on price competition, as they would in a market for homogeneous products, firms engage extensively in "nonprice competition." Here they compete by offering variations of style, quality and packaging, and by offering various ancillary services with the product. Ancillary services would include such items as rapid delivery, assistance in setting the product up and training the buyer in its use, favorable warranty conditions and the availability of prompt repair and spare parts services. There are strong efforts to establish brand loyalties in markets with differentiated products, and the use of advertising can be extensive. It is even possible for "two-way" trade to develop, as when automobiles are exported from the United States to Germany at the same time that automobiles of a different brand are exported from Germany to the United States. Obviously, the different makes of automobiles offer different qualities and features, and therefore really represent different products, aimed at different segments of the market.

CARTELS

We have seen that oligopolistic market structures are often characterized by differentiated products and extensive nonprice competition among the rival firms. However, this does not mean that price competition is absent. Price competition can be just as fierce among oligopolistic firms as it can among firms operating under other market structures, especially when the products are relatively homogeneous. Price wars, in which rival firms competitively slash prices, can and do erupt, resulting in reduced profits for all firms. Because of this threat of mutually destructive price competition, firms have an incentive to collude in making their price and quantity decisions.

To avoid price competition in the world market, oligopolistic firms may form a *cartel*, which is a formal organization of producers of a given commodity. One of the objectives of a cartel is to transfer price and quantity decisions from the individual firms to a central decision-making body, representing all firms in the industry.

Particular cartel arrangements differ according to the degree of collusion among the firms. With perfect or "ideal" collusion, the objective of the cartel is to maximize total industry profit and the level of prices and total output are determined by the central decision-making unit. Since the price and quantity decisions are made on an industry level by a single decision-making unit, the decisions are essentially those of a monopolist. Industry profits will be maximized where industry marginal revenue equals industry marginal cost. In Figure 4–5, industry marginal revenue (MR_I) would equal industry marginal cost (MC_I) at point E, with the industry producing Q_1, and setting a price equal to P_1. A mechanism must then be established by which total cartel output (and profits) is distributed among the member firms. Arriving at a distribution satisfactory to all members is probably the most difficult task the cartel must face.

This "ideal" monopoly solution is not often achieved in practice, however. Decisions are often made by negotiation, with each member

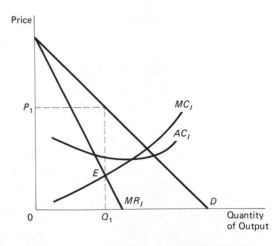

FIGURE 4-5 "Ideal" Monopoly Solution Under a Cartel

firm or country pressing for its own individual objectives. The differences in individual goals will require compromise if a result approximating the ideal solution is to be attained.

Once a cartel is established, incentives arise for individual member firms to leave the cartel and operate independently. If a single firm were to price below the common cartel price, this would attract additional sales to that firm (at the expense of the other members), possibly increasing its profits above what they would be under the cartel. However, if other cartel members follow suit and reduce their prices, all firms will receive both lower prices and profits than they enjoyed under the cartel arrangement. Because of the incentive for individual members to leave the cartel and establish prices independently, the life span of most cartels has been short.

Organization of Petroleum Exporting Countries[6]

Perhaps the most successful international cartel in recent history is OPEC, whose members control a large proportion of the world's petroleum production. Although OPEC was organized in 1960, it did not really operate as a cartel at first. During the early 1970s, however, the members of OPEC, acting in concert, began raising the price of oil. By 1981 the price had been pushed to approximately $34 per barrel, a dramatic increase when compared to the 1969 price of $1.84. The fact that OPEC was able to impose price increases of this magnitude and garner hundreds of billions of dollars in additional oil revenues attests to its market power. Although there is some evidence that the power

[6]In Chapter 3 we discussed the impact of OPEC on the terms of trade of both oil-exporting nations (OPEC nations) and oil-importing nations. In this section we concentrate on the price and output policies of OPEC as it operates as an international cartel.

of OPEC may be waning during the 1980s, there is no question that it has been enormously successful.

An intersting question is why OPEC was able to achieve such success, when attempts to cartelize the production and sale of other commodities has been notably unsuccessful. There are several reasons, the foremost being the nature of the world market for oil. During the 1960s and 1970s, world demand for petroleum products increased dramatically. Because the non–OPEC nations only accounted for a small fraction of world oil production, the result was an increased dependence by the oil-importing nations upon OPEC oil. As an example, in 1970 the United States imported 23.3 percent of its total oil consumption. This percentage skyrocketed to 44.7 percent by 1979, and most of this increase came from OPEC. Because of the limited competition from nonmember producing nations, OPEC was able to set and maintain high prices, and individual members were able to maintain their lofty profits. Under these circumstances, there was little incentive for members to break away from the cartel in hopes of increasing individual profits.

The outlook for OPEC's continued success, however, is more clouded. In the long run, we would expect that OPEC's high oil prices would attract greater competition, both from the non–OPEC oil-producing nations and from alternative energy sources. It should also stimulate efforts on the part of consumers to conserve petroleum. In fact, these long-run effects are beginning to appear in the 1980s. The increase in the price of petroleum has stimulated non–OPEC oil production throughout the world, most notably in Mexico and in the North Sea area. Also, regions that were previously deemed to be noneconomical for petroleum production are now being extensively explored. Meanwhile the world demand for petroleum actually declined in 1980 from its 1979 level, and stood at its lowest point since 1976. Although this was partially due to a slowdown in the rate of economic growth in the industrialized countries (the main consumers of oil), there are clear indications that conservation efforts, stimulated by the OPEC–induced price increases, have begun to reduce petroleum demand. The greater fuel efficiency of automobiles and the additional energy-saving features of new homes are examples of these conservation efforts. World petroleum demand is also declining due to the fact that many consuming nations are steadily shifting to alternative forms of energy to meet their needs. Increasing use of coal, nuclear power, and natural gas, as well as other alternatives, signals a declining dependence on OPEC–produced oil.

The largest producing member of OPEC, Saudi Arabia, has recognized the long-run effects of high petroleum prices, and in 1981 attempted to convince its fellow members to hold the line on oil prices to prevent the consuming nations from shifting to other sources of energy. When it became clear to the Saudis that the other OPEC members would not cooperate in this strategy, they deliberately set production levels high enough to create a surplus of oil on the world market. At the same time, the Saudis began to set prices below those of their fellow members, which placed further pressure on the other OPEC members to reduce their prices.

This disagreement over pricing represented the most serious division within OPEC since its inception. Whether or not OPEC will continue to operate as a successful international cartel will depend on the ability of its members to resolve differences peacefully, as well as on the ability of consuming nations to reduce their dependence on OPEC oil.

QUESTIONS AND EXERCISES

1. How might the presence of a monopolist in one trading nation alter the pattern of trade between two nations that would exist under perfect competition? Is it necessarily the case that the pattern of trade will change? Use graphical models to answer these questions.

2. Suppose you were assigned by the President to arrive at a policy decision on whether he should take action to discourage foreign firms from dumping their products in the United States. Present arguments on both sides of the issue, making sure that the viewpoints of all relevant segments of society are considered.

3. The United States both exports and imports computers from Japan. How is this possible? Is this trade pattern a violation of the law of comparative advantage?

4. What are the advantages to a group of producers of cartelizing their output on the world market? What conditions would favor the achievement of these benefits? Relate your answer to the experience of OPEC.

5. If exporters in your country belonged to a successful international cartel, would you recommend a policy which attempted to eliminate their participation? Be sure to consider the effects of a cartel on the prices of traded goods and the trade patterns of your nation.

6. What is the impact of transportation costs on the price of a traded good? Using graphical analysis (partial equilibrium), show how the introduction of transportation costs could completely eliminate trade (i.e., move the two countries back to their pretrade positions).

7. Answer this question on the basis of the following information:

	MOC of Computers	MOC of Automobiles
U.S.	1/4 auto	4 computers
Japan	20 autos	1/20 computer

Assume a constant exchange rate between the U.S. dollar ($) and Japanese yen ($Y$) of $10Y = \$1.00$. Select money prices for autos and computers in the United States and Japan which are consistent with the above information on MOC. Then determine the pattern of trade between the United States and Japan on the basis of money prices. Is it consistent with the pattern predicted on the basis of MOC alone?

Dynamic Aspects of International Trade 5

Up to this point our analysis of international trade has been conducted in a static framework, one which examines trade patterns at a point in time with the forces that determine trade patterns held fixed. Under these assumptions, once international equilibrium is attained the volume and direction of trade, as well as the international terms of trade, will not change. In actuality, it is clear that the patterns of international trade are undergoing constant change. Thus, if we are to obtain a more accurate picture of world trade patterns, we must consider the dynamic aspects of trade—that is, how the determinants of trade change over time. In this chapter, then, we shall expand our analysis and consider the effects of changing factor endowments, changing technology, changing demand patterns and random disturbances on the pattern of international trade.

ECONOMIC GROWTH

Factor Growth and Factor Prices

Even if factors of production were perfectly immobile internationally, we would find that the resource base of most countries undergoes constant change. This, in turn, affects the costs of the various goods being produced by a country and the country's ability to compete in world markets for these goods. The Heckscher–Ohlin framework (discussed in Chapter 3) provides some guidance in analyzing the effects of changes in factor endowments on the cost of producing tradeable goods, and on trade patterns themselves. Although the Heckscher–Ohlin theorem itself was developed under an assumption of fixed factor endowments, it did suggest that a country would have relatively lower costs (compared to its foreign trading partner) in producing those goods that require intensive use of the factors of production in which that country is relatively abundant. The relative abundance of a given factor would cause it to be relatively cheap. This, in turn, would permit relatively cheap production of these goods requiring heavy inputs of that factor. If the price of a factor is inversely related to its abundance, then an increase in its supply would *(ceteris paribus)* lower its relative price. This, in turn, would alter relative international production costs and could change existing international trade patterns.

Whether or not growth in a particular factor of production increases or decreases a country's volume of trade will depend upon whether it is used intensively in the country's import-competing sector or in its export industry.[1] To illustrate this point, suppose that a nation is exporting fish, which are relatively capital-intensive and importing coconuts, which are relatively labor-intensive. An increase in the quantity of capital in that nation will lower the cost of capital, which, in turn, will lower the cost of fish production. This will further strengthen the country's comparative advantage in fish, and will cause its production of fish to expand. There are now more fish available for export, which increases the volume of international trade.[2]

---

[1] We are assuming that the relative demand for the two goods remains constant or, in other words, that the two goods are consumed in the same proportion as before growth.

[2] T. M. Rybczynski has shown that if all the Heckscher–Ohlin assumptions hold, and if the country being analyzed is so small as to be a price-taker for both goods in the world market, an increase in the factor used intensively in one good will cause an absolute increase in the output of that good and an absolute decline in the output of the other. If the expanding good is the export good and the contracting good is the import good, the country will have more of the export good available for trading, and will become even more dependent upon foreign supplies of the imported good.

Growth based on expansion of the factor used intensively in the production of the export commodity is thus referred to as *protrade biased growth*.

On the other hand, if the expanding factor of production is the one used intensively in the import-competing industry, the country's output of this good will rise. In our above example, if the nation's labor force were to increase, lowering the relative price of labor, then the cost and price of coconuts, its imported good, will decline. The nation will shift its demand toward domestically produced coconuts, making the country less dependent on imports of coconuts and thus reducing the volume of trade. In addition, if the expanding import-competing industry draws resources away from the export industry, the export industry will have to contract. Growth based on expansion of the factor used intensively in the import-competing industry is thus called *antitrade biased growth*.

In the likely circumstance that both factors of production are growing over time, the outcome will depend on the relative rates of growth of the factors and the relative intensities with which they are used in the two industries. A more detailed analysis of the relative degree of pro- or antitrade biased growth is left to advanced texts. For our purposes, it is easy to see how changing factor endowments can affect the relative costs and production levels of traded goods and, in turn, the patterns of international trade. Now let us briefly examine the impact of protrade biased factor growth on the relative prices of the traded goods.

Factor Growth and the Terms of Trade

Our present discussion will be limited to the case in which growth occurs only in the factor used intensively in the production of the export commodity. This will lead to an increase in the production of the exportable good, resulting in an excess supply of the exportable good at the prevailing international terms of trade. If the country is large enough to be able to influence world price, the price of exports relative to the price of imports will decline. That is, protrade biased growth will result in a worsening of the country's terms of trade. Recalling from earlier chapters, a deterioration in the terms of trade, by itself, would move the country to a lower community indifference curve. The extent of such a deterioration depends on several factors, including the price elasticities of foreign and domestic demand and supply for the two goods.

Protrade biased growth, then, will have two effects on the welfare of the country in which the factor growth is taking place: (1) the total output of the country will be expanding, with export production increasing relatively more than import production and (2) the price of exports relative to the price of imports will be declining. Whether the benefits of increasing output exceed the losses associated with the deterioration of the terms of trade will determine if the country is better or worse off because of growth. If the negative terms of trade effect outweighs the positive effect of increased production, the growth that generated this outcome is termed *immiserizing growth*.

Immiserizing growth is particularly relevant to the situation of the less-developed countries which frequently desire to improve their economic well-being by means of economic growth based on expanding exports. The gains from such growth might be foiled, however, if it is accompanied by a worsening of the terms of trade. Chapter 19 will discuss the evidence regarding the long-term movements in the terms of trade of the less-developed countries. For the present, it is important to understand how changing factor supplies can affect trade patterns and the prices of traded goods.

INTERNATIONAL MOBILITY OF PRODUCTIVE FACTORS

So far, we have discussed the possibility of changes in factor endowments within a country while maintaining the assumption that factors are perfectly immobile between countries. Relaxing this assumption provides yet another source of change in factor endowments. For example, if labor migrates from country A to country B, there will be a simultaneous reduction in the supply of labor in country A and an increase in the supply in country B. This will alter the relative resource endowments and will change the relative costs of producing traded goods in both countries.

Once again, the Heckscher–Ohlin framework offers a useful starting point in analyzing these results. Suppose there are two countries, Bali and Hai, each producing two goods, fish and coconuts, using two factors of production, capital and labor. Also assume that fish production is relatively capital-intensive and coconut production is relatively labor-intensive and that Bali is relatively capital abundant and Hai is relatively labor abundant. This assures that the ratio of the price of capital to the price of labor will be lower in Bali than in Hai. Now suppose trade opens between the two countries. According to the Heckscher–Ohlin analysis, in which factors are perfectly immobile between countries, Bali would specialize in and export fish to Hai, and Hai would specialize in and export coconuts to Bali.

Suppose, however, that labor and capital were mobile internationally. Under such conditions, labor would begin migrating from Hai, where it is relatively cheap, to Bali, where it is relatively expensive. Likewise, capital would begin migrating from Bali to Hai. This migration of factors would change the relative factor supplies in both countries. This, in turn, would change the relative factor prices; the ratio of the price of capital to the price of labor would rise in Bali and fall in Hai. This would occur as capital became more scarce in Bali and more abundant in Hai, and as labor became more scarce in Hai and more abundant in Bali. In the limiting case of perfect international factor mobility, the migration would continue until relative factor prices in the two countries became equal.

Under perfect competition, a factor's relative price reflects its relative marginal productivity. This means that the relatively low price of capital in Bali, prior to migration, reflects the relatively low productivity of capital in Bali. Likewise, the relatively low price of labor in Hai reflects the relatively low productivity of labor in Hai. The migration of capital from Bali to Hai and the migration of labor from Hai to Bali means that each factor would be moving from the country in which its marginal productivity is relatively low to the country in which its marginal productivity is relatively high. This international reallocation of resources toward areas of higher productivity would produce a more efficient international distribution of resources, and would result in a higher output of fish and coconuts in both countries. Thus, international mobility of factors of production can increase the joint output of the two countries, just as international specialization and trade can when factors are perfectly immobile internationally. In this sense, international factor mobility can be viewed as a substitute for international trade in producing the gains from specialization (although trade between the countries can still occur). The "gains" would be captured through a more efficient allocation of resources *across* countries, rather than through specialization and resource reallocation *within* countries, as under the Heckscher–Ohlin assumptions.

In the real world, factors of production do have some international mobility, although it is far from perfect. Labor does migrate internationally, as when, for example, unskilled guest workers from Greece, Yugoslavia and Italy find temporary work in German and Swiss factories, or when multinational corporations send skilled labor or management specialists to work abroad in a foreign subsidiary. In fact, the international mobility of not only skilled and managerial labor, but also of capital and technology, has been increased by the spread of the multinational enterprise. We will have more to say about multinational enterprises in Part VIII, but for now it is important to recognize that MNEs are increasingly sensitive to opportunities to transfer factors of production worldwide to obtain improvements in productivity.

MORE RECENT THEORIES OF TRADE

By incorporating economic growth into our analysis of international trade, we have made a significant extension of our earlier static analysis. However, our analysis of economic growth, although dynamic in nature, has still been couched in terms of the traditional Heckscher–Ohlin comparative cost framework. Dissatisfaction with the Heckscher–Ohlin framework has resulted in the development of several new theories of trade. Although these newer theories differ in specifics, they do share several common strains of thought. In particular, they emphasize that the development of trade patterns is a dynamic process, with trade relationships among countries changing over time. Although these more recent theories were developed as alternatives to the Heckscher–Ohlin comparative-cost approach, it will be argued that they should be viewed as complements to, rather than replacements of, traditional trade theory.

Income and Tastes as Determinants of Trade

In traditional trade theory, comparative advantage is based on differences in relative production costs, which rest, in turn, on differences in relative factor prices. If relative factor prices were identical across countries, no trade would occur at all; or, conversely, the greater the divergence in relative factor prices, the greater would be the scope for trade. This would imply that the volume of trade should be greater among countries having greater differences in relative factor prices. If this were true, we would expect to find a larger flow of trade between highly industrialized countries and less-developed countries than among the highly industrialized countries themselves. This would follow from the fact that the ratio of the cost of labor to the cost of capital tends to be much lower in less-developed countries than in highly industrialized countries.

Real world observations suggest that exactly the opposite is true; the volume of trade among industrialized countries far outweighs the volume of trade between industrialized and less-developed countries. One possible explanation is that the industrialized economies have such enormous capacities to produce, as well as to consume, that a large volume of trade can occur among the advanced countries on the basis of relatively small differences in relative factor costs. The huge demand for imports by the industrialized countries simply cannot be met by the non-industrialized countries and must be largely met by trade among the industrialized countries themselves.

Another explanation has been offered by Staffan B. Linder, who argues that trade in manufactured goods that are nonhomogeneous depends more upon similarities in tastes across countries than upon differences in production costs. Firms within a country are primarily oriented toward producing goods for which there is a large home market. This determines the set of goods these firms will have to offer when they begin to export. The most promising foreign markets for such exports will be found in countries with similar tastes. The menu of goods demanded within an economy, as well as the quality of these goods, depends largely on the country's per capita income and its state of development. If an exporting country is highly industrialized, it is more likely to find attractive markets in other countries with similar preferences; that is, in other industrialized countries rather than in less-developed countries. Thus it is not surprising that the majority of world trade occurs among the industrialized countries.

The Linder thesis, in addition to helping to explain a given pattern of world trade, offers some insight into changing trade patterns. As per capita income grows within a country, its residents will be able to afford a larger quantity of the goods offered on world markets, and their tastes will tend to move closer to those in the more advanced economies. As a result, both the volume and the characteristics of foreign goods demanded by this country will change. Thus the very process of economic growth and development can affect the volume and composition of world trade by affecting the demand preferences of trading nations.

In addition to experiencing changes in per capita income, growing countries typically undergo changes in population itself. Rapidly increasing population can produce a rapid increase in the demand for goods, including foreign goods, even if per capita demand remains constant. In addition, the structure of a country's population tends to shift over time, with changes occurring in the percentage of persons in different age groups, in different occupations, and in urban versus rural locations. Because people within these different groups demand somewhat different sets of goods and services, shifts in the sizes of these groups can produce shifts in the set of goods demanded from abroad.

Technology Gaps as a Basis for Trade

Technology can be defined as the body of knowledge and skills available for use in the production of goods and services. Technological change affects world trade by constantly bringing new goods into the market and by improving the methods used to produce existing products. However, technological change does not affect all nations equally. New technology is generated primarily in the industrialized countries, where the size of markets and the scale of output permit significant outlays for research and development. Although technology, once developed, can spread rapidly, it is not always readily applicable to the less-developed economies. Even among industrialized countries the spread of technology can be inhibited by the time required for foreign firms to recognize and imitate it, and by the existence of patents and other legal constraints on its diffusion.

Because technology is not equally accessible to all countries, "technology gaps" emerge in which the most advanced technology is concentrated in relatively few countries. Not surprisingly, these countries tend to develop strong comparative advantages in high-technology items. As the more advanced countries concentrate in the production of high-technology goods, the comparative advantage in lower technology items may pass to countries further behind in the development process. Having established the importance of technology in determining comparative advantage, let us examine several recent propositions regarding the influence of changing technology on trade patterns.

Product Life Cycle Theory of Trade

Recognition of the importance of technology in determining world trade patterns has led to the development of a theory in which shifts in comparative advantage are based explicitly on the spread of technology. The *product life cycle theory,* as it is called, was first advanced by Raymond Vernon. It examines the trade patterns that evolve from the time a new product is introduced by a particular country to the time when the technology required for its production is available on a worldwide basis. According to Vernon, a newly developed product will pass through several stages of development, each stage having a different effect on trade patterns. The theory is most applicable to trade in manufactured products. Our discussion will categorize a product's development into three stages.

new product stage

Vernon begins with the proposition that entrepreneurs located within a particular market are more likely to be aware of the opportunity of introducing a new product in that market than producers located elsewhere. This is because of their proximity to the market and their familiarity with local demand conditions. Using the United States as his frame of reference, Vernon suggests that because of the relatively high per capita income level and high per-unit labor costs in the United States, the most likely candidates for new products will be found among those consumer goods that appeal to high income levels and among labor-saving capital goods. The product, in its earliest stage, will typically be unstandardized, meaning that the producer is attempting to develop the product characteristics that best satisfy consumer preferences. Production of the newly developed product will more than likely be located in the country of origin, since there is an overwhelming advantage, early in the product's life, in maintaining close communications with both customers and input suppliers.

maturing product stage

As the domestic market for the product expands, and domestic producers become familiar with the characteristics of the market, the product's design becomes more standardized. Standardization will enable the producers to achieve economies of scale through mass production.

Although the primary market for the product will initially be in the home country, demand for the product will eventually spread to foreign markets. The principal foreign markets will be those having demand patterns similar to those of the home country. If the new product is suited for high-income preferences, or is essentially a labor-saving innovation, Vernon argues that the most likely foreign markets would be those with high income levels and high labor costs. Thus, a product that is first developed in the United States will find its most likely foreign markets in such places as the Western European nations and Japan. The emphasis on demand characteristics as determinants of the pattern of trade should be recognized as an offshoot of Linder's hypothesis.

During this stage, producers begin to perceive the costs of production as an important consideration in determining the location of production. In fact, as the foreign markets develop, those countries themselves become prime candidates for production locations. If the original producers calculate that the commodity can be produced at a lower cost abroad than at home (taking account of transportation costs), the competitive position of the domestic producers may be enhanced by a relocation of production. With any such relocation there will be a displacement of exports from the home country. In fact, if the discrepancy in costs is substantial, the product may be produced in the foreign country and exported to third countries and even back to the originating country itself.

During this stage, it is probable that foreign producers will recognize the opportunities for gain and will also enter into the production of the commodity. This will, of course, displace home country exports even further. It should be noted that Vernon's emphasis on the influence of relative costs in determining the production locations suggests that the product life cycle theory is not totally divorced from the traditional, comparative costs theory of trade.

standardized product stage

As the product reaches an advanced stage of standardization, costs of production will become the predominant determinant of the location of production. By this time producers are quite familiar with the market for the product, so that the need for close communication between producers and consumers is diminished. In this situation, less-developed countries may provide the most attractive production locations, especially if production is relatively labor intensive, because of their relatively lower labor costs. If such a shift in production location occurs, exports from less-developed countries will further displace the production of the commodity in the home country.

The trade pattern of a newly developed product, as predicted by the product life cycle theory, is displayed in Figure 5–1. This figure shows the production and consumption of the new product, over time, by the country of origin. As is evident in Figure 5–1, the quantity of exports (production minus consumption) is at its peak during the middle of the mature product stage, when foreign demand first appears. As the mature product stage proceeds, and some home producers move production abroad, both home production and exports begin to decline. Finally, as the standardized product stage is reached, home country production declines significantly, until the country becomes a net importer of the product.

the role of technology in the product life cycle

The driving force behind the product life cycle theory of trade is the transmission of the technology associated with the new product, either in product design, quality, or production technology, from one country to another. Vernon thought the primary mechanism for transferring technology was the relocation of productive fa-

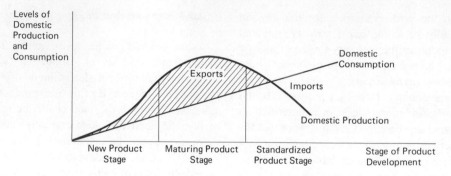

FIGURE 5-1 The Trade Patterns of the Originating Country During the Product's Life Cycle

cilities by the original, home country firms. Others have emphasized that technology is often directly transferred to foreign producers.

Such a transfer can be brought about by licensing arrangements (whereby use of the technological knowhow is sold to the foreign firm), joint ventures between home and foreign producers, direct imitation, and even industrial espionage. The interval between the innovating country's initial production and the initial production by the imitating country is referred to by M.V. Posner as the "imitation lag." Gary C. Hufbauer, in a meticulous study of the trade patterns of synthetic materials, found that, on average, the imitation lags for new products in this group has declined during the period between 1910 and 1960. Since Hufbauer's study, it is likely that the imitation lag has been shortened even further, due to the proliferation of multinational firms and their subsidiaries which facilitate the international transmission of technology.[3] If imitation lags are in fact becoming shorter, the implication is that, if a country is to maintain a net export position through innovation, that innovation must be an ongoing process.

[3]More will be said about the role of the multinational enterprise in the international transmission of technology in Part VIII.

The process of innovation and export would require that a country which exports technologically-advanced products maintain substantial levels of research and development within its export industries. Evidence of this was found by Donald Keesing in his study regarding the concentration of skill levels in export industries of selected countries (see Table 3–3). Keesing found a greater proportion of the type of skilled labor involved in research and development efforts (scientists and engineers) in export industries of the industrialized countries (exporters of high-technology goods) than in those of other countries.

the product life cycle theory—an example

Insight into the role of the transfer of technology can be obtained by considering individual cases. Although the patterns of technology transfer and shifts in production location will vary from product to product, the development of trade in assembled monochrome (black and white) television receivers provides an example, in which the trade pattern seems to have followed the path suggested by the product life cycle theory.

Television receivers were first introduced by U.S. producers in the late 1940s, and until the late 1950s the United States accounted for the vast majority of world production. During this period, the United States was a net exporter of television receivers, mostly to Western Europe and Japan, countries with high income levels and thus similar demand characteristics. In the late 1950s and early 1960s, foreign production of television receivers began to accelerate, particularly in Japan. The result was displacement of U.S. exports to those countries; this trend continued until in 1962 the United States began importing receivers from Japan. Imports continued to grow during the 1960s, and by 1970 they exceeded domestic production and accounted for 52 percent of total U.S. consumption.

The pattern of U.S. television receiver imports warrants closer investigation. Through the mid-1960s essentially all receiver imports by the United States came from Japan (99 percent in 1965). These developments suggest that Japan had imported U.S. production technology, improved upon it, and become a dominant force in the world market for television receivers. In fact, throughout the 1960s, U.S. producers had difficulty meeting the price of the Japanese products.

As time passed, and the product became more standardized in quality and production technique, cost conditions became the most important determinant of production location. As a result, U.S. manufacturers began to locate their own television assembly operations in the low-wage areas of the Far East in an effort to lower costs and become more price competitive. By 1970, Japan's share of U.S. imports had dropped to 73 percent, while imports from Taiwan and Korea accounted for 20 percent. The vast majority of imports from the latter two nations were produced by subsidiaries of multinational enterprises headquartered in the United States. Although there may be minor discrepancies between the development of trade in television receivers and the pattern predicted by the prod-uct life cycle theory, the parallels do appear to be quite strong.

Product Life Cycle and Traditional Trade Theory

In the introduction to this section, we mentioned that the more recent theories of international trade are best interpreted as complements to the traditional comparative-cost approach. In fact, in discussing the later phases of the product life cycle theory, we made particular note of the influence of relative production costs in determining the location of the production of a standardized product.

There are other ways in which the newer theories of trade tie in with earlier trade theory. An implication of the product life cycle is that a country will export a new product if it holds a competitive edge in the technology associated with the product. Since one of the most important factors underlying the development of technology is human capital (a country's stock of skills and knowledge), we would expect the countries exporting technologically advanced goods would be those that are relatively abundant in human capital. After a particular technology has been transmitted to another country, the innovating country may no longer be relatively abundant in those particular skills and therefore will lose its comparative advantage in the product. Once the trading partners obtain the technology necessary to produce a product, as well as the human capital needed to implement the technology, the relative costs of production (determined by the relative endowments of capital and unskilled labor) will largely determine the pattern of trade. Thus these more recent theories of trade do not appear to be in conflict with the more traditional theories as one might first think. They might more accurately be perceived as logical extensions of previous theory into a dynamic setting, with a greater emphasis on the role of technology or human capital as a factor of production.

QUESTIONS AND EXERCISES

1. How can you account for the fact that comparative advantage patterns seem to shift over time?

2. Suppose there is an increase in the quantity of a particular factor of production, say capital, available to an economy. Maintaining all of the Heckscher–Ohlin assumptions, trace the effects of this increase through changes in relative factor prices and relative production costs to the effect on the nation's pattern of trade. Be explicit about whether the imported good or the exported good is capital-intensive.

3. Discuss the ways in which the spread of technology can affect international trade patterns.

4. Evaluate the proposition that, because of the rapid transmission of technology, the United States will soon lose its comparative advantage in high-technology items.

5. Discuss the effects of rapid population growth on the composition of goods a country will demand on world markets.

6. How would you account for the fact that there is a much larger quantity of trade among industrialized countries than between industrialized countries and nonindustrialized countries?

7. Comment on the following statement. The Heckscher–Ohlin explanation of trade patterns should probably be dismissed completely since we now have other theories of trade, completely unrelated to H–O, which provide better insights as to why nations trade various goods.

8. A new product recently developed by Japanese entrepreneurs is the industrial robot, which is intended to perform industrial tasks previously performed by labor. Currently, Japan is the world's dominant producer and exporter of robots. To whom do you think Japan is exporting the robots, and why? Also, present a scenario of how international trade in robots might proceed in the future.

The Foreign Exchange Market 6

In chapters 2 through 5, much of the analysis of international trade was developed without reference to currency units; Bali bartered fish to Hai in exchange for coconuts. In this chapter, we shall examine the role of money and exchange rates in international economic relations. The focus will be on the foreign exchange market, a worldwide market in which currencies of the various nations are traded. *Foreign exchange* itself is a term applied to foreign currency in general. From the point of view of a U.S. resident, the Japanese yen, the British pound sterling, and the German deutsche mark are foreign exchange. From the point of view of a resident of Germany, the dollar, the pound, and the yen are foreign exchange.

An exchange rate is the rate at which one currency trades for another on the foreign exchange market. Thus, if $2.00 are selling for £1, the exchange rate is $2.00 per pound, or £.50 per dollar. The exchange rate not only states the price of one currency in terms of another, it also serves as a medium for translating prices of goods and services quoted in one currency into prices expressed in another. Thus a potential U.S. importer can take the sterling price of a given British good and multiply it by the dollar-sterling exchange rate (expressed in dollars per pound) to obtain the dollar price of the British good. This facilitates comparison of home and foreign prices in deciding where to buy a given commodity. To illustrate, suppose a case of British scotch whiskey costs £60 in London, and a case of comparable whiskey costs $130 in the United States. This information, alone, would be of little value in comparing British and U.S. liquor prices. However, if the exchange rate between the dollar and the pound is $2.00 per pound, we can multiply the British price, £60, by the exchange rate and find that the British price expressed in dollars is $120; the British whiskey is cheaper than the U.S. whiskey. Note that the dollar price of British goods will change if the exchange rate changes even if the pound-price of British goods remains constant.

ORGANIZATION AND PROCEDURES IN THE FOREIGN EXCHANGE MARKET

In principle, the foreign exchange market encompasses all transactions involving the exchange of currencies. Unlike some financial markets, such as the New York Stock Exchange, the foreign exchange market is not located in any one place. Instead, it is more analogous to the over-the-counter securities market in that transactions are conducted primarily over the telephone or teletype, and the market is spread over financial centers throughout the free world. The major participants in the market consist of large commercial banks, their customers, and a network of brokers, who specialize in trading specific currencies, and who frequently intermediate in transactions between banks within a given financial center.

The commercial banks, by far the largest dealers in the market, act primarily on behalf of their customers, who are engaged in trading goods, services and assets with foreigners. Transactions among banks and brokers make up what is known as the "wholesale market," whereas transactions between banks and their customers make up the "retail market." The banks make a profit by charging slightly more for foreign exchange than they have to pay for it. There is, thus, a small difference between the "buying" and "selling" prices of foreign currency.

Commercial Bank Functions in Clearing International Payments

Since commercial banks play such an important role in almost all international financial transactions, we should have a closer look at how they serve their customers in providing facilities for making international payments. To service international customers, a bank will enter a *correspondent* relationship with other banks around the world. These banks agree to cooperate in clearing international payments among customers in each of the countries. When a U.S. bank enters a correspondent relationship with, say, a British bank, each will establish, in the other, a demand deposit denominated in the currency of the other country. The U.S. bank will thus hold a sterling demand deposit in the British bank, and the British bank will hold a dollar demand deposit in the U.S. bank.[1]

Suppose, now, that a U.S. importer buys £200 worth of goods from a British exporter and that he must pay for these goods in sterling. There are a number of ways by which payment could be made: by check, by a draft drawn on one of the banks (roughly the equivalent of a cashier's check) or by telegraphic transfer. Since the telegraphic transfer is the most common way of making international payments, let us assume that this is the method used. The U.S. importer will contact his bank and purchase a telegraphic transfer in the amount of £200. Assuming the exchange rate is $2.00 per pound, the U.S. bank will charge the importer's account in the amount of $400 (the dollar equivalent of £200 at an exchange rate of $2.00 per pound; the importer has thus paid for the goods). (Follow these transactions in the T-accounts in Figure 6–1[a].) The U.S. bank will now cable its correspondent bank in Britain with instructions to shift £200 from its account to the British exporter's account. Accordingly, the British bank will debit the sterling account of the U.S. bank in the amount of £200; this transfers the funds from the U.S. to the British bank. Simultaneously, the British bank will credit the British exporter's account

[1]These deposits might be established by a simple "swap" arrangement whereby each bank credits the other with deposits of equal value according to the going exchange rate.

FIGURE 6-1 Clearing of International Payments: U.S. Importer

(a)

U.S. Commercial Bank			British Commercial Bank		
Assets		Liabilities	Assets		Liabilities
Value of £ deposit in British bank	− $400* (3)	− $400 (1) Importer's account		− £200 (2)	U.S. bank's account
				+ £200 (4)	British exporter's account

(1) U.S. bank lowers U.S. importer's account by $400.
(2) British bank lowers U.S. bank's pound deposit by £200.
(3) This is also recorded in dollars on the U.S. bank's books.
(4) British bank raises British exporter's account by £200.

(b)

U.S. Commercial Bank			British Commercial Bank		
Assets		Liabilities	Assets		Liabilities
	− $400 (1)	Importer's account	Value of $ deposit in U.S. bank	+ £200 (3)	+ £200 (4) British exporter's account
	+ $400* (2)	British bank's account			

(1) U.S. bank lowers U.S. importer's account by $400.
(2) U.S. bank raises British bank's dollar deposit by $400.
(3) This is also recorded in pounds on the British bank's books.
(4) British bank raises British exporter's account by £200.

with £200, and the exporter is thus paid for the goods. The final effect is that the British exporter is paid £200 for his goods, the U.S. bank's sterling deposit in the British bank is reduced by £200, and the U.S. importer has paid $400 to the U.S. bank. The transaction might well have been payable in dollars, the currency of the importer. In this case, the U.S. importer would pay his bank $400, the U.S. bank would then credit the dollar account of the British bank by $400 (thereby transferring the funds to the British bank), and the British bank would then credit the British exporter with £200, the equiv-

alent of $400 at the $2.00 per-pound exchange rate.[2] (See Figure 6–1[b].)

If a U.S. exporter were to sell, say, $600 worth of goods to a British importer, a similar set of transactions would occur. (See Figure 6–2[a].) If the transaction is payable in dollars, the British importer would pay £300 to his bank

[2]These examples all assume that the exporter and importer wish to hold only their domestic currencies. It is possible, under current banking arrangements, for a home resident to hold foreign currency deposits, and vice versa.

FIGURE 6-2 Clearing of International Payments: U.S. Exporter

(a)

U.S. Commercial Bank				British Commercial Bank			
Assets		Liabilities		Assets		Liabilities	
		− $600* (2)	British bank's account	Value of $ deposit in U.S. bank	− £ 300 (3)	− £300 (1)	British importer's account
		+ $600 (4)	U.S. exporter's account				

(1) British bank lowers British importer's account by £300.
(2) U.S. bank reduces British bank's dollar deposit by $600.
(3) This is also recorded in pounds on the British bank's books.
(4) U.S. bank raises U.S. exporter's account by $600.

(b)

U.S. Commercial Bank				British Commercial Bank			
Assets		Liabilities		Assets		Liabilities	
Value of £ deposit in British bank	+ $600* (3)	+ $600 (4)	U.S. exporter's account			− £300 (1)	British importer's account
						+ £300 (2)	U.S. bank's account

(1) British bank lowers British importer's account by £300.
(2) British bank raises U.S. bank's pound deposit by £300.
(3) This is also recorded in dollars on the U.S. bank's books.
(4) U.S. bank raises U.S. exporter's account by $600.

in London (assuming, again, that the exchange rate is $2.00 per pound). The British bank would then cable the U.S. bank to transfer $600 to the U.S. exporter, and in order to transfer the funds between banks, the British bank's dollar account in the U.S. bank would be reduced by $600. Again, the transaction does not have to be payable in the currency of the exporter. If it were payable in sterling, the British importer would pay £300 to the British bank; the British bank would, in turn, add £300 to the account of the U.S. bank. The U.S. bank would then credit the U.S. exporter with $600. (See Figure 6–2[b].)

Note that, as a general rule, U.S. imports result in an increase in U.S. commercial bank liabilities to foreigners or a decrease in U.S. commercial bank claims (assets) on foreigners. On the other hand, U.S. exports result in an increase in U.S. commercial bank claims on foreigners, or a decrease in U.S. commercial bank liabilities to foreigners.[3] (These effects are marked * in figures 6–1 and 6–2.)

[3]Foreign currency deposits in a foreign bank held by a U.S. bank constitute a claim by the U.S. bank on foreigners; dollar deposits held in a U.S. bank by a foreign bank constitute a liability by the U.S. bank to foreigners. This information will be useful in the discussion of the balance of payments in Chapter 7.

Commercial Bank Operations in the Foreign Exchange Market

Through experience, banks operating in international currency markets come to know how much of each foreign currency they should keep in inventory to service their customers. They will typically try to maintain their foreign currency balances at about that level. If, during a given day, the addition to a bank's holdings of a particular foreign currency, through acquisition from exporter customers, matches the reduction of the bank's holdings of that currency, through sales to importer customers, there will be no change in the bank's net position in that currency. (Such a situation is depicted in Figure 6–3[a].) Should sales to importers outweigh receipts from exporters during the day, the bank will find its inventory of that particular currency depleted below the desired level. (See Figure 6–3[b].) In order to restore the inventory to the desired level, the bank will attempt to purchase the necessary balances on the foreign exchange market. If there happens to be some other bank or banks in the market trying to dispose of a surplus of the same currency, these positions

FIGURE 6-3 Effect of Clearing International Payments on Banks' Foreign Assets and Liabilities (exchange rate: $2/£)

(a)

U.S. Commercial Bank			British Commercial Bank		
Assets		Liabilities	Assets		Liabilities
$ value of £ deposit in British bank	+ $400 (2) − $400 (4)			+ £200 (1) − £200 (3)	U.S. bank's account

(1) U.S. bank's holdings of pounds increase through acquisition from U.S. exporters.
(2) Item (1) recorded on U.S. bank's books.
(3) U.S. bank's holdings of pounds decrease through provision of pounds to U.S. importers.
(4) Item (3) recorded on U.S. bank's books.

(b)

U.S. Commercial Bank			British Commercial Bank		
Assets		Liabilities	Assets		Liabilities
$ value of £ deposit in British bank	+ $400 (2) − $600 (4)			+ £200 (1) − £300 (3)	U.S. bank's account

(1) U.S. bank's holding of pounds increase through acquisition from U.S. exporters.
(2) Item (1) recorded on U.S. bank's books.
(3) U.S. bank's holdings of pounds decrease through provision of pounds to U.S. importers.
(4) Item (3) recorded on U.S. bank's books.

can be matched or "married."[4]

If desired sales in the market just happen to match desired purchases at any given point in time, there will be no excess supply or demand in the market and no resultant pressure on the exchange rates. If desired purchases and sales are unmatched, however, there will be pressure for the exchange rate between the home and foreign currencies to adjust. Exchange rates, the prices of currencies in terms of other currencies on the foreign exchange market, will adjust to supply and demand pressures just as will the price of a company's stock in the stock market. Excess demand for sterling, in exchange for dollars, on the foreign exchange market will cause sterling to gain in value (appreciate) vis-à-vis the dollar. Excess supply of sterling will cause it to lose value (depreciate) against the dollar.[5]

A SIMPLE MODEL OF THE FOREIGN EXCHANGE MARKET

We are now in a position to construct a very simple supply and demand model of the foreign exchange market. This model will help us to analyze the effects of changes in economic con-

[4]As mentioned above, interbank purchases and sales of foreign exchange are often made through brokers, who specialize in dealing in particular currencies. As specialists in a limited number of currencies, brokers are better able to provide up-to-the-minute information on the market for these currencies. In addition, by dealing through brokers, banks are able to remain anonymous up until the point that the transaction is closed. This helps protect the banks' bargaining power in dealing with each other.

[5]The terms *appreciation* and *depreciation* are applied to movements of the value of a currency in response to buying and selling pressures in the foreign exchange market. The terms *revaluation* and *devaluation* are applied to changes in the value of a currency through deliberate adjustment of a parity or exchange rate peg by the governments involved. Devaluation and revaluation are discussed in detail in Chapter 8.

ditions within countries on the exchange rates and the balance of payments between countries. As with other markets, the forces of supply and demand interact within the foreign exchange market to produce an equilibrium price (exchange rate) and quantity of currency traded. Suppose there are two countries, the United States and Britain. The residents of these countries are trading goods, services and assets with each other and regularly buy and sell foreign exchange to be used in making payment. The demand for sterling on the foreign exchange market is derived primarily from the demand by U.S. residents for British goods, services and assets. The demand for dollars is derived primarily from the demand by British residents for U.S. goods, services and assets.[6]

The demand for dollars in this market is the same thing as the supply of pounds; in order to buy the dollars, one must offer sterling. Likewise, the demand for pounds is equivalent to the supply of dollars. We could thus analyze the market either in terms of the supply and demand for sterling or in terms of the supply and demand for dollars; the two would be equivalent. Let us elect to analyze the market in terms of the supply and demand for sterling.

The Demand for Foreign Exchange

In Figure 6–4, the exchange rate (the price of pounds in dollars, $/£) appears on the vertical axis, and the quantity of sterling traded per time period appears on the horizontal axis.[7] Schedule

[6]One can think of exceptions. A U.S. resident who has been holding British bonds, but wishes to repatriate his funds, would sell the bonds for pounds sterling and then convert the sterling to dollars, adding to the demand for dollars in the market.

[7]Let us stress, at this point, the importance of carefully specifying whether the exchange rate is expressed in dollars per pound ($/£), or pounds per dollar (£/$). Although either is legitimate for expressing the exchange rate, $/£ is the appropriate

(1)	(2)	(3) ([1] × [2])	(4)	(5) ([1] × [4])
Price per case in £	Exchange Rate	Price per Case in $	Quantity of Cases Demanded	Quantity of £ Demanded
£50	$3.00/£	$150	200	£10,000
50	$2.00/£	100	300	15,000
50	$1.00/£	50	400	20,000

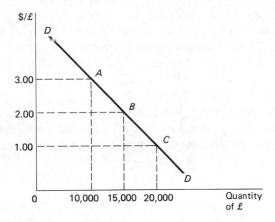

FIGURE 6-4 The Demand for Sterling

DD is the demand for sterling in the foreign exchange market by U.S. residents who wish to buy British goods, services and assets. The *DD* schedule slopes downward to the right, reflecting the fact that as the pound becomes cheaper, British goods will become cheaper to U.S. residents, inducing them to increase their purchases of British goods. As U.S. residents buy more British goods, they must increase their purchases of pounds with which to buy these goods.

Suppose that a case of Scotch whisky costs £50 in Britain and that this sterling price remains constant. If the exchange rate were $3.00 per pound, the price of a case in dollars would be

specification in a model in which the variable on the horizontal axis is "quantity of pounds," as in Figure 6–4. On the other hand, £/$ would be appropriate if the variable on the horizontal axis were "quantity of dollars."

$150; ($3.00/£ × £50 = $150). Let us say that U.S. residents would buy 200 cases at that price. They would have to buy £10,000 on the foreign exchange market in order to buy the 200 cases. Thus at the exchange rate of $3.00 per pound U.S. residents would demand £10,000. This is represented by point *A* in Figure 6–4.

If the exchange rate were to change to $2.00 per pound, the price of a case in dollars would fall to $100; ($2.00/£ × £50 = $100). U.S. residents, responding to the lower dollar price, would increase their purchases of Scotch; let us say they would now buy 300 cases. To do so, they would buy £15,000 on the foreign exchange market, since each case costs £50. The fact that U.S. residents would demand £15,000 if the exchange rate were $2.00 per pound is represented by point *B*.

If the exchange rate were to change to $1.00 per pound, the price of a case in dollars would become \$50; (\$1.00/£ × £50 = \$50). U.S. residents would buy even more Scotch, say 400 cases, at this price. They would now have to buy £20,000 on the foreign exchange market to buy the 400 cases, since each case costs £50. The fact that, at \$1.00 per pound, U.S. residents would demand £20,000 is represented by point C.

It is clear, then, that as British goods become cheaper to U.S. residents as a result of a depreciation in sterling, U.S. residents will buy a greater quantity of sterling with which to buy additional British goods. In other words, there is an inverse relationship between the price of pounds (the exchange rate in terms of \$/£) and the quantity of sterling demanded on the foreign exchange market; the demand curve slopes downward to the right.

The Supply of Foreign Exchange

Schedule *SS* in Figure 6–5 is the supply of sterling offered on the market by British residents to obtain dollars with which to buy U.S. goods, services and assets. This schedule is drawn sloping upward to the right to reflect the fact that as the pound rises in value (or, equivalently, as the dollar falls in value) U.S. goods become cheaper to British residents, inducing them to increase their purchase of U.S. goods.[8] As British residents increase their purchases of U.S.

[8]It is important to note that movement up the vertical axis represents an appreciation of the pound, or a depreciation of the dollar. Movement down the axis represents a depreciation of the pound or appreciation of the dollar.

(1)	(2)	(3) ([1] ÷ (2)])	(4)	(5) ([1] × [4])	(6) ([5] ÷ [2])
Price per Tire in \$	Exchange Rate	Price per Tire in £	Quantity of Tires Demanded	Total Quantity of \$ Demanded	Quantity of £ Offered
\$100	\$1.00/£	£100.00	100	\$10,000	£10,000
100	\$2.00/£	50.00	300	30,000	15,000
100	\$3.00/£	33.33	600	60,000	20,000

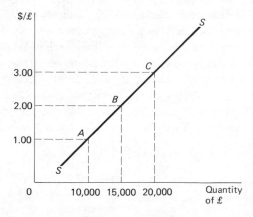

FIGURE 6-5 The Supply of Sterling

goods, they must increase their purchases of U.S. dollars (i.e., increase their offerings of pounds) with which to buy these goods.[9]

Suppose that U.S. automobile tires cost $100 each in the United States and that this dollar price remains constant. If the exchange rate were $1.00 per pound (equivalent to £1 per dollar), the price of U.S. tires in Britain would be £100; (£1/$ × $100 = £100). Let us say that British residents would buy 100 tires at this price. They need to obtain $10,000 on the foreign exchange market to make this purchase. They would have to offer £10,000 for the dollars, since the exchange rate is $1.00 per pound. This establishes point A on the supply-of-pounds curve, SS. The quantity of pounds offered is recorded on the horizontal axis in Figure 6–5.

If the exchange rate were to change to $2.00 per pound (equivalent to £.50 per dollar), the price of a U.S. tire in pounds would fall to £50 (£.50/$ × $100 = £50). British residents, responding to the lower sterling price, would increase their purchases of U.S. tires; let us say they would now buy 300 tires. To do so, they would have to obtain $30,000 (300 tires at $100 each). They would obtain the $30,000 on the foreign exchange market by offering £15,000 for it, since the exchange rate is $2.00 per pound. This establishes point B on the supply-of-pounds curve.

If the exchange rate were now to change to $3.00 per pound (equivalent to £.3333 per dollar), the price of a U.S. tire in pounds would fall to £33.33 (£.3333/$ × $100). British residents would again increase their purchases of U.S. tires and now buy, say, 600 tires. To do so, they would have to obtain $60,000 (600 tires

[9]The upward-sloping supply curve implies that the demand for U.S. goods and services by the British is elastic. As we shall see, if the demand for U.S. goods and services were inelastic, the supply of sterling would bend backward toward the northwest.

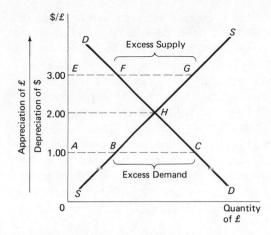

FIGURE 6-6 Supply and Demand for Sterling

at $100 each) on the foreign exchange market by offering £20,000 for it, since the exchange rate is $3.00 per pound. This establishes point C on the supply-of-pounds curve.

This example (which assumes that the British demand for U.S. tires is elastic) shows that as the pound *appreciates,* British residents will offer *more* pounds on the foreign exchange market to obtain dollars with which to buy greater quantities of U.S. goods. There is thus a positive relationship between the exchange rate, expressed in dollars per pound, and the quantity of pounds supplied on the foreign exchange market.

Exchange-Market Equilibrium

In Figure 6–6, the supply and demand curves for foreign exchange are combined. The equilibrium exchange rate and the quantity of pounds traded on the foreign exchange market are given by the intersection of the SS and DD schedules. Only at that particular exchange rate (which we assume to be $2.00 per pound) will the exchange market be cleared. At exchange rates lower than $2.00 per pound (say, $1.00 per pound) there will be an excess demand for sterling. Here, the quantity of sterling demanded *(AC)* will exceed the quantity supplied *(AB)*. The excess demand *(BC)* will cause sterling to appreciate until it reaches $2.00 per pound. On the other hand, at exchange rates higher than $2.00 per pound (say, $3.00 per pound) there will be an excess supply of sterling. In this case, the quantity of sterling supplied *(EG)* exceeds the quantity demanded *(EF)*. The excess supply *(FG)* will cause sterling to depreciate until it reaches $2.00 per pound. Point *H* thus represents a stable equilibrium toward which the market exchange rate will adjust.

A Special Case: The Backward-Bending Supply Curve for Foreign Exchange

In deriving the supply curve in Figure 6–5, we made the assumption that British demand for U.S. tires was elastic. This assumption was incorporated in the price and quantity magnitudes we used in that example; when the sterling price

of tires fell from £100 to £50 (a 50 percent decrease) the quantity of tires demanded increased from 100 to 300 (a 200 percent increase); when the sterling price fell from £50 to £33.33 (a 33.3 percent decrease) the quantity of tires demanded increased from 300 to 600 (a 100 percent increase). Since in each case the percentage increase in the quantity demanded was greater than the percentage decrease in the price, the demand was, by definition, elastic.

Now we shall show that if the British demand for U.S. tires were inelastic, this would generate a supply-of-pounds curve that "bends backward," sloping to the northwest. Note that in Figure 6–7 we have assumed that the percentage increase in the quantity of tires demanded is smaller than the percentage decrease in price, implying that demand is inelastic; when the sterling price of tires falls from £100 to £50 (a 50 percent decrease) the quantity demanded increases from 100 to 140 (a 40 percent increase); when the price falls from £50 to £33.33 (a 33.3 percent decrease), the quantity demanded in-

Price per Tire in $	Exchange Rate	Price per Tire in £	Quantity of Tires Demanded	Total Quantity of $ Demanded	Quantity of £ Offered
$100	$1.00/£	£100.00	100	$10,000	£10,000
100	$2.00/£	50.00	140	14,000	7000
100	$3.00/£	33.33	180	18,000	6000

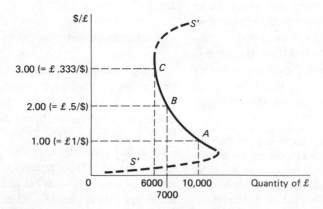

FIGURE 6-7 The Supply of Sterling (British Demand for U.S. Goods Inelastic)

creases from 140 to 180 (a 28.5 percent increase). In this case, we can see that if the exchange rate is $1.00 per pound, the British will want to buy 100 U.S. tires and will have to offer £10,000 to get the dollars to buy them. This establishes point A on the supply-of-pounds curve, SS. If the exchange rate changes to $2.00 per pound, the British will want to buy 140 tires and will have to offer £7000 to get the dollars to buy them; this establishes point B on the supply-of-pounds curve. Finally, if the exchange rate changes to $3.00 per pound, the British will want to buy 180 U.S. tires and will have to offer £6000 to get the dollars to buy them; this establishes point C on the supply-of-pounds curve. We can see that between points A and C, the SS curve slopes in a northwesterly direction.

It can be argued that the British demand for U.S. tires will not remain inelastic as their sterling price becomes either very high or very low. If the price were to rise to extremely high levels, the British would turn more and more readily to domestic substitutes; if the price fell to extremely low levels we would expect the British to substitute U.S. tires for British tires at an increasingly rapid rate. Either extreme would produce a fairly high elasticity of demand. This would imply that the slope of the supply-of-pounds curve would eventually turn back toward a southwest–northeast direction, as shown by the dashed portions at either end of SS in Figure 6–7.

Although this example deals with the demand for a single product, the results can be generalized as follows: if the overall demand by the British for the whole set of U.S. exportable goods is inelastic, the supply-of-pounds curve will be backward bending.[10]

[10]While the elasticity of demand for a single good could very well be inelastic, there is good reason to believe that the overall foreign demand for the whole set of a country's exports will be elastic, due to the broader range of available substitutes.

A backward-bending supply curve produces some interesting possibilities for equilibrium in the foreign exchange market. If the demand by the British for U.S. goods is *very* inelastic (so that the supply-of-pounds curve bends back severely), and if the demand for British goods by U.S. residents is also very inelastic (so that the demand curve for sterling is very steep), it is possible to have multiple equilibria, as shown in Figure 6–8 as points A, B and C. If the exchange rate stands at either $1.80, $2.00 or $2.20 per pound, it will remain there unless disturbed. The foreign exchange market will be cleared, since the quantity of sterling demanded will be equal to the quantity supplied.

However, A and C represent *stable equilibria*, while B is an *unstable equilibrium*. An equilibrium is said to be stable if the exchange rate will automatically *return* to that point when disturbed. An equilibrium is unstable if the exchange rate tends to move *away* from the equilibrium point when disturbed. Suppose the exchange rate is in equilibrium at $2.00 per pound, the unstable equilibrium. The quantity of pounds demanded and the quantity supplied are both equal to KB, and there is no pressure for the exchange rate to change. Now suppose

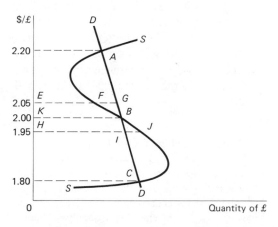

FIGURE 6-8 Stable and Unstable Equilibria in the Foreign Exchange Market

the exchange rate is somehow disturbed to $2.05 per pound. Here, the quantity of sterling demanded *(EG)* exceeds the quantity supplied *(EF)* and this puts upward pressure on the pound, causing it to appreciate; the exchange rate thus moves upward, farther *away* from the initial equilibrium rate of $2.00 per pound. By the same token, if the exchange rate were disturbed from the original equilibrium of $2.00 per pound to a lower level—say, $1.95 per pound—there would be an excess supply of pounds equal to *IJ*. Here, the exchange rate would move downward, farther *away* from $2.00 per pound. It is left as an exercise for the reader to demonstrate that disturbances from equilibria *A* or *C* will produce pressures that will *return* the exchange rate to the original equilibrium.

You might wonder just how low the elasticities of demand for British goods by the Americans and the demand for U.S. goods by the British would have to be to produce an unstable equilibrium of the kind depicted in Figure 6–8. These conditions have been worked out, and are known as the *Marshall–Lerner conditions,* named after the economists who derived them. Simply put, the Marshall–Lerner conditions state that if the sum of the elasticities of demand-for-British-goods-by-Americans and the demand-for-U.S.-goods-by-British is equal to or greater than 1.0, the exchange market equilibrium will be stable. If the sum of these two elasticities is less than 1.0, the equilibrium will be unstable.[11] We shall have more to say about unstable equilibria and the Marshall–Lerner conditions in chapters 8 and 24.

[11]Symbolically, equilibrium will be stable if $n_1 + n_2 \geq 1.0$ and unstable if $n_1 + n_2 < 1.0$, where $n_1 =$ the elasticity of demand for British goods by U.S. residents and $n_2 =$ the elasticity of demand for U.S. goods by British residents. The Marshall–Lerner conditions assume that the elasticity of supply of exports by both countries is infinite.

DISTURBANCES TO THE MARKET UNDER FREELY FLUCTUATING EXCHANGE RATES

Changes in the equilibrium exchange rate are brought about by forces that shift the *SS* and *DD* schedules. These forces include anything (other than a change in the exchange rate itself) that causes a change in desired purchases of foreign goods, services and assets by home residents, or that causes a change in desired purchases of home goods, services and assets by foreigners.[12]

Disturbances Involving the Trade of Goods and Services

In analyzing the forces that shift the supply and demand curves for sterling, let us consider changes in the demand for goods and services separately from changes in the demand for assets. If we abstract from the demand for assets, shifts in the demand and supply for sterling reflect changes in U.S. demand for British goods and services and British demand for U.S. goods and services. The supply and demand of U.S. and British goods and services, in turn, are influenced by changes in macroeconomic conditions within the two countries. The major macroeconomic variables identified as having an effect on the supply and demand of goods and services across countries are the relative prices of home and foreign goods (usually represented by the ratio of home to foreign price levels) and the level of real income within the countries. However, one can think of other disturbances such as seasonal effects, changes in productive capacity, harvest

[12]Changes in the exchange rate itself will generate movements *along* the curves, but not shifts in the curves themselves. This is because the exchange rate is the variable that has been placed on the vertical axis.

conditions, strikes and many others that would also have an effect on the supply and demand for foreign and home goods.

Let us see how disturbances in relative price levels and real income would affect the supply and demand for home and foreign goods, the supply and demand for sterling and ultimately the exchange rate between the two currencies. In this analysis, we shall assume that the demand for both U.S. and British exports is elastic; this means that the supply and demand curves for sterling will slope in the ordinary directions.

relative price-level changes

Beginning at an equilibrium position in Figure 6–9(a), with DD and SS representing the demand and supply curves for sterling and $2.00 per pound the equilibrium exchange rate, assume that U.S. prices of goods and services rise relative to British prices. The increase in U.S. prices relative to British prices will have the effect of making British goods more attractive to both U.S. and British residents. This will cause some switching of demand from U.S. to British goods. As U.S. residents buy more British goods, they will have to buy more sterling

with which to purchase these imported goods. This increase in the demand for sterling is shown as a rightward shift in the DD schedule, in Figure 6–9(a), to D'D'. Meanwhile, British residents will demand fewer U.S. goods, will require fewer dollars to buy U.S. goods and thus will offer less sterling for dollars on the foreign exchange market. This is shown as a leftward shift in the supply curve from SS to S'S' in Figure 6–9(b). The combined effect of the increase in the demand for and the decrease in the supply of sterling (shown in Figure 6–9[c]) is to put upward pressure on the dollar price of sterling. Here the pound is shown to appreciate from $2.00 to, say, $2.10.

The increase in U.S. prices vis-à-vis British prices, in this example, has caused a shift in both the supply and demand schedules for sterling. This is because the incentives of residents in both countries are affected by the relative price change. The excess demand for sterling (AB) generated by the supply and demand shifts has caused sterling to appreciate to $2.10 per pound. An increase in the British price level relative to that of the United States would have the opposite effect; it would increase the supply and decrease the demand for sterling and cause

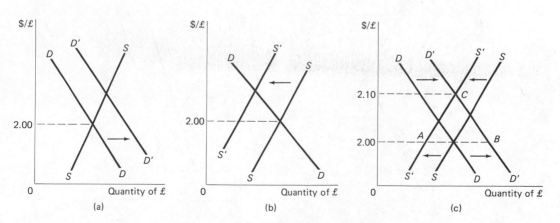

FIGURE 6-9 Disturbances of the Supply and Demand for Sterling: Price-Level Changes

a depreciation of the pound against the dollar. This analysis suggests a systematic relationship between relative rates of inflation within countries and movements in exchange rates. Over time the country with the higher rate of inflation will, *ceteris paribus,* experience a depreciation in its currency on the foreign exchange market.[13]

income changes

An increase in real income within a country will tend to raise the demand for goods and services, including foreign goods and services, by residents of that country. An increase in U.S.

income will thus generate an increase in the demand for British goods, and Americans will demand more sterling with which to buy those goods. This is reflected in a rightward shift in the *DD* schedule, in Figure 6–10(a), to *D'D'*. An excess demand for sterling *(BC)* will ensue, and this will drive the price of sterling upward toward the new equilibrium, which we assume to be $2.10 per pound.[14]

By similar logic, an increase in British income will generate an increase in British demand for U.S. goods. British residents will offer more sterling on the foreign exchange market in order to obtain the dollars needed to buy the additional U.S. goods. This is reflected in a rightward shift in the *SS* schedule, in Figure 6–10(b), to *S'S'*. An excess supply of sterling *(EF)* is generated, and this will drive the price of sterling down to the new market equilibrium, which we assume to be $1.90 per pound.

[13]Empirical evidence suggests a close correspondence between exchange rate movements and movements in relative price levels over long periods of time. Over shorter periods, the correspondence is not so close. There is a theory, known as *purchasing-power parity theory,* which relates exchange rates to the relative purchasing powers of the currencies. The "relative" version of this theory holds that, over time, there will be a close correspondence between percentage changes in relative price levels across countries and percentage changes in the respective exchange rates.

[14]As a "second-round effect," the increase in demand for British goods could put upward pressure on British income and prices, which could generate further shifts in the *SS* and *DD* schedules. For simplicity, we shall abstract from such second-round effects and focus strictly on initial effects.

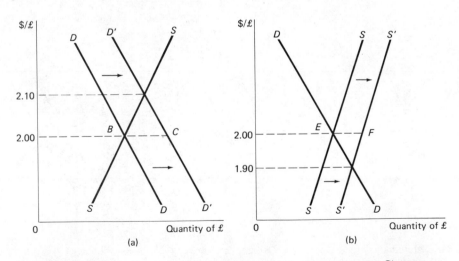

FIGURE 6-10 Disturbances of the Supply and Demand for Sterling: Income Changes

Disturbances Involving International Capital Flows

So far, we have concentrated on the supply and demand for sterling generated by the trade of goods and services. A second component of the supply and demand for foreign exchange is associated with international capital flows. *Capital flow* or *capital movement* are terms applied to the international flow of funds for the purpose of buying foreign assets. If a U.S. resident transfers funds to London to buy British bonds, he generates a capital outflow from the United States to Britain. To buy the foreign assets, he must first buy sterling on the foreign exchange market, which adds to the demand for sterling on that market. If a British resident buys U.S. bonds, this constitutes a capital inflow to the U.S. from Britain. The British resident must, of course, buy dollars (sell pounds) in order to buy U.S. assets, and this adds to the supply of sterling on the foreign exchange market.[15]

We shall have much more to say about the various categories of capital movements and their determinants in Part III.

The demand and supply of foreign exchange for purposes of buying foreign short- and long-term assets can be added to the demand and supply derived from trade of goods and services to obtain the overall demand and supply of foreign exchange. It is the interaction between the overall demand and supply on the foreign exchange market that determines the exchange rate between two currencies. The exchange rate is thus influenced not only by trade transactions, but also by long-term and short-term capital transactions.

[15]Our discussion of the relationship between the exchange rate and the supply and demand for sterling for purposes of buying foreign assets is cast in terms of the *flow* of funds between countries. Some recent exchange-market models relate the exchange rate to *stocks* of home and foreign assets (including money) demanded by home and foreign residents.

Exchange rates fluctuate almost continuously on the foreign exchange market, at least among the major currencies. This reflects a continuous shifting in the demand and supply of foreign exchange, caused by the changing incentives to buy foreign goods, services and assets.

THE MECHANICS OF EXCHANGE-RATE STABILIZATION

Until now we have assumed that the exchange rate is free to adjust to its new equilibrium level after a disturbance to the supply or demand for currencies on the foreign exchange market. Frequently, however, the authorities of one or both of the countries involved will attempt to inhibit or prohibit exchange-rate fluctuations. If exchange rates are rigidly fixed by the authorities, shifts in the supply and demand for foreign exchange will result in variations in the country's *international reserves* rather than variations in the exchange rate. To understand these relationships, let us explore the mechanics of official exchange-rate stabilization and the effects of disturbances to the market under fixed exchange rates.

We shall begin by assuming that the British government has a policy of maintaining a rigidly fixed exchange rate between the U.S. dollar and the pound sterling.[16] The object of this policy is to keep the dollar–sterling exchange rate from moving upward or downward from a predetermined level, known as a *peg*, or *parity*. If the dollar value of the pound should begin to rise above the peg, the British central bank, the agent that conducts exchange market intervention for the British government, would sell sterling on the foreign exchange market (thereby augment-

[16]Actually, either or both governments could participate in the stabilization activities. In fact, a third country could act to influence the dollar–sterling exchange rate if it should so choose.

ing the supply of sterling on the market) in sufficient quantity to halt the pound's appreciation. Should the pound begin to depreciate below the peg, the central bank would buy sterling on the foreign exchange market (thereby augmenting the demand for sterling on the market) in sufficient quantity to keep the pound from falling. The central bank would place its orders to buy or sell sterling through commercial banks that deal regularly in the market.

The Use of International Reserves

When the British central bank buys sterling on the foreign exchange market, it must pay for it with foreign exchange. In our example, the bank would pay for the sterling with U.S. dollars.[17] The central banks of the various countries maintain stocks of foreign exchange and other foreign assets for the purpose of making just such payments. This stock of foreign assets, plus the country's gold holdings, are known as the country's international reserves.[18] Activity by the British central bank to support sterling in the foreign exchange market would entail a reduction in Britain's international reserves, since some of the dollars in the reserves must be used to purchase the sterling. On the other hand, if the British central bank were to intervene in the market to prevent sterling from appreciating, the result would be an increase in Britain's international reserves, as the central bank would receive dollars in exchange for the sterling it sells on the foreign exchange market. Intervention to support one's home currency thus involves a reduction in home international reserves, while intervention by the home central bank to support the value of a foreign currency, vis-à-vis the home currency, has the effect of increasing the home country's international reserves.

Figure 6–11 provides a hypothetical picture of the intervention by the British central bank in pegging the exchange rate, along with the effects of intervention on Britain's international reserves. Here, we are assuming that the British central bank is maintaining a rigid exchange rate peg at $2.00 per pound. The dashed line represents the equilibrium exchange rate, or the path the exchange rate would follow, over time, if it were allowed to fluctuate freely on the foreign exchange market. To hold the pound at $2.00, the Bank of England must purchase sterling on the foreign exchange market when the equilibrium exchange rate starts to fall below $2.00 and sell sterling when it starts to rise above that level.

[17]Technically, the British could buy the sterling with any regularly traded foreign currency and rely on arbitrage to bring about the desired adjustment between the dollar and the pound. For simplicity, and because it is the most common practice, we shall assume the British buy and sell dollars when intervening on the foreign exchange market to stabilize the pound.

[18]Although only currencies are traded on the foreign exchange market, other highly liquid foreign assets are included in international reserves, since they earn interest and can still be readily exchanged for currencies.

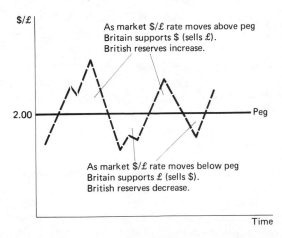

FIGURE 6-11 Government Intervention to Peg the Exchange Rate

Market Disturbances Under Fixed Exchange Rates

We are now in a position to analyze the effects of disturbances in the foreign exchange market under exchange rates that are fixed by the government. In Figure 6–12, assume that the exchange market is initially in equilibrium at $2.00 per pound and that the British central bank is maintaining a rigid peg at that level. In this initial equilibrium situation, *AB* is the quantity of pounds being bought and sold by U.S. and British private residents. It is important to underscore an important assumption at this point: the supply and demand curves are assumed to reflect activity by British and U.S. *private* residents, respectively. The buying and selling of sterling by the central bank to maintain the peg at $2.00 is *not* included in the supply and demand curves.

Beginning from the initial equilibrium, suppose the demand for pounds by U.S. residents now increases. This would reflect an increase in the demand for British goods, services or assets by U.S. residents, as outlined earlier in the chapter. The increase in the demand for sterling is shown by a rightward shift in *DD*, to *D'D'*, just as in the analysis depicted in Figure

6–10(a). Ordinarily, under freely fluctuating exchange rates, the pound would appreciate to, say, $2.10 per pound. However, the British central bank acts so as to hold the exchange rate at $2.00 per pound. It does this by selling sterling on the foreign exchange market.

How much sterling must the British central bank sell to peg sterling at $2.00 per pound? To answer this question, note that at $2.00 per pound the quantity of pounds demanded by U.S. private residents after demand has shifted to *D'D'* is *AC*, while the quantity supplied by British private residents remains at *AB*. There is, thus, an excess private demand for sterling in the market equal to *BC*. It is this excess demand that would ordinarily push the exchange rate up to $2.10 per pound and that the Bank of England must counteract if it wishes to keep sterling from appreciating. The Bank of England must therefore sell sterling in the amount *BC*. It must, in other words, "fill the gap" between the quantity of pounds supplied and demanded by private U.S. and British residents. Note that in selling sterling in the amount *BC*, the British would accumulate dollar reserves in the amount of $2.00 × *(BC)*.

If, beginning with the initial equilibrium, the British had experienced an increase in demand

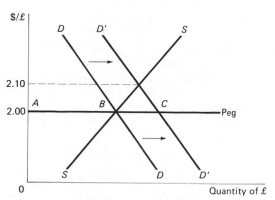

FIGURE 6-12 Exchange-Market Intervention: British Support the Dollar

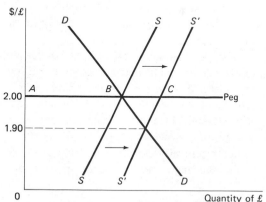

FIGURE 6-13 Exchange-Market Intervention: British Support the Pound

THE FOREIGN EXCHANGE MARKET **83**

for U.S. goods, services or assets, the result would have been a rightward shift in the supply of sterling, as shown in Figure 6–13. Supply would shift to the right as British residents offer additional sterling in the foreign exchange market to obtain dollars with which to buy the additional U.S. goods. If the exchange rate were free to fluctuate, the pound would depreciate to $1.90 per pound. To maintain an exchange-rate peg at $2.00 per pound, the British authorities would have to buy sterling in the amount *BC*. They would, in other words, have to take the excess supply of sterling off the market. This means depleting dollar reserves in the amount of $2.00 × *(BC)*.

Exchange-Market Intervention in Practice

The foregoing example assumed that the British government was maintaining the peg rigidly at $2.00 per pound. Actually, even under "fixed" exchange-rate regimes, some leeway is allowed for minor fluctuations. Under the Bretton Woods system of the 1950s and 1960s, in which exchange rates were generally fixed, the rules permitted free fluctuations within a band of 1 percent on either side of parity. There was, thus, a 2 percent range within which the dollar price of a foreign currency could fluctuate freely. The authorities were required to intervene only if the exchange rates exceeded the upper or lower limits of the band.[19]

Under a "managed" floating exchange-rate system, such as we have today, governments do not undertake to peg the exchange rate at any particular level or to keep it within any pre-specified range. On the other hand, the exchange rates are not allowed to fluctuate freely. Governments generally permit market forces to determine the major movements in the exchange rates, but intervene to maintain "orderly market conditions." This might involve intervention to iron out seemingly random short-term fluctuations or to retard the rate of appreciation or depreciation of some currency. A number of European countries even attempt to bind their currencies together in a joint float against the dollar. These arrangements will be discussed in much more detail in Chapter 18.

QUESTIONS AND EXERCISES

1. Suppose that U.S. exports to Canada increase during a given period of time. Analyze the possible effects on U.S. short-term bank claims and liabilities. Consider cases in which payment for the exports is denominated in Canadian dollars and in which it is denominated in U.S. dollars. Conduct the same exercise for an increase in U.S. *imports* from Canada.

2. Construct a simple model of the foreign exchange market, showing the supply and demand for foreign exchange. Assuming freely fluctuating exchange rates, use this model to analyze the effects of the following disturbances on the exchange rate between home and foreign currency. In each case, be explicit about the assumptions you make regarding movements in other variables in the system.

  a. an increase in home income
  b. an increase in foreign income
  c. an increase in the home inflation rate
  d. an increase in the foreign inflation rate

3. Repeat the exercises in question 2, but now assume that the exchange rate is rigidly fixed by the home authorities. In each case, identify the amount by which the home country's international reserves will change as a result of maintaining the exchange rate peg.

4. Suppose that the elasticities of supply and demand for foreign exchange are so low that there is an unstable equilibrium on the foreign exchange market. Construct a model to depict such a case and label the unstable equilibrium as point *B* (see Figure 6–8). With the initial equilibrium

[19]The Smithsonian agreements of 1971 widened the bands to 2 1/4 percent either side of parity. See Chapter 24.

at point *B*, and assuming freely fluctuating exchange rates, analyze what would happen to the exchange rate if there were a *slight* increase in the demand for foreign exchange.

5. Carefully distinguish between the following sets of terms:

   a. wholesale and retail foreign exchange market
   b. appreciation and revaluation
   c. depreciation and devaluation
   d. long-term and short-term capital movements
   e. freely fluctuating exchange rates and managed floating exchange rates

The Balance of Payments   7

A country's balance of payments is a record of its economic transactions with the rest of the world. It is useful not only as a historical record of international transactions, but also as a basis for analyzing current international economic relations and evaluating international economic policy.

Actually, there are two distinct balance-of-payments concepts that are useful in analyzing international economic relationships. The first, the *accounting balance of payments,* records transactions between home and foreign residents during some specific period of time. It is thus a historical record of international purchases and sales of goods, services and assets. Trends in these figures can serve as a basis for forecasting future movements in the balance of payments.

The second concept, the *market balance of payments,* focuses on the balance of payments as of a specific point in time, rather than over a span of time. This concept is useful in analyzing equilibrium or disequilibrium conditions in the balance of payments. Because payments between countries usually entail the purchase or sales of foreign currency, the market balance of payments corresponds closely to events on the foreign exchange market.[1] In this chapter, we shall concentrate on the accounting balance of payments, and then in Chapter 8 we shall discuss the market balance and tie it into the foreign exchange market.

[1]The distinction between the accounting and the market balance-of-payments concepts was introduced by Fritz Machlup. See Fritz Machlup, *International Payments, Debts and Gold* (New York: Scribner's, 1964), Chapter 3.

THE ACCOUNTING BALANCE
OF PAYMENTS

The accounting balance of payments, as mentioned above, is a historical record of the purchases and sales of goods, services and assets between home and foreign residents for a given time period. The basic accounting period is usually one year, although quarterly balance-of-payments reports are common, and some components of the balance of payments are even reported monthly. Balance-of-payments data are collected and compiled by the Department of Commerce in the United States and by comparable agencies in other countries. This is the source of the balance-of-payments information that is reported by international agencies such as the International Monetary Fund, and discussed in the financial press.

Format for Balance-of-Payments
Record Keeping

Balance-of-payments transactions are recorded in a format based on double-entry bookkeeping. The double-entry system recognizes that there are two sides to any transaction: the transfer of goods (or services or assets), on the one hand, and the transfer of money in payment for the goods on the other. To record these two sides, the balance-of-payments sheet is divided into two columns, which are headed by the labels "debit" and "credit." As we shall see, the debit column is used to record independently motivated transactions that would lead to a money payment to foreigners, while the credit column is used to record independently motivated transactions that would lead to a money receipt from foreigners. Of the two sides of any given transaction, the *independently motivated* or *autonomous* side is the actual transfer of the good, service or asset from the seller to the buyer. The *payments* or *financing* side is the transfer of money or an IOU from the buyer to the seller.

For each international transaction, one of the two sides is recorded in the debit column and the other side in the credit column. If a U.S. firm exports $1000 worth of goods to a British firm, for example, an entry of $1000 is made in the credit column to record the fact that the goods were shipped out; a corresponding $1000 entry is made in the debit column to record the fact that the goods were paid for. The fact that each time an entry is made in one column, an equal entry will be made in the other, means that when all purchases from and sales to foreigners have been entered, total debits must equal total credits.

Just as the balance of payments is divided vertically into the debit and credit columns, it is divided horizontally into different "accounts." These accounts delineate various kinds of transactions that can occur between home and foreign residents. The *merchandise trade account,* for example, records purchases and sales of tangible goods. The *services* account records purchases and sales of intangible services, as well as earnings on foreign investments, and is sometimes called the *invisibles* account. The *unilateral-transfers* account records gifts between home and foreign residents, and the *capital* account records purchases and sales of assets.[2] Finally, a *money-payments* account records current money payments (the transfer of cash balances to pay for goods, services and assets) between home and foreign residents.[3]

---

[2]Formerly, capital account transactions were divided so as to segregate long-term capital transactions (which involve assets having a maturity of one year or more) from short-term capital transactions (which involve assets having a maturity of less than one year). This distinction is no longer as prominent in balance-of-payments reporting.

[3]Technically, money payments are short-term capital transactions, and the Department of Commerce lumps them with other short-term capital items in its balance-of-payments accounts. We choose to segregate money payments in order to illuminate the relationship between the balance of payments and the foreign exchange market.

FIGURE 7-1 Balance-of-Payments Format

	Debits	Credits
Merchandise trade account	Receipts of tangible goods from foreigners (imports)	Transfers of tangible goods to foreigners (exports)
Services account	Receipts of services from foreigners	Provision of services to foreigners
Unilateral-transfers account	Transfers of gifts to foreigners	Receipts of gifts from foreigners
Capital account	Receipts of assets from foreigners	Transfers of assets to foreigners
Money-payments account	Receipts of money payments from foreigners	Transfers of money payments to foreigners
Total debits and credits		

Rules for Making Entries

Figure 7–1 shows a balance-of-payments sheet divided vertically into the debit and credit columns and horizontally into the various accounts. Entries into the balance of payments are recorded on the basis of the market value of the transactions and are entered according to certain rules. These rules will first be presented in summary form, and will be followed by examples to illustrate each one. The rules are as follows:

Record the following as debits:

1. receipts of tangible goods from foreigners (merchandise imports)
2. receipts of services from foreigners (service imports)
3. transfers of gifts to foreigners
4. receipts of assets from foreigners (i.e., increases in claims on foreigners or reductions in liabilities to foreigners)
5. receipts of current money payments from foreigners

Record the following as credits:

1. transfers of tangible goods to foreigners (merchandise exports)
2. provision of services to foreigners (service exports)
3. receipts of gifts from foreigners
4. transfers of assets to foreigners (i.e., increases in liabilities to foreigners or reductions in claims on foreigners)
5. transfers of money payments to foreigners

Note that each of these rules corresponds to one of the cells in the balance-of-payments format in Figure 7–1. Figure 7–1 will serve as a convenient guide in placing various transactions in the balance of payments in the exercises that follow.[4]

Applications of Rules

The application of these rules can be illustrated by the following series of hypothetical transactions:

1. Suppose that a U.S. firm sells $1000 worth of computer parts to a firm in Britain and that

[4]This method of exposition was developed by James C. Ingram. See James C. Ingram, *International Economic Problems,* 3rd ed. (New York: Wiley, 1978), Chapter 4.

the parts are paid for in dollars by telegraphic transfer. The exporting of the parts is the independently motivated side of the transaction and the transfer of funds is the payments side of the transaction. The actual export of the parts is a transfer of goods to foreigners and, according to the rules in Figure 7–1, goes in the merchandise trade account in the credit column. The transfer of funds from the British firm to the U.S. exporter is a current money payment and goes in the money-payments account on the debit side. The entries in this example are shown in Figure 7–2 as item (a). Note that, as of this point, $1000 has been entered in the debit column and $1000 in the credit column.

2. Suppose that the next transaction is the importing of $800 worth of wine from France. The independently motivated side of the transaction is the importing of the wine itself, and the entry goes in the merchandise trade account in the debit column. Let us assume that payment is by check. The U.S. importer writes a check on his U.S. bank and sends it to the French exporter. In this case the payment goes on the credit side of the money account. This transaction is recorded as item (b) in Figure 7–2.

3. Next, suppose that a U.S. engineering firm sells professional services to a Japanese firm for $600 and is paid by telegraphic transfer. The independently motivated side of the transaction, the provision of the services, goes in the services account on the credit side. The payments side of the transaction goes in the money account on the debit side. This appears as item (c) in Figure 7–2.

4. Now suppose a U.S. traveler buys an airline ticket for $300 from Air France. Airline services are intangible, and the independently motivated side of the transaction goes in the services account on the debit side. Payment, let us say by check, goes on the credit side of the money account. This is item (d) in Figure 7–2.

5. Suppose that, next, a U.S. resident buys a bond for $1000 from the Swiss government. Here an asset, the bond, is received from a for-

FIGURE 7-2 U.S. Balance of Payments Showing Individual Entries

	Debits	Credits
Merchandise trade account	800 (b) 200 (j)	1000 (a) 600 (i)
Services account	300 (d)	600 (c)
Unilateral-transfers account	600 (i)	200 (j)
Capital account	1000 (e) 500 (h)	700 (f) 800 (g)
Money-payments account	1000 (a) 600 (c) 700 (f) 800 (g)	800 (b) 300 (d) 1000 (e) 500 (h)
Total debits and credits	6500	6500

eigner, so the independently motivated side of the transaction is entered on the debit side of the capital account. Assuming payment is by check, the payments side of the transaction is entered on the credit side of the money account. This is item (e).

6. Now suppose that a Japanese resident buys some General Motors stock for $700 and pays by check. Capital stock is an asset, so the independently motivated entry goes in the capital account on the credit side (we are transferring the stock to the Japanese buyer), and the payment goes on the debit side of the money account. This is item (f) in Figure 7–2.

7. If a British resident were to buy $800 worth of U.S. Treasury bills and pay by check, the independently motivated side of the transaction would be entered as a credit in the capital account of the U.S. balance of payments. Payment is recorded as a debit to the money-payments account. This is labeled as item (g) in Figure 7–2.

8. If a U.S. resident were to buy $500 worth of German Treasury bills, the capital account would be debited and the money account credited in that amount (item [h]).

9. So far, we have ignored the unilateral-transfers account. This account is used to record gifts given to and received from foreigners. Suppose the U.S. government were to provide grain to Mauritania, as a gift. In this case, grain would be leaving the country, just as it would if the grain had been sold rather than given away. The independently motivated side of the transaction would thus be recorded as a credit to the merchandise trade account, just as for any export. In recording the "payments" side of the transaction, however, the grain is not actually paid for, so we cannot make the entry in the money-payments account. Instead, it is entered in the unilateral-transfers account, in this case as a debit. The unilateral-transfers account is thus a receptacle for the payments side of transactions involving gifts. Note that this is consistent with the rules described above and in Figure 7–1. In this case, if the value of the grain donation were $600, the transaction would result in a $600 credit to the merchandise trade account and a $600 debit to unilateral transfers (item [i] in Figure 7–2).

10. Finally, suppose that an Italian resident were to give a $200 pair of shoes to his brother in New York. An entry of $200 would be made on the debit side of the merchandise trade account to record the fact that the shoes entered the country. Simultaneously, $200 would be entered on the credit side of the unilateral-transfers account to record the fact that the shoes were a gift (item [j] in Figure 7–2). Note that when all these entries have been made, total debits ($6500) are equal to total credits ($6500), as they must be under the double-entry bookkeeping system.

Reporting Various "Balances" in the Balance of Payments

Figure 7–3 consolidates the figures within each of the accounts in Figure 7–2 and provides a convenient summary from which to illustrate several different "balances" reported by the Commerce Department, the International Monetary Fund and other reporting agencies. The most widely reported balances are computed as follows.

merchandise trade account

If we draw a line under the merchandise trade account, as shown by line AA in Figure 7–3, and find the difference in the sum of the debits and the sum of the credits down to that line, we find that credits exceed debits by $600. We thus have a $600 "credit balance" in the merchandise trade account. A credit balance above the line is called a "surplus," so in this case we have a merchandise trade surplus of $600. A debit bal-

FIGURE 7-3 U.S. Balance of Payments Showing Consolidated Figures Within Accounts

		Debits	Credits	
Merchandise trade account		1000	1600	
	A			A
Services account		300	600	
	B			B
Unilateral-transfers account		600	200	
	C			C
Capital account		1500	1500	
	D			D
Money-payments account		3100	2600	
Total debits and credits		6500	6500	

Computing Balances:

Total credits above line *AA*	1600	Total credits above line *BB*	2200
Total debits above line *AA*	− 1000	Total debits above line *BB*	− 1300
Credit balance above line *AA*	600	Credit balance above line *BB*	900
Merchandise trade surplus		*Goods-and-services* surplus	
Total credits above line *CC*	2400	Total credits above line *DD*	3900
Total debits above line *CC*	− 1900	Total debits above line *DD*	− 3400
Credit balance above line *CC*	500	Credit balance above line *DD* (equals debit balance below line *DD*)	500
Current account surplus		*Money-payments* surplus	

ance above the line is called a "deficit." Thus, if we had had a debit balance of, say, $200 in the merchandise trade account, this would represent a $200 merchandise trade deficit.

It is useful to note that the credit balance above the line must always be equal to the debit balance below the line. This follows from the fact that total debits over the entire balance-of-payments sheet must equal total credits. We could, therefore, just as well have measured the $600 merchandise trade surplus in the above example as the debit balance below line *AA* instead of as the credit balance above the line. In fact, the traditional view of the balance of payments was that the deficit or surplus balance above the line was being "financed" by the corresponding credit or debit balance below the line.

goods-and-services account

A second balance reported by the Commerce Department is the goods-and-services balance. It is obtained by drawing the line below the services account (line *BB* in Figure 7–3) and finding the difference in the sum of the debits and credits down to that line. Note that the goods-and-services account contains all of the information in the merchandise trade account as well as the information in the services account. In Figure 7–3, we have a credit balance of $900, or a "goods-and-services account surplus" of $900, meaning that exports of goods and services are greater than imports. On the other hand, if the sum of debits had exceeded the sum of credits down to line *BB*, we would have had a goods-and-services account deficit. Once again, notice that the credit balance above line *BB* is exactly equal to the debit balance below line *BB*.

current account

Another widely reported account is the current account. The current account is obtained by drawing the line below the unilateral-transfers account (line *CC* in Figure 7–3) and finding the difference in the debits and credits down to that point. In our example, we have a $500 credit balance, or a $500 surplus on current account. The current account surplus means that the home country is exporting more goods and services than it is importing, after making allowance for gifts to and from foreigners. It also implies that this surplus is being financed by a net capital outflow as indicated by the debit balance below the line.

overall balance of payments

There has been considerable controversy, over the years, as to how to measure the *overall balance of payments*. Ideas as to how to compute the overall balance have varied with changing views as to what information the balance of payments *ought* to reflect. During the late 1950s and early 1960s the prevailing view was that the balance of payments ought to reflect fundamental long-run international economic activity, and the *basic balance,* as it was called, was used as the overall balance of payments. The basic balance segregated long-term and short-term capital account transactions, placing the long-term capital items above the line and the short-term items below. The basic balance thus showed the balance on purchases and sales of goods, services and long-term assets. This arrangement reflected the view that trade of goods and services, unilateral transfers and purchases and sales of long-term assets were "independently motivated" transactions, whereas the short-term capital transactions, below the line, were essentially payment items.

During the 1960s, the United States became increasingly concerned about the level of its international reserves and the effects of its balance of payments on those reserves. The view began to emerge that the balance of payments should be constructed so as to emphasize the actual and potential claims on U.S. reserves that resulted from international transactions. Accordingly, the overall balance of payments was redesigned, beginning in 1963, to reflect these pressures. The new balance of payments divided the capital account into finer subdivisions and put those short-term items that represented official and private claims against U.S. reserves below the line. Official gold transactions, which constituted actual reserve changes, were also put below the line. All other short-term transactions were put above the line along with the merchandise, service and long-term capital items. This arrangement was called the *liquidity basis* for reporting the balance of payments. On two subsequent occasions, the short-term capital items again were reshuffled above and below the line to produce the *official-reserves-transactions basis* (1965) and the *net-liquidity basis* (1971). After the advent of floating exchange rates in the 1970s, the reporting of claims against U.S. reserves was no longer felt to be of such great importance,[5] and these various bases for reporting the overall balance of payments were abandoned. The Department of Commerce now regularly reports the merchandise trade, the goods-and-services and the current account balances.

A final method of defining and computing the overall balance of payments can be called the *money-payments* balance. While this method has not received official sanction, it is especially useful for analyzing international monetary relations and linking the balance of payments to the foreign exchange market. It is obtained by drawing the line between the capital account and the money-payments accounts, as with line *DD* in Figure 7–3. This has the effect of isolating, below the line, the actual money payments between the home country and the rest of the world during the reporting period. In our example, we would have an overall money balance-of-payments surplus of $500, which could be measured either by the excess of credits over debits down to line *DD*, or by the excess of debits over credits below line *DD*. The $3100 worth of debits below line *DD* represents money actually paid to foreigners during the reporting period, and the $2600 worth of credits represents money received from foreigners. The difference, $500,

[5]Since international reserves no longer had to be used to maintain exchange-rate pegs, there was no longer a danger that a balance-of-payments deficit could deplete a country's reserves to the point that the country was forced to devalue its currency against a key currency or gold. In the case of the United States, there was no longer the danger that the U.S. deficit would strip U.S. gold reserves and thereby threaten the entire gold exchange standard system.

represents the excess of receipts over payments to foreigners, and is the amount of the surplus.

total debits and credits

From the foregoing discussion, it can be seen that the relevant information consists of balances within specific accounts, which are subsets of the total set of entries in the balance of payments. "The line" was drawn so as to isolate various subsets of entries, or accounts, and the focus was on the balances within those accounts. The total of all debits and credits ($6500 in the example in Figure 7–3) is of little interest. The fact that total debits equals total credits is the trivial result of the fact that every debit entry had to be matched by a corresponding credit entry. Asking whether the balance of payments is in balance thus does not focus on whether total debits equal total credits over the whole balance-of-payments sheet, but whether the sum of debits equals the sum of credits within some specified account.

Special Treatment in Recording Certain Transactions and Presenting Data

The foregoing examples covered most of the important relationships in balance-of-payments accounting. There are a few additional points that should be made, however, to complete the picture.

earnings on foreign assets and labor services

First, we have established that the services account records transactions involving intangible items such as transportation, insurance, engineering and legal services, along with all the other transactions one would normally classify under services. The services account includes one other set of transactions, however, which may be rather surprising. Interest, dividends and royalties received as the result of holding foreign bonds, stocks and other assets are counted as payment for an export of services. The provision of these services is recorded on the credit side of the services account, while the money receipts are entered as a debit in the money account. Likewise, interest, dividends and royalties paid by U.S. residents to foreigners are counted as payment for an import of services. The receipt of these services is recorded on the debit side of the services account, while the money payments are recorded as a credit in the money account.

The rationale is that by leaving capital abroad, instead of bringing it home, a U.S. resident is providing a service to the foreign firm for which he is paid a fee. Thus, when a U.S. resident receives $100 interest on a British bond, $100 would be entered on the credit side of the services account to record the fact that the service was provided (the independently motivated side of the transaction). A corresponding $100 would also be entered on the debit side of the money-payments account to record the payments side of the transaction.

Just as earnings on foreign assets enter the services account, so do earnings on labor services performed in a foreign country. Thus if U.S. residents work abroad and send their wages home, there would be a credit entry in the services account to reflect the provision of labor services to the foreigners. The money payment itself would enter as a debit in the money-payments account.

entries in the capital account

One might have thought, before reading the preceding section, that current earnings on foreign investment would be placed in the capital account. The capital account, however, is reserved for the acquisition or sale of assets across borders, not for earnings on those assets. Thus if a U.S. resident had bought a British bond for $1000 in 1978, this transaction would have been entered in the capital account for the year 1978. If he received $100 in interest during 1979, 1980, 1981 and 1982, a $100 entry would be made in the services account for each of the years, 1979–1982. There would be no capital account entry for 1979–1982, since no bond was bought or sold during that period. If the U.S. resident were then to sell his bond back to a British resident in 1983, an entry would be made in the capital account in 1983 to record the sale of the bond.

As is clear from the foregoing example, the balance of payments is a *flow* statement, not a *stock* statement. It records the "flow" of the bond from Britain to the United States in 1978 and from the United States to Britain in 1983. It does not record the stock of foreign bonds held by home residents at any given point in time. There would be no capital account entries, in other words, during the years 1979–1982.

While the capital account is reserved for entries that record the international purchase and sale of assets, the term *assets* is very broadly defined. It includes any financial instrument, security or title that represents any kind of claim against foreigners, whether long term or short term. It includes items ranging from titles to real estate and long-term government bonds to corporate commercial paper and ordinary commercial bank demand deposits.

Along this line, we might note that, frequently, international sales are made on credit, which involves exchanging goods for an IOU. These IOUs take the form of short-term claims on foreigners, and therefore would be entered in the capital account. In the example in Figure 7–2, if the $1000 worth of computer parts (item [a]) had been sold on credit, the independently motivated side of the transaction would still have been entered as a credit to the merchandise trade account, just as before. However, the payments side (the receipt of the IOU) would have been entered as a debit to the capital account, since this represents an increase in claims on foreigners. (Check the consistency of these entries with the rules displayed in Figure 7–1). If the British importer subsequently paid off the IOU, this would be recorded in a separate set of entries. There would be a credit to the capital account in the amount of $1000, to reflect the fact that the IOU was returned to the British importer (a reduction in claims on foreigners), and a debit of $1000 to the money-payments account to record the fact that money was received in return.

Commercial bank demand deposits are regarded as short-term assets. As we know, actual money payment for goods, services and other assets typically involves the transfer of the ownership of demand deposits. It is clear, therefore, that what we have been calling the "money-payments account" is technically a subset of the capital account. It is merely useful, as we mentioned earlier, to separate the money-payments entries for analytical purposes.

A final comment on the capital account has to do with some of the terminology surrounding international capital flows. If a U.S. resident buys a British bond for, say, $1000, the U.S. resident receives the bond from Britain and, in exchange, transfers $1000 to the British seller. This transaction is said to involve a *capital outflow* or *capital export* from the United States. It is a *capital inflow* or *capital import* from the British point of view. Even though there is a transfer of bonds into the United States, the focus of the term *capital flow* is on the direction of flow of money in payment for the bonds. Thus a *long-term capital outflow* from the United States means that U.S. residents are acquiring long-term foreign assets in exchange for a flow of money to the foreign sellers. A U.S. short-term capital outflow means that U.S. residents are buying short-term foreign assets in exchange for the money outflow.

questions of residency

Questions sometimes arise as to the residency of parties involved in international transactions, and the answer can govern whether or not certain transactions are to be included or excluded from the balance of payments. While it is usually clear who is a resident of what country, ambiguities can arise. As you would expect, any U.S. individual, U.S. firm, U.S. institution or U.S. government agency physically located within the U.S. border is treated as a U.S. resident for balance-of-payments purposes. On the other hand, it is not so obvious how a subsidiary of a U.S. firm operating in, say, Brazil or a branch of a New York bank operating in London should be treated—or the International Monetary Fund located in Washington, D.C., or the United Nations in New York.

While the rules applied to cases such as these may sometimes seem arbitrary, rules have to be adopted. Any arbitrary aspect of the rules becomes unimportant as long as they are applied consistently over time. A subsidiary of a U.S. firm operating overseas, even if it is wholly owned by the U.S. parent, is deemed to be a foreign resident. Thus, if the parent company were to ship spare parts to its subsidiary, the transaction would be treated as an export and would enter the balance of payments. If the subsidiary were to buy office supplies in the foreign city in which it is located, this would be treated as a transaction between two foreigners and would not enter the balance of payments.

A *branch* of a U.S. firm operating overseas, on the other hand, is treated as a U.S. resident.[6] The transfer of items between the home office and the foreign branch would never enter the balance of payments, since this is deemed to be

[6]A branch is an office or operating unit which is an integral part of the home company. This is in contrast to a subsidiary, which is legally a separate entity and issues its own stock.

a transaction between two U.S. residents. However, transactions between the branch and foreign residents *would* be regarded as international transactions. Thus, if the foreign branch of the U.S. company were to buy office supplies in the foreign city, the transaction would enter the balance of payments, since it is deemed a transaction between a home and a foreign resident.

Foreign embassies, consulates and other official agencies physically located in the United States are treated as foreign residents, as are international institutions such as the International Monetary Fund, the World Bank and the United Nations. A U.S. tourist abroad is treated as a U.S. resident and, when he sits down to a meal in Rome, he is deemed to be importing food and wine.

errors and omissions, or statistical discrepancy

As you might expect, the data collection process that forms the basis for the published balance-of-payments figures is far from perfect. The cost of collecting balance-of-payments information is immense, and a perfectly accurate procedure would be prohibitively expensive, even if it were technically feasible. As a result, the Department of Commerce bases its figures partly on information gathered and partly on estimates. Perhaps the most accurate information is to be found in the merchandise-trade data, which is based largely on customs records. Capital account information, as well as information on money payments, is based on reports by commercial banks and other financial institutions stating changes in their claims and liabilities to foreigners. This data is in summary form, and is not matched with specific current account transactions. Since the Department of Commerce does not have a system by which it can simultaneously record the debit and credit sides of each transaction, the debit and credit figures for any given transaction are likely to come from different sources. Many transactions simply fail to get recorded at all, and sometimes the debit side will be recorded while the credit side will not (or vice versa).

Not surprisingly, when the Commerce Department adds up its debits and credits, the two totals are not likely to be equal. Since in principle total debits must match total credits, the Department of Commerce arbitrarily inserts a figure to make them equal. This correcting entry is called "errors and omissions," or "statistical discrepancy," and is labeled as such in the balance of payments. If, for a given year, the Commerce Department's figure for total debits were, say, $1 million, while its figure for total credits were $1.2 million, an additional entry of $200,000 would be made in the debit column (the lower of the two) to make it equal to the total in the other column. For purposes of analyzing the balance of payments, errors and omissions are usually treated as part of the capital account, since short-term capital transactions arc the most likely to be overlooked in the data collection process and are thus most likely to be the source of error.

government transactions

Thus far, little has been said about the role of government in the balance of payments. Government, of course, has a great deal of influence on the economic climate within a country through the application of monetary, fiscal and other policies. This, in turn, has an indirect effect on the balance of payments through its effects on the incentives for private transactions. Government also has an effect on the balance of payments through its own direct international transactions. Official international transactions can be divided into two classes. The first, which we will call *ordinary government transactions,* includes all international purchases, sales and gifts of goods, services and assets other than those designed to influence the level of exchange rate;

in other words, all international transactions that do not directly involve the accumulation or depletion of international reserves. For ordinary transactions, government agencies are included as "home residents" and their international purchases and sales would enter the balance of payments in the same manner as those of a home firm or individual.

The second class of official transactions, which we shall call *exchange-market intervention,* involves the use of international reserves to intervene on the foreign exchange market. This type of activity was discussed in Chapter 6 and will be explored at length in subsequent chapters. Basically, changes in international reserves enter the balance of payments according to the same rules that apply to other transactions (see the discussion surrounding Figure 7–1). Suppose the U.S. government were to sell $1000 worth of its sterling reserves for $1000 on the foreign exchange market in order to support the value of the dollar. U.S. sterling assets would be transferred to the foreign buyer (a credit to the capital account) and payment for the sterling would be received (a debit to the money-payments account). Some reporting agencies segregate official reserve movements into a separate account, in which case the credit would be made to the official-reserves account instead of to the capital account. Segregation of official-reserve movements was especially common during the 1960s and early 1970s when the main focus of the balance of payments was on international reserves.

SOME BALANCE-OF-PAYMENTS STATISTICS

Now that we have developed the basic principles of balance-of-payments accounting, let us have a look at some balance-of-payments figures. Before presenting the figures, comments on some of the conventions associated with presentation

of balance-of-payments data are in order. First, debits are typically designated by a minus sign, as are deficit balances within specific accounts. A positive number (usually indicated by the absence of a sign) designates a credit entry, or a surplus balance within a particular account. The capital account is divided into two broad categories: "U.S. assets abroad," representing changes in holdings of foreign assets by U.S. residents, and "Foreign assets in the U.S.," representing changes in holdings of U.S. assets by foreigners. These broad categories are further subdivided as shown in Figure 7–4. "Allocations of SDRs" is a separate account used to

FIGURE 7-4 U.S. Balance of Payments, 1980 (billions of dollars)

Merchandise exports	$224.0
Merchandise imports	−249.3
Merchandise Trade Balance	−25.3
Net military transactions	−2.5
Net investment income	38.9
Receipts	82.8
Payments	−43.9
Net travel and transportation receipts	−0.8
Other services	0.6
Balance on Goods and Services	10.8
Unilateral transfers	−7.1
Balance on Current Account	3.7
U.S. assets abroad, total	−84.8
U.S. official reserve assets	−8.2
Other U.S. government assets	−5.2
U.S. private assets	−71.5
Foreign assets in the U.S., total	50.3
Foreign official assets	15.5
Other foreign assets	34.8
Allocations of SDRs	1.2
Statistical discrepancy	29.6

Source: U.S. Department of Commerce, *Survey of Current Business,* June 1981.

record the distribution by the International Monetary Fund of special drawing rights. These are special instruments used in balance-of-payments settlement among countries. SDRs will be discussed in some detail in Chapter 24.

Figure 7–4 presents U.S. balance-of-payments data for 1980. During that year, the merchandise trade balance was in deficit in the amount of $25.3 billion. This deficit had been in excess of $25 billion since 1977, and is attributable, in part, to the huge increases in the price of oil imports during the 1970s, and in part to fluctuations in the United States vis-à-vis foreign economic activity. The goods-and-services account showed a surplus of $10.8 billion; this reflected a surplus in the services account of roughly $36 billion, which more than offset the merchandise trade deficit. The United States typically runs a surplus in its services account, primarily due to earnings on the rather large holdings of foreign investments by U.S. residents. Note that U.S. receipts of investment income from abroad outweighed similar payments to foreigners by some $39 billion in 1980.

Adding the $7.1 billion debit balance in the unilateral-transfers account to the balance in the goods-and-services account yields a current account surplus of roughly $3.7 billion.

Within the capital account, the $84.8 billion debit figure for "U.S. assets abroad" means that foreign assets held by U.S. residents rose by that amount during 1980. Of that amount, official reserve assets rose by $8.2 billion, other government assets by almost $5.2 billion and privately held assets by over $71 billion. Included in this latter figure are bank deposit claims received in payment for the sale of goods, services and other assets. In other words, the "receipts" side of the money-payments account (see Figure 7–2) is included here. Foreign holdings of U.S. assets rose by $50.3 billion during 1980. Of this amount, $15.5 billion went into official holdings and $34.8 billion into private holdings. The payments side of the money-payments ac-

count is included here. As a final point, note that errors and omissions, or statistical discrepancy, was almost $30 billion in 1980, a record high figure. Although the source of this discrepancy is actually unknown, there is a fairly high probability that much of it represents unrecorded increases in U.S. assets held by foreigners.

For a more detailed breakdown and discussion of U.S. trade and balance-of-payments relationships, see the March, June, July, September and December issues of the *Survey of Current Business,* published by the U.S. Department of Commerce. In the following chapter, we shall establish the link between the balance of payments and the foreign exchange market.

QUESTIONS AND EXERCISES

1. Distinguish between the "accounting" and "market" balance-of-payments concepts. Identify situations in which each would provide useful information for policy purposes.

2. What is the rationale for double-entry bookkeeping in balance-of-payments record keeping?

3. Construct a balance-of-payments ledger sheet and record the following transactions, observing the rules set forth in this chapter.

   a. A U.S. firm buys $2000 worth of Scotch whisky from a British firm and pays by check.

   b. A U.S. firm sells $5000 worth of machinery to its wholly owned subsidiary in Brazil. Payment is by check.

   c. The U.S. government gives $3000 worth of wheat to Pakistan.

   d. A U.S. firm buys $1000 worth of auto parts from a Canadian firm on credit (no current payment is made).

   e. A U.S. petroleum engineering firm sells $2000 worth of its services to Mexico. Payment is by check.

   f. A U.S. resident buys $4000 worth of British bonds. Payment is by check.

g. The United Nations secretariat in New York buys $3000 worth of office equipment in New York. Payment is by check.

h. A U.S. resident receives $500 in interest payments on a Canadian bond which he bought three years ago.

4. Using the entries you made in question 3, compute the following balances. Identify whether there is a surplus or deficit in each case.

a. the merchandise trade balance

b. the goods-and-services balance

c. the current account

d. the overall "money" balance of payments.

5. What is the "errors and omissions" or "statistical discrepancy" entry in the balance of payments?

6. Given that total debits must, in principle, always equal total credits, what is meant by balance-of-payments surplus or deficit?

The Market Balance of Payments 8 and Balance-of-Payments Adjustment

Now that we have established the principles of balance-of-payments bookkeeping, we are in a position to analyze the "market" balance of payments and balance-of-payments adjustment. The market balance of payments, as mentioned in Chapter 6, focuses on international transactions as of a point in time (say, the current moment) whereas the accounting balance of payments summarizes transactions that occurred during some historical span of time (say, last year).

Because it depicts international payments at a point in time, the market balance of payments is closely related to activity on the foreign exchange market at that particular instant. If foreigners are trying to buy $1000 more of U.S. goods, services and assets than U.S. residents are trying to buy of foreign goods, services and assets, this describes a $1000 surplus in the U.S. market balance of payments. It also implies an excess demand for dollars on the foreign exchange market in the amount of $1000; foreigners will be trying to buy $1000 more dollars (to buy U.S. items) than U.S. residents are trying to sell (to obtain foreign currency with which to buy foreign items). Equilibrium or disequilibrium in the market balance of payments thus corresponds to equilibrium or disequilibrium on the foreign exchange market.

It should be emphasized that the concepts of equilibrium or disequilibrium, in the sense of a system which is at rest or disturbed, apply to the market but *not* to the accounting balance of payments. Balance-of-payments equilibria or disequilibria apply to situations in which payments to and receipts from foreigners are either matched or unmatched at a point in time. Because the data in the accounting balance cover a span of time, they reflect situations at many different, generally uncomparable, points in time.

Although we can think in terms of "balance" and "imbalance" or "surplus" or "deficit" in the accounting balance of payments, this balance depends upon where we choose to draw "the line" in adding up debits and credits. In terms of format—that is, where the line is drawn—the accounting balance that would come closest to the market balance of payments concept is the overall money balance of payments. In fact, one way of describing the market balance of payments is that it is the overall money-balance concept applied to a point in time.

Henceforth, in discussing the balance of payments, we will be referring to the *market* balance of payments unless otherwise specified.

LINKING THE BALANCE OF PAYMENTS AND THE FOREIGN EXCHANGE MARKET

To further establish the link between the market balance of payments and the foreign exchange market, consider the U.S. balance of payments transactions summarized in Figure 8–1. Suppose these transactions were all happening at the present moment. The overall money balance of payments would stand at a $500 surplus. This is measured by the excess of credits over debits above line *DD* or, equivalently, by the excess of receipts over payments to foreigners, measured by the excess of debits over credits below line *DD*. The balance below line *DD* is, of course, the balance in the money-payments account, and is what we are calling the market balance of payments.

FIGURE 8-1 U.S. Balance of Payments

	Debits	Credits
Merchandise trade account	$ 800	$1000
Services	300	600
Unilateral transfers		
Capital account	1500	1500
D ——— *D*		
Money payments	3100	2600
Total debits and credits	$5700	$5700

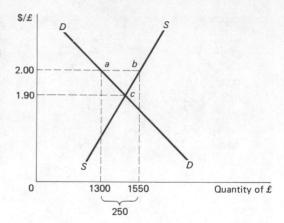

FIGURE 8-2 Supply and Demand for Sterling on Foreign Exchange Market

Designating the home country as the United States and the foreign country as Britain, let us assume that payments for international transactions have to be made in the currency of the exporting country.[1] To make payment for its purchases of U.S. goods, services and assets, British residents would have to buy $3100 on the foreign exchange market. If the going exchange rate is $2.00 per £1, this means the British would be offering £1550 on the foreign exchange market to obtain these dollars. Meanwhile, to make payment for their foreign purchases, U.S. residents would have to buy $2600 worth of sterling, which at the $2.00 per £1 exchange rate would amount to £1300. Thus, at an exchange rate of $2.00 per £1, we have the British supplying £1550 and U.S. residents demanding £1300, with the result that there is an excess supply of £250. This situation is shown in Figure 8–2, where *SS* and *DD* are the supply and demand curves for sterling on the foreign ex-

[1]This is strictly a simplifying assumption. It was established in Chapter 6 that the effect on the foreign exchange market would be the same whether the transactions are denominated in home or foreign currency.

change market. As we can see, the situation is one of disequilibrium, since at the going exchange rate, $2.00 per pound, there is an excess supply of sterling. This excess supply of sterling corresponds to the excess of British purchases from U.S. residents over U.S. purchases from British residents as shown in Figure 8–1.

Exchange-Rate Adjustment and the Balance of Payments

Balance-of-payments "adjustment" is the process by which balance-of-payments disequilibria are removed once they appear. If the authorities did nothing to interfere with movements in the exchange rate in the example depicted in Figures 8–1 and 8–2, the excess supply of sterling would drive the price of sterling downward. The depreciation of sterling would have the effect of stimulating U.S. purchases of British goods and would thus increase the quantity of sterling demanded on the foreign exchange market. Meanwhile, the appreciation of the dollar (which is equivalent to the depreciation of the pound) would choke off some of the British purchases of U.S. goods. These effects would be shown in Figure 8–2 as a movement along the supply and demand curves from points a and b to point c. Assuming that the intersection of the supply and demand curves happens to lie at a level of $1.90 per pound, the exchange rate would move to that level, at which point the excess supply of sterling would be eliminated.

The effects of this on the balance of payments are shown in Figure 8–3. Suppose that the depreciation of sterling raises the purchase of British goods by U.S. residents by $200, thereby increasing the debits in the merchandise trade account from $800 to $1000. This is accompanied by an increase of $200 in the credit column of the money-payments account to reflect payment for these additional purchases. Meanwhile, suppose the appreciation of the dollar curtails British purchases of U.S. goods by $300,

FIGURE 8-3 U.S. Balance of Payments

	Debits	Credits
Merchandise trade account	$1000	$ 700
Services	300	600
Unilateral transfers		
Capital account	1500	1500
D		D
Money payments	2800	2800
Total debits and credits	$5600	$5600

lowering the credits in the merchandise trade account to $700. This, of course, is accompanied by a $300 reduction of debits in the money-payments account to reflect the cutback in payments by the British. Assuming no other account in the balance of payments is affected, we now have a situation in which U.S. money receipts are equal to U.S. money payments, a situation consistent with the equilibrium at point c in Figure 8–2. The particular numbers selected in this example are arbitrary, of course; the exact amount by which the depreciation of sterling would affect payments by British to U.S. residents, or by U.S. to British residents, would depend on the price elasticities involved. Nevertheless, the effects of the depreciation in sterling would be to bring foreign payments and receipts into balance.[2]

Fixed Exchange Rates and Balance-of-Payments Imbalance

Instead of letting the exchange rate move from $2.00 per pound to the new equilibrium, the authorities of one or both countries could

[2]This makes the assumption that the Marshall–Lerner conditions are met (see Chapter 6); this is not an unreasonable assumption when applied to the general menu of exports by the two countries. The effects of currency devaluation when the Marshall–Lerner conditions are not met are discussed below.

intervene on the foreign exchange market, as described in Chapter 6, to hold the exchange rate at $2.00 per pound. Let us suppose the British central bank elects to do this. In Figure 8–2, this means that it will have to buy £250 per period on the foreign exchange market. This is equal to the amount of the British deficit (or U.S. surplus), which at the $2.00-per-pound exchange rate is equal to the $500 imbalance shown in Figure 8–1. We can generalize this and say that in order to keep the exchange rate from moving, the authorities would have to intervene on the foreign exchange market in an amount equal to the balance-of-payments surplus or deficit. The British government, in our example, is "financing" the British balance-of-payments deficit by paying out dollar reserves equal to the deficit. This has the effect of providing sufficient additional dollars to British residents to enable them to buy $500 more goods from the United States than the Americans are buying from them. "Financing a balance-of-payments deficit," thus, consists of intervening on the foreign exchange market to keep the exchange rate from moving.

In our example, we could have had the U.S. instead of the British government intervene to maintain the exchange rate at $2.00 per pound. The United States would have had to buy up the excess £250, paying out $500 in exchange for it. Here, the U.S. central bank would be providing the additional $500 required by the British residents to finance their balance-of-payments deficit. In the process, of course, U.S. sterling reserves would increase.

BALANCE-OF-PAYMENTS ADJUSTMENT

Balance-of-payments adjustment is the process by which imbalances in the overall balance of payments are eliminated, once they appear. It is useful, at the outset, to divide balance-of-

payments adjustment mechanisms into two classes: automatic mechanisms and policy-induced mechanisms. The *automatic* mechanisms are propelled by forces which are automatically set in motion by the balance-of-payments surpluses or deficits themselves. If left to operate freely, these mechanisms will eliminate the surplus or deficit. The balance of payments will therefore automatically gravitate toward equilibrium following a disturbance, provided there is no interference with the process. As we will see, it is quite common for the authorities to interfere with this process, for a variety of reasons, and as a result balance-of-payments imbalances can persist for long periods of time.

The *policy-induced* adjustment mechanisms include a number of measures that can be undertaken by the authorities to restore balance to the balance of payments. These measures are applied when the authorities think the automatic mechanisms are operating too slowly, or when the authorities are for some reason blocking the automatic mechanisms, but still wish to eliminate a surplus or deficit.

AUTOMATIC BALANCE-OF-PAYMENTS ADJUSTMENT MECHANISMS

Automatic balance-of-payments adjustment mechanisms can be divided into three broad groups, distinguished by the variables through which they operate to eliminate an imbalance. We can identify these as (1) the exchange-rate adjustment mechanism, (2) the income adjustment mechanism and (3) monetary adjustment mechanisms. The monetary adjustment mechanisms can be further divided into three subgroups: (a) the price-level adjustment mechanism, (b) the interest-rate adjustment mechanism and (c) the cash-balance adjustment mechanism. Let us see how each of these mechanisms operates.

The Exchange-Rate Adjustment Mechanism

The principles of the exchange-rate adjustment mechanism have already been covered in the discussion surrounding Figure 8–2, which is reproduced nearby as Figure 8–4. A balance-of-payments surplus or deficit can persist only if the market exchange rate is being maintained at some level other than the equilibrium exchange rate. In Figure 8–4, if the market rate is maintained at $2.00 per pound, while the equilibrium rate lies at $1.90 per pound, a U.S. surplus (i.e., British deficit) equal to *ab* will ensue. If the authorities allow the exchange rate to seek its equilibrium level, the pound will depreciate toward $1.90 and the surplus will be squeezed out. If, as an alternative example, the market exchange rate were held at $1.80, while the equilibrium is at $1.90, a U.S. balance-of-payments deficit (i.e., a British surplus) equal to *de* would ensue. Again, the deficit could be eliminated by allowing the exchange rate to seek its equilibrium level.

It should be noted that it may take some time for an exchange-rate movement to restore full, long-run equilibrium to the balance of pay-

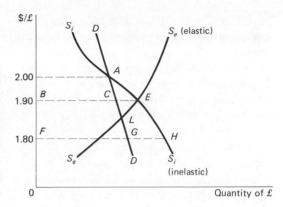

FIGURE 8-5 Adjustment Under Very Low Elasticities

ments. The elasticities of supply and demand are likely to be lower in the short run than over longer periods, as time is required for home and foreign residents to adjust their purchases to exchange-rate movements. In fact, if the elasticities are extremely low, exchange-rate movements can produce the opposite of the expected effects. Such a situation is depicted in Figure 8–5. Here the elasticity of supply of sterling is so low that we have the "backward-bending supply curve" phenomenon described in Chapter 6. Supply curve S_iS_i bends backward toward the northwest instead of lying in the normal southwest–northeast direction. If the elasticity of demand for sterling is so low that the Marshall–Lerner conditions are not met, we will have an unstable equilibrium at point A.[3] Suppose the equilibrium exchange rate is $2.00 per pound, while the actual market rate is $1.90 per pound. At $1.90 per pound, the quantity of sterling supplied is BE and the quantity demanded is BC. This means there is a British balance-of-

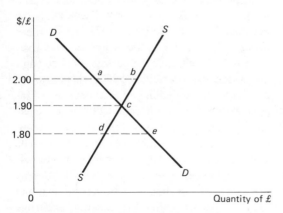

FIGURE 8-4 Supply and Demand for Sterling on Foreign Exchange Market

[3]Recall that for the Marshall–Lerner conditions to be met, so as to ensure a stable equilibrium, the sum of the elasticities of demand reflected in the curves must be greater than or equal to 1.0.

payments deficit of *CE* and an excess supply of sterling on the foreign exchange market of equal amount.

With a freely fluctuating exchange rate, sterling would depreciate in response to the excess supply pressure. As it moves down toward $1.80, however, we see that the excess supply of sterling and the British balance-of-payments deficit is increasing, not decreasing (observe that the deficit of *GH*, at $1.80 per pound, is greater than the deficit of *CE*, at $1.90 per pound). What is happening is that, with very low elasticities, the depreciating pound does not have much effect on the physical quantity of British imports. As the pound loses value relative to the dollar, British residents will have to pay more sterling per unit of imports, with the result that they have a higher import bill. This means a greater balance-of-trade deficit unless British export revenues are increased sufficiently. The latter is precluded by the low elasticity of demand for British goods by Americans; as the pound declines in value, Americans will not significantly increase their imports of British goods.

We might note, at this point, that if the exchange rate had initially been *pegged* at $1.90 per pound, and the British faced a deficit equal to *CE,* the usual remedy would be for the British to devalue the pound. However, the devaluation of the pegged exchange rate from $1.90 to $1.80 would *increase* the deficit from *CE* to *GH*.

The low elasticities are not likely to persist indefinitely, however. Over time, British importers will have time to respond to the now higher cost of imported goods by cutting back on the physical quantity of imports. This will lower the import bill, and the British trade deficit will decrease. In terms of Figure 8–5, as elasticities increase, the supply curve will tend to "unbend" and assume an elastic confirmation as indicated by curve S_eS_e. Actually, the demand

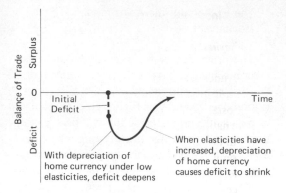

FIGURE 8-6 The J-Curve Effect

curve would also become more elastic, and thus flatter, but we shall ignore this point to keep Figure 8–5 as simple as possible. With supply curve S_eS_e in effect, the depreciation of the pound from $1.90 (or, in the case of a pegged exchange rate, the devaluation from $1.90) will move the exchange rate toward stable equilibrium *L* and *reduce* the balance-of-payments deficit. At point *L,* the deficit will be completely eliminated in that the horizontal distance between curves *DD* and S_eS_e will become zero.

A number of economists argue that a phenomenon of this kind occurred following the devaluation of the dollar in 1971. At first, the lower value of the dollar deepened the U.S. trade deficit, but after the passage of time (during which the elasticities had a chance to increase) the trade deficit began to decrease. This phenomenon has been called the "J-curve effect" because of the path the balance of trade would follow over time (see Figure 8–6). The 1971 episode is described further in Chapter 24.

Since the perverse case involving extremely low elasticities is likely to be rare, and is not likely to persist, a freely fluctuating exchange rate, given a sufficient amount of time, will eliminate a balance-of-payments imbalance.

The Income Adjustment Mechanism

a keynesian model

To understand the income adjustment mechanism, it is helpful to think in terms of a simple Keynesian model that shows the determinants of the national income level. Imagine a spending stream flowing from the household sector of the economy to the business sector (see Figure 8–7) as the household sector purchases goods and services. In addition, imagine a payments stream flowing from the business sector to the household sector, as the business sector pays wages, interest, rent and profits (factor payments) to the households in compensation for labor, capital, land and entrepreneurial inputs. The flow of payments from the business to the household sector represents the households' income; this income is then either saved or spent on goods and services. The whole circular flow of income is known as the national income stream.

There are certain leakages from and injections to the income stream as it flows from the business sector to the household sector and back again. Beginning at the top of the diagram in

Figure 8–7, we identify national income (Yn) as the total amount of factor payments being made by the business sector.[4] Before these payments reach the household sector, however, they are taxed, and this represents the first leakage from the income stream. The amount of taxes is labeled T. This leaves a smaller stream, known as disposable income (Yd), actually flowing to the households.

Now let us see what the household sector does with its disposable income. First, a certain proportion is saved; this represents another leakage from the income stream, since it will not be spent by the households on goods and services. Most of these funds will probably be placed in banks or other financial institutions, although some may be stashed away in vaults or mattresses. Saving is represented by S in Figure 8–7.

Another fraction of household disposable income will be spent on imports (M). This is also a leakage from the home income stream, since it is not paid to the home business sector for goods and services. As we can see, the three leakages, taxes, saving and imports, tend to reduce the level of national income; as funds flow out of the national income stream through one of the leakages, the size of the circular income stream will shrink. The flow of spending by the household sector on goods and services produced by the home business sector is known as consumption and is labeled C in Figure 8–7.

Just as there are leakages from the national income stream, there are also some injections. First, the government will spend at least some of its tax revenues. As the government spends funds (either directly or indirectly) for goods and services, these payments reenter the income stream, as represented by item G in Figure 8–7.

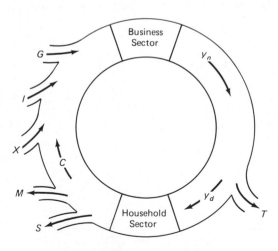

FIGURE 8-7 The National Income and Spending Stream

[4]For simplicity, we abstract from the depreciation of plant and equipment.

The government, of course, does not have to spend the exact amount of its tax revenues during any given period of time. It can spend more, thereby running a budget deficit, or it can spend less, thereby running a budget surplus. If it spends the exact amount of its tax revenues, it is said to have a balanced budget.

A second injection can come in the form of export sales to foreigners (item X in Figure 8–7). When foreign residents buy goods and services from the home business sector, payment for these goods and services enters the home income stream. Of course, export injections may not be equal to import leakages. If imports exceed exports, the country is running a balance-of-trade deficit; if exports exceed imports, it is running a trade surplus. If imports exactly equal exports, then trade is said to be in balance.

A third injection consists of spending by the business sector, itself, on new plant and equipment. This is known as *investment* and is labeled I in Figure 8–7. The business sector obtains the funds for these expenditures by borrowing them from financial institutions. If all household savings are placed in financial institutions and if the business sector borrows exactly that amount, then the savings leakage will be equal to the investment injection. This may not be the case, however; during any given period of time the business sector may end up borrowing more or less than the exact amount of savings.

Figure 8–7 provides insight into an important feature of the national income stream. If total injections ($I + G + X$) equal total leakages ($S + T + M$), the flow of income around the circuit will remain constant. If this is the case, income is said to be in "equilibrium." If total leakages are greater than total injections, however, the size of the income stream will shrink, and if total injections are greater than total leakages, the size of the national income stream will expand.

determinants of leakages and injections

To complete our model, let us specify the items that will cause the injections and leakages to increase or decrease. First, with regard to the saving leakage, let us assume that a given proportion of any change in income will be saved. If this proportion is, say, 10 percent, then an increase in income from $10 billion to $20 billion would result in an increase in saving of $1 billion. The proportion of a change in income that is saved is known as the *marginal propensity to save*. Under this specification, saving is a positive function of income, as shown in Figure 8–8(a) by line S. As we have depicted

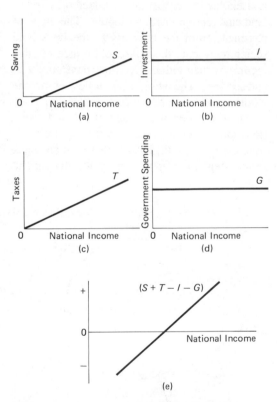

FIGURE 8-8 Domestic-Sector Leakages and Injections

the saving function, the actual level of saving will be negative at very low levels of income (implying that households are either borrowing funds or using up prior savings) and positive at higher levels of income. At all levels, saving increases as income increases.

Second, with regard to the investment injection, we assume that the level of investment is *exogenous* (determined by variables that exist "outside" the model). These would include business expectations and the interest rate. In particular, we assume that the level of investment would *not* be affected by the level of income. Line *I* in Figure 8–8(b) represents the level of investment, and its horizontal position reflects the fact that it will not change as income changes. Increases in interest rates or a more pessimistic business outlook would cause the level of investment to shift downward, while a decrease in interest rates or a brighter business outlook would cause investment to shift upward.

Third, with regard to the tax leakage, we assume that taxes vary positively with income. If the marginal tax rate is, say, 20 percent of income, a $10 billion increase in income will be accompanied by a $2 billion increase in taxes. The level of taxes is represented by line *T* in Figure 8–8(c), and its upward slope reflects the positive relationship between taxes and income.

Fourth, with regard to the level of government spending, we assume that it is independent of the level of income, as indicated by its horizontal position in Figure 8–8(d). Increases in government spending would cause an upward shift in line *G*, while decreases would cause a downward shift in line *G*.

Fifth, with regard to the level of imports, we assume that these are positively related to the level of income. As home income rises, home residents will spend a fraction of the increase on foreign goods; this fraction is known as the *marginal propensity to import*. The positive re-

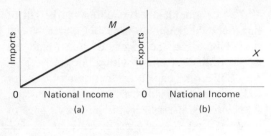

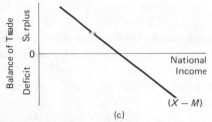

FIGURE 8-9 Foreign-Sector Leakages and Injections

lationship between imports and income is shown by the upward slope of line *M* in Figure 8–9(a).

Finally, with regard to the export injection, we assume that exports are independent of the level of home income (in fact, they are determined by the level of *foreign* income), as depicted by the horizontal position of line *X* in Figure 8–9(b). An increase in exports would appear as an upward shift in line *X*, while a decrease would appear as a downward shift.

domestic-sector and foreign-sector leakages and injections

Now let us identify saving, investment, taxes and government spending as "domestic-sector" leakages and injections, since they represent activity that involves exclusively domestic residents or the domestic government. If we add up the domestic-sector leakages and subtract the domestic-sector injections, we will have what we can call "net domestic-sector leakages." This can be expressed symbolically as $(S + T - I$

− G), or graphically by adding the height of line S and the height of line T in Figure 8–8 and then subtracting the height of line I and the height of line G. The resulting line, $(S + T - I - G)$, can be called the "net domestic-sector leakage function" and is shown in Figure 8–8(e). Its positive slope reflects the positive slopes of curves S and T; leakages increase as income increases. Note that this function will lie above the zero axis at levels of income at which total domestic-sector leakages exceed total domestic-sector injections; it will lie below the zero axis at income levels at which total domestic-sector injections exceed total domestic-sector leakages.

In similar fashion, we can identify imports and exports as "foreign-sector" leakages and injections, since they involve foreign residents and affect the balance of payments. If we subtract the import leakage from the export injection, we will have what can be called "net foreign-sector injections." Note that $(X - M)$ represents the balance of trade of goods and services, and if there are no gifts or capital movements, it represents the overall balance of payments. Graphically, net foreign-sector injections can be shown by subtracting the height of line M in Figure 8–9 from the height of line X; this yields line $(X - M)$ in Figure 8–7(c). Its negative slope reflects the fact that imports increase with income. Note that line $(X - M)$ will lie above the zero axis at levels of income at which exports exceed imports and will lie below the zero axis at levels of income at which imports exceed exports. In fact, the height of line $(X - M)$ above the zero axis indicates the amount of a balance-of-trade surplus, and the distance of this line below the zero axis indicates the amount of a balance-of-trade deficit.

Earlier, in our discussion of Figure 8–7, we established that for national income to remain at a steady level, total injections must exactly

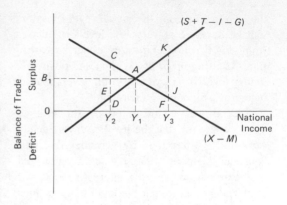

FIGURE 8-10 National Income Equilibrium

equal total leakages. In other words, the following conditions must be met:

$$(S + T + M) = (G + I + X)$$

or, equivalently,

$$(S + T - I - G) = (X - M)$$

Graphically, the height of the $(S + T - I - M)$ function must be equal to the height of the $(X - M)$ function. This will occur where the two functions intersect, as shown by point A in Figure 8–10. With the two functions equal at point A, national income will be steady at point Y_1. This is the equilibrium level, since it is the only level at which total leakages equal total injections. If income were somehow displaced to point Y_2, net foreign-sector injections, DC, would exceed net domestic-sector leakages, DE, and the level of income would rise toward Y_1. If income were somehow displaced to Y_3, net domestic-sector leakages, FK would exceed net foreign-sector injections, FJ, and the level of income would fall toward Y_1. Thus the level of income at which $(X - M) = (S + T - I - G)$ is a stable equilibrium toward which the actual level of income will always move.

disturbances to the balance of payments

In Figure 8–10, at the equilibrium level of income Y_1, note that $(X - M)$ stands at a positive level, and is represented by point B_1 on the vertical axis. Point B_1 represents a balance-of-payments surplus (assuming no gifts or capital movements) since it is equal to the amount of exports minus imports. If the intersection of $(X - M)$ and $(S + T - I - G)$ were to lie below the zero axis, the value of B would be negative, indicating a balance-of-payments deficit.

If one or both of the functions should shift, creating a new intersection of $(X - M)$ and $(S + T - I - G)$, income would adjust to the level consistent with the new intersection. The functions themselves would shift in response to changes in the injections and leakages they comprise. In particular, we can note the following.[5]

1. An increase in exports will shift $(X - M)$ upward, while a decrease in exports will shift it downward.

2. An increase in investment will shift $(S + T - I - G)$ downward, while a decrease will shift it upward.

3. An increase in government spending will shift $(S + T - I - G)$ downward, while a decrease will shift it upward.

4. An increase in taxes will shift $(S + T - I - G)$ upward, while a decrease will shift it downward.

income adjustment mechanism in the Keynesian model

Now let us see how the income adjustment mechanism will operate to reduce an imbalance in the balance of payments. The basic idea is that if a balance-of-payments surplus or deficit

[5]Verification of the direction of these shifts, by tracing their effects through Figures 8–8 and 8–9, is left as an exercise for the reader.

develops at a given level of income, forces will be generated that will cause the level of income to change. The change in income, in turn, will at least partially reduce the payments imbalance. In illustrating the income mechanism, we shall assume that the authorities are maintaining a *rigid exchange-rate peg,* so that the exchange-rate adjustment mechanism is completely inoperative. However, we shall assume that any effects of the pegging operations on the country's money stock are neutralized by the government. In addition, to simplify the analysis, we shall assume that capital movements are absent, so that the overall balance-of-payments surplus or deficit will be equal to the surplus or deficit in the trade account. Finally, we shall assume that the balance of payments is initially in balance. This is reflected in Figure 8–11(a) by the fact that the $(X - M)_1$ and $(S + T - I$

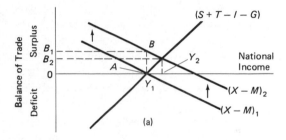

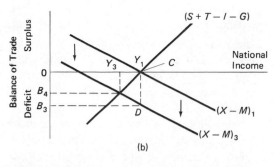

FIGURE 8-11 The Income Adjustment Mechanism

$- G)$ curves intersect at a point on the income axis; in other words, $B = 0$. The initial equilibrium level of income is Y_1.

Now suppose there is a disturbance to the balance of payments in the form of an increase in exports. This shifts the $(X - M)$ curve upward to $(X - M)_2$, and at the initial level of income, Y_1, a balance-of-payments surplus is created equal to OB_1. Now the income adjustment mechanism comes into the picture to reduce this deficit. With the $(X - M)$ curve in its new position, Y_1 is no longer the equilibrium level of income; total injections exceed total leakages by the amount AB. This causes the national income stream to increase, which is shown by a movement in Y up to the level Y_2. Here, total leakages are once again equal to total injections, since at that point $(X - M)_2$ intersects with $(S + T - I - G)$. With the upward movement in income, and the consequent rise in imports, the balance-of-payments surplus is reduced from OB_1 to OB_2. Although the surplus is not eliminated, it has been substantially reduced.

If the initial disturbance had come in the form of a decrease instead of an increase in exports, the $(X - M)$ curve would have been shifted downward to $(X - M)_3$, as shown in Figure 8–11(b). At initial income equilibrium level Y_1, a balance-of-payments deficit is created equal to OB_3. However, Y_1 is no longer the equilibrium level of income; total leakages exceed total injections by the amount CD. This causes income to fall from Y_1 to Y_3. At that point, total injections and leakages are once again equal. With the decline in income, imports decrease and the balance-of-payments deficit is reduced from OB_3 to OB_4.

Using this same model of the relationship between national income and the balance of payments, we can analyze the effects of other kinds of disturbances. These would include an in-crease or decrease in investment or government spending, or exogenous shifts in imports, saving or taxes. These exercises would start with an initial equilibrium as in the preceding examples, and then would shift the curve which is affected by the disturbance in the appropriate direction. The effect on the balance of payments can then be observed, and the effect of the income adjustment mechanism can be traced. Analysis of these other disturbances is left as an exercise for the reader.

The Monetary Adjustment Mechanisms

One shortcoming of the income adjustment model that we have been examining is that it ignores the effects of a balance-of-payments deficit or surplus on the country's money stock. The payments imbalance *will* affect the quantity of money in circulation (unless the authorities take specific steps to offset it) and this, in turn, will affect such variables as the country's interest rate, its price level and the amount of cash balances being held by the public. The changes in these variables will themselves serve to reduce the payments deficit or surplus. In fact, the monetary mechanisms will not merely reinforce the income mechanism of the preceding section; unless interfered with, they will completely eliminate the payments imbalance.

the effects of payments imbalance on a country's money stock

To understand how the price-level, interest-rate and cash-balance mechanisms work, we must first understand the effects of a balance-of-payments surplus or deficit on a country's money stock. In general, under a *pegged exchange-rate system,* a balance-of-payments surplus will increase the money stock and a deficit will de-

FIGURE 8-12 Monetary Effects of Exchange-Market Intervention under Balance-of-Payments Surplus

Federal Reserve				New York Commercial Bank			
Assets		Liabilities		Assets		Liabilities	
Value of foreign currency deposits	+$1 billion (4)	+$1 billion (1)	Deposit liability to N.Y. commercial bank	Deposit held in Federal Reserve	+$1 billion (2)		
				Value of foreign currency deposits	−$1 billion (3)		
					+$1 billion (5)	+$1 billion (6)	Dollar deposit held by foreign commercial bank

(1) Federal Reserve creates $1 billion in new deposits; credits this to New York commercial bank.
(2) This appears as $1 billion asset on New York commercial bank's books.
(3) New York commercial bank transfers $1 billion worth of foreign currency deposits to Federal Reserve.
(4) This appears as an increase in foreign currency deposits owned by Federal Reserve.
(5) New York commercial bank buys $1 billion worth of foreign exchange from foreign commercial banks to replenish its foreign currency holdings.
(6) To pay for this foreign currency, New York bank credits foreign commercial banks with $1 billion in dollar deposits.

crease the money stock of the country that is conducting the pegging operations.[6]

Suppose the United States is running a balance-of-payments surplus of $1 billion. To keep the dollar from appreciating, the U.S. central bank (the Federal Reserve) would have to sell $1 billion on the foreign exchange market. In exchange, of course, it would receive foreign currency balances. The Federal Reserve would operate through one or more of the large New York commercial banks and would follow steps similar to those outlined in Figure 8–12. First the Federal Reserve would create a new deposit liability on itself in the amount of $1 billion and credit this to the New York commercial bank. In exchange, the commercial bank would transfer to the Federal Reserve $1 billion worth of foreign currency, which the commercial bank has been holding as deposits in a foreign bank (or banks). This depletes the New York commercial bank's inventory of foreign exchange, and the bank will replenish this inventory by buying additional foreign currency deposits on the foreign exchange market; it will, of course,

[6]Balance-of-payments imbalances would not cause changes in the money stock under *freely* fluctuating exchange rates since there would be no intervention by the central bank. In that case, however, the exchange-rate adjustment mechanism would be fully operative and would itself act to remove the payments imbalance.

offer dollars to buy the foreign exchange. It is this step that augments the supply of dollars on the foreign exchange market and keeps the dollar from appreciating.[7]

During this process, an important monetary development has occurred; the U.S. money base has been expanded. Deposits held at the Federal Reserve by a commercial bank (e.g., item 2 in Figure 8–12) constitute part of that bank's "reserves," and bank reserves (along with cash held by the banks) constitute the country's *money*

base. Note that the expansion of the money base in this case is equal to the amount of the balance-of-payments surplus. The commercial banking system, through a process of lending and re-lending, can create new deposits equal to a multiple of any new reserves. As a result, the overall U.S. money stock can expand by a *multiple* of the original balance-of-payments surplus. To summarize, then, the money base will expand by an amount equal to the balance-of-payments surplus,[8] and the overall money stock can be expanded by a multiple of the expansion of the money base.

[7]This scenario of central bank intervention is highly simplified. Actual intervention operations may be more complex, but they are analytically equivalent in their effects on the foreign exchange market and the money stock.

[8]Assuming there is no sterilization. This is explained below.

FIGURE 8-13 Monetary Effects of Exchange-Market Intervention under Balance-of-Payments Deficit

Federal Reserve				New York Commercial Bank			
Assets		Liabilities		Assets		Liabilities	
Value of foreign currency deposits	− $1 billion (1)	− $1 billion (3)	Deposit liability to New York commercial bank	Value of foreign currency deposits	+ $1 billion (2)		
				Deposit held at Federal Reserve	− $1 billion (4)		
				Value of foreign currency deposits	− $1 billion (5)	− $1 billion (6)	Dollar deposit liabilities to foreigners

(1) Federal Reserve transfers $1 billion worth of foreign currency deposits to New York commercial bank.
(2) This appears as an increase in foreign currency deposits held by New York commercial bank.
(3) Federal Reserve reduces New York commercial bank's dollar deposit in Federal Reserve.
(4) This appears on New York commerical bank's books as a reduction in reserve assets.
(5) New York commercial bank sells $1 billion worth of foreign exchange holdings to foreign buyers.
(6) This is paid for by a reduction in New York commercial bank's dollar liabilities to foreigners.

The effects would be exactly the opposite if the United States were running a balance-of-payments deficit of $1 billion. The Fed would now have to buy $1 billion on the foreign exchange market to keep the dollar from depreciating. In this case, the Federal Reserve would transfer to the commercial banks $1 billion worth of foreign currency which it holds as deposits in foreign banks. In return, the Federal Reserve would reduce the New York commercial banks' dollar deposits at the Federal Reserve by $1 billion (these steps are shown in Figure 8–13). The commercial banks would now hold more foreign exchange than they previously did, and to reduce these holdings back to the prior level (which was presumably the amount the banks preferred to hold to service their customers and to satisfy their portfolio requirements), they would sell the surplus foreign exchange on the foreign exchange market. They would buy dollars in return, and this last step would augment the demand for dollars and support the value of the dollar on the foreign exchange market.

Once again, there has been an important effect on domestic bank reserves. The reduction in the commercial bank deposits at the Federal Reserve by $1 billion (item 4 in Figure 8–13) reduces bank reserves by that amount. With commercial bank reserves now lowered by $1 billion, the commercial banking system will have to contract its loans and deposits by a multiple of that amount. Note that the money *base* shrinks by an amount *equal* to the balance-of-payments deficit, and the overall money *stock* shrinks by a *multiple* of the reduction in the money base.

sterilization

Incidentally, the Federal Reserve could offset any expansion or contraction of commercial bank reserves caused by balance-of-payments imbalances. This would be accomplished by conducting opposing open market operations. Suppose the Federal Reserve had bought $1 billion on the foreign exchange market to support the dollar, and wished to offset the resulting reduction in commercial bank reserves. It would do this (in an entirely separate operation) by buying $1 billion worth of government securities on the open securities market. The Federal Reserve would pay for these securities by creating a new deposit liability on itself in the amount of $1

FIGURE 8-14 Sterilization through Open Market Operations

Federal Reserve				New York Commercial Bank		
Assets		Liabilities		Assets		Liabilities
Security holdings	+ 1 billion (2)	+ $1 billion (3)	Deposit liabilities to New York commercial bank	Security holdings	− $1 billion (1)	
				Deposit held in Federal Reserve	+ $1 billion (4)	

(1) New York commercial bank transfers $1 billion worth of securities to Federal Reserve.
(2) This appears as an increase in security holdings by Federal Reserve.
(3) Federal Reserve credits New York commerical bank with new $1 billion deposit.
(4) This appears on books of New York commercial bank as increase in deposits held at Federal Reserve.

billion and crediting this to the banks from which the securities are bought. In exchange, the banks would transfer $1 billion worth of securities to the Federal Reserve (see Figure 8–14). The key step is the creation of $1 billion in new reserves for the commercial banking system (step 4 in Figure 8–14). This $1 billion expansion in reserves just offsets the reduction in reserves (step 4 in Figure 8–13) that resulted from exchange-market intervention activity.[9] This process by which the central bank neutralizes the effects of balance-of-payments imbalances on the country's money base is called *sterilization*.

Now that we have seen how exchange-market intervention by a country's central bank will alter the country's money base, we can see how the price-level, interest-rate and cash-balance mechanisms would operate. In discussing these mechanisms, we will assume that sterilization does not occur.

the price-level adjustment mechanism

To trace the steps by which the price-level mechanism would operate, let us assume that the United States moves from an initial position of balance-of-payments balance to a deficit of $1 billion per month. The U.S. central bank is maintaining a policy of rigid exchange-rate pegs, so that the exchange-rate adjustment mechanism is inoperative. As outlined above, the interven-

[9]If the Federal Reserve had bought the securities from the general public instead of directly from a bank, the outcome of the process would have been the same, although more steps would have been involved. The Federal Reserve would have written checks on itself in the amount of $1 billion and issued them to the public in exchange for $1 billion worth of securities. When the public deposited these checks in their commercial banks, the commercial banks would obtain ownership of deposits at the Federal Reserve in that amount. Commercial bank reserves and thus the money base would have risen by $1 billion.

tion by the Fed on the foreign exchange market to hold the dollar at its initial level would have the effects of reducing the U.S. money base by $1 billion and the money stock by a multiple of $1 billion per month. With the shrinking money stock, the U.S. price level would begin to fall relative to foreign prices,[10] causing U.S. goods to become increasingly more attractive to foreigners and causing foreign goods and services to become increasingly less attractive to U.S. residents. Both home and foreign residents would begin to switch from buying foreign goods and services to buying U.S. goods and services. This would result in an increase in U.S. exports and a reduction in U.S. imports and a consequent reduction in the U.S. deficit.

the interest-rate adjustment mechanism

The interest-rate adjustment mechanism is triggered by the fact that the contracting money stock in the United States has the short-run effect of raising interest rates. As U.S. interest rates rise relative to foreign rates, both U.S. and foreign wealth holders will shift some of their existing holdings from foreign to U.S. assets. In addition, a larger portion of any ongoing stream of newly created wealth will find its way into U.S. assets and a smaller portion will flow into foreign assets. This activity helps to generate surplus in the U.S capital account and serves to reduce the original balance-of-payments deficit.

the cash-balance adjustment mechanism

The cash-balance adjustment mechanism also stems from the fact that the U.S. deficit of $1 billion per month will reduce the U.S. money stock by a multiple of that amount. U.S. resi-

[10]The fall in U.S. prices relative to foreign prices could very well take the form of a slowing in the United States relative to the foreign rate of inflation.

dents will permit their cash balances to dwindle only so far before they will do something about it. When cash balances begin to fall below tolerable levels, residents of the United States, the deficit country, will begin to retrench on spending for goods and services (to curtail the decline in cash balances) and this will tend to reduce imports. They will also work to restore cash balances to the desired level by pushing sales of goods and services to foreigners; this will tend to increase exports. In addition, U.S. residents may seek to augment cash balances temporarily by selling off assets to foreigners; this will contribute to a surplus in the capital account. All of these actions will serve to reduce the original deficit.

Although the Keynesian income adjustment mechanism was found to be "incomplete" in that it could come to a halt before balance-of-payments balance was completely restored, the price-level, interest-rate and cash-balance mechanism, if allowed to operate, will continue until the deficit is eliminated. This is because the money stock of the deficit country will continue to shrink for as long as the deficit continues.

Repercussions through the Foreign Economy

So far, we have ignored the effects of the U.S. payments imbalance on foreign economies and the effects of foreign repercussions on the adjustment mechanisms. It turns out that the effects on the foreign economies will typically reinforce the adjustment mechanisms just described. Suppose, as in our foregoing example, the U.S. central bank is acting to maintain the exchange-rate peg by buying dollars on the foreign exchange market. The fact that the Federal Reserve is buying dollars means that it must be selling foreign currency from its stock of reserves. The sale of foreign currency by the U.S.

central bank will not of itself increase the stock of foreign money (a country's money base can be affected only by the acquisition and disbursement of that country's money by its *own* central bank); it will merely pass the ownership of these balances from the Federal Reserve to whatever parties happen to buy them on the foreign exchange market. Although there is no actual expansion of the foreign country's money base, the rate of spending abroad will tend to increase as foreign currency is moved from idle balances held by the Federal Reserve to active circulation by the foreign residents. Any such increase in foreign spending will tend to increase U.S. exports and help to reduce the original deficit.

If we were to alter our example to have the *foreign* central bank do all the exchange-rate pegging while the Federal Reserve did none, the automatic balance-of-payments adjustment mechanisms would still operate. In this case, however, it would be the *foreign* money stock that would be systematically altered. In the case of a foreign surplus—the counterpart to the U.S. deficit—the foreign money stock would be expanded as the foreign central bank created and sold its own currency to keep it from appreciating. Foreign prices would rise relative to those in the United States, foreign interest rates would fall, and the cash balance constraint on foreign spending would be loosened. All of these developments would serve to reduce and ultimately eliminate the original U.S. deficit.

All of the automatic balance-of-payments adjustment mechanisms we have discussed tend to operate simultaneously and to reinforce each other. One might wonder, then, how balance-of-payments surpluses and deficits can persist for as long as they do. In large measure, the answer lies in the fact that the authorities frequently interfere with the operation of the adjustment mechanisms, sometimes deliberately, sometimes inadvertently, but usually in pursuit of competing policy objectives.

POLICY-INDUCED BALANCE-OF-PAYMENTS ADJUSTMENT

If a balance-of-payments imbalance persists for longer than is considered desirable, there are a number of deliberate measures the authorities can take to reduce the imbalance. These policies can be divided into two broad categories: those aimed at switching home and foreign purchases between home and foreign goods so as to improve the balance of payments; and those aimed at adjusting the overall level of home spending upward or downward as necessary to rebalance the balance of payments. These are known as expenditure-switching and expenditure-changing policies, respectively.

Expenditure-Switching Policies

Expenditure-switching policies are designed to redirect the patterns of spending among countries. They include such measures as devaluation, exchange controls and trade restrictions. To reduce a deficit, for example, the home authorities might devalue home currency with the idea that this would give home goods a greater competitive edge in world markets and thereby stimulate exports. At the same time, foreign goods would become more expensive to home residents, and this would reduce imports. The devaluation is thus aimed at redirecting both home and foreign purchases more toward home goods.

Exchange controls consist of requirements that all home residents selling goods, services or assets to foreigners turn over their foreign exchange proceeds to the government. In return, these parties receive home currency in an amount determined by the official (pegged) exchange rate. By acquiring control of all foreign exchange earnings, the government can control the rate at which foreign exchange is spent for imports of goods, services and assets, and can

therefore control the size of the balance-of-payments deficit.[11]

Exchange controls have the disadvantage that they suspend the free market for trading the home country's currency and are expensive to operate. They do, however, relieve the home authorities of having to use their international reserves to support home currency on the foreign exchange market. Exchange controls are typically applied by governments that are maintaining an exchange rate that overvalues home currency on the foreign exchange market, but whose reserves are running so low that there is a threat that the government might have to abandon the practice of overvaluing the home currency.

Trade restrictions can also be applied to divert international trade flows. Import tariffs, for example, increase the price that home residents have to pay for foreign goods and can cause home residents to switch purchases from foreign to home goods, thus reducing imports. Import quotas place an outright limit on the physical amount of various goods that can be imported, while "nontariff" barriers make importing more difficult and expensive.

Expenditure-Changing Policies

Expenditure-changing policies began to receive attention when it was realized that expenditure-switching policies, taken alone, might be insufficient to remove balance-of-payments imbalances. Suppose, for example, that a country is running a balance-of-payments deficit at the same time that its resources are fully employed. Such a situation is shown in Figure 8–15(a). Here, Y_f is assumed to be the full-employment level of income. It is also the initial equilibrium income level, since total leakages and injections are equal at that level. The initial

[11]Through exchange controls, the government can also control *which* goods are imported.

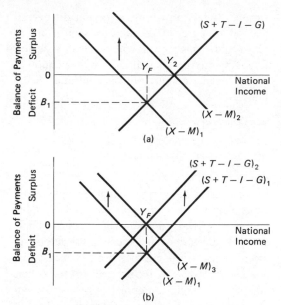

FIGURE 8-15 Coordination of Income-Switching and Income-Changing Policies

balance-of-payments deficit is equal to OB_1. Now suppose the country tries to remove the deficit by devaluing home currency. The devaluation switches both home and foreign purchases to home goods, as intended, increasing exports and decreasing imports. This appears as an upward shift in $(X - M)$ to $(X - M)_2$. Now, however, the new equilibrium level of income, Y_2, is greater than the full-employment level. The primary effect of the additional demand for home goods is thus to drive home prices upward. The rising home prices (relative to foreign prices) will serve to counteract the effects of the devaluation. As home prices rise, traders will switch back into foreign goods, causing the $(X - M)$ curve to recede back toward its original position, and the deficit will continue.

If upward pressure on home prices is to be avoided when home currency is devalued, it is necessary to reduce the overall level of spending by home residents. This can be accomplished through expenditure changing (in this case, expenditure-reducing) policies. Expenditure reduction through curtailment of investment or government spending will cause the $(S + T - I - G)$ curve to shift upward. If sufficiently strong expenditure-reducing policies are applied, the $(S + T - I - G)$ curve can be shifted to $(S + T - I - G)_2$ as in Figure 8–15(b). Now a devaluation in an amount sufficient to move $(X - M)_1$ to $(X - M)_3$ will establish both balance-of-payments balance and an equilibrium income level equal to the full-employment level.

The Absorption Approach

Insight into the importance of expenditure-changing policies can be gained by considering the *absorption approach* to balance-of-payments problems. The absorption approach recognizes that, in order for the trade account to balance, a country's absorption of goods and services (i.e., its consumption, investment and government spending) must equal the country's output of goods and services. This can be seen by considering the following equation, which relates total sources of goods and services available to the economy to the ways in which they are absorbed by the economy.

$$Y + M = C + I + G + X$$

On the left-hand side we see that the goods and services available to the economy must come from either home output (Y) or imports (M). On the right-hand side we see that these goods and services must be absorbed by domestic consumption (C), domestic investment (I), government spending (G) or sales to foreigners (X). Now let us move M to the right-hand side to obtain

$$Y = C + I + G + (X - M)$$

We can now identify $C + I + G$ as domestic absorption (A), and $(X - M)$ as the balance of trade (B), where positive values of B represent a trade surplus and negative values a trade deficit. Our equation now reads

$$Y = A + B$$

or

$$B = Y - A$$

In this latter form, we can see that the balance of trade will be in surplus if domestic output exceeds domestic absorption, and in deficit if domestic absorption exceeds domestic output. Trade will be in balance if domestic absorption and output are equal. In other words, if absorption exceeds output, the difference is being met by imports, and there will be a deficit in the trade account. If output exceeds absorption, the excess is being exported and there must be a surplus in the trade account. Since a trade surplus or deficit is the result of an imbalance between output and absorption, removing a payments imbalance requires bringing output and absorption back into line with each other. This can be accomplished by reducing or increasing overall domestic expenditures (absorption) as necessary to adjust it to the level of output. From this came the notion of expenditure-changing policies.

The specific measures that can be taken to implement expenditure-changing policies are the standard ones by which a country's authorities attempt to regulate the level of aggregate demand within the economy: expansionary or contractionary monetary and fiscal policies. In most cases, a combination of expenditure-switching and expenditure-changing policies is required to eliminate a balance-of-payments imbalance. If the country is running a balance-of-payments deficit while the economy is at full employment, a devaluation coupled with expenditure reduction will be required, as in the above example. If the country is running a balance-of-payments

surplus, but is unwilling to permit an overall decline in aggregate demand for fear of unemployment (as might occur with revaluation alone), removing the surplus will require revaluation of home currency coupled with expenditure-raising policies.

THE HIERARCHY OF BALANCE-OF-PAYMENTS ADJUSTMENT MECHANISMS

In considering the various balance-of-payments adjustment mechanisms, one can envision a hierarchy of defenses against payments imbalance. When an imbalance occurs, the automatic mechanisms will begin to operate to remove it. Almost immediately, the currency of the deficit country will begin to depreciate on the foreign exchange market. If the authorities are maintaining a rigid exchange-rate peg, however, the exchange-rate mechanism will be completely blocked; under a managed floating exchange-rate system, in which the authorities allow the exchange rate to adjust partially, the exchange-rate mechanism will be partially blocked. With the exchange-rate mechanism blocked, the other automatic mechanisms come into play, most of them propelled by the effects on the money stock of exchange-market intervention. Frequently, however, the authorities will not allow the automatic fixed-exchange-rate mechanisms to operate either. Governments seldom like it when domestic monetary conditions are upset by variations in the balance of payments, and will often act to sterilize these effects. Complete sterilization would neutralize the price-level, interest-rate and cash-balance mechanisms. This leaves only the Keynesian income mechanism operative and, as we saw earlier, it will not ordinarily bring about complete adjustment. There is even a question as to whether *any* lasting effect can be obtained from the income mechanism if the money stock is not allowed to change; income cannot very well rise if the money stock cannot increase sufficiently to support a higher level of income.

With the automatic adjustment mechanisms blocked by the authorities, the balance-of-payments surplus or deficit can continue. Eventually, a country running a deficit will find its international reserves running low. If they run out, the authorities can no longer peg the currency on the foreign exchange market, and the exchange-rate adjustment mechanism will begin to operate. Typically, it is at this point that countries begin to consider the deliberate adjustment measures described above.

If the country is running a surplus, there is no danger of its running out of international reserves. After all, it is intervening on the foreign exchange market to hold down the price of its own currency, and this requires buying up foreign currencies which are *added* to its international reserves. The fact that the country is having to pour its own currency into circulation, however, can be highly inflationary. If the inflationary effects of pouring money into the economy through exchange market intervention cannot be sterilized, the country might find itself resorting to some of the deliberate policies. Germany and Switzerland, for example, found that their balance-of-payments surpluses during the 1970s were highly inflationary and imposed measures to restrict capital inflows into their countries. Unwilling to let the exchange rates float freely and unwilling to let the automatic adjustment (especially the price-level) mechanisms operate, these countries resorted to a deliberate policy of trying to block capital inflows.

THE MONETARY APPROACH TO THE BALANCE OF PAYMENTS

The monetary approach to the balance of payments offers an alternative way of viewing the forces that determine balance-of-payments surpluses or deficits. In this view, balance-of-payments imbalances result from imbalances between the supply and demand of money within the economy. If the home supply for money exceeds the home demand, the excess funds will be spent abroad on foreign goods, services and assets. This produces an overall balance-of-payments deficit. If the home demand for money exceeds the supply, home residents will augment domestic money balances by stepping up sales of goods, services and assets to foreigners and by decreasing purchases from foreigners. This produces an overall balance-of-payments surplus.

Now let us consider the determinants of the demand and supply of money. The demand for money is assumed to be a stable function of real income, the price level and the interest rate. If prices rise, the public will wish to hold a larger amount of money balances to cover their economic transactions. At lower price levels, the public will demand smaller money balances. As the economy grows (i.e., as real income increases over time), the demand for money will grow proportionately. The interest rate represents the opportunity cost of holding money, so that at high interest rates the public will demand smaller money balances and at lower interest rates it will demand larger money balances. The demand for money can be expressed as follows:

$$M_d = f(P, y, r)$$

where

M_d = demand for money by the public
P = general price level
y = real income level
r = interest rate

The supply of money is equal to the money base multiplied by the deposit expansion multiplier. The money base is divided into two components. The first, the domestic-credit component, is that part of the money base that is deliberately created by the central bank for the purpose of expanding the home money supply. This component is increased or decreased primarily through open market operations (the purchase and sale of securities on the open market by the central bank). The second component of the money base is known as the international-reserves component. It is that part of the money base that results from central bank intervention on the foreign exchange market. The way in which exchange market intervention would affect the money base was discussed earlier in this chapter. The supply of money can be expressed as

$$M_s = A(D + R)$$

where

M_s = total supply of money in the economy
A = deposit expansion multiplier
D = domestic-credit component of the money base
R = international-reserves component of the money base

Now let us consider an example of how an imbalance between money supply and money demand can lead to imbalance in the overall balance of payments. Let us assume the home country is a small, open economy in which the home monetary authorities are pegging the exchange rate; foreign macroeconomic variables are fixed. Suppose further that the home economy is growing steadily over time, while prices and the interest rate remain constant. The demand for money will increase in proportion to economic growth. If the money supply grows at the same rate as money demand, no imbalance between money supply and money demand will result.

However, let us say that the central bank begins to expand the domestic-credit component of the money base at a faster rate by stepping up the rate at which it buys securities from the public. The overall money supply will now increase faster than money demand, and home

residents will spend the excess money balances on goods, services and assets. Buying items from fellow home residents does not relieve the excess supply of money, however; it merely shuffles it among home residents. On the other hand, purchases from foreigners does relieve the excess supply of money, and the overseas spending will continue until the entire excess supply of money has been dissipated through purchases from foreigners. Of course, the increase in foreign purchases pushes the overall balance of payments into deficit. Under this scenario, then, the balance-of-payments deficit results from an excess supply of money within the economy, which stems from the fact that the authorities are expanding the money supply faster than the rate of growth in the demand for money. The deficit will continue for as long as money-supply growth exceeds the growth in money demand.

As an alternative example, suppose the authorities were to slow the rate of growth in the money supply so that it becomes lower than the rate of growth in money demand. Excess demand for money will begin to build, and the public will try to meet the excess demand by drawing in funds from overseas. They will do this by stepping up sales of goods, services and assets to foreigners and cutting back on foreign purchases. This, of course, produces a balance-of-payments surplus—a surplus that will continue for as long as money demand is growing faster than the money supply.

The deficit or surplus generated by excessive or deficient growth in the money supply can be related to our discussion of the market balance of payments in earlier sections of this chapter. Recall that in our analysis of the market balance of payments, the below-the-line items represented money payments to and from foreigners, and that this corresponded to the excess demand or supply of foreign currency on the foreign exchange market. In Figure 8–1, which is reproduced nearby as Figure 8–16, the $500 debit balance in the money-payments account repre-

FIGURE 8-16 U.S. Balance of Payments

	Debits	Credits
Merchandise trade account	$ 800	$1000
Services	300	600
Unilateral transfers		
Capital accounts	1500	1500
D —————— *D*		
Money payments	3100	2600
Total debits and credits	$5700	$5700

sents an increase in overseas sales, as home residents attempt to draw in funds from abroad to meet an excess demand for money within the domestic economy. Above line *DD* in Figure 8–16, we can see the effects of this increase in overseas selling activity in the excess of credit entries over debit entries in the combined goods, services and capital accounts. In Figure 8–2, which is reproduced as Figure 8–17, this activity shows up as an excess supply of sterling, reflecting the outlay by foreign (British) residents to buy the additional U.S. goods.

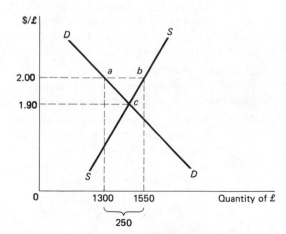

FIGURE 8-17 Supply and Demand for Sterling on Foreign Exchange Market

Balance-of-Payments Policy under the Monetary Approach

The implications for balance-of-payments adjustment policy under the monetary approach are clear. Since balance-of-payments deficits are caused by the fact that the money supply is growing faster than the demand for money, the remedy for the payments deficit is to slow the rate of growth in the money supply until it is brought back into line with the rate of growth in the demand for money. If the problem is a balance-of-payments surplus, which reflects a deficiency in the rate on growth in the money supply relative to the demand for money, the remedy is to increase the rate of growth in the supply of money until it reaches the rate of growth in the demand for money.

Domestic Policy under the Monetary Approach

It is interesting to consider the effects of domestic monetary policy under the monetary approach, given the assumptions of our preceding examples. Suppose the home authorities wish to conduct an expansionary monetary policy and thus step up the rate at which they are buying securities from the public. This means increasing the rate of growth in the domestic-credit component of the money base. The overall money stock will increase by a multiple of this amount as determined by the deposit expansion multiplier. However, home residents are not content to hold the additional money balances since the demand for money has not increased. They expend the surplus funds on foreign goods, services and assets. This puts downward pressure on home currency on the foreign exchange market, and to maintain the exchange-rate peg, the home central bank must buy home currency on the foreign exchange market. This reduces the international-reserves component of the money base. The net result is that any increase in the domestic-credit component of the money base generated by open market operations will be offset by contraction in the international-reserves component of the money base through exchange market intervention, and the overall size of the money base will not change. Of course, the balance of payments will be pushed into deficit in the process. An implication is that under this particular set of assumptions, monetary policy cannot work since the money stock cannot be effectively changed. Attempts to alter the rate of growth in the money supply only result in balance-of-payments imbalances.

Under a more relaxed set of assumptions, monetary policy might be more effective, in that the authorities *could* change the size of the money base. If the price level and the interest rate were flexible, an increase in the rate of growth in the money supply would affect these variables as well as the balance of payments. It would raise prices and lower interest rates, thereby raising the demand for money. Home residents would be induced to hold a greater portion of any increase in the money supply. Contractionary monetary policy would tend to lower prices and raise interest rates, so that home residents would be content to have their money holdings increase at a slower rate.

If the exchange rate were flexible instead of fixed, attempts to change the domestic-credit component of the money base would not be offset by subsequent exchange market intervention, and monetary policy would be even more effective. Of course, the exchange rate itself would move in response to internal monetary changes. Home currency would depreciate whenever the rate of expansion in the home money supply exceeded the rate of growth in money demand. Likewise, home currency would appreciate whenever the rate of expansion of the home money stock fell short of the rate of growth in money demand. We shall have more to say about the relationship between money supply, money demand, the balance of payments and the exchange rate in chapters 9 and 10.

QUESTIONS AND EXERCISES

1. What is meant by balance-of-payments equilibrium or disequilibrium? Discuss the applicability of these terms to the *accounting* and *market* balance-of-payments concepts.

2. Explain the connection between the market balance of payments and the foreign exchange market.

3. Explain the relationship between balance-of-payments surpluses or deficits and change in international reserves under a regime of fixed exchange rates.

4. What is meant by balance-of-payments adjustment? Distinguish between automatic and deliberate adjustment mechanisms.

5. How do movements in the exchange rate toward equilibrium on the foreign exchange market serve to bring the balance of payments into balance? Can you identify circumstances in which it would not?

6. How does the income adjustment mechanism operate? Is it possible for the level of national income to be in equilibrium at the same time that there is a payments imbalance? Explain.

7. What is "sterilization"? Explain how it affects the various automatic balance-of-payments adjustment mechanisms. Why would a government choose to use sterilization, given its effects on balance-of-payments adjustment?

8. Distinguish between expenditure-switching and expenditure-changing policies. How does each contribute to balance-of-payments adjustment?

9. Identify the particular combination of expenditure-switching and expenditure-changing policies that would be required to establish balance-of-payments equilibrium with full employment for a country which is running a payments surplus and is already operating at full employment. Justify the policy choices you specify.

10. Evaluate the statement that balance-of-payments surpluses or deficits are the result of policy choices made by governments, and that they would not persist in the absence of these policies.

INTERNATIONAL ECONOMIC INTERDEPENDENCE: THE EFFECTS OF INTERNATIONAL LINKAGES ON MACROECONOMIC ANALYSIS AND POLICY

INTRODUCTION:
Expanding Linkages among the World's Economies

The traditional approach in macroeconomic analysis, especially in the classroom, has been to focus on the individual national economy as an isolated entity. International economic relations and interdependencies are tacked on after the isolated economy has been thoroughly explored. While this approach may be useful for expository purposes, international linkages must play a central role in analyzing real world macroeconomic problems. Policy measures based on analysis that focuses too narrowly on the home economy and overlooks important international repercussions can produce unwanted effects both at home and abroad.

During the 1970s a series of major international economic disturbances, including the collapse of the international monetary system and the international oil crisis, underscored the interdependent nature of the world's economic system. One result is that the public, especially in the United States, has become much more aware of connections between conditions in the home economy and events in the rest of the world. This is not to say that the public had been entirely unaware of international economic problems. During the 1960s, U.S. balance-of-payments problems were widely reported, as were the several currency crises that erupted during that decade. But the United States is a vast, largely self-sufficient country, and international economic crises seemed to have few discernible effects on the daily lives of most Americans. Concern over international economic relations was left to those economists and government officials who specialized in such matters.

The economic shocks during the 1970s were to change that view. The oil crisis of

1973 and 1974 and its aftermath shattered any illusions that Americans could live in comfortable economic isolation. Their personal lives were touched by shortages and price increases that stemmed either directly or indirectly from the oil crisis. As it turned out, oil price increases not only added to existing inflationary pressures, but also generated a massive redistribution of wealth among countries and had a marked effect on international trade and capital flows.

In contrast to the Americans, residents of smaller, more highly open economies— economies for which exports and imports account for a large proportion of overall economic activity—have historically been more aware of international economic dependencies. These countries, which include Japan, Great Britain and many of the European countries, are less self-sufficient in terms of raw materials, semimanufactured goods and even finished goods. In addition, the international monetary arrangements adopted at the end of World War II placed the primary burden of maintaining exchange-rate stability on the non–U.S. members of the system. This meant that the internal monetary systems of these countries were more sensitive to foreign disturbances. Indeed, by the end of the 1960s, most European countries were convinced that greater international economic cooperation was imperative, and they adopted a resolution to form a common monetary system by the 1980s.

While the oil crisis may have been the most dramatic event in recent years to underscore the interdependence of the world economic system, other developments have been steadily strengthening the linkages among the various economies. Since the late 1950s, international trade and financial transactions have undergone enormous expansion. Industrial economies have become increasingly dependent on their trading partners, not only as sources of raw materials, intermediate products and final goods, but also as markets for their own output. National financial markets have become more closely linked with improvements in communication, with the lowering of official restrictions on capital movements and with the removal of exchange controls. The emergence of the Eurodollar market as an international money market with close ties to financial markets in individual countries has provided a conduit for more rapid transmission of short-term capital between countries.

Inflation is now seen as a global problem rather than as a problem whose cause and cure can be found solely within the structure of the afflicted economy. It has become clear that traditional domestic economic policy tools, such as monetary and fiscal policies, do not work the same way in an open economy as they do in relatively isolated economies. It has also become evident that monetary and fiscal policies applied for domestic purposes in one country can spill over and affect other economies in ways that may not be welcome.

As the linkages among the economies within the system expand, it will become increasingly important to understand how these linkages work. Otherwise it will become impossible to formulate sensible policies to control the international transmission of economic disturbances, or even to deal effectively with internal economic problems. The following two chapters are designed to provide insights into these linkages and mechanisms. Chapter 9 will explore channels through which inflation and other economic disturbances are transmitted among countries. Chapter 10 will examine the effects of macroeconomic policy in an open economy.

INTERNATIONAL TRANSMISSION 9
of ECONOMIC DISTURBANCES

No country in today's world exists in complete economic isolation. The very process of specialization and trade produces a vast array of mutual dependencies. A country heavily involved in international trade comes to rely on foreign sources for those goods in which foreign producers have a comparative advantage, while at the same time it becomes dependent upon foreign markets for sales of its own output. Beyond these normal trade dependencies, countries have become increasingly sensitive, in recent years, to macroeconomic conditions and disturbances from abroad. Cycles in output and unemployment can pass rapidly between countries that have closely tied goods and capital markets, and the transmission of inflation has become a truly global phenomenon.

In this chapter we shall identify a number of linkages that join the national economies. We shall also examine the important mechanisms by which economic disturbances can be transmitted from one country to the next. Our primary focus will be on the international generation and transmission of inflation because of its importance as a current international problem. We should bear in mind, though, that the mechanisms that transmit inflation between countries can also transmit other disturbances, including cycles in output and unemployment.

Until recently, inflation was regarded as a problem whose effects were confined, by and large, to the country in which it was generated. The concept of "imported inflation" (in which inflation seeps into the home economy from abroad) was well known, but was considered primarily to be a problem that arose when a country undervalued its currency on the foreign exchange market. A currency is "undervalued" if the government pegs the exchange rate at a level that makes the currency artificially cheap on the foreign exchange market. This causes an artificially high demand for home goods on world markets and can put upward pressure on home prices. As we shall see, an undervalued currency can certainly contribute to home inflation, but economists have begun to probe further for mechanisms and linkages that can produce inflation on a global scale.

Interest in inflation as an international phenomenon was heightened by the price increases that arose concurrently in a large number of countries in the late 1960s and in the 1970s. Figure 9–1 shows the comparative rates of inflation for three major industrial countries between 1964 and 1980. Note the upward trend in inflation between 1967 and 1974, and the downward trend between 1974 and 1976. The trends diverged between 1976 and 1978, but by 1979 they were all headed upward. A number of hypotheses have been advanced to explain this phenomenon. It is possible, for example, that the individual countries could be generating independent, home-grown inflations at the same time. This could occur by sheer coincidence, or it could occur in response to some set of developments that affects all of the countries simultaneously. Another possibility is that inflation is generated within a few key countries and then transmitted through various channels to other nations. Much of the recent work on international inflation has been aimed at identifying possible transmission channels and assessing their relative importance in spreading inflation.

THE GENERATION OF INTERNATIONAL INFLATION

In analyzing the sources of world inflation, it is useful to make a distinction between domestically generated inflation and what we are calling "international inflation." By international infla-

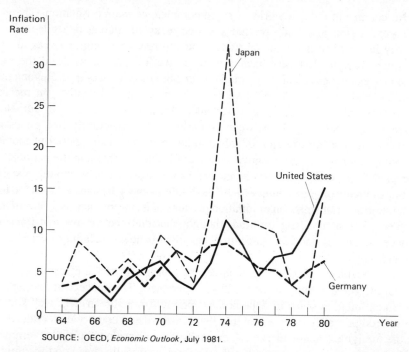

SOURCE: OECD, *Economic Outlook*, July 1981.

FIGURE 9-1 Comparative Inflation Rates in Three Leading Industrial Countries (Period-to-Period Percentage Change in Consumer Prices First Half of Year, Annual Rates)

tion, we mean inflation that is generated by the *interaction* among economies, as opposed to inflation that is generated entirely within countries. Let us now explore several possible explanations of the causes of worldwide inflation.

Coincidental Inflation in Separate Countries

As suggested above, one possible explanation of recent worldwide inflation is that individual countries have begun, by sheer coincidence, to inflate their economies independently. This seems unlikely in light of the fact that global inflation seldom occurred, prior to the late 1960s, except in time of war. There is little reason to expect, in the absence of some international development that affects all of the economies in the same way, that practically all of the countries in the system would pursue inflationary policies at the same time.

Common Pressures to Maintain Full Employment

A second possibility is that individual countries have begun to inflate in response to common social and political pressures. Most industrialized countries have commitments to maintain full employment, and come under pressure to implement expansionary monetary and fiscal policies whenever unemployment begins to develop. The expansionary response by the government can provide the impetus for domestic inflation. While such policies could certainly be inflationary, this argument leaves unanswered why unemployment should have occurred simultaneously on a global scale. It also fails to take account of the fact that many countries did choose restrictive monetary policies to dampen inflation during the 1970s even when it meant a rise in unemployment.

Rising Prices in Key Resources

A third possibility is that rapid increases in the world price of critical imports, such as food, oil, and other primary products, could have affected all the countries in the system at the same time. The first large-scale curtailment in oil supplies began in late 1973. Because the price elasticity of demand for oil is fairly low, at least in the short run, a small percentage reduction in supply resulted in a large percentage increase in price. The higher oil prices were "passed through" to the user economies, substantially raising the prices of those goods that use petroleum energy as a direct or indirect input. There seems to be little doubt that the increase in the world price of oil contributed to the severity of world inflation in the 1970s. There is also reason to believe that the income transfers from the user to the producer nations contributed to the global recession in the mid-1970s. We shall have more to say on the effects of the oil crisis toward the end of this chapter.

Removal of "Balance-of-Payments Discipline"

A fourth possible explanation of worldwide inflation is that changes in international monetary arrangements during the early 1970s reduced some of the antiinflationary constraints inherent in the old fixed-rate system. Under fixed exchange rates, it is argued, overly rapid monetary expansion within a country will lead to a balance-of-payments deficit and a depletion of international reserves. Since governments generally do not want to have their international reserves depleted, this serves as a constraint on monetary expansion and therefore on inflation. In addition, if a balance-of-payments deficit did develop, there would be pressure to employ a contractionary monetary policy to reduce it, thereby adding an additional restraint on monetary expansion. With the transition to managed floating exchange rates, so the argument goes, this "balance-of-payments discipline" was severely weakened and governments have felt freer to engage in monetary expansion.

As a counterpoint, others argue that a flexible exchange rate exerts an antiinflationary discipline of its own. Overly rapid monetary expansion will cause home currency to depreciate on the foreign exchange market. This imposes highly visible costs on many home residents, causing them to bring pressure to bear on the authorities to curtail monetary expansion. Whether either of these "disciplines" has much practical effect in constraining monetary expansion has never been established empirically.

Ratchet Effects

A fifth possible explanation of world inflation is that fluctuating exchange rates produce a "ratchet effect," which systematically pushes prices within the participating countries in an upward direction. The ratchet effect works as follows. Suppose the exchange rate between two countries is fluctuating. When home currency *depreciates*, home prices of imports increase, raising the average level of prices in the home country. Home workers, facing higher living costs, demand and may get higher wages. The higher wages, in turn, become built into overall home production costs, and cost-push inflation results. On the other hand, when home currency *appreciates*, there is not a corresponding deflation at home. Appreciating home currency will cause a decline in home import costs, and this will initially lower the average level of home prices. Home workers are not willing to accept lower money wages, however, and there is no related reduction in overall home production costs. As a result, production cost increases that occur when home currency depreciates are not offset by production cost decreases when home currency appreciates. The movement from fixed

to fluctuating exchange rates in the early 1970s, it is argued, may thus have introduced an inflationary bias into the system.

Whether the advent of flexible exchange rates and the ratchet effect have contributed significantly to worldwide inflation is debatable. First, the inflation of the 1970s was well under way before 1973, the year in which fixed rates were finally abandoned. In addition, some observers argue that fixed rates themselves contain a ratchet effect, so that there should be little change in the inflationary bias when the system moves from fixed to flexible exchange rates.

The ratchet effect under fixed exchange rates would work as follows. As we know, forces that cause a country's currency to depreciate under flexible exchange rates would produce a balance-of-payments deficit under fixed exchange rates. Conversely, forces that cause a country's currency to appreciate under flexible exchange rates would produce a balance-of-payments surplus under fixed exchange rates. In the absence of sterilization, a country running a balance-of-payments deficit will (*certeris paribus*) experience a contraction in its money stock. This will put downward pressure on wages and prices. Because wages and prices are resistant to downward pressure, however, the full deflationary effects of the deficit will not be felt. In fact, the authorities may ultimately be forced to expand the money stock to avoid unemployment. When the balance of payments is in surplus, the country's money stock will be automatically expanding, putting upward pressure on wages and prices. Wages and prices are not so resistant to upward pressure, and the full inflationary effect of the surplus *will* be felt. Just as upward and downward swings in the exchange rate create net upward pressure on wages and prices under flexible exchange rates, so will swings between balance-of-payments surpluses and deficits create upward pressure on wages and prices under fixed exchange rates.

Inflation as a Contagious Disturbance

A final explanation of world inflation is that, instead of being generated simultaneously within the various countries, inflation is generated within a few specific countries and is then spread abroad through a number of channels. Some observers maintain that the United States has been the major source of recent world inflation, and that this was especially true during the 1960s and early 1970s when exchange rates were essentially fixed. The following section explores the channels through which inflation can be transmitted between countries.

INTERNATIONAL TRANSMISSION OF INFLATION

It is well established that, for sustained inflation to occur within a country, there must be a sustained increase in the country's money supply relative to its money demand. This is true whether the inflation is being generated entirely within the country, or whether it is being transmitted from abroad. In the case of imported inflation, the necessary monetary expansion can occur as a direct result of exchange-market intervention, as the local authorities try to maintain a fixed exchange rate in the face of a balance-of-payments surplus that results from foreign inflation; or it can occur when the authorities expand the money supply to avoid any domestic unemployment that may be produced by the transmission process. The link between foreign inflation and home monetary expansion can be powerful under fixed, or even managed, floating exchange rates. Because this linkage frequently accompanies and reinforces other transmission mechanisms, it will be useful to review its operation before proceeding to a discussion of the other mechanisms.

The Monetary Mechanism

To set the stage for our discussion of the monetary transmission mechanism, let us suppose that there are two countries, the United States and Britain. The United States is the key-currency country. This means that, under fixed exchange rates, the British authorities peg the pound to the dollar while the U.S. authorities do not intervene on the foreign exchange market at all. These were the circumstances, incidentally, that prevailed under the Bretton Woods system between World War II and 1971, and which would be likely to prevail under any future system in which a large number of currencies are pegged to a single key currency. Given this set of assumptions, we will examine situations in which the key country is generating inflation and potentially passing it to the other country and situations in which the non-key-currency country is generating inflation and potentially passing it to the key country. We shall also consider the effects on the monetary transmission mechanism of moving from fixed to floating exchange rates.

Case 1: inflation generated within key country; other country maintains rigid exchange-rate peg

Starting from a position of balance-of-payments equilibrium, in which the British authorities are maintaining a rigid exchange-rate peg at $2.00 per pound, suppose that inflation begins to develop within the United States. As U.S. prices rise, U.S. and British residents alike begin to switch their purchases from U.S. to British goods. The greater demand for British goods creates an excess demand for sterling on the foreign exchange market. This, in turn, exerts pressure for sterling to appreciate against the dollar. Suppose that the excess demand for sterling amounts to £1 million per day. To hold the exchange rate at $2.00 per pound, the British authorities must sell £1 million per day on the foreign exchange market. In exchange, they will receive 2 million *dollars* per day, which will be added to British foreign exchange reserves. The sterling sold by the British authorities is newly created money and, as it moves into circulation, it adds £1 million per day to the British money base.

To help visualize the effects of this 1-million-pound monetary injection into the British economy, consider Figure 9–2. Intervention by the country's central bank on the foreign exchange market (item 1) will affect both the level of the country's international reserves (item 2) and the international-reserves component of its money base (item 3). Unless the central bank makes offsetting changes in the money base through open market operations (item 4) (sterilization), a change in the overall size of the money base will result. The total quantity of money in circulation (item 5) will tend to change by a multiple of the change in the money base. Changes in the quantity of money in circulation will, in turn, have an impact on the level of aggregate demand for goods and services (item 6), and ultimately on the level of output and prices in the economy (item 7).

The effects of British intervention on the foreign exchange market in this case (in which the British are selling pounds on that market) are expansionary. If unemployment is widespread in Britain, the primary effects would be to increase output, income and employment. If re-

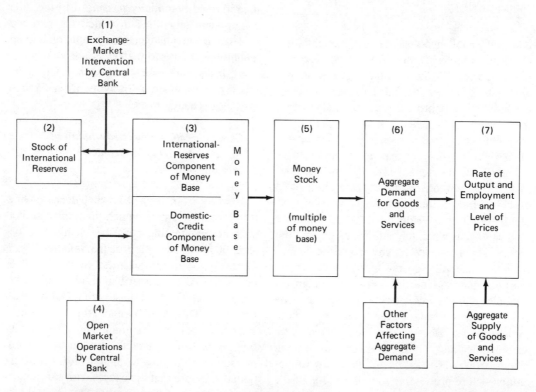

FIGURE 9-2 Relationship between Exchange-Market Intervention, Monetary Magnitudes, and Economic Activity

sources are fully employed, the primary effect would be inflation; inflation that began in the United States would now be spreading into Britain. As a possible remedy, Britain could sterilize the monetary effects of its exchange-market intervention by selling £1 million worth of securities to the British public. The pounds taken in by the central bank for the securities would offset the pounds paid out by the central bank in exchange for the dollars. In practice, many countries have been incapable of fully sterilizing the monetary expansion caused by exchange-market intervention. During the early 1970s, even West Germany and Switzerland, countries with well-developed capital markets, were unable to cope with the monetary expansion induced by attempts to peg the exchange rate. These countries had been facing prolonged balance-of-payments surpluses to begin with, and when speculation into their currencies surged in 1971 and again in early 1973, the monetary expansion resulting from their exchange-market intervention proved to be too heavy to sterilize and too inflationary for their home economies. As a result, these countries chose to abandon the exchange-rate pegs.

Returning to our example involving the United States and Britain, the $2 million U.S. balance-of-payments deficit does not contract the U.S. money base. A country's money base is altered only if the *home* central bank takes in or pays out home money. Because there is no intervention by the U.S. central bank, there is no change in the international-reserves component of the U.S. money base. While it is true that the British authorities have purchased $2 million on the foreign exchange market, this does not itself affect the size of the U.S. money base. Only if the British authorities were to turn these dollars over to the U.S. central bank would the U.S. money base be affected. This could happen as the result of an arrangement whereby the U.S. central bank is obligated to accept any dollars offered by the British central bank in exchange

for gold or other assets. The United States did have such an obligation under the Bretton Woods system, but this was renounced in 1971.

This example has established an especially important relationship. Under fixed exchange rates, the country actively pegging the exchange rate will experience a change in its money base (assuming the monetary effects of the exchange-market intervention are not sterilized), while the nonintervening country will experience no change in its money base. As a result, inflation can be passed from the key-currency country to the other country through expansion of the latter's money base, as its authorities intervene on the foreign exchange market to maintain the exchange-rate peg.

Case 2: inflation generated within country that is pegging exchange rate

Now let us change the example and let the inflation originate in Britain. Britain is still maintaining a rigid exchange-rate peg at $2.00 per pound, while the United States, the key-currency country, does not intervene on the foreign exchange market. The inflation within Britain causes both U.S. and British residents to switch their purchases from British to U.S. goods. The greater demand for U.S. goods creates an excess supply of sterling (i.e., an excess demand for dollars) on the foreign exchange market. This excess supply of sterling, which we shall assume is in the amount of £1 million per day, exerts pressure for sterling to depreciate against the dollar.

To hold the exchange rate at $2.00 per pound, the British central bank must spend $2 million per day from its foreign exchange reserves to buy £1 million on the foreign exchange market. This would reduce British international reserves by $2 million per day, of course, and would also reduce the international-reserves component of the British money base by £1 million per day (refer again to Figure 9–2). The British money stock would contract by a multiple of that amount, with contractionary effects on the British economy. Unless this monetary contraction is sterilized, it would serve to reduce the original inflationary pressure in Britain.

Meanwhile, the U.S. money stock is unaffected by the British pegging operations, so that there would be no lasting inflationary pressures within the United States.[1] If the dollar reserves of the British government had originally been held as idle balances, the act of returning these to active circulation would tend to increase the rate of turnover (the velocity) of the *existing* U.S. money stock. This might be mildly inflationary for the U.S. economy, but would not have the inflationary impact of a sustained $2 million expansion in the U.S. money base, as would have occurred if the United States had been doing the pegging.

We can see, then, that inflation originating in the country which is actively pegging the exchange rate is not readily transmitted to the nonpegging, key-currency country. In fact, the contractionary effects of the pegging operation tend to counteract the inflation in the originating country.

Case 3: exchange rate freely floating

If neither country is pegging the exchange rate, there is no tendency for inflation to be transmitted through the monetary mechanism. This is because neither country is altering the international-reserves component of its money base through exchange-market intervention. Suppose inflation first develops in the United States. As before, both U.S. and British residents will have an initial incentive to switch into

---

[1]Unless, of course, the British are able to borrow new dollars from the U.S. central bank to be spent on the foreign exchange market to support the pound. Any new dollars so created would add to the U.S. money base.

British goods, and the excess demand for sterling on the foreign exchange market will create pressure for the pound to appreciate. In this case, since the exchange rate is free to float, the pound will, in fact, appreciate against the dollar. As we know from our discussion of balance-of-payments adjustment in Chapter 8, the appreciation of the pound will reduce the payments imbalance, and will ultimately eliminate it. Meanwhile, neither central bank is intervening on the foreign exchange market, and the British money base is not being altered. Both economies are insulated from the effects described in Cases 1 and 2.

This is not to say that the initial surge in demand for British goods will have no effect on the two economies. If the pound does not appreciate rapidly enough to choke off all of the new demand for British goods as soon as it appears, the result will be upward pressure on British exports, output and prices. These direct-demand effects will be discussed in greater detail in a later section. The point to be made here is that the monetary mechanism itself is inoperative if exchange rates are allowed to float freely.

Case 4: managed floating exchange rates

The examples, so far, have dealt with the extreme cases of rigidly fixed or freely fluctuating exchange rates. In today's world, we have a system of managed floating exchange rates—a hybrid of both floating and intervention by the central banks. Under a managed floating system, the international-reserves component of a country's money base will be affected to whatever extent its own central bank intervenes on the foreign exchange market. If the British central bank sells a half-million pounds simply to retard rather than to halt the appreciation of sterling, the British money base will be expanded by the half-million pounds. It is also possible to have a situation in which *both* central banks are intervening to stabilize or to manage the dollar–sterling exchange rate. Here, the effects on each country's money base will be determined by the amount of its own currency that its own central bank buys or sells in the process of intervening.

CURRENT ACCOUNT TRANSMISSION MECHANISMS

Along with the monetary linkage, a number of other mechanisms can operate to transmit inflation among countries. The mechanisms to be discussed in this section can be called "current account mechanisms" since they operate through the current account of the balance of payments. These include the tradeable-goods-price mechanism and the Keynesian direct-demand-pressure mechanism.[2]

Tradeable-Goods-Price Mechanism

The *tradeable-goods-price mechanism* is based on the proposition that a homogeneous good, traded under competitive conditions with zero transportation costs, will have the same price everywhere in the world. If price discrepancies were to develop, traders would buy the good where it is cheap and sell it where it is dear, thereby eliminating any such discrepancy. This is the so-called *law-of-one-price*. Under these conditions, an increase in the world price of traded goods means that the prices of these goods must rise within all of the countries in the international trading system. Inflation in the rest of the world can thus be transmitted to the home

country as home prices of traded goods are pulled upward along with world prices. The increase in home prices of traded goods triggers a chain of events that can put upward pressure on the home prices of nontraded goods as well, resulting in a general inflation in the home country. As we shall see, the outcome depends crucially on the reaction of the home monetary authorities.

Let us illustrate the tradeable-goods-price mechanism with an example. Suppose that imports make up an important proportion of Britain's consumption basket, and that inflation begins to increase the price of tradeable goods on world markets. According to the law-of-one-price, the price of imported goods within Britain must rise proportionately. The fact that imports are an important component in British consumption means that the overall cost of living in Britain will rise. As the prices of imported goods increase, British residents will begin to switch their demand to domestic substitutes. This puts upward pressure on the prices of the substitutes, adding further to the home inflation. In addition, as the British import-competing industries expand, they will bid up the prices of factors of production within the country. Meanwhile, the higher world prices being realized by the British export industries will induce expansion by that sector. This will also add to the upward pressure on factor prices within Britain. The increase in factor prices means higher costs for other British industries, including those nontradeable goods industries that draw on the same resource base. Upward pressure on prices now develops in the nontradeable sector of the economy. Inflationary pressures, which originated abroad, have now permeated the British economy.

As we have suggested previously, a sustained rise in the average level of British prices would require a sustained increase in the British money stock relative to money demand. If there were no change in the British money supply, and if

[2]These mechanisms are explored at length in R. J. Sweeney and T. D. Willett, "The International Transmission of Inflation: Mechanisms, Issues and Evidence," *Bank Credit, Money and Inflation in Open Economies.* Supplement to *Kredit und Kapital* (Berlin: Duncker & Humblot).

the prices of nontraded goods were flexible in a downward direction, the higher import bill would draw British purchasing power away from nontraded goods, and the price of the latter would fall. With import prices rising and the prices of nontraded goods falling, the effects would tend to be offsetting; there would be little or no change in the overall cost of living in Britain.

If there were no change in the British money supply, and if the prices of nontraded goods were *inflexible* in a downward direction, the higher import bill would still draw British purchasing power away from nontraded goods. Since the prices of nontraded goods cannot fall, however, the decline in demand would create unemployment in the nontraded goods industries. In a situation in which the British government is committed to avoiding unemployment, it could be forced to expand the money stock to stimulate output. This, in turn, would reinforce inflationary pressures.

Keynesian Direct-Demand-Pressure Mechanism: Fixed Exchange Rates

Like the tradeable-goods-price mechanism, the *Keynesian direct-demand-pressure mechanism* operates through the current account. Whereas the tradeable-goods-price mechanism focuses on the tie between home and foreign prices of traded goods, the Keynesian direct-demand-pressure mechanism focuses on the fact that foreign inflation can cause an increase in the aggregate demand for goods and services in the home country. This, in turn, puts upward pressure on home prices. Suppose that (starting from an initial position of balance-of-payments equilibrium in which there is no inflation in either the United States or Britain) inflation begins to develop within the United States. Both U.S. and British residents begin to find U.S. goods less attractive and British goods more attractive than before and, as a result, begin to switch some of

their purchases from U.S. to British goods.[3] From the British point of view, the increase in exports and the decrease in imports add to the aggregate demand for home goods and services. If British resources are at or near full employment, the increase in aggregate demand will begin to drive up prices in Britain.

The extent to which U.S. inflation would cause U.S. and British residents to switch into British goods would depend on the elasticity of substitution between U.S. and British goods; the greater the substitutability, the greater the impact of U.S. inflation on British aggregate demand. The effects of U.S. inflation on the overall British economy would also depend on the linkages between the British export industry and the rest of the British economy. The stronger these linkages (the greater the "multipliers" associated with a change in the demand for British exports), the greater the impact on the overall British economy, and the greater the transmission of inflation between the United States and Britain.

For economies that are very closely linked, forces generating inflation in one country can generate inflation *simultaneously* in the other. Forces pushing upward on prices in the United States, for example, are likely to push upward on Canadian prices at the same time; prices would not necessarily have to rise in the United States *before* prices rise in Canada. Suppose that as a result of an increase in U.S. income, U.S. res-

---

[3]Here we are not assuming that the law-of-one-price holds as in the preceding section. In the present example, the prices of U.S. goods rise while those of Britain *initially* remain unchanged. The widening differential in prices is what causes residents of both countries to substitute British for U.S. goods. In the preceding section, in which the law-of-one-price held, there was no substitution of British for U.S. goods since the prices of tradeable goods were marked up in Britain right along with prices in the rest of the world.

idents begin to spend more for goods and services. If U.S. and Canadian goods are close substitutes, this additional spending will fall partly on U.S. goods and partly on Canadian goods. This would cause aggregate demand and prices to rise simultaneously in both countries. Here, it would be more correct to say that inflation-generating *impulses* were transmitted from the United States to Canada, than to say that inflation itself was transmitted.[4]

A similar result can occur if industries in one country depend heavily on inputs from both countries. Suppose the U.S. automobile industry, which uses parts and subassemblies manufactured in both Canada and the United States, begins to expand as a result of an increase in demand. As the U.S. demand for automobile parts and subassemblies increases, these latter industries will begin to expand in both countries. If both economies are at or near full employment, resource prices will rise in both countries, forming the basis for simultaneous cost-push inflation.

Keynesian Direct-Demand-Pressure Mechanism: Flexible Exchange Rates

Flexible exchange rates can offer a substantial degree of insulation against the international transmission of inflation through the Keynesian direct-demand-pressure mechanism, although this insulation may not be complete. Suppose that U.S. and British goods are highly substitutable, and that inflation begins to develop in the United States. Any additional purchases of British goods by U.S. residents will require that they buy ster-

[4]Note that the increase in Canadian prices in this case results from an increase in the demand for Canadian goods. Canadian prices are not simply being marked up in lock step with world prices. This example thus falls under the Keynesian direct-demand-pressure mechanism rather than under the tradeable-goods-price mechanism.

ling on the foreign exchange market; this will cause the pound to appreciate. The appreciating pound will itself diminish the attractiveness of the British goods, thereby lowering the additional quantity of British goods that U.S. residents will want to buy. British aggregate demand is at least partially shielded from the surge of spending in the United States.

If the rate of appreciation of the pound is equal to the difference in the rates of inflation in the two countries, the exchange-rate movement will completely offset the incentive to switch into British goods, and the Keynesian direct-demand-pressure mechanism will be inoperative. Suppose that the U.S. inflation rate is 10 percent per year, the British inflation rate is zero, and the pound is appreciating at 10 percent per year. Even though British goods are becoming relatively cheaper by 10 percent per year due to the difference in the inflation rates, the 10 percent appreciation in sterling is exactly offsetting this price advantage. If all markets operate very efficiently, there will be pressure for the currency of the country with the lower inflation rate to appreciate at the same rate as the difference in inflation between the two countries. As long as sterling is appreciating at less than 10 percent per year, in our example, while the difference in inflation rates remains at 10 percent, the incentives to switch to British goods will steadily increase. This, in turn, will generate heavier purchases of sterling on the foreign exchange market, pushing the rate of appreciation in sterling upward toward 10 percent.

As we have seen, imported inflation might not stem solely from higher foreign inflation rates. It could stem from an increase in foreign income. Suppose U.S. income were to increase while U.S. prices remain constant. If the U.S. marginal propensity to import is greater than zero, part of the increase in U.S. income would be applied to additional purchases of British goods. If Britain is at or near full employment this would create inflationary pressures in Britain. To buy the additional British goods, however, U.S. residents would have to increase their purchases of sterling. Under floating exchange rates, the resulting appreciation in sterling would choke off some of the additional demand for British goods. Again, the floating exchange rate would at least partially shield British aggregate demand and prices from foreign disturbances.

The United States, incidentally, will experience "imported deflation," in this case, even though no deflation is "exported" from Britain. Failure on the part of a country to revalue its currency in the face of a persistent balance-of-payments surplus will have a similar effect; the surplus reflects a situation in which the country's currency is being pegged below its equilibrium value.

UNDERVALUED CURRENCY AND IMPORTED INFLATION

As we have seen, the phenomenon of imported inflation depends critically on the behavior of the exchange rate. If the exchange rate can move rapidly in response to rising foreign inflation rates, there will be substantial insulation against any imported inflation that would otherwise occur through the monetary, the tradeable-goods-price or the direct-demand-pressure mechanisms. If for some reason the exchange rate cannot adjust rapidly, imported inflation is likely to occur. As a matter of fact, imported inflation is likely to occur at any time the foreign exchange value of a currency is held below its equilibrium level. Suppose that the dollar–sterling exchange rate is initially *at* its equilibrium level, the U.S.–British balance of payments is in balance and there are no inflationary pressures in either country. Now suppose the British authorities devalue the pound and peg it, say, 10 percent below its equilibrium value. This undervaluation of sterling will make British goods 10 percent cheaper to U.S. residents and will make U.S. goods 10 percent more expensive to British residents. The result will be a switching in spending toward British goods. This will add to British aggregate demand and generate inflationary pressures in that country. Inflation has been "imported" to Britain even though none has been exported from the United States.

EMPIRICAL EVIDENCE ON THE INTERNATIONAL TRANSMISSION OF INFLATION

What do the available data suggest about the international transmission of inflation and the various transmission mechanisms? In short, the empirical findings, to date, are inconclusive. A fundamental problem in trying to assess the importance and direction of the international transmission of inflation is the very fact that the prices of tradeable and nontradeable goods (within the individual countries as well as across countries) tend to move in the same direction at the same time. This makes it difficult to detect directions of causality and thus to draw inferences about the importance of specific mechanisms that may be operating.

Many observers would argue that, under fixed exchange rates, the transmission mechanisms are so powerful that it is difficult for individual countries to maintain rates of inflation that diverge very far from the average world rate of inflation. Most would argue that, under flexible exchange rates, individual countries have a greater degree of independence in choosing their own inflation rates than under fixed exchange rates. Indeed, some would argue that, under a system of freely fluctuating exchange rates, there would be no "world inflation rate" per se, but a set of individual, independent inflation rates within countries.

INTERNATIONAL TRANSMISSION OF CYCLICAL FLUCTUATIONS

The foregoing sections have concentrated on the international transmission of inflation, largely because of its importance as an issue in today's world. Other important kinds of disturbances are also transmitted internationally, however, including cycles in business activity. The international transmission of cyclical activity is best explained by the Keynesian direct-demand-pressure mechanism. Let us see how a cyclical downswing in the United States could generate a similar downturn in another country (say, Britain) which is closely linked in trade.

As the United States enters a recession, U.S. residents, faced with falling incomes, begin to curtail their overall spending, including spending on British imports. With the reduction in U.S. imports, British export industries begin to curtail their output. The contraction in British export industries is, in turn, passed on to the rest of the British economy through various linkages. The recession which began in the United States has now been transmitted to Britain. As the cycle is reversed, and spending in the United States turns upward again, part of this spending will fall on British goods, increasing aggregate demand and output in that country.

If time is required for the initial decline in U.S. spending to have a significant impact on British export industries, or for the fall in demand for British exports to work its way through to the rest of the British economy, the cyclical fluctuations in Britain could follow those in the United States by a considerable lag. If ties between the countries are sufficiently strong, as between the United States and Canada, the cycle could occur almost simultaneously in the two countries. Also, if U.S. industry is a heavy user of raw material exports from a second country, a decline in output in U.S. industry will have a direct and immediate impact on the economy of the second country, especially if the raw-material export industry is an important component of the second country's economy. In general, the stronger and more direct the trade ties between two countries, the greater we would expect the correlation to be between their business cycles.

PRICE INCREASES FOR CRUCIAL IMPORTS

Let us now examine, somewhat more closely, a disturbance we referred to briefly at the outset of this chapter: the effects of an increase in the world price of crucial imports upon the economies of the importing countries. We can define a *crucial import* as one which absorbs a large proportion of the income of the importing country and for which the price elasticities of demand and supply are low. In other words, the commodity is regarded largely as a necessity, and the importing country has little capability of increasing its production. A relatively small reduction in the world supply of such a good can result in a substantial increase in its price. This, in turn, can cause severe dislocations in the importing economy. Food and petroleum are items that often fall into this category.

Consider the effects of an increase in the world price of oil on a country that depends heavily on petroleum imports. First, the fact that oil is a critical input into the manufacture of a large number of goods means that the costs of production will rise for a large segment of the country's industry. These higher costs will become translated into higher prices for manufactured goods. There will also be upward pressure on the prices of transportation services, and the combined effect will be an increase in the overall cost of living in the importing country.

Second, the fact that oil prices are higher means

that the importing country will have to pay a larger proportion of its income for oil and for goods that use oil as an input. This leaves a smaller proportion of income for expenditure on other goods, which means that the demand for these other goods must fall. A decline in output and employment will therefore develop in the industries producing these other goods (assuming that prices in this other sector are not sufficiently flexible in a downward direction to maintain demand in the face of failing real income). A decline in output and employment in the oil-importing countries also means that they will not be able to import as much from each other as before. This adds another dimension to declining aggregate demand within the user countries.

These first two effects can contribute simultaneously to both inflation and unemployment in the importing economies. Many observers, in fact, are convinced that the large increases in oil prices in 1974 were a key factor in the combination of recession and inflation that hit the United States and other industrial countries in 1974–1975. A third possible effect of an oil price increase is to put deficit pressure on the balance of payments or downward pressure on the exchange rate of the importing country. This is especially true if the oil imports have to be paid for in some currency other than that of the importing country. During the 1970s and early 1980s, OPEC required payment in U.S. dollars. This meant that a country like Italy had to obtain dollars, or dollar credits, before it could import oil.

Suppose that Italy is maintaining a rigid exchange-rate peg and that its balance of payments is initially in balance. Now suppose the world price of oil increases. Every unit of Italian exports now commands fewer units of imports; in other words, the terms of trade have turned against Italy. Because the elasticity of demand is low, at least in the short run, Italy will not be able to reduce the quantity of its oil imports by as large a percentage as the price increase. This

means that oil imports will now use up a larger proportion of Italy's foreign exchange earnings than before. If Italy cannot increase its foreign exchange earnings through an increase in exports (this would not appear to be likely, considering that the cost of production in Italy will also have risen as a result of the oil price increase) it will face increasing shortages of foreign exchange. In other words, Italy's trade balance will move into deficit.

The Italian authorities now face a dilemma. If they should try to maintain the exchange-rate peg, their foreign exchange reserves could soon be depleted. If they let the lira float downward, this could accelerate the rate of internal inflation. The falling dollar–lira exchange rate would make the lira price of every barrel of oil all the higher and would make the lira prices of all other imports higher as well. One hope is that the oil-exporting countries would spend some of their additional oil earnings on Italian exports, thereby raising Italian foreign exchange earnings and providing more support to the lira on the foreign exchange market. This did not prove to be a reliable source of foreign exchange for most oil-importing countries during the 1970s, however.

Another hope is that the petroleum exporting countries would place their surplus dollar earnings in the Eurodollar market, or other international money markets to which Italy has access, and that Italy would be able to reborrow these funds to be used for further oil imports. (This process became known as "petrodollar recycling" in the 1970s.) This would require that the oil-importing country's creditworthiness be sufficiently strong to enable it to obtain these credits. Even if the credits could be obtained, continuous borrowing to finance oil imports would steadily increase the country's debt burden. This in itself would begin to sap a larger and larger proportion of the importing country's foreign exchange earnings. Dilemmas of this kind were faced by many oil-importing countries during the 1970s and 1980s and gave rise to special international monetary arrangements, such as the IMF's special Oil Facility, which was established in the mid-1970s to provide credits at favorable terms to countries caught in such circumstances as these.

In this chapter we have focused primarily on the transmission of economic disturbances through monetary and current account mechanisms. As we shall see in Chapter 10, economies are also linked through the capital account. Changes in interest rates and other capital market variables in one country can generate international capital flows that have an important effect on the economies of other countries.

QUESTIONS AND EXERCISES

1. Some observers have argued that a ratchet effect can operate to generate inflation under fixed as well as under flexible exchange rates. Outline and compare the ratchet effects under fixed and flexible exchange rates.

2. Some observers have argued that balance-of-payments discipline is lost in moving from a system of fixed to a system of flexible exchange rates, and that this promotes inflation within countries. Outline and evaluate this argument.

3. Contrast the operation of the *monetary* mechanism by which inflation can be transmitted from country A to country B under the following circumstances:

   a. Country B is pegging the exchange rate.
   b. Country A is pegging the exchange rate.
   c. Neither country is pegging the exchange rate.

4. How would the adoption of a common currency by the European Economic Community affect the transmission of inflation and cyclical activity among the EEC countries?

5. How might a country use sterilization to inhibit the transmission of inflation from abroad? What difficulties might a country encounter in attempting to use sterilization to block imported inflation?

6. What role does the *level* of the exchange rate play in the phenomenon of imported inflation?

7. It has been argued that the rapid increase in world oil prices during the 1970s produced pressures for both inflation *and* a slowdown of economic activity within oil-importing countries. What is the rationale of this argument?

8. It has been argued that in a world in which there are strong linkages among economies, it is difficult for an individual country, especially a small country, to maintain a rate of inflation that is substantially different from that in the rest of the world. Suppose that country A is a small country which is maintaining a fixed exchange rate. The rate of inflation within country A as well as in the rest of the world is initially 15 percent per year. Now country A tries to reduce its internal inflation rate to 5 percent through tighter monetary policy. Describe the forces that will come into play to oppose country A's attempt to accomplish this.

Domestic Economic Policy 10
in an Open Economy

In Chapter 9, we saw how economic interdependence among countries can foster international transmission of inflation and other economic disturbances. Economic interdependence can also have important effects on a country's ability to control its internal economic activity. As we shall see, the standard macroeconomic policy tools, monetary and fiscal policy, operate quite differently in an open economy than they would in a closed economy. In an open economy, the effectiveness of domestic policy depends crucially on such considerations as exchange-rate flexibility and the international mobility of financial capital.

To provide background for our discussion of domestic economic policy in an open economy, let us briefly review two important items. First, let us recall some of the basic principles governing international capital movements, since these will play an important role in the analysis. Then let us outline the way in which monetary and fiscal policy are supposed to operate in a *closed* economy. At that point we should be in a position to examine the operation of these policy tools in an open economy, under varying conditions, and to compare the open- with the closed-economy cases.

INTERNATIONAL CAPITAL MOBILITY

International capital *movements* consist of the international flow of funds for the purpose of buying and selling financial assets across national boundaries. International capital *mobility* can be defined as the sensitivity with which capital movements respond to changes in rates of return in the different countries. Capital mobility is said to be high if a given change in the relative interest rates across countries generates a large international flow of capital.

Capital mobility is said to be low if the given change in relative interest rates generates but a small international flow of capital.[1]

Capital mobility is said to be "perfect" if the slightest divergence between home and foreign interest rates generates such massive capital flows that the divergence is eliminated instantly. To illustrate, suppose there is perfect capital mobility between the United States and Britain, and that the interest rate in both countries is initially 10 percent. Now suppose interest rates in Britain begin to rise. As a result of the emerging interest-rate differential, a flood of capital will move from the United States to Britain, causing interest rates in the United States to rise and those in Britain to fall. This process will continue until the interest rates in the two countries are equalized once again. Under these circumstances, interest rates would always appear to be identical in the two countries, since any incipient divergence would be immediately wiped out. For capital mobility to be perfect, investors would have to regard home and foreign assets as perfect substitutes.

MONETARY AND FISCAL POLICY IN A CLOSED ECONOMY

Monetary and fiscal policy are the primary tools by which government can control (or attempt to control) the level of economic activity within a country. If the level of aggregate output is too low and the level of unemployment too high, the standard policy prescription is for government to raise the level of aggregate demand for goods and services through expansionary mon-

[1]Bear in mind that there is an array of interest rates in each country, applying to a wide variety of financial instruments and maturities. For simplicity, we shall assume, from now on, that there is a single interest rate in each country. This assumption is warranted if movements in the various individual interest rates are highly correlated.

etary and fiscal policies. This would help to stimulate output and employment.

If inflation is the problem, it is likely to be because the level of aggregate demand is too high for the rate of output that can be sustained by the country's resources at constant prices. The standard prescription in this case is for the government to lower the level of aggregate demand through contractionary monetary and fiscal policies. This helps to relieve the upward pressure on prices caused by the excess aggregate demand.

This rather simple set of prescriptions assumes that *either* unemployment *or* inflation is the problem facing the economy, and that to correct it, government has simply to adjust aggregate demand in the appropriate direction and by the appropriate amount. The situation becomes much more complicated when a country is facing unacceptable levels of unemployment and inflation at the same time. Emerging analysis also suggests that manipulating aggregate demand may not be sufficient, by itself, to cope with unemployment and inflation; it may also be necessary to give attention to conditions affecting the aggregate supply of goods and services.

Monetary Policy

Monetary policy consists of expanding or contracting the country's money supply in order to influence the level of aggregate demand. To stimulate aggregate demand, the monetary authorities would expand the money stock (see Figure 10–1) through open market operations, or through any of the other methods available to them. Expanding the money supply would lower interest rates within the country and this, in turn, would stimulate investment and other components of private spending. Aggregate demand would also be affected directly by the fact that the public would have a larger quantity of real money balances available to spend. If there

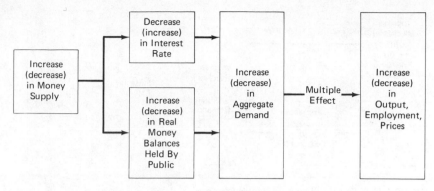

FIGURE 10-1 Monetary Policy in a Closed Economy

are idle resources in the economy, the increase in aggregate demand would generate a *multiple* increase in output and employment. If resources are at or near full employment, the increase in demand would bring about an increase in prices.

Contractionary monetary policy would work in exactly the opposite direction. As the authorities contract the money supply, by selling bonds in the open market, interest rates would rise. The increase in interest rates would choke off investment and other components of private spending, thereby lowering aggregate demand. Aggregate demand would also be reduced directly by the fact that the public would have a smaller quantity of real money balances available to spend. The decline in aggregate demand would result in a multiple reduction in the equilibrium level of output and would reduce any excess demand pressure on prices.

Fiscal Policy

Fiscal policy works either through changes in the level of government spending or through changes in the level of taxes in the economy. Because government spending is itself a component of aggregate demand, government can directly influence the level of aggregate demand by increasing or decreasing its own level of spending (see Figure 10–2). By raising or low-

ering taxes, government can alter the amount of disposable income in the hands of the public. Raising taxes lowers disposable income, thus lowering the amount of spending the private sector is willing or able to do. Lowering taxes raises disposable income, thus raising the amount of spending the private sector is willing or able to do.

Joint Use of Monetary and Fiscal Policies

Monetary and fiscal policies can be more effective if they are coordinated. For example, an expansionary fiscal policy (say, an increase in government spending with no changes in taxes) accompanied by no change in the quantity of money would initially have a tendency to stimulate aggregate demand, as outlined above. The government spending would have to be financed by borrowing from (selling bonds to) the public, however, and this would drive the interest rate upward. In addition, any increase in income generated by the policy would increase the demand for money, which, in the face of the fixed money supply, would reinforce the upward pressure on the interest rate. The increase in the interest rate would choke off investment and other components of private spending, offsetting the initial attempt to stimulate aggregate demand through an increase in government

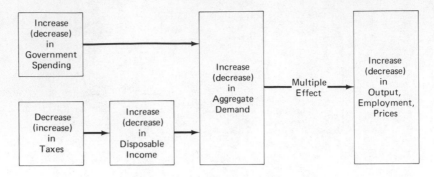

FIGURE 10-2 Fiscal Policy in a Closed Economy

spending. This is the widely discussed "crowding-out effect" in which increases in government spending "crowd out" spending by the private sector, without necessarily increasing the overall level of output in the economy.

If the authorities were to pursue an expansionary monetary policy in conjunction with the expansionary fiscal policy, the increase in the money supply would mitigate any increase in the interest rate. If the expansion in the money supply is fully adequate to finance the expansion in government spending, there need be no increase in the interest rate at all. Because the interest rate would not rise to choke off investment and other components of private spending, the increase in government spending would have its full, intended effect on aggregate demand.

MONETARY AND FISCAL POLICY IN AN OPEN ECONOMY: GENERAL ASSUMPTIONS

We turn, now, to an analysis of monetary and fiscal policies in an open economy. In order to simplify our analysis, we shall adopt the following assumptions.

1. There are two countries, Britain and the United States. Britain is the "home" country; the United States represents the rest of the world.

2. Britain is so small relative to the United States that Britain can take the U.S. interest rate as given.

3. The U.S. interest rate is constant.

4. The level of prices in both countries is constant.

5. The marginal propensity to import (the proportion of any increase in home income that is spent on foreign goods) is greater than zero, but less than 1.0. This means that part, but not all, of any increase in income will be spent on imports.

6. All government spending is financed through borrowing from the public and not through the creation of new money. This maintains a clear distinction between the effects of monetary policy and the effects of pure fiscal policy.

7. The demand for money within the home economy is positively related to the level of money income. This implies that a permanent increase in the level of income must be accompanied by a permanent increase in the quantity of money in circulation (or by a permanent increase in velocity—the rate at which money is turned over by the public). Otherwise the increase in income would increase the demand for money, which would drive the interest rate upward. This, in turn, would choke off certain components of private spending, forestalling any permanent increase in income.

8. The British money multiplier is 1.0, so that any change in the country's money base will result in an identical change in the country's overall money stock.

9. In cases in which the exchange rate between the pound and the dollar is fixed, the pegging is done by the British authorities. The U.S. authorities do not intervene on the foreign exchange market at all.

10. The British authorities do not sterilize any change in the money base brought about by exchange-market intervention.

11. International capital mobility is high. This is consistent with relationships among most of the developed countries in the free world and the observation by many experts that capital mobility is increasing.

While some of these assumptions might seem overly restrictive, they will permit a fairly simple analysis which will provide important insights into the operation of macroeconomic policy in an open economy. In the cases to follow, the home authorities will be attempting to increase the level of domestic output and income through expansionary monetary and fiscal policies. (For cases in which the authorities are pursuing *contractionary* policies, the mechanisms would be essentially the same, although the variables in the system would move in the opposite direction.) In the following discussion, we shall first consider monetary policy under both fixed and flexible exchange rates, and then we shall examine fiscal policy under each of the two exchange-rate regimes.

Case 1: monetary policy, fixed exchange rates

For purposes of our analysis, let us define monetary policy as the deliberate expansion or contraction of the *domestic credit* component of the country's money base. As we know, the money base can also be altered by changes in the *international-reserves* component. The lat-

ter will occur, in our examples, only in conjunction with balance-of-payments surpluses or deficits, and will be the result of exchange-market intervention by the authorities as they attempt to peg the exchange rates.

Suppose the British authorities wish to raise the level of national income through expansionary monetary policy. If Britain were a closed economy, the process would work as we outlined in Figure 10–1. If Britain were an open economy in a world of high international capital mobility, however, the process would operate as outlined in Figure 10–3. Here, the British authorities initially expand the domestic-credit component of the money base, which causes a corresponding increase in the money supply (item 1). As in the closed-economy case, this lowers the interest rate (item 2), which produces an increase in investment and aggregate demand (item 3). With capital highly mobile between countries, however, the declining interest rate causes a rapid capital outflow (item 5), which pushes the balance of payments into deficit (item 6). To keep the pound from depreciating in the face of the capital outflow and payments deficit, the British authorities must purchase sterling on the foreign exchange market (item 7). This causes a contraction in the international-reserves component of the money base and a corresponding contraction in the overall money supply (item 8). The final contraction in the money supply in item 8 counteracts the initial expansion (item 1) that was intended to stimulate the economy. Under fixed exchange rates and high international capital mobility, then, the effectiveness of monetary policy is weakened.[2]

[2]We should note that the relationships depicted in Figure 10–3 and the figures to follow are basically "simultaneous." This means that there may be feedback effects among the variables and that many of the changes occur concurrently. Nevertheless, the figures in this chapter reflect the principal causal sequences, while keeping the analysis relatively simple.

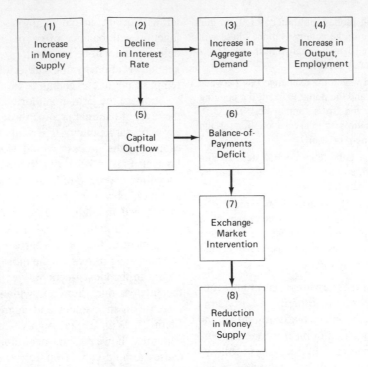

FIGURE 10-3 Monetary Policy—Fixed Exchange Rates

In the extreme case in which capital is perfectly mobile between countries, the downward pressure on the interest rate would cause such a massive outflow of capital that the initial monetary expansion in item 1 would be completely offset by the monetary contraction in item 8. There would be no net expansion in the money supply and thus no stimulation of economic activity. We can see, then, that monetary policy would be completely ineffective for a small country in a world in which capital is perfectly mobile between countries and in which the home authorities maintain a rigidly fixed exchange rate.

A few additional points need to be made. We have been assuming that Britain is a small country. If it were a large country, the capital outflow might cause interest rates in the United States to decline along with those in Britain. Not only would this affect the U.S. economy (a point to be discussed later in this chapter), it would also reduce the incentives for capital to flow out of Britain and would thus preserve more of the initial monetary expansion in that country. A larger country, therefore, has a greater chance of exercising an effective monetary policy under high capital mobility and fixed exchange rates than does a smaller country.

A second point is that there are steps the British authorities could take to reduce the tendency for a capital outflow to cause a contraction of the money supply. One step would be to impose official restrictions on capital outflows. Then, when the home interest rate is reduced through expansionary monetary policy, private residents would not be free to switch funds overseas to capture the relatively higher foreign interest rate. If this policy were successful (attempts to dam up the flow of capital through official regulations are *not* always successful, although attempts by government to control the inflow and outflow of capital are quite common), it could reduce the balance-of-payments deficit and the exchange-market intervention that would cause a recontraction of the money supply.

A second step the authorities could take would be to relax, somewhat, the rigidity with which they are pegging the exchange rate. If they are willing to accept some exchange-rate depreciation, they can reduce the amount of exchange-market intervention required in item 7, and thereby minimize the reduction in the money stock in item 8. Here, of course, the authorities would be moving away from a system of rigidly fixed exchange rates toward one of greater exchange-rate flexibility. Let us see how monetary policy would work under freely fluctuating exchange rates.

Case 2: monetary policy, flexible exchange rates

In this case, the British authorities wish to raise the level of home income through expansionary monetary policy, just as in case 1. Here, however, the exchange rate is perfectly flexible;

the authorities do not intervene at all on the foreign exchange market. Figure 10–4 outlines the effects of expansionary monetary policy under flexible exchange rates and high international capital mobility. (As the discussion proceeds, it will again be helpful to compare the process with the closed-economy case shown in Figure 10–1.)

The British authorities initially expand the domestic-credit component of the money base, which causes a corresponding increase in the money supply (item 1, Figure 10–4). As in the closed-economy case, this causes the interest rate to decline (item 2), which in turn stimulates investment and aggregate demand (item 3).

Because capital is highly mobile between countries, however, the declining interest rate causes a rapid capital outflow (item 5). The capital outflow pushes the capital account of the balance of payments into deficit (item 6). The capital account deficit causes sterling to depreciate on the foreign exchange market (item 7). This stimulates exports and curtails imports until the balance of trade is pushed into a surplus (item 8). The trade surplus will be exactly equal to the capital account deficit (item 6). This keeps

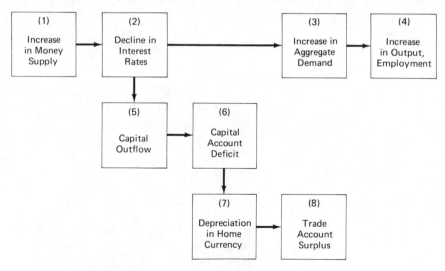

FIGURE 10-4 Monetary Policy—Flexible Exchange Rates

the overall balance of payments in balance, as is necessary under perfectly flexible exchange rates. The trade account surplus adds to the aggregate demand for British goods, reinforcing the expansionary effects of the reduction in interest rates in item 2. It thus reinforces the initial attempt by the authorities to expand output and employment.

An important feature of this case is that the capital outflow keeps the home interest rate from declining by as much as it would in the closed-economy case. This means that the interest-rate-induced stimulation to investment and aggregate demand will be weaker. Nevertheless, the addition to aggregate demand through the trade account will make up the difference.

If capital were *perfectly* mobile between countries, *all* of the increase in aggregate demand would come through the trade account surplus. This is because the capital outflow, item 5, would be so massive that the British interest rate could not fall at all relative to the U.S. interest rate. Since the U.S. interest rate is fixed, the British interest rate would have to remain

fixed also, and there would be no stimulation of investment or aggregate demand by that route.

Note that, under a flexible exchange rate, monetary policy remains effective because of the capital outflow and its effects on the exchange rate and the trade account, even though interest rates are not as sensitive to monetary changes as in a closed economy. Under a fixed exchange rate, monetary policy is *hampered* by the capital outflow and its effects on the balance of payments and exchange-market intervention.

Let us now see how fiscal policy would operate in an open economy with high international capital mobility.

Case 3: fiscal policy, fixed exchange rates

Suppose the authorities wish to increase national income through fiscal policy rather than monetary policy. For simplicity, we shall assume that fiscal policy takes the form of an increase in government spending to a permanently higher level while the tax rate is held constant. (Expansionary fiscal policy could very

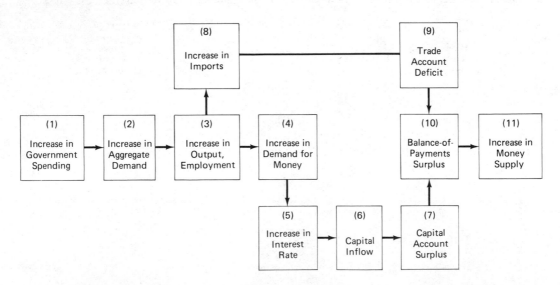

FIGURE 10-5 Fiscal Policy—Fixed Exchange Rates

well take the form of a reduction in the tax rate while government spending is held constant; the outcome would be similar, although somewhat weaker, than with an increase in government spending.) The process is outlined in Figure 10–5.

The increase in government spending (item 1) directly increases the level of aggregate demand (item 2), which increases the level of output and employment (item 3). These first three steps are similar to those in the closed-economy case shown in Figure 10–2. The increase in output and income would increase the demand for money by the public, which in a closed economy would drive the interest rate upward. This would choke off investment and other components of private spending.[3]

In an open economy with high international capital mobility, the increase in the demand for money (item 4 in Figure 10–5) and the increase in the interest rate (item 5) would cause a rapid capital inflow (item 6). This would push the capital account of the balance of payments into surplus (item 7). Meanwhile, the increase in output and employment (item 3) would cause an increase in imports (item 8), which would push the trade account into deficit (item 9). The effect on the overall balance of payments (item 10) would depend upon whether the trade account deficit (item 9) or the capital account surplus (item 7) were larger. Since capital is highly mobile, it is more likely that the capital account surplus would outweigh the trade account deficit, with the result that the overall balance of payments would move into surplus (item 10). Since the authorities are committed to a fixed exchange rate, they will intervene on the foreign exchange market and sell home currency to keep it from appreciating. This amounts to an expansion of the international-reserve component

of the money base, which generates an expansion in the overall money supply (item 11).

A key point in this case is that the capital inflow (item 6) keeps the home interest rate from rising by as much as it would in the closed-economy case. The expansion of the money supply in item 11 means that the increase in the demand for money in item 4 will be at least partially satisfied, and this forestalls the tendency for the interest rate to rise. As a result, investment and private spending will not be choked off as readily, and the attempt to stimulate overall economic activity through an increase in government spending will be at least partially successful. Fiscal policy aimed at increasing output and employment is thus more effective in an open economy with fixed exchange rates than it is in a closed economy.

We might note that if the trade account deficit (item 9 in Figure 10–5) were to outweigh the capital account surplus (item 7), the overall balance of payments would move into deficit, and the authorities would have to *buy* home currency on the foreign exchange market to keep it from depreciating. This would cause the money stock to decrease, driving the interest rate upward even more rapidly than in the closed-economy case. Here the choking off of investment and other private spending could be severe. In the end the level of output would actually decline (assuming, still, that prices are constant) since the total money stock would be smaller. Thus if capital mobility is low and the marginal propensity to import is high, the attempt to stimulate the economy through fiscal policy could backfire.

If capital were *perfectly mobile* between countries, the capital inflow (item 6) would be so massive that the home interest rate would not rise at all relative to the foreign interest rate. Since the foreign (U.S.) interest rate is fixed, the home interest rate would remain fixed also. The increase in the money stock (item 11) would completely satisfy any increase in the demand for money that arises in item 4. There will be

---

[3]Bear in mind that the money supply is constant at this point, since the authorities are not exercising monetary policy. They are making no effort to expand the domestic-credit component of the money base.

no choking off of investment and other private spending, and the attempt to stimulate output and employment through fiscal policy will be fully successful. Thus the higher the international mobility of capital, the greater the effectiveness of fiscal policy under a fixed exchange rate.

Case 4: fiscal policy, flexible exchange rates

In this case the British authorities again attempt to raise the level of home income by increasing government spending to a permanently higher level. Now, however, the exchange rate is perfectly flexible.

As Figure 10–6 suggests, the effects of an expansionary fiscal policy are largely the same up through item 7 (the capital account surplus) and item 9 (the increase in imports), as under fixed exchange rates. The difference comes in the effects on the trade deficit (item 10). The capital account surplus (item 7) causes home currency to appreciate on the foreign exchange market (item 8). This, in conjunction with the

income-induced increase in imports (item 9), pushes the trade account into deficit (item 10). The increase in imports and decrease in exports associated with the trade deficit cause aggregate demand to decline (item 11). The decrease in aggregate demand in item 11 will tend to offset any increase in aggregate demand in item 2. Attempts to increase output and employment through expansionary fiscal policy will thus be weakened in an open economy with high capital mobility and flexible exchange rates.

If capital were *perfectly* mobile between countries, the trade deficit (item 10) would offset any increase in government spending, rendering fiscal policy wholly ineffective. Until the point is reached that the trade deficit does rise enough to offset the increase in government spending, aggregate demand and therefore output and income will be elevated above their original levels. So will the demand for money. As long as the demand for money lies above its original level (recall that the *supply* of money remains constant at its original level), capital will continue to flow into the country, home currency will continue to appreciate and the trade

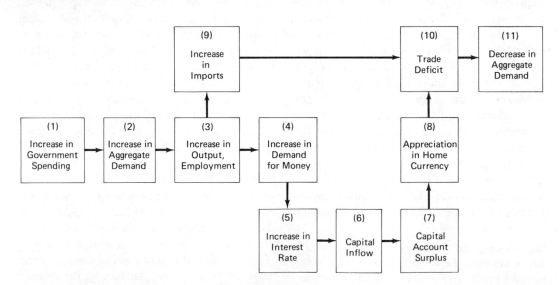

FIGURE 10-6 Fiscal Policy—Flexible Exchange Rates

deficit will continue to deepen. The process will come to a halt only when the trade deficit has risen to match the increase in government spending. Then, of course, aggregate demand will once again stand at its original level, as will output, income and employment. Under perfect capital mobility, the process would work so rapidly that the trade deficit would increase more or less in tandem with government spending, so that there would not even be much *transitory* increase in income. Fiscal policy would thus be completely ineffective under freely fluctuating exchange rates and perfect international capital mobility.

AN ALTERNATIVE PERSPECTIVE: FOCUS ON THE MONEY SUPPLY

The processes outlined in cases 1 to 4 can be viewed from a slightly different perspective. This alternative perspective is fully consistent with (and complementary to) the foregoing analysis and provides a strong clue to the outcome in each case. This view focuses on the fact that if prices and the velocity of money (the rate at which the public turns over the money stock) are constant, the level of output and income in the economy will vary with the money supply; there can be no permanent increase in output and income without an increase in the money supply. Let us see the implications of this view for each of the above cases.

Case 1: monetary policy, fixed exchange rates

Here, the initial attempt by the authorities to expand the money supply will be reversed by subsequent exchange-market intervention. Since the actual monetary expansion will be smaller than originally intended, the increase in output and income will not be as great as was anticipated. In the extreme case of perfect international capital mobility, the authorities will be contracting the international-reserves component of the money base just as rapidly as they are expanding the domestic-credit component, so that the money supply itself remains unchanged. Output and income, therefore, will not rise permanently.

Case 2: monetary policy, flexible exchange rates

Here, the expansion of the domestic-credit component of the money base is not offset by exchange-market intervention, since exchange rates are left free to fluctuate. The larger money stock will support a higher level of output.

Case 3: fiscal policy, fixed exchange rates

Here, there is no initial expansion of the domestic-credit component of the money base to accompany the increase in government spending. However, the international-reserves component is expanded as the authorities intervene on the foreign exchange market to keep home currency from appreciating. This provides the necessary monetary support for an expansion in income and output.

Case 4: fiscal policy, flexible exchange rates

Here, there is no expansion of the domestic-credit component of the money base to accompany the government spending, nor is there a subsequent expansion of the international-reserves component due to exchange-market intervention. There is, thus, no expansion of the money stock to support any permanent increase in income and output.

The effectiveness of monetary and fiscal policy in an open economy under high international capital mobility is summarized in Figure 10–7. In analyzing these various cases, we have been

FIGURE 10-7 Effectiveness of Monetary and Fiscal Policy in an Open Economy with High International Capital Mobility

Home Macroeconomic Policy	Home Exchange Rate Policy	Effect on Home Money Supply	Effectiveness of Home Macroeconomic Policy
Monetary policy	Fixed exchange rates	Attempt to change domestic-credit component of money base offset by change in international-reserves component of money base	Monetary policy weakened
Monetary policy	Freely fluctuating exchange rates	Attempt to change domestic-credit component of money base *not* offset by change in international-reserves component of money base	Monetary policy remains effective
Pure fiscal policy	Fixed exchange rates	International-reserves component of money base changes so as to support fiscal policy	Pure fiscal policy strengthened
Pure fiscal policy	Freely fluctuating exchange rates	No change in either domestic-credit component or international-reserves component of money base	Pure fiscal policy ineffective

assuming that the velocity of money is constant. The analysis could be amended to allow for variations in velocity by noting that an increase in velocity would produce effects similar to an increase in the money supply, while a decrease in velocity would produce effects similar to a decrease in the money supply. It may well be that an *increase* in the money supply will be accompanied by a slight *decrease* in velocity, which means that the intended effects of the monetary expansion will be partially offset. In general, however, any decrease in velocity that occurs as a reaction to an increase in the money stock will not be sufficient to offset fully the effects of the monetary expansion, and the major thrust of our conclusions will not be altered.

We have also been assuming that prices are constant. If they are not, a monetary expansion could result in upward pressure on the price level as well as upward pressure on income and output. With flexible prices, the conclusions reached above would still hold, in general, if we relate increases in the *nominal* money supply to increases in *money* income.

MACROECONOMIC POLICY UNDER MANAGED FLOATING

Our discussion, so far, has assumed that exchange rates are either rigidly fixed or are allowed to fluctuate freely. While these are extreme cases, they convey the more important implications about the effectiveness of macroeconomic policy in an open economy. To round out our analysis, let us now consider how these policies would be affected under managed floating exchange rates.

Under managed floating, a country can vary the extent to which it intervenes on the foreign exchange market. Heavier intervention moves the country closer to the fixed exchange-rate case, while intervening less heavily moves the country closer to the flexible exchange-rate case.

This has several implications for policy. First, if a country wishes to implement monetary policy in an open economy with high international capital mobility, it can enhance the effectiveness of this policy by reducing its exchange-market intervention and allowing the exchange rate to float more freely. This minimizes changes in the international-reserves component of the money base which might offset the deliberate changes in the domestic-credit component.

Second, if a country wishes to implement monetary policy in an open economy with high international capital mobility, but wishes to keep the exchange rate stable, it may have to resort to controlling capital inflows and outflows in order to preserve the intended effects of monetary policy. Of course, the authorities must be willing to accept the costs of imposing controls on capital flows, which would include a potentially serious misallocation of financial capital and ultimately a misallocation of real resources.

Third, if a country wishes to implement pure fiscal policy (in which there is no change in the domestic-credit component of the money base) in an open economy with high international capital mobility, it can increase the effectiveness of this policy by stepping up its exchange-market intervention as necessary to keep the exchange rate stable. This will produce changes in the international-reserves component of the money base that will support the intended fiscal policy.

INTERNATIONAL REPERCUSSIONS OF MONETARY AND FISCAL POLICY

In the preceding sections, we saw how international capital movements can interfere with or reinforce attempts by the home government to apply monetary and fiscal policy. In this section, we shall see how monetary and fiscal policy applied in one country can have significant spillover effects on economic activity in other countries. Our analysis will draw upon the relationships established in Chapter 9 regarding the international transmission of economic disturbances as well as upon the relationships established earlier in this chapter regarding the domestic effects of monetary and fiscal policy in an open economy.

As before, we shall assume that Britain is a relatively small country which has the choice of either pegging its exchange rate or letting it float freely. The United States will be conducting monetary and fiscal policy for its own internal purposes, and we shall see how the U.S. policy actions can affect the British economy.

Let us assume that, at the outset, the rates of inflation and unemployment prevailing in Britain are exactly those that the British prefer. Any disturbance emanating from the United States that raises the level of British spending will generate unwanted inflation; any disturbance that lowers the level of British spending will generate unwanted unemployment. Meanwhile, the United States is experiencing unwanted unemployment and has decided to pursue expansionary monetary and fiscal policies to raise the level of its own income, output and employment.[4] As before, we shall consider cases in which monetary and fiscal policy are applied under fixed and floating exchange rates in a world of high capital mobility.

Case 1: monetary policy, fixed exchange rates

This case begins as the United States, the large country, initiates an expansionary monetary policy. The effects of this policy on the U.S. economy will be to lower the U.S. interest

[4]We could also examine cases in which the United States is experiencing unwanted inflation and has decided to pursue contractionary monetary and fiscal policies. The mechanisms would be the same, but would work in the opposite direction.

rate, raise U.S. aggregate demand and raise the level of U.S. income and output. The increase in income will have the further effect of increasing U.S. imports.

The impact of these developments on the British economy will come through two channels: the increase in U.S. imports and the flow of capital that will arise as U.S. interest rates fall. Figure 10–8 traces these effects. The increase in U.S. imports, of course, represents an increase in exports by the British. The increase in British exports (item 1) generates a trade surplus (item 2) which increases the level of aggregate demand for British goods and services (item 3). The trade surplus also pushes the overall balance of payments into surplus (item 6).

Meanwhile, the British economy is also being affected through the capital account. The declining U.S. interest rate generates a capital flow from the United States to Britain (item 4). This drives the British interest rate downward (item 8), as investors buy British securities in large quantities. The capital flow into Britain also creates a capital account surplus (item 5), which coupled with the trade surplus creates an overall

balance-of-payments surplus (item 6). To maintain the exchange-rate peg, the British authorities must sell sterling on the foreign exchange market. This will expand the international-reserves component of the money base and hence the money supply (item 7).[5] Meanwhile, the declining British interest rate stimulates investment (item 9), which combines with the trade surplus to raise aggregate demand (item 3). The increase in aggregate demand is financed by the monetary expansion (item 7) and the result is strong inflationary pressure in Britain (item 10).

It is interesting to compare the effects of the U.S. monetary expansion on Britain under high and low capital mobility. With low capital mobility the stimulus to British aggregate demand would stem primarily from the increase in U.S.

[5]We shall continue to assume in this, and in all the following cases, that Britain does not sterilize changes in the international-reserves component of the money base. We shall also continue to assume that the money multiplier is 1.0, so that a change in the money base will be accompanied by an equal change in the money stock.

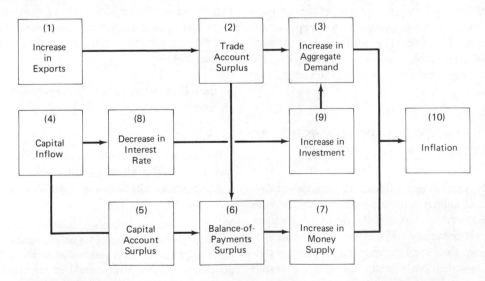

FIGURE 10-8 U.S. Monetary Policy—Fixed Exchange Rates: Effects on British Economy

imports, which is but a fraction of the increase in U.S. income generated by the U.S. monetary policy. The inflationary effect in Britain would be fairly modest. With very high capital mobility, however, the capital inflow to Britain would be massive, and the pegging activity by the British authorities would pour huge amounts of sterling into circulation. The intended expansionary effect of U.S. monetary policy within the United States would be diminished, since many of the new dollars created by the U.S. central bank would be absorbed by the British central bank in the process of pegging the exchange rate. Meanwhile, there would be strong inflationary pressure in Britain.

If the United States is very large and Britain relatively small, a modest monetary expansion from the U.S. perspective (i.e., relative to the preexisting quantity of money in the United States) can result in a disproportionately large monetary expansion from the British perspective (i.e., relative to the preexisting quantity of money in Britain). A small country attempting to maintain an exchange-rate peg in a world of high international capital mobility may thus find itself faced with monetary tidal waves from abroad. If, because of its small size, it does not have the resources to sterilize the domestic monetary repercussions, such a country may be forced to abandon attempts to conduct an independent monetary policy, to abandon its fixed exchange-rate policy, or to restrict the flow of capital into or out of the country.

Case 2: monetary policy, flexible exchange rates

As we saw in the preceding chapter, flexible exchange rates can provide a substantial degree of insulation against foreign economic disturbances. This applies to shifts in foreign monetary and fiscal policy as well as to other phenomena.

Let us again assume that the U.S. central bank has initiated an expansionary monetary policy to raise the level of U.S. economic activity. The main external effect will again be to raise the level of U.S. imports and to generate a flow of capital from the United States to Britain. In this case, the increase in U.S. demand for British exports (item 1 in Figure 10–9) causes sterling to appreciate on the foreign exchange market (item 2).

Meanwhile, the declining U.S. interest rate creates a capital inflow into Britain (item 3), which pushes the capital account into surplus (item 4). This reinforces the tendency for the increase in exports (item 1) to cause sterling to appreciate on the foreign exchange market. Under a flexible exchange rate, the overall balance of payments must remain in balance, so the appreciating pound must diminish exports and increase imports until the point is reached that the capital account surplus (item 4) is matched by a trade account deficit (item 5). Although the exogenous increase in exports (item 1) would, by itself, push the balance of trade toward surplus, this is more than offset by the curtailment in exports and increase in imports as British currency appreciates under the capital inflow.

By itself, the development of a trade deficit (item 5) would mean a decline in aggregate demand. However, the capital inflow (item 3) depresses the British interest rate (item 6), which stimulates investment (item 7). The increase in investment will tend to offset the trade deficit (item 5) in its effects on aggregate demand (item 8), so that aggregate demand need not be changed. In fact, since there is no change in the British money supply in this case, there can be no permanent change in the level of British income.[6]

The flexible exchange rate thus helps to insulate the overall level of British aggregate demand, and therefore income, output and employment from the effects of U.S. monetary policy. There may, however, be a shift in British

[6]Again, we ignore the effects of any change in the velocity of money.

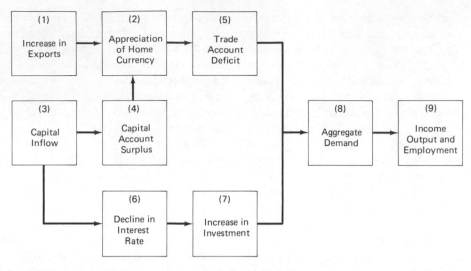

FIGURE 10-9 U.S. Monetary Policy—Flexible Exchange Rates: Effects on British Economy

production away from tradeable goods toward internal investment goods.

Case 3: fiscal policy, fixed exchange rates

Suppose, now, that the United States attempts to increase output and employment through expansionary fiscal policy, with no accompanying increase in the supply of money. The major external effects of an expansionary U.S. fiscal policy will be an increase in the U.S. interest rate and an increase in U.S. imports. From the British point of view, this means an increase in exports (see item 1 in Figure 10–10) and a capital outflow (item 3) large enough to cause the British interest rate to rise (item 7). The capital outflow (item 3) will also generate a capital account deficit (item 4). With high international capital mobility, the capital account deficit is likely to outweigh the trade account surplus (item 2), so that the overall balance of payments will be pushed into deficit (item 5). The overall balance-of-payments deficit means a contraction in the international-reserves component of the British money base and thus a contraction in the money

supply (item 6). This reinforces the increase in the British interest rate (item 7). Because of the rising interest rate, investment will fall (item 8), lowering aggregate demand (item 9). The tendency for aggregate demand to fall as a result of falling investment will be opposed by the balance-of-trade surplus (item 2). A clue to the final outcome lies in the decline in the money stock (item 6). The final amount of money in active circulation will not support a level of income as high as the original level. As a result, British income output and employment (item 10) will decline. In this case, the U.S. fiscal policy may have raised the level of U.S. output and employment, but it was accomplished at the expense of a decline in British output and employment.

By contrasting the outcome under low and high international capital mobility, we can gain insights into the effects of increasing capital mobility. With very low capital mobility, the British trade surplus would outweigh the capital account deficit and would generate a surplus in the overall balance of payments. This would lead to an increase in the money supply and an

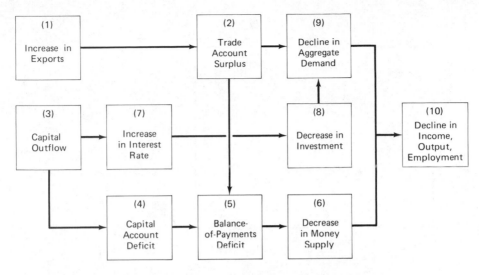

FIGURE 10-10 U.S. Fiscal Policy—Fixed Exchange Rates: Effects on British Economy

expansionary effect on the British economy. As capital mobility increases, the deficit pressure on the overall balance of payments through the capital account will increase. At some point, the deficit pressure through the capital account will exactly match the surplus pressure through the trade account. Here, the balance of payments will be in balance and there will be no effect on the money supply. As capital mobility continues to increase, the deficit pressure through the capital account will begin to outweigh the surplus pressure through the trade account. Now the British money supply will contract and there will be contractionary effects on the British economy.

Case 4: fiscal policy, flexible exchange rates

Let us now see what would happen to Britain if the United States attempts to raise the level of its output and employment through fiscal policy under floating exchange rates. The major external effects of U.S. fiscal policy again include an expansion of U.S. imports and an in-

crease in the U.S. interest rate. The effects on the British economy are traced in Figure 10–11. The increase in imports by U.S. residents represents an increase in exports (item 1) from the British viewpoint. Because capital is highly mobile, the British will also experience a capital outflow (item 2), which will raise the British interest rate (item 6). The capital outflow also pushes the capital account into deficit (item 3). The floating exchange rate (item 4) keeps the overall balance of payments in balance, however, adjusting the trade account so that the trade surplus (item 5) is just equal to the capital account deficit (item 3). Meanwhile, the rising British interest rate (item 6) reduces investment (item 7). Because there is no change in the money stock, there will be no permanent change in the level of British income; the increase in aggregate demand due to the increase in net exports (item 5) just offsets the reduction in aggregate demand due to the decline in investment (item 7). The end result is that exports have crowded out investment, while the overall level of economic activity remains unchanged.

The effects of foreign monetary and fiscal

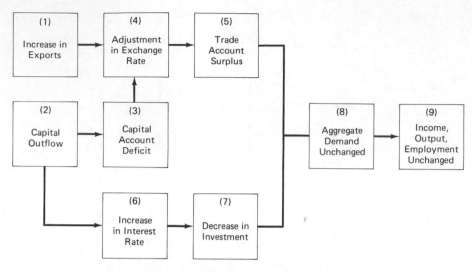

FIGURE 10-11 U.S. Fiscal Policy—Flexible Exchange Rates: Effects on British Economy

policy on the home economy under high international capital mobility are summarized in Figure 10–12.

MACROECONOMIC SPILLOVER EFFECTS UNDER MANAGED FLOATING

While the foregoing analysis assumed that exchange rates were either rigidly fixed or freely fluctuating, the spillover effects of domestic macroeconomic policy can be substantial under managed floating exchange rates. Any domestic policy that affects the magnitude of international trade or capital movements is bound to have an impact on foreign economies, no matter what exchange-rate regime is in effect.

During 1981, for example, the United States was pursuing a tight monetary policy in an effort to curb inflation that had been building in the U.S. economy for a number of years and that had reached double-digit rates. The tight monetary policy coupled with persistent inflationary expectations pushed the U.S. prime interest rate

(the rate charged by banks to their best customers) to over 20 percent. The high U.S. interest rates attracted capital from abroad, especially from countries which had well-developed banking sectors and as a result had become depositories for large amounts of foreign funds. As capital flowed to the United States, the currencies of these countries came under heavy downward pressure on the foreign exchange market.

A number of foreign countries, especially West Germany and the countries linked to the mark through the European Monetary System, complained that the U.S. policy was forcing them either to accept currency depreciation or to adopt tighter monetary policies themselves in order to stem the capital outflow. The Bank for International Settlements in Basel, Switzerland, an institution that acts as a clearing house for many of the central banks in the system, and that frequently reflects the views of the central banks, admonished the United States not to pursue an overly stringent monetary policy because of the spillover effects on other countries.

Interestingly, some observers have suggested that the outcry from many of the European coun-

FIGURE 10-12 Effects of Expansionary (Contractionary) Foreign Monetary and Fiscal Policy on Home Economy Under High International Capital Mobility

Foreign Macroeconomic Policy	Home Exchange-Rate Policy	Effect on Home Economy
Expansionary (contractionary) monetary policy	Fixed exchange rates	Inflation (deflation and unemployment)
Expansionary (contractionary) monetary policy	Freely fluctuating exchange rates	Little or no change in price level or overall level of economic activity
Expansionary (contractionary) fiscal policy	Fixed exchange rates	Deflation or unemployment (inflation)
Expansionary (contractionary) fiscal policy	Freely fluctuating exchange rates	Little or no change in price level or overall level of economic activity

tries (which up until that point had been criticizing the United States for failing to bring inflation under control) was largely for political purposes. Actually, many of the European governments believed that greater monetary restraint was appropriate for their own economies, but had been unwilling to face the political costs of pursuing tighter monetary policies. With the high U.S. interest rate causing capital outflows from their countries, the foreign central banks could claim that they had no choice but to pursue tighter monetary policies to keep their currencies from losing value on the foreign exchange market. Blame for pursuing a tight domestic policy could thus be laid at the door of the United States. As it turned out, most of the European countries affected by the tight U.S. policy accepted a combination of consequences, letting their currencies depreciate, somewhat, against the dollar, while pursuing tighter monetary policies at home.

QUESTIONS AND EXERCISES

1. Suppose that country A is a small country which is experiencing a high rate of inflation. The authorities wish to curb inflation by implementing a contractionary monetary policy. Assuming that capital mobility is very high among countries, contrast the effects if country A implements this policy while

a. rigidly pegging its currency to foreign currencies on the foreign exchange market.

b. allowing the exchange rates to float freely.

2. Suppose country A attempts to curb inflation through pure fiscal policy. Trace the effects of this policy, assuming

a. country A rigidly pegs the exchange rates.

b. exchange rates are allowed to float freely.

3. Evaluate the following claim: In a world of high international capital mobility, it is difficult for a small country to implement a rate of monetary expansion that differs greatly from the rate of monetary expansion in the rest of the world. Of what significance is the exchange-rate policy being pursued by the country?

4. During the early 1980s the United States was pursuing a restrictive monetary policy in an effort to reduce the rate of home inflation. Using the simplified models developed in this chapter, trace the effects of this policy on a small country closely tied to the United States in trade and finance. Assume, first, that the foreign country is vigorously stabilizing its exchange rate with the dollar. Then assume that the exchange rate is allowed to float freely.

5. Many European countries have argued that if the United States is going to pursue a tight monetary policy, it should at least intervene on the foreign exchange market to keep foreign currencies from depreciating against the dollar as a result of this policy. Analyze the effects of such a suggestion on U.S. efforts to curb inflation through restrictive monetary policy.

6. Many observers argue that international capital mobility is increasing over time. If so, what are the implications for the spillover effects of macroeconomic policy among the countries in the system?

7. Suppose a small country is experiencing spillover effects from a contractionary monetary policy being implemented by a large trading partner. The small country is pursuing a policy of managed floating exchange rates. How should the small country vary the degree to which it stabilizes the exchange rate with the larger country if:

   a. the small country is already facing an economic slowdown and does not wish to experience further contraction in its economy?

   b. the small country is facing internal inflation which it wishes to curb?

CLOSING ESSAY:
Policy Choices in an Interdependent World

We live in a world of tradeoffs. There is no question that modern transportation and communications technologies, as well as liberalization of international trade and financial arrangements, have done much to improve access by all countries to international markets. Closer international ties in markets for goods have added substantially to the abundance and variety of goods and services available to residents of the trading countries. Greater international integration of capital markets has broadened investment opportunities and has helped to ensure that investment funds will find their way to places in which they are in greatest demand.

On the other hand, the more closely countries are linked by trade and financial relations, the stronger are the channels through which economic disturbances can pass among the countries. Stronger international economic linkages make it more difficult for countries to regulate their own economies through the traditional tools of monetary and fiscal policy. They also make each country more sensitive to monetary and fiscal measures taken abroad. The economic benefits of an integrated world require sacrifice in terms of economic independence.

Still, countries are not without some control over the repercussions of foreign economic disturbances on their own economies. As we have seen, the choice between fixed and flexible exchange rates can affect the extent to which foreign inflation or foreign policy measures can impact on the home country. The optimum degree of exchange-rate flexibility for trying to neutralize disturbances from abroad will depend on the degree of international capital mobility as well as the nature of the disturbances themselves.

In similar fashion, the effectiveness of monetary and fiscal policy tools for regulating the home economy depend critically on the degree of exchange-rate flexibility and the degree of international capital mobility. The optimum mix of monetary and fiscal policy for dealing with purely domestic problems will depend both on the degree of international capital mobility and the degree of flexibility in exchange-rate movements.

In Chapter 9, we saw that flexible exchange rates offer more insulation against foreign inflation than do fixed rates. This is because, under flexible rates, the monetary authorities will not be intervening on the foreign exchange market and thereby expanding the home money stock, and because the flexible exchange rate can offset foreign price changes, thereby weakening the tradeable-goods-price mechanism and the Keynesian direct-demand-pressure mechanism. A fixed exchange rate, on the other hand, enhances the transmission of inflation through all of these channels. In fact, a fixed exchange rate that undervalues home currency can generate "imported inflation" even when none is being exported from abroad.

This does not mean that a flexible exchange rate is neutral in its impact on the economies within the system. As we saw in Chapter 9, depreciating home currency, if not matched by an equal percentage decline in foreign prices, can generate inflationary pressures within the home economy. The depreciating home currency not only directly raises the prices of imported goods, raw materials and intermediate products, but also induces labor to press for higher wages to protect its standard of living. This, in turn, feeds into home production costs.

In Chapter 10, we saw that attempts to apply monetary and fiscal policy to regulate the home economy would meet with varying degrees of success, depending on the exchange-rate regime in effect and the degree of international capital mobility. With high capital mobility, monetary policy works relatively better than does fiscal policy if exchange rates are flexible, while fiscal policy works relatively better if exchange rates are fixed. If a country is managing the flexibility of its exchange rate, therefore, it may wish to reduce its exchange-market intervention during periods in which it is trying to reduce home inflation through contractionary monetary policies.

We also saw, in Chapter 10, that the repercussions on the home economy of monetary and fiscal policies applied in other countries can be reduced by appropriate exchange-rate policies. In general, the home country can resist the repercussions of foreign monetary and fiscal policies (or other, autonomous changes in foreign spending) by reducing intervention on the foreign exchange market. With high capital mobility, rigidly fixed exchange rates can translate foreign monetary expansion into strong inflationary pressures at home and translate expansionary foreign real expenditures, including government expenditures, into deflationary pressures at home.[1]

Many observers argue that, during the 1960s and early 1970s, most inflation of the international variety originated in the United States and radiated overseas. This view is consistent with the fact that the other countries in the system were doing the bulk of the intervening on the foreign exchange market, making them especially vulnerable to imported inflation. Exchange-market intervention by the United States during this period was minimal.

Since 1973, most of the larger countries have adopted managed floating exchange rates. Each country's sensitivity to foreign inflation under these circumstances depends in large measure on the extent to which its authorities intervene on the market. Resisting inflationary pressures from abroad is, of course, but one of many considerations a country would weigh in setting its exchange-rate policy. Many countries have opted to hold down the values of their currencies on the foreign exchange market in order to protect the international competitiveness of their exports, even at the cost of imported inflation.

Speculation against the dollar during the 1970s made the exchange-rate management problem especially difficult for countries on the receiving end of speculative capital flows. Such capital inflows can cause intense pressure for the currencies in these countries to appreciate. Letting one's currency appreciate will make home goods less competitive on international markets, yet intervening to forestall appreciation will add to internal inflationary pressure. During the 1970s some countries, including Italy, France and Belgium, tried to deal with this problem by holding down the values of their currencies for transactions involving the trade of goods, while letting the exchange rate float for financial

---

[1]The implications of this discussion for fixed versus flexible exchange rates have to be weighed along with other considerations that bear on this issue. A more complete discussion of the pros and cons of different exchange-rate regimes appears in Chapter 25.

transactions. Others, including Switzerland and Germany, sought to discourage speculative capital inflows by imposing restrictions on foreign investment in domestic assets.

There seems to be little reason to doubt that the international integration of goods and capital markets will continue. If it does, not only inflation but the overall business cycle may begin to assume global dimensions. Moreover, there seems to be little prospect, at least in the near future, for reductions in international dependencies for vital primary products, such as food and petroleum. In a world in which international economic dependencies and linkages are increasing, an understanding of the likely effects of foreign disturbances on the home economy and of the policy choices available to deal with them will become all the more important.

INTERNATIONAL CAPITAL FLOWS AND INTERNATIONAL CREDIT MARKETS III

INTRODUCTION:
International Capital Flows: A Source of Efficiency or a Source of Instability?

Each year, billions of dollars of financial capital flow among the countries that make up the international economic system. These flows perform the essential function of transmitting purchasing power among the countries, allocating it to locations where it is in greatest demand. This helps to facilitate the international trade of goods and services and helps to finance the transfer of real capital among countries.

Financial capital flows make up a significant part of total international payments. As an example, U.S. net private capital inflows recorded in the balance of payments ran about $31 billion during 1980, while net private capital outflows were about $71 billion. In addition, the statistical discrepancy, widely believed to measure unrecorded capital account transactions, showed an inflow well in excess of $30 billion. While these figures might seem small compared to the $341 billion worth of U.S. goods-and-services exports during the year, and the $334 billion worth of goods-and-services imports, the quantity of funds involved is still enormous. The relative importance of capital flows becomes even more apparent when you consider that the *imbalance* in recorded net private capital inflows and outflows was $40 billion while the imbalance in exports and imports of goods and services was only about $7 billion. Because they are an important component of international payments, capital flows have a major impact on exchange-rate movements and the balance of payments of the countries within the system.

Much of the international movement of funds takes the form of short-term capital flows. Short-term capital flows can be especially volatile; evidence suggests that during the 1970s large quantities of short-term funds moved back and forth among countries in response to changes in national interest rates and changes in expectations about future exchange rates. This was seen as being especially disruptive, not only to the foreign exchange market, but also to the monetary sectors of the countries within the system.

It is widely believed that the volatility of short-term capital flows was made worse by the presence of an international money market that was without adequate controls. The Eurocurrency market, it is alleged, not only served to channel existing funds more rapidly among countries, but also generated large volumes of new liquidity that could wash in and out of countries, creating monetary havoc. A great deal of effort has been devoted to analyzing the liquidity producing capacity of the Eurocurrency market and the effects of such a phenomenon on the economies of individual countries. A number of proposals have been advanced to bring the Eurocurrency market under control. If the Eurocurrency market is in fact capable of creating money and credit at a faster rate than is desired by the monetary authorities within the various countries, then steps to regulate the market would certainly seem warranted. Whether the Eurocurrency market actually operates this way, however, is a matter of dispute.

In the following two chapters, we shall explore these issues. We begin by analyzing the forces that generate international capital flows in general. We then examine the mechanisms by which the Eurocurrency market transmits and possibly creates liquidity, and we evaluate arguments for imposing controls on international money markets.

INTERNATIONAL CAPITAL MOVEMENTS 11

Exchange-market pressure is pressure for a currency's exchange rate to change. Such pressure is the result of an imbalance between the demand for and supply of the currency in question and is associated with an imbalance (surplus or deficit) in the country's international transactions. The immediate result of such pressure must be either an exchange-rate change, a change in the level of accommodating transactions (more specifically, a faster or slower rate of change in the country's international reserves) or both. Because of their volume and variability, private international capital flows are an important source of variation in exchange-market pressure. An understanding of the behavior of exchange rates or the balance of payments thus requires an understanding of the forces that generate international capital movements.

International capital movements can be defined as the movement of funds from one country to another for the purpose of purchasing assets in the second country. Assets, here, are broadly defined to include long-term as well as short-term securities; debt as well as equity instruments; and physical assets, such as plant, equipment and real estate.

SOME ESSENTIAL FUNCTIONS OF CAPITAL MARKETS

International capital markets, like the capital markets found within countries, facilitate the transfer of money from those who wish to defer expenditure on goods and services to those who wish to spend more on goods (including investment goods) and services during the current period. Those wishing to obtain greater current purchasing power borrow funds by entering the capital market and selling instruments that represent future claims on the borrower. Those wishing to defer expenditures lend funds by buying these debt instruments.

169

Typically, there is a secondary market for these financial instruments. If the lender decides that he does not wish to hold the instrument to maturity, he can sell it to another party for an amount that is determined in the financial market at that point in time. A network of financial institutions, including investment banking houses, securities brokers, commercial banks, savings and loan companies, insurance companies and pension funds act as middlemen to facilitate the transfer of funds from lenders to borrowers.

Borrowers include firms that want to obtain funds for working capital, as well as for long-term investment. They include government, which obtains funds to pay for current public goods and services and to pay for public investment projects such as roads, waterways and public buildings. Borrowers also include private residents who are investing in housing or consumer durable goods, or who simply wish to borrow in order to increase current consumption levels. Lenders include households, who wish to save by deferring spending from the current to a future period, and firms whose income happens to exceed costs, taxes and dividend payments.

The debt instruments themselves range from very short-term drafts that mature whenever the lender calls for repayment, to bonds that mature in many years. Some instruments never mature at all. These would include equity issues such as common or preferred stock, which represent a participation in the ownership in the firm that issues them.

In well-organized, active markets, the rates of return on the various credit instruments are determined by competitive forces. Borrowers attempt to attract funds by offering a more attractive rate of return than is being offered by competing instruments. Efficient financial markets thus help to ensure that savings (and the resources that these savings command) are allocated to sectors of the economy in which the resources are in greatest demand.

INTERNATIONAL VERSUS PURELY DOMESTIC FINANCIAL MARKETS

Financial markets frequently extend across national boundaries. Lenders often find that borrowers in foreign countries offer higher rates of return for the amount of risk involved than do domestic borrowers. Likewise, borrowers often find that funds are available at more reasonable rates in foreign countries. Those subsets of transactions (in various assets) which are international in nature make up what can be called the *international financial market,* and the international transfer of funds associated with these transactions are known as *international capital movements.*

Forces that determine international capital movements are much the same as those that determine movements of capital within countries. Lenders will allocate funds to instruments that offer an attractive rate of return for a given level of risk, while taking account of their liquidity needs. There are some features of international financial markets that differ from those of a purely domestic market, however. The very fact that transactions are conducted across national borders means that in most cases the borrower, the lender, or the financial intermediary will have to convert funds from one currency into another, and that one of the parties will have to take exchange risk into account. *Exchange risk* is the risk that the exchange rate between the two currencies will change between the time of lending and the time of repayment, and thereby confer a capital loss on one of the parties.

A second feature of international financial markets is that different countries have different political systems and different sets of regulations governing international capital flows. International lenders may therefore face what is known as *political risk*. This is the risk that the government of the borrowing party will impose regulations that partially or wholly freeze payments of interest or principal. As we shall see, special markets have evolved that help participants in international transactions to reduce and sometimes eliminate political and exchange risk.

LONG-TERM VERSUS SHORT-TERM CAPITAL MOVEMENTS

Most analysis of international capital movements makes a distinction between long-term and short-term capital flows. Long-term capital flows involve investment in long-term instruments—those that have a maturity of a year or more. Short-term capital movements involve investment in short-term instruments—those that have a maturity of less than a year.

Long-Term Capital Movements

Long-term international capital flows result from the buying and selling of long-term debt or equity instruments across national borders. In analyzing long-term capital movements, we shall distinguish between portfolio investment and direct foreign investment. These distinctions are useful because each of the categories reflects a somewhat different motive for moving funds between countries.

portfolio investment

Portfolio investment involves the purchase of assets strictly for the purpose of earning a rate of return that is attractive for the given level of risk; there is no acquisition of control of the institution that issues the asset. Portfolio investment would include the purchase of government securities and corporate bonds. It would also include the purchase of equity instruments, so long as the acquisition does not involve a controlling interest in the firm issuing the instrument.

direct investment

Unlike portfolio investment, direct investment involves acquisition of a controlling interest in the foreign firm or facility. A typical case would involve a firm in the home country acquiring sufficient common stock in a foreign corporation to give the home firm voting control. The home firm would then become the *parent* company and the foreign firm the *subsidiary*. If the home firm were to acquire all of the controlling interest in the foreign firm the latter would become a *wholly owned subsidiary*. Direct foreign investment can also involve the acquisition or construction of new plant and equipment. If a home firm has a manufacturing subsidiary abroad and moves funds overseas to finance an expansion of the subsidiary plant, this falls into the category of direct foreign investment. Finally, direct foreign investment includes the overseas reinvestment of foreign subsidiary earnings.[1]

Short-Term Capital Movements

Short-term international capital flows result from the buying and selling of short-term instruments across national borders. These transactions include the extension of trade credit and the transfer of working capital within companies that do business in several countries. In addition, other holders of liquid wealth frequently transfer funds out of the short-term securities of one country and into the short-term securities of another. As an example, some of the oil-exporting countries hold large amounts of wealth which they have derived from the sale of oil. Large portions of these funds have been invested in the short-term government securities of var-

[1]Recall from Chapter 7 that if foreign subsidiary earnings are repatriated, they are counted as earnings on services provided to foreigners in the balance of payments.

ious industrial countries. The finance ministers of the oil-exporting countries are very sensitive to changes in relative rates of return in various countries as well as to changes in the exchange risk associated with holding a given country's assets. In this setting, if U.S. interest rates were to rise relative to, say, British interest rates, or if fears began to arise that sterling would depreciate on the foreign exchange market, the finance ministers would respond by shifting funds out of British securities into U.S. securities.

By the same token, national central banks, which hold international reserves in the form of the liquid assets of other countries, have incentives to make similar shifts. Commercial banks, whose customers include firms doing business across national borders, hold inventories of various national currencies and other foreign short-term assets. These banks also have incentives to shift funds in response to perceived changes in risk and return. Indeed much of the short-term capital flow that occurred during the 1970s and 1980s has been attributed to changes in relative interest rates and changes in expectations about exchange-rate movements.

The trade of goods and services gives rise to a large volume of international short-term financial transactions, since funds must be transferred or credit extended to pay for internationally traded goods. When credit is extended by the exporter to the importer, the importer is in effect borrowing funds from the exporter across national borders. Here, the borrower (or the borrower's bank) issues a debt instrument to the lending exporter. These are typically short-term instruments with payment due in 30, 90 or 180 days, as is typical in most domestic credit transactions.

As we can see, there are a number of variables to which wealthholders might respond, causing them to move funds from one country to another. In the following section, we want to take a closer look at the role of portfolio adjustment in determining international capital flows.

PORTFOLIO INVESTMENT AND PORTFOLIO THEORY

The framework within which international portfolio investment is analyzed is known as *portfolio theory*. Portfolio theory was developed to explain investment behavior in general and has been found to be useful in explaining the portfolio-investment component of international capital movements. In discussing portfolio theory, we shall initially assume that we are observing the behavior of a single wealthholder in making decisions as to how to allocate his wealth among available assets. The term *wealthholder* will be broadly construed to encompass all managers of wealth. Wealthholders would thus include commercial banks, insurance companies, pension funds, industrial firms, individuals and even governments. The portfolio manager's wealth is the total value of the assets in his portfolio; this wealth can then be divided among available assets as the wealthholder chooses. The variables that affect the wealthholder's choice of assets include expected rates of return, risk and changes in wealth. Let us see how these items affect portfolio investment decisions.

expected rates of return

Assume that our wealthholder has a given amount of wealth, W. Let us also assume that there are 3 different assets, A_1, A_2, and A_3, in which he could place his wealth. Each of these assets has an expected rate of return, r_1, r_2, and r_3, respectively. The expected rate of return on an asset includes not only the interest rate that the asset will pay, but also any expected capital gain or loss. Capital gain or loss would result if the market price of the asset changes between the time the wealthholder buys it and the time he sells it. For example, a wealthholder might be able to buy a bond having a face value of $1000 for a market price of $900 if he buys it several years before maturity. If he holds the bond to maturity and receives the $1000 face value, he will realize a capital gain of $100. Any expected capital gain or loss has to be factored into the wealthholder's expected rate of return on the asset.

Another source of capital gain or loss is change in the home currency value of an asset that is denominated in foreign currency. This would occur if there is a change in the exchange rate between home and foreign currency during the time the asset is being held. Suppose an American wealthholder buys a £1000 British bond for $1000 (assuming the exchange rate between the dollar and sterling to be $1.00 = £1). Then suppose the dollar depreciates against sterling to $2.00 = £1. When the £1000 instrument matures and the £1000 is converted back to dollars, the U.S. wealthholder will receive $2000— a gain of $1000. Of course, if the dollar had *appreciated* against sterling, the wealthholder would have suffered a capital loss.

To summarize, then, the expected rate of return associated with an asset consists of three components: the interest earnings, the expected capital gain or loss due to a rise or fall in the market price of the asset and the expected capital gain or loss due to a change in the exchange rate. We should note that at the time the investment decision is made, the wealthholder is usually aware of the rate of interest he will receive on the asset. If he knows for certain that he will hold the asset to maturity, he can also calculate the capital gain (or loss) as the difference in the face value of the instrument and the price he pays for it. If there is some chance he will sell the asset before maturity, he can only estimate the capital gain or loss he will incur. Since he does not know in advance what the

exchange rate will do during the time he holds the asset, he can only guess at that also. For these reasons, r_1, r_2 and r_3 are properly called *expected* rates of return.

perceived risks

We shall designate the risks associated with holding assets A_1, A_2 and A_3 as ρ_1, ρ_2 and ρ_3, respectively. Risk, itself, has several components. It includes the risk that the institution issuing the asset will default in whole or in part on either the interest or the principal. It includes *exchange risk,* the risk that the exchange rate might move against the wealthholder and confer a capital loss. It also includes *political risk*— the risk that the government of the foreign country might impose restrictions that tie up the wealthholder's funds abroad. Because the probabilities of default, exchange-rate change and adverse political decisions are unknown in advance, the evaluation of the risk element is entirely subjective and reflects the wealthholder's personal assessment of the probabilities at the time the investment decision is made.

tradeoff between risk and return

At this point, let us consider the tradeoff between risk and expected return facing the wealthholder as he decides how much wealth to place in a given asset. All things being equal, the wealthholder would prefer to have the highest possible rate of return for a given level of risk, or the lowest possible level of risk for a given rate of return. Consequently, if we wished to induce the wealthholder to accept a higher level of risk, we would have to offer him a higher rate of return as compensation. By the same token, we could induce him to accept a somewhat lower rate of return if we were to lower the level of risk associated with the investment.

We can formalize our argument in the following form:

(1) $$\frac{A_1}{W} = f_1(r_1, \rho_1)$$

where

W = the wealthholder's fixed stock of wealth

A_1 = the amount of wealth allocated to asset A_1

r_1 = the expected rate of return on asset A_1

ρ_1 = the subjective risk associated with asset A_1

This equation states that the proportion of wealth allocated to asset A_1 is a function of the expected rate of return and risk associated with asset A_1. Here A_1/W is positively associated with the rate of return on asset A_1 and negatively associated with the risk attributed to holding that asset.

the portfolio allocation decision

But there is more to the investment decision than that. In deciding how to divide his wealth among the *three* available assets, the wealthholder will take the risks and expected rates of return on all of these assets into account simultaneously. A 20 percent rate of return on asset A_1 will be a lot more attractive if the alternative available rates of return are 10 percent than if the alternative available rates are 25 percent, or even 15 percent. Comparative risk levels are also important. Suppose that asset A_1 has had an expected rate of return of 20 percent while assets A_2 and A_3 have expected rates of return of 10 percent. The relative attractiveness of asset A_1 will be greater if the risks associated with assets A_2 and A_3 are high than if they are low.

Since the proportion of wealth to be placed in asset A_1 will depend not only on the risk and expected rate of return of asset A_1, but also on the risks and expected rates of return of assets A_2 and A_3, equation (1) should be expanded to:

(2) $$\frac{A_1}{W} = f_1(r_1, r_2, r_3; \rho_1, \rho_2, \rho_3; X_1)$$

$$\frac{A_2}{W} = f_2(r_1, r_2, r_3; \rho_1, \rho_2, \rho_3; X_2)$$

$$\frac{A_3}{W} = f_3(r_1, r_2, r_3; \rho_1, \rho_2, \rho_3; X_3)$$

Here we have an expanded and more realistic model of the wealthholder's behavior. This set of equations states that the proportion of wealth allocated to any one asset will depend on the expected rates of return and risks not only of the asset in question, but of other assets as well. The variable X stands for all other factors that might affect the wealthholder's decision.

There is one additional aspect of the allocation decision that we should emphasize. Suppose that the expected rate of return on asset A_1 were greater than the expected rates of return on the other two assets, while the risks on all three assets were the same. Would the wealthholder allocate *all* of his wealth to asset A_1 in order to maximize his earnings? The answer is generally no. Although the individual risks associated with assets A_1, A_2 and A_3 may be equal, there is an additional risk, known as *portfolio risk*, associated with putting all the eggs into one basket. The wealthholder can lower his portfolio risk by *diversifying* his holdings—spreading his wealth among several assets whose prices do not typically vary according to the same pattern.

Portfolio Equilibrium

Now let us assume that the wealthholder, having a fixed stock of wealth and facing a given array of expected rates of returns and risks, has allocated his wealth among the available assets so that he is satisfied with the distribution. Since he has no desire for further reallocations, the shifting of funds among assets is at a halt. In this state, the wealthholder's portfolio is said to be in *equilibrium* or in *balance*.

shifts in portfolio equilibrium

If, starting from portfolio equilibrium, there were to be a change in one of the variables (say, an increase in the expected rate of return on asset A_2 to a higher level), the portfolio would no longer be in balance, since the wealthholder would now have an incentive to reallocate his wealth among the assets. This portfolio disequilibrium would give rise to a flow of funds among assets as the wealthholder shifts funds out of assets A_1 and A_3 and into asset A_2. After a certain amount of wealth has been reallocated, the flow of funds among assets would come to a halt, as portfolio risk (the risk of putting too many eggs in one basket) rises to offset the benefits of *further* reallocations. When the wealthholder reaches the point that he does not desire any further reallocation, the portfolio will once again be in equilibrium, though with a different distribution of wealth among the different assets. The increase in r_2, in this example, has caused the wealthholder to shift from one portfolio equilibrium position to another, and the higher level of r_2 has produced an equilibrium in which a higher proportion of wealth is allocated to A_2. Given the wealthholder's set of preferences for risk and return, there is a particular equilibrium allocation associated with each possible combination of risks and expected returns, and a change in one of these variables will generate a flow of funds among assets as the wealthholder moves from one portfolio equilibrium to another.

changes in wealth

So far, we have assumed that wealth is constant. What would happen if wealth were to grow over time? To analyze the effects of a change in wealth, let us take one more step with our model and multiply both sides of equation (2) by W. This yields:

$$A_1 = f_1(r_1, r_2, r_3; \rho_1, \rho_2, \rho_3; X_1)\, W$$

$$(3) \qquad A_2 = f_2(r_1, r_2, r_3; \rho_1, \rho_2, \rho_3; X_2)\, W$$

$$A_3 = f_3(r_1, r_2, r_3; \rho_1, \rho_2, \rho_3; X_3)\, W$$

Now, instead of having the *proportion* of wealth the wealthholder wants to allocate to each asset on the left-hand side, we have the *amount* of wealth he wants to allocate to each asset. It is easy to see that as W increases, A_1, A_2 and A_3 will all increase. Equation (3) suggests that if wealth were to double, the amount of wealth allocated to each asset would also double, as long as the risk, the return and the X variables remain constant. Only if there were changes in one or more of the allocation variables would the *proportion* of wealth allocated to each asset change as wealth increased.[2]

Application of Portfolio Theory to International Capital Movements

Everything we have said up to this point would apply to portfolio investment decisions in general, whether foreign assets were involved or not. To see how the model is valuable in explaining and understanding international capital movements, let us assume that one of the assets, A_1, is a foreign (British) asset, while A_2 and A_3 are home (U.S.) assets. The wealthholder is a U.S. resident who holds both home and foreign assets in his portfolio.

Let us assume that our wealthholder's portfolio, as well as the portfolios of all other wealthholders, is initially in equilibrium and that

[2]We refer to the items in parentheses in equation (3) as *allocation variables* since they determine the allocation of the wealthholder's wealth among the various assets.

the amount of wealth in all portfolios is fixed. Since no wealthholder is reallocating funds among assets, there will be no international portfolio capital flow. Now suppose that r_1 rises due to an increase in the British interest rate. Wealthholders will now begin to reallocate funds from assets A_2 and A_3 to asset A_1. This will entail a flow of funds from the United States to Britain. After a point, the capital flow to Britain will cease as wealthholders reach new portfolio equilibria. This will occur when portfolio risk has risen enough, U.S. interest rates have risen enough and British interest rates have receded enough to offset the benefits of any further shifting of funds into British assets. U.S. interest rates will rise in this example because the selloff of U.S. assets will tend to lower their prices and consequently raise the rates of return on them. British interest rates will tend to recede (from the level to which we initially assumed that they rose), because the increased demand for British assets will drive up their prices and consequently lower the rate of return on them.

We might mention that not all wealthholders will shift the same amount of funds in response to the change in r_1. They will tend to have differing assessments of the risks and expected rates of return on the assets. They will also tend to have differing preferences for risk-taking or avoidance and they may start out with different amounts of wealth invested in the available assets. Nevertheless, they will still tend to act in the same *direction* in response to a change in one of the variables, and they will all tend to move from one portfolio equilibrium position to another.

In this example, we let the British interest rate rise while the other variables remained constant. If we had let the other expected rates of return, r_2 and r_3, rise by as much as r_1, there would have been little incentive for any international shifting of funds since there would be little or no increase in the *relative* attractiveness of asset A_1. For this reason, some analysts prefer

to focus on differentials in expected rates of return across countries in explaining the distribution of wealth among assets. In other words, instead of using r_1 and r_2 separately as variables explaining asset selection, these analysts would use the differential $(r_1 - r_2)$.

As another example, let us suppose that, beginning from a position of portfolio equilibrium, wealthholders begin to fear that the British government will impose restrictions on the movement of funds out of Britain. This means that the political risk component of ρ_1 has risen. Now wealthholders will begin to shift funds out of British into U.S. assets and will continue to do so until portfolio risk has risen, the British interest rate has risen and the U.S. interest rate has fallen so as to offset the benefits of further reallocation of funds. Again, the shifting of funds will cease when the wealthholders reach new portfolio equilibria.

As a final example, let us support that, starting from portfolio equilibrium, wealth begins to increase in the United States while British wealth remains unchanged. U.S. wealthholders will begin to allocate the additions to their wealth into assets A_1, A_2 and A_3 in proportions dictated by the relative magnitudes of the allocation variables. Since some of these funds will be flowing into asset A_1, there will be a capital flow from the United States to Britain. This will continue for as long as U.S. wealth continues to increase.

Stock Adjustments and Continuous Flows

As we can see from the foregoing examples, international capital flows can have both a *stock-adjustment* component and a *continuing-flow* component. The stock adjustment arises as wealthholders shift their funds among assets in various countries due to changes in the allocation variables. This is called a stock-adjustment phenomenon since it entails the reallocation of the existing stock of wealth among available assets; it comes to a halt when the reallocation is completed. The continuing-flow component, on the other hand, results from steady additions to the stock of wealth, and it will continue for as long as the level of wealth increases.

If there should be a change in the allocation variables at the same time that a continuous flow is in progress, the effect would be twofold. Stock adjustment would be added to the wealth-induced flows, and the proportion of the wealth-induced flows flowing into each asset would be altered. For example, suppose that during a given period the allocation variables are constant and that U.S. wealth is increasing by $6 million per month. Of this, $2 million per month is being allocated each to assets A_1, A_2 and A_3. There is thus a $2 million per month capital flow from the United States to Britain. Now let r_1, the expected rate of return on British assets, rise relative to r_2 and r_3. There will be an adjustment in which previously existing amounts of wealth will be moved from assets A_2 and A_3 into asset A_1. This stock adjustment will be added to the continuous flow being generated by U.S. wealth increases. In addition to that, there will be an alteration in the proportion of the new additions to wealth allocated to the three assets. Now, perhaps $4 million of the $6 million monthly increment in wealth will be allocated to A_1 and only $1 million each to assets A_2 and A_3.

In actual world financial markets, expected rates of return and risks undergo frequent changes. The levels of wealth held by individuals, firms and institutions also vary. As a result, portfolio equilibria are continuously being disturbed, and wealthholders are constantly adjusting toward new equilibria. This produces an ongoing, varying flow of portfolio capital among countries.

The Role of Real Versus Nominal Interest Rates

As a final point, we should note that in making long-run international portfolio adjustments, wealthholders tend to compare real interest rates rather than nominal interest rates. (The real in-terest rate is defined as the nominal [or market] interest rate minus the expected rate of inflation.) This is because any gain that can be captured by moving funds to a country with a high nominal interest rate (that is, in turn, being boosted by high inflationary expectations) is likely to be offset by depreciation of that country's currency on the foreign exchange market.

FOREIGN DIRECT INVESTMENT

While portfolio theory is useful in analyzing capital flows in which wealthholders shift funds among countries in response to changes in expected rates of return and risk, it is not very useful for analyzing flows generated by direct foreign investment. Foreign direct investment, as we mentioned earlier, involves a transfer of funds to a foreign enterprise over which residents of the investing country have effective control, or acquire effective control, as a result of the investment.

Direct foreign investment is determined more by factors peculiar to the firm or industry involved than by rates of return on assets in the home and foreign countries. Largely because the motivations are specific to the firm or industry, attempts to form general models to explain direct foreign investments have so far proven to be unsuccessful. A more detailed discussion of direct foreign investment appears in Chapter 21.

THE FORWARD EXCHANGE MARKET

As we mentioned earlier, wealthholders placing funds abroad face the risk that foreign currency will depreciate while funds are invested in foreign securities. For short-run investments, wealthholders can protect themselves against exchange risk by making use of the forward exchange market. Here, the wealthholder would enter a forward contract with his bank, in which the bank agrees to buy a specific amount of foreign currency from the wealthholder at a specific future date at a prespecified exchange rate. (We, of course, assume that the bank is in the international banking business and offers forward contract services to its customers.) This removes any uncertainty over how much home currency the wealthholder will receive when he repatriates his funds. The act of eliminating exchange risk through the forward exchange market in this fashion is known as "covering" one's position or obtaining *forward cover.*

The exchange rate specified in the forward contract is known as the *forward exchange rate,* and it is determined in an active market for forward contracts; when a bank and its customer enter a forward contract, the forward exchange rate specified in the contract will be the forward rate prevailing in the market at the time the contract is entered. Forward contracts can be drawn up for different maturities. If the wealthholder wishes to keep his funds invested in foreign securities for 30 days, he would enter a 30-day forward contract; if he wishes to keep his funds abroad for 180 days, he would enter a 180-day contract. Most contracts have maturities of 30, 90 or 180 days, as these correspond to the periods for which trade credit is ordinarily extended. Occasionally, however, contracts are issued for up to a year, and sometimes longer.

The forward exchange rate may, and probably will, be different from the spot exchange rate and is likely to be different for each maturity. These differences are governed primarily by differences in interest rates in the two countries involved, as well as by differences in interest rates associated with different maturities. The spot and forward markets are linked by an arbitrage mechanism that keeps the percentage differential between spot and forward exchange rates consistent with differentials between home and foreign interest rates. We shall see how this mechanism works at a later point.

Parties who move funds from one country to another to capture higher interest rates and cover their positions while their funds remain abroad are known as *covered interest arbitragers.* The forward exchange market facilities are useful to other parties as well. These include *traders of goods and services* who wish to cover exchange risk between the time goods are bought or sold and the time payment is made. They also include *currency speculators* who can use the forward exchange market to profit from expected exchange rate changes, and *governments* which can use the forward market to control movements in the spot exchange rate. Let us see how each of these parties would make use of the forward exchange market.

Traders of Goods and Services

importers

To see how a trader of goods and services can use the forward market to avoid exchange risk between the time goods are bought or sold and the time payment is made, consider the following example. Suppose a U.S. resident orders some goods from a British exporter. The goods cost £1000; payment is to be made in sterling and is due in 180 days. Suppose, further, that the spot exchange rate at the time the order is placed is $1.00 = £1. The U.S. importer faces the risk that the dollar might depreciate during the 180 days so that he would have to pay more than $1000 to buy the £1000 to pay his debt when it comes due. To protect himself against exchange risk, he would buy £1000 forward from his bank (i.e., enter a forward contract in which the bank agrees to sell him the £1000 in 180 days at a specified exchange rate). Let us say the forward exchange rate at the time the contract is drawn up is $1.03 per pound. For his part, the importer obligates himself to pay $1.03 per pound for the sterling when the contract matures (instead of the $1.00 he would have had to pay in the spot market). He has, however, eliminated any *uncertainty* over what he will have to pay, while delaying payment for 180 days.

Note that the British exporter does not face exchange risk in this example. The U.S. importer is to pay him exactly £1000 in 180 days in sterling, the exporter's home currency, no matter what happens to the exchange rate in the interim. In general, the party whose *home* currency is specified as the medium for payment will not face exchange risk, while the party for which *foreign* currency is to be used for payment *will* face exchange risk. Thus, if payment had been specified in dollars in this example, the U.S. importer would face no exchange risk while the British exporter would. The British exporter would run the risk that sterling would appreciate so that the $1000 would buy fewer than £1000 after the 180 days had passed. The currency in which payment is to be made is a matter for negotiation between the trading parties.

forward premium and discount

Returning to the case in which payment is to be made in pounds sterling, the 3¢ premium in the price of forward sterling is called the *forward premium* on sterling. It is often expressed as a percentage, so that in this example there would be a 3 percent forward premium on sterling for 180-day contracts. A 3 percent *premium* on forward sterling is equivalent to a 3 percent forward *discount* on the dollar; if the forward exchange rate expressed in dollars per pound stands at 3 percent *above* the spot rate expressed in dollars per pound, then the forward exchange rate expressed in pounds per dollar must stand at (approximately) 3 percent *below* the spot rate expressed in pounds per dollar.

As mentioned earlier, the forward premium reflects the difference in interest rates in the two countries. It does not represent the bank's profit on the transaction, nor does it reflect a charge made by the bank for accepting the exchange risk from the trader. The bank makes its profit on a small spread between the buying and selling price on forward sterling. The manner in which the bank handles the exchange risk will become clear in a moment.

exporters

Consider, now, the case of a U.S. exporter selling goods to a British importer. Once again, suppose that the spot exchange rate is $1.00 = £1 at the time the goods are sold, that the goods cost £1000 and that payment is to be made in sterling. The British importer faces no exchange risk, but the U.S. exporter, of course, does. He faces the risk that sterling might depreciate against the dollar so that he would receive fewer dollars for his £1000 than would otherwise be the case. To avoid this risk, the U.S. exporter would sell £1000 forward; his bank would agree to buy £1000 from him in 180 days at the price of $1.03 per pound, the prevailing forward exchange rate. Here, the U.S. exporter has transferred his exchange risk to the bank.

the bank's position

We can now see how the bank handles the exchange risk it accepts from its trader-customers. Let us say that the same bank serves the U.S. importer and the U.S. exporter in the two preceding examples. Let us also assume that these two transactions take place on the same day. The bank agrees to buy £1000 from the U.S. exporter in 180 days for $1.03 per pound; it also agrees to sell £1000 to the U.S. importer in 180 days for $1.03 per pound. At this point the bank will have no net exchange risk; its obligations to buy and sell sterling in 180 days are offsetting. Thus we have a situation in which both the U.S. exporter and the U.S. importer have neutralized their exchange risk by transferring it to the bank, and in which matching contracts have eliminated exchange risk for the bank. It is clear that exchange risk can actually be eliminated, not merely transferred, through the forward market facilities.

Suppose that, on a given day, the bank's forward purchases do not match its forward sales for a given maturity. The bank will then seek out other banks in the market that have offsetting positions. Thus if bank A has an excess of £5000 forward purchases over forward sales during the day, it will attempt to find another bank (or banks) that has an excess of forward sales over purchases. These banks can then enter forward contracts among themselves to "marry" their positions, thereby eliminating any residual exchange risk that might exist. Suppose that after all of the banks in the system have married their positions to the fullest extent possible, there is still an excess of forward purchases over forward sales of sterling. This market-wide excess demand for forward sterling would *(ceteris paribus)* then drive the forward exchange rate (in dollars per pound) upward until the market clears.

Covered Interest Arbitrage

the arbitrage mechanism

A second set of users of the forward exchange market are wealthholders who place funds abroad for short periods of time and cover their positions through the forward exchange market. To see how covered interest arbitrage works, let us consider how a U.S. wealthholder would respond to interest-rate incentives in the United States and Britain. Assume that, initially, both the spot and the 180-day forward exchange rates are $1.00 = £1. Also assume that the interest rate for 180 days is 10 percent in both the United States and Britain. Assume further that there is no political risk as perceived by the wealthholder, and that the wealthholder's portfolio is initially in equilibrium. These initial conditions are recorded in column (1) of Table 11–1.

Now let us assume that the British 180-day interest rate rises to 15 percent while the U.S. interest rate and the spot and forward exchange rates remain unchanged. These are shown as the "secondary conditions" in column (2) of Table 11–1. Now the wealthholder will have an incentive to shift funds from U.S. to British assets to capture the higher British interest rate. Let us say that the wealthholder under these circumstances will want to transfer $1000 to British assets. To accomplish this, and to protect himself from exchange risk, he will perform the following steps:

1. Take $1000 from U.S. assets at a cost of 10 percent in interest earnings.
2. Convert the $1000 to £1000 at the spot exchange rate of $1.00 = £1.
3. Invest the £1000 in British assets at 15 percent interest.

TABLE 11-1

	Covered Interest Arbitrage Example		
	Initial Conditions (1)	*Secondary Conditions* (2)	*Final Conditions* (3)
180-day interest rate in U.S.	10%	10%	10%
180-day interest rate in Britain	10%	15%	15%
Spot exchange rate	$1.00 = £1	$1.00 = £1	$1.03 = £1
180-day forward exchange rate	$1.00 = £1	$1.00 = £1	$ .98 = £1

4. Buy $1150 forward (i.e., sell £1150 forward) at the forward exchange rate of $1.00 = £1.

All of these steps would be performed more or less simultaneously. Entering the forward contract to sell £1150 forward for $1150 assures the wealthholder that he will be able to convert his £1000 principal plus his £150 interest earnings back to dollars at $1.00 per pound when the 180-day maturity is up. Here, the wealthholder has captured the higher British interest rate while avoiding any possible loss due to exchange rate change during the 180-day period. In this example, the wealthholder comes out ahead by 5 percent. He earns 15 percent on British assets while he foregoes the 10 percent which he could have earned on U.S. assets. He is able to buy dollars forward at the same exchange rate as he is able to sell them spot, so that there is no cost of forward cover in the form of a forward premium on the dollar.

effects of covered interest arbitrage

Covered interest arbitragers, in pursuing the steps outlined above, produce some important effects in the foreign exchange market. Consider, first, the effects of step 2. Here, wealthholders are selling dollars for sterling in the spot market. This causes sterling to appreciate from the initial $1.00 = £1. Let us say that the spot rate is pushed to $1.03 = £1. This information is recorded in column (3) in Table 11–1. Meanwhile, in step 4, wealthholders are *selling* sterling forward for dollars. This causes the forward pound to depreciate below the initial $1.00 = £1. Let us say that the forward rate declines to $.98 = £1. This is also recorded in column (3) of Table 11–1.

Further effects are also possible. The selling of U.S. assets in step 1 is likely to raise U.S. interest rates above the initial 10 percent, and the buying of British assets in step 3 is likely to lower British interest rates below the 15 per-

cent level. For the sake of simplicity, let us assume that covered interest arbitrage has no measurable effect on U.S. or British interest rates.

Consider, now, the incentives for covered interest arbitrage in the final conditions listed in column (3) of Table 11–1. What would happen if the wealthholder now tried to take advantage of the higher British interest rate? It is true that by transferring funds from U.S. to British assets he could capture 5 percent more in interest earnings over the 180-day period. However, there is now a 5 percent premium in the cost of buying dollars on the forward exchange market to cover his position. Whereas it costs him $1.03 to buy each pound on the spot market when he transfers funds to British assets, he gets only $.98 for each pound he sells forward in covering his position. The 5 percent gain he would realize due to the interest rate differential is exactly offset by the 5 percent premium on the forward dollar. At this point there is no further incentive for covered interest arbitrage.

It is useful to recap our example in the following terms. In the initial conditions (column [1]) there was no incentive for covered interest arbitrage: the interest-rate differential (zero) was exactly equal to the percentage forward premium on the dollar (zero). In the secondary conditions, the interest-rate differential (5 percent) was greater than the percentage forward premium on the dollar (zero) so that incentives for covered interest arbitrage arose. The arbitrage, itself, had the effect of causing the forward dollar to appreciate and the spot dollar to depreciate. This activity continued until the point was reached that the forward premium on the dollar had risen to match the interest-rate differential of 5 percent. At that point, the incentives for further arbitrage disappeared, since the forward cover cost as much as the gain in interest earnings. Covered interest arbitragers thus have an incentive to act when there is a discrepancy between the percentage forward premium (in the exchange market) and the differential in interest rates between the two countries. The arbitrage itself will drive the spot and forward exchange rates to the point that the forward premium is equal to the interest-rate differential. *Interest parity* is a name given to the conditions in which the percentage forward premium is equal to the interest-rate differential.[3]

Note that covered interest arbitrage will cause the spot and forward exchange rates to move in directions that put the currency of the country with the lower interest rate (the U.S., in our example) at a forward premium. The currency of the country with the higher interest rate will stand at a forward discount. In our example, the 5 percent forward premium on the dollar is equivalent to a 5 percent forward discount on the pound.

link between spot and forward markets

Once the foregoing mechanisms are understood, it is easy to see that covered interest arbitrage tends to transmit variations in the forward exchange rate to the spot exchange rate, and vice versa. If the pound were to appreciate on the forward exchange market while the interest-rate differential remained constant, this would create incentives for covered interest arbitragers to move funds out of U.S. assets into British assets to make a profit due to the cheaper forward cover on the dollar. The act of buying sterling on the spot exchange market would cause the spot pound rate to appreciate. The initial upward variation in the forward rate would have been transmitted to the spot rate. Similar examples would show that an initial variation in the spot exchange rate would be transmitted to

[3]The reader might find it instructive to reinforce these points by analyzing the incentives and the effects of covered interest arbitrage under different assumptions about the levels of interest rates in the two countries and the spot and forward exchange rates.

the forward exchange rate. As a result, the time paths of the spot and forward exchange rates tend to follow a similar pattern and tend to be separated by a percentage amount approximately equal to the interest-rate differential.

effects of political risk

Our discussion, so far, has assumed that political risk is absent. The presence of political risk would mean that the wealthholder could not be certain of getting his funds out of the foreign country when he wishes. In this case he would require a somewhat higher rate of return to compensate for the additional risk, as suggested by portfolio theory. Under these circumstances, interest-parity conditions might not hold even after arbitragers have acted. The incentives for arbitrage may vanish before arbitrage has caused the percentage forward premium to adjust to match the interest-rate differential.

covered arbitrage and portfolio theory

As a final point, it is useful to view covered interest arbitrage in the context of the portfolio theory we discussed earlier in the chapter. The wealthholder still bases his decisions on the expected rates of return and risks of all available assets. However, he views the expected rate of return on short-term foreign assets as the covered foreign interest rate. That is to say, he considers the relevant rate of return on the foreign asset to be the foreign interest rate minus the percentage forward premium that it will cost him to cover his position. The wealthholder faces no exchange risk in this case, since this will be eliminated by the forward cover.

Political risk, of course, may still remain. Many observers argue, however, that while political risk exists in transferring funds from one national money market to another, it is virtually absent in transferring funds among Eurocurrency deposits denominated in different currencies. This is because governments generally do not regulate or control Eurocurrency deposits since, by definition, a Eurocurrency deposit is a deposit in a bank located *outside* the country of the currency in question. Thus a U.S. resident could place funds in Euromark deposits in London for a 180-day period with no fear that the German government would tie up the funds; the German government has no control over mark deposits in London banks. With virtually no political risk, any discrepancy between the Eurocurrency deposit-rate differential between two currencies, on the one hand, and the percentage forward premium or discount prevailing between these two currencies, on the other, will trigger vigorous arbitrage activity that will quickly eliminate the discrepancy. We shall have more to say about the Eurocurrency market in the following chapter.

Currency Speculation

A third group of users of the forward exchange market are currency speculators. Currency speculation can be defined as deliberately taking an uncovered position in foreign currency in anticipation of a change in the exchange rate. It involves the deliberate assumption of exchange risk, and the speculator can incur a loss if the exchange rate moves against him instead of in his favor.

Currency speculation can, of course, take place through the spot exchange market. Suppose that a U.S. resident believes that sterling will appreciate over the next, say, 90 days, and wishes to speculate that this will happen. He can transfer funds out of U.S. assets into British assets for the 90-day period, converting dollars into pounds (spot) in the process. He will not cover his long position in sterling with a forward purchase of dollars, as would a covered interest arbitrager, since he wishes to *accept* exchange risk. If sterling does in fact appreciate by the time he coverts his holdings back into dollars,

he will realize a profit. Of course, if sterling has depreciated, he will incur a loss. Any difference in interest rates between the two countries would have to be taken into account (as an opportunity cost) in calculating the speculator's profit or loss, and the speculator would take this into account in deciding whether to act in the first place. Note that spot market speculation amounts to an "uncovered" interest arbitrage transaction. In other words, it could be characterized as a covered interest arbitrage transaction *plus* an "uncovering" (speculative) forward market transaction.

the forward speculative process

Currency speculation is a much simpler process if conducted through the forward exchange market. Here, all the speculator would have to do is to buy or sell foreign currency forward by entering a contract with his bank. This avoids having to go through the process of selling home assets, converting the funds to foreign currency on the spot foreign exchange market, investing the funds in foreign securities (about which the speculator's information may be severely limited) and then reversing the whole process at the end of the period of speculation. In speculating through the forward exchange market, the procedure would be as follows. Suppose a U.S. resident wishes to invest $1000 in a speculation that sterling will appreciate over the next 90 days. The prevailing 90-day forward exchange rate is, say, $2.00 per pound, and the speculator believes that sterling will appreciate to $2.10 per pound. The speculator enters a forward contract with his bank in which the speculator agrees to buy (the bank agrees to sell) £500 in exchange for $1000 in 90 days. If, at the end of the 90 days, the actual spot exchange rate has risen above the $2.00-per-pound forward rate that was written into the contract, the speculator will make a profit. Let us say that the actual spot exchange rate moves to $2.10 per pound as the speculator had expected. He can buy sterling at $2.00 per pound through his forward contract and then sell this sterling in the spot market for $2.10 per pound. If, instead of rising, the actual spot rate had fallen below the contractual $2.00-per-pound forward exchange rate, the speculator would have incurred a loss.

Note that in deciding whether to bet that sterling will appreciate or depreciate, the speculator would compare the *expected future spot exchange rate* with the *prevailing forward exchange rate* that is to be written into the forward contract. He would not compare the expected future spot rate with the prevailing *spot* exchange rate. Thus, if the prevailing spot rate were $1.90 per pound, while the forward rate were $2.00 per pound, and the speculator expected the spot rate to move to $1.95 per pound, he would *sell* sterling forward, rather than buy it, even though he expects sterling to appreciate by 5 cents. Comparing the expected future spot exchange rate to the prevailing forward exchange rate, rather than to the prevailing spot exchange rate, implicitly takes account of differences in interest rates in the two countries, since the differential between spot and forward exchange rates is governed by the differential in interest rates.

effects of currency speculation

A primary effect of currency speculation through the forward exchange market will be to drive up the forward exchange rate of the currency which the speculator thinks will appreciate. This results from the excess demand for forward contracts in the favored currency. A further effect is that the upward movement in the forward exchange rate will be translated to the spot exchange rate, as described in the section on covered interest arbitrage. Thus the favored currency will appreciate on the spot market as well as on the forward market.

Government Intervention on the Forward Market

A fourth set of users of forward exchange market facilities consists of government agencies, typically central banks, that intervene on the *forward* market to control currency fluctuations on the *spot* exchange market. As we established in our discussion of covered interest arbitrage, arbitrage will translate fluctuations in the forward exchange rate into fluctuations in the spot exchange rate. By the same token, if the authorities can stabilize fluctuations in the forward exchange rate, arbitrage will transmit this stabilizing effect to the spot market.

the stabilization mechanism

Suppose that sterling were under downward pressure on the spot exchange market due to deficit pressure in Britain's balance of payments. Suppose further that the British government does not want the pound to depreciate and wishes to hold the exchange rate at its original level of, say, $2.00 per pound. One option—the most familiar—would be for Britain to enter the spot market directly and buy pounds in sufficient quantity to prevent its decline. An alternative approach would be for the British government to buy sterling forward in sufficient quantity to keep the *forward* exchange rate stable. Since covered interest arbitrage would maintain the differential between the spot and forward exchange rates at a magnitude consistent with the interest-rate differential, the spot rate would also remain stable (assuming the interest-rate differential remains unchanged). The British government would thus accomplish indirectly through the forward market what it could have accomplished directly through the spot exchange market.

The major advantage of attempting to peg the exchange rate by intervening on the forward exchange market is that the government does not have to make any immediate expenditure of international reserves. Whereas intervention on the spot market to support home currency would require the direct expenditure of reserves, forward market intervention merely involves entering contracts for future purchases. This may be useful if the authorities fear that reductions in reserve levels are likely to trigger speculation against the home currency.

The use of forward market facilities to support home currency, of course, assumes that the deficit balance-of-payments pressure which is putting downward pressure on the spot exchange rate is temporary, that in time this pressure will be reversed and that in the end the equilibrium value of home currency will not have declined. If the price of home currency has not fallen when the forward contracts mature, the government can sell the home currency for as much as it has to pay for it under the forward contracts.

The major disadvantage of pegging home currency through the forward exchange market is that if the initial downward pressure on spot home currency is not temporary, home currency may depreciate between the time the government enters the forward contracts and the time the contracts mature. If this happens, the government will incur a loss in international reserves, as it will have to pay more for home currency under the forward contracts than the prevailing price on the spot exchange market. Of course, the government would have lost reserves anyhow if it had attempted to peg the exchange rate through the spot market, only to have home currency decline in the end. There is the danger, however, that the government could lose more reserves in attempting to peg through the forward market. The government does not know in advance how much home currency will depreciate on the spot market and therefore does not really know how great its reserve losses might turn out to be when the forward contracts mature. Home currency could depreciate by more than the government expects, with the result that it might cost far more reserves to buy each unit of home currency under the forward contracts than anyone had anticipated. At least with spot market intervention, the government knows exactly how much the intervention activity is costing it in terms of international reserves. There is, in addition, the fact that the government might be tempted to be more bold in intervening through the forward than through the spot market, since there is no direct, immediate depletion of reserves. The ultimate loss in reserves might thus be greater than if attempts to peg the exchange rate had been conducted through the spot market.

Forward Exchange Market Equilibrium

The interaction of all participants in the forward market produces upward or downward pressure on the forward exchange rate as it adjusts to clear the market of excess supply or demand. Forward exchange market equilibrium can be defined as a state in which the forward exchange rate has adjusted to a level that clears the market, and in which all participants have adjusted their positions to the desired levels. Note that equilibrium in the forward exchange market requires simultaneous equilibrium in the spot exchange market (and vice versa), since any further change in the spot market will stimulate further covered interest arbitrage activity, which will have further impact on the forward market. Since disturbances are constantly occurring in both the spot and the forward markets, the markets are seldom at rest in an equilibrium position.

The classification of users of the forward exchange market, as presented in the preceding section, is designed to give a picture of the kinds of activity that go on in that market. They are not air-tight compartments containing separate groups of people. Hence a single multinational firm might act simultaneously as a trader, buying forward marks to cover a commitment to pay for goods it is importing from Germany; as an arbitrager, moving working capital from Britain to the United States to capture favorable interest earnings while covering its position by buying forward sterling; and as a speculator, moving other working capital balances from Italy to the United States in anticipation of a depreciation in the lira.

All of these activities represent actions taken in the course of managing the firm's overall portfolio, with the portfolio manager evaluating changes in the expected rates of return and risks of all available investment options. International capital flows occur as portfolio managers shift stocks of funds among the assets of various countries in response to changes in these risk and expected return variables. They occur as the level of wealth and thus the quantity of investable funds rises or falls in the various countries and as firms make decisions regarding direct foreign investment. These capital flows underlie an important component of the supply and demand for currency in the spot exchange market as well as for contracts in the forward exchange market. They also constitute an important component of a country's balance of payments.

QUESTIONS AND EXERCISES

1. Distinguish between direct foreign investment and portfolio investment. Give examples of each type.

2. What are the components of the expected rate of return on a foreign asset? Provide examples of each component.

3. What kinds of risk would an investor have to take into account in deciding whether to invest in a foreign asset?

4. Suppose the expected rate of return on U.S. assets were to rise well above the expected rates of return on the assets of all the other countries in the system. Would foreigners be likely to move all of their funds into U.S. assets? Explain.

5. What is meant by the term *portfolio equilibrium?* Describe the process that would ensue if, starting from portfolio equilibrium, the expected rate of return on a single asset in a single country were to increase. (Assume this asset is traded internationally.)

6. Distinguish between the stock-adjustment and continuing-flow components of international portfolio capital flows.

7. Identify the principal participants in the forward exchange market. Describe the incentives to which each would respond. Describe the effects that operations by each of these participants would have on both spot and forward exchange markets.

8. What is meant by interest parity? Describe the process that would ensue if interest-parity conditions were upset by a rise in home interest rates.

9. If intervention through the forward exchange market in order to peg the spot exchange rate does not require any immediate expenditure of foreign exchange resources, why do governments not make wider use of forward exchange-market intervention?

International Credit Markets: 12
Operations and Issues

In Chapter 11 we examined international capital movements, giving particular attention to conditions that stimulate the shifting of funds among countries. In this chapter we want to look more closely at a specific sector of the international market for funds, one that has been growing rapidly in importance in international monetary affairs: the Eurocurrency market. As we shall see, this market has become the center of considerable controversy in recent years.

While most observers agree that the Eurocurrency market has added greatly to the efficiency with which funds can be transmitted among countries, some are convinced that the market also creates severe problems. In this view, the Eurocurrency market is capable of generating vast amounts of new money and credit, a phenomenon that fuels worldwide inflation and undermines independent exchange-rate and monetary policies on the part of individual countries. Before attempting to analyze these issues, let us first establish just what a Eurocurrency is and how the Eurocurrency market operates.

ORGANIZATION OF THE EUROCURRENCY MARKET

Eurocurrencies and Eurodollars

A *Eurocurrency* is a time deposit denominated in the currency of one country, but placed in a bank located in some other country. If, for example, a U.S. resident were to remove funds from a deposit in a New York bank and place them on deposit (in dollars) in a London bank, the London deposit would be a Eurocurrency (in this case, a Eurodollar) deposit. Since Eurocurrency deposits are *time* deposits, the depositor relinquishes the right to use or draw upon the deposit for a specified period of time. In exchange for this, he receives an attractive rate of interest. The maturities on these deposits are short term, seldom running more than six months. Banks that accept these deposits are known as *Eurobanks*. The Eurobanks, in turn, lend out these balances to borrowers who have use for funds denominated in that particular currency.

One frequently sees the term *Eurodollar market* applied to the Eurocurrency market as a whole. This is a holdover from an earlier period in which the market dealt almost exclusively in U.S. dollars. In our discussions, we shall use the term *Eurocurrency* to apply collectively to all of the national currencies being traded in this market, and the term *Eurocurrency market* to apply to the market as a whole. We shall use the terms *Eurodollar* and *Eurodollar market* when referring specifically to transactions in dollars.

The prefix *Euro* has also become something of a misnomer, since the practice of accepting foreign currency deposits has spread from London and Europe to other parts of the world. The Caribbean has become an important center for Eurodollar operations in the Western hemisphere, for example, while Singapore has become an important center in Asia. Still, the prefix *Euro* is retained in most discussions of these markets.

Euro Versus Traditional International Money Markets

In traditional international banking, if a resident in one country wished to obtain the currency of another country, he would either have to buy it on the foreign exchange market or borrow it from a bank located in the country that issued that currency. He could not simply borrow the foreign currency from a bank located in his own country or in some third country.

Thus, if a British resident wished to borrow dollars, he would have to enter the New York money market to obtain the funds. With the advent of the Eurocurrency market, foreign residents can now borrow dollars in London or any of the other Eurocurrency centers around the world. Borrowing dollars in London is often more convenient for European firms than borrowing in New York, especially since European business hours coincide with banking hours in London, but not with those in the United States. In addition, it is often more economical to borrow in the Eurocurrency market, since the Eurobanks can usually offer a more favorable interest rate to both borrowers and lenders than banks in the various domestic money markets. This is because the Eurobanks typically have lower operating costs as a result of a lower degree of regulation by government authorities. The British government, for example, imposes greater restrictions, including reserve requirements, on the purely domestic transactions of banks operating in London than they do on the Eurocurrency transactions of the same banks.

The Eurobanks, like all financial intermediaries, make a profit on the difference between the interest rate they pay for deposits and the interest rate they charge for loans. While this differential is ordinarily only a fraction of a percent, the volume of currency they handle is so large that Eurocurrency operations are quite profitable. Eurocurrency transactions seldom involve sums of less than $5 million.[1]

Eurobanks as Financial Intermediaries

In addition to acting as a simple conduit between ultimate lenders and borrowers, the Eurobanks serve as financial intermediaries. One important function of a financial intermediary is

[1]G. Dufey and I. Giddy, *The International Money Market* (Englewood Cliffs, N.J.: Prentice-Hall, 1978), p. 51.

to substitute its own creditworthiness for that of the ultimate borrower. If a resident of the United States were to lend dollars directly to a European firm, the U.S. lender would have to rely on the creditworthiness of the European borrower. If the European borrower were to default, the U.S. lender would suffer a loss. On the other hand, if the U.S. lender were to place his funds with a Eurobank, and the Eurobank, in turn, were to lend to the European borrower, the U.S. lender would accept the liability of the Eurobank and would suffer a loss only if the bank itself were to default. This is unlikely, and at any rate the creditworthiness of the Eurobank is easier to determine than that of potential foreign borrowers.

A second service the Eurobanks can offer as financial intermediaries is to repackage funds to fit the needs of borrowers. The European firm may wish to borrow $20 million, whereas the U.S. lender may have only $5 million to lend. The Eurobank does not have to match up its loans with specific deposits, however, and can make the $20 million loan out of a common pool of funds obtained from many depositors.

A third service provided by the Eurobanks as financial intermediaries is to reconcile the maturity preferences of lenders and borrowers. Typically, depositors wish to commit their funds for fairly short periods of time, while borrowers wish to have use of the funds for longer periods. The Eurobanks are in a position to accommodate these divergent wishes. Since the Eurobanks accept one liability from the ultimate borrower and issue a separate liability to the depositor, these instruments can carry different maturities. This kind of operation is known as *maturity transformation;* it, of course, requires that the bank have an ongoing stream of shorter term deposits to "back" the longer term loans, and that it be able to borrow Eurocurrencies itself to cover any shortfall between deposit renewals and loans outstanding. A more common form of reconciling the maturity preferences of borrowers and lenders is to *match* maturities. The flow of funds into and out of the market is very sensitive to interest rates, and, by slightly raising the borrowing rate, Eurobanks can usually attract sufficient funds to match any demand for loans of a given maturity.

Necessary Conditions for Eurocurrency Operations

For a currency to be included in Eurocurrency transactions, it must meet several criteria. First, of course, there must be substantial demand for it by participants in international trade and finance. It must be fully convertible with other currencies, and commercial banks in the currency's originating country must be able to provide *nonresident convertibility.*[2] Nonresident convertibility means that the banks are willing and able (i.e., not prohibited by government regulations) to transfer ownership of the demand deposits on their books from one foreign resident to another. This facilitates the free transfer of Eurocurrency among nonresidents.

the effect of regulation on Eurobank location

The location of Eurocurrency centers is strongly influenced by the degree of regulation imposed on Eurocurrency operations by the local authorities. In general, the market will tend to expand in locations in which the political climate is relatively stable and in which regulation by the local government is at a minimum. Regulations such as reserve requirements on deposits, insurance requirements, interest-rate ceilings and various taxes raise the costs of operation. Since the Eurocurrency markets are

---

[2]By "originating country," we mean the country from which the currency originally came. Thus the United States is the originating country for Eurodollars, Germany is the originating country for Euromarks, etc.

highly competitive, banks located in countries that impose these kinds of controls are unable to compete effectively with banks located in countries in which regulations are less stringent.

To escape these costs, banks located in high-regulation areas, such as the United States, often open branches and subsidiaries in foreign locations where the controls are not as heavy. U.S. branches and subsidiaries are very active in Eurocurrency transactions in London as well as in such "offshore" locations as Nassau and the Cayman Islands. As of the end of the 1970s, there were no Eurobanks inside the United States.

international banking facilities

In 1981, however, the Federal Reserve Board took steps to encourage Eurobanking in the United States by authorizing U.S. banks to set up *International Banking Facilities (IBFs)*. Through the IBFs, U.S. banks (and branches of foreign banks located in the United States) can make loans to and receive deposits from foreign banks and nonbank foreign residents, as well as from other IBFs, under much less stringent rules than are applied to ordinary U.S. banking operations. In particular, transactions by the IBFs are exempt from reserve requirements and ceilings on interest rates that can be paid to depositors. The intent is to lower the cost of U.S. bank transactions with foreigners, thereby enabling U.S. banks to compete effectively for Eurocurrency business.

The likely effect of this change in policy is that U.S. banks will capture a substantial portion of the Eurocurrency market, since New York already enjoys several advantages that make it a highly competitive banking center. These include a high concentration of banking facilities and expertise and a large volume of banking business that enables it to capture economies of scale. As Eurocurrency business shifts to resident U.S. banks, it is likely that many of the Eurcurrency facilities in such offshore locations

as Nassau and the Cayman Islands will shrink, since they were established explicitly to escape the costs of just such regulations as reserve requirements and interest-rate ceilings. It may be that these offshore locations will be able to retain some Eurocurrency business if they continue to impose lower tax burdens and keep other regulatory costs lower than are found in New York and other major banking centers.

Frequently, offshore Eurobanks will perform intermediation between U.S. residents. They will accept Eurodollar deposits from one U.S. resident and lend them to another. Their lower operating costs enable them to offer more favorable interest rates to both depositor and borrower than financial institutions located within the United States itself. Because transactions between IBFs and U.S. (non-IBF) residents are still subject to the traditional reserve requirements and interest-rate ceilings, the offshore banks should still be able to intermediate between U.S. residents, especially when U.S. equilibrium interest rates exceed official ceilings.

The Eurobond Market

A separate financial market, which is distinct from the Eurocurrency market but in which large international banks sometimes participate, is the Eurobond market. As the name implies, the securities traded in this market are long-term instruments which are sold in countries other than the one whose currency denominates the security. Securities issued in this market are usually underwritten by syndicates or consortia of several large international banks and involve extremely large sums of money.

An important distinction between the Eurobond market and the Eurocurrency market, other than the difference in maturities, is the fact that financial intermediation per se does not occur in the Eurobond market. The lender accepts the liability of the ultimate borrower directly and thus accepts the risk that the borrower might default. The fact that the lender accepts the debt instrument of the borrower also means that there is no maturity transformation; the borrower must thus find lenders whose preference for maturity corresponds to his own.

GROWTH OF THE EUROCURRENCY MARKETS

Early Developments in the Eurocurrency Market

The Eurocurrency market first began to develop in the late 1950s after universal currency convertibility had been established. Expansion of business in the newly formed European Economic Community helped to expand the demand for dollar balances and contributed to the growth in the market in the early years. Nevertheless, the market grew rather slowly through the early 1960s.

During the mid-1960s, the market began to expand rapidly. By 1969, gross Eurocurrency deposits had risen to $57 billion, as estimated by the Bank for International Settlements, while net Eurocurrency deposits had risen to $44 billion. The gross figure measures all foreign currency deposits, whether held by other banks or by nonbank entities. The net figure subtracts out interbank deposits. Most observers argue that the net figure is the relevant magnitude, since it comes closer to measuring the actual amount of purchasing power in the market. Table 12-1 provides a picture of how the market has grown over the years. These figures are very rough estimates at best, since there is no systematic, official record of Eurocurrency transactions.

The rapid expansion in the mid-1960s has been attributed by some observers to regulations within the U.S. money market and to restrictions that were imposed on capital outflows from the United States during that period. For example,

TABLE 12-1

BIS Estimates of Size of Eurocurrency Market ($ billions, end of period)

	Gross	Net
1965	14	12
1967	23	18
1969	57	44
1971	98	71
1973	191	132
1975	259	205
1977	310[a]	262[a]
1979	900[a]	450[a]

Sources: G. Dufey and I. Giddy, *The International Money Market* (Englewood Cliffs, N.J.: Prentice-Hall, 1978); and Bank for International Settlements, *Annual Report*, 1980 and 1981.
[a]Midyear estimates.

U.S. Banking Regulation Q put a ceiling on the interest rate that could be paid to depositors by U.S. financial institutions. When deposit rates in the Eurocurrency market rose above the U.S. ceiling, U.S. residents began to transfer balances from the U.S. domestic market to the Eurodollar market. Many U.S. borrowers then turned to the Eurodollar market for loans, since that is where the funds were now to be found. Regulation Q thus had the effect of shifting a substantial portion of financial intermediation between U.S. lenders and U.S. borrowers from U.S. financial institutions to Eurobanks located abroad.

Restrictions on capital outflows from the United States helped to bolster the Eurodollar market by making it harder for Europeans and other foreign residents to borrow dollars in New York. Because the dollar was the chief vehicle currency for international trade and financial transactions, it remained in strong demand by foreign firms and financial institutions. With access to U.S. markets restricted, foreign residents turned increasingly to the Eurodollar market, and the volume of transactions in that market expanded accordingly.

Rapid Growth During the 1970s

The Eurocurrency market surged again in the early to mid-1970s. Growth in the market during this period was probably due, in large measure, to growth in the overall supply and demand for money and credit within the individual countries in the system. As the quantity of money and credit within individual countries grew, a proportion of the new funds found their way into the Eurocurrency system, just as portfolio theory would suggest. An alternative view would reverse this direction of causality. It holds that a major source of expansion of world liquidity during the 1970s was the Eurocurrency market itself: the Eurocurrency market generated large quantities of new money and credit which spilled back into the individual countries. The latter view is highly questionable, however; as we shall see in the following section, the Eurocurrency market per se does not readily generate *new* money or credit.

A second element in the expansion of the Eurocurrency market during the 1970s was the rapid increase in the world price of oil and the transfer of large amounts of wealth from oil-importing to oil-exporting countries. The oil-exporting countries required payment in dollars, for the most part, and the price increases meant that non-U.S. importers had to raise much larger quantities of dollars to pay their oil bills. Many of these countries turned to the Eurodollar market for these funds, adding to the quantity of transactions in that market.

Meanwhile, the oil-exporting countries acquired dollar balances at a much more rapid rate than in the past. While some of the OPEC countries spent their funds for current imports, others accumulated enormous quantities of dollars. Many of these dollars (which became known as

petrodollars) were placed in the Eurodollar market, which offered an attractive rate of return. This process of receiving petrodollars from the OPEC countries as deposits and lending them out again to oil-importing countries became known as *petrodollar recycling*.

Following the oil-price increases of 1973 and 1974, and again in 1979, there was widespread concern over whether existing financial institutions would be capable of channeling funds smoothly from those countries that were accumulating petrodollars to those in need of dollar loans to finance further oil imports. A number of plans and programs were discussed that would marshal efforts by official agencies and international institutions to cope with the petrodollar recycling problem. Some of these programs, such as the IMF's *Special Oil Facility* and programs of direct loans by OPEC governments to less-developed oil-importing countries, were actually put into place. As it turned out, private financial markets, including the Eurocurrency market, proved to be surprisingly efficient in intermediating between petrodollar lenders and borrowers.

A third feature of the Eurocurrency expansion, especially in the late 1970s, was the rapid growth in Eurocurrency balances denominated in currencies other than the U.S. dollar. The German mark and the Swiss franc were prominent among the Eurocurrencies that came under heavier demand during this period. Lower interest rates on Euromark and franc assets stimulated stronger borrowing of these currencies relative to the dollar. On the supply side, a surge of deposits, which stemmed from widening OPEC balance-of-payments surpluses, bolstered the supply of these currencies in the market. Of course, the OPEC surpluses bolstered the supply of dollars at the same time. By the end of the 1970s, total credit outstanding in the market, net of interbank deposits, was estimated at over $450 billion in dollar equivalents. At that point the U.S. dollar accounted for approximately 75 percent of all Eurocurrency deposits, while the German mark accounted for some 12 percent and the Swiss franc about 5 percent.[3]

DIFFERING VIEWS OF THE CAUSES OF EUROCURRENCY GROWTH

The rapid growth in the Eurocurrency market in the 1970s caused alarm among some observers, particularly officials at the various national central banks, who feared that the expansion of international liquidity was running out of control. Steps to bring market growth under control required that the causes of growth be identified, and this led to much speculative theorizing about the causes of Eurocurrency expansion. Unfortunately, the absence of any reliable data on the Eurocurrency market severely hampered efforts to analyze the market. Nevertheless, several hypotheses were put forth.

Growth Through Eurocurrency Credit Expansion

One hypothesis, perhaps the most alarming of all, was that the Eurocurrency market was expanding liquidity in the same way a commercial banking system within a given country could expand money and credit. Proponents of this view feared that because reserve requirements were absent, the Eurobanks could go on expanding credit almost without limit. If the Eurocurrency market could expand indefinitely, then the amount of liquidity that could be generated would lie beyond the effective control of the monetary authorities within the individual countries. The quantity of Eurodollar deposits

and the amount of world dollar credit could go on expanding, for example, even in the face of efforts by the U.S. authorities to tighten domestic dollar credit.

However, these fears were based on the mistaken notion that the Eurocurrency system can create money in the same way that a domestic banking system can. While a domestic banking system can create new money and credit as it takes in deposits and makes loans, the Eurocurrency system does not do this. The contrast can be illustrated in the following example. If you were to deposit $5 million (say, in the form of a check written to you by the government) in a *domestic* commercial bank, the bank could lend out a large percentage of it to other customers. Let us say it lends out $4 million; it does this by creating a *new* demand deposit in favor of the borrower. This new deposit represents new medium-of-exchange in that it is readily spendable by the borrower. Meanwhile, your $5 million deposit is still readily spendable to you. The total amount of readily spendable demand deposits (money) is now $9 million. As the borrower spends the proceeds of the loan, writing checks which get deposited in other banks, the banking system as a whole, through further lending, can expand the total amount of readily spendable deposits to a multiple of the $5 million you originally deposited.[4]

Now, in contrast, suppose you were to make a $5 million deposit in the Eurocurrency market. You do this by writing a check on a dollar demand deposit you hold in a U.S. bank (say, the First New York Bank) and depositing it in a Eurobank (say, the London Eurobank). Your check transfers ownership of the $5 million deposit in the First New York Bank to the London Eurobank; in turn, the London Eurobank credits

[3]Bank for International Settlements, *Annual Report*, 1980.

[4]See any principles of economics textbook for the mechanics of the process through which banks create money.

you with a $5 million Eurodollar deposit. Here the analogy with the domestic banking system breaks down. The Eurodollar deposit you now own is not a demand deposit; it is a time deposit. This means you have relinquished use of this deposit until the London Eurobank repays it to you at a specified future date. Your Eurodollar deposit is no longer countable as part of the medium of exchange since you cannot draw on it. The London Eurobank can lend the $5 million out to borrowers, which may be other Eurobanks or non-Eurobank borrowers. When the London Eurobank lends the $5 million to others, it does not create a new demand deposit liability on itself; it merely passes the ownership of the $5 million deposit in the First New York Bank on to the borrower. If one were now simply to add up all Eurodollar deposits (including the $5 million by you as well as subsequent redeposits [in other Eurobanks] of the funds loaned out by the London Eurobank) one would come up with a figure much larger than $5 million. Still, the only spendable money (medium of exchange) in the picture is the $5 million deposit in the First New York Bank, control of which has been passed on from you to others. No new money has been created, as was the case with the domestic bank loan.

To recap, then, demand deposits placed in domestic banking systems constitute part of the money supply (defined as medium of exchange) and are readily spendable by the original depositor. Deposits placed in the Eurobanking system are time deposits, are not spendable by the depositor and are thus not part of the medium of exchange. Domestic banks create new money, when they make loans, by creating new demand deposit liabilities on themselves. Eurobanks do not create new money when they lend; they merely pass the use of already *existing* deposits on to the borrower. The specter of autonomous, unlimited credit expansion by the Eurocurrency market has therefore been a false alarm, at least under present institutional arrangements.

Growth Due to Regulations on Capital Movements

A second hypothesis is that the Eurocurrency markets have expanded largely because of controls placed on capital movements among countries. As we mentioned earlier, this argument has been applied in particular to the surge in activity in the mid-1960s. Skeptics argue that, while U.S. controls on capital outflows might have aided the development of the Eurodollar market during the 1960s, it does not offer an explanation of the market's sustained growth. Indeed, When U.S. controls on capital outflow were *removed* in 1974, there was no noticeable decline in the rate of growth in the Eurodollar market.[5]

Growth Due to U.S. Balance-of-Payments Deficits

A third hypothesis is that growth in the Eurodollar market is tied to the U.S. balance-of-payments deficit. A U.S. deficit usually means that foreigners are receiving dollars faster than they are spending them, and accumulations of foreign-held dollars can easily show up as increases in the Eurodollar market base. The fact that the U.S. payments deficit was so heavy, especially during the 1970s, thus contributed to the rapid growth in the Eurodollar market.

This view overlooks several key points. First, acquisition of dollar balances by foreigners does not depend on a U.S. balance-of-payments deficit. Even if the balance of payments were balanced, foreigners would still receive dollars for the goods, services and assets they sell to Americans, and they could still choose to place these dollars in the Eurodollar market. Second, when foreigners are paid by Americans for goods, services and assets, they receive payment in the

[5]Dufey and Giddy, *The International Money Market*, p. 111.

form of dollar balances located in U.S. domestic banks. These are not Eurodollars. It requires a separate, deliberate act to transfer these dollars to the Eurodollar market. This would tend to happen only if foreign holders of dollars found the risk and rate of return in the Eurodollar market to be more attractive than in the U.S. domestic money market.

As a matter of fact, a higher rate of return in the Eurodollar market would attract funds from both foreign *and* U.S. owners of domestic dollar balances. Such a shift in funds would contribute to a U.S. balance-of-payments deficit, of course, and one could argue that conditions in the Eurodollar market were, in this case, *causing* the U.S. payments deficit, instead of the other way around.

Growth Due to Increases in World Supply and Demand for Credit

A fourth hypothesis about expansion in the Eurocurrency market is steadily finding wider acceptance. This is the view that Eurocurrency growth is determined primarily by growth in the supply and demand for credit in that market.

the supply of funds to the market

According to portfolio theory, the amount of wealth held in the form of Eurodollar deposits would depend on both the total outstanding stock of dollars in circulation and the relative risk and rate-of-return variables in the Eurodollar, the U.S. and other foreign money markets. If the overall stock of dollars increases, a certain proportion of this increase could be expected to flow into the Eurodollar market, even if risks and rates of return remain constant. On the other hand, if rates of return rise in the Eurodollar market (relative to other rates of return), one would expect the proportion of the overall stock of dollars held in the Eurodollar market to increase, and for a larger proportion of any new

increases in dollars to flow into the Eurodollar market. By the same token, a decline in the Eurodollar rate relative to U.S. interest rates should cause a shift of dollars back toward the U.S. money market.

As mentioned at an earlier point, Eurocurrency interest rates tend to be more favorable to both borrowers and lenders because of the lower costs of operation in the Eurocurrency market as compared to the domestic money markets. These lower operating costs stem from lower levels of regulation by national governments. In addition, the Eurocurrency market tends to be more competitive than the national money markets, and therefore tends to operate on a narrower margin between deposit and lending rates. In the absence of controls, the Eurodollar deposit rate has historically been equal to or higher than comparable deposit interest rates available in the U.S. money market, while Eurodollar loan rates have been equal to or lower than comparable loan interest rates in the U.S. money market.

the demand for Eurocurrency credit

On the demand side, increases in the volume of international trade and investment give rise to an increase in the demand for credit. As overall credit demand expands, the amount sought through the Eurocurrency market will also expand, even if lending rates remain constant. In addition, the *proportion* of credit sought through the Eurocurrency market will increase as this market is able to offer more favorable lending rates than the competing national markets.

the interaction of supply and demand for Eurocurrency credit

The Eurocurrency rate is the interest rate that adjusts to regulate the inflow and outflow of funds to the Eurocurrency market and to reconcile the quantity of funds demanded and supplied within that market. (There is a Eurocurrency rate for every currency and for every maturity traded in the market.) In simple terms, an exogenous increase in demand for Eurocurrency loans will drive the Eurocurrency rate upward. The rising Eurocurrency rate, in turn, will draw funds in from the national money markets, thereby providing the liquidity to meet the increase in demand. On the other hand, an exogenous increase in the supply of funds to the Eurocurrency market will depress the Eurocurrency rate, making the market more attractive to borrowers, thereby increasing the total quantity of funds borrowed in the market. The Eurocurrency market thus expands in concert with the overall world demand and supply for credit, and it is able to increase its share of overall financial intermediation as it is able to offer more attractive interest rates. The market is not, however, the *source* of new liquidity; any new liquidity has to originate in the *national* money and credit markets.

PERCEIVED PROBLEMS AND PROPOSED REGULATIONS FOR THE EUROCURRENCY MARKET

Most national money and credit markets are highly regulated by government, usually through the country's central bank. The size of the money base is controlled by the buying and selling of government securities in the open market (open market operations), the buying and selling of foreign currency (exchange-market intervention) and the lending of reserves to commercial banks. The size of the money multipler (the extent to which the commercial banking system can multiply the money base into a larger overall money stock) is controlled by setting reserve requirements. The setting of reserve requirements is an extremely powerful tool. By raising reserve requirements high enough—to 100%—

the central bank can eliminate the ability of the commercial banking system to expand the money supply altogether.

In addition to controlling the size of the money base and the money multiplier, the central bank also regulates the lending practices of the commercial banks. Lending practices are controlled by regulations governing the kinds of assets financial institutions can hold, the types of deposits they can accept and the interest rates they can pay. In addition, the banks are periodically audited to ensure that they engage in "sound banking practices."

The Eurocurrency market escapes this kind of regulation; exemption from regulation is the basis of the cost advantage which enables the Eurocurrency market to compete effectively with the national credit markets. Nevertheless, as we have seen, there are those who believe that controls should be placed on the Eurocurrency market similar to those imposed on domestic banking systems. Not surprisingly, the primary advocates of controls over the Eurocurrency market are the monetary authorities within the various national governments.

Let us examine, now, the major complaints about the Eurocurrency market and evaluate the associated proposals to regulate it.

Autonomous Expansion of World Liquidity

Perhaps the strongest complaint about the Eurocurrency market, especially in the 1970s, was that it could create new money and credit without limit. These fears have led to proposals that reserve requirements be placed on Eurocurrency deposits, just as they are on domestic bank deposits. As we have seen, however, the Eurocurrency market cannot itself increase the amount of available credit, so that controls to contain such activity would be misplaced. Imposing reserve requirements would only serve to limit the efficiency with which the market can transmit credit among countries.

The Undermining of Domestic Monetary Policy

A second complaint is that the Eurocurrency market undermines the ability of the national monetary authorities to control money and credit within their *own* countries. Here, there are two possibilities to be considered: whether the Eurocurrency market reduces control of a country's money *base,* and whether it reduces control over the domestic money *multiplier.* A related issue is whether the Eurocurrency market undermines a country's choice as to the exchange-rate policy it will pursue.

By increasing international capital mobility, the Eurocurrency market strengthens the channels through which foreign monetary expansion or contraction can affect the home money base under a regime of fixed exchange rates (see Chapter 10). Some observers fear that rapid expansion of money in the Eurocurrency market could be transmitted through these channels to the domestic money base, making it difficult for the home authorities to control its growth.

In a similar fashion, attempts by the authorities to expand the country's money base can generate a capital outflow that can counteract the attempt to expand the money base, as the authorities seek to keep the exchange rate pegged.

One remedy for the tendency for capital flows to counteract the effects of monetary policy under a system of fixed exchange rates is to let the exchange rate float. It is at this juncture that the complaint arises that unconstrained capital inflows and outflows deprive the country of an independent choice of exchange-rate policy. In a world of high capital mobility, countries that cannot effectively sterilize the effects of capital flows (and this would include most of the smaller countries in the system) are forced to choose

between a fixed exchange rate, on the one hand, and control of the money base, on the other. If they opt for control over the money base, they lose the option of having the exchange rate remain fixed.

An alternative remedy for the tendency for capital flows to offset intended monetary policy is to choke off the capital movements themselves. There were numerous instances in the late 1960s and the 1970s of attempts by governments to limit capital movements in order to reduce their impact on local monetary conditions. During the early 1970s, for example, Germany and Switzerland were the frequent targets for heavy speculative capital inflows. This caused strong upward pressure on the mark and franc on the foreign exchange market, and attempts by the German and Swiss central banks to stabilize the exchange rates resulted in rapid increases in the money base in each country. Unable to counteract the effects adequately through sterilization, these governments imposed special restrictions and taxes on capital inflows.

The contention that the Eurocurrency market has increased the efficiency with which *existing* funds can be passed among countries does have merit. To the extent that the market adds to the international mobility of capital, it does make it more difficult for the local authorities to control fluctuations in the country's money base, especially if they are also attempting to control the exchange rate. Even if the increase in capital mobility brought about by the Eurocurrency market does contribute to the difficulties of the monetary authorities, however, the following question remains: Should the efficiency of the Eurocurrency market, and the cost saving that this represents, be sacrificed to make the job of the monetary authorities easier? One could argue that this would not be unlike abolishing credit cards because they make it more difficult for the authorities to control the amount of credit being extended within the economy.

Eurocurrency Transactions and the Domestic Money Multiplier

While there is no effective money multiplier within the Eurocurrency market, there are still ways in which Eurocurrency transactions can affect the money multiplier within a given country. Suppose there is an increase in the world demand for dollars. If the U.S. banking system is not "all loaned up" (if the domestic money multiplier has not reached its maximum potential), the additional demand could cause domestic banks to increase their loans and thereby expand the outstanding quantity of demand deposits on their books. This could occur even if the U.S. money base itself remains fixed. To the extent that the Eurocurrency market provides a more efficient conduit for international financial flows, it may intensify the impact of foreign demand for dollars on the U.S. banking system.

The size of the money multiplier within a country can also be affected by Eurocurrency transactions in the following way. If there is a lower reserve requirement on domestic demand deposits owned by foreign residents than there is on similar deposits owned by home residents, then a transfer of funds to the Eurocurrency market by home residents (a transfer of ownership of a domestic demand deposit from a domestic resident to a foreign bank) will "free up" banking reserves to back further domestic money expansion. This represents a once-and-for-all increase in the domestic money multiplier, however; it cannot generate any kind of sustained increase in the home money multiplier or money supply.

Danger of International Monetary Collapse

A final concern, one that became prominent during periods of economic recession in the 1970s, is that a significant increase in loan defaults might cause a chain reaction of bankruptcies among the Eurobanks. This, it is feared, could lead to a collapse of the entire international monetary network.

A chain reaction of bankruptcies is most likely to occur when there is "pyramiding" of credit (as occurs among commercial banks within a domestic banking system) coupled with a run on the banks. A collapse could come as follows. If an important borrower were to default on a loan, the lending bank might not have sufficient funds to honor its liabilities to its depositors, and might go bankrupt. This bank's depositors, including other banks, would in turn find themselves short of funds, and a chain reaction of defaults could get started. Meanwhile, the public, perceiving that the banking system is in trouble, would rush to withdraw its deposits. Since the banks have loaned out a large percentage of their deposits, large numbers of them would have insufficient funds to cover their withdrawals; the whole banking system could then collapse.

Banking panics of this kind have occurred in the past. Several runs occurred within the United States, for example, during the late nineteenth century and early twentieth century. Since that time, two institutions have been established that have reduced the probability of bank panics in the United States to practically zero. The first is the Federal Reserve System, which, among other functions, serves as a "lender-of-the-last-resort" to the commercial banking system. If the commercial banks find themselves in danger of not being able to meet their deposit liabilities (or, even prior to that, if they find themselves with insufficient reserves to meet reserve requirements) the Federal Reserve System will lend funds to the banks that are under pressure. In a panic situation, this would enable the banks to cover deposits until the crisis subsides. The second institution is the *Federal Deposit Insurance Corporation (FDIC)*, which insures the safety of deposits and thereby removes the incentive for the public to withdraw funds in a wholesale fashion when banks do come under pressure.

To protect the international monetary system from collapse, some observers have felt that it is imperative to establish a lender-of-the-last-resort for the Eurocurrency market. Perhaps the ultimate lender would be some supranational institution, or perhaps the individual national central banks would serve in that capacity for Eurobanks chartered in their countries.

Like many of the other concerns about the Eurocurrency market, this particular set of fears is at least partially based on a mistaken analogy between the Eurocurrency system and a domestic commercial banking system. Even if a number of important borrowers were to default, and the Eurobanks were to suffer a substantial reduction in the funds available to cover deposits, the depositors could not rush to withdraw their funds from the market in a wholesale fashion as they could from commercial banks; because Eurocurrency deposits are time deposits, they cannot be withdrawn until maturity.

Perhaps even more important is the fact that credit is not pyramided in the Eurocurrency market as it is in a domestic banking system. In a domestic system, the withdrawal of, say, $5 million in cash from the banks by a nervous public can force a multiple contraction in the amount of outstanding money and credit. This is because cash withdrawals reduce the money base itself and can force a much larger absolute contraction in the money stock that has been pyramided on top of the base. In the Eurocurrency market, because credit is not pyramided in this fashion, it is unlikely that the withdrawal of $5 million would force a multiple reduction in credit.

There is one way that a Eurobank could find itself short of funds even when dealing in time deposits. This could occur if the bank were to let the average maturity of its loans get too "long" in relation to the average maturity of its deposits, and then were to experience a drastic slowdown in the rate at which it receives new deposits or redeposits. If the average loan maturity were, say, one year, while the average deposit maturity were three months, and if the rate at which new deposits are being received were to drop, the bank could reach a point that it has insufficient funds to pay off its maturing deposits prior to the time the longer term loans mature. Partially in recognition of this possibility, the Eurobanks generally limit the maturity of their loans to six months. If a borrower wants a longer term loan, the bank will ordinarily "roll over" (extend) the loan at the end of each six-month period. Because the loan maturities are limited to fairly short periods, the danger of being caught short due to a slowdown in new deposits is minimized, and the need for a lender-of-the-last-resort is diminished.

The principal remaining purpose for having a lender-of-the-last-resort would be to provide ultimate protection to individual banks that incur an unexpectedly heavy series of loan defaults. It is true that in the Eurocurrency system a large proportion of total deposits are interbank deposits. If an ultimate borrower were to default on a loan, the Eurobank (say, bank Z) that made the loan to the defaulting borrower would have to absorb the loss out of its other assets. If it could not, and went bankrupt, the bank that lent the money to bank Z (say, bank Y) would have to absorb the loss. The only way the system as a whole could collapse would be for every bank along the chain to be unable to absorb this loss out of its other assets. In other words, every bank along the interbank-deposit chain would have had to have made faulty decisions in making up its overall loan portfolio.

The question at this point is whether the Eurobanks are more likely to be irresponsible or to use bad judgment in making Eurocurrency loans than in making ordinary domestic loans, or in making direct home currency loans to foreigners. Experience does not seem to suggest that they are. Even if a small proportion of Eurobanks did act more irresponsibly in their Eurocurrency operations, it is not clear that it is necessary to have a lender-of-the-last-resort, or a set of controls over lending practices, to protect the system as a whole. Because of the time-deposit nature of the system and the absence of the pyramiding of credit, steps to protect the overall integrity of the system do not appear to be urgent.

The Importance of Institutional Arrangements

Throughout our discussion of proposals to regulate the Eurocurrency market, we have argued that much of the concern surrounding the market is based on a faulty analogy between the Eurocurrency market and a commercial banking system. The fact that the Eurocurrency market deals exclusively in time deposits and transmits existing credit from one party to another distinguishes it from a commercial banking system, which deals largely in demand deposits and creates new credit through its deposit and lending process.

There is still an unanswered question, however. What if the Eurocurrency system were to begin accepting demand deposits and making loans by creating new demand deposits in favor of the borrower? Under these circumstances, the Eurobanks *would* have the capacity to create new liquidity. Credit could then be pyramided, and the possibility of panics and the potential collapse of the system would become real. Arguments for controls over the expansion of Eurocurrency credit would become more cogent.

What are the chances that such institutional changes would occur? We should note, first, that they are not occurring spontaneously under current conditions. As long as the Eurocurrency system is able to attract time-deposit balances from the national money markets to meet increases in demand for Eurocurrency loans, there should be little incentive to start accepting demand deposits (and thus face greater uncertainty over when the deposits will be withdrawn) or creating demand deposit liabilities against themselves. As long as operating costs are lower in the Eurocurrency market than in domestic money markets, Eurobanks should be able to attract funds when needed by offering higher interest rates on deposits than are available in domestic markets. Only if it became more difficult to compete for deposits by offering more attractive interest rates would the Eurobanks be likely to compete by offering demand deposits. Ironically, such an outcome could result from attempts to regulate the Eurocurrency market.

On the other hand, if the costs of operating in the Eurocurrency market were raised to the point that the Eurobanks could no longer offer competitive interest rates, much of the business being done throughout the Eurocurrency market would revert to the domestic money markets. It would appear, then, that cost advantage is a *sine qua non* for the Eurocurrency market, and that as long as the cost advantage remains, the Eurobanks are not likely to undergo institutional changes that could foster new credit creation.

Under present arrangements, it would appear there is little need for regulation of the Eurocurrency market. A major effect of regulation would be to raise the costs of operation and reduce the efficiency with which the market can serve those engaged in international trade and investment. If the institutional structure should change, however, so that international banking institutions began creating new liabilities, many of the problems associated with domestic banking systems would appear and steps to protect the integrity of the system as a whole might be appropriate.

QUESTIONS AND EXERCISES

1. How is the Eurocurrency market able to compete with the national money markets in attracting depositors and borrowers of credit?

2. What bearing does the fact that the Eurocurrency market deals exclusively in time deposits have on the market's ability to create new money and credit?

3. Of what significance is the fact that in making loans, a Eurobank does not credit the borrower with a new demand deposit, drawable on the Eurobank, but transfers to the borrower a claim to the existing Eurocurrency base?

4. What have been the major factors underlying the growth of the Eurocurrency market? How did each of these factors promote growth in the market?

5. What do you think would happen to the Eurocurrency market if national governments were to impose identical regulations on domestic and Eurocurrency banking activities? Explain.

6. Evaluate the argument that the Eurocurrency market helps to undermine the ability of the national monetary authorities to control national money aggregates.

CLOSING ESSAY
The Mixed Blessings of High International Capital Mobility

It is clear that international capital flows perform some essential functions in international economic relationships. They help to finance the international trade of goods and services and provide a vehicle for transferring real capital among countries. They also represent the shifting of short-run funds to locations that offer higher returns and greater protection against loss.

While the benefits of international capital movements are clearly recognized, there are aspects that generate a great deal of concern among the monetary authorities of individual countries. After all, capital flows create pressure for exchange rates to change, since they generate an increase in the demand for the currency into which capital is flowing. This pressure can become massive at times. When this happens, the authorities face the choice of letting the exchange rate respond to the capital flows, resisting the pressure of the exchange rate to change by intervening on the foreign exchange market, or by imposing restrictions on international financial transactions. The first alternative can damage the competitiveness of the country's traded goods, or generate internal inflationary pressures; the second alternative makes it more difficult to control internal monetary conditions and the third directly interferes with international trade and investment.

During the 1970s the world faced rapid inflation that affected nearly every nation in the free world. While this global inflation appeared to be caused, in part, by steady increases in the world price of oil and perhaps by shortages of foodstuffs and other key resources, it seemed that, for many countries, inflation was being forced upon them by an excessive growth in liquidity in the rest of the world. It became evident that an individual country, especially a small country, could have a difficult time maintaining a rate of monetary expansion and price inflation that was out of step with the rest of the world. In addition, it was widely believed that the international money markets, particularly the Eurocurrency markets, were generating new liquidity at an excessive rate, thereby compounding the problem. The fear began to spread that unless something were done to bring this liquidity expansion under control, international inflation could run rampant while individual countries stood helplessly by.

Recent analysis strongly suggests that these fears were largely misplaced. The Eurocurrency market is not capable of generating large, sustained increases in money and credit on its own accord. Policies aimed at curtailing liquidity creation within this market would thus appear to be ill advised, first because they are unnecessary and, second, as a side effect, because they would diminish the efficiency with which the market can serve the needs of international trade and investment. Since the real sources of liquidity expansion are to be found within the individual countries within the system, efforts to curtail the rate of expansion of global liquidity would have to be aimed at those sources.

On the other hand, there are ways in which the Eurocurrency market does reduce the ability of individual countries to pursue independent monetary and exchange-rate policies. Because of its very efficiency, the Eurocurrency market helps to transmit the effects of monetary growth in one country to other countries in the system. Attempts by one country to pursue an independent rate of monetary expansion can generate capital inflows and outflows that will force the country's monetary expansion back into line with the rest of the world. This process is also intensified by the efficiency of the Eurocurrency market. While countries may understandably wish to counteract the monetary effects of capital inflows and outflows, these efforts should not include policies aimed at restricting growth in the international money market. The problem of the international transmission of liquidity is essentially different from the problem of international liquidity creation itself, and policies should be chosen accordingly. The international transmission of monetary expansion, as well as other economic disturbances, is discussed at some length in Part II.

INTERNATIONAL COMMERCIAL POLICY: THEORY AND APPLICATION $\quad$ IV

INTRODUCTION

Few economic issues raise the emotions of the general public more than the threat to domestic industry posed by foreign imports. Domestic residents resent the thought of domestic jobs being lost at the expense of foreign imports. Of course, the philosophy of a market-oriented economy is that competition is healthy, and necessary, to achieve maximum production in the most efficient manner. Yet when the source of that competition lies outside the country's borders, the favorable view of competition often falls by the wayside. The failure of a domestic firm that results from the success of another domestic firm is viewed differently than if that failure results from the success of a foreign firm. The difference in attitude toward foreign and domestic sources of competition arises primarily out of a feeling of nationalism held by domestic policymakers and residents. This feeling of nationalism often dominates purely economic considerations in the formation of international trade policy.

Historically, in all trading nations, domestic import-competing firms and the factors of production they employ have never been reluctant to ask government policymakers for protection from the threat of foreign import competition. In more cases than not, policymakers have shown an aversion to the potential damage to domestic firms that may result from foreign imports and as a result have granted protection. After the War of 1812, President James Madison raised the level of protection afforded the cotton textile industry of New England in order to protect it from an influx of textile imports from England. In 1983, approximately one hundred and seventy years later, the cotton textile industry of the United States remains one of the most highly protected industries in the economy; cotton imports are subject not only to higher-than-average tariffs but also to outright quantity limitations. This illustrates the fact that, although the specifics of trade policy may have changed over the years, the general approach taken by most nations has remained remarkably steady. The objective of the following chapters is to analyze the economic impact of restrictive trade policy, to discuss why countries would employ restrictive trade measures and finally to outline the history of U.S. commercial policy over the past fifty years and examine its effect on the pattern of trading relations.

Our discussion of protection begins by first examining the economic effects of the instruments of trade policy most frequently used by trading nations. Particular attention is focused on tariff policy, which has been the most widely used method of protecting the domestic economy. We shall also examine a group of trade policy measures known as "nontariff barriers." Although the details may differ, we shall see that each type of policy is designed to increase the output of domestic firms at the expense of foreign imports. This objective, taken alone, may seem admirable from the point of view of the domestic country; however, these policies also entail adverse effects for domestic consumers, such as price increases. The overall welfare effect of the protective trade measures on the domestic economy will be shown to be generally negative.

Despite the fact that protective trade policies tend to reduce overall welfare, nations continue to employ such policies. In Chapter 15, we present arguments that might be made in favor of trade protection along with counterarguments to this protectionist logic.

Our discussion of trade policy concludes by examining the history of the international commercial policy of the United States and the effects of that policy on international trade patterns. In Chapter 16, we shall see that the major trading nations of the world have periodically made attempts to dismantle mutual trade barriers. In fact, they have formed an international organization and negotiated an agreement, known as the General Agreement on Tariffs and Trade (GATT), to facilitate this process. U.S. commercial policy has at times been consistent with this move toward a negotiated free trade, while at other times it has run counter to this movement. In fact, recent developments in the trade policy of not only the United States, but also of the other major trading nations, have raised serious questions as to whether the international community is ready to subordinate the interests of import-competing industries to the goal of achieving free trade. Let us, now, turn to the opening chapter of this section, which examines the economic effects of tariff policy.

Tariffs: Their Structure 13 and Economic Effects

Historically, the most important instrument of trade policy has been the tariff. A tariff is a tax imposed on goods and services traded across national borders and can be applied to either imports or exports. Although as a matter of practice, tariffs are applied mainly to imports, many less developed countries do apply duties to a significant number of their export products. The motivation behind a nation's tariff policy has generally been twofold. First, tariffs can serve as a means of raising revenue to finance the activities of government; second, tariffs can serve as a device to protect domestic industries from foreign competition. The revenue-generating function of tariffs today is relatively insignificant, particularly for the industrial nations, although this was not always the case. The decline in the importance of tariffs as a source of revenue is illustrated for the United States in Figure 13–1, where the percentage of total federal revenue collections accounted for by tariffs is shown to have declined substantially over the course of the last two centuries. In contrast to the more industrialized countries, the tariff policies of many of the developing nations often serve as a significant source of revenue. In fact, according to one estimate, revenue collected from import and export tariffs accounted for approximately 32 percent of the total tax revenue of 47 developing nations during the period, 1969–1971.[1] Although revenue-generating tariffs cannot be ignored, the primary role of tariff policy in recent times has been as a means of protecting domestic industry from foreign competition.

---

[1] Raja J. Chelliah, Hessel J. Baas and Margaret R. Kelly, "Developing Countries Tax Effort Continues to Rise, Study Shows," *IMF Survey,* June 3, 1974, pp. 162–164.

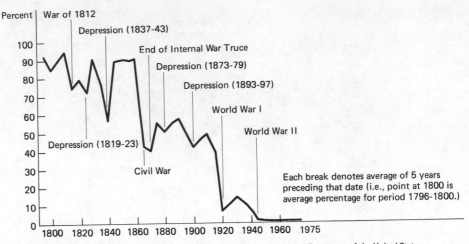

Source: John M. Dobson, *Two Centuries of Tariffs: The Background and Emergence of the United States International Trade Commission* (Washington, D.C.: U.S. Government Printing Office, 1976.)

FIGURE 13-1 Percentage of Federal Revenue Generated by Customs Duties:1790–1975

TYPES OF TARIFFS

Tariffs are applied in either one of two ways, as an *ad valorem* duty or as a *specific* tax. An ad valorem tariff is expressed as a percentage of the dutiable value of the traded good—say, 35 percent of the value—while a specific tariff is a designated amount per unit of quantity of the good—say, 10 cents per pound. For a small number of traded goods a *compound* tariff is applied which combines a specific and ad valorem tariff—say, 10 cents a pound plus 35 per-

TABLE 13-1[a]

Examples of Tariffs under the U.S. Tariff System				
Ad Valorem Tariffs		Specific Tariffs		Compound Tariff
Automobiles, passenger	2.9%	Lamb	$ .05 per lb.	Dried mushrooms, 2.7¢ per lb. + 8.5%
Still cameras (over $10)	6.4%	Pork sausage	$ .06 per lb.	Perfume, 6¢ per lb. + 6.9%
Transistor radio	9.3%	Sugar cane	$2.50 per short ton	Safety razor blades, 9¢ each + 2.7%
Toys	14.9%	Grapefruit juice	$ .25 per gallon	Knitted wool hats, 29¢ per lb. + 15.9%

Source: U.S. International Trade Commission, *Tariff Schedule of the United States Annotated 1981* (Washington, D.C.: U.S. Government Printing Office, 1981).

[a]These are the most-favored nation rates (the lowest rates applicable).

cent of the good's dutiable value. In Table 13–1, examples of the various types of tariffs under the U.S. tariff system are presented for several products.

Both types of tariffs offer particular advantages and disadvantages in their application. Specific tariffs are much easier to administer than ad valorem tariffs. Suppose that a specific tariff equal to $200 per unit is applied to imported automobiles. Under such a tariff, any imported automobile, regardless of value, will be taxed $200, a relatively simple task. If, on the other hand, imported automobiles are taxed according to an ad valorem rate—say, 10 percent—the task of determining the amount of payable duty becomes somewhat more complicated since the customs official must appraise the dollar value of the automobile. Obviously, this appraisal is quite important since the amount of duty payable will vary directly with the dollar size of the appraised value. The problems inherent in obtaining an accurate valuation are reflected by the complex system of valuation employed by U.S. custom officials. This system involves nine possible methods of valuation, including the controversial American Selling Price system (to be discussed in Chapter 14).[2] The valuation of imports will also depend on whether the valuation is made on a c.i.f. basis (costs, insurance and freight), which includes the costs of transportation and insurance, or on an f.o.b. basis (free on board) which excludes those costs. Both the valuation of an imported good and the ad valorem tariff obligation associated with that

good will be greater using the c.i.f. method. Traditionally, the United States has used the f.o.b. method while the European nations have relied primarily on the c.i.f. approach.

Although use of the specific tariff may eliminate problems of valuation such a tariff is not without problems. First, a specific tariff cannot discriminate between different qualities of a product. For instance, if automobiles were subject to a specific tariff—say, $500 per unit—a Toyota and Mercedes-Benz would be assessed identical duties, $500 each, despite the divergence in value arising from their different qualities. If the Toyota and Mercedes were valued at $5000 and $20,000, respectively, the $500 specific tariff as a percentage of the value of the automobiles (ad valorem equivalent) would equal 10 percent for the Toyota and 2.5 percent for the Mercedes. Obviously, the lower priced Toyota will bear a much heavier tariff burden than will the Mercedes. This disparity would not arise under an ad valorem system, since each make of automobile would be subject to an identical percentage duty. Because of this problem, the vast majority of specific tariffs under the U.S. tariff system are applied to products that are homogeneous in quality (and thus close in value), such as agricultural products (see Table 13–1).

A related problem associated with the specific tariff is its inability to maintain a constant rate of protection for a traded good whose price is rising over time. No matter how much the price of the commodity might change, the amount of payable duty under a specific tariff will remain constant. With an ad valorem tariff, on the other hand, the amount of collectable duty will increase as the price (and valuation) of the commodity increases. In fact, the general rise in prices over time has caused the U.S. system of tariffs to move from one based mainly on specific tariffs to one based primarily on ad valorem tariffs.

[2]The Tokyo Round of multilateral trade negotiations (completed in 1979) arrived at an international customs valuation code, designed to simplify and standardize the valuation procedures of trading nations. The code "simplifies" the process by providing five explicit methods of valuation. The United States has agreed to abide by the code and eventually to eliminate the American Selling Price system.

THE ECONOMIC IMPACT
OF TARIFFS—THE STATIC EFFECTS

The Small Country Case

In the preceding section, we mentioned that there were two motives for imposing a tariff: (1) as a means of generating revenue and (2) as a device to protect domestic import-competing industries from foreign competition. Let us now examine more formally the revenue-generating and protective functions of tariff policy, as well as the other effects that accompany such a policy. The impact of tariff policy will be analyzed within a two-country, partial equilibrium framework assuming perfectly competitive conditions. It will also be assumed, initially, that the foreign producers' import supply curve to the domestic country is perfectly elastic (horizontal). This means that the foreign industry is willing to supply as large a quantity as the home country wants to buy at the world price (the price received by the foreign producers). This assumption implies that the domestic country is too small a purchaser of the product on the world market to affect the world price by varying its demand for imports. The assumption of a horizontal import supply curve is thus referred to as the "small country assumption."

This situation is depicted in Figure 13–2, which shows the foreign import supply curve under free trade (S_F^F), as well as the supply (S_D) and demand (D_D) conditions of the domestic country. It is assumed that the foreign producers are willing to supply the imported good—say, fish—at a world price equal to $3.00 per unit.

Prior to the imposition of the tariff, domestic producers of fish will be unable to establish a price exceeding the world price, $3.00, since domestic consumers would shift their demand for fish away from domestic toward foreign supplies of fish. Thus the home country price under free trade (P_D^F) would equal the world price, $3.00 per fish, and would be the price faced by domestic producers and consumers. At that price the domestic industry would supply Q_1 fish while domestic consumption would equal Q_2. The amount by which domestic consumption ex-

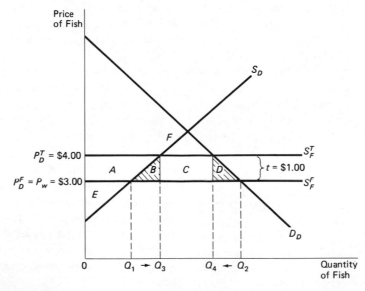

FIGURE 13-2 The Economic Effects of a Tariff: The Small Country Case

TABLE 13-2

Welfare Effects of Tariff Policy	
Welfare Losses	*Area*
Decrease in Consumers' Surplus	A + B + C + D
Welfare Gains (Transfer from Consumers to Producers and Government)	
Increase in Producer's Surplus	A
Increase in Tariff Revenue (Revenue Effect)	C
Net loss	B + D
Production Effect	B
Consumption Effect	D

ceeds domestic production, $Q_2 - Q_1$, would of course equal the quantity of fish imports.

Now let us introduce a specific tariff $(t)^3$ equal to $1.00 per fish. A tariff, of course, is a tax on imports from foreign producers and can be considered an additional cost to the foreign producers.[4] To cover the costs of the tariff, foreign producers will require a higher selling price. In our example, the foreign producers must receive $3.00 per fish (after the tariff) to be willing to supply fish to the domestic country. With a $1.00-per-fish tariff, foreign producers will thus charge a price of $4.00 to domestic consumers, $3.00 of which will remain with the foreign producer, while $1.00 will be paid as duty to the domestic customs officials. Graphically, the foreign import supply curve will shift upward by $1.00, the amount of the specific tariff. In Figure 13–2 this is shown by the upward shift of the import supply curve from S_F^F ($3.00) to S_F^T ($4.00).

With the increase in the price of imports, domestic consumers will turn to domestic supplies. They will bid the domestic price upward until it is just equal to the price of imports, $4.00 per fish. The tariff, by raising the price of competitive imports, allows domestic producers to raise their price to the new, higher level. Unlike the foreign producers, however, the entire price

increase is garnered by the domestic producers since they are not subject to the tariff. One effect of the tariff, then, is to establish a difference between the price received by foreign producers ($3.00) and that received by domestic producers, the difference being equal to the amount of the specific tariff ($1.00). Also, domestic consumers face a higher price for fish ($4.00) than do foreign consumers ($3.00) who are not faced with the tariff. The increase in the domestic price will lead to an increase in domestic production, from Q_1 to Q_3, and a decrease in domestic consumption, from Q_2 to Q_4. This implies that the quantity of imports will decline from $Q_2 - Q_1$ to $Q_4 - Q_3$. It should be noted that, even though the quantity of imports supplied by foreign producers declines, the price they actually receive (the world price) remains equal to $3.00. Thus the tariff offers protection to the domestic import-competing industry since it results in both an increase in domestic production, at a higher price, and a decrease in imports. The most extreme case of protectionism would be a tariff set at a level greater than (or equal to) the difference between the free trade price and the pretrade price; this tariff would

---

[3]The results using an ad valorem tariff would be identical.

[4]We are assuming that the tariff-imposing government collects the tariff from the foreign producers.

[5]By the welfare effects of a tariff, we are referring to the economic well-being of the trading countries as a whole. The degree of the economic well-being of a nation may be thought of as being represented by the community indifference curve upon which the nation is operating.

eliminate imports. Such a tariff is called a *prohibitive* tariff.

Welfare Effects of Tariff Policy—Small Country Case

Although we have examined the impact of tariff policy on the levels of domestic consumption and production, world and domestic prices, and on the flow of imports, we have yet to address the question of whether the economic welfare[5] of the tariff-imposing country, as a whole, is improved or worsened. Intuitively, it would appear that domestic producers have benefited from the tariff while domestic consumers (who are paying a higher per-unit price and consuming a smaller quantity than under free trade) have become worse off economically. To analyze the welfare effects more rigorously, we shall first introduce the concepts of producers' and consumers' surplus and then apply those concepts to a welfare analysis of tariff policy.

consumers' surplus

To aid the discussion of consumers' surplus, we shall refer to Figure 13–3(a), which portrays the market demand schedule for a good—say, fish. Assume that the equilibrium price of fish equals $3.00. The market demand schedule indicates that some individual consumers are *willing* to purchase units of fish at prices exceeding $3.00. For example, at the price $5.00 per fish, some consumers would be willing to purchase Q_1 of fish. However, under perfectly competitive conditions, there is only one price of the good that all consumers encounter, the equilibrium price. Thus, even though there are individual consumers who are *willing* to pay prices greater than the equilibrium price, those consumers will only *have* to pay the lower equilibrium price. This benefit, accruing to those consumers who would be *willing* to pay a higher price, is referred to as *consumers' surplus*. Con-

sumers' surplus can be formally defined as the difference between the amount consumers are willing to pay (the area under the demand curve, area $A + B$) and the amount they would actually pay (area B [$3.00 \times Q_E$]). In Figure 13–3(a), then, consumers' surplus would equal area A. It should be noted that the higher the equilibrium price facing consumers, the smaller will be area A and the lower will be the size of consumers' surplus.[6]

producers' surplus

Producers' surplus is based on a line of reasoning similar to that for consumers' surplus. In Figure 13–3(b), an industry supply curve of fish is depicted with an assumed equilibrium price of $3.00 per fish. The industry supply curve indicates that some individual firms within the industry are willing to supply a quantity of fish at a price less than $3.00; for example, at $1.00, the quantity that firms are willing to supply equals Q_1. However, all firms operating under perfect competition receive a single price; the equilibrium price. Because the equilibrium price applies to all firms in the industry, those firms *willing* to supply a quantity of the good at a price less than the equilibrium price will benefit; this benefit is called *producers' surplus*. If the industry supply curve were thought of as the industry marginal cost curve (which it would be in the short run under perfect competition), then the benefits of producers' surplus can be interpreted as the fact that some firms will be receiving a price greater than the additional costs of producing an extra unit of the good.

[6]The propriety of using consumers' surplus as a measure of a nation's economic welfare has been a point of controversy in economics. Strictly speaking, its use is justified only under certain assumptions. Most intermediate price theory texts contain a discussion of the topic. In particular, see Jack Hirshleifer, *Price Theory and Applications*, 2nd ed. (Englewood Cliffs, N.J.: Prentice-Hall, 1980), Chapter 7.

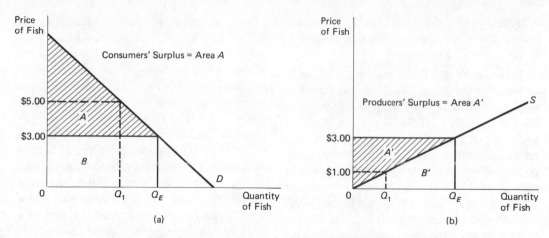

FIGURE 13-3 Consumers' and Producer's Surplus

Specifically, producers' surplus is defined as the difference between the amount producers *actually* receive ([$3.00 × Q_E], area $A' + B'$), and the minimum amount they would be *willing* to receive (the area under the supply curve, area B'). In Figure 13–3(b), then, producers' surplus would equal area A'. Finally, it should be recognized that an increase in the equilibrium price will increase the size of producers' surplus.

Applying Consumers' and Producers' Surplus to Tariff Analysis

Returning to our tariff analysis, we can now identify the areas representing consumers' and producers' surplus in Figure 13–2. Under free trade, with an equilibrium price equal to $3.00, consumers' surplus is represented by area $A + B + C + D + F$; upon the tariff-induced increase in domestic price to $4.00, consumers' surplus will equal the area represented by F. The reduction in consumers' surplus, then, equals the area $A + B + C + D$.

Producers' surplus under free trade, at a price equal to $3.00, is represented by the area E; with the tariff-induced increase in price to $4.00, producers' surplus would equal area $A + E$. Thus producers' surplus increases by the area

represented by A. As a result of the tariff policy, then, there has been a transfer of welfare within the tariff-imposing country from domestic consumers to domestic producers. Consumers, because they now *pay* a higher price for *domestically* produced output, lose a portion of consumers' surplus equal to area $A + B$. Domestic producers, on the other hand, because they *receive* a higher price for their output, *gain* an amount of producers' surplus equal to the portion of the loss in consumers' surplus applying to domestic production; this gain is equal to area A.

There is still another transfer of economic welfare that results from the tariff policy; this transfer is called the *revenue effect*. The total amount of tariff revenue collected by the importing country is equal to the per-unit tariff, $1.00, multiplied by the quantity (units) of imports under the tariff, $Q_4 - Q_3$. This is represented graphically by the area of rectangle C in Figure 13–2. This increase in tariff revenue has been at the expense of a portion of consumers' surplus equal to area C. In other words, the tariff-induced increase in the price of imports has resulted in consumers paying more for the quantity $Q_4 - Q_3$ of imports; this increased expenditure is equal in value to the tariff revenue collected by the government (area C). Thus there is a transfer of welfare from domestic customers to the domestic government.

It should be noted that the tariff revenue is collected by the domestic government from foreign producers. In our example, the domestic government extracted $1.00 per fish from the $4.00 import price. Let us assume that the domestic government uses this revenue to purchase goods and services or to reduce taxes in such a manner so as to just offset the loss in consumer surplus by area C. The net change in the overall welfare of the nation, then, is equal to the difference between the loss in consumers' surplus $(A + B + C + D)$, on the one hand, and the increase in producers' surplus (A) and tariff revenue (C), on the other. Since the reduction in consumers' surplus is greater than the increase in producers' surplus plus tariff revenue, the tariff-imposing nation will suffer an overall loss in economic welfare equal to the areas of the two triangles B and D. Triangles B and D are referred to as the "deadweight welfare loss" of tariff policy. The welfare results of tariff policy are summarized in Table 13–2.

The welfare loss triangles lend themselves to a more direct interpretation. The triangle B is referred to as the *production loss* to the economy, in that it represents the amount by which the domestic cost of producing $Q_1 - Q_3$ exceeds the cost at which $Q_1 - Q_3$ could have been obtained through imports under free trade. That is, more domestic resources are being devoted to the production of fish than is optimal. The triangle D, on the other hand, represents the *consumption loss* to the economy, in that some consumers who were willing to pay more than $3.00 per fish for the quantity $Q_2 - Q_4$ under free trade, but only had to pay $3.00, are denied that benefit when the price rises to $4.00. In this case the loss to those consumers is not compensated by a gain to other sectors of the economy.

We can see, then, that the imposition of a tariff will result in a redistribution of economic welfare from domestic consumers to domestic producers and to the domestic government. In addition, there will be a net welfare loss since not all of the reduction in consumers' surplus is offset by the gains to producers and to the government. The loss may even be greater than our analysis has so far indicated. This is so, because we have omitted the administrative costs of tariff policy. These costs, which include the maintenance of a customs department and a tariff court which judges disputes on such matters as the valuation of imports, may be considerable. Also, policymakers must devote considerable amounts of their resources to the formation of tariff policy, resources which could be used for other productive endeavors. Let us now see whether the same conclusions are reached when the importing country is large enough to influence the world price of the traded good.

Large Country Case—The Terms of Trade Effect

So far, we have shown that if the supply curve of imports is perfectly elastic (the small country assumption) the imposition of a tariff will have no effect on the price received by foreign producers—that is, the world price. However, for some traded goods, the supply curve is not perfectly elastic; foreign producers will require a higher (lower) price in order to offer a greater (smaller) quantity of imports to the domestic market. This means that the supply curve of imports will be upward sloping. An upward-sloping supply curve, in turn, implies that the importing country is large enough so that changes in the quantity of imports demanded by that country will influence the world price of the product. Hence, the use of an upward-sloping import supply curve is referred to as the *large country case*. As might be expected, the imposition of an import tariff by a large country will result in a change in the world price of the import good.

Let us examine the effects of a tariff for the large country case more closely, concentrating on the world price effects, with the aid of Figure 13–4. The left-hand panel of Figure 13–4 depicts the supply (S_D) and demand (D_D) schedules for fish of the domestic, importing country. The right-hand panel, on the other hand, depicts the *world market* for fish, where the world market concentrates on the quantity traded of the good and its world price.[7] The world market includes the domestic import demand curve (D_M) for fish

[7]For the right-hand panel truly to represent the world market for the good, import demand and supply of all countries should be considered. In our example, however, we are assuming a two-country world with one exporter of fish and one importer.

and the foreign import supply curve (S_F) which is assumed to be upward sloping. The import demand curve is obtained from the information provided in the left-hand panel and is derived by simply taking the difference between the quantity demanded and the quantity supplied in the domestic market at every price. The price of fish is determined in the world market at the point where import demand equals import supply. Because we are primarily concerned with the effect of tariffs on the world price, our attention will focus on the world market.

Under free trade, international equilibrium will occur at point E, in Figure 13–4, the point of intersection of the import supply and demand curves. The world and domestic price will be $3.00 with the quantity of fish imports equal to OQ_M. From the left-hand panel, it can be seen that the levels of domestic production and consumption at $3.00 will equal Q_1 and Q_2, re-

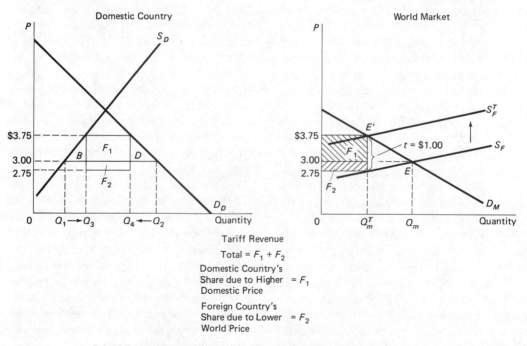

Tariff Revenue

Total = $F_1 + F_2$

Domestic Country's
Share due to Higher = F_1
Domestic Price

Foreign Country's
Share due to Lower = F_2
World Price

FIGURE 13-4 The Economic Effects of Tariff Policy: Large Country Case

spectively, the difference being equal to OQ_M.

A specific tariff equal to $1.00 per fish will have the same effect upon the import supply curve as it did in the small country case; an upward shift in the curve equal to the amount of the tariff, from S_F to S_F^T in Figure 13–4. To reiterate, this upward shift reflects the fact that foreign producers under the tariff require a higher selling price at every level of output to cover the $1.00-per-unit duty that they are assessed. Equilibrium under the tariff policy will occur at point E' where the tariff-distorted import supply curve (S_F^T) intersects the import demand curve. The domestic price, the price faced by domestic producers and consumers, will equal $3.75 per fish under the tariff while the quantity of imports will fall to OQ_M^T. As a result of the rise in the domestic price, domestic production will rise and domestic consumption will fall to Q_3 and Q_4, respectively, in the left-hand panel.

What happens to the world price received by foreign producers as a result of the tariff? Just as in the small country case, the price of imports to domestic consumers will equal the price of domestic production; in our example, $3.75 per fish. Foreign producers will not garner the entire selling price since they must pay domestic customs officials a duty equal to $1 per fish, meaning that the price they actually receive equals $2.75 per fish. This price, the world price under the tariff, however, is lower than the free trade world price, $3.00 per fish. That is, because the domestic-importing country is assumed to be a large country, the tariff-induced decrease in the quantity of fish demanded will result in a decline in its world price. This result is in contrast to that obtained in the small country case, where the tariff left the world price unchanged.

The welfare effects of a tariff will be similar to those in the small country case with the exception of the revenue effect. Because of the rise in the domestic price of fish, consumers' surplus will be reduced and will be partially offset by an increase in producers' surplus and government tariff revenue. Just as in the small country case, these changes yield a net welfare loss equal to the production and consumption losses; triangles B and D, respectively, in the left-hand panel of Figure 13–4. The revenue effect is depicted in the right-hand panel. Tariff revenue collected is, of course, equal to the per-unit tariff, $1.00, times the number of units of imports, OQ_M^T; and is represented by the rectangle, $F_1 + F_2$, in the right-hand panel of Figure 13–4.

Let us address the question of how the $1.00 per-unit tariff burden is allocated between the domestic and foreign country. The foreign producers are unable to "pass" the entire $1.00 tariff on to domestic consumers in the form of a $1.00 increase in the domestic price. Specifically, the price facing domestic consumers increased by only $.75 from its free trade level of $3.00. Foreign producers were forced to absorb a portion of the cost of the tariff equal to $.25. This is indicated by the fact that the price actually received by foreign producers declined from $3.00 per unit to $2.75. The division of the tariff costs are represented by area F_1, the domestic country's portion, and F_2, the foreign country's portion. Under the small country case, it should be remembered that the entire cost of the tariff was absorbed by domestic consumers as foreign producers passed on the entire amount of the tariff in the form of a price increase to domestic consumers.

Another way to view the situation is that the price of imports to the domestic country has fallen. Even though domestic consumers do face a higher price ($3.75), only a portion of that price is received by foreign producers ($2.75), as $1.00 of the price stays within the nation's borders as tariff revenue. It should be recalled that if the price of imports decreases, while the price of exports remains unchanged, the importing country's terms of trade will improve, enhancing the economic welfare of the country. The reduction in the world price of imports in the large country case is called the *terms of trade effect*. If the terms of trade effect is great enough (i.e., if the price of imports declines enough), it is possible that the positive welfare effects of that decline may more than offset the negative welfare effects of a tariff which result from the volume of trade being restricted (triangles *B* and *D*), leading to a net benefit from tariff policy. This particular outcome, as well as its implications for trade policy, will be discussed in more detail in Chapter 15. For now, it is sufficient to understand the difference in tariff analysis between the small and large country case.

MEASURES OF THE LEVEL OF TARIFF PROTECTION: NORMAL VERSUS EFFECTIVE PROTECTION

By increasing the price of competitive imports and thereby allowing domestic producers to raise their prices, tariffs offer a degree of protection to domestic import-competing producers. The protection afforded the value or price of the final output of domestic producers is referred to as *nominal protection*. The magnitude of that protection is measured by *nominal tariff rates,* which are those rates listed in the importing country's tariff schedule.

However, it is questionable whether the nominal tariff is the most accurate measure of the actual degree of protection afforded to domestic producers. Domestic producers are not so concerned with the protection offered the value of their final output as they are with the protection offered to their value-added; *value-added* is defined as the difference between the value of final output and the value of inputs used to produce that output. The protection afforded by the tariff system to a domestic firm's value-added is referred to as *effective protection,* and the degree of that protection is measured by *effective tariff rates*.

To illustrate the difference between the two concepts of protection, consider the effects of a particular tariff arrangement on a producer of a final good—say, automobiles—which uses a single input—say, steel. Suppose that under free trade the price of the quantity of steel used in the production of an automobile is $2000, while the final price of the auto itself is $5000; this implies that the value-added by the automobile manufacturers equals $3000. Now suppose Congress is considering establishing a protective tariff scheme for domestic automobile manufacturers. The auto manufacturers will not be concerned so much with the protection afforded the total value of the automobile as with the protection afforded to their value-added, since this represents the dollar value of the income (wages, profits, rents and interest) generated by their activity. Any protection afforded the $2000 of steel input by the tariff system is of little concern to the automakers, since steel is simply an input which they purchase to produce their output. In fact, if the domestic price of steel were to increase because of tariff protection, this would represent an increase in costs to automakers, reducing their value-added.

If Congress were to enact a 20 percent nominal tariff on imported automobiles, the domestic price of automobiles would increase to $6000 (assuming the small country case). This action alone, by raising the price of automobiles, will also raise the amount of value-added by the auto industry from $3000 to $4000 (assuming the price of steel is not affected). Now suppose that this tariff were coupled with a nominal tariff on *steel* inputs equal to 10 percent; this would raise the domestic price of steel to $2200. Since the increase in the price of steel represents an increase in costs to the automakers, the nominal tariff on steel, by itself, would lower the value-added of the auto manufacturers. To determine the protective effects on the automakers of the *total* tariff package, it is necessary to compare their value-added before and after the imposition of this tariff arrangement. These calculations are

TABLE 13-3

		Calculation of the Effective Rate of Protection		
		Free Trade Price	Nominal Tariff	Price Under Tariff
Final product:	Automobile	$5000	$t_n = 20\%$	$6000
Input:	Steel	2000/car	$t_i = 10\%$	2200
	Value-added	$3000		$3800

$$\text{Effective rate of protection, } t_e = \frac{\$3800 - \$3000}{\$3000} = 26.6\%$$

presented in Table 13–3, where the value-added is shown to have increased under this tariff package from its free trade value of $3000 to $3800.

The effective rate of protection is defined as the percentage change in value-added resulting from a system of tariffs:

$$t_e = \frac{v' - v}{v}$$

t_e = effective rate of protection

v' = value-added under protection

v = value-added under free trade

In our example, the effective rate of protection of automobiles would equal approximately 26.6 percent, which exceeds the nominal tariff rate for automobiles (20 percent). This implies that the protective effect of the nominal tariff on automobiles more than offsets the reduction in protection resulting from the nominal tariff on steel. In general, the following relations between the nominal tariff on output (t_n) and input (t_i), and the effective rate of protection (t_e) will exist:

$$(1)\ t_e > t_n \text{ if } t_n > t_i$$

$$(2)\ t_e = t_n \text{ if } t_n = t_i$$

$$(3)\ t_e < t_n \text{ if } t_n < t_i$$

It should be emphasized that it is the effective rate of protection which must be increased if the objective of trade policy is to attract resources into a productive activity and increase its level of output. Thus if an industry is to be truly protected from foreign competition, the relationship between the nominal tariff on its output and the nominal tariff on its inputs must be considered in developing a protective tariff package.

Offshore Assembly Provision

One interesting and generally overlooked aspect of U.S. tariff policy is the *offshore assembly provision (OAP)*. Under the OAP, tariffs on manufactured products assembled in foreign countries are applied only to the value added in the assembly process, provided that U.S.–made components were used by the foreign producers in their assembly operations. Table 13–4 shows the dollar value of imports entering the United States under the OAP in 1978. The magnitude of such imports is substantial, totaling about $9.8 billion or 5.6 percent of the value of all U.S. imports in 1978. The volume of OAP imports has increased almost tenfold from its 1966 level of $.95 billion, and has been growing at

TABLE 13-4

	Imports under Offshore Assembly Provisions of the United States—1978 and 1966			
	OAP Imports—1978		*OAP Imports—1966*	
	Value of OAP Imports—1978 ($ million)	*% of Total 1978 Imports*	*Value of OAP Imports—1966 ($ million)*	*% of Total 1966 Imports*
Total	9,735.3	5.6	953.0	3.8
From developed countries	5,447.0	3.1	895.8	3.6
From developing countries	4,288.3	2.5	57.2	.2

Source: U.S. International Trade Commission, *Import Trends in TSUS Items 806.30 and 807.00*, USITC Publication 1029 (Washington, D.C.: U.S. Government Printing Office, 1980).

a faster rate than imports as a whole. The rapid growth of OAP imports is reflected by the fact that the percentage of total imports accounted for by OAP imports has increased from 3.8 percent in 1966 to 5.6 percent in 1978.

There are important economic implications associated with the OAP. First, this policy encourages foreign manufacturing firms (assemblers) that desire to export to the United States to use U.S.–made components since their tariff burden will be reduced accordingly. Second, the policy encourages the import of products assembled by foreign producers. Thus, the OAP offers potential benefits to both the United States and its trading partners. Such a policy has special significance to those less developed countries who are attempting to increase their manufacturing operations and need available export markets for their products. The manufactured exports of those nations can become more competitive in the United States if they use American–made components in their assembly operations. More will be said about the role of the OAP as an aid to the economic growth process of the developing countries in Chapter 20.

INTERNATIONAL COMPARISONS OF MEASURES OF TARIFF PROTECTION

At this point it may prove useful to take a brief look at the relative patterns of tariff protection, both nominal and effective, of several industrialized nations. Table 13–5 shows a country-wide comparison of the average nominal tariff rates for selected industrial product groups prior to the recently completed Tokyo Round of multilateral trade negotiations (MTN), 1979, and also the reduced rates which were negotiated during the Tokyo Round. These reduced rates will be implemented gradually and will be completely installed by the late 1980s.

It is interesting to note the variability of the nominal rates both within product groups and between countries. Although this list provides at best sketchy information concerning the relative levels of protection worldwide, it does provide some indication as to what are the import-sensitive product groups, and thus the most protected, in each country. For example, textile products in the United States receive a relatively high degree of tariff protection, while the Eu-

TABLE 13-5

Average Nominal Tariff Rates (percent) of Selected Industrial Products, 1979
(reduced rates negotiated in Tokyo MTN)

			European Economic Community					
Product Group	U.S.		(EEC)		Canada[a]		Japan[a]	
Textiles and apparels	22.2%	(17.5)	10.8%	(8.8)	22.8%	(20.7)	5.5%	(5.4)
Ferrous metals and products (steel)	4.6	(3.4)	4.2	(3.2)	7.9	(5.2)	0.7	(.6)
Office and computing equipment	4.6	(3.0)	7.7	(5.7)	10.3	(1.4)	15.0	(5.1)
Scientific and controlling instruments	11.5	(6.1)	9.8	(6.4)	6.8	(3.6)	6.8	(5.2)
Automotive equipment	3.3	(2.6)	11.6	(9.6)	10.5	(6.4)	6.3	(3.1)
All industrial products excluding petroleum	6.1	(4.2)	6.3	(4.6)	10.1	(6.9)	3.2	(2.3)

Source: office of the U.S. Trade Representative, *Twenty-Fourth Annual Report of the President of the United States on the Trade Agreements Program 1979* (Washington D.C.: U.S. Government Printing Office, 1980.)
[a]Canada and Japan have hundreds of tariffs which are applied at a lower rate than the rates listed in their tariff schedules as permanent rates. The rates listed above refer to the lower applied rates.

TABLE 13-6

Average Protection of Manufactured Goods for Selected Countries[a]

Tariffs

	Average Tariff Rates on All Manufactured Imports		Average Tariff Rates on Manufactured Imports from Developing Countries	
Country	Nominal	Effective	Nominal	Effective
U.S.	6.8%	11.6%	12.4%	23.9%
European Economic Community (EEC)	6.6	11.1	14.1	27.6
Japan	9.4	16.4	11.7	20.2
All developed market economy countries	6.5	11.1	11.8	22.6

Source: United Nations Conference on Trade and Development, *The Kennedy Round Estimated Effects on Tariff Barriers* (New York: United Nations Publications, 1968).
[a]The nominal rates listed here may differ from the average rates on all industrial products listed in Table 13-5. This situation arises because of: (1) differences in the dates the calculations were made, (2) differences in the products covered in the calculations and the methods of calculations and (3) for Japan, Table 13-6 uses the listed rates rather than the applied rates as in Table 13-5.

ropean Economic Community offers a substantial degree of tariff protection to its automotive industry.

From the discussion in the previous section, we know that to obtain a true idea as to the degree of protection afforded an industry by a particular tariff package, we must examine the effective rates of protection. Table 13–6 portrays the aggregate average nominal and effective rates on manufactured products after the implementation of the tariff reductions negotiated in the Kennedy Round of multilateral trade negotiations (approximately 1972) for several countries. The rates of protection of these countries are shown both for total manufactured imports and those manufactured goods imported solely from developing countries.

It is obvious from Table 13–6 that the de-veloped countries tariff structures on manufactures are more protective than the nominal rates alone would indicate. We know that such a pattern of protection will occur because the nominal tariffs applied to inputs of manufactured goods are less than the nominal tariffs applied to the final manufactured product. A tariff structure in which the effective rate of protection is higher than the nominal rate is referred to as *tariff escalation*. Tariff escalation is even more pointed with regard to the manufactured imports from the developing countries.

In Table 13–7, this pattern of tariff escalation is demonstrated more explicitly. Table 13–7 shows the nominal and effective rates for several products at various stages of production. The message portrayed by Table 13–7 is clear; the less advanced the stage of production, the lower

TABLE 13-7

Nominal and Effective Rates on Selected Products (post-Kennedy Round, 1972)

	Country					
	U.S.		EEC		Japan	
Product	Nominal	Effective	Nominal	Effective	Nominal	Effective
Leather						
1. Hides and skins	1.1%	1.1%	0 %	0 %	0 %	0 %
2. Leather	4.7	12.0	4.8	12.3	11.6	34.7
3. Shoes	14.9	26.3	11.9	19.3	22.9	36.5
Pulp and Paper						
1. Pulpwood	0	0	2.1	2.1	0	0
2. Woodpulp	0	−1.1	3.3	5.0	5.0	7.5
3. Paper and paper articles	2.5	5.0	6.1	13.0	7.7	17.2
Wool						
1. Wool, raw	11.4	11.4	0	0	0	0
2. Wool yarn	20.7	49.5	5.7	17.5	5.0	14.7
3. Wool fabrics, woven	20.7	60.9	16.0	38.1	10.0	21.3
Aluminum						
1. Bauxite	0	0	0	0	0	0
2. Alumina	0	0	5.6	5.6	0	0
3. Aluminum, unwrought	4.0	6.0	5.8	5.6	10.4	11.4
4. Aluminum, wrought	5.9	11.5	12.8	29.3	13.6	29.0

Source: United Nations Conference on Trade and Development, *The Kennedy Round Estimated Effects on Tariff Barriers.* (New York: United Nations Publications, 1968).

the nominal tariff, resulting in a higher effective rate at the more advanced stages of production.

Tariff escalation has serious consequences, particularly for those developing countries that wish to industrialize by using the developed countries as an export market for their manufactured goods. Instead of encouraging manufactured exports from the less-developed countries, tariff escalation provides an incentive for the developing countries to continue to produce and export products associated with the less-advanced stages of production, such as raw materials. More will be said on this matter in Chapter 19, which deals with the trade problems of the developing countries.

QUESTIONS AND EXERCISES

1. Explain the meaning of both specific and ad valorem tariffs. Present arguments for and against the use of each type of tariff.

2. Comment on the validity of the following statement. Under a tariff policy, domestic and foreign producers receive identical prices for sales to the domestic consumer.

3. Suppose you were an economist for a consumer group and Congress was considering legislation raising the tariff on Japanese automobiles. Would you support the legislation? Why or why not? Would it make any difference to you if some members of your group were employed as autoworkers?

4. a. Suppose that under free trade the price to domestic consumers for imported color televisions were equal to $300 per set and that a specific tariff equal to $50 per set were imposed. Would the price of sets to domestic consumers be greater than, equal to or less than $350 if the importing country were small? If it were large?

b. If the price of sets to domestic countries increases to, say, $340, as a result of the tariff, what will be the price received by foreign producers? Why would a tariff result in a world price (the price received by foreign producers) less than the free trade price?

c. Show, graphically, the welfare effects of this tariff policy on the importing country, assuming it is a large country.

5. Answer this question on the basis of the following information:

		Free Trade Price	Nominal Tariff
Final product:	Shoes	$30/pair	$t_n = 10\%$
Input:	Leather	$15/pair	$t_i = 20\%$
	Value-added		

Calculate the effective rate of protection for shoes. How is the effective rate different from the nominal rate of protection? If you were a shoemaker, which measure of protection would you be more concerned with, and why?

6. What is meant by tariff escalation, and does it occur in the real world? Suppose you were the Secretary of Economic Development for a less-developed country, hoping to industrialize with the aid of trade. What arguments would you present to the more advanced countries to convince them that their tariff structures were restricting such development? Would you approve of the offshore assembly provision?

APPENDIX 13A
A General Equilibrium Analysis of Tariff Policy

In Chapter 13, the economic effects of tariff policy were analyzed within a partial equilibrium framework, a framework which concentrates on the effects of tariff policy on only one traded good. Let us now examine the impact of a tariff within a general equilibrium framework, making use of trade offer curves, and assuming that the two trading partners are large countries.

In Figure 13A–1, trade offer curves under free trade are shown for the United States ($TOC_{U.S.}$) and Japan (TOC_J). It is assumed that the United States exports wheat to Japan, while Japan exports automobiles to the United States. Under free trade, equilibrium will occur at point A (where $TOC_{U.S.}$ and TOC_J intersect) which will yield the terms of trade represented by the slope of the line TOT_1. Trade, of course, is balanced with the U.S. exporting OW_1 of wheat to Japan in exchange for OA_1 of automobile imports.

Now suppose that the United States imposes a tariff on imports of automobiles, and that this tariff is collected by the U.S. government from U.S. automobile importers in the form of wheat. The effect of this policy will be to shift $TOC_{U.S.}$ inward to $TOC_{U.S.}^T$. The shift in the trade offer curve reflects the fact that U.S. importers are now willing to offer less wheat exports for a given quantity of automobile imports since they must also pay a quantity of wheat to the government for importing autos. For example, prior to the imposition of the tariff, U.S. importers would be willing to offer OW_0 of wheat exports to Japan in exchange for OA_2 of autos (point C on $TOC_{U.S.}$). However, after the imposition of the tariff, those importers would only be willing to offer OW_2 bushels of wheat in exhange for OA_2 units of autos. This is so, because, having made the payment of OW_2 bushels of wheat to the Japanese, the American importers would then have to pay W_2W_0 bushels of wheat to the American government as a tariff payment. The tariff rate, in terms of wheat, can be expressed as BC/A_2B. This ratio represents the tariff payment ($BC = W_2W_0$) as a percentage of the price of automobile imports ($A_2B = OW_2$), expressed in terms of wheat.

The new equilibrium point will occur at point B, the intersection point of $TOC_{U.S.}^T$ and TOC_J. The new terms of trade are represented by TOT_2, which depicts a relatively lower (higher) price for automobiles (wheat). In other words, after the imposition of the tariff, the terms of trade of the export good, wheat, has increased. This favorable movement in the terms of trade of the United States, by itself, implies that the economic welfare of the United States has improved. On the other hand, the decrease in the relative price of Japan's export good, automobiles, implies that Japan has been made worse off by this policy.

However, we know from previous discussions that in order to make a judgment about the change in the economic welfare of a trading nation, we must also examine the changes in the nation's volume of trade. In Figure 13A–1, it can be seen that even though the United States pays a lower per-unit price for automobile imports, its quantity of imports has declined (OA_1 to OA_2). Also, U.S. sales of wheat exports have declined (OW_1 to OW_2). The reduction in wheat exports reflects the fact that the tariff policy of the United

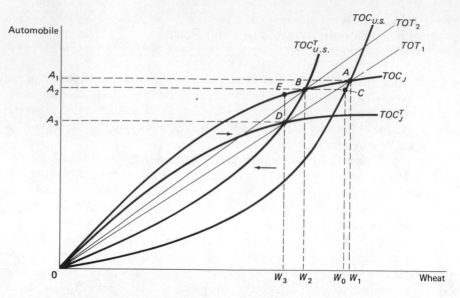

Figure 13A-1 General Equilibrium Analysis of Tariff Policy

States has resulted in a transfer of resources from the relatively efficient wheat export industry to the relatively inefficient automobile industry, which results in a reduction in the level of overall output and income of the United States.

In Japan, the effects of the U.S. tariff unambiguously lower its economic welfare, as both its terms of trade and volume of trade (and output) have been reduced. Thus, even though it is *possible* for the economic welfare of the United States to increase, this can only occur at the expense of its trading partner.

Because the economic welfare of Japan has been reduced as a result of the U.S. tariff on automobiles, it might be expected that Japan would undertake a trade policy designed to increase its welfare. Japan may retaliate against the United States by imposing a tariff on wheat imports from the United States, in the hopes of improving its terms of trade with the United States. In Figure 13A–1, suppose Japan imposes a tariff (as expressed in terms of automobiles) equal to DE/DW_3. Such a tariff will shift TOC_J to TOC_J^T and move the equilibrium point from point B to D; at point D the terms of trade will be represented by TOT_1, the free trade value. Japan's retaliation has achieved its objective in the sense that its terms of trade have improved (the price of autos has increased) compared to the terms of trade prevailing at point B. However, its volume of trade has declined, which offsets the benefits of the terms of trade improvement. Of course, the United States is worse off economically at point D than at the previous equilibrium point, point B.

This trade "war," in which one trading partner attempts to improve its economic well-being by imposing an import tariff, which, in turn, provokes the other country to retaliate with its own tariff, can possibly result in reduction of both countries' economic welfare, compared to their free trade position. This situation is depicted in Figure 13A–1. At point D, the equilibrium point after the retaliation, the terms of trade are equal to their free trade value, TOT_1. However, the volume of each nation's trade is lower than the level prior to the tariff policies. The reduced volume of trade is reflective of the lower level of output and income of each nation. Thus a large country which plans to impose a tariff in an effort to improve its terms of trade, and thus its economic welfare, must consider the possibility that its trading partner may retaliate with its own tariff. If its trading partner is also a large country, then both nations may be worse off, compared to their free trade position, after this round of tariff increases.

Nontariff Barriers to Trade: 14
Theory and Policy

Nontariff trade policies can be thought of as any trade instrument other than a tariff that causes the flow of internationally traded goods and services to be distorted from its free trade pattern. The list of nontariff barriers to trade (NTBs) consists of a vast array of policy measures. Some of those measures, such as import quotas and export subsidies, are specifically designed to restrict or encourage the flow of traded goods. Other measures, such as health and safety requirements or domestic tax arrangements, are designed to achieve domestic aims, but nonetheless have an effect on international trade patterns.

Until recent years most of the attention regarding trade policy has been focused on tariff policy. However, since successive rounds of trade negotiations have resulted in a considerable reduction in the level of tariffs (and thus their influence on trade patterns), the relative importance of NTBs has grown, as has interest in the analysis of their economic impact. This chapter, then, will examine the economic effects of NTBs.

Specifically, we will look at several groups of nontariff barriers, beginning with quantitative restrictions. We will then turn to an examination of export policies, domestic policies that affect trade patterns and, finally, policies designed to retaliate against the trading behavior of foreign firms and governments.

QUANTITATIVE RESTRICTIONS

Import Quotas

Of the almost innumerable list of NTBs, import quotas are probably the most readily identified. Import quotas are unilaterally imposed by the importing country and place an upper limit on the physical quantity of the product that may be imported during a specified

TABLE 14-1

| Example of U.S. Import Quotas (1981) | |
Product	Quantity/Time Period
Clothespins (escape clause action)	125,000 units/90 days
Peanuts	1.7 million lbs./year
Butter substitutes	1.2 million lbs./year
Fibers of cotton, processed, but not spun	1000 lbs./90 days

Source: U.S. International Trade Commission, *Tariff Schedule of the United States Annotated 1981*. (Washington, D.C.: Government Printing Office, 1981).

time period. Table 14–1 presents several examples of products whose import level into the United States is limited by import quotas.

allocation of the quota quantity

Because the import quota is a physical restriction on the quantity of imports, usually less than the free trade quantity, some domestic importers of the product will be unable to obtain the quantity of imports that they could under free trade. The upshot of this situation is that there must be a method of allocating the limited supply of imports among domestic importers. One method used in the United States is to allocate the rights to the available import quantity on a pro rata basis. If the total quantity of the import good demanded by importers exceeds the quota quantity, the individual importers receive a percentage of their demand equal to the ratio of the quota to the total quantity demanded collectively by the importers. Another method sometimes used is to issue import licenses (rights to a specified quantity of imports) to importers on the basis of their historical levels of imports; this method is used by the U.S. Department of Agriculture in allocating import quotas for dairy products. Licenses have even been issued directly to the foreign producers of the commodity in an attempt not only to regulate total imports

of the commodity, but also to control the particular sources of supply. The most equitable of these methods is probably the pro rata system, where equal access among importers is permitted. Allocation on a historical basis, on the other hand, discriminates against those importers wishing to import the product for the first time. The economic importance of gaining access to the limited quantity of imports under a quota system will be seen in the ensuing discussion of the economic effects of a quota.

The Economic Impact of an Import Quota

Let us now examine the economic effects of an import quota within a partial equilibrium framework, assuming that the importing nation is a small country. This situation is depicted in Figure 14–1, where under free trade the domestic country will consume and produce Q_2 and Q_1, respectively, of the product, say fish, with the difference between consumption and production $(Q_2 - Q_1)$ representing the quantity of imports. The world and domestic prices are equal under free trade; let us say $3.00 per fish as shown in Figure 14–1.

Assume an import quota is now imposed equal to the quantity ED, which is less than the amount which would be imported under free trade. The imposition of the quota will directly affect the

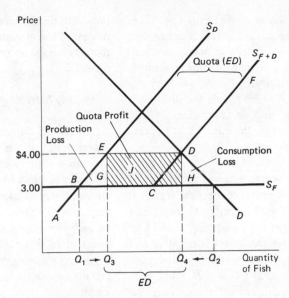

FIGURE 14-1 Economic Effects of a Quota

supply of the commodity available to the importing country. Under free trade, the importing nation could obtain any quantity of fish it desired at the world price of $3.00. However, because imports are limited under the quota, the supply of the product available to the importing nation will be restricted to the domestically produced output plus the quantity of imports permitted by the quota. We can derive the total supply curve (domestic plus foreign supply) facing the importing country by horizontally summing the quantity supplied by domestic producers at each price (represented by the domestic supply curve) and the quantity of imports that are permitted under the quota, ED. The resulting total supply curve S_{F+D}, is represented by the line $ABCDF$[1] in Figure 14–1. It should be noted that at every price the total supply curve exceeds the domestic

[1]For prices below $3.00 the total supply curve is simply equal to the domestic supply since foreign producers are unwilling to supply any quantity of fish for a price less than $3.00 per fish.

supply curve by the distance, ED, the quota quantity.

Equilibrium under the quota occurs where total supply to the domestic country equals total demand; this occurs at point D in Figure 14–1. Here the domestic price has increased to $4.00 per fish. At the higher domestic price, domestic consumption will decline to Q_4 while domestic production will increase to Q_3. The quantity of imports falls to $Q_4 - Q_3$, which of course equals the amount of the import quota, ED.

What is the effect of the import quota on the domestic importers? Suppose import licenses are issued, free of charge, by the government to domestic importers. The importers, having the right to purchase a designated quantity of imports from foreign producers, can do so at the world price, $3.00, since foreign producers remain willing to supply imports at that price. However, they can then turn to the domestic market and sell those imports at the higher domestic price, $4.00. That is, domestic importers who receive the right to import under a quota system can earn a *quota profit;* a quota profit is the profit accruing to domestic importers that results from the divergence in world and domestic prices. The amount of the quota profit is represented graphically in Figure 14–1 by the area of rectangle *J* which equals the difference between the world and domestic price ($4.00 − $3.00) multiplied by the quantity of imports permitted under the quota *(ED).*

Because of the increase in the domestic price under the import quota, the welfare effects of the quota will, with one exception, be identical to those associated with a tariff. These effects are labeled in Figure 14–1, where it should be noted that the net welfare effect is negative and equal to the sum of the production and consumption losses (triangles *G* and *H*), just as in the case of the tariff. The difference between the two policies is that the tariff revenue collected on imports under a tariff policy is replaced by the quota profit under a quota policy. If the import quota is allocated to domestic importers by the issuance of free licenses, then the quota will have the effect of redistributing economic welfare from domestic consumers to domestic producers and to holders of the import licenses.

It is possible, however, that the government could itself garner a portion or even all of the quota profit, either by selling the import licenses or by auctioning them off to the domestic importers. The quota profit is an incentive for domestic importers to compete for the right to import goods that are subject to an import quota. If domestic importers were perfectly competitive, an individual importer would be willing to pay a per-unit price for a license to the government, just below the difference between the domestic and world price. In Figure 14–1, the domestic importers would be willing to pay a price just below $1.00 per unit of imports, since the available quota profit is equal to $1.00 per unit of imports. Under such an arrangement, the quota profit would be transferred from the importers to the domestic government. In practice, however, the system of selling licenses for the imported good is not widely used by governments.

Orderly Marketing Arrangements

An import quota, strictly defined, is a unilateral action taken by the government of the importing country to limit the quantity of imports of a product from its trading partners. Any unilateral action taken in the international arena may result in either economic or political retaliation by countries affected by the action. The threat of retaliation by foreign countries in response to import quotas, coupled with the fact that import quotas are viewed unfavorably under international trade agreements, has led to an alternative method of quantitatively restricting imports: *Orderly Marketing Arrangements (OMAs),* or, as they are sometimes called, *Voluntary Export Restraints (VERs).*[2] OMAs are similar to quotas in that they represent a physical limitation on the quantity of imports. However, OMAs are not unilaterally imposed, but are either bilaterally negotiated between the importing and exporting countries or multilaterally negotiated among several countries on each side. The mere fact that OMAs are achieved by international consultation and negotiation—although the negotiations are usually accompanied by the threat of unilateral action (see the following section)—makes OMAs a more acceptable policy in the

[2]There is a technical difference between Orderly Marketing Arrangements and Volunatry Export Restraints (although their economic effects are identical). OMAs are typically imposed as a result of an escape clause action (see section on escape clauses) and are negotiated under formal provisions of the Trade Act of 1974. VERs, on the other hand, are typically negotiated directly between the Office of the U.S. Trade Representative and the foreign exporting country, and the negotiation process is not as formal.

TABLE 14-2

	Examples of OMAs and VERs	
Product	Principal Countries Involved	Type of Accord and Date
Textiles and garments (Multifiber Agreement)	Over 40 importing and exporting countries	Five-year pacts set import and export quotas and annual growth rates (first negotiated in 1962; most recent version applies to the years 1982 through 1986)
Specialty steel	U.S., Japan, Common Market, Sweden, Canada	Japan negotiated quota in U.S. market, U.S. imposed quotas on others (1969–1971)
Carbon steel	Common Market, Japan, South Africa, Spain, South Korea	Japan voluntarily restrains exports to the Common Market, which sought similar curbs by others (1970)
TV sets, radios, calculators	European countries, Japan	Japan voluntarily restrains exports to Benelux, Britain (1973)
Shoes	U.S., Taiwan, Korea, Italy, Brazil, Spain	U.S. has negotiated OMA with Taiwan to limit 1977 imports to 122 million pairs, a 34% decrease from 1976 levels. Similar 4-year OMA negotiated with Korea to limit imports to 33 million pairs in 1977, a 25% decrease from 1976 levels
TV sets	U.S., Japan, Taiwan, Korea	U.S. has negotiated OMA with Japan restricting imports for 1977 to 1.56 million sets plus 190,000 knockdown sets, a 40% decrease from 1976 levels (1977–1981)
Meat	U.S. and 12 exporting countries	U.S. negotiated constrained export levels for total meat products equal to 1.57 billion pounds in 1979
Textiles and apparel	U.S. and China	Three-year negotiated pact beginning in 1980 set maximum export level of textile product groups from China, allowing an annual rate of growth (1980–1981)
Automobiles	U.S. and Japan	Three-year pact was negotiated establishing limits on Japanese auto exports to the U.S. beginning in 1981. For the first year Japanese exports are not to exceed 1.68 million cars. For the second and third years exports can increase by an amount equal to 16.5 percent of the growth in the domestic market

Source: U.S. International Trade Commission, *Report of the President of the United States on the Trade Agreements Program* (Washington, D.C.: U.S. Government Printing Office, various issues).

eyes of the international community. Table 14–2 presents examples of products whose import quantities have been restricted by OMAs (and VERs) in recent years.

The impact of an OMA on price and quantity is identical to that of an import quota of equal size. The primary distinction between OMAs and import quotas is the manner in which the two policies are administered; this, in turn, determines the distribution of the available quota profit. The responsibility of controlling the flow of the traded good under an OMA is usually that of the foreign exporting country. Foreign exporting firms are issued export licenses by the foreign government; these permit the firms to export a certain amount of the product. Because the foreign exporting firms directly control the flow of goods to the importing country, it is more likely that they will sell the good at the higher domestic price and thus capture the quota profit. Thus the quota profit may be transferred from the domestic country to the foreign exporting country when an OMA is used in place of an equivalent import quota. Even though OMAs may be more attractive to the international trading community, they may be economically more costly to the importing country than would be an import quota of equal size.

the political economy of OMAs and VERs

It was suggested in the previous section that OMAs and VERs are preferable to the international community because they are negotiated among the trading nations, instead of being unilaterally imposed by the importing nations as in the case of import quotas. Thus OMAs and VERs would seem to embody a sense of international cooperation and diplomacy. However, when the circumstances surrounding the implementation of an OMA or VER are examined more closely, it becomes apparent that the notions of cooperation and diplomacy may be more imagined than real.

Most OMAs and VERs are implemented under the threat of unilateral import quotas. Unless a quantitative restriction were negotiated or imposed "voluntarily" by the exporting country, imports of the good will, typically, be unilaterally restricted by the importing country. Thus world leaders, in an effort to avoid political friction, either domestically or internationally, have increasingly in recent years imposed quantitative restrictions under the labels of OMAs or VERs. Although the names may differ, OMAs and VERs remain quantiative restrictions on trade, just as import quotas.

An example which clearly illustrates the nature of these "bilateral" trade restrictions is the negotiated VER between Japan and the United States, in 1981, which restricted exports of automobiles from Japan to the United States. During 1980, domestic automakers in the United States were experiencing financial difficulties as a result of low sales volume. One of the primary reasons for lagging sales, the industry and its workers contended, was the substantial rise of import sales to the United States, particularly from Japanese producers. The share of Japanese imports had risen to almost 25 percent of the U.S. market in 1980, up from 12 percent in 1978.

In early 1981, the protests of the industry were answered by its supporters in Congress in the form of legislation calling for a quota on Japanese imports equal to 1.6 million units for a period of three years. This figure represented an approximately 200,000-unit decrease from the 1980 level of imports (1.82 million). The Reagan administration was in a political vise; on the one hand, they wanted to minimize the domestic political damage that might result if they decided not to go along with the sentiment of Congress, while on the other hand they wanted to minimize international friction between itself and a valued ally. In addition, President Reagan had just been elected to office a few months earlier on the philosophy of free enterprise. If he were to support a restrictive trade agreement, just a few months after entering office, the credibility of his convictions would suffer.

The solution to the dilemma came in the form of a negotiated "voluntary" export restraint between Japanese and American trade officials. Japanese auto exports were to be restricted to a 1981 level of 1.68 million units (see Table 14–2). Although the figure was higher than the proposal lingering in Congress, it was restrictive enough to convince the congressional supporters of a quota to withdraw their proposal. Of course, the Japanese automakers were far from pleased with the agreement. However, most realized that the VER was preferable to the congressional alternative, and they reluctantly accepted the arrangement.

This example is fairly typical of the manner in which VERs are implemented. The VER concerning automobiles was not so much an act of international diplomacy and cooperation, or even a voluntary act on the behalf of Japanese auto producers, as it was a reaction to the protectionist sentiment prevailing in the United States. Although the final agreement was less restrictive than the congressional proposal, it was nonetheless a quantitative restriction on automobile imports to the United States, similar to a quota. Most of the agreements listed in Table 14–2 came about under similar circumstances.

Quantitative Restrictions versus Tariffs

Our analysis has suggested that, with the exception of the difference between the quota profit and tariff revenue, the static economic effects of quantitative restrictions and tariffs are similar. However, there are several other ways in which the two types of trade measures differ. One difference (usually cited as an advantage of quotas over tariffs) is that the effect of a quota on the quantity of imports is certain. When a tariff rate is increased (or decreased), the exact effect of such an action on the quantity of imports cannot be precisely predicted since the response by producers and consumers to a change in price is uncertain. Thus, if a policymaker's chief concern is keeping imports below a certain level, an import quota can guarantee that imports will not exceed the predetermined level.

A second difference is that quantitative barriers are more restrictive in a dynamic sense. The essence of a tariff is that it raises the price of imports to the domestic market, making them less competitive with domestic production. Foreign producers, however, can possibly offset the effects of this tax if they were to reduce their costs of production—say, by increasing their efficiency—which would in turn allow them to reduce their selling price and thereby increase their sales of imports. With quantitative restrictions, the quantity of imports supplied by foreign producers is strictly limited, regardless of the selling price, and thus there is little incentive for foreign producers to attempt to reduce the costs of producing imports in an effort to increase sales to the importing country. Thus, because quotas restrict imports on the basis of quantity rather than price, they will discourage efficient behavior on the part of foreign producers, and reduce the long-term competitive forces within the world market.

EXPORT POLICIES

Our discussion of trade policy so far has been limited to trade measures which restrict imports. Often, however, the objective of trade policy is to control the flow of exports for reasons relating either to balance of trade conditions or to the state of the internal domestic economy. Let us consider two particular export policies, one which is designed to encourage exports, and another which is intended to restrict such a flow.

Export Subsidies

A subsidy is the opposite of a tax in that a subsidy represents a payment to a firm or consumer from the government. *Export* subsidies are subsidies paid to firms for export activities or to foreign consumers of exports, and are intended to encourage export sales abroad. Subsidies may assume any number of forms ranging from direct cash payments to reduced taxes. Export subsidies, however, are often more subtle in nature, often appearing on the surface as something other than a subsidy. Regardless of their form, export subsidies amount to either a reduction in the firm's costs of producing output for export or to a reduced price for foreign consumers of exports.

The economic impact of an export production subsidy is examined in Figure 14–2, which depicts the world market for a traded good—say, fish. Under free trade the quantity of fish exports will be equal to Q_1, with a selling price equal

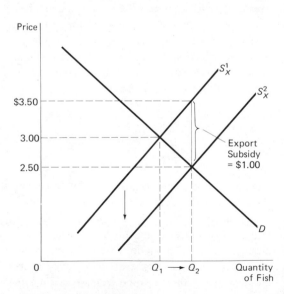

FIGURE 14-2 Economic Effects of an Export Subsidy (World Market for Fish)

to \$3.00 per unit. The cost-reducing effects of an export subsidy—say, equal to \$1.00—will result in a downward shift of the export supply curve by \$1.00 from S_x^1 to S_x^2. Such a downward shift reflects the fact that because of the subsidies offered to export production, exporters are willing to accept a lower price from consumers for each unit of export than they were under free trade. As is evident from Figure 14–2, the effect of the export subsidy will be (as anticipated) to increase the quantity of exports—from Q_1 to Q_2. The price of the export good to foreign consumers will fall from \$3.00 to \$2.50 as a result of the export subsidy. However, when the \$1.00 per-unit subsidy is added to the selling price of the exporting firms, the actual receipts accruing to those firms will increase (to \$3.50 in our example). Thus an export subsidy is a policy instrument which can result to an increase in output and employment in the export sector.

It should be noted that, although export subsidies accomplish these particular objectives, they are not achieved without cost to the exporting country. First, the subsidy payment is a cost to the government and the public it represents. Second, the price actually received from the foreign country for exports (\$2.50) has fallen from its free trade level (\$3.00). This decline in the price of exports, of course, implies that the nation's terms of trade will have worsened, lowering the welfare of the exporting country.

Examples of Export Subsidies

subsidized export credit

As mentioned above, export subsidies are quite often veiled, assuming a form that makes it difficult to detect the policy as an export subsidy. An example of such an export subsidy, and one which is used quite frequently, is the subsidization of export financing. In the United States, the Export-Import Bank facilitates the financing of purchases of U.S. export produc-

234   NONTARIFF BARRIERS

tion by either providing private banks with guarantees on credit they extend to foreign consumers, or by directly financing such purchases with credit granted to foreign consumers at below the private market rates of interest. All major trading nations have similar arrangements. Clearly, increasing the availability of credit to foreign purchasers of exports, and easing the terms upon which that credit is granted, will lead to greater sales of exports than would otherwise be the case.

The subsidization of export credit led to a serious dispute among the major industrialized countries in 1981. Because of the high interest rates prevailing at that time, many of those nations were lending money for export sales at rates well below the market rates of interest that they had to pay to acquire the funds. Thus these lending agencies were losing money, and consequently the agencies themselves had to be subsidized by their governments. To reduce its losses, the U.S. Export-Import Bank raised its lending rate to 10 3/4 percent. This rate was approximately 2 percentage points higher than the European nations were offering and almost 4 percentage points higher than the rates offered by the Japanese. Obviously, U.S. exporters were at a competitive disadvantage in the contest for sales to third countries.

The Reagan administration placed strong diplomatic pressure, as well as threatening an all-out export credit war, on the European nations and Japan to raise their rates closer to the market rates of interest. A compromise between the United States and Europe was reached in late 1981 which called for the European nations to raise their rates to the levels of the U.S. Export-Import Bank. However, Japan, which had market interest rates several points below those prevailing in the United States and Europe, refused to increase its export-credit rates to the levels prevailing in the United States and Europe. This problem will probably remain unsettled as long as the level of interest rates differs worldwide.

tax policies toward export earnings

Another U.S. program designed to promote export performance through "indirect" subsidization, has been a provision of the Revenue Act of 1971 that permits U.S. exporters to establish export subsidiaries known as DISCs (Domestic International Sales Corporations). DISCs are essentially paper corporations which can be allocated a significant portion of the export-related income of the parent firm. Income allocated to a DISC is given favorable tax treatment, as payment of taxes on one-half of the export-related profits allocated to a DISC can be deferred. Such favorable treatment reduces the costs to U.S. firms of export activity, and will increase their ability to compete in the world markets.

As might be expected, export subsidies in any form will be quite unpopular with other nations whose domestic industries must compete against such subsidies. In fact, export subsidies on industrial products are strictly forbidden under GATT provisions, and partially with regard to agricultural trade. As a result, importing countries whose industries must compete against subsidized foreign production have frequently countered with retaliatory trade restrictions. The nature of these retaliatory trade measures will be discussed in detail in a later section of this chapter.

Export Restrictions

Although the majority of export trade policies are directed toward the promotion of export sales, there have been frequent instances of government efforts to restrict the flow of exports leaving their borders. What possible reasons would a national government have for reducing the flow of employment-generating exports? There exist several possible motivations, both economic and noneconomic, for restricting export sales. First, a nation may wish to reduce the inflationary effects of abnormally high foreign demand. By restricting export sales, the supply of the good within the domestic market will rise, holding down the price faced by domestic consumers. Second, by restricting the export of a good and thereby reducing its world supply, the world price of the export product may be driven upward, improving the exporting nation's terms of trade. Third, a nation may desire to conserve limited supplies or avoid physical shortages of an export good. There exists a fourth motive for restricting exports, which is particularly important to nations that wish to develop domestic processing industries and which are dependent on raw materials that are exported. Export restrictions on raw materials would guarantee the domestic industry access to the raw materials needed in processing, as well as hold down the cost of the inputs to the domestic industry.

Controls on exports can also be employed for foreign policy motives. If an exporting nation wishes to "punish" a foreign nation for what it views as unacceptable foreign policy behavior, the nation may restrict the supply of an important commodity to that nation. In so doing, the exporting nation may evoke political concessions from the foreign nation. For example, the oil embargo that the Arab oil-producing nations imposed against the United States and the Netherlands in 1973–1974 was an attempt to punish those countries for their support of Israel in the Middle East.

DOMESTIC POLICIES THAT INFLUENCE TRADE PATTERNS

Frequently, policies that are directed primarily at purely domestic objectives have an indirect and sometimes significant impact on international trade. In this section let us briefly examine two examples of such policies.

Domestic Subsidies

Domestic subsidies granted to domestic producers are usually intended to increase the total output of the domestic producers without concern as to whether such a policy affects trade patterns. However, just as in the case of explicit export subsidies, domestic subsidies, because of their cost-reducing effects, will enhance the worldwide competitiveness of the domestic producers, possibly leading to an increase in export sales. If the country is a net importer of the subsidized commodity, the resulting increase in domestic output will tend to displace imports of the product.

Differing Domestic Tax Structures

The United States and the European governments employ quite different tax systems to collect revenue to finance their operations. The United States system is based primarily on corporate and individual income taxes, which are "direct" taxes, while the European nations depend primarily on a national value-added tax system, which is an "indirect" tax. According to economic theory, indirect taxes, including the value-added tax, are passed on to consumers in the form of higher prices, while income and other direct taxes reduce profits without raising prices. Because of the alleged difference in the effect of the two types of taxes on the prices of the final goods, there are provisions in the GATT that permit *destination principle border tax adjustments*. With destination border tax adjustments, exports that are subject to indirect domestic taxes may have those taxes rebated to the domestic producer. In addition, imports are subject to the indirect national taxes of the importing country (as well as existing import tariffs). However, no such adjustments are permitted for direct taxes. Obviously, adjustments by countries that employ a system of indirect taxes (such as the European nations) will enhance the competitiveness of their exports and reduce the competitiveness of foreign imports. On the other hand, nations relying on direct taxes will not realize these advantages.

Critics of the existing rules note that experience suggests that both direct and indirect taxes result in higher prices in the long run. If so, they argue, goods subject to direct taxes should also be eligible for border tax adjustments. Under the present system, U.S. producers must bear the burden of U.S. income taxes and still attempt to compete with foreign producers, who are relieved of the burden of their value-added taxes. This issue has yet to be resolved, and, because of its complexity, probably will remain unresolved for the foreseeable future.

RETALIATORY TRADE POLICIES

When the flow of imports into a country increases, the losing sector in the importing nation will be the domestic import-competing industry. Sometimes the increase in imports is a result of normal economic developments (increased efficiency of foreign production, for instance), while at other times it may result from "unfair" trading practices of the foreign-exporting firms or governments. In response to the economic injury that the domestic import-competing sector might incur as a result of increased import competition, many trading nations have established mechanisms to address such a situation. These mechanisms involve trade measures which are to be imposed in retaliation against the increased flow of imports. Let us examine several of the retaliatory trade policies commonly used by the United States.[3]

[3]The United States is not the only nation having a set of retaliatory trade policies. Almost all industrialized nations have retaliatory policies similar to those of the United States.

Escape Clause Action

Domestic industries in the United States have recourse if they feel that an increase in import competition is a substantial cause of material injury to their operations. Such industries may present their case to the U.S. International Trade Commission (USITC). The USITC investigates the industry's claim and then reports its findings to the President. If the USITC finds that material injury has occurred, the President must determine what remedy is in the nation's economic interest; the remedy may be in the form of tariff increases, import quotas or "orderly marketing arrangements." The President may also refuse to implement an affirmative decision by the USITC, in which case Congress may force implementation of a remedy. As of 1981, there were six escape clause actions in effect. These are listed in Table 14–3, along with the retaliatory trade measure employed to restrict import competition.

Countervailing Duties

In an earlier section, we saw that the imposition of export subsidies by a foreign country will increase the quantity of foreign exports. The increase in foreign exports, of course, represents an increase in imports to the domestic-importing country. Because of the harmful economic impact of foreign export subsidies on the domestic import-competing industries, the United States has established a procedure to retaliate against imports which are subsidized by foreign countries. Basically, the procedure is for the affected domestic industry to petition the Commerce Department and the USITC to initiate a formal investigation. If the Commerce Department determines that, in fact, the designated imports are being subsidized and the USITC also determines that such imports are a cause of material injury to the domestic industry, a Countervailing Duty

TABLE 14-3

| Trade Measures Resulting from Escape Clause Actions, in Effect as of 1981 | |
Product	Retaliatory Trade Measure
Color television	Orderly Marketing Arrangements
Citizens band radio	Increased duties
High carbon ferrochromium	Increased duties
Industrial fasteners	Increased duties
Clothespins	Quota
Steel cookware	Increased duties

Source: U.S. International Trade Commission, *Tariff Schedules of the United States Annotated 1981* (Washington, D.C.: U.S. Government Printing Office, 1981).

Order is issued which directs the assessment of a countervailing duty on the imported good in question, equal to the amount of the export subsidy. The Countervailing Duty Order will be revoked once the practice of export subsidization by the foreign country is abandoned. Table 14–4 presents several examples of Countervailing Duty Orders issued during 1979 against imports found to be subsidized.

Antidumping Duties

The practice of dumping was discussed in Chapter 4 in the context of a monopolistic exporting firm attempting to maximize total profits through price discrimination; specifically, establishing a lower price for the sale of its goods to its export market than for sales to its own home market. Often, the motivation behind the practice of dumping by foreign exporters is suspected to be something other than simple profit maximization. For instance, foreign exporters are sometimes suspected of *predatory dumping,* whereby foreign producers set a lower price in their export markets only temporarily in an effort to drive out domestic competitors. Once the competitors in its export market are forced to leave, the foreign producer will then raise its price to some higher level. It is also thought that foreign producers may establish a lower export price in an effort to eliminate temporary surplus production by increasing sales in the

TABLE 14-4

| Examples of Countervailing Duty Orders Issued by the United States in 1979 | | |
Country	Product	Rate of Duty
European Economic Community	Tomato products	62.3%
Japan	Industrial fasteners	.2
Argentina	Nonrubber footwear	.9
Spain	Ampicillin	2.2
Canada	Optic sensing systems	9.0

Source: Office of the U.S. Trade Representative, *Twenty-Fourth Annual Report of the President of the United States on the Trade Agreements Program 1979* (Washington, D.C.: U.S. Government Printing Office, 1980).

TABLE 14-5

Examples of Antidumping Action Taken in 1979 by the United States		
Country	Imported Product	Trade in Millions $
France	Viscose rayon staple fiber	1.7
Canada	Methyl alcohol	14.7
Korea	Bicycle tires and tubes	14.5
Belgium	Sugar	.3
Italy	Perchlorethylene	1.7

Source: Office of the U.S. Trade Representative, *Twenty-Fourth Annual Report of the President of the United States on the Trade Agreements Program 1979*, (Washington, D.C.: U.S. Government Printing Office, 1980).

export market rather than disrupting the existing price structure in their own home market. Whatever the reason for dumping, firms in the importing country may be economically injured by the lower priced foreign goods.

Under U.S. law, domestic firms have an avenue of appeal to obtain trade measures to protect them from the practice of foreign dumping. Antidumping duties will be imposed if (1) the Department of Commerce judges that a competitive foreign good is being sold at less than fair value (usually the price set by the foreign exporter in its own home market) and (2) the USITC also determines that such imports are causing or threatening to cause material injury to the domestic industry. Table 14–5 presents a partial list of antidumping actions taken by the United States against foreign imports in 1979.

trigger price mechanism for steel products

During the 1970s, a considerable number of antidumping petitions were filed which were concerned with a variety of steel products imported from a number of countries. Although the cases definitely had their own individual characteristics, it became clear that the problem of dumping was related to the entire steel industry and to imports from many countries. In response to this situation, the *Trigger Price Mechanism (TPM)*, or reference price system, as it is sometimes called, was established in 1978 to protect the U.S. steel industry from foreign dumping. The TPM established a minimum price for imports of twenty-two steel mill products; the minimum price is called the reference price. If the price of imported steel is less than the reference price, an antidumping investigation is automatically initiated (or triggered) by the Commerce Department. The reference prices, although applied to imports from all countries, were constructed on the basis of production data from the world's most efficient steel producers, the Japanese, and are adjusted quarterly to reflect the changing costs of producing steel.

The intended aim of the TPM, obviously, is to placate domestic steel producers by artificially raising the price of imported steel. In so doing, imported steel will be discouraged as the higher priced domestic production will become more competitive. Has the intended effect of the TPM been realized? During its first two years of operation, government officials, as might be expected, contended that the TPM had been quite effective in achieving its goal of import reduction, as steel imports declined from 21 million tons in 1978 (18 percent of domestic consumption) to 17.5 million tons in 1979 (15 percent of domestic consumption). Most steel industry officials, although not entirely satisfied with the TPM, would agree that the TPM did lead to a stabilization in the industry's profit. In fact, one study suggests that domestic steel prices were 2 percent greater during 1979 than they would have been without the TPM.

The U.S. Steel industry, however, has rarely been satisfied with the manner in which the Commerce Department has administered the trigger price mechanism, and has periodically attempted to obtain even stronger restrictions on steel imports. In fact, in early 1982, domestic steel producers attempted to circumvent the TPM by filing for individual antidumping and countervailing duties against a number of foreign countries. As a result of the filing of these private cases, the Commerce Department suspended the TPM.

As these individual cases worked their way through the antidumping procedure (along with several countervailing duty cases against foreign steel producers), tensions between the United States and the affected foreign nations increased (particularly with the European nations). In an effort to diffuse these tensions, and at the same time arrive at a plan designed to handle the longer-term problems of steel imports, the U.S. Commerce Department in mid-1982 negotiated a voluntary export restraint with European nations that will limit their exports to a level equal to 5.75 percent of the U.S. market (their current share is 6.4 percent). In exchange for this agreement, the Commerce Department wanted U.S. complainants to drop their antidumping cases. Although the matter was not resolved as of September 1982, indications are that the U.S. producers will not accept the negotiated arrangement and will continue on with their complaints until the USITC makes a final decision.

Even when these cases are resolved, it is unlikely that the saga of steel imports into the United States will be resolved. The problems of the U.S. steel industry are not limited to foreign competition, and until these other problems are addressed, it is likely that the U.S. industry will continue to be in poor financial health. If recent history is any indication, the industry will attempt to solve these problems by seeking further protection from foreign competitors.

OTHER NTBs RESTRICTING IMPORTS

Government Procurement

Government bodies are major purchasers of goods and services. In 1979, for example, government agencies accounted for the purchase of 20 percent of the goods and services produced in the United Kingdom, 20 percent in West Germany, 10 percent in Japan and 20 percent in the United States. Even allowing for the fact that these totals include services which for the most part are nontradeable, the magnitude of these spending levels represents large potential markets for foreign producers. In their efforts to penetrate these markets, however, foreign producers often find themselves discriminated against by domestic governments that favor domestic producers. In most countries some form of preferential treatment seems to be extended to domestic producers in the contest for government sales. With the exception of the United States, most countries do not have explicit laws to deal with government procurement practices. Instead, they discriminate in a more indirect manner. For example, governments might simply limit the number of firms permitted to bid on sales, or they might publicize a government contract in such a manner so as to make it difficult for foreign producers to gain equal access to the sale.

The policy of the United States is unique only in that it is explicitly set in law, in the form of the Buy American Act of 1933. As it stands today, the Buy American Act requires government agencies to make purchases from domestic firms unless their cost exceeds the price of a competitive foreign good by 6 percent (12 percent if the domestic items are supplied by small firms or are produced in areas where substantial unemployment prevails). Also, an executive order allows department heads to reject those guidelines and impose their own standards. The Department of Defense has taken such action and has granted domestic producers a preference of 50 percent.[4]

Valuation and Technical Procedures

From our earlier discussion of ad valorem tariffs, we know the importance of the method of valuation of imports in determining the amount of collectible duty. Trading nations often employ methods of valuation that are clearly intended to protect domestic industries from foreign competition. One of the most blatant culprits in recent years was the American Selling Price (ASP) system of valuation,[5] which was applied by the United States, primarily to imports of benzoid chemicals and rubber-soled footwear. Under this system the ad valorem tariffs on these products were applied not to the value of the foreign import, but to the price of the domestic output. Since the price of the domestic output usually exceeded the price of competitive import products, the ASP system increased the tariff

[4]During the Tokyo Round of multilateral trade negotiations (completed in 1979), a Government Procurement Code was negotiated by the participating countries, to which the United States was party. To conform to this code, certain aspects of the Buy American Act will become inoperable. More will be said on the Tokyo Round and the Government Procurement Code in Chapter 16.

[5]It should be recalled from the previous chapter that under the Valuation Code negotiated in the Tokyo Round, the United States agreed to drop the American Selling Price procedure. However, it has been replaced by a procedure which, although it conforms to the code, still is quite restrictive for the products formerly covered by the ASP.

burden on the imported goods. More will be said regarding the ASP, as an issue in trade negotiations, in Chapter 16.

Health and Safety Regulations

Many countries, in recent years, have legislated health and safety standards for a vast array of traded products. As might be expected, the stringency of these laws varies considerably between countries, as does the application of the laws. In fact, importing nations often apply the standards in a manner designed to curb the flow of imports. In 1981, U.S. exporters of pharmaceuticals complained bitterly about the elaborate safety standards test imposed by the Japanese. It was not uncommon for the process to take up to two years to complete, even though the U.S. products had previously achieved U.S. and world safety approval. In fact, the exporters charged that the procedure seemed to drag out just long enough for Japanese companies to develop competing goods.

QUESTIONS AND EXERCISES

1. How do the economic effects of a tariff differ from those of an import quota? In the long run, do you believe that import quotas or tariff policy will be the most effective instrument in restricting trade? Why?

2. Is there a difference between an import quota and an Orderly Marketing Arrangement? If so, explain. Do you believe that OMAs (or VERs) offer a more attractive trade policy instrument (from a diplomatic point of view) than import quotas?

3. What are the economic motives of a nation that imposes policies designed to restrict exports?

4. How might the pollution control requirements imposed on automobiles sold in the United States affect the flow of imports into the country?

5. An important input in the production of polyester fibers is natural gas. Natural gas prices in the

United States are subject to price controls which artificially maintain its price below world levels. Do you believe that such price controls are non-tariff barriers to trade? Why or why not?

6. How do export subsidies affect the pattern of world trade? Cite a specific example of an export subsidy, and how would it affect the flow of trade.

7. Explain how the following policies may act as a nontariff barrier to trade:

   a. domestic subsidies
   b. valuation of imports
   c. differing domestic tax systems

8. Define the following:

   a. countervailing duties
   b. antidumping duties
   c. escape clause actions

9. What do you think are the attitudes of trading partners of the United States toward the policy of escape clause action?

10. Describe three ways in which import quantities may be allocated under an import quota. Make sure you present the differences among the methods. Which of the methods do you believe is most equitable?

Arguments for and Against 15
Trade Restrictions

One of the central messages of the previous two chapters was that the application of restrictive trade measures would generally lower the economic well-being of the nation imposing those policies. That is, the gains obtained from specialization and exchange under free trade will be diminished by a restrictive trade policy. Given the costs involved with restricted trade, why is it that governments continue to impose new trade measures and resist the dismantling of existing trade barriers? In this chapter, some of the more common arguments offered by countries to justify their restrictive trade policies will be presented along with various counterarguments. In most instances, it will be seen that, on the basis of the economic welfare of the entire country, trade restrictions are difficult to justify. Before proceeding to those arguments, let us obtain an idea of the magnitude of the economic costs of restrictive trade policy by examining an estimate of the costs of U.S. trade restrictions.

THE COSTS OF U.S. PROTECTION

It should be recalled that the economic costs of tariff policy result from both the substitution of higher priced domestic output for imports (the production loss) and the decrease in the level of domestic consumption resulting from the higher prices that consumers face (the consumption loss). The combination of an increase in domestic output and a decrease in domestic consumption is reflected by a reduced volume of trade.

The *net* welfare losses resulting from either a tariff policy or a quota policy are shown in Figure 15–1, for the small country case, where the production loss is represented by the area of triangle B and the consumption loss by triangle D. If a quantitative restriction

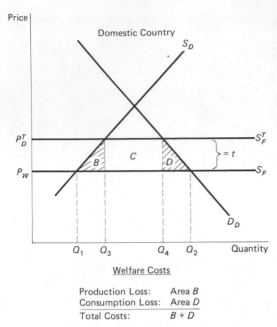

Price

Domestic Country S_D

P_D^T

P_W

S_F^T

S_F

$\} = t$

B

C

D

D_D

Q_1 Q_3 Q_4 Q_2 Quantity

Welfare Costs

Production Loss: Area B
Consumption Loss: Area D
Total Costs: $B + D$

FIGURE 15-1 The Welfare Costs of Tariff Policy: The Small Country Case

of imports were administered by the exporting country, as in the case of Orderly Marketing Arrangements, there would be an additional loss since a portion of the quota profit (area C) would likely be garnered by the foreign exporting firms.

Stephen Magee attempted to measure empirically the welfare costs to the United States of maintaining the system of import tariffs and

quantitative restrictions that was in place in 1972 (after the Kennedy Round of trade negotiations), by estimating the dollar size of the production and consumption loss triangles. Specifically, Magee estimated the annual benefits that would accrue to the United States if the import restrictions on three categories of imports were removed: (1) imports subject to a tariff and which were directly competitive with domestic products, (2) imports subject to a tariff and which had no domestic competition and (3) imports subject to quantitative restrictions. The results are summarized in Table 15–1.

According to Magee's estimates, the total annual welfare cost to the United States of maintaining its 1972 level of tariffs and quantitative restrictions was approximately $4 billion. It should be noted that the $4 billion estimate does not include the costs of NTBs other than quantitative restrictions, of which there are many, nor does it include the administrative costs of trade policies.

It is interesting to note an updated estimate of the costs of U.S. protection developed by Dale W. Larson.[1] Following the exact meth-

[1]See Dale W. Larson, "The Cost of Import Protection in the United States," Discussion Paper Series, Department of Treasury, May 25, 1979 (unpublished manuscript).

TABLE 15-1

Estimated Costs (annual, 1972) to the United States of Import Restrictions (billions of dollars)			
	Directly Competitive Imports (tariffs)	Noncompetitive Imports (tariffs)	Quantitative Restrictions	Total
Total welfare costs ($B + D$)	.29	.2	3.6[a]	4.09
Consumption loss (D)	.11	.2		
Production loss (B)	.18			

Source: Stephen Magee, "The Welfare Effects of Restrictions on U.S. Trade," *Brookings Papers on Economic Activity,* August 1972, pp. 645–705.
[a]$1.2 billion of this amount is accounted for by the loss of the quota profit to foreigners.

odology of Magee, Larson estimated that the net welfare costs of the U.S. protective scheme that was in place in 1978 equaled approximately $4.2 billion. If the welfare-increasing effects of the elimination of oil import quotas are ignored, Larson estimates that the social cost of protectionism increased between 1972 and 1978 on the order of 225 percent, compared to the growth in GNP of 200 percent.

Thus it is evident that the trade restrictions of the United States are quite costly to society and these costs do not appear to be diminishing. The United States is not alone, as all trading nations maintain a system of restrictive trade measures, and thus incur the costs of protection as well. Let us now turn to the question of why governments insist on undertaking restrictive trade policies despite the economic costs of such policies.

TERMS OF TRADE ARGUMENTS

Import Restrictions and the Terms of Trade Effect

In Chapter 13 it was demonstrated that if the domestic importing country is assumed to be a large country, then the imposition of a tariff on an imported good would lead to a fall in its world price,[2] the price received by foreign producers. Both the free trade situation and the price and quantity effects of tariff policy under the large country assumption are depicted in Figure 15-2 (which is reproduced from Figure 13-3).

Upon the imposition of a $1.00 specific tariff

[2] Under the large country assumption NTBs to imports will also lead to a fall in the world price.

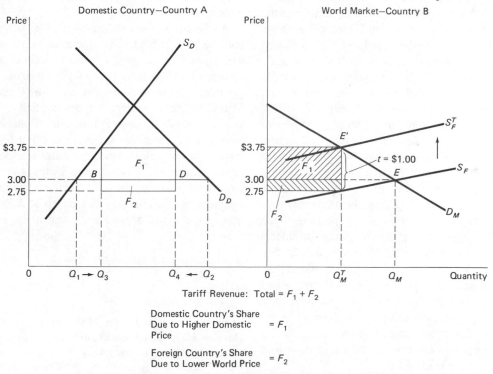

FIGURE 15-2 Economic Impact of a Tariff: Large Country Case

by country A (the domestic, importing country), the price received by foreign producers of country B will fall from $3.00 per fish to $2.75 per fish. The tariff-inclusive price encountered by domestic consumers in country A will of course equal $3.75. Because $1.00 per unit of fish imports is collected by the government of country A in the form of tariff revenue, the quantity of imports to country A under the tariff ($Q_4 - Q_3$) will be obtained from country B at a lower price ($2.75) than under free trade ($3.00). If the prices of country A's exports remain unchanged, the decline in the price of its imports implies that country A's terms of trade (the ratio of export prices to import prices) will increase. From previous chapters we know that an increase in a country's terms of trade will, by itself, result in an improvement in the economic welfare of that country.

We can determine the exact magnitude of the gains to country A that result from its improved terms of trade. In the right-hand side of Figure 15–2, total tariff revenue is equal to the area F_1 + F_2 ($1.00 \times Q_M^T$). The burden of this tariff payment is divided between country A and country B. Although the $1.00-per-unit tariff is collected from foreign producers, they have shifted a portion of the tariff burden to domestic consumers by raising their selling price by $.75 to $3.75 per unit. Thus consumers, by paying a higher price for imports, are absorbing the portion, F_1 ($.75 \times Q_M^T$), of the total tariff payment. However, the remaining portion of the tariff payment, F_2, is borne by foreign producers who receive a price ($2.75) which is $.25 less than their free trade price. That is, country A, by paying a lower price to country B, has shifted a portion of the tariff costs to country B. The area F_2 represents the gains to country A resulting from the reduced import price that it actually pays foreign producers; this gain is called the *terms of trade effect*.

To determine the *net* change in the economic welfare of the tariff-imposing country, the gains resulting from the improvement in the terms of trade, area F_2, would have to be weighed against the production and consumption losses associated with the tariff, areas B and D, respectively, in Figure 15–2. Policymakers in the large country case, then, should set a tariff level that maximizes the gains associated with the improvement in the terms of trade relative to the loss in welfare caused by the reduced volume of trade; such a tariff is referred to as the *optimum tariff*. The optimum tariff rate will lie between a zero tariff rate and a prohibitive tariff rate. If a tariff were set so high that imports were eliminated (a prohibitive tariff), there would be no tariff revenue collected (or import price reduction) and thus no terms of trade effect. If, on the other hand, a zero tariff rate were set, there would again be no import price reduction or tariff revenue collected, and thus no terms of trade effect.[3]

As the large country label suggests, a country must be large enough to be able to influence the world price of the good if it is to employ an optimum tariff policy. One of the most likely candidates for large country status is the United States, which is a large importer, relative to world demand, of several products. Examples include such consumer products as color televisions and bicycles. Also, the European Economic Community, which establishes a common tariff policy for its members against nonmember imports, may as a group be able to influence the world price for some of its im-

[3]The optimum tariff rate, t^*, is equal to:

$$t^* = \frac{1}{\varepsilon_s^m},$$

where ε_s^m is equal to the elasticity of import supply. This implies that the optimum tariff rate will be greater (lower), the more inelastic (elastic) is foreign import supply. Recall that in the small country case the ε_s^m is infinite (perfect elasticity). This implies that the optimum tariff in that case would equal zero.

ported products. Although examples of the large country case may exist for individual traded products, one would be hard pressed to discover a single country, which by its tariff policy alone, could alter the prices of a large enough portion of its import bundle to significantly improve its overall terms of trade.

Although optimum tariff policy does provide a justification, on the grounds of economic welfare, for an importing nation to raise tariffs, such a policy is only beneficial to the importing country; any gain accruing to the importing country because of a lower import price implies a loss to the foreign exporting country. This is so since the decline in the price of the traded good represents a fall in the price of the foreign country's exports. If the foreign nation recognizes the transfer in economic welfare from itself to the tariff-imposing nation, the foreign country may respond in kind; imposing a retaliatory optimum tariff on its imports from the domestic country. As a result of this retaliation, both countries may be worse off than they were prior to this round of tariff increases. The threat of retaliation and its welfare effects are analyzed in detail in Appendix 13A. Even from this discussion, however, it is clear that the threat of retaliatory trade policy reduces the potential benefits to a nation applying an optimum tariff policy.

Export Restrictions and the Terms of Trade Effect

Another instrument of trade policy that may lead to improved terms of trade is an export restriction (either in the form of an export quota or tax). As described in Chapter 13, a country which supplies a large proportion of the world's total production of a particular product, could raise the world price of the product by restricting its export sales. By raising the price of its export good, the nation's terms of trade would improve, raising its level of economic welfare.

Export restrictions, however, would also en-tail economic costs to the country imposing them. The reduced volume of exports would result in a decrease in producers' surplus greater than the gain in domestic consumers' surplus. To determine the net welfare effect of an export restriction, the benefits of an improved terms of trade would have to be weighted against the costs of a lower volume of exports. Policymakers, then, would desire to establish an export restriction (either a tax or a quota) which maximized the net benefits of the improved terms of trade.

The use of export restrictions for the purpose of improving a nation's terms of trade is much more common in practice than the use of optimum import tariff policy. This results from (1) the fact that the exports of many countries are concentrated in fewer products than is their menu of imported goods and (2) the fact that many exporting nations are large enough producers of a product to be able to influence the world price of the commodity. Thus it is more likely that a single nation will be able to influence the price of an export product that accounts for a substantial proportion of its export bundle, than for a single nation to be able to influence the price of an import product that accounts for a significant proportion of its total imports.

This situation is particularly true in the case of many developing nations, for whom a significant portion of their exports are accounted for by a few products. For example, in Jamaica, only three products, alumina, bauxite and sugar, account for over three-fourths of the total value of export sales. Also, Jamaica is one of the world's largest suppliers of bauxite, and thus could increase the price of bauxite by reducing its supply. Thus, many developing nations, faced with situations that are similar to that of Jamaica, have attempted to control the flow of their export products to the world market, either individually or collectively, in an effort to improve their terms of trade. We will have much more to say (in Chapter 20) concerning the exact methods employed by the developing nations to control export flows. For now it is important to understand that the use of export restrictions by a nation, to improve its terms of trade, is another economic justification for trade restrictions.

DOMESTIC EMPLOYMENT OBJECTIVES

One of the effects of a restrictive trade policy is to increase the level of output of the domestic import-competing industry. If, as should be expected, employment in the industry varies directly with output, policymakers could use trade policy to achieve domestic employment goals. The justification for pursuing such a policy would be that the benefits associated with the employment gains would more than offset the welfare loss associated with restrictive trade policy.

Given that an increase in employment in a particular industry is a desirable objective, the question policymakers must ask is: Does there exist a policy alternative that will also result in an increase in employment in the designated domestic industry, but in a less costly (economically) manner than trade policy? In fact, such a policy does exist in the form of a domestic production subsidy for the industry. From our discussion of subsidies in Chapter 13, it should be recalled that the effect of a production subsidy is to reduce the costs of production to the industry. This situation is shown graphically in Figure 15–3, where it is assumed that the country is importing the traded good, and is a small country.

Under unsubsidized free trade, equilibrium will occur at $3.00 per fish with the free trade levels of domestic output and consumption equal to Q_1 and Q_2, respectively. Imports, of course, would equal $Q_2 - Q_1$ prior to the subsidy.

If a domestic production subsidy is now enacted—say, equal to $1.00 per fish—the domestic supply curve would shift downward from

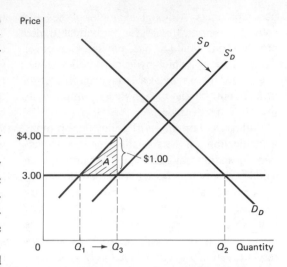

Figure 15-3 Economic Effects of a Domestic Subsidy

S_D to S_D'. The vertical distance between the two curves equals the amount of the production subsidy. Such a shift implies that, at every level of output, domestic producers require a lower price from consumers by an amount equal to the subsidy paid by the government. As a result of the subsidy, domestic production would rise to Q_3. The price to domestic consumers would remain unchanged at $3.00 per fish, and thus domestic consumption would remain at its free trade level. Furthermore, the price received by foreign producers for import sales would also remain unchanged, although the quantity of imports would decrease because of the increase in domestic production. The price actually received by domestic producers, however, has increased. In addition to the $3.00 per fish received from consumers, domestic producers will also receive the $1.00 per fish subsidy payment from the government, meaning that domestic producers will receive a total of $4.00 per fish.

The protection afforded the domestic industry is not without costs. The subsidy payment is a financial cost to the government (and the taxpayers it represents). In fact, the cost of the subsidy will exceed the gain to the domestic producers by an amount equal to the area of triangle *A* in Figure 15–3. This loss is a *production loss* in the same sense as the production loss that resulted from tariff policy. That is, the importing country has substituted higher cost domestic output for an equal quantity, $Q_3 - Q_1$, of lower cost imports. However, unlike tariff policy, there is no consumption loss associated with a domestic production subsidy since the price faced by domestic consumers remains at its free trade level. These results suggest that equivalent gains in domestic output and employment can be achieved by either domestic production subsidies or by import restrictions, but by employing the subsidy the welfare losses associated with reductions in consumption can be avoided.

It should be noted that, although domestic production subsidies may be preferable to tariffs or quotas in achieving domestic employment goals in import-competing industries, alternatives such as fiscal and monetary policy may be even more effective and less costly than either subsidies or trade policy in attempting to attain economy-wide employment goals. However, the point of the preceding discussion is to illustrate that there are often less costly policy measures than trade restrictions that can be employed to realize domestic economic objectives.

INFANT INDUSTRY ARGUMENT

Another argument in favor of using a restrictive trade policy is the so-called *infant industry argument*. According to the infant industry argument, temporary protection is needed to insure the competitiveness of a newborn domestic industry. Even though the domestic industry may not be competitive with foreign industry in its early years, the argument continues, as time proceeds the industry will be able to reap the benefits of growth and economies of scale. Once such a stage has been reached, the need for protection will have been eliminated, since the domestic industry will now be competitive with foreign producers on its own. Thus the infant industry argument suggests that protection will only be needed temporarily. This argument, however, suffers on several accounts.

Suppose that in fact the importing country is endowed with factors of production in such a fashion that, given temporary protection from import competition, the infant industry in question could eventually become competitive in the world market. During the period of time that the protective trade measures are in effect, however, we know that the domestic country will suffer losses in economic welfare. The analysis of the previous section demonstrated that equivalent protection could be offered the domestic industry in a less costly fashion if domestic production subsidies had been employed. Thus, given that policymakers deem that temporary assistance is needed for the long-term development of the industry, *trade policy* may not be the best means available to provide that protection.

If the newborn industry is truly capable of achieving long-term profitability, then neither tariffs nor subsidies should be needed to keep the industry afloat during its infancy. The industry, instead, should be able to borrow against future profits, in the capital markets, during the beginning stages of its operation. If conditions in the capital markets prohibit such borrowing, then government policies should be directed at improving the efficiency of those markets so that the future profitability of the industry is capitalized.

The infant industry argument for protection has traditionally been used by countries that are in their developing stages and that are attempting to achieve economic development through import substitution. The United States, in its formative years, attempted to protect its fledgling industries from European imports. For example, in the early 1800s the newly established New England cotton textile industry received special protection from British import competition. Nations which are less developed today continue to protect neophyte manufacturing industries from the imports of the developed nations. More will be said about the use of trade restrictions for economic development in Chapter 20, but for now let it suffice to say that such protection has not usually yielded the desired results. The primary reason for this lack of success has been the fact that, typically, the industries being protected do not enjoy a comparative advantage in production and therefore never become truly competitive, regardless of the level of protection. Because those industries never leave the infancy stage, the protection must be left in place on a permanent basis so those industries can sustain their operations.

INCOME DISTRIBUTION

In the discussion of the Heckscher–Ohlin explanation of trade in Chapter 3, it was argued that the opening of free trade would result in a redistribution of income from the factor used intensively in the production of the import-competing good, the scarce factor, to the factor used intensively in the production of the export commodity, the abundant factor. For example, if a country exported capital-intensive goods, a movement toward free trade would result in an increase in the returns to the owners of capital relative to the returns accruing to the scarce factor—say, labor.

On this basis, it might be anticipated that owners of the factor of production used intensively in the production of the import-competing product will have an interest in restricting free trade through protectionist trade measures. Protection, of course, would result in an increase

in the relative domestic price of the import-competing product, causing resources to be transferred from the export to the import sector. In the process, the price of the factor used intensively in the production of the import-competing good will be bid up. If the scarce factor of production were labor, one method of protecting its wages, then, would be to restrict imports through a protectionist trade policy.

BALANCE OF PAYMENTS

A trade policy that restricts imports has a side effect of improving the nation's balance of trade and payments; this effect is generally viewed quite favorably by policymakers. Upon closer observation, however, the impact of such a trade policy may not be quite so straightforward. Specifically, an import restriction, by raising the relative price of imports, may attract resources from the production of exports to the import sector, reducing the quantity of exports available to sell abroad. Such a development obviously would diminish any improvement in the balance of trade brought about by a reduction in imports.

A related argument for protection is based on the notion that an outflow of domestic currency is equivalent to a decrease in the nation's wealth. Thus a trade restriction on imports, by reducing the outflow of domestic currency expended on foreign produced goods, will, the argument contends, result in an increase in the nation's wealth. This argument sounds quite similar to that put forth by the mercantilists (see Chapter 2) and really is a vestige of that time. However, this argument is clearly fallacious. The real source of wealth in world trade lies in the gains from specialization and exchange accruing to those nations that engage in free trade. The flow of currency between countries serves only as a medium of exchange to accommodate the international flow of goods and services.

TRADE RESTRICTIONS AS A TOOL OF FOREIGN POLICY

Because international trade is a crucial link between the world economies, a disruption of that trade can cause serious economic injury to a trading nation. This is particularly true when the traded good is one which a nation must import because of a lack of domestic capacity to produce it. As mentioned in Chapter 14, nations that export goods to other countries heavily dependent on them as a source of supply have on occasion restricted the flow of the traded good for foreign policy reasons. The economic damage to the importing nation can be substantial. Because of this potential injury, trade restrictions on exports have been increasingly employed as a means by which exporting nations can "punish" foreign countries for "unacceptable" behavior—either politically or militarily. Recent examples of export restrictions that were imposed for foreign policy reasons include the oil embargo, in 1973–1974, that the Arab oil-producing nations imposed on the United States and the Netherlands for their support of Israel, and the 1980–1981 grain embargo that the United States imposed on the Soviet Union because of their invasion of Afghanistan.

WHY RESTRICT TRADE? NATIONALISM AND POLITICS

The analysis of Chapters 13 and 14 demonstrated that, with few exceptions trade restrictions will result in a lower level of economic welfare for the country which restricts trade. In this chapter we have presented the arguments that nations frequently use to justify their application of trade restrictions. In most cases,

those arguments were shown to be weak, either in logic or on economic grounds. Why, then, do nations continue to impose new restrictions and resist dismantling existing restrictions?

Most arguments for protection boil down to the economic interests of a particular sector within the domestic country. If the interests of that sector are threatened by foreign competition, the obvious cure is to restrict that competition through trade policy. However, many domestic firms and their workers are frequently threatened by *domestic* competition. In those cases, policy actions are not taken against the domestic competitors, and in fact such competition is frequently viewed as healthy. Why the difference in opinion concerning domestic and foreign competition? It is primarily a result of nationalism. To have a domestic firm injured by another domestic firm is somehow more acceptable to domestic residents and policymakers than to have the firm injured by a foreign firm. Because of this nationalistic attitude, domestic policymakers have traditionally been willing to sacrifice the economic well-being of the entire nation for the interests of an individual sector of the economy, by imposing trade restrictions.

Domestic residents outside the protected sectors seem almost unaware of the harmful effects that such protection may have on them. This was clear during the negotiations between the United States and Japan, in 1981, on the VER concerning automobile exports from Japan to the United States. The majority of the media coverage of the negotiations concentrated on the plight of the American auto industry, and how a VER would aid their plight. Very little mention was made of a study that estimated that a VER might raise the price of automobiles by 3 percent to domestic consumers. As long as domestic consumers, as a whole, remain unaware or are unconcerned about the price-increasing effects of restrictive trade policy, trade policy will provide a convenient tool to policymakers in their efforts to aid domestic industries that are being injured by foreign competition.

QUESTIONS AND EXERCISES

1. If an importing nation is a large country, what will be the welfare effects if the nation imposes an import tariff? What would the relative welfare effects have to be in order to justify the use of the tariff? Answer graphically.

2. How might a nation use its export trade policy to improve its economic welfare? Are there any costs involved with such a policy? If so, explain. Under what conditions would a country be able to employ such a policy?

3. Explain the infant industry argument for import restrictions. Do you believe this argument is valid? Explain.

4. Suppose you were asked to recommend a policy which would result in an increase in output and employment for an import-competing industry. Would you recommend import restrictions or domestic production subsidies? On what basis would you make your decision?

5. Explain why unskilled labor in the United States might favor import restrictions (use the Heckscher–Ohlin framework in your answer). Suppose a trading partner is willing to reduce its trade barriers to U.S. exports in return for a reduction in U.S. import restrictions. Would this fact lessen U.S. labor's desire for import restrictions? Why or why not?

6. Present two arguments for trade restrictions that are not based on economic motives. Do you believe these arguments are valid? Why or why not?

7. Suppose there is a national debate on whether the level of tariffs on steel imports should be raised. On one side in the issue are the United Steel Workers and U.S. Steel. On the other side of this issue is a major purchaser of steel products, General Motors. Present the arguments that each group would offer on this issue. Which group's argument is correct? In other words, if you were to make the final decision, what would you recommend?

8. Given that restricted trade generally lowers the economic welfare of the country that imposes the restrictions, why do you think nations continue to resist lowering trade barriers?

The Trade Policy of the United States: 16
Its effect on International Relations

The previous chapters have demonstrated that, despite strong arguments for unimpeded international trade, government policymakers continue to find reasons to apply restrictive trade measures. The trade policy of the United States is no exception. From its earliest days, the United States, as well as most other countries, has not been reluctant to impose trade measures for any variety of reasons. However, the overriding objective of U.S. trade policy has traditionally been to protect domestic industries from foreign competition. In 1789 Congress passed and President Washington signed a trade bill designed both to generate revenue and to protect the newborn industries of the United States. More recently, the Reagan administration, in 1981, negotiated a voluntary export restraint agreement with Japan that limited the quantity of Japanese automobile exports to the United States, in an effort to protect American automobile interests. Thus, despite the passage of two hundred years, U.S. trade policy has continued to be characterized by an aversion to allowing a domestic import-competing industry to be severely injured by foreign competition. Let us now examine the commercial policy of the United States in more detail and see how that policy has affected the trading relationships of the United States with the rest of the world.

THE TRADING ENVIRONMENT OF THE WORLD PRIOR TO WORLD WAR II

As Figure 16–1 shows, U.S. tariffs reached their highest levels during the early 1930s. These steep tariff levels were a result of the Smoot–Hawley Tariff Act, a protectionist piece of legislation passed in 1930. The tariff legislation that eventually evolved into the Smoot–Hawley Act was intended originally only to raise tariffs on agricultural goods.

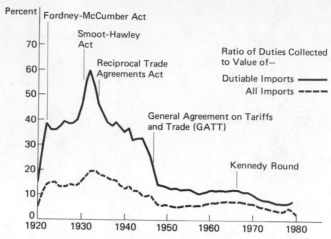

Percent

Fordney-McCumber Act

Smoot-Hawley Act

Reciprocal Trade Agreements Act

Ratio of Duties Collected to Value of—

Dutiable Imports ——————

All Imports ─ ─ ─ ─ ─

General Agreement on Tariffs and Trade (GATT)

Kennedy Round

Sources: John M. Dobson, *Two Centuries of Tariffs, The Background and Emergence of the United States International Trade Commission,* Figure 4, p. 34 (Washington, D.C.: U.S. Government Printing Office, 1976). Office of U.S. Trade Representative, *Twenty-Fourth Annual Report of the President of the United States on the Trade Agreements Program 1979,* Table 13, p. 157 (Washington, D.C.: U.S. Government Printing Office, 1980).

FIGURE 16-1 Ratio of Duties Collected to Value of U.S. Imports, 1930–1979

Although the 1920s had been a period of economic prosperity for the economy in general, the agricultural sector had wallowed in a depressed condition. In an effort to aid agriculture, by protecting it from foreign competition, congressional legislators representing agricultural districts pressed for higher duties on agricultural imports. In order to obtain the support from urban legislators needed to pass the higher agricultural duties, supporters of the agricultural duties had to agree to support an increase in tariffs on many industrial products as well. Thus a seemingly limited piece of tariff legislation evolved into the all-encompassing Smoot–Hawley Act that raised approximately eight hundred tariff rates on both industrial and agricultural products. The act resulted in an increase in the average ad valorem rate on dutiable imports from 38.5 percent for the years 1922–1929 to approximately 52.8 percent for the years 1930–1933.

During the 1920s the United States had grown into the world's largest market for traded goods. With the introduction of the Smoot–Hawley Tariff Act, access to this market was severely dimin-

ished. The heightened tariff levels of the United States, coupled with the arrival of the global Depression in the early 1930s, led to the deterioration of the trade balances of the trading partners of the United States, particularly those in Europe, and worsened the already depressed state of those nations' economies. The response to the Smoot–Hawley Act was a worldwide movement to impose retaliatory tariffs against U.S. exports.[1] The economic impact of these actions on the United States was, as expected, to worsen the effects of the Depression by reducing U.S. export sales; export sales declined in value from $5.4 billion in 1929 to $1.6 billion by 1932. In fact, the volume of all world trade dropped dramatically as a result of the low income levels and the high levels of protection that existed at that time.

[1]Foreign nations reacted in other ways to protect domestic production from foreign competition during the Depression. In particular, currency controls were frequently imposed, and many nations devalued their currencies to make their exports more competitive.

RECIPROCAL TRADE AGREEMENTS ACT OF 1934

The economic environment faced by the Roosevelt administration when it took office in 1932 was characterized by both depressed income levels and highly restricted trade. Despite the protective effects offered to individual sectors of the economy, the Roosevelt administration viewed these protective trade policies as a factor compounding the bleak economic conditions prevailing at that time. Although advocating an increase in free trade was but a minor factor in the overall philosophy of Roosevelt's New Deal, his administration (particularly, Secretary of State Cordell Hull) viewed trade as an avenue to recovery and a means to insure world cooperation and peace.

It was this line of reasoning that led the Roosevelt administration to introduce legislation to Congress that was intended to liberalize trade. The legislation that finally emerged from Congress in 1934 was the *Reciprocal Trade Agreements Act (RTAA)*. The most important provision of the RTAA was the transfer of the authority to reduce tariff levels from Congress to the executive branch. Under the RTAA the executive branch was granted authority to engage in bilateral trade negotiations. The President or his trade representative was permitted to negotiate tariff reductions of up to 50 percent in exchange for tariff concessions by trading partners of the United States. The method of negotiation was to be on an item-by-item basis, meaning that tariff concessions would be negotiated individually for all traded products. The trade negotiators were also to use the *most-favored nation* principle, whereby if a tariff reduction should be negotiated with one country, it would be extended to all "most-favored" nations.

The authority granted the executive branch under the RTAA was originally to be for a three-year period, but it was periodically renewed until it was replaced by the Trade Expansion Act of 1962. The RTAA, although not intended to dismantle tariff restrictions completely, nonetheless did lead to a significant reduction in tariff levels. Between the years 1934 and 1947, the United States negotiated separate trade agreements under the RTAA with twenty-nine foreign countries; these resulted in a decrease of the average ad valorem tariff rate on dutiable imports from 48 percent to 25 percent.[2] In addition, the RTAA provided a crucial first step toward the establishment of a negotiating framework which would lead to further reductions in tariffs in the future.

GENERAL AGREEMENT ON TARIFFS AND TRADE

As the major trading nations realized the gains from the liberalization of trade brought about by the tariff reductions of the 1930s and 1940s, there developed an increasing interest in attaining further reductions. It was evident, however, that the method of bilateral negotiations used to achieve the earlier tariff reductions contained some serious drawbacks. The most serious defect associated with the bilateral negotiations was the use of the most-favored nation (MFN) principle. To reiterate, under the MFN principle once country A had reached a bilateral agreement with country B on reciprocal tariff reductions, those tariff concessions would automatically be extended to country A's other trading partners which held MFN status. So, as a result, when country A entered into bilateral negotia-

[2]This decrease overstates somewhat the decline in tariffs directly resulting from negotiations under the RTAA. Because many of the tariffs at that time were specific tariffs, increases in the prices of traded goods accounted for a significant portion of the percentage decrease in protection.

tions with another MFN trading partner—say, country C—negotiators of country A had little to offer in the way of concessions to country C, in return for tariff reductions on its export sales to country C, since country C had previously been extended such concessions under the MFN provision. Because of this defect in the existing system of negotiations, as well as the increased use of nontariff barriers by some countries, it became clear to the major trading nations that a new, comprehensive approach to international commercial policy was needed.

The first attempt to create an international framework designed to facilitate a comprehensive, multilateral approach to trade policy was an effort by the United Nations. In 1948 a conference sponsored by the United Nations produced a charter for the International Trade Organization (ITO), which was to provide the ground rules for international trade and oversee its regulation. The ITO was to be an affiliate of the United Nations. The charter of the ITO was long and complicated and kindled fears among foes of free trade within the United States that U.S. domestic economic policy would be regulated by some of the provisions of the ITO. Because of a lack of support for the ITO in Congress, the Truman administration withdrew it from consideration in 1950.

However, the United States was anxious to get the process of trade liberalization under way. Knowing that the ratification of the ITO charter by Congress would be time-consuming, if it were ratified at all, the United States, in 1947, organized a conference of eighteen nations[3] with the objective of negotiating a comprehensive agreement on trade policy. The conference participants agreed that any pact reached would be temporary in nature, pending the creation of the ITO.

[3]By the end of this conference the number of participants had grown to twenty-three.

The negotiations for tariff reductions within this group were conducted bilaterally on a product-by-product basis. The results of these negotiations were then brought together to form a comprehensive, multilateral agreement, which became known as the *General Agreement on Tariffs and Trade (GATT)*. The GATT was formally adopted by the conference in 1947. The provisions contained in this agreement did not require the approval of Congress, since the President was already empowered to negotiate reductions in tariffs.

The results of this first round of negotiations under the auspices of the GATT were quite impressive in the area of tariff reductions, affecting nearly forty-five thousand traded products, or two-thirds of world trade. Equally important, the agreement reached by the participating countries contained general provisions governing the conduct of international trade, as well as specific codes regarding the use of certain nontariff barriers. Let us briefly discuss the main principles of the GATT.

1. Trade is to be conducted in a nondiscriminatory manner, meaning that a nation's trade policy should be applied equally to all countries. To guarantee adherence to the principle of nondiscrimination, GATT requires member nations to use a most-favored nation policy when applying tariffs.

However, the GATT does permit discrimination under the guise of preferential trading agreements (to be discussed in Chapter 17), whereby a group of countries may completely eliminate trade restrictions between them, yet maintain trade restrictions against nonmember nations. An example of such an arrangement is the European Economic Community.

2. GATT also bans the use of quantitative restrictions on trade. However, exceptions are made for countries experiencing balance-of-payments difficulties and for those countries which use similar quantitative restrictions on

domestic production. Also, developing countries may employ quantitative restrictions to aid their future development if they receive approval from GATT.

3. Although GATT has no power to insure compliance with its provisions, it does provide a framework within which disputes between two countries over trade practices may be negotiated. Also, GATT members are obligated to notify GATT of trade measures which they adopt unilaterally. In the latest round of negotiations, there has been an attempt to strengthen the role of GATT as a mediator in trade disputes. The GATT mechanism for presenting grievances has been employed by the United States on several occasions, such as the complaint lodged against Japan in 1979 regarding its restraints on the marketing of U.S. tobacco exports.

As mentioned earlier, the GATT was originally intended to be temporary, but with the failure of the ITO to materialize, it soon became apparent that the GATT was the only viable alternative that could act as an organization to deal with matters of international trade. Thus GATT became both an international agreement and an organization whose objective was to deal with issues of international trade. The importance of GATT is reflected by its growth in membership from twenty-three original members to over eighty nations today. The GATT member countries now account for over 80 percent of the value of world trade.

As an organization, GATT's primary contribution has been to provide a forum for periodic multilateral trade negotiations (MTNs) with the objective of negotiating the dismantlement of existent trade barriers. Between 1947 and 1962, five "rounds" of MTNs have been held under the auspices of GATT with the primary result (and intention) being the reduction of worldwide tariff rates. Table 16–1 shows both the scope (the percentage of dutiable imports whose tariffs were reduced) and depth (the av-

TABLE 16-1

U.S. Tariff Reductions in the First Five Rounds of MTNs, 1947–1962

GATT Conference	Scope (%)[a]	Depth (%)[b]
First Round, 1947	54	35
1949	5.6	35.1
1951	11.7	26
1956	16	15
1962	20[c]	20

Source: U.S. Tariff Commission, *Operation of the Trade Agreements Program:* First Round, *June 1934–April 1948,* Part IV; Second Round, *Third Report:* Third Round, *Fourth Report,* Table 1; Fourth Round, *Ninth Report,* Table 6; Fifth Round, *Fourteenth Report,* Table 1. Reprinted from John W. Evans, *The Kennedy Round in American Trade Policy–The Twilight of GATT?* (Cambridge, Mass.: Harvard University Press, 1971).
[a]Scope is the percentage of total dutiable imports whose tariffs were reduced.
[b]Depth is the average percentage tariff reduction.
[c]Estimated.

erage percentage tariff reduction) of the reductions in the U.S. tariff rates that came out of the MTNs. It is evident that these rounds of negotiations did result in a substantial decline in the overall levels of tariffs and probably contributed to a freer flow of goods and services. Since 1962, there have been two subsequent rounds of MTNs, the Kennedy Round and the Tokyo Round. Because of the special nature of those negotiations, they will be discussed in more detail below.

TRADE EXPANSION ACT OF 1962 AND THE KENNEDY ROUND

Up to 1962 the Reciprocal Trade Agreements Act had been the basis of the executive branch's authority to participate in multilateral trade negotiations. Rather than renewing the RTAA for a twelfth time in 1962, the Kennedy administration sought unprecedented power to negotiate a new multilateral trade agreement and toward that end submitted the *Trade Expansion Act (TEA)* to Congress. This act was passed in 1962.

There were several international economic developments at that time which precipitated the need for a new U.S. trade policy. Foremost was the emergence of the European Economic Community as an economic power. And with the pending membership of the United Kingdom, the economic strength of EEC would increase even further. With the United Kingdom included, the EEC at that time represented an economic union consisting of 160 million people and a level of output rivaling that of the United States. Moreover, the value of trade between the United States and the EEC members accounted for almost 90 percent of the value of world trade. Since many of the trade policies in effect or under consideration by the EEC had (or would have) a direct effect on the United States, it became clear to the Kennedy administration that negotiations were needed.

One of the policies of the EEC which concerned U.S. officials most was the preferential tariff arrangement established by the EEC. Under this arrangement, a common external tariff was applied by EEC member nations against nonmembers' exports. Meanwhile, substantially lower duties were placed on intracommunity trade. Obviously, such an arrangement discriminates against nonmember countries in favor of member nations' goods. Of equal concern was the EEC's common agricultural policy, which was being formulated at that time. Early indications as to the nature of that policy suggested that its impact on the agricultural exports of the United States could be quite detrimental. Since the U.S. trade position at that time had begun to worsen, any potential reduction in one of its primary export products was indeed a matter of concern.

The Trade Expansion Act of 1962 (TEA)

authorized the Kennedy administration to enter into the sixth round of multilateral trade negotiations under the auspices of GATT—these negotiations became known as the Kennedy Round. At this point let us briefly discuss the main provisions of the TEA of 1962.

The Provisions of the TEA

The tariff-cutting authority granted to the executive branch under the TEA was to last five years and permitted tariff reductions of up to 50 percent on an across-the-board or "linear" basis. That is, instead of negotiating tariff reductions on individual products, a negotiated reduction of tariff rates would be applied equally to all products. In addition, any existing tariffs of less than 5 percent could be completely eliminated, as could tariffs on products in which the EEC and the United States together accounted for over 80 percent of world trade. As in the past, tariff reductions agreed to by the United States were to be applied on a most-favored nation basis (which at that time excluded most Communist nations). All authority, of course, was dependent on reciprocal reductions in foreign tariffs that affected U.S. exports.

Another important aspect of the TEA was the provision regarding the treatment of factors of production dislocated by increased import competition brought about by tariff reductions. Previously, industries threatened by potential tariff reductions were protected by "peril points." *Peril points* were tariff levels (predetermined by the United States Tariff Commission), below which the duty could not be reduced by negotiators without congressional approval. The "peril points" themselves were based on potential material injury to the industry in question and clearly placed a constraint on U.S. negotiators. Under the TEA, domestic industries would not be able to escape the consequences of trade liberalization. Instead, the dislocated factors of production could either attempt to obtain special protection through escape clause action or be provided with adjustment assistance. Adjustment assistance to dislocated firms took the form of low-interest loans, free technical advice and tax allowances for losses resulting from increased trade liberalization. Workers affected would be aided through extended unemployment compensation, retraining for new occupations and relocation allowances to assist a worker's family in moving to where employment was available.

The Results of the Kennedy Round

The Kennedy Round of negotiations proved to be tedious and quite demanding on the participants, as it lasted almost up to the expiration date of the authority granted to U.S. negotiators by the TEA (May 1967). Questions as to whether the across-the-board method of reducing tariffs would have a differential impact on the EEC and the United States, as well as the negotiations involving sensitive industrial sectors (such as steel and chemicals), were among the factors

contributing to the extended duration of the talks. Also complicating the negotiations was the fact that the EEC did not finalize its own agricultural policy until midway through the negotiations. Many of its provisions regarding the treatment of agricultural imports proved to be unacceptable to the other negotiating countries. Since the United States insisted that negotiations on industrial and agricultural products proceed simultaneously, delays in agricultural negotiations prompted similar delays on the industrial front.

Despite these problems, the Kennedy Round of negotiations was concluded in May 1967 with some impressive results, particularly in the area of tariff reduction. Table 16–2 shows the average percentage tariff cuts on the nonagricultural imports of the major trading nations that were achieved in the Kennedy Round. The average reduction of the major industrial countries equaled about 35 percent. Tariff reductions on agricultural goods were not nearly as impressive, however. Difficulties in reducing agricultural tariffs arose because of such factors as the restrictive nature of the EEC's common agri-

TABLE 16-2

Average Tariff Reductions (percentage) Negotiated in the Kennedy Round on Nonagricultural Imports

Reduction Granted by	All Participants	On Imports from			
		U.S.	EEC	Japan	U.K.
U.S.	35	—	37	38	30
EEC	33[a]	33	—	36	—
Japan	NA	35	NA	—	NA
U.K.	NA	33	—	NA	—
Total	35	NA	NA	NA	NA

Source: John W. Evans, The Kennedy Round in American Trade Policy—The Twilight of the GATT? (Cambridge, Mass.: Harvard University Press, 1971). Reprinted from Chapter 15, Table 6.
[a]Including agricultural imports.

cultural policy and the fact that trade in agricultural products is restricted to a large extent by nontariff barriers. Even though the reduction of trade restrictions on agricultural products was quite limited, the participating countries were able to negotiate the International Grain Agreement, which established a minimum world selling price for wheat and obtained commitments from producing countries on food aid to developing countries.

The volume of trade affected by concessions in the Kennedy Round was approximately $40 billion, which represented about a quarter of world trade. Of the goods traded between industrial countries about 40 percent were affected by the concessions. The United States itself reduced tariffs on approximately 54 percent of its dutiable imports.

As noted above, the Kennedy Round failed to confront adequately the problem of nontariff barriers, for both agricultural and industrial products. In fact, the only significant action that was taken on NTBs was the passage of an antidumping code, which basically permitted a nation to impose antidumping duties only if it could prove that the practice of foreign dumping is a direct cause of material injury.[4]

The Kennedy Round was the first round of negotiations to recognize explicitly the special problems of trade confronting the developing countries. Specifically, the trade concessions negotiated between the advanced countries were extended to the exports of the developing countries without requiring them to lower their own import restrictions. However, the benefits accruing to those countries were minimal, since

the major tariff cuts were made on industrial products while the majority of the developing countries' exports were nonmanufactured goods.

POST–KENNEDY ROUND DEVELOPMENTS

The tariff reductions negotiated in the Kennedy Round were implemented gradually over the five-year period 1967–1972. During that time the economic situation of the United States, as well as its economic relations with the rest of the world, had changed. For the first time in this century, in 1971, the United States experienced a balance-of-trade deficit, with imports exceeding exports by approximately $2 billion. This worsening of the U.S. trade position had been developing throughout the 1960s. Particularly disturbing was the growing weakness exhibited in the trade performance of key manufactures. The trade positions of commodities such as motor vehicles, steel products, textiles, footwear and consumer electronics had shifted from surplus to deficits during the 1960s and early 1970s. There is no single explanation for the failure of American exports to maintain their earlier position. Factors such as domestic inflation, an overvalued dollar, the increased internal trade of the EEC and the increased competitiveness of Japanese production undoubtedly combined to worsen the trade position of the United States.

As might be expected, those sectors of the economy most affected by increased foreign competition were anything but in favor of further trade liberalization. In fact, they clamored for increased protection. This increase in protectionist sentiment surfaced in the trade policy of the United States. Because the United States was bound by the tariff reductions negotiated during the Kennedy Round, most of the new protectionist measures assumed the form of nontariff barriers such as bilaterally "negotiated" voluntary export restraints.

[4]The U.S. negotiators had also agreed to eliminate its American Selling Price system of evaluating chemical imports in return for an additional 30 percent cut by the EEC on its import tariffs on chemicals. However, the U.S. Congress failed to abolish the ASP so the agreement was never implemented.

TRADE ACT OF 1974 AND THE TOKYO ROUND

The international economic situation facing the Nixon administration in the early 1970s was characterized by a deteriorating balance-of-payments position and increased protectionist sentiment. Particularly disturbing to the administration, which basically adhered to a philosophy of free trade, was the increased use of nontariff barriers, not only by the United States, but by all trading nations. However, any efforts to liberalize trade further were not likely to succeed in such an atmosphere.

The balance-of-payments deficit, and particularly the balance-of-trade deficit, continued to worsen in the early 1970s (see Chapter 25). The problem became so acute that on August 15, 1971, President Nixon announced several drastic unilateral steps to deal with the situation. One of those measures was a temporary 10 percent surcharge on imports. Although the administration's actions were clearly protectionist in nature, they did provide the impetus for two necessary developments. First, they helped to bring about a much needed devaluation of the dollar, which by itself would lead to an improvement in the U.S. trade position. Second, Nixon's actions served as a catalyst for a new round of multilateral trade negotiations that began within a year. Prior to those negotiations, the United States dropped its surcharge, while its trading partners relaxed the retaliatory measures they had imposed on the United States. In fact, a few countries even granted some unilateral tariff concessions to the United States in an attempt to show their commitment to broader negotiations with the United States.

All that was needed to begin a new round of negotiations was American legislation granting negotiating authority to the administration. With the help of the lobbying support of business and the realization by Congress that the United States was becoming more and more dependent on export sales, authority was granted in the form of the Trade Act (TA) of 1974. However, the Trade Act was not totally removed from the protectionist sentiments prevailing at that time. It will prove useful, in understanding the restraints that United States negotiators were operating under, to examine the main provisions of the Trade Act.

1. The TA granted the President five-year negotiating authority to reduce tariffs by up to 60 percent. Tariffs of less than or equal to 5 percent could be eliminated. On the other hand, tariffs could be increased by 20 percent, ostensively to harmonize duty levels internationally, but really to give U.S. negotiators a bargaining weapon. The tariff reductions agreed upon were to be implemented over a ten-year period.

2. The President was authorized to negotiate reductions, eliminations or harmonizations of nontariff barriers to trade (NTBs). The agreements reached by the President on NTBs were subject to congressional approval. However, the ability of Congress to disapprove was constrained by the amount of time permitted for congressional consideration.

3. Import relief, in the form of escape clause procedures and adjustment assistance, was substantially liberalized. Increased imports now had to be a *substantial* cause or threat of material injury to the domestic competing industry for the U.S. International Trade Commission to recommend escape clause action. Previously, increased foreign competition had to be deemed the *major* cause of material injury. In response to an affirmative decision, the President could now raise the duty on the imports, impose an import quota, negotiate an Orderly Marketing Arrangement, offer adjustment assistance or take no action at all.

Adjustment assistance was detached from escape clause actions so that firms and workers injured by import competition could now apply directly to the Commerce and Labor departments, respectively, for relief. Assistance to workers could now extend up to fifty-two weeks at 70 percent of the worker's average weekly wage. Training, job search and relocation expenses were also provided. Qualified individual firms could receive technical assistance, loan guarantees and direct loans.

4. Retaliation was authorized against unfair or illegal trade practices by foreign countries. Procedural changes and time limits were changed to make retaliatory policies, such as antidumping action and countervailing duties, more effective.

5. Authority was granted to the President to extend most favored nation status to Communist countries—partially in response to the Nixon administration's efforts at detente. However, the granting of such status was limited by an amendment introduced by Senator Henry Jackson, which prohibited MFN status to those countries restricting Jewish emigration from their countries.

6. Authorization was granted to establish preferential tariff rates for imports from developing countries. The U.S. system of preferential tariffs and its effect on the developing countries will be discussed in detail in Chapter 20.

Tokyo Round—Negotiations and Results

With the Trade Act in hand, the United States could enter into a seventh round of multilateral trade negotiations—the Tokyo Round. The Tokyo Round began formally in 1973 with substantive negotiations starting in 1975. Just as the Kennedy Round proceeded at a painstakingly slow pace, so did the Tokyo Round (and for many of the same reasons). This round was finally concluded in April of 1979.

industrial products

The approach to negotiating tariff reductions on industrial products was based on the premise that the higher tariffs should be reduced proportionately more than the lower rates of duty. The rationale behind this approach was obviously to achieve a greater degree of harmonization between lower and higher rates. This objective was of particular importance to the EEC, which argued, correctly, that even though the average U.S. tariff on industrial products was not significantly different from that of the EEC, individual industry tariffs varied substantially, with the United States imposing rates of duty much higher than the average tariff rate on a number of products.

Thus, with the exception of certain import-sensitive products, industrial tariffs were reduced using a formula designed to achieve greater uniformity of rates across countries. The tariff reductions negotiated covered about $120 billion, or 90 percent of industrial trade among the major industrial nations. The average tariff rate reductions on all industrial trade are shown in Table 16–3 for the four major industrial trading blocs. These concessions are, for the most part, to be implemented in eight annual stages, beginning on January 1, 1980.

agricultural trade

With respect to agricultural products, all countries negotiated on the basis of direct responses to specific requests, submitted by their trading partners, for concessions on both tariff and nontariff barriers for particular products. Under this request/offer system, the average tariff reduction worldwide affected approximately 25 percent of world agricultural trade ($12 billion). The average tariff reductions on agricultural products are shown in Table 16–3 for the

TABLE 16-3

Average Percentage Reduction in Tariffs on Dutiable Imports, Tokyo Round

Country	All Dutiable Imports	Dutiable Agricultural Imports	Dutiable Manufactured Imports	Other Dutiable Imports
United States	29.6	17.2	30.9	51.2
EEC	29.3	30.0	29.0	31.4
Japan[a]	10.7	3.6	11.8	5.9
Canada[a]	28.0	20.0	28.1	48.8

Source: U.S. Congress, Congressional Budget Office, *The Effects of the Tokyo Round of Multilateral Trade Negotiations on the U.S. Economy: An Updated View* (Washington, D.C.: Government Printing Office, 1980).
[a]For Canada and Japan, the figures shown represent a reduction in applied rates.

four major trading nations. The negotiations resulted in reduced tariff rates or liberalized quotas that applied to about $4 billion of United States agricultural exports, or 25 percent of such exports. On the import side, the United States granted tariff reductions covering imports of $2.6 billion.

nontariff barriers

The one feature that distinguishes the Tokyo Round of multilateral trade negotiations from all earlier rounds is the emphasis placed on reducing NTBs. Since the level of tariffs has declined as a result of the earlier rounds of negotiations, the importance of NTBs in restricting trade has gradually increased. In an attempt to circumvent the effects of the reduced tariff levels, trading nations have increased their use of NTBs in both number and kind, particularly since the Kennedy Round. Participants in the Tokyo Round recognized this development and addressed the problem by negotiating codes regarding the use of various categories of NTBs. Because of the qualitative nature of NTBs, the codes are general legal documents; specific regulations will not emerge in many instances until

bilateral negotiations between the concerned countries result in a resolution, or until disputes between countries are brought before a GATT panel.

A multilateral code was also negotiated regarding import licensing practices, as was a code eliminating trade barriers on civilian aircraft. However, the countries were unable to reach agreement on a code governing safeguard measures (such as escape clause actions). Finally, an agreement was reached on formalizing procedures by which international disputes on trade practices could be resolved within the GATT framework. Any bilateral disagreement between member nations is to go before a GATT panel which will render a decision on the dispute.

Effects of Tokyo Round Negotiations on the United States

Obviously, any multilateral reduction in trade restrictions that is based on reciprocity will result in both winners and losers within each of the participating countries. Those sectors of the economy that compete heavily with imports will suffer to some extent by any reduction in protection, while the export-oriented sectors are likely to gain as a result of any reduction of trade barriers protecting their foreign markets. It is possible to identify, based on estimates, those individual sectors in the United States most likely to experience significant gains in output and employment as a result of the negotiated pact. By far the largest gains in output and employment will accrue to the agricultural sector and to those industries that employ sophisticated technology and highly skilled workers. Included in that group are the aircraft, the electrical machinery and components and the chemical industries. The U.S. industries in which output and employment are most likely to fall are generally those using labor-intensive production techniques and employing older, well-known technology. This group would include the apparel, the plastics and the china industries. This pattern of losers and winners is what might have been expected. Table 16–4 shows in more detail the estimated employment effects over the life of the tariff reductions (approximately eight years) for several U.S. industries, including both winners and losers.

It should be mentioned that special consideration was given by U.S. negotiators to those industries that are particularly sensitive to import competition. For example, the tariff reduc-

tions on textile imports were much lower (9.5 percent) than the overall average reduction on manufactured imports (31 percent), in an effort to protect the vulnerable U.S. domestic textile industry. In addition, many of the quantitative restrictions on textile imports were tightened to offset the reduction in tariffs. As a result of these considerations, job losses in the textile industry were minimized; the Department of Labor estimates that these losses will be equal to .3 to .5 percent of the current textile industry labor force over the course of the tariff reduction. Other import-sensitive domestic industries receiving special treatment included the rubber footwear industry and the leather industry.

Estimates of the effects of the tariff reductions on total employment in the United States suggest that the net effect will be small. The Department of Labor estimates a net loss of 300 jobs, while a study by Alan Deardoff and Robert Stern[5] puts the estimate at a net *gain* of 2300

[5]*An Economic Analysis of the Effects of the Tokyo Round of Multilateral Trade Negotiations on the United States and the Other Major Industrialized Countries,* Report to the Subcommittee on International Trade, U.S. Senate Committee on Finance, 96:1 (June 1979), pp. 92–108.

TABLE 16-4

Estimated Employment Effects of Tariff Reductions (in percentage changes of current labor force)			
Gains		Losses	
Industry	Percentage Change	Industry	Percentage Change
Semiconductors	3.2	Pottery and food utensils	− 22.7
Computing machines	3.0	Lace goods	− 5.8
Aircraft equipment	2.5	Jewelry	− 4.8
Electronic components	1.7	Motorcycles	− 3.2
X-ray apparatus	1.6	Optical instruments	− 1.7

Source: U.S. Department of Labor, *Trade and Employment Effects of Tariff Reduction Agreed to in the MTN* (Washington, D.C.: U.S. Government Printing Office, 1979).

jobs over the course of the tariff reductions. When Deardoff and Stern incorporate the effects of the negotiated changes in nontariff barriers into their analysis, they estimate the United States will experience a net gain of 15,000 jobs (only .02 percent of the current labor force in the United States).

THE NEW PROTECTIONISM

The protectionist sentiment characterizing trading relations prior to the Tokyo Round has not diminished significantly; in fact, some would argue that it intensified during the late 1970s and into the early 1980s. During this time there has been a proliferation of both unilateral and bilateral protectionist measures. The United States' part in this trend is reflected by the imposition of trade restrictions resulting from escape clause actions. At the end of 1981 escape clause relief had been afforded to six different products in the United States. Some of these were quite important and all were instituted since 1974. The escape clause actions in effect at the end of 1981 are shown in Table 16–5 (reproduced from Table 14–3), along with the dates that they were implemented and the trade policy taken to provide relief.

As it turned out, passage of the Trade Act of 1974 was something of a stimulus to the increased use of the escape clause mechanism. It should be recalled that the Trade Act of 1974 liberalized the conditions under which an escape clause action could be taken; now import competition has to represent only a *substantial* cause of injury to the domestic industry rather than the *major* cause of injury. As negotiations led to reductions in trade restrictions, escape clause actions provided a convenient means of maintaining special protection for import-sensitive sectors of the economy and, not surprisingly, their use has increased.

Other highly visible examples of recent protectionist acts on the part of the United States include the establishment in 1978 of the "trigger price mechanism," which sets a minimum price for steel imports (see Chapter 14) and the VER on automobiles that was negotiated between the United States and Japan in 1981. Even the Reagan administration, which has publicly espoused the virtues of free trade, has been guilty of participating in the new wave of protectionism. In addition to the voluntary export restraint pact applying to automobiles, that was negotiated with Japan in 1981, the Reagan administration extended (along with fifty other nations), in 1981, the Multifiber Agreement, which reg-

TABLE 16-5

Trade Measures Resulting from Escape Clause Actions, 1981

Produce	Retaliatory Trade Measure	Dates Implemented
Color television	Orderly Marketing Arrangements	1977
Citizens band radio	Increased duties	1978
High carbon ferrochromium	Increased duties	1978
Industrial fasteners	Increased duties	1979
Clothespins	Quota	1979
Steel cookware	Increased duties	1980

Source: U.S. International Trade Commission, *Tariff Schedules of the United States Annotated 1981* (Washington, D.C.: U.S. Government Printing Office, 1981).

ulates global trade in textiles (see later section) and imposed import quotas on sugar in 1982. The protectionist actions of the United States during the late 1970s and early 1980s have not, as might be expected, sat well with the trading partners of the United States, which have voiced their complaints loudly.

The United States, however, is by no means the only participant in the recent surge of protectionism. In 1980 and 1981, there was an abundance of restrictive trade measures that were instituted worldwide. Britain imposed import quotas on United States polyester and nylon yarns. The French government vetoed a French company's purchase of Japanese cargo ships and offered instead a $40 million subsidy so that the company could buy ships built in France. Also, French customs officials intentionally delayed the official certification of Japanese produced automobiles on technical grounds (such as safety and emission standards), even though unofficial certification was granted prior to the time the autos left Japan. And the Italian automobile maker, Fiat, tried to block a deal between Alfa-Romeo and Japan's Nissan Motors, a deal that would have opened the door of the Italian auto market to Nissan. Also, France and Italy placed quotas on Japanese automobile imports equal to 3 percent and 11 percent, respectively, of total domestic market sales.

In many ways, the final version of the agreement reached in the Tokyo Round is a reflection of the recent trends in international trade relations. Although advertised as a step toward freer trade, the pact on closer examination embodies many hidden aspects of protectionism. For example, many governments deviated from the tariff-reducing formula when it came to tariff reductions for their own import-sensitive sectors. In the previous section, we saw that the United States limited tariff reductions in several import-competing sectors, including textiles and footwear. Also, the negotiations failed to obtain a safeguards code to regulate such policies as

escape clause cases. As a result, countries remain free to impose discretionary trade restrictions under the banner of escape clause actions. There is the danger that unrestricted use of escape clauses or safeguard measures can largely offset the negotiated reductions in trade barriers. Finally, even though a number of specific quantitative restrictions were removed or reduced, no attempt was made to negotiate or establish guidelines for the eventual elimination of those types of policies. Even the nontariff codes that were adopted to cover quantitative restrictions have no provisions for further negotiated reductions in their use.

The recent increase in protectionism has had a very special impact upon the developing countries. In many cases the recent trade restrictions have been applied to products that account for a substantial portion of the developing countries' manufactured exports—such as textiles, footwear and television sets. Because many of the more advanced developing countries are emerging as major exporters of manufactured goods, it can be expected that, as their exports begin to threaten established industries in the developed countries, those exports will encounter similar restrictions. If so, any further spread of protectionism may be borne disproportionately by the developing countries.

What lies at the root of this recent surge in protectionism? Clearly, the general economic slowdown during this period of time contributed to the increased calls for protection. Also, a few protectionist measures can actually mushroom into a trend, if they are followed by retaliatory trade measures by the affected countries. In fact, the rules of GATT actually encourage such behavior. For example, if a nation imposes a unilateral quota on imports of a product from a particular country, that country, under GATT rules, is free to retaliate with import restrictions against products from the nation originally imposing the quota. Whatever the reasons, this recent trend is quite disturbing to advocates of free trade. Before concluding this chapter, let us examine in more detail recent developments in international commercial policy that have special significance for the future course of international trading relations.

Multilateral Quantitative Restrictions on Manufactures: The Multifiber Agreement

In Chapter 14 we saw that, in recent years, Voluntary Export Restraints and Orderly Marketing Arrangements have been used increasingly to restrict the quantity of imports. One characteristic of VERs and OMAs is that they are negotiated between the importing and exporting countries. These agreements, typically, are bilateral in nature when they are first negotiated, involving only one importing country and one exporting country. Because the exports of third countries are not included in these agreements, exports of these countries have typically increased as they replace the restricted exports of the country involved in the agreement. As a result, the importing country may have to extend the VER to include other exporting nations if it is to protect its domestic industry. Thus a bilateral agreement might possibly evolve into a multilateral agreement that controls a substantial quantity of the world's trade in a particular product.

This process of expanded coverage has occurred with several negotiated OMAs between the United States and a trading partner. For example, in 1977 the United States negotiated an OMA with Japan, limiting Japanese exports of color television receivers to the United States. In response to the void created by the restrictions on Japanese sales, Taiwan and South Korea increased their export sales to the United States. To continue to protect U.S. producers from foreign competition, the United States was forced to extend the OMA to cover sales from Taiwan and South Korea. Thus, what started out to be

a bilateral agreement expanded into a multilateral agreement that restricted the flow of much of the world's trade in color television receivers.

The most all-encompassing multilateral agreement, however, is the Multifiber Agreement (MFA), which applies to the world trade in textiles. The Multifiber Agreement includes over forty countries, and provides a framework for the "orderly" expansion of world trade in textiles. This framework allows nations to negotiate bilateral quantitative restrictions on textile trade. Under the MFA, importing nations are supposed to allow textile imports to grow about 2 percent annually. The United States had such agreements with twenty-one exporting nations in 1980.[6]

Trade Adjustment Assistance (TAA)

Trade Adjustment Assistance was described earlier in the chapter. The objective of TAA is to provide aid to workers and firms that are hurt by liberalized trade. In the case of workers who are dislocated because of freer trade, TAA can take the form of monetary compensation, training and payment for relocation costs. Firms, on the other hand, may be eligible for technical assistance, loan guarantees and direct loans.

TAA is viewed by many as an alternative to trade restrictions in the effort to protect import-competing industries. As trade is liberalized, resources that are temporarily dislocated by free trade can be financially aided by adjustment assistance until they move to the more efficient sectors of the economy. Or if these resources do not have the skills required in those sectors, TAA can provide those skills by offering training programs. Trade can thus be liberalized and

[6]The MFA was renegotiated in December of 1981. The new pact will govern world trade through July 1986. The new version is even more restrictive than its predecessor, as it gives the importing nations more latitude to restrain imports.

resources can be allocated to their most efficient use. Although such a program will be a cost to the government, it is argued that over the long run the benefits of free trade and the resulting efficient allocation of resources will outweigh those costs. Let us take a brief look at the experience of TAA in the United States.

As discussed earlier, TAA was first introduced in the United States by the Trade Expansion Act of 1962 (TEA). Under the TEA, the applicant had to prove that the "major" cause of its material injury was an increase in imports that was caused "in major part" by a reduction in trade barriers. The procedure for establishing eligibility was lengthy and complex. Because of its administrative complexity and strict wording, it was not until November 1969 that the first group of workers received TAA. Between that time and April 1975, when the act expired, thirty-six firms and approximately fifty-four thousand workers were certified as eligible for TAA (although only thirty-five thousand actually received aid). Total outlays under the TAA for that period equaled approximately $85 million.

The Trade Act of 1974 greatly liberalized both the criteria for eligibility and the size of the TAA benefits. Under this act, it was only necessary to demonstrate that increased imports contribute "importantly" to material injury, not that imports were a "major" cause of injury, as under the TEA. Under these liberalized terms, it is not surprising that in the first two years after the passage of the Trade Act of 1974 more than five hundred thousand worker requests for TAA were received by the Labor Department, four times as many as had applied during the previous twelve years under the TEA. Between April 1975 and May 1981 worker payments totaled almost $2.7 billion and were concentrated in such import-sensitive industries as automobiles, steel, apparel and textiles and footwear. These figures do not include training and relocation expenses, or the approximately $250 million in financial assistance to firms.

Because of its costliness, TAA fell under the Reagan administration's budget ax in 1981. Criteria were made stricter, as imports now had to be a "substantial cause" of injury instead of a contributing cause, and benefits were significantly reduced. Most union leaders were quite displeased, and vowed to protect their membership by lobbying for protectionist trade restrictions. Thus, in its twenty years of existence in the United States, TAA does not appear to have fulfilled its original objective.

THE ROLE OF JAPAN IN INTERNATIONAL TRADING RELATIONS—"TRADE RECIPROCITY LEGISLATION"

One of the most heated issues in recent years has been the role of Japan in international trading relations. Japan's trade position with other industrialized nations has been in surplus, and this surplus has been increasing in size over the past decade. During the 1970s, the United States incurred a cumulative deficit with Japan equal to about $47 billion. And in 1981 alone the bilateral deficit reached $15 billion. The story is quite similar in regard to the trade balance between Japan and the European nations. As might be expected, such a situation has generated much friction among the industrialized nations.

Why has Japan been able to accrue large trade surpluses with the United States? Have they resulted primarily from increased export sales or from restrictions on imports? It is true that the volume of Japan's export sales during the 1970s has risen faster than that of any other industrialized country (103 percent). This surge in exports has consisted primarily of high-technology, manufactured products. The next question, then, is: Have Japanese exports increased because of "unfair" trade practices, such as export subsidies or dumping, or because Japanese producers are becoming more efficient than their American counterparts? Although cases of unfair export trade practices have occurred, they are not as widespread as might first be thought. And when such practices have been identified by the United States, they have been met with retaliatory trade policies.

The overriding reason for Japan's impressive export performance is their increased competitiveness in the world markets. Japan's firms are typically much more export oriented than are U.S. firms. The general consensus by Japanese industry on the need to export is facilitated by a vast commercial–information gathering network that makes firms aware of export opportunities. Part of this network is sponsored by the government, while private trading companies, established by Japanese firms, also provide a vital link to world export markets. Another factor is the Japanese "industrial policy" since World War II. This policy has encouraged the development of key priority industries. These industrial policies in the past have included government credit allocation to priority industries in an effort to aid their capital investment.

It is interesting to note that Japan has not traditionally been an innovator in technology, but an imitator. Once having acquired the needed technology, they have improved it, and become a dominant force in the world market for products incorporating such technology. Whatever the reasons, Japanese exports of high-technology items have increased dramatically, and are quite competitive on the basis of price and quality.

Criticism of Japanese export policy has not been overly loud. Most observers recognize that, for many items, the Japanese are simply the world's most efficient producers (although this has not stopped the imposition of trade restrictions on Japanese export products). On the other hand, Japanese import policy has been subject to much criticism. U.S. exporters argue that one reason for the huge Japanese surplus with the United States is Japanese import restrictions. They contend that their products would be competitive in the Japanese market if those markets were open.

Although Japan's average tariff levels are among the world's lowest, exporters to Japan claim that their products are blocked by nontariff barriers. For example, U.S. producers of medical equipment and pharmaceuticals claim that their products are subject to an elaborate and time-consuming standards test, after they have already been tested for health and safety characteristics in the United States under equally stringent standards. The delay can be expensive, and often the delays seem to last just long enough for Japanese competitors to enter the market with their own products. Also, U.S. petrochemical producers argue that sales in the Japanese market are negotiated on an established basis among Japanese companies, with no opportunity for U.S. bidding, and semiconductor exporters continually complain about the discriminatory purchasing practices of the quasi-public agency, Nippon Telegraph and Telephone Corporation (NTT).

The Japanese respond that many of the barriers are more imagined than real. They contend that the real reasons for the lack of success of U.S. exporters is that their products are either noncompetitive in price or inferior in quality. Also, U.S. exporters are inflexible, unwilling to change the features of their product to accommodate Japanese consumers.

The view of the U.S. Congress is that the trade policy of the Japanese is, in fact, the dominant factor causing the U.S. deficit with Japan. This view is reflected by the so-called *trade "reciprocity"* legislation, directed at Japan, that was introduced in Congress in 1982. The reciprocity legislation would require U.S. trade retaliation against a country which maintains levels of protection on U.S. products greater than the levels imposed by the United States on similar foreign products. The concept of such reciprocity legislation is a significant departure from previous trade policy. In past trade negotiations, the trading nations have attempted to win concessions from trading partners by offering to lower their own trade barriers. "Reciprocity" legislation, on the other hand, attempts to obtain concessions, not by the promise of reciprocal reductions in barriers, but by the threat of greater barriers if the foreign markets are not opened. The implications of such a policy on global relations are staggering. Not only would it violate the principles of GATT, but it would, in all likelihood, lead to retaliatory reactions from the foreign countries affected by such a policy, potentially resulting in a global trade war.

The Japanese, in 1982, have attempted to diffuse this protectionist fever, by granting numerous unilateral concessions to U.S. products. The package of concessions included an easing of customs and product-testing, as well as advancing by two years the tariff reductions negotiated in the Tokyo Round. However, the Japanese steps are generally viewed as insufficient by U.S. trade negotiators and Congress. Specifically, the U.S. complains that the package does not go far enough in reducing agricultural trade barriers or simplifying the distribution system for foreign products.

As long as the bilateral imbalance between Japan and the United States exists, there is always the potential for a trade war between two of the world's major trading nations. If, as seems likely, the export-oriented producers of Japan continue to make inroads into the U.S. market in the future (with such products as semiconductors, robots and aircraft) and if the United States lags behind competitively, the imbalance will remain, regardless of trade policy. U.S.–Japanese trading relations loom as one of the most serious trade issues of the 1980s, an issue that will not likely be resolved in the foreseeable future.

QUESTIONS AND EXERCISES

1. Describe the following pieces of U.S. trade legislation:
   a. Smoot–Hawley Act
   b. Reciprocal Trade Agreements Act
   c. Trade Expansion Act
   d. Trade Act of 1974
2. What is the GATT? Describe how it came into being. In the area of tariff reduction, do you feel GATT has achieved its objectives? Why or why not?
3. What was the economic incentive to the United States of entering into the Kennedy Round of multilateral trade negotiations?
4. What was the most serious problem with the method of negotiating used under the Reciprocal Trade Agreements Act? How was that method changed?
5. What were the most successful results of the Kennedy Round of trade negotiations? In which two areas of trade liberalization did the Kennedy Round fall short?
6. Did all sectors of the U.S. economy accept the idea of increased trade liberalization in the years immediately following the Kennedy Round? Why or why not? Cite some specific examples of economic events to support your views.
7. Describe two provisions of the Trade Act of 1974 that significantly changed U.S. trade policy.
8. In what important way did the efforts in the Tokyo Round toward trade liberalization differ from those in all previous rounds? Do you believe the Tokyo Round was successful in those efforts? Why or why not?
9. Comment on the following statement: All sectors of the U.S. economy benefited from the results of the negotiations at the Tokyo Round.

10. Evaluate the following statement: With the tremendous success of the Tokyo Round in liberalizing the international trade environment, all trading nations have been enthusiastically undertaking actions designed to implement a free trade environment since the conclusion of those negotiations.

11. Select a recent development in trade world and describe its impact on trade policy. Do you think this situation will contribute to the further liberalization of trade?

CLOSING ESSAY:
The Future Course of International Trade Policy

The history of international trading relations projects mixed signals as to the future direction world trade policy may follow. Some of those events, such as the impressive reductions in worldwide tariff levels negotiated under the auspices of GATT, suggest that the trading nations of the world adhere to a philosophy of free trade and may be expected to push for further trade liberalization. On the other hand, such events as the recent surge in protectionist policies indicate that, in fact, policymakers of trading nations are unwilling to make the necessary changes that would make trade truly "free." With such ambivalent signals it is impossible to make any precise forecasts about the future course of trade policy. Rather than making such predictions, let us simply put forth some observations regarding trade policy in general and how future developments in international trade might affect trade policy.

First, it should be noted that, historically, protectionism has been at its height during periods of depressed economic conditions. Since the 1970s was a period characterized by unprecedented (at least since the Depression) disturbances and upheavals in economic conditions, it would follow that such a period would be one of heightened protectionism. If the economic conditions of the 1980s are also volatile, it can be expected that there will be periodic episodes of protectionism. A prediction on the future course of trade policy, then, would depend on the future course of general economic conditions.

Second, the pattern of past trade liberalization suggests that future liberalization may be quite difficult. Specifically, the present level of tariffs on the vast majority of manufactured products is quite low, implying that further reductions may not contribute greatly to an increase in the international flow of goods and services. Any tariff reductions of significance, then, would have to be for those import-sensitive sectors which have thus far escaped the full impact of trade liberalization—a politically difficult task. It also follows that any significant trade liberalization would have to occur through a reduction in nontariff barriers. However, nontariff barriers are usually qualitative in nature and are often not easily recognizable as trade barriers, making any future meaningful reduction a difficult task.

Also, past trade liberalization has been directed primarily toward manufactured goods rather than agricultural products. As a result, the agricultural sector is today the most highly protected of all traded product groups. Future liberalization of agricultural trade seems no more likely than in the past for two reasons: (1) many of the domestic support programs for agriculture are complemented by restrictive trade measures and (2) the agricultural sector of most nations is viewed by policymakers as a politically sensitive one, as well as a sector important to domestic security.

Third, the future course of trade policy will depend on the future problems of international trade. Included among these future problems are trade in services, such as banking and insurance, and the emergence of many of the developing countries as key participants in the trade of manufactures. It is estimated that trade in services accounts for approximately one-fourth of the value of all international trade. Furthermore, the growth rate of service trade is much greater than it is for trade in goods. Moreover, there is a growing link between trade in services and trade in goods. Sales of computers, for example, are often accompanied by trade in software and service contracts. It can be expected that this link will strengthen as new, technologically advanced goods emerge that require accompanying support services.

Already, there are strong hints of protectionism in the service trade. For example, in 1981, Argentina required car importers to insure shipments with local insurance companies and West Germany requires that foreign firms who wish to advertise in German magazines hire models through German agencies. Thus as service trade grows, protectionism might also grow, creating another roadblock to trade liberalization.

We previously noted that the recent surge in protectionist measures by the developed countries has been disproportionately aimed at those manufactured products which constitute a significant portion of the exports of the developing countries. Undoubtedly, any future increase in the exports of the developing countries that threatens the established industries of the developed countries can be expected to be met with demands within the developed nations for protectionist measures.

A fourth factor which may determine the future course of international trading relations is the type of exchange-rate system in use. If flexible exchange rates are employed, problems in international competitiveness may be resolved through adjustments in exchange rates rather than trade policy. A final factor may be the growth of the trading sectors of the nations of the world, particularly the U.S. export sector. In the United States, exports account for only about 7 percent of output, but this has been growing in recent years. As that share increases and U.S. industry becomes more export oriented, it may dawn upon U.S. lawmakers that the United States has much to gain from free trade based on reciprocity. That is, trade policy will not be viewed only as a means to protect domestic import-competing industries, but also as a means to promote export-oriented industries.

What will be the role of GATT in determining the future of international trade policy? GATT will continue to provide a forum for future rounds of multilateral trade negotiations. Also, the latest round of negotiations has attempted to strengthen the role of GATT as a mediator in bilateral trade disputes with the intent of discouraging unilateral trade measures. However, the role of GATT can only be as strong as its members choose to make it. If its members are truly dedicated to the further liberalization of trade, then the institutions of GATT will prove quite valuable in achieving that aim. If not, GATT will merely represent a gathering place for the trade representatives of the world.

If the recent developments in international trade are indicators of the future, proponents of free trade will be quite disappointed. In order to reverse this trend, the trading nations of the world are going to have to base trade policy more on consideration for the overall economic well-being of their populace, than on the interests of a few import-competing sectors. For the reasons documented above, this task may prove to be even more difficult in the future than in the past.

REGIONAL ECONOMIC INTEGRATION V

INTRODUCTION

In Part Four we saw that since World War II, barriers to trade have been substantially reduced, particularly the levels of tariffs. Partially as a result of these reductions in trade barriers, the volume of trade among nations has grown substantially, increasing the degree of economic interdependence among nations. Households and businesses both depend increasingly on foreign sources of supply for consumption goods and raw materials. Firms no longer view their market as being constrained by national borders, but also look toward foreign nations as potential markets.

In addition, there have been other factors that have contributed to the rise in economic interdependence among the nations of the world. The tremendous growth in multinational enterprises (MNEs) since World War II has been one of those factors. MNEs facilitate the international transmission of goods, services, technology and financial capital, since these items can be transferred within a single firm across national borders, rather than between two or more separate firms.

International capital markets have further contributed to a more closely linked world economy. With the development of international banking and brokerage houses, investors can take advantage of financial opportunities on a global scale. The growth of the Eurocurrency market and other such currency markets facilitates the international payments mechanism for goods, services and assets. Thus nations in the world economy are much more closely interrelated than they were twenty or thirty years ago.

One of the most explicit efforts at increasing the degree of international economic interdependence has been the formation of regional economic blocs. The formation of such blocs is termed *economic integration*. The nations engaging in economic integration desire to capture the economic benefits associated with the dismantlement of the barriers between their economies and the international economy.

The forms of economic integration are many. Some nations have established regional trading blocs, in which restrictions on mutual trade are reduced below the levels imposed on trade from outside the bloc. However, economic integration involves more than simply the free flow of trade on a regional level. Groups of nations have also made attempts to liberalize intercountry factor movements, to establish fixed exchange rates on a regional basis and to harmonize and coordinate national fiscal and monetary policies. All of these efforts have been based on a desire by the participating nations to capture the potential economic benefits associated with regional economic integration.

Some of the attempts at regional economic integration have been notably successful while others have failed. Why has this been the case? As nations become more economically interdependent, greater economic and political cooperation is required. The degree of cooperation can range from the lifting of restrictions on free trade to coordination of national monetary policies. All cooperation involves some sacrifice by the individual nations of a portion of their autonomy in economic policymaking. For example, a nation participating in a regional economic agreement may be prohibited from imposing import restrictions on another participating nation even if those imports threaten a domestic import-competing industry. Or, under an expanded form of regional economic integration, a nation may be prohibited from devaluing its currency vis-à-vis other participating nations' currencies in an effort to cure a payments deficit. Thus it can be suggested even at this early stage of discussion that there are both benefits and costs associated with regional economic integration. While countries might desire to attain the economic benefits of integration, they may also be reluctant to make the necessary sacrifice in terms of economic autonomy. The extent to which countries are willing to accept the sacrifice of autonomy that accompanies integration will determine the success of the integration efforts.

Our discussion of economic integration is composed of two chapters, each addressing different aspects of regional economic integration. Chapter 17 begins by examining the economic effects of liberalizing trade and lifting restrictions on the movement of factors of production among a group of nations. This is followed by a discussion of several specific attempts at regional integration, concentrating on the most complete—the European Economic Community. The forms of integration addressed in Chapter 17 require the participants to lower barriers that inhibit the free flow of goods and factors of production. The effect of this action is to create a bloc of countries which are more closely linked among themselves than with the rest of the world. It will be seen that the European effort at these forms of integration have been relatively successful.

Chapter 18 concentrates on the more advanced stages of economic integration, when countries engage in extensive monetary and political coordination. Again, the European attempts to achieve these advanced levels of integration are discussed in detail. It will be seen in this chapter that the degree of cooperation required to make these more advanced stages of integration successful is much greater than for the forms of integration examined in Chapter 17. In these stages, the participating nations become more closely linked, not by the dismantlement of barriers, but by the creation of policies and institutions which encourage closer ties between the participants. It is necessary for the success of these stages that the participants forego a significant degree of economic autonomy. For this reason, the more advanced stages of integration have been much more difficult to achieve than those discussed in Chapter 17. The European efforts at establishing the more advanced stages of integration reflect the reluctance of nations to sacrifice a degree of economic autonomy, despite the potential economic benefits that may accrue.

CUSTOMS UNION 17
AND COMMON MARKET

Economic integration occurs when two or more nations undertake policies that result in greater mutual economic interdependence. By increasing economic interdependence it is hoped that the productive capacity and efficiency of the member nations will be increased. The degree of interdependence can vary widely—from a reduction in trade barriers on a limited number of products to the establishment of a unified monetary policy. Some attempts at economic integration have been more successful than others. And even for those more successful efforts, not all aspects of integration were implemented smoothly.

In this chapter, the economic effects of two forms of integration, the *customs union* and the *common market*, are examined. We will also take a look at those factors which determine whether or not economic integration will be successful for a group of nations. Then we shall turn our attention to actual attempts by nations to achieve economic integration, concentrating on the European experience.

TYPES OF ECONOMIC INTEGRATION

Economic integration among nations can occur in varying stages, representing various degrees of economic cooperation between the participants. The stages of integration can be separated into two broad categories: (1) those which encourage the free movement of goods and services as well as factors of production between participating nations and (2) those which, in addition to free trade and factor movements, involve increased cooperation in the areas of monetary and fiscal policy. Let us now define more precisely the specific forms of economic integration.

Of the types of integration that involve liberalization of trade between the participating nations, the most limited in scope are *preferential trading agreements*. Participants in a preferential trading agreement reduce restrictions on trade between themselves, while maintaining a higher level of restrictions on goods imported from nations outside the agreement. Frequently, the reductions in trade restrictions are one-sided, in that only a small group of the participants reduce their trade barriers on imports from the other member nations. The other group may not reciprocate with a reduction in its barriers. Examples of preferential trading arrangements include the favorable tariff treatment granted by the European nations to imports from many of the developing countries.

The next stage of integration is the *free trade area*. With the establishment of a free trade area, member nations agree to completely dismantle trade barriers on products traded among themselves, while maintaining their own, individual trade restrictions on goods imported from nonmember nations. In practice, certain product groups are frequently excluded from the elimination of mutual trade barriers.

A *customs union* represents the next stage of economic integration and involves an even greater degree of cooperation among its members. Under this arrangement a group of nations will remove all trade restrictions on goods traded within the union and, in addition, will adopt a system of common trade restrictions to be applied to goods imported into the union from the outside. When the member nations extend the arrangements of the customs unions to include the free movement of factors of production—labor and capital—between the participating nations, those nations have established the next degree of integration, a *common market*.

All of the stages of integration discussed so far involved the lowering of restrictions on the movement of goods and services or factors of production among the participating nations. Under these arrangements the member nations remain free to undertake their own monetary and fiscal policies to achieve their domestic macroeconomic objectives—such as inflation and employment goals. However, in the most advanced stage of integration, an *economic union,* the freedom of individual nations to engage in independent macroeconomic policy is diminished. Specifically, an economic union not only has all the characteristics of a common market, but in its most complete form it also involves the transfer of the responsibility for economic policy from the individual member nations to a supranational decision-making unit representing all members. Such an arrangement would involve the establishment of a single monetary and banking system, a unified monetary and fiscal policy and a government body to establish and implement economic policy for the entire union. A less complete form of an economic union is a *monetary union,* which involves the establishment of fixed exchange rates between nations (a currency area) along with a harmonization of monetary and fiscal policy. It should be noted that an economic union differs from a monetary union since it represents an actual forfeiture by individual nations of their right to form domestic economic policy; not just a harmonization of policies as in a monetary union. The stages of economic integration are summarized in Table 17–1, along with the characteristics associated with each stage.

THE ECONOMIC EFFECTS OF A CUSTOMS UNION

Static Effects

Because the various forms of economic integration involve a reduction in the level of trade barriers between member nations, they may be interpreted as a step toward free trade. However, this movement toward free trade is limited since the member nations continue to impose restrictions on imports from nonmember nations.

TABLE 17-1

Stages of Integration and Associated Characteristics

Characteristics Stages of Integration	Reduction of Mutual Trade Barriers	Elimination of Mutual Trade Barriers	Common External Trade Barriers	Free Movement of Factors of Production	Harmonization of Fiscal and Monetary Policy (and Fixed Exchange Rates)	Unified Monetary and Fiscal Policy That Is Determined by Central Authority
Preferential trading agreements	X					
Free trade areas	X	X				
Customs union	X	X	X			
Common market	X	X	X	X		
Monetary union	X	X	X	X	X	
Economic union	X	X	X	X	X	X

Clearly, a move toward economic integration by a group of nations will provide member countries with a competitive edge over nonmember nations in trade with other member countries. Let us now examine more formally the economic effects of economic integration by analyzing the impact of the establishment of a customs union on both member and nonmember nations.

Suppose that the world trade in wheat involves three countries—say, the United States, France and Belgium. Further assume that Belgium is a small country which imports wheat from either the United States or France. The situation is depicted graphically in Figure 17–1 where the supply (S_B) and demand (D_B) conditions for wheat in Belgium are portrayed along with the import supply curves of the United States $(S_{U.S.})$ and France (S_F). According to Figure 17–1, the United States is the world's low-cost producer of wheat, since wheat producers in the United States are willing to supply a bushel of wheat for $2.00 as compared to the French price of $3.00.[1] Under free trade, Belgium will

[1]The price of wheat in Belgium is expressed in U.S. dollars ($) for convenience.

import wheat from the United States at a price equal to $2.00

Suppose that Belgium imposes a specific tariff of $2.00 per bushel in a uniform manner; that is, the tariff is applied equally to wheat imports from both the United States and France. Such a policy will result in an upward shift of the import supply curves of both the United States and France to $S_{U.S.}^T$, $4.00 per bushel, and S_F^T, $5.00 per bushel, respectively. With a uniform tariff, Belgium will continue to import wheat from the United States, which remains the low-price source of wheat. Belgium will produce Q_1 bushels of wheat and consume Q_2 bushels at a price of $4.00 per bushel. The difference between consumption and production, $Q_2 - Q_1$, represents the quantity of wheat imports from the United States.

Now suppose that Belgium and France join together to form a customs union. Under such an arrangement all trade barriers between Belgium and France will be abolished while the two countries will maintain a common set of trade restrictions against the nonmember nation, the United States. If the $2.00-per-bushel tariff continues to be applied to wheat imports from the United States the pattern of wheat trade will be significantly altered. The price to Belgium of wheat produced in the United States will remain equal to $4.00 per bushel. However, the price of wheat produced in France will be reduced to its free trade level of $3.00 per bushel. Belgium will now turn to France as its source of wheat imports.

In Figure 17–1 the price of wheat imports faced by Belgium will fall from $4.00 to $3.00 per bushel. At the lower price, production of wheat by Belgian farmers will decrease to Q_3, while consumption in Belgium will increase to Q_4. As a result, the quantity of imports to Belgium will increase to $Q_4 - Q_3$. Thus not only is the source of imports altered with the formation of a customs union, but the quantity of imports is increased as well. These changes in

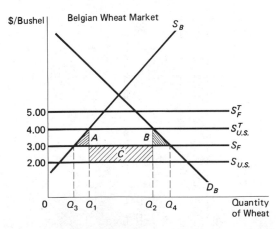

FIGURE 17-1 The Static Effects of Customs Union Formation

trade patterns are not surprising, given the discriminatory nature of tariff policy under a customs union. Since imports from member nations are treated more favorably than those originating outside the union, it can be expected that trade between member nations will increase at the expense of nonmember trade. In addition, the price-reducing effects of lower tariff rates can be expected to result in an increase in the quantity of trade.

Welfare Effects of a Customs Union

So far, our discussion has focused on changes in trade flows and import prices as well as on the changes in the output and consumption levels of the importing country. Let us now investigate the question of whether the importing nation, Belgium, benefits from joining a customs union.

There are two types of welfare effects that must be considered. The first is known as the *trade creation* effect. Trade creation represents the improvement in the economic welfare of the importing nation, resulting from the lower import price and the consequent increase in the quantity of imports associated with customs union formation. The trade creation effects are depicted graphically in Figure 17–1 by triangles A and B. These are known as the production and consumption effects, respectively. The production effect is a welfare gain since it represents the savings to Belgium resulting from the replacement of high-cost domestic wheat production with low-cost wheat imports (France) by an amount equal to Q_1Q_3. Similarly, the consumption effect is a positive change in Belgium's economic welfare since it measures the gains to Belgain consumers, who increase their consumption by Q_2Q_4, when the import price falls from $4.00 to $3.00.

The second welfare effect of customs union formation is known as *trade diversion*. Trade diversion occurs when, because of customs union

formation, imports from a low-cost nonmember nation are replaced by imports from a high-cost member nation. In our example, trade diversion has occurred since Belgium has replaced wheat imports from the United States, the low-cost producer, with those from France, the high-cost producer. Before the union was formed, wheat imports equal to $Q_2 - Q_1$ were obtained from the United States at a price equal to $4.00 per bushel. It should be recalled, however, that the $4.00 price included the $2.00-per-bushel tariff which, of course, was paid to Belgian customs officials and thus remained in the country. The actual price paid by residents of Belgium for wheat produced in the United States was thus $2.00 per bushel. When Belgium and France formed a customs union, Belgium substituted French for American wheat imports at a price equal to $3.00 per bushel. Since the $3.00-per-bushel price excludes any tariff payments, it represents the actual cost of a bushel of French wheat imported into Belgium. Thus the replacement of wheat imports from the United States by imports from France has resulted in an increase in the cost of wheat imports to Belgium equal to $1.00 per bushel; this applies to the quantity $Q_2 - Q_1$. The loss in economic welfare for Belgium is represented by area C in Figure 17–1; this area represents the additional cost of the import quantity, $Q_2 - Q_1$, to Belgium after customs union formation.

To determine the net welfare effects of customs union formation, the trade creation effects (areas $A + B$) must be compared to the trade diversion effects (area C). If the trade diversion effects are greater than the trade creation effects, then it is possible for the establishment of a customs union to result in a reduction in the economic welfare of the importing nation. On the other hand, if the trade creation effects outweigh the trade diversion effects, there will be a net increase in the economic welfare of the importing nation.

If the formation of a customs union is viewed

as a step toward free trade, as suggested previously, then any potential for a decrease in economic welfare seems contrary to the expected impact of free trade. The potential for an adverse effect on economic welfare arises because of the discriminatory nature of the member nations' tariff policy under a customs union arrangement. As was demonstrated, such an arrangement may lead to a displacement of imports from the low-cost nonmember nation in favor of imports from high-cost member nations, resulting in trade diversion.

factors affecting the net welfare effects of customs union formation

Several factors will influence whether or not the net welfare effect of customs union formation will be positive or negative. First, trade diversion will be eliminated completely if the importing nation continues to import from the low-cost world producer after entering into a customs union agreement. This would occur if the low-cost producer were a partner in the customs union. In our example, trade diversion would have been avoided if Belgium had formed a customs union with the United States instead of France, since Belgium would have continued to import wheat from the low-cost producer, the United States. Obviously, the likelihood of a customs union including the low-cost producer will increase as the number of nations joining the customs union increases.

Even when the low-cost producer is not a member of the union, trade diversion can be avoided if the common external tariff is so low that the low-cost nonmember nation can still offer a selling price below that of the member nations. In our example, if the common external tariff applied to wheat imports from the United States had been $.50 per bushel instead of $2.00 per bushel, the selling price of U.S. wheat would have been $2.50 per bushel compared to the tariff-free French price of $3.00 per bushel. Un-

der these circumstances, Belgium would have continued to import wheat from the United States and trade diversion would have been avoided.

Given that trade diversion and trade creation exist under a customs union agreement, several factors will determine the relative size of the two welfare effects. A particularly important factor is the differential between the cost of producing in the home country, the other member country and the outside country. In our example (see Figure 17–1), if wheat produced in the United States had a free trade price equal to $1.50 per bushel the size of rectangle C, the measure of trade diversion, would have been greater. In addition, the size of the triangles A and B, the measures of trade creation, would have been smaller. On the other hand, the magnitude of the trade creation effects will be greater and the trade diversion effects lower, the lower the cost of imports from the member nation. Referring to Figure 17–1 once more, if France had a free trade price of less than $3.00 per bushel, the size of the triangles A and B would have been greater, while the size of the rectangle C would have been smaller.[2]

Dynamic Effects

The impact of economic integration on the price, quantity and source of imports, and thus on economic welfare, is known as the "static effects." However, the effects of customs union formation extend beyond these static effects.

[2]The relative size of the trade creation and trade diversion effects are also influenced by the elasticities of supply and demand of the home country. The more (less) elastic is its supply and demand, the greater (lower) will be the trade creation effects of customs union formation. That is, as the price of imports decline upon formation, the quantity of output of domestic producers will decline more and the quantity consumed by domestic residents will increase more, the greater are the home country's elasticities of supply and demand.

Over time, the formation of a customs union may cause fundamental changes in the economic structure of the member countries; these changes are referred to as the *dynamic effects* of customs union formation.

With the reduction in trade restrictions between member nations, it follows that many industries previously protected from foreign competition will have to adjust to a new competitive environment. An increase in competition can be expected to have the usual effect of stimulating efficiency in the previously protected industries by encouraging cost-cutting and technological improvements in those industries. Those firms in the economy which fail to adjust may fall by the wayside with their dislocated resources being transferred to the more competitive sectors of the economy. The end result will be an economy whose resources are more efficiently employed, and this will tend to increase the economic well-being of the nation.

Second, the formation of a customs union may increase the size of the markets available to firms operating within the union. As a result, those firms will be able to increase their level of production and in so doing realize economies of scale; economies of scale are defined as a reduction in the per-unit costs of production as output increases. As a result, the productive efficiency of the firm will increase.

Other factors may also stimulate investment expenditure within the union. If the increased efficiency in production is accompanied by an increase in profits (say, because of lower costs), firms would have more funds available for investment in capital goods. Or the growth of the firm's market area may generate prospects for higher future profits, stimulating investment expenditure. Investment expenditure from outside the union may also be stimulated. Business firms in nonmember nations that are discriminated against by the union's external barriers may attempt to circumvent those barriers by moving production facilities within the union. The effect of expenditure on new capital goods is to increase both the productive efficiency and capacity of the economy.

All of the dynamic effects will increase the productive efficiency of the member nations either through improved resource allocation, better production techniques or increased investment expenditure on new capital goods and technology. The net effect of these events, over the long run, will be to increase the productive capacity of the member nations, and thus the potential economic well-being of those nations. In fact, many believe that the gains from a customs union result not so much from trade creation, but from the longer term, dynamic effects. Both the static and dynamic effects of customs union formation will be discussed later in the chapter in reference to the experience of the European Economic Community.

THE ECONOMICS OF A COMMON MARKET

We have seen that a customs union involves the elimination of restrictions on the free movement of traded goods among a group of nations. A *common market* takes economic integration a step further by not only liberalizing trade, but also liberalizing the movement of factors of production among the member countries. This section will be limited to defining factor mobility and considering why an association of nations might wish to promote it.

First, let us see how the movement of factors of production is ordinarily inhibited. In the case of labor, there are several barriers to mobility: (1) many nations maintain quotas restricting the number of foreign workers that may be employed in that nation, (2) information regarding the availability of employment in foreign nations is oftentimes limited and (3) for skilled labor, certifications of competency (e.g., diplomas and licenses) are often unacceptable outside the country of certification. To implement the free movement of labor, these and other barriers would have to be eliminated.

Capital mobility, both physical and financial, is inhibited primarily by national legislation, although information costs and institutional barriers can also play a role. As an example of legislative barriers, national governments sometimes limit capital outflows by imposing a tax on the returns earned on foreign investment or by placing outright quantitative limitations on capital movements.[3] Institutional barriers would include an absence of financial facilities through which to conduct an international transfer of funds. For instance, if commercial banks of different nations are unwilling or unequipped to accept foreign assets or liabilities or to handle international payments, then the international flow of capital will be severely impaired.

Why would an association of nations wish to promote factor mobility? The primary reason is that factor mobility would lead to a more efficient allocation of labor and capital within the association (see Chapter 5). Both labor and capital would move from their least productive locations (with the lowest wages, profits and interest payments) to the areas of greatest productivity (with the highest wages, profits and interest payments). As a result, the association's total level of production and income (and economic welfare) would be enhanced.

EUROPEAN ECONOMIC INTEGRATION

Unquestionably, the most recognizable and far-reaching attempts at economic integration have been those of the European nations. The estab-

[3]Examples of such controls that the U.S. government has imposed were the Interest Equalization Tax of 1963, which applied a tax to income earned on foreign capital (except Canada), and the "voluntary" control program of 1965, which established ceilings on permissible capital outflows.

lishment of the European Free Trade Area and European Economic Community represent the most successful effort yet by a group of sovereign nations to increase both their economic and political interdependence. The European Economic Community, in particular, has already attained a significant degree of integration and is currently involved in efforts to reach an even more advanced stage of integration by forming a monetary union. Accompanying the move toward economic integration is a movement toward political integration. In this section, the discussion of European integration will be limited to the efforts aimed at liberalizing the movement of goods and services and factors of production among the participating nations. Europe's efforts at monetary and political integration will be the subject of the following chapter.

European Economic Community (EEC)

The EEC had its origin in the mid-1950s. At that time the European nations were undergoing an economic recovery from the effects of World War II. Production levels were increasing from their depressed levels immediately following the war, as was the volume of trade among the European nations. To sustain this growth, many European leaders perceived a need for closer economic and political cooperation among the European nations.

Specifically, the European economies at that time were faced with two problems that might be solved by economic integration. First, the individual European markets were quite fragmented on a national basis because of restrictive trade barriers among the nations. As a result, European firms were producing for small-sized markets and thus were unable to achieve economies resulting from high levels of production. The small scale of the European firm was particularly apparent when compared to the size of the typical U.S. firm. Producers in the United

States, who were realizing substantial economies of scale, were viewed by Europe as a competitive threat to their smaller, less efficient firms. By establishing a customs union, the European countries hoped to achieve the benefits of a larger European market and at the same time to provide themselves with protection from the competitive pressure of U.S. firms.

In addition to the potential economic benefits, there were political gains to be attained by a more closely united Europe. After the war, the European nations, individually, were unable to guarantee security against potential threats to the newly established peace. An economically and politically united Europe could offer a much stronger deterrent to any potential outside disruption. In fact, it was this aspect that offered the strongest incentive to the United States to support the formation of the EEC. Moreover, the Europeans felt that their interests in the world political arena could be more effectively represented by a united Europe.

The first step toward integration was the establishment of the European Coal and Steel Community (ECSC) in 1952. The ECSC consisted of six members: Belgium, France, West Germany, Italy, Luxembourg and the Netherlands. Each of these countries relinquished, to the central authority of the ECSC, its sovereign powers concerning the economic activity of their coal and steel industries. The ECSC established free trade in coal and steel among the members and encouraged competitive market conditions in these industries throughout Europe. Furthermore, the founders of the ECSC hoped that it would provide the cornerstone for a more complete integration of the economic activities of Europe.

The dream of an economically integrated Europe moved closer to reality in 1958 with the Treaty of Rome which established the European Economic Community. The six original members of the EEC (the same nations that formed the ECSC) resolved to establish a common market over a twelve-year transitional period. All trade restrictions on industrial goods, including both tariff and nontariff barriers, were to be eliminated, in staged reductions, on intra–Community trade. In addition, the Community was to establish a common external tariff on imports from outside the EEC; the tariff was to be based on the arithmetic average of the existing duties of each of the individual members. These objectives, as stated in the Treaty of Rome, were accomplished in less time than originally planned; both the elimination of internal tariffs on industrial goods and the establishment of a common external tariff against nonmember imports were completed by July 1968. At this point, the EEC had achieved customs union status, at least as far as industrial trade was concerned.

the common agricultural policy

The agricultural trade of Europe did not accommodate to economic integration as smoothly as did industrial trade. Prior to integration, the prices of agricultural production in Europe had been supported by national price support schemes, and domestic production had been protected from import competition by a system of tariffs and quotas; these individual policies varied considerably among the nations. The objective of the EEC, according to the Treaty of Rome, was to eliminate intra–Community barriers to agricultural trade and replace the national price support policies with a Common Agricultural Policy (CAP).

Under the CAP, which is still operational today, it was agreed that a Community-wide guaranteed price level (target price) would be established for agricultural products. These prices are supported by the Community authorities, who intervene on the market to buy or sell a commodity in whatever quantity is necessary to maintain the target price.

It is interesting to note that the establishment

of common target prices almost resulted in the withdrawal of France from the Community. Disagreement was intense among member nations as to what the common level of target prices should be. The dispute was especially intense between France and Germany. France possessed the most efficient agricultural sector in the Community, and therefore could sell its products at relatively low prices. Germany, on the other hand, had traditionally protected the income of its farmers with a high-price support policy. Germany, therefore, was against low target price levels, since its farmers would have to accept a severe price reduction for their products if they were to compete with the more efficient French farmers. France objected to high target prices, arguing that it would eliminate the competitive advantage that its agricultural sector had over the other members. The issue became so heated that France made serious threats of withdrawal from the Community if the German wishes were adopted. In 1964 a compromise was struck, and the Community adopted a set of target prices that lay between the French and German pre-union domestic prices.

These target prices could not be maintained, however, unless foreign competition were restricted. The key to insulating the EEC agricultural market from foreign competition is a system of variable import levies. Under this system a "threshold" price, which is a minimum price for agricultural imports, is established. Imports entering at prices less than the threshold price are subject to a variable duty, which is set at a level that increases the price of the import to the threshold price. Thus, agricultural imports are, in essence, prohibited from competing with Community agricultural production on the basis of price. As a result, agricultural imports have been effectively limited to filling any shortfall in Community production relative to Community demand. The elimination, in stages, of the intra–Community barriers to agricultural trade and the establishment of a variable levy system

was achieved by the mid-1970s; by this time the CAP covered more than 95 percent of the agricultural production of the member nations.

The EEC as a Common Market

As stated previously, the EEC was intended to be more than a customs union. The Treaty of Rome, in fact, contained an explicit provision calling for the establishment of a common market. Has factor mobility been achieved within the EEC? The EEC has indeed made substantial progress in reducing the obstacles to the inter-country flow of labor and capital. Labor mobility within the Community has been encouraged by several pieces of legislation. For example, labor mobility is enhanced by legislation which requires that migrants receive social security benefits equal to those of residents of the host country. In addition, social security rights can be retained if the migrant should move from one EEC member country to another. Thus a German who has been working for a year in France is entitled to the same social security benefits when he returns home as if he had never been away. The establishment of the European Coordination Bureau, which publicizes employment opportunities available throughout the Community and attempts to match vacancies in the Community job markets with unemployed workers, has also encouraged the intra–Community movement of labor.

The free movement of capital within the EEC has also been encouraged. However, safeguards were built into the Treaty of Rome which allow a member country to impose controls if capital movements disrupt that country's capital market. Obviously, the effect of such safeguards is to inhibit the free flow of capital. Despite these impediments, there have been developments that have promoted capital flows. These include the development of a Community–wide bond market, the tremendous growth of the Eurocurrency market, increased collaboration among European commercial banks and the growth of Community–wide firms with subsidiaries in several member nations.

European Free Trade Association

On January 4, 1960, seven European nations joined together to form a free trade area. Charter members of the European Free Trade Association (EFTA) included Austria, Denmark, Norway, Portugal, Sweden, Switzerland and the United Kingdom. The motives behind the formation of the EFTA were twofold. First, the European nations that were not included in the EEC were concerned that their exclusion could result in a loss to their economies. Establishment of a free trade area among those nations was viewed as one way to mitigate any potential economic injury. Second, the formation of the EFTA was an attempt to establish an entity which could negotiate effectively with the EEC on issues of mutual interest.

The scope and purpose of the EFTA was much more limited than that of the EEC. Its primary objective was to gradually reduce internal trade restrictions on trade in industrial goods. The dismantlement of trade restrictions on industrial trade within the EFTA was completed by the end of 1967. However, the EFTA did not establish a common external tariff nor did they attempt to include agricultural trade in their plans. The EFTA also differed from the EEC in that its members did not contemplate any move toward more advanced stages of integration.

The Changing Structure of the EEC and EFTA

The structure of the two trading blocs of Western Europe and their relations with one another have shifted from time to time. In fact, the membership of both the EEC and EFTA has changed significantly. In 1973 three of the original members of the EFTA, the United Kingdom, Ireland and Denmark, became members of the EEC. Their membership into the Community was phased in over a period of five years, which culminated in 1977 when tariffs were eliminated between the three new members and the six original members. By that time, the new members had also established common external tariffs identical to those of the original members, and were participating fully in the other aspects of the EEC. Meanwhile, Iceland joined the EFTA in 1970 and is now a full participant in that organization.

The membership of the EEC has continued to expand. Greece became the tenth EEC member in 1981 and will gradually lower its trade barriers with the other member countries over a period of five years, at which time they will be eliminated. Also, slated for future membership, sometime in the mid-1980s, are Portugal and Spain.

Just as important as the reshuffling of membership between the EFTA and the EEC is the agreement on trading relations that has been negotiated between the two trading blocs. The main provision of this agreement called for the elimination of tariffs on industrial goods traded between the EEC and EFTA nations; this became fully implemented on July 1, 1977. This agreement resulted in the creation of the world's largest free trade area, encompassing some 22 percent of world trade.

The Economic Effect of European Economic Integration

Earlier in this chapter we discussed the economic effects, both static and dynamic, upon countries that enter into customs union arrangements. In this section, we will see how joining these associations affected the countries of both the EEC and EFTA.

One effect of moving from a uniform tariff situation (where a tariff is applied equally to all

TABLE 17-2

EEC and EFTA Imports of Manufactured Products, by Member and Nonmember Shares, Selected Years, 1953–1965 (dollar amounts in millions)

Source of Imports	Value			Trade Shares (percent)		
	1953	1958[a]	1965	1953	1958[a]	1965
Total imports of EEC	$4841	$8910	$25,138	100.0	100.0	100.0
Imports from members	2270	4455	14,645	46.9	50.0	58.3
Imports from nonmembers	2571	4455	10,493	53.1	50.0	41.7
EFTA countries	1385	2174	4680	28.6	24.4	18.6
United States	620	1132	2850	12.8	12.7	11.3
Others	566	1149	2963	11.7	12.9	11.8
Total imports of EFTA	4792	8555	17,385	100.0	100.0	100.0
Imports from members	1270	1933	4213	26.5	22.6	24.2
Imports from nonmembers	3522	6622	13,172	73.5	77.4	75.8
EEC countries	2022	4047	7589	42.2	47.3	43.7
United States	508	864	2032	10.6	10.1	11.7
Others	992	1711	3551	20.7	20.0	20.4

Source: U.N., *Commodity Trade Statistics,* Vols. III, VIII, IX and XV. Reprinted from Lawrence B. Krause, *European Economic Integration and the United States* (Washington, D.C.: Brookings Institution, 1968), Table 2-2.
[a]1959 for EFTA data.

trading partners) to a customs union arrangement is that the source of imports to the domestic country may change. Because of the discriminatory nature of the tariff system associated with a customs union, a tendency will develop for member nations to shift import demand toward fellow members and away from nonmember nations. To what extent has the source of imports to the European nations been altered by economic integration? Table 17–2 shows the volume and composition (in terms of source country) of manufactured imports into EEC and EFTA nations for certain years preceding and following integration. For both the EEC and EFTA the share of imports from member nations increased between 1958 and 1965, as integration proceeded; while the share of nonmembers declined during the same period. The impact of European economic integration on trade with the United States, however, shows mixed results.

Imports from the United States into the EEC as percent of total imports decreased from 1958 to 1965, while imports from the United States captured a larger share of total EFTA imports in 1965 than in 1958.

agricultural trade

Much the same pattern holds true for trade in agriculture. As the common agriculture policy of the EEC was implemented during the 1960s, the share of agriculture imports coming into EEC nations from other EEC nations increased, rising from 20 percent in 1961 to 35 percent in 1969. It is also interesting to note that because the CAP has maintained high agricultural prices (generally above world agricultural prices) by protecting European farmers from foreign competition with a variable levy system, the EEC has become self-sufficient in over 90 percent of the agricultural products its residents consume. In fact, the EEC's only major agricultural import requirements are for certain grains, fresh citrus fruit and soybean oils and fats.

For some products, the EEC's price policies have even resulted in vast quantities of surplus production. This has been especially true for such products as soft wheat, sugar, poultry and pork, although nowhere is the situation more pronounced than for dairy products; EEC authorities are literally storing mountains of surplus butter and cheese. Not surprisingly, countries outside the EEC have directed harsh criticism at the agricultural trade policies of the EEC. It is evident that the variable levy system has protected EEC producers at the expense of agricultural sales of nonmember countries to the EEC.

The friction is becoming even more intense because of another aspect of the EEC's agricultural trade policy. As EEC agricultural production began to outstrip EEC consumption, a method was needed to "dispose" of these surpluses. The method used most frequently is for the EEC to subsidize the export of these surpluses to nations outside the Community. Subsidization is often necessary because the domestic support prices (target prices) of EEC agriculture are higher than world prices. Thus not only are agricultural sales by nonmembers to the EEC severely restricted by the variable levy system but the non–EEC nations must also compete with subsidized EEC exports in third-country markets.

This policy of subsidizing agricultural exports has led to serious disputes between the EEC and other agricultural exporting nations, particularly the United States. The U.S. poultry industry has charged the EEC with raising chicken export subsidies to $100 million in 1980, up from a 1970 level of $5 million. U.S. poultry exporters argue that the EEC's share of third-country poultry markets more than doubled during the 1970s. It is clear that while the CAP has certainly supported community agricultural interests, it has done so at the expense of free trade.

the trade creation and diversion effects of European integration

How has the formation of regional economic blocs affected the domestic welfare of the member nations of the EEC and EFTA? Have the importing nations experienced trade diversion, switching their purchases of imported goods to high-cost member nations and away from low-cost nonmember producers? Has there been trade creation, and have the trade creation effects been large enough to offset any trade diversion effects? A number of studies have attempted to estimate the relative magnitude of these effects and these studies seem to agree in their findings. Evidence suggests that the CAP of the EEC has resulted in significant trade diversion in agricultural trade. With regard to trade in manufactured products, the general conclusion seems to be that the trade creation effects of integration, for both the EEC and EFTA, have outweighed any trade diversion effects. A study by Mordechai Kreinin, for example, estimates that the trade creation effects for the EEC were four times greater than the trade diversion effects in 1967–1968 and eight times greater for the period 1969–1970.

dynamic effects

In addition to the static effects of economic integration, we suggested at an earlier point that integration will increase the competitive pressures on the member nations because of liberalized trade within the union. As a result, the productive efficiency of firms within the union will tend to increase as will the level of investment expenditure. These developments would

TABLE 17-3

Growth of Gross Domestic Product of the EEC and EFTA Countries and the United States, Before and After Integration, in 1958 Prices[a] (in percentages)

Country	Compound Annual Rate of Increase		
	1953 to 1958–1959	1958–1959 to 1964	Change in Growth Rates
EEC			
Belgium–Luxembourg	2.7	5.1	2.4
France[b]	4.7	5.6	0.9
Germany	6.9	7.1	0.2
Italy	5.2	6.0	0.8
Netherlands	4.5	5.6	1.1
EFTA			
Austria	6.7	4.8	−1.9
Denmark	2.9	5.8	2.9
Norway	2.9	5.3	2.4
Portugal	4.0	6.7	2.7
Sweden	3.9	5.1	1.2
Switzerland	4.6[c]	5.7	1.1
United Kingdom	2.4	3.8	1.4
United States	2.1	4.1	2.0

Sources: Organization for Economic Cooperation and Development, *Statistics of National Income Accounts, 1950–61* (Paris, 1963), and *National Accounts Statistics, 1955–64* (Paris, 1960). Reprinted from Lawrence Krause, *European Economic Integration and the United States* (Washington, D.C.: Brookings Institution, 1968), Table 2-3.
[a]At factor costs.
[b]At market prices.
[c]1954 to 1958–1959.

stimulate the productive capacity and thus the income and output levels of the member nations.

Dynamic benefits of this kind seem to have accrued to members of both the EEC and EFTA in the form of increases in their annual rate of growth of domestic production. This is indicated in Table 17–3 which shows that, with the exception of Austria, the growth rates of the member nations increased after integration. It should also be noted that prior to integration, the European nations were experiencing historically high rates of growth. This suggests that factors other than integration were also causing economic growth. However, the fact that these rates increased to even higher levels after integration suggests that economic integration may have provided an additional stimulus to economic growth in Europe.

QUESTIONS AND EXERCISES

1. Define the six stages of economic integration discussed in Chapter 17. List the stages according to the degree of integration, and point out how each stage differs from the stage which is one step below it in terms of the degree of integration.

2. Suppose that Mexico and the United States are considering forming a customs union for trade in grain. Assume that Mexico is a small country which can either import grain from Canada at $1000 per ton or from the United States at $1100 per ton. Prior to customs union formation, Mexico applies a uniform tariff to grain imports equal to $200 per ton. Under the customs union arrangement, Mexico would eliminate the tariff on imports from the United States, and continue to apply it to Canadian imports.

   a. Would Mexico benefit from forming a customs union with the United States? Answer this graphically, showing both the costs and benefits of customs union formation.

   b. Suppose that the tariff applied to Canadian grain was $50 per ton instead of $200. Under these conditions would Mexico's economic well-being be affected by customs union formation with the United States? (Assume that under a uniform tariff policy the tariff also equaled $50 per ton.) Show your answer graphically.

   c. Suppose instead that Mexico joined Canada in forming a customs union, where the preunion tariff of $200 per ton was applied uniformly. Would Mexico benefit economically from joining such a union? Show graphically.

3. Define trade creation and trade diversion. If trade diversion is greater than trade creation for a country joining a customs union, is it necessarily the case that the economic well-being of the nation will be reduced, particularly in the long run?

4. What are the economic arguments for a group of countries to form a common market? Why might countries (or sectors within individual countries) resist joining a common market arrangement?

5. Do you believe that the countries belonging to the European Economic Community have benefited economically from membership? Have the benefits been shared equally by all sectors of the economies of the EEC? Provide evidence to support your argument.

6. Explain the basic framework of the Common Agricultural Policy (CAP) of the EEC. Place special emphasis on the trade policy aspects of the policy, both toward imports and exports. Has the CAP been viewed favorably by nonmember nations that export agricultural goods?

7. Suppose the United States, Canada and Mexico are considering forming a customs union, and that you are asked to submit to the President a recommendation on whether membership is in the best interests of the United States. What would be the factors that you would have to consider in making your recommendation? Do you think that *all* sectors of the U.S. economy would benefit or be injured equally by membership? Cite several examples of the effects on individual sectors (consumers and producers).

Monetary Integration: 18
The European Experience

In the previous chapter we described a monetary union among nations as a form of economic integration involving the establishment of fixed exchange rates between the currencies of the member nations, along with a harmonization of monetary and fiscal policies. In this chapter the nature and economic effects of a monetary union will be discussed, assuming that the participating nations have also established a customs union and a common market. In fact, it will be argued that the free movement of goods, services and factors of production is a necessary prerequisite for a successful monetary union. Our discussion will begin by examining the rationale for a monetary union and then proceed to examine the European efforts at monetary integration. To facilitate the presentation, we must first address the concept of currency areas.

CURRENCY AREAS

A *currency area* is an economic region where a single currency is employed or, equivalently, two or more currencies are locked together in value so as to be in effect a single currency. For two currencies to function as one, they must have a rigid and irrevocably fixed exchange rate and be freely convertible.[1] Also, the monetary authorities involved must coordinate their policies in a manner which facilitates the fixed value between the indi-

---

[1]By "rigidly fixed," we mean that the exchange rate is not allowed to fluctuate in the slightest amount. Unlike the adjustable peg of the Bretton Woods System, it cannot even fluctuate within a narrow band.

vidual currencies. Separate currency areas are segregated from one another by the fact that their currency exchange rates are not rigidly and permanently fixed. The establishment of a *monetary union*, then, represents the merger of two or more formerly separate currency areas into one unified currency area.

The most common example of a currency area is an individual nation, where a single currency applies to all regions within the nation, but fluctuates in value against outside national currencies. For example, the United States is a single currency area, since its currency unit, the dollar, is universally accepted at a constant value in all regions. A dollar is a dollar whether used to purchase goods in New York or California, and its value is not rigidly fixed to currencies of other nations.

However, currency areas need not be defined by national boundaries. If the currencies of two individual nations have a rigid, irrevocably fixed exchange rate, and if the governments guarantee convertibility, then the two nations represent a single currency area. For example, suppose the value of the West German deutsche mark (Mk.) were rigidly fixed to the French franc (Fr.), at a rate equal to Fr. 2 = Mk. 1. If the permanency of this rate of exchange was unquestioned and the ability to convert one currency into another was assured, then a German deutsche mark would be an equally acceptable monetary unit in France as the French franc (and vice versa). Suppose a French bottle of wine had a franc price equal to Fr. 10. An individual in France holding deutsche marks, who desired to purchase the wine, could sell Mk. 5 for Fr. 10 and then proceed to purchase the wine. Or the individual might be able to purchase the wine by paying Mk. 5 to the French storekeeper, who then could readily convert the deutsche marks into Fr. 10. As long as the rate of exchange and convertibility between the franc and deutsche mark were guaranteed, individuals and firms operating in France (or West Germany) would be indifferent as to whether they hold francs or deutsche marks for transaction purposes.

The two currencies can be considered as one currency, and the currency area would include both France and West Germany. This currency area would be no different than the currency area defined by a single nation—say, the United States where two nickels in one region of the nation can be freely exchanged for a dime from another region of the nation, at a rigidly fixed exchange rate (2 nickels = 1 dime).

What, then, is the ideal composition of a currency area? Should they be formed according to national boundaries, as has traditionally been the case, or should they be established on some basis other than national boundaries? In the following section we shall examine the factors that determine the composition of an optimum currency area.

The Principle of Optimum Currency Areas

Optimum currency areas can be roughly defined as currency areas that afford the most efficient adjustment process in response to both internal and external disturbances. As suggested in the previous section, a currency area may or may not correspond to national borders. In fact, separate, independent currencies for each nation may not lead to the most desirable economic consequences. The following example will serve to demonstrate a few of the problems that can arise when a currency area is established on a national basis.

Suppose that a nation, say the United States, has two economically distinct regions; let us call them East and West. By "economically distinct" we mean that each region specializes in the production of distinct and separate goods, and that factors of production are immobile between regions. Also, assume that the United States has a single currency which is unquestionably accepted in both the East and West.[2]

Given this situation, let us see what happens when there is a shift in the demand patterns of the residents of the United States from the goods produced in the East, say steel, to the goods produced in the West, say semiconductors. Such an economic disturbance will initially result in an increase in unemployment in the eastern section of the United States. Meanwhile, the shift in demand toward semiconductors can be expected to place upward pressure on the price of semiconductors. Let us suppose that the general cost of living in the West is linked to the price of semiconductors; this means that inflation will begin to develop in the West.

How might this situation of inflation in the West and unemployment in the East be remedied? If labor were mobile, we might expect to see a migration of unemployed workers from the East to the West where semiconductor production is on the increase. Such a movement might also dampen the inflationary pressures in the West by slowing down wage increases or possibly even lowering wage levels. However, this solution has been eliminated by our assumption that factors are immobile between regions.

A second alternative might be for the national monetary authority to employ monetary policy. However, the monetary authorities would face a dilemma. If they were to direct their efforts toward the unemployment problem in the East by undertaking an easy monetary policy, they take the chance of worsening inflation in the West. Conversely, if they were to undertake a tight monetary policy in an effort to reduce the inflationary pressure in the West, they run the risk of worsening unemployment in the East. Thus monetary policy designed to improve the situation in one region would worsen the situation in the other region. The crux of the dilemma lies in the fact that the East and the West are part of the same currency area.

A possible solution would be to divide the two regions into separate currency areas, with each region having its own currency which can fluctuate in value against the other region's currency. In other words, each region would become an autonomous economic region with its own currency and freedom to pursue its own monetary policy. With flexible exchange rates between the two regions, the adjustment process in both regions would be smoother. If demand were now to shift from steel to semiconductors, the East would experience a balance-of-trade deficit with the West since eastern residents would be purchasing a greater quantity of semiconductors from the West, and western residents would be purchasing less steel from the East. Under a system of flexible exchange rates, the eastern currency would depreciate against the western currency, thereby increasing the price of semiconductor imports to eastern residents and lowering the price of steel for western residents. As a result, there would now be a change in demand away from semiconductors toward steel, mitigating the unemployment problems in the East. Since the appreciation of the western currency would relieve some of the demand pressure on semiconductors, this would serve to reduce the inflationary pressures in the West. Thus the adjustment of each region to the change in demand patterns would be easier if each region had its own currency and these currencies were allowed to fluctuate against each other, than if the two regions had a common currency.

It is clear, then, that national boundaries may not be the best criterion for establishing currency

---

[2]This presentation of how to determine an optimum currency area is derived from an article by Robert A. Mundell, "A Theory of Optimum Currency Areas," *American Economic Review,* 51 (September 1961), 657–665. This article provided the foundation for much of the analysis of optimum currency areas.

areas. In our example, smaller regional currency areas turned out to be superior to a national currency area. In many instances, however, optimum currency areas *would* extend beyond national borders to include several nations. If formerly autonomous national currency areas join together to form a single currency area, then a *monetary union* has been established. Now let us consider several factors that will influence the size of an optimum currency area.

Factors Influencing the Size of an Optimum Currency Area

One consideration that will influence the size of an optimum currency area is the degree of mobility of factors of production. One could argue that a currency area should correspond to regions within which factor mobility is high. If the factors of production are mobile, then regional imbalances can be resolved by the movements of factors from one region to the other. For instance, in the preceding example, it was suggested that the problem of divergent employment conditions might have been eliminated by a movement of labor from the region with high unemployment to the region with expanding output and employment. In this situation, there would have been no need for an adjustment in exchange rates between the two regions in order to eliminate the imbalance.

The size of an optimum currency area would also depend on the degree of capital mobility, particularly financial capital. For capital to be highly mobile within a union, it would be necessary for financial and monetary systems to be highly integrated. Under such an arrangement, the slightest divergence in interest rates between regions within the union would induce sizeable flows of capital between the regions. As a result, balance-of-payments imbalances between the regions could be easily accommodated by capital flows from surplus regions to deficit regions.

For example, if one region were experiencing a deficit on current account, capital inflows would be attracted to offset the current account deficit by fractionally increasing the interest rate on financial instruments. In effect, the surplus regions of the currency area would be lending funds to the deficit regions to finance their payments deficit. The greater the degree of integration of the financial and monetary systems of the union (the greater the mobility of capital), the more easily this transfer of funds would be accomplished. The payments imbalance, therefore, could be handled without resort to exchange-rate adjustments.

It should be noted that the financing of payments imbalances through capital flows from surplus to deficit regions is properly viewed as a temporary measure. In order for the deficit region to make a true adjustment in its payments position, the underlying causes of the imbalance (such as low productivity or high inflation) must be corrected. Selling financial instruments to borrow funds from a surplus nation is only a stopgap measure for payments adjustment.[3]

The degree of factor mobility is not the only criterion affecting the size and composition of an optimum currency area. For example, the greater the size of a country's foreign trade sector, the more beneficial it will be for that nation to form a currency area with its trading partners than to maintain separate national currencies with fluctuating exchange rates. This argument follows from the fact that the larger the international trade sector of a domestic economy, the greater the potential impact on the economy of any change in the exchange rate. For instance,

---

[3]However, it is often pointed out that if the deficit country uses these borrowed funds to increase its capital stock and thus to increase its productivity and international competitiveness, then these borrowings may be viewed as a permanent solution to the causes of its payments imbalances.

a depreciation of home currency will have a much greater impact on the domestic price level (increase) of a nation which imports a considerable portion of its consumption goods, than it will for a country which imports only a small fraction of its consumption goods. A trade-dependent country would be better off in terms of price stability if it were to form a currency area (with fixed exchange rates) with its trading partners.

Finally, it is clear that two nations or regions that desire to form a currency area must have similar economic objectives, particularly in regard to levels of inflation and employment. Suppose one member of the union assigns a higher priority to employment goals than its partner, and is willing to sustain a higher rate of inflation in order to achieve these objectives than its partner would be willing to endure. In pursuing the expansionary policies necessary to attain high employment, that nation can be expected to incur a payments deficit with its trading partner. If the two nations are joined together in a monetary union in which exchange rates are fixed, several problems can arise. First, in order to support the fixed rate of exchange, the central banks of the participating nations will be forced to engage in large-scale intervention on the foreign exchange market. From Chapter 6 we know that such intervention is dependent on the adequacy of available reserves. Also, if the effects are not sterilized, exchange market intervention will lead to changes in the money supply of the intervening country, thereby disturbing economic conditions in that nation. Second, although the payments imbalance could be corrected by proper monetary and fiscal policy adjustments in each nation, this would require that the deficit nation undertake contractionary macroeconomic policy or that the surplus country inflate its economy. Both of these policies result in exactly the opposite effects desired by policy authorities. It would thus be very difficult

for two countries to maintain a common currency area while pursuing divergent policy objectives.[4]

The formation of an optimum currency area depends on all of the above factors, taken in combination. In practice, there have been several attempts to combine individual, national currency areas into a monetary union that transcends national borders. Let us now turn to examine the most well-known of these efforts: the European Monetary System.

THE EUROPEAN MONETARY SYSTEM

The most far-reaching efforts to organize several national currency areas into one large currency area have been those of the European nations, culminating in the formation of the European Monetary System (EMS). As mentioned previously, one of the long-standing goals of the EEC has been the establishment of a closer economic union among its members; steps to forge a monetary union represent major efforts in that direction.

These efforts by the EEC countries have been less successful, however, than their earlier attempts to form a common market. This can be explained by the difference in the nature of the two processes. Establishing the free flow of trade and factors of production requires that existing intercountry barriers be dismantled; this is sometimes referred to as "negative" integration. Establishing a monetary union, on the other hand, requires that exchange rates be stabilized and that national monetary and fiscal policies be highly coordinated. The increase in international cooperation which is required is referred to as "positive" integration and involves developing extensive economic linkages among countries.

[4]The effects of macroeconomic policy under fixed exchange rates are discussed in detail in Chapter 8.

Not surprisingly, the latter type of integration has proved more difficult to attain than the former. Let us see how this process has proceeded in the case of the European Monetary System.

Early European Efforts at Monetary Integration

In 1970 the central authorities of the EEC received the Werner Report, which advocated the formation of a monetary union by the EEC member nations. The Werner Report also provided a blueprint for the organization of the monetary union, which it viewed as a springboard to a full economic and political union of Europe. As a first step toward monetary union, the member nations of the EEC, in 1972, formed the "European snake", which was a scheme to stabilize European exchange rates. Under the "snake" arrangement, the exchange rates between the currencies of the member nations were to be held within a narrow band of values around a parity rate. During the first year of operation the value of the members' currencies were also pegged to the U.S. dollar, but within a wider range of values.[5] However, in March 1973, when the worldwide system of pegged exchange rates collapsed (see Chapter 24), the European nations ceased to limit the fluctuations of their currencies against the dollar. By continuing to

[5]Under the Smithsonian agreements (1971), the European currencies were pegged to the dollar and allowed to fluctuate $2^1/_4$ percent above and below their pegged dollar value. When the bilateral European rates were calculated from their respective values against the dollar, however, the European currencies could actually fluctuate against one another by twice that amount (plus or minus $4^1/_2$ percent). Under the snake arrangement, however, the bilateral European currency rates were only to fluctuate by plus or minus $2^1/_4$ percent. This lower band of fluctuations of the European currencies within the wider Smithsonian band accounted for the arrangement's name—a snake in a tunnel.

maintain pegged rates among EEC member currencies, the EEC had, in effect, established a "joint float" of their currencies against the dollar and other nonparticipating currencies.

A few nations within the snake—specifically, the United Kingdom, Italy and France—had great difficulty maintaining the value of their currencies within the predetermined range. These countries were experiencing higher rates of inflation than the other members, and as a result were incurring balance-of-payments deficits. This placed severe downward pressure on their exchange rates with other snake currencies. To maintain their parity values, either the central banks would have to intervene massively on the foreign exchange market to purchase the currency of the deficit countries, or the deficit countries would have to impose contractionary monetary and fiscal measures on their economies. The deficit countries were either unable or unwilling to undertake those measures, and as a result were forced to leave the snake. The United Kingdom was the first to depart, allowing the pound to float against the other European currencies in late 1972. In fact the United Kingdom, Italy and Ireland all left the snake prior to the time the joint float began in early 1973. France participated in the joint float for a short while, but withdrew in January 1974. Norway and Sweden, though not EEC members, entered the joint float in 1973. However, by 1979 both of these nations had also withdrawn from the snake.

Efforts at Restoring Monetary Integration: The Formation of the European Monetary System

With the departure of so many important countries from the joint float, much of Europe was operating, for all intents and purposes, with a system of flexible exchange rates during the mid- to later 1970s. Still, most of the European nations were convinced that the costs of intra–European exchange-rate flexibility far outweighed the benefits. The size of the exchange-rate fluctuations was viewed as disruptive to community trade as well as upsetting to many of the EEC's specific programs for economic integration, such as the common agricultural policy. Accordingly, the EEC nations renewed their efforts to return to a system of fixed exchange rates among their currencies. As a result, the *European Monetary System* was established in March 1979 with the objective of creating a zone of monetary stability. With the exception of the United Kingdom, all members of the EEC elected to participate in the EMS.

The efforts to revive monetary integration within Europe were spearheaded by France and Germany. Each viewed the EMS as a device that would be supportive of its own economic goals. France's economy has historically been plagued with relatively high rates of inflation, which has resulted in a depreciation of the franc against most other European currencies, particularly the German deutsche mark. France's president during the late 1970s, Valerie Giscard d'Estaing, was attempting to impose an antiinflation discipline on the French economy. Linking the value of the franc to the stronger German mark would reinforce his efforts, since France would be forced to impose contractionary fiscal and monetary policy should the franc depreciate too much against the mark.

Germany's economic problems were just the opposite. Because of the antiinflationary bias of German economic policy, the deutsche mark was viewed by outsiders as a more attractive outlet for foreign exchange holdings than were the other EEC currencies. Thus when the dollar was depreciating during the 1970s, holders of dollar assets diversified their portfolios by shifting much of their wealth into assets denominated in marks. This caused the mark to appreciate relative to other EEC currencies which, in turn, made German exports less competitive. Concern over the continuing appreciation of the mark

and its effect on German exports prompted German Chancellor Helmut Schmidt to strongly push for the EMS, and the fixed exchange rates that went along with it.

Major Features of the EMS

The principal feature of the EMS is the establishment of central exchange rates—the official, fixed exchange rates among the various currencies. The values of the currencies are permitted to fluctuate around their central rates within margins of plus or minus $2^1/_4$ percent. The currency of Italy, however, is permitted, on a temporary basis, to fluctuate within margins of plus or minus 6 percent. The central rates are to be reviewed periodically, and an individual currency's central rate is to be changed if pressures on that currency indicate a fundamental change in its relative value. Thus the EMS is not a true monetary union, since its exchange rates can fluctuate within a narrow band.

The agreement that inaugurated the EMS also established the European Currency Unit (ECU). The ECU is a unit of account whose value is determined by a weighted average of the values of the currencies of the member nations. Each member's currency has a central rate against the ECU. The primary purpose of the ECU is to serve as a denominator for the intervention transactions to be undertaken by the central banks in their efforts to maintain the central rates. If a member's exchange rate, vis-à-vis the ECU, deviates too far from the central rate, then its authorities must act to correct the situation. In addition to serving as the denominator for the currency pegs, the ECU is intended to serve as a means of settling accounts between central banks.

ECUs are to be issued to central banks by the *European Monetary Fund (EMF)* in exchange for gold and dollar reserves. The EMF has not been formally established and the creation of ECUs has been implemented by swap arrangements (ECUs for gold and dollars) among individual central banks.[6]

A number of facilities have been established under the EMS to aid members that are experiencing payments deficits with other member nations and that must therefore support their central rate on the foreign exchange market. Intervention by an EMS country in the foreign exchange markets to support its central rate is to be undertaken using other participating currencies. Thus, if the Italian lira is declining in value vis-à-vis the German deutsche mark, the central bank of Italy would be expected to support its central rate by purchasing lira using deutsche marks. If Italy's central bank were short of the deutsche marks needed to support the lira, the EMS has established an arrangement whereby Italy's central bank could borrow deutsche marks automatically for a short period of time. These borrowings would then be repaid by Italy using gold, foreign exchange reserves or ECUs as the means of payment.

The EMS has also established facilities for countries burdened with a more serious and longer term payments problem. A $30 billion intervention fund has been established that will be used for medium or long-term loans to member nations that must give longer term support to their central rates while internal macroeconomic adjustments are being worked out.

The reader may have noticed that the EMS appears to be quite similar to the former "snake." Both arrangements attempted to stabilize intra–European exchange rates and also called for periodic review of the central exchange rates. However, there are some important differences between the two monetary arrangements. First,

the EMS has created a much larger intervention fund for deficit nations to draw upon in attempting to support the value of their currencies. This allows the deficit nations a longer period of time to implement the internal adjustments necessary to eliminate their payments imbalances. Second, the EMS has the long-term objective of moving toward a more advanced stage of monetary and economic union, whereas the snake was never intended to be anything more than a fixed exchange-rate system. Because of its greater financing capacity and its long-term commitment to an economically unified Europe, the EMS is a far more ambitious attempt at integration than was the snake.

Performance of the EMS

In its first two years, the EMS was fairly effective in minimizing exchange-rate fluctuations between the currencies of its members. With the exception of a handful of central rate changes, the EMS exchange rates were relatively stable, and remained within the specified margins. In fact, in its first year of operation, fluctuations among the exchange rates of the participating countries were the lowest in eight years.

Whether the EMS will move toward its goal of a true monetary union or whether it will even be able to maintain a zone of monetary stability is unclear, as several problems continue to plague the system. First, Britain has continued to keep the pound out of the EMS. Because of the importance of the United Kingdom among the European economies, and its interrelationship with the participating members of the EMS (Britain is, of course, a member of the EEC), any meaningful move toward a full economic union of Europe would have to include the United Kingdom. Second, the EMS has as yet been unable to establish the European Monetary Fund as a clearing mechanism for transactions between central banks. Third, the economic ob-

[6]Physically, ECUs take the form of credits on the books of the European Monetary Fund (for now, the central banks of the members). When one country transfers ECUs to another, those credits are transferred from the account of the first country to that of the second on the books of the fund.

jectives of the individual member nations, in terms of employment and inflation, remain as diverse as ever. As a result, it is unclear whether those nations suffering payments deficits with the rest of the Community would be willing to undertake the contractionary fiscal and monetary policies (with their adverse employment effects) to eliminate their payments imbalances. This question is even more clouded since the election of the Socialist government in France in 1981, which places a higher priority on full employment. Recall that the reluctance to undergo internal deflation in order to cure external deficits was what led to the demise of the snake. Finally, the sensitivity of the EMS to fluctuations in the value of the dollar remains a problem. In fact, such fluctuations have placed strains on the exchange-rate structure within the EMS during the early 1980s. High interest rates in the United States were attracting funds from Europe, placing downward pressure on the European currencies, with greater downward pressure falling on the weaker currencies.

EUROPE: AN ECONOMIC AND POLITICAL UNION

An *economic union* was defined in the previous chapter as the most advanced stage of economic integration. In its most complete form, the responsibility for economic policy is transferred from the governments of the individual member nations to a central authority representing the entire union. In other words, a sovereign nation would be expected to relinquish its right to form national economic policy. Such an arrangement obviously involves a much greater degree of cooperation than a monetary union. While the success of a monetary union, which involves simply the joining together of national currency areas into one large currency area, requires that national economic policies be harmonized, it does not necessarily imply a forfeiture of poli-

cymaking prerogatives by national governments to a supranational authority.

Because of the degree of cooperation needed for the successful operation of an economic union, both financial and political institutions representing the entire union would have to be established. For example, it would be necessary to create a unified banking system with a single central bank for the entire union. In addition, a governing body representing the entire union would have to be established to implement a common fiscal policy. Thus any discussion of economic union would have to involve a discussion of political union, as well.

The founders of the EEC had as their ultimate objective an economically and politically unified Europe. Many observers thought progress toward a greater degree of economic integration would occur automatically as the first stages of integration were implemented. For example, it was thought that, as trade barriers within the Community were dismantled, harmonization of national policies governing such matters as subsidies on the production of traded goods and of tax systems (which could otherwise disrupt free trade) would naturally follow. Likewise, it was thought that regulations governing the movement of capital and labor within the Community would be reconciled. For example, if corporate profit taxes were allowed to remain lower in one nation than in another, it could cause capital to move to the low-tax nation even if this did not entail the most productive use of capital. A more efficient allocation of resources could be obtained by coordinating national tax policies. Thus, it was believed that the participating countries would have strong incentives to coordinate their national policies in order to capture all of the benefits of economic integration.

As a matter of fact, the EEC member nations have undertaken efforts to at least coordinate many of their national policies. These efforts include the establishment of Community–wide value-added tax systems, greater coordination of national social security schemes and the common agricultural policy. Although these efforts have not resulted in identical policies within all of the countries, they have brought them much closer together.

Probably the most sensitive area of economic policy coordination has been that of macroeconomic policy—the use of fiscal and monetary policy to achieve employment and inflation objectives. There were high hopes that the formation of the EMS in 1979 would encourage policy coordination in this area. As mentioned earlier in the chapter, macroeconomic policy harmonization is almost a prerequisite for a successful monetary union, since divergent policies will lead to divergent inflation rates, which will put severe pressure on the fixed exchange rates. Still, the members of the EMS seem to have divergent views on the levels of inflation they are willing to endure. Not surprisingly, when there is a conflict, member nations give priority to their national objectives over policies to support the EMS. This reflects the traditional responsibilities of national governments in the areas of employment and inflation. It can therefore be expected that, for the foreseeable future, national governments will be reluctant to subject their policies to the discipline required by a monetary or economic union.

QUESTIONS AND EXERCISES

1. Define an optimum currency area and a monetary union. Does a monetary union necessarily have to be an optimum currency area? Explain. Also, discuss a manner in which an optimum currency area may be established, other than by a monetary union.

2. Suppose two countries are considering forming a monetary union, and you are asked to provide a recommendation on whether the union should be established. You are given the following information: (a) labor and capital are relatively immobile between the two countries, (b) mutual trade accounts for a substantial portion of their respective GNP and (c) they have similar views on tolerable domestic inflation rates. Present your recommendation, making sure you address all relevant considerations.

3. Evaluate the following statement: Optimum currency areas necessarily correspond to national currency areas. It might be useful to present a counterexample if you doubt this statement.

4. Describe the snake arrangement of the European countries. Why did the arrangement fail? Were the European nations satisfied with a situation where intra–European exchange rates were permitted to fluctuate? Why or why not?

5. Describe the principal features of the European Monetary System, making sure you address the following aspects:

   a. exchange-rate structures
   b. a system-wide currency unit
   c. foreign exchange intervention procedures
   d. credit facilities

6. Do you believe that the European Monetary System will be more or less successful than the snake arrangement? Why or why not? What are some of the problems that the EMS must circumvent to ensure its future success?

7. Suppose two countries—say, country A and country B—have divergent views on inflation and employment goals. Specifically, country A is willing to endure high rates of inflation to attain its employment objectives, while country B places a higher priority on reducing inflation. What problems would arise if these two countries joined together to form a monetary union?

CLOSING ESSAY:
The Nature of Future European Monetary Integration

Take a moment to imagine a Europe in which all the individual nations have been subsumed within a federation under one supragovernment. Formerly independent nations would simply be economic and political regions within a unified Europe. Under such an arrangement, there would be common prices for all goods and services and factors of production throughout the Community, as well as a common money.

On a more mundane level, such an arrangement would imply that a Frenchman planning to take a vacation in Italy would not need to acquire a passport or make plans to convert his francs into lira. Such a vacation would be no different than a New Yorker traveling to California. Or a German–based firm wishing to establish a subsidiary in Belgium would find it no more difficult than an Ohio–based firm wishing to establish a subsidiary in Texas. An unemployed Irish welder would think no more of seeking employment in Germany than an unemployed welder in Michigan would think of seeking employment in Florida. All of these economic "tasks" are undertaken within the United States many times daily with minimum inconvenience. If Europe were to establish a true economic union, these tasks would become no more difficult than they are within a single nation such as the United States.

Can a United States of Europe ever evolve from the current European Monetary System? Can the economic tasks described above become as straightforward when undertaken across national boundaries in Europe as they are when undertaken across regional boundaries within a single country. The previous two chapters have addressed many of the economic and political aspects of that question, examining the degree of success achieved thus far, as well as the problems remaining in attaining greater degrees of integration. This closing essay will extend that discussion by examining how the EMS might overcome some of the obstacles to reaching the status of a monetary union, and how such a monetary union may operate in practice.

Obviously, one prerequisite for Europe to assume such a status would be bilateral exchange rates that are unquestionably stable, not like the current situation where exchange rates can fluctuate around a central rate which itself can be changed. What would guarantee stability in exchange-rate values? Some argue that perfect mobility of capital between the European nations will assure such stability. Suppose France were experiencing a balance-of-payments deficit with Germany on a current account basis, placing downward pressure on the mark/franc exchange rate. France might intervene on the exchange market to support the franc by purchasing francs using its stock of deutsche mark reserves. If short of deutsche marks, France under the EMS system may automatically receive a credit of deutsche marks from Germany. However, there may be no need for intervention if capital is perfectly mobile. With a truly integrated financial system in Europe, France could sell securities in the European financial market by simply offering a fractionally higher interest rate, yielding an inflow of capital large enough to offset the payments deficit, which would eliminate the downward pressure on the franc. Such a situation would be equivalent to the situation in the United States when, say, Ohio, is running a trade deficit with California, and funds are being transferred from Ohio banks to California banks. There is little difficulty adjusting to such a situation, as Ohio banks will sell securities in the New York money market, while California banks will use their surplus funds to purchase interest-yielding securities in that market. The key to this smooth adjustment is that financial markets between regions within a monetary union are fully integrated, so that securities from one region are acceptable in another region. As stated in Chapter 18, the European money markets do seem to be becoming more closely linked with the establishment of the European bond market, the proliferation of the Eurocurrency market and branch banking that transcends national borders. Thus it is possible that greater financial integration may increase the chances of exchange-rate stability in Europe.

Suppose a truly fixed exchange system were established. How would an individual nation adjust to internal imbalances, such as excessive unemployment? If there were individual nations experiencing excessive unemployment, those workers who are unemployed might migrate to areas within the union where employment is available. Such movements of labor have occurred in limited numbers within the Community (primarily from Italy and Greece), although not enough to eliminate regional imbalances.

Individual nations may attempt to employ national monetary policy to correct internal disturbances. However, if capital is mobile within the monetary union, then the efficacy of national monetary policy becomes doubtful. For example, an attempt by an individual central bank to increase its money supply in an effort to stimulate employment may be negated because of the downward pressure such a policy will place on national interest rates. With fixed exchange rates, a decline in the interest rate in one nation will result in an outflow of funds from its borders to more attractive assets in other European nations, causing the domestic money supply to fall and interest rates to rise, frustrating the monetary authorities. The development of the Eurodollar market has accentuated the interdependence of national monetary policies in Europe.

Will national fiscal policies be any more effective in correcting internal disturbances than monetary policies, or will national governments completely relinquish their policymaking ability in a monetary union? National fiscal policy, it is argued by some, will remain effective, in the short run, under a monetary union. For example, a nation experiencing unemployment may undertake increased expenditures designed to reduce the problem. In fact, those expenditures could be financed by issuing bonds in the Community capital market (which would also help the nation's payments position). However, for the expenditures made possible by bond issues in the Community bond market to be effective in the long term, those expenditures should be designed to increase the productive capacity of the nation (public investment) rather than just to maintain expenditure levels. Once such an adjustment has been made, the nation should be more competitive and its employment and payments position improved, eliminating the need for borrowing.

Fiscal policy designed to maintain income in depressed regions—such as unemployment compensation and welfare payments—might be more effective if implemented by a Community–wide government from a Community budget. Such payments would involve a transfer of income from the more prosperous nations to those experiencing economic difficulties as in the case of payments made under Common Agricultural Policy. However, a considerable amount of friction exists among the members because of the question of how equitable are the disbursements from the Community budget.

The development of a common monetary policy for the Community is the key prerequisite for the establishment of a successful monetary union. The proposed second stage of the EMS would attempt to institutionalize common monetary policy by establishing the European Monetary Fund (EMF). Currently, the European Monetary Cooperation Fund has the responsibility of issuing ECUs against 20 percent of the reserves held by central banks and recording the volume of transactions between individual central banks. However, the issuance of credit to nations with deficits is undertaken bilaterally between central banks. The creation of the European Monetary Fund might centralize the task of granting credit. Member nations would transfer reserves to the EMF, and endow it with the authority to grant credit to other member nations. Such a step would be a significant move toward true economic integration. This is demonstrated by the fact that, if the EMF has the power to grant credits in ECUs, it would have the power to create liquidity or money. In other words, the proposed European Monetary Fund, as described above, would represent a Community monetary institution with the power to create liquidity and thus establish a monetary policy for the entire Community.

If the ECU does, in fact, become a widely used common currency in the EMS, then it might be anticipated that the European Monetary Fund would also assume the responsibility of establishing and implementing an intervention policy regarding the ECU/dollar exchange rate. Thus the proposed EMF, as described above, has many of the characteristics of a European central bank.

The preceding discussion was speculation on how a European monetary union in the future might function. All of the aspects addressed implied that a great deal of cooperation between the nations would be required. The need for cooperation is not new; it has been the prevailing message throughout the previous two chapters. The greatest demand placed on the individual nations is that they relinquish to Community authority their responsibility for establishing important aspects of economic policy. As might be expected, independent nations with divergent characteristics and economic aims will find it difficult to forfeit that responsibility to an authority representing the entire Community, despite the desire to obtain the benefits of a monetary union. It is this ambivalence which presents the principal roadblock to the attainment of the long-term goal of an economically united Europe.

INTRODUCTION

Throughout the previous chapters, frequent references have been made to the less-developed countries (LDCs). A formal description of what is meant by the term "less developed" will be postponed until the main body of this section, but for now let it suffice to say that the less-developed nations can be thought of as those countries characterized by low levels of economic development; that is, the poor nations of the world. These nations comprise a distinct bloc of nations with economic and social characteristics quite different from those of the rich nations.

The chief concern of this section is how the economic problems of the less-developed nations differ from those of the more advanced nations, and, more specifically, how those problems are affected by their international economic relations. The economic problems of poor nations are of immense proportions, and are reflected by the absolute poverty that the majority of their residents must endure. The problems cannot be viewed as exclusively the concern of the poor nations. The less-developed countries constitute well over one-half of the world's population, and the economic difficulties affecting that proportion of the world's population must be the concern of all nations, rich and poor alike.

The interests of the rich and poor nations are interwoven in a vast network of international trading and monetary relations, as well as political and military associations. Because of this complex system of economic relations between the less-developed nations and advanced nations, the latter group has a deep-seated economic interest in understanding those problems and taking the appropriate action which best serves those interests.

Often, the advanced nations will undertake actions which aid the plight of the LDCs, while other actions they may take are viewed by the LDCs as detrimental to their condition.

As will be shown, the uneven distribution of income and wealth among the world's nations places the poorer nations of the world in a position of dependency on the rich nations in many instances. The less-developed nations desire to escape such a dependency, and to attain a level of economic development which will place them on a more equal footing with the advanced nations, providing the opportunity to their residents to improve their quality of life. One avenue of escape is through greater participation in world commerce. However, the dominant position of the industrialized nations in production and marketing inhibits many of those efforts. As a result, the LDCs in recent years have clamored for a change in the manner in which international economic relations are conducted, and advocated procedures that will place the LDCs in a more equitable position.

This section begins by examining the characteristics of developing countries that set them apart from other nations, and then proceeds to detail their economic relations with the more advanced nations. This discussion is followed by an examination of the particular economic problems resulting from the economic characteristics of the LDCs.

Chapter 20 begins by tracing the rising dissatisfaction among LDCs regarding their economic position in the world economy—a dissatisfaction that culminated in 1974 with their call for a New International Economic Order. The chapter then turns to a discussion of a number of proposals and actions that have been undertaken by the various blocs of nations to improve the conditions of the LDCs. As will be seen, the plight of LDCs is quite severe, and this will no doubt be one of the burning international economic issues of the future.

Economic Problems 19
of the Developing Countries

The nations of the world present quite a heterogeneous mix of economic, political and social characteristics. In this chapter we shall focus on the economic differences among the nations of the world. In particular, we shall examine the economic relations among two distinct blocs of nations—the rich and the poor. The difference in economic conditions between these two groups of nations creates a number of problems for international economic relations; these problems are highlighted in this chapter. The chapter begins by examining the economic characteristics of the poor nations, relative to those of the richer nations, and then proceeds to discuss the specific problems faced by the poor nations in their efforts to improve their economic well-being. Throughout the chapter, we attempt to emphasize the interrelationships between rich and poor nations, and how they affect the economic plight of the poor nations.

DEVELOPED AND LESS-DEVELOPED NATIONS

The most striking economic disparity among the various nations of the world is to be found in the level of their economic development. Using per capita gross national product as a measure of economic development, Table 19–1 illustrates the difference in development for selected nations, as of 1978. For example, an intercountry comparison of the GNP figures would suggest that an average individual in the United States had an income level approximately 54 times the level of an individual in India. A broader view of the worldwide disparity of income levels is presented in Table 19–2, which categorizes the nations of the world into per capita income groups and also shows the population of each group.

TABLE 19-1

Per Capita GNP of Selected Nations and Other Demographic Characteristics
(1978)

Country and Rank	GNP per Capita	Adult Literacy Rate (%)	Life Expectancy
Kuwait (1)	$15,970	60	69
United States (6)	9,770	99	73
Italy (22)	4600	98	73
USSR (26)	3710	99	70
Argentina (37)	2030	94	71
Republic of Korea (48)	1310	93	63
Guatemala (60)	930	47	57
Bolivia (75)	510	63	52
Pakistan (99)	240	21	52
India (107)	180	36	51
Bangladesh (117)	90	26	47

Source: World Bank, *World Development Report, 1980,* and *1980 World Bank Atlas* (Washington, D.C.: World Bank Publications, 1980).

According to those figures, almost one-half of the world's population earns less than $300 annually and approximately three-fourths earn less than $3000 per year.

The validity of such intercountry comparisons, however, is questionable. One problem is simply the practical limitations of obtaining accurate income data for the poorer nations. Also, the differing structures of the economies of the world—the upper income level nations have highly organized markets, while the poorer nations generally have many economic transactions taking place outside the marketplace—make dollar-for-dollar comparisons of income levels difficult. For example, it would be difficult for a resident of the United States to conceive of

TABLE 19-2

Per Capita Income Group	Number of Countries	Population mid-1978 (millions)	Cumulative Percentage of World Population (%)
Less than $300	36	2,008	48.3
$300 to $699	38	493	60.1
$700 to $2999	50	571	73.8
$3000 to $6999	29	536	86.7
$7000 and over	25	552	100.0

Number of Countries and Population by Income Groupings

Source: World Bank, *1980 World Bank Atlas* (Washington, D.C.: World Bank Publications, 1980).

an individual surviving on an annual income of $180, the average in India; especially considering that the poverty level in the United States is defined for a family of four as approximately $6000 per year. However, for residents of India, many goods and services, such as housing, food and clothing, are self-produced or obtained in barter exchange, and thus would not be included in official calculations of output or income levels. This qualification, however, is not intended to nullify intercountry comparisons of per capita GNP as a legitimate means of contrasting world economic conditions. Even if an accurate calculation of the per capita GNP level of India were obtained, and the per capita income calculation increased, say, 10 times to $1800, the United States per capita income figure would still be more than five times greater, which is still a significant disparity.

Finally, it should be noted that the stages of economic development are not only distinguished by divergent income levels, but also by many economic and demographic characteristics. For example, the poorer nations of the world are generally more dependent on agriculture, relative to industrial production, than are the rich nations. Also, as Table 19–1 indicates, the poorer nations of the world are typically hindered by low levels of education, as measured by literacy rates, and lower health and medical standards, as measured by life expectancies.

Traditionally, the nations of the world have been divided into two groups—the developed countries (DCs) and the less-developed countries (LDCs), with per capita income levels serving as the criterion for assigning a particular nation to one or the other category. However, the LDC–DC dichotomy is not entirely representative of the range of levels of economic development throughout the world. Individual countries within each of the two groups can be quite different in many respects. For example, on the basis of per capita income alone, several

of the members of OPEC[1] would be included in the DC category. However, these nations differ from the other rich nations in almost every remaining economic and demographic characteristic. In fact, the nonincome characteristics of those nations more closely resemble the characteristics of the LDCs.

Non-oil-exporting nations that are categorized as LDCs also display a vast array of characteristics. For example, both Brazil and Bolivia are traditionally grouped together as LDCs, and relative to, say, the United States, such a classification is appropriate. However, those two nations themselves are quite different economically. In Brazil, over the past two decades, income has grown more than twice as rapidly as it has in Bolivia (4.9 percent annually versus 2.2 percent), and in 1978 the level of per capita income in Brazil was three times that of Bolivia. There are a number of other LDCs, including Hong Kong, Taiwan and Korea, that although quite poor today, are currently experiencing high rates of growth in income, and like Brazil, they are moving farther away from other LDCs whose economies are much less vibrant in terms of growth.

Despite the inherent difficulties in making such distinctions, we shall follow the traditional procedure of classifying a country as either developed (DC) or less developed (LDC). In addition, references will be made to a third group of nations—the oil-exporting nations—that derive a substantial portion of their income from petroleum exports. As mentioned above, many of these nations have high per capita income levels, yet in all remaining aspects are more appropriately identified with the LDCs. Nations that are typically considered to be developed include the Western European countries, Canada, the United States, Japan, New Zealand and

[1]Those nations would include Kuwait ($15,970/year), Libya ($7210/year) and Saudi Arabia ($6590/year).

Australia; most of the remaining nations are considered as either less developed or oil exporting. In our ensuing discussion, the diversity within each group should be kept in mind.

ECONOMIC GROWTH VERSUS ECONOMIC DEVELOPMENT

Without a doubt, many, if not most, of the problems facing the LDCs stem from their relatively (and absolutely) low levels of income. It is thus not surprising that one of the foremost objectives of the developing nations is to achieve a higher rate of growth in per capita income.

It should be noted, however, that economic growth is often accompanied by many other changes, some desirable, others of more questionable worth. It is generally agreed that improvements in education, nutrition and health go hand in hand with economic growth. At the same time, as a country grows, changes in the fundamental structure of its economy and society can be expected. These typically include a high degree of urbanization, shifts in foreign trade patterns and changes in the composition of the nation's production, usually a shift from agriculture to manufacturing. Developing countries, then, must be concerned with more than simply the rate of increase in income; they must also be prepared to deal with the complex economic and social effects that accompany economic growth. Economic growth in combination with these structural changes is referred to as *economic development*. While the developing nations clearly desire to raise their economic growth rates, they wish to do so in a manner which yields a satisfactory form of economic development.

While many different strategies for economic development have been formulated and prescribed for the LDCs, a thorough discussion of these theories and strategies is beyond the scope of this text. Instead, our discussion will focus on those aspects of economic development that affect and are affected by international trade and monetary relations.

The Impact of Trade on Economic Growth

As we saw in Chapter 5, economic growth can lead to changes in the volume and pattern of trade. In addition, the converse relation can also hold. Expanding trade can lead to both a fuller employment and a more efficient allocation of existing resources. As we saw in Chapter 2, a nation can improve its economic well-being through free trade; that is, by specializing in the production of the commodities in which it enjoys a comparative advantage and trading those commodities for other goods in the world market.

Many LDCs believe that they can achieve economic growth by increasing the sale of exports. The idea is that expanding output and employment in the export sector will stimulate output and employment in other sectors of the economy. Export expansion may also have a number of dynamic effects on the domestic economy. For example, if the increase in export sales is accompanied by an increase in profits in the export sector, investment expenditure on capital equipment for that sector may be expected to expand. This will raise the productive capacity of the economy. Also, growth in the export industries could generate a demand for more advanced labor skills to handle the international transactions, stimulating the domestic economy to provide the human capital (education and training) needed to prepare workers for those positions. Finally, the additional foreign exchange earned through greater export sales might be used to increase imports of capital goods that would add to the productive capacity of the economy.

For these reasons, some observers believe that free trade and export expansion are vehicles through which the LDCs can achieve their desired level of economic development. As we shall see shortly, there are several reasons why economic development via trade expansion might be more difficult than it first appears.

CHARACTERISTICS OF LDC TRADE

Table 19–3 depicts the pattern of imports to and exports from the developing nations in 1979. The most striking feature is the overwhelming dependence by the LDCs on the developed countries, both as a source of imports (70 percent of LDC imports originated in the DCs) and as a market for their exports (74 percent of LDC exports were to the DCs). It follows, then, that trade among the LDCs themselves is quite limited in volume, accounting for only about a quarter of total LDC trade.

Another prominent feature is the composition of LDC exports. Primary products (see the product definitions in footnote b, Table 19–3) account for some 77 percent of the total value of LDC exports. This implies that, despite efforts by the LDCs to industrialize and expand their exports of manufactures, they remain dependent on nonmanufactures as a source of export earn-

[2]The dominance of primary product exports over manufactured exports may be exaggerated since fuel exports are included in the primary product calculation. Because the OPEC nations are considered LDCs in these calculations, the substantial rise in petroleum prices in the 1970s will increase the value of primary product exports relative to manufactured exports.

TABLE 19-3

World Trade Patterns: 1979 (billions of U.S. dollars) Excluding Communist Bloc Nations			
	Imports of:		Total Exports
Exports from	Developed[a]	Developing	
Developed Primary[b]	191.64	37.68	229.32
Manufactures	587.28	197.55	784.83
Developing Primary	236.21	70.72	306.93
Manufactures	58.77	32.46	91.23
World Trade (Total) Developed	778.92	235.23	1014.15
Developing	294.98	103.18	398.16
Total imports	1073.90	338.41	1412.31

Source: United Nations, *Monthly Bulletin of Statistics* (New York: United Nations Publications, July 1981).

[a]Developed countries include all Western European nations, the United States, Canada, Japan, Australia and New Zealand; the remaining nations are considered developing nations. The trade of the centrally planned economies is excluded completely.

[b]Primary products are defined according to the Standard International Trade Classification (SITC) which considers commodity categories, 0–4, as primary products and includes agricultural products, raw materials and fuels. Manufactures are considered products in SITC categories 5–9 and include chemicals, machinery and other manufactures.

ings.[2] Moreover, the manufactures that the LDCs do export, such as textiles and apparels, generally are labor intensive and require low levels of technology in production. The heavy dependence of LDCs on low-technology exports is illustrated by the fact that, in 1980, 39 percent of the value of total clothing imports by the DCs came from non-oil-exporting LDCs, while only 6 percent of total imports of engineering products came from non-oil-exporting LDCs.

It should be noted, however, that the dominance of primary products in the export trade of LDCs was diminishing during the 1960s and 1970s. This trend is indicated in Table 19–4, which shows the percentage of the value of total LDC exports, excluding fuel products (see footnote 2), accounted for by manufactures. Although the percentages are overstated because of the exclusion of fuel products (a primary product) from the total value of exports, the trend is apparent; LDCs as a group have increased their exports of manufactures relative to primary products during the past twenty years. However, this does not suggest that the LDCs have been transformed from economies based on primary products to economies based on manufactures. The LDCs' share of manufactured exports remains quite low relative to that of the DCs, as does the absolute value of manufactured goods produced in the LDCs.

Moreover, the increase in exports of manufactured goods has not been distributed evenly among the LDCs; indeed, most of the increase has been concentrated in a handful of the more rapidly developing countries within that group. This disparity is depicted in Table 19–5, which shows the change in the share of manufactures in total nonfuel exports for selected LDCs between 1960 and 1975. In 1975, manufactured exports in South Korea and Hong Kong accounted for over 80 percent of those countries' total exports, and this proportion has increased substantially since 1960. On the other hand, for countries like Chad and Mali, the percentage of manufactures decreased during this period, from the already low percentages that prevailed in 1960.

Finally, it should be pointed out that the exports of many LDCs are concentrated in a small number of commodities. This is particularly true for the LDCs that depend heavily on exports of primary products. This is evident in Table 19–6, which shows a recent sample of selected LDCs, along with the percentage of exports accounted for by the country's three leading export com-

TABLE 19-4

Share (%) of Manufactures in Total Nonfuel Exports for LDCs

Year	Manufactures Share (%) of Exports (excluding fuel), all LDCs
1960	19.9
1965	25.9
1970	37.3
1975	44.5
1978	51.8

Source: United Nations, *Monthly Bulletin of Statistics* (New York: United Nations Publications, various issues).

TABLE 19-5

Share (%) of Manufactures in Total Nonfuel Exports of Selected LDCs

Country	Year 1960 (%)	1975 (%)
Argentina	4.1	24.3
Brazil	4.0	25.6
Chad	8.6	3.8
Hong Kong	82.6	93.3
Mali	3.2	1.2
Mexico	23.8	40.4
Pakistan	18.0	54.4
South Korea	60.9	81.5
Sudan	.1	1.2

Source: United Nations, *Yearbook of International Trade Statistics, Trade by Country* (New York: United Nations Publications, various issues).

TABLE 19-6

Concentration of Exports of Selected LDCs (1980)

Country	Products	% of Total Export Value
Bangladesh	Jute Goods, Raw Jute	64.0
Botswana	Diamonds, Copper–Nickel, Meat	86.6
Burma	Rice, Teak, Oilcakes	65.2
Burundi	Coffee, Cotton	88.6
Chile	Copper, Iron Ore	45.9
Costa Rica	Coffee, Bananas, Beef	50.8
Dominican Republic	Sugar, Ferronickel, Coffee	51.1
Guatemala	Coffee, Sugar, Cotton	53.4
Honduras	Bananas, Coffee, Frozen Beef	62.4
Ivory Coast	Coffee, Wood, Cocoa	65.5
Jamaica	Alumina, Bauxite, Sugar	75.7
Liberia	Iron Ore, Rubber, Diamonds	74.2
Malawi	Tobacco, Tea, Sugar	71.8
Paraguay	Timber, Cotton, Soybeans	69.1
Rwanda	Coffee, Tin, Tea	90.1
Somalia	Live Animals, Bananas, Hides and Skins	90.5
Sudan	Cotton, Gum Hashab, Groundnuts	77.1

Source: International Monetary Fund, *International Financial Statistics* (Washington, D.C.: International Monetary Fund, May 1981).

modities. In one of the most extreme cases, the nation of Rwanda depends almost exclusively (90 percent) on three products for its export trade. The problems arising from the concentration of exports in a limited number of products will be explored in the following section, along with the problems created by several other pertinent characteristics of LDC trade.

THE INTERNATIONAL ECONOMIC PROBLEMS OF LDCs

Export Price Instability

As we saw in the preceding section, a substantial percentage of LDC exports consists of primary products such as agricultural commodities and raw materials. Many observers believe that the supply and demand characteristics of these products create special problems for the LDCs, particularly with regard to the stability of export prices.

The elasticity of supply of many primary products, especially agricultural products, can be quite low in the short run. After an agricultural crop has been planted, for example, the quantity of the product is essentially fixed for the subsequent marketing period (prior to the completion of the next growing season), regardless of how the price of the commodity might move.

In the face of low supply elasticities, a change in demand can lead to a substantial movement in the price of the product. Suppose that the supply of a primary product, say coffee, is perfectly inelastic as shown in Figure 19–1. If the world demand for coffee exports were to decrease (say, because of a U.S. government report claiming that coffee is a carcinogen), the resulting leftward shift of the demand curve (from D_1 to D_2) would cause a substantial decline in price (from P_1 to P_2). This decline is greater than would be the case if the supply curve were upward sloping (reflecting greater price elasticity). For the exporting country, the combination of a lower price and unchanged quantity means a lower level of revenue and smaller foreign exchange earnings.

On the other hand, a substantial increase in price (and export earnings) would result if the demand for coffee were to increase. The implication is that, because the LDCs depend so heavily on the DCs as markets for their exports, a change in demand by the DCs for LDC exports will lead to wide fluctuations in their export prices and earnings.

Just as shifts in demand will produce wide variations in price when supply is inelastic, so will shifts in supply produce wide variations in price when demand is inelastic. Because many of the primary commodities exported by LDCs have few substitutes (at least in the short run), as in the case of important mineral products such as tin, the demand for those products tends to be relatively price inelastic. As a result, supply-side disturbances often lead to substantial changes in LDC export prices.

Such a situation can best be illustrated in a two-period framework. Figure 19–2 depicts the hypothetical market supply and demand conditions in the market for an LDC export, say coffee. The export supply curve is depicted as perfectly inelastic while the demand curve is portrayed as relatively price inelastic. Suppose that in time period 1, after the quantity of coffee supplied (S_1) has been determined, the DCs increase their demand for coffee, shifting the demand curve from D_1 to D_2. This causes a substantial increase in price, from P_0 to P_1. Because

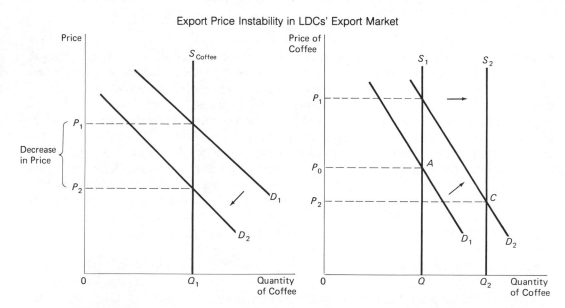

Export Price Instability in LDCs' Export Market

FIGURE 19-1 World Market for Coffee (Decrease in Demand)

FIGURE 19-2 World Market for Coffee (Increase in Demand and Supply)

of the attractive price received by producers in time period 1, the quantity of coffee planted in the following time period will probably increase, shifting the supply curve from S_1 to S_2. Because of the relatively inelastic demand, the resulting decline in price in time period 2 (from P_1 to P_2) will be substantial. It is easy to see, then, how inelastic supply and demand conditions for primary products, coupled with the fact that primary products make up a significant proportion of LDC exports, creates the potential for substantial fluctuations in LDC export prices and earnings.

Wide swings in export prices and earnings can have a significant, adverse impact on the overall economies of the LDCs. One possible effect is an inefficient allocation of resources within the LDCs. For example, a high price for a primary product that is only temporary in nature will attract investment resources and factors of production from other sectors of the economy. Later, when the price of the commodity declines to a level more consistent with the long-term value of the product, a larger quantity of resources will have been irrevocably committed to the production of the product than is called for on the grounds of efficiency. Or, on the other hand, the uncertainty generated by price fluctuations may deter resources from entering the export sector (even when they otherwise would), as producers shy away from the possibility of future price declines.

Empirical evidence on the degree of instability in LDC export prices is inconclusive. In one of the best known and most widely cited studies of the stability of commodity prices, Alasdair MacBean concludes that on average the export prices of the LDCs do not show any greater instability than do the export prices of the DCs. MacBean also found little evidence to suggest that the prices of primary products are significantly more unstable than the prices of manufactures. However, another study, by Ben-ton Massell, estimates that between 1950 and 1966 the export prices of LDCs showed 50 percent greater instability than the export prices of DCs.

Declining Terms of Trade

Another problem related to LDC export prices is the long-term movement in the LDCs' commodity terms of trade, defined as the ratio of the price of exports to the price of imports $\left(\dfrac{P_x}{P_m}\right)$. In particular, the LDCs are greatly concerned about their terms of trade vis-à-vis the DCs. As we saw in Chapter 2, a worsening of the terms of trade for an individual nation implies (other things being equal) a decline in the economic welfare of that nation. Some observers argue that a systematic decline in the terms of trade of the LDCs, vis-à-vis the DCs, has generated a transfer of income to the DCs from the LDCs, increasing the already substantial income gap that exists between the two blocs of nations.

Several arguments are offered as to why one should expect a secular deterioration in the terms of trade of the LDCs. First, it is generally thought that the income elasticity of demand for primary products is less than that for manufactures. Thus, as the DCs and LDCs experience growth in per capita income, they will increase their demand for manufactures relative to their demand for primary products. The result will be to place upward pressure on the prices of manufactures, the dominant imports of the LDCs, relative to the prices of primary products, the dominant export commodity of the LDCs.

Second, the DCs have demonstrated a propensity, when primary product prices *do* increase over the long run, to employ technology to develop synthetic substitutes for the primary products. This has the effect of increasing the competition facing the primary products and possibly even lowering their prices as a result of a reduction in demand. A recent example of the development of synthetic substitutes for primary products exported by the LDCs is to be found in synthetic fibers (such as polyester); synthetic fibers compete directly with such natural fibers as cotton, an important export for many LDCs.

Third, it has been argued that the terms of trade of the LDCs will decline because of a difference in the world market structure for manufactures and primary products. In the highly competitive primary product industries, reductions in demand, or reduction in costs due to improvements in production techniques, will be readily translated into reductions in price. In the less competitive manufacturing industries, on the other hand, price-setting producers are in a better position to resist such downward pressure on prices.

A number of attempts have been made to estimate the movement in the terms of trade of the LDCs over time. These estimates have been the subject of much controversy for a variety of reasons. As is clear in Figure 19–3, which depicts the movement of the commodity terms of trade $\left(\frac{P_x}{P_m}\right)$ of the LDCs since 1953 (the solid line), the LDCs have experienced periods of both increasing and decreasing terms of trade. During the 1950s there was a gradual decline in the LDCs' commodity terms of trade, followed by a leveling off during the 1960s. Then there was a sharp increase in 1974 followed by a decline in the late 1970s. Although Figure 19–3 shows an increase in the commodity terms of trade over the twenty-five-year period covered, it would be a mistake to conclude that many of the individual LDCs have experienced an improvement in their terms of trade. This is because the increase is accounted for almost entirely by a boom in commodity prices during the mid-1970s, much of which was concentrated in petroleum.

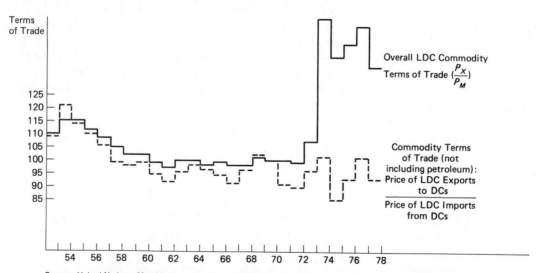

Source: United Nations, *Monthly Bulletin of Statistics* (New York: United Nations Publications, various issues).

FIGURE 19–3 Terms of Trade of the LDCs, 1953–1978 (1970 = 100)

A more interesting exercise might be to examine the time path of the terms of trade between the LDCs and the DCs, that excludes the exports which benefit only a handful of LDCs such as petroleum. In Figure 19–3, the dashed line shows the movement in the ratio of the price of exports from LDCs to DCs, excluding petroleum, to the price of imports of the LDCs from the DCs. This trend suggests that events may not have been as favorable to the non-oil-exporting LDCs as the overall commodity terms of trade would suggest. In fact, the declining trend implies that there may have been a redistribution of income from the LDCs to the more advanced nations.

It is thus difficult to reach an unambiguous conclusion as to whether the LDCs as a whole have experienced an improvement or a deterioration of their terms of trade. Further complicating the matter are methodological problems with using the commodity terms of trade as a measure of welfare. Factors such as the development of new tradeable products and improvements in product quality seriously impair the interpretation of a trend when the calculated terms of trade are based simply on the prices of tradeable goods. For example, if a newly developed computer is imported by an LDC and the price of the new computer is twice that of the computer it replaced, then the calculation of the commodity terms of trade would obviously be lower. However, if the computer is five times as productive as the original computer, then the economic welfare of the LDC is actually improved.

Trade Policy of the DCs toward the Exports of the LDCs

In Part IV, we mentioned several aspects of world trade policy which specifically affected the LDCs. This section will consolidate those earlier thoughts and add some further insights on the impact of world trade policy, particularly that of the DCs, on the trade position of the LDCs. As we shall see, many of the policies of the DCs toward the LDCs create considerable difficulties for the LDCs in their attempt to expand their exports.

Despite their efforts to increase the role of manufactures in their export trade (efforts that have been successful for some LDCs), the developing nations, for the foreseeable future, will continue to depend heavily on exports of primary products, especially agricultural products. Since the DCs represent the largest market for LDC agricultural exports, there is clearly an interest on the part of the LDCs to have open access to those markets.

However, the protectionist measures applied by the DCs to agricultural products are quite extensive. These restrictive trade policies imposed on agricultural imports by the DCs are often designed to support their national agricultural policies, whose objective is to guarantee price and income levels for the agricultural sectors of their economies. One such policy, previously discussed, was the Common Agricultural Policy of the European Economic Community. This policy restricts agricultural imports through the use of the "variable levy," a flexible tariff that raises the price of imports to match the price of domestic production. In addition, a disproportionate share of nontariff barriers (NTBs) applied by the DCs are imposed on agricultural products.

As we mentioned earlier, many developing nations have sought to expand their manufacturing exports in an effort to offset the uncertainties associated with the primary product markets and also to stimulate industrialization within their economies. Here again their efforts are often frustrated by the trade policies of the developed countries, who constitute the primary market for manufactured LDC exports. In this case, the tariff structure of the DCs discriminates against imports of manufactures from the LDCs. In Chapter 13, it was shown (see Table 13–6) that the tariff structure of the DCs favors the manufactured imports of other DCs over those originating from LDCs; in 1972, the effective rate facing all manufactures (11.1 percent) was less than half the rate facing manufactures from the LDCs (22.6 percent).

It is also apparent from our earlier discussion that the tariff structures of the DCs are characterized by *tariff escalation* (see Chapter 13), whereby the nominal tariff on primary inputs is less than the nominal tariff on the more advanced stages of production, raising the effective rates of protection on final products. As we saw earlier, the effect of tariff escalation is to encourage the LDCs to export primary products, such as raw materials, and to discourage their export of the more advanced manufactured goods. Thus tariff escalation makes it difficult for LDCs to use exports as a foundation upon which to build their manufacturing sectors.

Efforts by the LDCs to expand their manufactured exports have been most successful in labor-intensive industries in which production techniques have low technological requirements. These include such industries as textiles, clothing, footwear and light manufactures such as consumer electronics. Imports of these products by the DCs typically compete with traditional, well-established industries in which the DCs are losing their comparative advantage. The DCs have historically protected these industries with tight restrictions on competing imports. For example, textile imports to the DCs are not only saddled with some of the highest tariff rates of any product group, but they also face severe quantitative restrictions (e.g., the Multifiber Agreement).

It is quite likely that in the future, as the production technology associated with other manufactures is obtained by LDCs, LDC exports of those products to the DCs will also encounter trade restrictions.[3] Such a trend will, of course, thwart the LDCs' future efforts at industrialization. An indication of such a trend was the reaction of the United States in the late 1970s to Korean and Taiwanese exports of color television receivers, a manufactured product that Korea and Taiwan had recently begun to produce and export. Because Korean and Taiwanese production became a threat to U.S. producers of color television receivers, the U.S. government negotiated an orderly marketing arrangement (resulting from an escape clause action) limiting the quantity of those exports. Other manufactured export products of the LDCs have been met with similar restrictions by the importing DCs. Thus, if the past actions of the DCs are any indication of future policy, the LDCs can expect that their attempts to expand exports of manufactured goods in the future (such as steel and chemicals) will continue to meet with frustrating trade barriers.

Moreover, the LDCs feel as though they are defenseless in countering these restrictions. Because the LDCs are small purchasers of most products exported by DCs, they have little ability to retaliate with restrictions of their own. In addition, only a small proportion of LDCs participate in the GATT, and therefore they do not have an official forum to voice their displeasure of the trade practices of the DCs.

Trade Deficits and Their Financing

A recent development of great concern to the LDCs is the substantial increase in the size of their trade deficits with the rest of the world.

[3]Many of these more technologically advanced manufactures are produced in the LDCs by multinational corporations (MNCs) headquartered in the DCs. Typically, the MNCs will locate their assembly operations in the LDCs to take advantage of the lower labor costs and they will import various components from abroad.

After remaining stable, though sizeable, for many years, these deficits suddenly began to explode in the mid-1970s. Factors contributing to this development were the increase in petroleum prices during the 1970s, the decline in the price of many primary products following the commodity boom of the mid-1970s and the generally low level of world economic growth, which depressed the demand for many LDC exports (particularly industrial raw materials). As a result, the trade deficits of the non-oil-exporting LDCs increased from $18.3 billion in 1973 to $73.2 billion in 1979 (which, incidentally, was equal to 30 percent of the total value of LDC exports).

The upshot is that the LDCs have had to borrow huge sums in order to finance these rising trade imbalances. By 1978, Brazil had accumulated $27.2 billion of foreign debt, Mexico $24.8 billion and South Korea $12 billion. In total, by 1978, the non-oil-exporting LDCs had accrued foreign debt equal to $210 billion, up from $74 billion in 1973.

Where have the LDCs borrowed these funds? Prior to the surge in the size of the trade deficits, most of the funds borrowed by the LDCs were obtained from official sources, such as multilateral development banks (MDBs). This group includes the World Bank, the Inter-American Development Bank and the Asian Development Bank. The primary purpose of the MDBs is to act as financial intermediaries to facilitate the growth of the LDCs. They obtain funds from the paid-in capital of member DCs or by borrowing in the private capital markets, using the guarantee of the member DCs as "collateral." The funds are then loaned to the LDCs at highly concessional interest rates.[4] In principle, MDB loans are supposed to be extended to LDCs for specific development projects in such areas as

industry, energy, health, agriculture and population planning. The funds are generally not supposed to be used by the LDCs to finance payments deficits.

Lately, however, with the mounting payments deficits, the LDCs have had to borrow directly in the private capital markets, usually from private banks in the DCs. In 1972, private creditors accounted for approximately one-third of the outstanding debt of the non-oil developing nations; by 1978, this share had increased to almost one-half.

The sheer magnitude of their foreign debt imposes a considerable burden on the LDCs. It is estimated that, in 1979, Brazil had to use 66 percent of its export earnings to meet principal and interest payments on its foreign debts. The burden of foreign debt is even greater for some of the lowest income nations; for example, it is estimated that Cameroon's debt service obligations run 1.36 times its export earnings, while those of Malawi and Somali run 1.82 and 2.87 (respectively) times their export earnings. As might be expected, the international banking community is becoming increasingly concerned over the ability of the LDCs to carry their current debt. There is also concern about the financial risks to the banks that have issued the loans should the LDCs default on payment. As a result, unless the outlook for the LDCs' payments position improves, it seems likely that the private financial market will attempt to reduce its role in the financing of the deficits of the LDCs.

The effect on the LDCs of a reduction in the availability of private financing is immense. If the LDCs cannot find adequate financing for their deficits, their deficits will have to be reduced. One alternative available to the LDCs under these circumstances would be to reduce imports. However, many imports, such as petroleum (which in 1980 totaled 20 percent of the export earnings of the LDCs) and high-technology industrial goods, are crucial to the de-

[4]In 1979, for example, the interest rate on World Bank loans to the LDCs was around 8 percent, while the market rate was closer to 15 percent.

velopment process of these countries. Another alternative would be for the LDCs to expand their volume of exports. However, we have just seen how difficult export expansion will be for the LDCs. A final alternative would be to borrow greater amounts of funds from MDBs or to obtain outright aid from the DCs. The prospects for these alternatives do not appear bright, as the MDBs, whose policy is determined largely by the DCs, have traditionally been hesitant to issue loans for balance-of-payments purposes. Meanwhile, foreign aid as a source of funding is quite unpredictable. The following chapter will have more to say about the debt-servicing problems of the LDCs and the efforts by these countries to resolve the problem.

QUESTIONS AND EXERCISES

1. What are the primary differences between developed and less developed countries? Are all individual countries within each group identical? If not, explain how they differ.

2. Describe the nature of the international trade patterns of the LDCs. What problems do their trade patterns create in terms of their efforts at economic development?

3. What is one of the primary economic objectives of the LDCs? How might the LDCs achieve that objective using international trade?

4. How does the nature of the world supply and demand conditions for LDC export products contribute to the instability in the prices of those products? How does export price instability affect the progress of the economic development of the LDCs?

5. Explain why the terms of trade of the LDCs might decline over the long run. What has been the actual movement of the terms of trade over the past twenty-five years?

6. In what ways does the trade policy of the developed countries discriminate against the LDCs' efforts at industrialization?

7. Do you believe that the developed countries will liberalize their trade policies toward the LDCs in the future? Why or why not? Make sure you mention future developments in trading relations between the rich and poor nations that may influence future trade policy.

8. How have the rising trade deficits of the LDCs affected their economic development plans? Make sure you mention several ways in which this deficit could be reduced, and how each of those solutions will affect the economic development plans of the LDCs.

THE NEW INTERNATIONAL ECONOMIC 20
ORDER AND OTHER GLOBAL EFFORTS
TO AID THE LDCs

In the preceding chapter, we presented a lengthy discussion of the international economic environment encountered by the LDCs and identified some of the specific problems that they face. It is not difficult to understand why the LDCs perceive the international economic environment to be quite unfavorable. The LDCs are dissatisfied with what is commonly referred to as the *international economic order,* which can be defined as the political and economic framework in which international economic relations among sovereign nations take place. One element of the international economic order is the international trading and monetary framework in which international economic relations transpire, including the international policies adopted by the world's trading nations. The framework also encompasses those international institutions that were established to facilitate world economic cooperation in the areas of trade, finance and investment. The central feature of the international economic order, however, is the distribution of economic power that results from this framework.

LDC dissatisfaction with the existing international economic order exists primarily for the following reasons: (1) the tremendous gap between the income levels of the DCs and LDCs and (2) the LDCs' heavy dependence on the DCs as an export market and as a source of imports of commodities, technology and capital. Furthermore, the LDCs believe that the DCs have parlayed their economic advantages into an institutional framework that compounds the problem. The LDCs believe that international organizations such as the International Monetary Fund, the World Bank and GATT, which are ostensibly intended to facilitate economic cooperation among all countries of the world, are, in fact, dominated by the DCs and thus are not capable of truly responding to the plight of the LDCs. For example, the voting structures of the IMF and the World Bank are based on the size of a nation's contributions to those organizations, which ensures that the DCs (the main contributors) will dominate the decision-making process.

Thus in recent years the LDCs have, collectively, called for a *New International Economic Order* (NIEO), one in which international economic relations are carried out in a more equitable manner between DCs and LDCs. This chapter will begin by presenting a brief history of the efforts by the LDCs to develop a collective demand for an NIEO. This will be followed by an economic analysis of several of the NIEO proposals, as well as the world's experience in attempting to implement them. In addition, other measures not explicitly called for in the NIEO, but which the LDCs have employed to improve their economic well-being, will be discussed.

HISTORICAL DEVELOPMENT OF THE CALL FOR AN NIEO

The LDCs have at various times attempted to organize a united front in an effort to add weight to their common demands on the DCs. The central issues surrounding the LDC movements have changed over time. Prior to the early 1960s, organized demands by the LDCs focused largely on political relations with the DCs, since many of the LDCs were just emerging as independent nations. For example, at the first conference of the Non-Aligned Movement (1961), whose membership consisted of LDCs not belonging to any political or military alliance with a DC, provisions were adopted calling for decolonization, noninterference in the internal affairs of sovereign states, peaceful coexistence among countries and a strengthening of the United Nations. Less attention was paid to measures dealing with the economic development of the participating nations.

In the early 1960s, however, the LDCs began to recognize the need for economic measures. In fact, the 1960s were designated as the First Development Decade by the United Nations and a program was adopted to promote the economic development of the LDCs. The program urged the DCs: (1) to take steps to ensure that the LDCs could sell their exports at stable prices, (2) to reallocate to the LDCs a larger share of profits from the raw materials industries that were owned by DCs' companies but located within the LDCs and (3) to take steps to increase the flow of capital to the LDCs on mutually acceptable terms. This program represented a dramatic change in the orientation of the UN, from world security issues to world economic issues. The change was partially attributable to the increasing percentage of UN membership accounted for by the LDCs during the 1950s and 1960s.

In conjunction with the UN resolution for the First Development Decade, the first United Nations Conference on Trade and Development (UNCTAD I) was held. The objective of the conference was to discuss the trading relations of the LDCs and DCs. UNCTAD provided a forum for the poor countries to express their views on international trading arrangements, as well as on the general economic policies of the DCs. The LDC–DC dialogue initiated at UNCTAD I accentuated the problems between the two blocs of nations as never before. The LDCs acted as a united front, collectively presenting their demands to the DCs, and became known as the Group of 77 (now actually exceeding 125 in number). UNCTAD I adopted a "Final Act" which embraced fifteen principles. Many of those principles were quite general in nature, addressing such issues as respect for national sovereignty, while others incorporated fairly specific demands such as calls for trade preferences and price stabilization schemes for LDC exports.

UNCTAD has since become institutionalized, and meets every fourth year to provide a forum for the interchange of ideas between LDCs and DCs. However, UNCTAD is dominated by the LDCs, which act more or less as a unit in presenting their views on the international economic order. The LDCs believe that this organization is essential as a counterbalance to such organizations as the IMF and GATT, which they perceive as being controlled by the DCs.

The success of UNCTAD in achieving concrete results for the LDCs, however, has been quite limited. Although the DCs did agree to adopt a system of trade preferences for LDC exports at UNCTAD II (these will be discussed later), few other results are discernible. The ineffectiveness of UNCTAD is partially attributable to its voting framework. UNCTAD works by consensus, and therefore resolutions passed by UNCTAD are not binding on those nations that do not concur. Resolutions designed to change the economic relations between DCs and LDCs will be implemented only if the DCs strongly favor the arrangement.

However, despite their lack of success with attaining concessions from the DCs (or perhaps because of it), the LDCs in the early 1970s began to assert themselves more forcefully. The UN General Assembly in 1970 concluded that the First Development Decade had been a failure and established even more ambitious goals for LDCs in the 1970s; the 1970s were to be the "Second Development Decade."

The position from which the LDCs pressed their demands was strengthened considerably by several economic developments of the early 1970s. The most important of those was a rise in the prices of many primary commodities, particularly petroleum. During 1973–1974, OPEC increased the price of a barrel of petroleum from $3.00 to $11.65. Such unilateral action by a group of LDCs and the resulting success was unique, and was viewed by other LDCs as both an inspiration and an example of the economic power that the LDCs could potentially wield over the DCs.

In terms of rhetoric, the new-found confidence of the LDCs reached its peak at the Sixth Special Session of the General Assembly of the United Nations in April 1974, the first session devoted entirely to economic development problems. The outcome of this session was a long list of demands by the LDCs, most of which had been rejected on previous occasions by the DCs. These demands were incorporated in the Declaration and Programme of Action for the Establishment of a "New International Economic Order."

The demands were quite bold, particularly since they were being sponsored by such a prestigious multilateral body as the United Nations. The DCs were uncharacteristically passive at the session, providing little formal opposition to the resolution. This passivity can be explained partially by the economic developments of the time, which had placed the LDCs in a more powerful bargaining position. Also, the developed countries knew that there was little chance that the demands could be implemented without their concurrence. It was virtually costless to let the LDCs pass paper resolutions, while it might have strained international political relations to oppose them openly.

What were the proposals embodied in the NIEO, and which if any of those proposals has been transformed into action? Rather than outlining the details of the proposals, suffice it to say that they called for concrete actions aimed at eliminating or at least reducing the special international economic problems that were discussed in the preceding chapter. It is questionable whether there has really been much significant change in the economic relations between LDCs and DCs as a result of the call for NIEO. While it is true that, since 1974, there have been a series of negotiations and conferences addressing the specific proposals, including the World Population Conference (1974) and the UN Conference on Technical Cooperation Between Developing Countries (1978), few substantive changes have actually occurred. While the NIEO proposals have largely gone unmet, measures have been taken by the LDCs themselves and in cooperation with the DCs, both before and after the call for a NIEO, to combat the international economic problems that inhibit their economic development. Let us now examine some of these measures.

EXPORT EARNINGS STABILIZATION SCHEMES

In the preceding chapter, it was argued that two of the most pressing problems confronting the LDCs were related to the price levels of their exports. One concern was with the short-term fluctuations in both export prices and earnings. The other was the belief that the long-term trend in the LDCs' commodity terms of trade was unfavorable to them. In response to these problems the LDCs, in cooperation with the DCs, have established export price stabilization schemes, known as commodity agreements. Besides commodity agreements, plans have been worked out between the DCs and the LDCs to finance short-term shortfalls in LDC export earnings. In addition, there have been several instances when the LDCs have implemented unilateral actions to stabilize or increase export prices.

Commodity Agreements

Commodity agreements bring together producers and consumers of particular commodities in an effort to stabilize prices, usually around the long-term price trend. Specifically, the contracting parties determine a range of values within which they wish to confine the price of the commodity. If the price of the commodity fluctuates or threatens to fluctuate outside that range, action will be taken to maintain the price within the predetermined range.

Most commodity agreements involve products that are, for the most part, produced by the LDCs and exported to the DCs. The agreements are intended to benefit both parties. The ex-

porters of the commodities, the LDCs, hope to gain by the guarantee of a stable price that cannot fall below a predetermined minimum level. The consuming nations, the DCs, also hope to benefit by a stable price, one that cannot exceed a predetermined maximum.

In addition to the economic motives for entering into commodity agreements, the DCs frequently have political motives. Commodity agreement participation can be a means to facilitate political goodwill with the LDCs, many of which are considered to be of strategic importance to the DCs. Also, if commodity prices are maintained at levels that exceed free trade market prices, the agreements have the effect of transferring resources from the DCs to the LDCs. Thus they can serve as a vehicle for foreign aid, an objective pursued to some extent by all DCs.

mechanisms used to implement commodity agreements

International commodity agreements can employ one or a combination of several mechanisms to achieve price stabilization. These mechanisms include buffer stocks, export quotas and production controls.

A buffer stock arrangement involves the establishment of an internationally held stock of funds that is used to purchase a commodity to stabilize its price. When the price of the commodity approaches or falls below the minimum, the manager can use the funds to purchase the commodity (bidding up its price). The buffer stock also holds a stock of the commodity itself. When the price approaches or exceeds the upper limit of the predetermined price range, the buffer stock manager can sell quantities of the commodity from the commodity stock in an effort to depress the price. Buffer stocks, however, present several practical problems. First, the commodity must be nonperishable so that it can be stored. This precludes many agricultural goods.

Second, the storage of the commodity itself is quite costly. Agreement among the participating nations as to how much of a share of the storage and administrative costs each should assume can be a point of severe contention. Finally, if the market price of the commodity exceeds the upper limit established by the agreement for a prolonged period of time, sales of the commodity from the buffer stock can deplete the stock itself, making future sales impossible.

Production controls and export quotas influence the price of commodities in a similar fashion—by affecting the world supply of the commodity. The total quantity of exports or production permitted under a commodity agreement is based on future price projections. If it is thought that the price of the commodity will decline in the future, the producing nations would be assigned a lower export quota or production level. Conversely, if it is predicted that the price of the commodity will rise in the future, so as to approach the upper limit of the predetermined price range, the producing nations will be permitted to increase their levels of production and exports.

A major problem in trying to place quantitative controls on exports and production is the allocation of the quota among the producing nations. For example, if a decrease in the total quantity of exports is required, how is that decrease to be allocated among individual producers? Small producers may be reluctant to reduce their levels of exports or production to still lower levels. A related problem is the appearance of new producers of the commodity, who are likely to be drawn into the market by the artificially high prices. Producing nations just embarking on the production or export of a commodity are likely to be unwilling to reduce their levels of production or exports at that juncture. Even large producers have an incentive to cheat on production quotas, and enforcement can become a problem.

At this point, let us examine a specific commodity agreement. This will provide an example of how export prices are stabilized and will illustrate some of the problems we have just discussed.

the international tin agreement

The International Tin Agreement (ITA), first instituted in 1956, is designed to control the price of tin through the use of buffer stocks. The agreement is administered by the International Tin Council (ITC), an intergovernment body composed of 7 tin-producing nations which account for 85 percent of world production and 22 consuming nations which account for approximately 95 percent of world consumption.

Although there seems to be widespread agreement that the ITA has been successful in stabilizing prices, recent problems have surfaced which threaten the effectiveness of the ITA. The leading problem is that the size of the tin buffer stock has been insufficient to moderate price changes, particularly during the late 1970s. During that period, the price of tin generally exceeded its upper limit, resulting in the depletion of the buffer stock as sales of tin were made in an attempt to moderate the price increases. As a result, the ITC has been forced to rely increasingly on export controls to defend the price range.

Another complicating factor is the recent action of the United States, a consuming member nation. The United States government has accumulated a huge stockpile of tin, and in 1981, began to gradually sell large quantities of tin from its stockpile to the ITC's buffer stock. If the price of tin continues to exceed its upper limit, the ITC will be required to sell the tin in the open market, in order to moderate its price. This action was not viewed favorably by the producing nations. Whether the strain in relations, caused by this display of consumer power by the United States, will destroy the ITA remains to be seen.

UNCTAD's Integrated Program for Commodities

In 1976, in response to the NIEO fever, UNCTAD IV passed a resolution launching the Integrated Program for Commodities (IPC). The centerpiece of the IPC was the establishment of a Common Fund ($3 to $6 billion) for financing buffer stocks to stabilize the prices of eighteen designated primary products exported predominantly by the LDCs.

The developed countries are greatly divided on the Integrated Program for Commodities, with the United States leading those who are skeptical of the plan. Their primary concern is with the establishment of a common fund prior to the negotiations of the commodity agreements themselves. The United States prefers to negotiate commodity agreements on a case-by-case basis and then to establish a common fund for each individual agreement. The rationale for this approach is that each commodity market has its own characteristics and thus is not best served by a blanket agreement. In fact, it is pointed out that several of the commodities designated by UNCTAD are already committed to individual agreements (e.g., coffee and tin).

However, by 1979, the essential elements of a limited common fund had been agreed upon, and negotiations to conclude an agreement were continuing. In the meantime, several commodity agreements had been concluded or were under negotiation under the auspices of the IPC (including sugar, rubber, cocoa and copper). However, the LDCs are hopeful that more commodity agreements can be negotiated within the IPC framework.

Questions About the Benefits of Commodity Agreements

Are commodity agreements truly in the best interests of the producing nations, specifically the LDCs? The answer to this question is not clear. If commodity agreements are intended to maintain (or raise) producer income, raising or maintaining prices will not serve this goal unless the demand for the product is inelastic. Although, as suggested in the previous chapter, demand for many primary products is price inelastic, there are a number of individual products for which the elasticity of demand is not as certain. For example, coffee drinkers can turn to tea in response to high coffee prices. Or users of copper can substitute aluminum if the price of copper were to increase significantly. In the longer run, substitutes for primary products may be more easily found, or new substitutes developed, in response to artificially high prices.

Finally, the commodity agreements negotiated thus far provide but a partial answer to the problem of stability of export earnings, since they apply to individual export commodities, and not to aggregate exports and export earnings. Despite the concentration of particular commodities in the export bundle of many LDCs, few depend exclusively on any one commodity. Thus, to assure a stable level of export earnings, a more comprehensive approach to the exports of the LDCs would have to be taken.

Cartels and Producers' Associations

Commodity agreements, it was shown, involve bilateral or multilateral cooperation among consuming and producing nations for the purpose of stabilizing the price of a particular commodity. Another method used by the LDCs to stabilize the prices of their export commodities is to establish cartels or, as they are sometimes called, producers' associations. Unlike commodity agreements, cartels involve unilateral attempts by the producing nations to stabilize or increase the price of a particular product by exerting their collective power.

Much of Chapter 4 dealt with the economic analysis of cartels in the context of imperfect competition. There we saw that the nations that produce a particular product will be better able to assure themselves of higher prices and profits if they act collectively, rather than separately, and try to maximize the total profits of the cartel. As pointed out, several conditions are necessary for a cartel to be successful. Most importantly, demand for the product must be relatively price inelastic (due to a lack of substitute goods) and producers must be willing to cooperate in the establishment of price and output levels.

We also saw that the most successful cartel in recent history has been the Organization of Petroleum Exporting Countries, whose actions have caused the price of petroleum to rise substantially during the 1970s. Other attempts by the LDCs to cartelize their export commodities have not been nearly as successful as OPEC. In fact, with the possible exception of the International Bauxite Association, the other attempts have failed to attain their goal of higher prices.

Although much of the difficulty experienced by cartels has resulted from a failure of the producing nations to cooperate, the overriding problem has been the ability of consuming nations (primarily the DCs) to find substitute commodities in response to the high prices established by the cartels. As a result, many of the primary product producing nations (primarily the LDCs) have abandoned their efforts at unilateral cartelization, and have opted instead for cooperating with the major consuming nations to establish multilateral commodity agreements.

TRADE POLICY OF THE DCs
TOWARD THE LDCs—
THE GENERALIZED SYSTEM
OF PREFERENCES

In the preceding chapter, it was argued that the trade policy of the DCs seemed to discriminate against the export products of the LDCs. Because the LDCs are so dependent on the markets of the DCs for export sales, it is not surprising that the LDCs have a strong interest in altering the structure of protection being maintained by the DCs. This interest was first put forward in 1964 (at the first United Nations Conference on Trade and Development) when the LDCs as a group proposed the adoption of a *Generalized System of Preferences (GSP)*. The GSP requires that the DCs grant preferential tariff treatment to imports of manufactured and semimanufactured products originating in the LDCs. In particular, eligible imports from the LDCs would be subject to lower tariffs than similar imports from other sources.

Progress toward the adoption of a GSP by the developed countries was initially quite slow. One inhibiting factor was that, prior to the Kennedy Round of multilateral trade negotiations, GATT provisions forbade any discriminatory application of tariffs, where discrimination was based on the origin of the goods. During the Kennedy Round, however, a provision was adopted that permitted the DCs to grant tariff reductions on imports from the LDCs without requiring reciprocity. This provision opened the door to the developed countries to implement GSP schemes. However, it was not until July 1971 that the first GSP scheme was adopted by the European Economic Community. This reluctance on the part of the DCs is understandable in light of the increased competition this would bring to their domestic industries. As we have mentioned on several occasions, imports of manufactured goods from the LDCs may be especially threatening to the DCs since these goods are generally labor intensive, have low technological requirements and therefore compete with the older, traditional industries of the DCs that employ predominantly low-skilled labor. It should also be noted that some of the LDCs themselves were less than enthusiastic about a GSP. For example, those African nations whose exports already received preferential treatment from the European Economic Community, were not excited about the prospect of having those trade preferences extended to all LDCs.

Among the developed nations considering adoption of a GSP, the United States was one of the last to institute a plan. Authority to initiate a GSP was granted by Congress in the Trade Act of 1974, and the United States finally implemented such a scheme in January 1976. The GSP of the United States grants duty-free entry to approximately 2800 tariff items from 137 LDCs.[1] However, the U.S. GSP may not be as all-encompassing and generous as it first appears, since it contains many qualifications and restrictions. First, many important manufactures of the LDCs are excluded; these include watches, selected steel products, electronics, glass articles, textiles and footwear, as well as most agricultural and fishery products. Second, limits are placed on the value of any one product that can be imported under the GSP. GSP benefits are suspended: (1) when the value of those imports either exceeds $41.9 million (in 1979 dollars) within a single year or (2) when imports of a good from a particular country account for over 50 percent of total imports of the product to the United States (provided total imports ex-

[1]Countries excluded from GSP benefits include the Communist nations and all but three members of OPEC (Indonesia, Venezuela and Ecuador).

TABLE 20-1

U.S. Imports from GSP–eligible Developing Countries, 1976–1978 (billions of dollars)					
	1976		1977		1978
Total Imports from Eligible Developing Countries	28.1		34.7		41.4
Most-Favored Nation Imports					
Duty-free	7.1		9.2		10.0
Dutiable	14.4		17.8		21.6
Eligible for Generalized System of Preferences	6.5		7.7		9.7
Less:					
Exceeds 50 percent limit[a]	−0.7		−0.8		−1.0
Exceeds dollar limit[a]	−1.2		−2.0		−2.2
Not granted GSP[b]	−1.5		−1.0		−1.3
Granted Generalized System of Preferences (% of total eligible imports)	3.2	(11.4)	3.9	(11.2)	5.2 (12.6)
Agriculture	0.5		0.6		0.6
Manufactures	2.6		3.3		4.6

Source: U.S. Congressional Budget Office, *Assisting the Developing Countries: Foreign Aid and Trade Policies of the United States* (Washington, D.C.: U.S. Government Printing Office, 1980), Table 18.
[a]Denied duty-free because of competitive need criteria limitations.
[b]Denied duty-free because insufficient share of value-added originated in the exporting country, or because of transshipment or other factors.

ceed $1 million). Also, products are not eligible for GSP treatment unless at least 35 percent of their value originated in the beneficiary nation.

Because of these limitations, only a small percentage of the imports from GSP–eligible countries actually enter the United States duty free. Table 20–1 shows the breakdown of imports from eligible LDCs into the United States for the years 1976, 1977 and 1978. During this period, only 11 to 12 percent of total imports from eligible LDCs were granted GSP treatment. It is clear, then, that the GSP program is somewhat limited in the extent to which it encourages the exports of the LDCs.[2]

Several recent studies suggest that another of the DCs' trade policies, the Offshore Assembly Provision (OAP), may be of more benefit to the LDCs than the GSP. As we saw in Chapter 13, under the OAP, import tariffs are applied only to the value-added by the LDCs in the assembly process, provided the LDCs use components obtained from the importing DC. Because the assembly of components for reexport constitutes a large and growing share of the manufactured exports of the LDCs, the OAP, by lowering the tariff payment on those products, provides a substantial benefit to the LDCs.

The evidence seems to support this contention. The rate of growth in LDC exports to the United States under the OAP is quite impressive. One study estimates that the dollar value of such imports increased almost eight times from 1970 to 1978 (from $540 million to $4.3 billion). In fact, the value of LDC manufactured imports entering the United States in 1978 under

the OAP ($4.3 billion) was almost equal to the amount entering under the GSP ($4.6 billion). With the tremendous growth of OAP imports, it is possible that in the near future OAP imports may exceed those entering under the GSP.

FOREIGN ASSISTANCE TO LDCs FROM DCs

Another key element in the LDCs' efforts at economic development is foreign aid received from the developed countries. Foreign aid can be broadly defined as all official grants and concessional loans (made at lower than market interest rates), issued as either monetary funds or in kind, which have the objective of transferring resources from the DCs to the LDCs to aid those countries in their developmental efforts. Basically, foreign assistance can be issued in one of two ways. Aid can be granted directly, from a single developed country to a single less-developed country. Or aid can be transferred multilaterally, as when a developed country contributes to a multilateral development bank, which then loans those funds to any number of less-developed countries.

One advantage of bilateral aid, from the viewpoint of the donor DCs, is that the DCs can target the aid to countries of their own choosing. In addition, the DCs can place constraints on how the aid is to be used by the LDCs.

The bilateral aid programs of the United States pointedly illustrate these advantages. The United States provides bilateral aid through three major programs, each having its own characteristics. The *Development Assistance* program issues loans and grants at concessional terms for specific development projects in such areas as education, health care and agricultural development. The *Economic Support Fund (ESF)* issues concessional loans and grants to countries of political importance to the United States in an effort to "promote economic and political stability" within those countries. Although the ESF program is

[2]In early 1982, the Reagan administration further reduced the impact of the GSP by revising the eligibility criteria. It is estimated that the revisions will cut the value of eligible LDC exports by 15 percent. In addition, GSP benefits were withdrawn on a substantial number of products exported from the more advanced developing countries such as Brazil, Mexico, Israel and South Korea.

intended to promote economic development, only about 30 percent of funds are used for such projects. In practice, most of these funds have been used by the recipient countries to support balance-of-payments deficits. Obviously, the ESF fund is intended to be used as an instrument of U.S. foreign policy, as the majority of the funds are directed to those LDCs of strategic importance to the United States (such as Egypt and Israel). The third assistance program of the United States is the *Food Aid Program,* which finances U.S. food exports to LDCs through grants and concessional loans.

It should be noted that most of the U.S. aid programs require the recipient countries to make their commodity purchases from the United States. In 1978, for example, 14 percent of U.S. wheat exports were to LDCs that purchased the wheat using the funds received through the Food Aid Program.

Multilateral aid, on the other hand, is not quite as convenient a tool to achieve the political objectives of the donor countries, since their contributions are made to international financial institutions that then administer the distribution of the funds to the LDCs. These institutions include the IMF and the various multilateral development banks, such as the World Bank and Inter-American Bank. The grants and loans issued by the IMF are generally for balance-of-payments purposes, while those administered by the multilateral development banks are generally for projects aimed at developing the LDCs' economic infrastructure.

The absolute dollar amounts of official bilateral and multilateral aid provided by the DCs has tripled between 1967 and 1978 (it equaled $18 billion in 1978), with the United States providing the largest single contribution. However, the volume of aid as measured as a percent of the DCs' GNP has been declining during the 1960s and 1970s. In 1960, foreign aid accounted for .52 percent of the total GNP of the DCs, and had dropped to .32 percent in 1978.

In the late 1970s, the OPEC nations, as a result of the increase in oil revenue, have become actively involved in foreign aid programs. In 1978, the OPEC countries contributed $3.7 billion (1.1 percent of their GNP). Although most of OPEC aid has been directed toward non-oil-producing Arab countries, project aid has increasingly been extended to non–Arab countries. The future of OPEC aid is, of course, tied directly to the future of oil revenues. If those revenues were to decline, as they have in the early 1980s, OPEC's level of foreign assistance could also be expected to decline.

The future course of foreign aid is unclear, particularly for multilateral aid. The Reagan administration has proposed substantial reductions in U.S. contributions to the multilateral development banks. In addition, the administration has called for an overhaul of the lending policies of the MDBs as well as those of the IMF. Specifically, they have recommended that interest rates on loans be more in line with market rates, and that loans and grants be tied to financing specific development projects. Supporters of multilateral aid worry that if the United States reduces its contributions, other nations will follow.

On the other hand, the Group of 77, in 1981, put forth a program calling for aid to quadruple between 1980 and 1990. The United States, of course, did not support this program. The French, however, did support an increase in aid and pledged to double their foreign assistance to the LDCs. With such divergent views, the issue of whether foreign aid will be expanded or reduced will be central in the DC–LDC dialogue for the future.

Many observers question whether foreign assistance is an effective instrument in promoting economic development of the LDCs. The critics of aid argue that aid may actually retard growth since it substitutes for domestic saving and investment projects. Also, foreign aid, in the form of loans, only worsens the balance-of-payments problems because of rising debt repayment obligations of the LDCs. Thus the future role and scope of foreign aid as an instrument of economic development will likely be a point of controversy among the nations of the world.

QUESTIONS AND EXERCISES

1. What is meant by an "international economic order"? Why are the LDCs dissatisfied with the existing international economic order?

2. Trace the development of the LDCs' call for a "New International Economic Order." Make sure the changing nature of the LDCs' concerns are pointed out.

3. Define a commodity agreement. Describe two mechanisms that can be used to implement the pricing scheme of a commodity agreement. Make sure you mention the problems that can arise when these mechanisms are employed.

4. Evaluate the following statements: In practice, commodity agreements have been instituted with little difficulty. An example of a problem-free commodity agreement is that applying to tin.

5. Do you believe the commodity agreements are in the best long-term interests of the LDCs? Why or why not?

6. Describe two other international arrangements designed to protect the export (or trade) position of the LDCs.

7. What is a Generalized System of Preferences? Does the U.S. system of preferences aid the export expansion efforts of the LDCs as much as one might at first think? Why or why not?

8. What are two forms of foreign assistance? Which form is more advantageous to the DC and which is more advantageous to the LDCs? Do you think that foreign aid is an effective tool in the development plans of the LDCs? Why or why not?

CLOSING ESSAY:
A Response to the NIEO Proposals

Chapters 19 and 20 explored some of the peculiarities of world trade relations that contribute to the problems of developing nations. There can be little doubt that the LDCs are faced with a serious situation, and they have put forth a number of programs and proposals to try to improve their positions. The underlying theme in the LDC demands is that economic development is impeded by the fact that the DCs hold a dominant position in the world economy; economic improvement will therefore be difficult unless the DCs offer concessions designed to change the manner in which international economic relations are conducted. However, many observers have expressed doubts as to whether the reasons most frequently put forth by the LDCs to explain their low level of development are valid. In particular, questions have been raised about the proposals embodied in the New International Economic Order. The remainder of this essay will present the viewpoint of those who are critical of the NIEO, and will include some solutions that this group would offer in place of the NIEO proposals.

The LDCs perceive the problem of export prices—instability in the short run and deterioration of their terms of trade over the long run—as one of the principal obstacles to their economic development. The prescribed remedy has been either the unilateral formation of cartels or multilateral commodity agreements—with the objective of stabilizing or even raising export prices. As we saw earlier, attempts by LDCs to cartelize commodity exports have met with limited success. In fact, OPEC probably represents the only cartel that has been fully successful. Even OPEC, the inspiration to the LDCs in the 1970s, has encountered difficulties. Why? For the same reasons other cartels have floundered: (1) the reduction in demand for the commodity by consuming nations as a result of the high price imposed by the cartel and (2) the failure of producers to cooperate. The combination of declining demand by the oil-importing nations and differences among OPEC members over pricing policy has resulted in a substantial surplus of oil in the world markets in the early 1980s, and this has put pressure on the oil producers to reduce prices.

The effectiveness of commodity agreements in stabilizing export prices and, more importantly, export earnings, can also be questioned. First, if an increase in price results from a decrease in supply, the increase in price will help stabilize export earnings by offsetting the reduced supply. The effort to reduce the price to its long-term trend would then be counterproductive since it would unambiguously cause export revenue to fall. Second, the practicality of using buffer stocks to implement the agreements is open to question. The holding of adequate stocks of the commodity to diminish price fluctuations can be financially burdensome to the participating nations. As a result, most attempts to use buffer stocks have failed because of insufficient stocks, which can be attributed in part to insufficient funds to purchase the necessary quantities of the commodity. Also, some critics argue that, if in fact the objective of the commodity agreements is to stabilize prices around the long-term trend, private speculators would do the job just as well as the buffer stock manager. If speculators believed that the current price of a commodity were higher than its long-term trend, then they will sell the commodity at the high price, thereby pushing the price downward toward the trend. If private speculators are as accurate in their forecasts of trends as buffer stock managers (and there is no a priori reason to believe they are not), they would be preferable on the basis of costs.

If, instead of maintaining prices around a long-run trend, commodity agreements are intended to raise prices above their free market levels, they will encounter, in the long run, the same difficulties that are faced by the cartels. Finally, the use of export quotas, as a means of implementing commodity agreements, has its own set of problems. Not the least of them is determining the manner in which the quotas are to be allocated among producers.

The call for an Integrated Programme for Commodities by the LDCs in 1976 formalized the demand for the use of commodity agreements. Its main feature is a call for the establishment of a common fund to finance buffer stocks for all commodities. Although the greater size of the common fund might eliminate some of the funding problems associated with buffer stocks, the other problems associated with commodity agreements would still exist.

What, then, are possible solutions to the problem of export price stability, and the long-term problem of the worsening terms of trade? The critics of the NIEO suggest addressing the source of the problem: unstable demand and supply conditions. Since the supply of many primary products (particularly agricultural products) cannot be controlled by policy, the best option for the LDCs would be to obtain stable markets for their exports. That is, encourage the DCs to undertake policies that will stabilize their own income and inflation levels, thereby eliminating the causes of fluctuating demand for the LDC exports. Critics also argue that if the LDCs would take a more active role in such multilateral organizations as the IMF and GATT, they could put forth their demands for open and stable export markets more effectively.

Finally, there is some skepticism over whether there is a long-term tendency for the terms of trade of primary products to fall. As the world's population increases disproportionately in the LDCs, the demand for agricultural products and raw materials will grow relative to the demand for manufactures, so that the terms of trade will improve. According to this view, the LDCs would be better off in the long run if they would concentrate on exporting primary products.

In regard to increasing the access of LDC exports to the DCs' markets, the NIEO has suggested that the DCs grant trade preferences to the LDCs. However, because of various domestic pressure groups acting on behalf of the import-competing industries in the DCs, these measures have had but a limited effect in increasing the LDCs' exports. In fact, the structure of the generalized system of preferences may actually serve as a disincentive for successful export performance, since the least developed nations often receive more reductions in trade barriers than do the more successful LDC exporters.

Even though the failure of the GSP is not the fault of the LDCs, but of the interest groups within the DCs, many observers suggest that the LDCs could achieve greater success if they would participate in the GATT–sponsored multilateral trade negotiations and push for multilateral, nondiscriminatory tariff reductions. Although such reductions do not provide trade preferences to the LDCs, they would be more permanent in nature and perhaps less subject to circumvention by escape clause actions, since they would be negotiated and agreed to by both the DCs and LDCs. The LDCs have substantial bargaining power in any two-way negotiations, since they are the dominant exporters of many products vitally needed by the DCs. Proper use of such power would help assure the permanence of any reductions in barriers to entry into DC markets. In addition, many LDCs do not require trade preferences in order to be competitive in the world markets for their exports; this is particularly true for products that are labor intensive. In those product groups in which the LDCs have attained the greatest success, the markets are far from saturated, and free trade, without the threat of retaliatory action, is the most promising avenue for future success.

Foreign debt created by increasing balance-of-payments deficits looms as a severe problem for the LDCs. Many LDCs have suggested that special international monetary arrangements be established to facilitate the servicing of this debt. One specific suggestion is that a greater proportion of SDRs issued by the IMF be allocated to the LDCs. Some LDCs have even gone so far as to suggest that a portion of this debt simply be canceled. These proposals, which would involve a transfer of resources from the DCs to LDCs, are viewed by many with considerable skepticism. First, the private capital markets have provided a vital service by financing the increasing LDC debt. To default on that debt would seriously impair future private lending to LDCs. Second, the many causes of the payments deficits, oil price increases and recession within the DCs, are of a temporary nature, so that there is no need for special financial arrangements of a permanent nature. Those nations with long-term deficit and financing problems can avail themselves of existing IMF facilities, which are intended to provide loans and to reschedule the debt-service obligations for members with payments problems.

Finally, many economists note that the trade strategies of the LDCs themselves often inhibit economic development. By placing high tariffs on consumer goods, domestic resources are diverted from export industries, which may represent the nation's true comparative advantage, to domestic production of substitutes for the restricted consumer goods. Also, taxes imposed by LDCs on their exports often discourage earnings from those exports and encourage inefficient resource allocation. Restrictive policies also shelter the domestic economy from competitive pressures that stimulate efficiency.

To conclude, the critics of the NIEO proposals contend that they are not in the best long-term interests of the LDCs. They argue that economic development would be best served not by a transfer of resources from the DCs to LDCs, but by full participation by the LDCs in the international forums on world economic relations and by the use of their existing bargaining power to guarantee that they receive equitable treatment. By sheltering themselves from competitive pressures, the LDCs are postponing their economic development.

THE MULTINATIONAL VII ENTERPRISE

INTRODUCTION

One of the most significant developments in the international economy in recent years has been the truly phenomenal growth of multinational enterprises. MNEs are, basically, corporations that operate in more than one country. Thus a country which is host to an affiliate of an MNE will have within its borders an economic entity which is controlled by managers located abroad. Just as liberalized trade barriers and economic integration lead to a more intertwined world economy, so too will the presence of MNEs. If the managers of the MNE decided, for example, to shift production from the foreign country to its home country, the employment level of the host nation would be adversely affected. Host governments are typically not pleased with the prospect that a foreign-owned business can potentially influence economic events within its jurisdiction, especially when it might counteract the economic policy of the host country.

Although many nations of the world believe that the increased integration brought about by MNEs is detrimental, particularly since it results in a loss of a degree of economic sovereignty for those nations in which MNEs locate their affiliates, many other nations view MNEs in a much more tolerant light. Some nations view the MNE as a potential source of capital that is needed to generate growth in the levels of output and employment. In fact, some argue that MNEs are the only economic entities that can recognize and take advantage of investment opportunities in prospective host nations on a global scale. That is, without MNEs, many countries without adequate domestic sources of capital might never obtain the capital called for by available investment opportunities. Thus, many nations welcome affiliates of MNEs within their borders. Even from this brief introduction, it is clear that the economic effects of the MNEs are mixed, with some nations viewing them favorably, others unfavorably. Accordingly, the policies adopted by nations throughout the world toward MNEs have been mixed.

What is the magnitude of the impact of the MNE on the world economy? Should countries be overly concerned about their presence? All evidence suggests that the role of the MNE in the world economy is substantial, and growing. In fact, an MNE can influence many facets of the economic activity of an individual nation—from employment levels to the balance of trade. As the role of the MNE increases, countries throughout the world will be forced to develop policies toward them, and in so doing they will have to measure the related costs and benefits of the MNE.

In Part VII, then, the factors that influence the policies of nations toward MNEs will be examined. Chapter 21 begins by detailing the nature of the MNE; that is, its characteristics which distinguish it from other firms. Data are presented that demonstrate the magnitude of the role of MNEs in the world economy. Having obtained an idea as to the scope of MNEs, we proceed in Chapter 22 to examine the costs and benefits of MNEs—for the world economy, and for both the investor and host country. That discussion is followed by a presentation of the policies that nations throughout the world have adopted toward MNEs. As will be seen, the subject of MNEs is quite interesting, as well as being one of the most controversial topics in international economics.

The Nature and Scope 21
of the Multinational Enterprise

Because of the vast array of characteristics exhibited by multinational enterprises, it is difficult to arrive at a single definition that provides a set of criteria that could be used to unambiguously determine whether a business firm qualifies as an MNE. As a result, there has been a proliferation of definitions of an MNE. Some definitions offer qualitative criteria that a firm must fulfill to be considered an MNE, such as whether the firm operates and controls income-generating activities in more than one country. Others put forth more pragmatic criteria, such as the number of countries in which a firm operates or the proportion of total assets or sales accounted for by foreign subsidiaries. For the purpose of having an operational definition of an MNE, let us define an MNE as an international business enterprise with production locations in more than one country. The foreign subsidiaries of the MNE must not only be owned (at least a substantial proportion of them) by the parent company, which is headquartered in the home country, but the operations of the subsidiary must also be ultimately controlled or supervised by the parent firm.

FOREIGN DIRECT INVESTMENT

The establishment of a foreign subsidiary is accompanied by *direct investment* in the host foreign country. Foreign direct investment can be defined as the establishment of a new business enterprise or the expansion or acquisition of an existing firm by residents of one country within the borders of another country. An important characteristic of direct foreign investment is that, typically, the investors not only maintain ownership of the foreign enterprise, but also maintain control over the operations of the foreign firm.

While foreign direct investment is similar to international portfolio investment (see Chapter 11), in that they both involve an international transfer of capital, there are fundamental differences. First, direct foreign investment is carried out to a much larger extent by corporations than by individual investors. Second, although both types of investments do involve ownership of capital in foreign nations, with portfolio investment, the actual management of the foreign firm is usually undertaken by managers whose residency is the same as the location of the project. Thus the foreign firm simply obtains its capital funds from abroad, while maintaining its managerial responsibilities. In contrast, with a direct investment, a firm located outside the country in which the project is located, not only provides the capital funds, but also assumes responsibility for controlling the operations of the project.

THE NATURE OF MNEs

The character of MNEs varies considerably—in the manner in which they are established, in the pattern of ownership, and in the objectives of their operations. Corporations can implement a direct foreign investment by either establishing a new affiliate abroad or by purchasing a foreign-owned firm located in a foreign nation. Foreign direct investment can also be undertaken by expanding the operations of an existing foreign affiliate. Such expansion can be carried out by not only increasing the physical capital of the firm, but also by having the parent firm transfer or sell to its foreign subsidiary nonfinancial assets, such as managerial services and licenses to technology.

The ownership arrangements of foreign affiliates differ significantly among MNEs. For a number of reasons (to be discussed later), the parent firm might desire to hold less than 100 percent equity in its foreign subsidiaries. Often,

the parent will enter into joint ventures—sharing ownership with residents of the host foreign country or even forming a partnership with the host country government. An example of the latter arrangement occurred in 1970 when U.S. Steel entered into a joint venture with the government of Brazil, in which the Brazilian government held a 49 percent share of an iron ore mining project located in Brazil. Foreign direct investments have even been undertaken by parent companies that are jointly owned by investors from more than one nation. For example, the Royal Dutch Shell petroleum company is an MNE whose ownership is composed of both Dutch and British investors.

The objectives and aims of MNEs, and the motives behind the foreign direct investment decision, are also quite diverse. One objective that a firm might have for going multinational is to expand vertically. That is, a parent corporation that produces processed goods may establish a foreign subsidiary for the purpose of having the subsidiary produce inputs for the parent or for the purpose of procuring raw materials located in the host nation for resale to the parent company. An example of vertical expansion on a global scale was the establishment, by the world's major petroleum companies, of foreign subsidiaries in countries where their raw material—crude oil—was located. MNEs are also established on a horizontal basis. Corporations may desire to set up foreign facilities that carry out much the same activities as the parent company, the only difference being the location of their activities.

THE DECISION TO BECOME AN MNE

The Premultinational Status of a Firm

Why would a business firm producing in a single country desire to expand its production location to another country—that is, become an MNE? And what factors would influence the foreign investment decision of the firm? Before exploring these questions, it would be useful to examine the status of a firm, in terms of conducting international business, prior to becoming an MNE.

For a business firm to consider producing abroad, it will typically have had some international business experience. That experience probably involves international trade; most likely, the export of its product(s) to a foreign country. If the company's export sales are successful over an extended period of time, it can be anticipated that the firm will devote more resources to export sales. The company might, for example, allocate more sales staff to the foreign market. At the same time, the firm might increase its research of its growing export market, in an effort to become more familiar with its characteristics. The company could even establish sales offices in the foreign nation to facilitate its export trade with that nation and to maintain closer contact with its foreign customers.

The firm could also penetrate its foreign market by establishing licensing arrangements with firms of the foreign nation. Under such arrangements, the firm might sell the right to distribute the product or the technology needed to produce the product to an established foreign firm. In addition, the domestic firm could sell a license to the foreign firm that allows the foreign firm to use the domestic firm's product name and trademark.

Eventually, the firm might consider establishing a production unit in the foreign country. However, such a step is an enormous undertaking, accompanied by substantial risks to the firm. The firm must feel comfortable about locating a huge capital investment within the borders of a foreign nation. Managers of the firm must fully understand the behavior and attitudes of both foreign customers and the foreign government. Their behavior and attitudes may be quite different than those of the home country. These considerations are but a small part of the overall social, political and cultural differences between two countries, which combine to make the foreign investment decision quite complex and generally more risky than a domestic investment decision. It follows then, that for a firm to produce internationally, there must be lucrative economic incentives which more than compensate for the associated risks. In the following section, the particular factors which influence the firm's decision to go multinational will be examined.

FACTORS INFLUENCING THE MULTINATIONAL DECISION

For convenience, let us assume that the foreign direct investment decision is based on one of two motivations or goals of the firm: either the maximization of profits or the maximization (or maintenance) of sales. The establishment of a foreign subsidiary can be perceived as a means of achieving one or both of these objectives.

Foreign Direct Investment and Sales Maximization

Given that a firm is attempting to increase or maintain its level of sales, there are several motivations for a firm to establish a foreign affiliate. If the firm is already supplying its foreign customers through exports, the firm might perceive a need to have closer contact with its customers in order to better understand the needs of the market, and therefore it may wish to establish a local subsidiary in that country. Also, a foreign subsidiary located in one country might be in closer proximity to other export markets, and thus it might provide a more efficient base from which to service those markets.

Another important determining factor in the competition for international sales is the quality of ancillary services offered by the firm. Many technologically advanced products, such as computers, require postsales service on a regular basis, and the ability to provide such service is a determining factor in many sales. Obviously, postsales service can be more easily administered, the closer the service unit is to the customers. In the case of foreign customers, service requirements would be more effectively accommodated by an affiliate located in the foreign market.

Exports to a foreign market can be disrupted by the imposition of trade restrictions by the foreign government. By supplying the foreign market with products produced locally, by an affiliate, a firm can avoid such restrictions. A related problem is the effect of fluctuations in exchange rates on export sales. For example, if the currency of the home country were to appreciate vis-à-vis the foreign country's currency, the foreign price of export sales would increase and the quantity of sales would decrease. Obviously, movements in exchange rates would not be a factor to a firm if sales to those foreign markets were from affiliates located within the foreign country.

Foreign Direct Investment and Profit Maximization

If the firm were attempting to maximize profits, there would be many incentives to the firm to undertake direct investment in a foreign nation. Most of these incentives involve differences in the costs of production that exist among nations. Many corporations are attracted to a nation because of what is perceived as lower costs of production, particularly labor costs. For example, it is generally the case that wage levels in many of the less-developed countries are lower then they are in the developed countries. This disparity provides an incentive to corporations to establish subsidiaries in such low-wage nations, particularly if their production process is labor intensive. In 1977, the average hourly compensation paid by foreign manufacturing af-

filiates of U.S.–based MNEs, located in less-developed countries, was $1.74. During the same year, the average hourly compensation for workers in manufacturing firms located in the United States was $5.81. Thus it appears as though many U.S.–based MNEs may have been attracted to LDCs by their relatively low wage levels.

Although relative wage costs are certainly an important factor in the foreign direct investment decision, other characteristics of labor must also be considered. Labor in the host foreign country, regardless of wage costs, must possess the skills needed in the productive process, and those skills must be of comparable quality to those possessed by workers in the home country of the MNE.[1] Firms are also attracted to countries with a labor force characterized by low absenteeism and low levels of strike activity.

Other cost factors may also influence the decision of the firm. By producing abroad, instead of exporting, the firm can avoid transportation costs, thereby improving its competitive position. Also, the corporate tax systems of individual nations differ widely. Obviously, a corporation will be more inclined to locate a foreign subsidiary in a country where the burden of taxation on its earnings is lower than in other nations, including its home country.[2]

As mentioned previously, corporations expand vertically across national borders in an effort to obtain direct control of raw materials that are located in foreign countries. This was the

[1]Studies suggest that the differences in labor productivity between parent and host countries (generally lower in the latter) are not nearly enough to compensate for the much lower wage levels in the host nation. For example, see Michael Sharpston, "International Sub-Contracting," *Oxford Economic Papers,* March 1975.

[2]In the following chapter, it will be pointed out that lower tax burdens in the host country are often offset by the treatment of foreign earnings by the home country tax system.

motivation for the multinational expansion of the large petroleum companies in the 1950s. Examples of vertical expansion outside the petroleum industry include the foreign bauxite mining operations of Alcan Aluminum and the foreign copper mining operations of Kennecott Copper, both MNEs headquartered in the United States. Not only will vertical integration on a global scale generally assure a more reliable supply of the raw material, but also the costs of those inputs might be lower if they were purchased from an affiliate, rather than from an outside foreign-owned firm.

noneconomic factors

Besides the purely economic and financial factors influencing the corporate decision to locate abroad, the social and political characteristics of the prospective host nation must also be considered. The firm contemplating foreign expansion must be concerned with the attitude of the host government toward the presence of foreign-owned firms within its borders. Host countries frequently impose regulations and controls on foreign subsidiaries operating within its jurisdiction. The nature of these regulations will be detailed in the following chapter. For now, let us point out two of the most common of these regulations. Host countries often place restrictions on the remission of profits by the subsidiary, from the host country to the country of the parent firm. Also, local content requirements are frequently imposed, whereby the foreign subsidiary is required to use a certain proportion of host-country labor and materials. Obviously, such controls by the host country will inhibit the operations of the MNE. The firm must consider the past history of the prospective host country's policy toward foreign affiliates, and also predict whether existing controls will be tightened or new controls imposed in the future.

In addition to the attitudes of the host government toward foreign direct investment, the MNE must be convinced that the government itself is stable. Any change in either the leadership of a nation or in the basic form of government, will, in all likelihood, affect the environment in which affiliates of MNEs operate. The MNEs operating in Iran prior to that country's revolution in 1979, and the subsequent change of leadership, might not have undertaken the original direct investment if such a development had been forecast. Precise forecasts of the long-term stability of a host government are difficult to make. Yet the foreign direct investment decision requires that the corporation make such a forecast, and then incorporate that prediction, along with the economic factors, into the final decision on the foreign direct investment.

When a corporation steps into the world of multinational operations, the entire nature of the firm is altered. The firm must view its operations from a global perspective. The tasks required of managers are compounded with foreign affiliates, and to be successful the multinational managers must acquire the skills necessary to operate on a global scale. Managers must not only be aware of economic developments and government policy in the home country, but now must be equally concerned with similar developments in the country where its subsidiaries are located. Although the risks of global expansion are substantial, many firms, which have been willing to view their activities on a global perspective, have seen their foreign direct investments pay off handsomely.

DATA ON MULTINATIONAL ENTERPRISES

For a number of reasons, worldwide data on the size and patterns of MNE activities are, at best, sketchy. Governments of both home and host countries have historically concentrated their efforts in international data collection on accumulating information on trade flows among nations. Much the same can be said for the multilateral international organizations such as the United Nations. Those data which are available are primarily concerned with the stocks and flows of foreign direct investment. Because the definitions of foreign direct investment employed by individual governments differ, the coverage and reliability of the data vary enormously both among countries and even within an individual country over time. As a result, conclusions drawn from these data must be considered with care.

However, the data on MNEs that do exist can be used to attain a rough idea of the scope of MNEs, as well as an idea as to their importance in international economic relations. The discussion will begin by examining the available evidence on MNEs and worldwide foreign direct investment, and then will analyze the pattern of foreign direct investment undertaken by parent companies based in the United States. Concluding this section will be a brief historical description of the development of MNEs worldwide, concentrating on the role of U.S.–based MNEs.

Multinationals—Their Worldwide Scope

As stated above, deficiencies in data make intercountry comparisons of foreign direct investment extremely risky. Remembering this caveat, let us examine the information contained in Table 21–1. Table 21–1 shows the world stock of foreign direct investment, as measured by the book value of parent firms' equity in foreign subsidiaries, at the end of 1967 and 1976. Total value of foreign direct investment equaled $299 billion at year end 1976, with the U.S. share far exceeding the shares of other individual investor nations. It should be pointed out that these figures underestimate the control that MNEs exert on the world economy in that they represent only the equity of the parent corporation in its foreign affiliates, not the value of assets that they actually control. Thus if a parent firm owned 51 percent of a subsidiary having $100 million of assets, the data would show a stock of foreign direct investment equal to $51

TABLE 21-1

World Stock of Foreign Direct Investment (book values in billions of U.S. dollars)

	1967		1976		Annual Rate of Change
United States	$ 59.5	55.1%	$137.2	45.9%	9.75%
United Kingdom	17.5	16.2	32.0	10.7	7.00
Switzerland	5.0	4.6	22.5	7.5	18.00
Japan	1.5	1.4	20.0	6.7	34.00
Germany	3.0[a]	2.8	19.7[a]	6.6	23.00
France	6.0	5.6	11.5	3.8	7.50
Canada	3.7	3.4	9.0	3.0	10.00
Netherlands	2.2	2.0	4.3	1.4	8.00
Sweden	1.5	1.4	4.3	1.4	12.00
Other	8.1	7.5	38.5	13.0	12.00
Total	$108.0	100.0%	$299.0	100.0%	

Source: United Nations estimates; 1976 figures are preliminary. Reprinted from Lawrence G. Franko's "Multinationals: The End of U.S. Dominance," *Harvard Business Review,* November/December 1978, Exhibit 11.
[a]Figure does not include retained earnings and may understate German foreign investment by as much as 50%.

million, yet the parent would control all of the subsidiaries' operating assets, since it is the majority owner. It is thought by many that, in fact, the size of foreign assets controlled by MNEs may be two to three times as great as the size of foreign assets actually owned.

To obtain a better grasp of the importance of MNEs in the world economy, it will prove useful to compare the value of production associated with the foreign subsidiaries of the world's MNEs (so-called international production) to the value of total world production. The data on the value of sales or output of affiliates of MNEs are limited. In order to make an estimate of the value of such production, let us borrow a technique from the United Nations, which estimates the value of international production as being equal to twice the book value of foreign direct investment.[3] Based on the $299 billion figure for the 1976 book value of foreign direct investment, the estimated value of international production would equal $598 billion. This figure was approximately 8 percent of total world output in 1976 ($7255 billion). Other estimates of international production have put forth even higher figures. One study, for example,[4] estimates that 15 percent of world production is accounted for by the output of affiliates of MNEs.

[3]The United Nations employed this technique in its frequently cited study, *Multinational Corporations in World Development* (New York, 1973).

[4]See Judd Polk, "The New International Production," *World Development*, May 1973.

TABLE 21-2

Twenty Largest Multinationals Worldwide:
On the Basis of Foreign Revenue, 1977

Company/Country	Foreign Revenue (millions)	Foreign as % of Total
Exxon/U.S.	$44,333	73.5%
Royal Dutch/Shell Group/Neth.–Britain	NA	—
British Petroleum/Britain	22,200	81.0
Mobil/U.S.	20,481	59.0
Texaco/U.S.	18,927	66.2
Ford/U.S.	14,985	35.0
General Motors/U.S.	14,172	22.4
Standard Oil of Calif./U.S.	14,150	60.9
Phillips Gloeilampenfabrieken/Neth.	13,592	90.0
Intl. Business Machines/U.S.	11,040	52.4
International Tel. & Tel./U.S.	10,023	51.7
Gulf Oil/U.S.	9,229	51.1
Unilever/Britain–Neth.	NA	—
Nestlé/Switzerland	NA	—
Bayer/Germany	8,030	70.6
Volkswagenwerk/Germany	7,717	58.0
Siemens/Germany	7,294	50.5
Compagnie Française des Petroles/France	NA	—
B.A.T. Industries/Britain	6,469	83.5
Daimler-Benz/Germany	6,321	52.4

Source: *Forbes*, June 25, 1979.

Although such estimates are admittedly rough, they do provide an idea as to the extent of international production. Those estimates, whether they be 8 or 15 percent, imply that the foreign affiliates of MNEs account for a significant portion of the world's economic activity.

The dispersion of MNEs on the basis of national ownership is shown in Table 21–2, which lists the twenty largest MNEs, on the basis of 1977 foreign revenue, along with the country of ownership. Although the number of U.S.–based MNEs (nine) is greater than for any other investor nation (West Germany and the United Kingdom are second with four each), it is evident that U.S. corporations have no monopoly on the ability to operate internationally.

Also, it is interesting to note the divergence among the MNEs listed in Table 21–2 in terms of the importance of their foreign operations in their overall operations. For example, although General Motors' total revenue is considerably greater than that of the Ford Motor Company, the amount generated abroad is less than that of Ford. This suggests that some corporations place relatively more emphasis on the international aspects of their operations than others.

The Foreign Direct Investment Position of the United States

Because of the dominant position of U.S.–based MNEs, and the fact that the data on U.S.–based MNEs are more extensive than those of other investor countries, a detailed examination of the foreign direct investment position of the United States and its historical development will prove interesting. The Commerce Department records show that, in 1977, 3540 U.S. corporations were parent corporations to a foreign affiliate—that is, they had a direct or indirect ownership interest of 10 percent or more of a foreign business enterprise. The number of foreign affiliates totaled 35,789, of which 24,666 accounted for over 99 percent of the total assets and sales of all U.S. affiliates. Of those 24,666 affiliates, 11,909 were majority owned by their parent firm. Finally, it should be noted that 96

TABLE 21-3

Stock of U.S. Foreign Direct Investment, Year End, by Industry (millions of dollars and percent of total)

Industry/year	1950	1957	1966	1979	Annual Rate of Growth (%) (1950–1979)
All industries	$11,788	$25,394	$51,792	$192,648	10.1%
Petroleum	3,390 (29%)	9,055 (27%)	13,893 (27%)	41,553 (22%)	9.0
Manufacturing	3,831 (32%)	8,009 (40%)	20,740 (40%)	83,564 (43%)	11.2
Other industries	4,566 (39%)	8,331 (33%)	17,160 (33%)	67,531 (36%)	9.7

Source: Bureau of Economic Analysis, U.S. Department of Commerce, "Trends in the U.S. Direct Investment Position Abroad, 1950–79," in *Survey of Current Business* (Washington, D.C.: U.S. Government Printing Office, February 1981).

percent of the foreign affiliates were nonbank affiliates of nonbank parents, although the nonbank affiliates accounted for only 59 percent of the total value of affiliate assets.

Table 21–3 shows the foreign direct investment position of the United States, as measured by the value of the stock of foreign direct investment, at year end for 1950, 1957, 1966 and 1979. Also depicted is the distribution of U.S. foreign direct investment by industrial activity.

Table 21–4 provides much the same information, except that the foreign direct investment totals are classified according to the area of the world in which they are located.

At year end 1950, the U.S. direct investment position abroad was $11.8 billion and by the end of 1979 this figure had grown to $192.6 billion. Over this period, 1950–1979, the average annual growth rate of U.S. foreign direct investment was 10.1 percent.

TABLE 21-4

Stock of U.S. Foreign Direct Investment by Area, Year End (millions of dollars and percent of total)

Area/Year	1950	1957	1966	1979	Average Annual Growth by Area (1950–1979)
Total	$11,788	$25,252	$54,562	$192,648	10.1%
Developed Countries	5,696	13,463	36,461	137,927	11.6
	(48%)	(53%)	(67%)	(72%)	
Canada	3,579	8,332	16,840	41,033	8.8
	(31%)	(33%)	(31%)	(21%)	
Europe	1,720	3,993	16,200	81,463	14.2
	(15%)	(16%)	(30%)	(42%)	
Australia, New Zealand and South Africa	378	957	2,665	9,656	
Japan	19	181	756	5,775	
	(.1%)	(.7%)	(1%)	(3%)	
Developing Countries	5,736	10,735	14,465	47,841	7.6
	(49%)	(43%)	(27%)	(25%)	
Latin America	4,735	8,805	9,854	36,835	7.5
	(40%)	(35%)	(18%)	(19%)	
Other	1,001	1,930	4,611	11,006	
Middle East	NA	NA	1,671	−375	
Africa	NA	NA	1,477	3,615	
Asia (Far East)	NA	NA	1,463	7,766	
International[a]	356	1,054	3,636	6880	10.8
(shipping)	(3%)	(4%)	(7%)	(4%)	

Source: U.S. Department of Commerce, *Survey of Current Business* (Washington, D.C.: U.S. Government Printing Office, various issues).

[a]The international category refers to U.S. direct investment unallocated to a particular nation. International shipping constitutes the majority of such investment.

RECENT TRENDS IN THE WORLDWIDE PATTERN OF FOREIGN DIRECT INVESTMENT

Although the foreign direct investment position of the United States is considerably larger than that of other investor nations, recent developments suggest that non–American MNEs may be challenging the dominant position of the United States. This trend is indicated by the information shown in Table 21–1, which presents a comparison of the foreign direct investment position of the leading investor nations for the years 1967 and 1976. During this period, it is evident that the dominant position of the United States was eroded somewhat, as its share of world foreign direct investment declined from 55 percent to 46 percent.

This decline in the American share, and the corresponding increase in the non–American share, was the result of the relatively higher rates of growth in foreign direct investment by the latter group of nations during the late 1960s and 1970s. While United States foreign direct investment grew at an annual rate of approximately 10 percent between 1967 and 1976, the foreign investment of many other nations grew at a considerably higher rate. For example, Japan's direct investment abroad grew at an average annual rate of 34 percent between 1967 and 1976, West Germany's at a 23 percent annual rate and Switzerland's at an 18 percent annual rate. Another illustration of the "non–American challenge" to the U.S. foreign direct investment position is one study's estimate that by 1971 the international production of affiliates of European–based MNEs exceeded the international production of the affiliates of MNEs headquartered in the United States.[5]

[5]See Robert B. Stobaugh, "Multinational Competition Encountered by U.S. Companies That Manufacture Abroad," *Journal of International Business Studies,* Spring/Summer 1977.

What are the factors behind this non–American challenge to the dominance of the U.S.–based MNEs? There does not appear to be a single, overriding explanation, but a combination of several factors. During this period, the industrial productivity of Japan and continental Europe increased more rapidly than that of the United States. As a result, the products of those nations became more competitive with those of the United States, a development which is reflected by the increasing share of world exports captured by those nations. Since foreign production typically follows the exporting stage of international business, the increased participation of non–American nations in the world trading system would be a natural steppingstone to their increased participation in international production.

Another factor might be that prior to the mid-1960s few non–American corporations operated according to a global strategy, probably due to a lack of experience in managing large, multidivisional organizations, much less a multinational organization. However, not only have European and Japanese corporate managers developed that capacity, but many believe that they have improved upon American managerial practices.

Despite recent trends, the U.S. foreign direct investment position continues to dominate that of other investor nations. However, it can be expected that in the future the extent of that dominance will continue to be reduced, as more non–American corporations extend their corporate outlook to a global scale.

THE UNITED STATES AS A HOST COUNTRY

An offshoot of the surge in non–American foreign direct investment during the 1970s was the increasing role of the United States as a host country to foreign direct investment. The rise of foreign direct investment in the United States is illustrated in Table 21–5, where the value of such investment is shown for the years 1971 to 1979. Foreign direct investment in the United States almost quadrupled from 1971 to 1979, when at year end it totaled over $52 billion. From a global perspective, the United States is currently host to more foreign direct investment than any nation except Canada.

This investment is highly concentrated, as the eight nations with the largest holdings of direct investments in the United States accounted for over 90 percent of the 1979 total. Those nations are listed in Table 21–6, along with the size of their 1979 holdings. Although not shown in Table 21–6, it is useful to point out the individual nations whose direct investments in the United States have grown most rapidly during the 1970s. The unquestionable leader was Japan, whose direct investment in the United States increased almost sixfold from 1975 to 1979. Following Japan in terms of growth were the Netherlands and West Germany, respectively. A final aspect of the national ownership of direct investment in the United States is the absence of any of the OPEC nations from

TABLE 21-5

Foreign Direct Investment in the United States (stock at year end)

Year	Value (millions)	Percentage Increase
1971	$13,914	—
1972	14,868	6.9%
1973	20,556	38.3
1974	25,144	22.3
1975	27,662	10.0
1976	30,770	11.2
1977	34,595	13.8
1978	42,471	22.8
1979	52,260	23.0

Source: U.S. Department of Commerce, *Survey of Current Business* (Washington, D.C.: U.S. Government Printing Office, August 1976 and August 1980).

TABLE 21-6

1979 Stock of Foreign Direct Investment in the United States, by Investor Country

Country	Value (billions)	Percentage
Netherlands	$12.4	23.7%
United Kingdom	9.2	17.6
Canada	6.9	13.2
West Germany	5.4	10.3
Japan	3.6	6.9
Netherlands Antilles	3.2	6.1
Switzerland	3.1	5.9
France	2.3	4.4
Other nations	6.2	11.9
Total	$52.3	100.0%

Source: U.S. Department of Commerce, *Survey of Current Business* (Washington, D.C.: U.S. Government Printing Office, August, 1980).

Table 21–6. In 1979, OPEC nations accounted for only about $400 million of foreign direct investment in the United States, or less than 1 percent of the total.[6]

What are the causes of this recent influx of foreign direct investment into the United States? First, the substantial depreciation of the dollar in the late 1970s reduced the foreign currency cost of acquiring U.S. companies and expanding existing facilities. Also, the costs of production in the United States, relative to those in other countries, were lowered by the dollar depreciation, making investment attractive. Second, the price of stocks in the United States was relatively low during those years, making acquisition of American firms less costly. Third, the periodic threats of increased protectionism by the United States against specific products seem to have prompted direct investment as a way for foreign companies to escape the protectionist

[6]Remember the $400 million refers to direct investment—investment involving a 10 percent or more ownership share. It excludes portfolio investments by the OPEC nations in the United States.

measures. Fourth, relative to the rest of the world, the United States has very few restrictions on foreign direct investments and a political system which is quite stable; both of these factors reduce the risks investors must consider. Finally, the growth in direct investment in the United States might be best explained as a natural consequence of the overall surge in non–American foreign direct investment. Given the attractiveness of the United States as a host country and the fact that many foreign companies already service their U.S. markets with exports, it would follow that much of the new wave in non–American direct investment would be channeled toward the United States.

QUESTIONS AND EXERCISES

1. Define a multinational enterprise. Also, define foreign direct investment. How does foreign direct investment differ from international portfolio investment?

2. Describe several ownership arrangements that an MNE may assume.

3. Evaluate the following proposition. Most business firms do not have any international business experience prior to becoming an MNE.

4. Describe three ways by which a firm might maximize its sales by establishing a foreign affiliate.

5. Describe two ways by which a firm might lower its production costs by establishing a foreign production unit.

6. What is meant by "vertical" foreign direct investment? What is the incentive for a firm to undertake such an investment?

7. What are several noneconomic factors that a firm must consider before undertaking a foreign direct investment?

8. Evaluate the following statement: Multinational enterprises do not seem to play a very significant role in the international economy. In fact, their role in the economy seems to have diminished over the past twenty years.

9. What have been the principal reasons for the increasing role of the United States as a host country?

The Economic Effects 22
of Multinational Enterprises and Public
Policy Toward MNEs

Our discussion in Chapter 21 indicated that the role of the MNE in the world economy is substantial. Obviously, any entity which controls assets the size of those controlled by MNEs and is also responsible for as much as 8 to 15 percent of the world's production (according to the estimates presented in the previous chapter) is going to have a significant impact on the world's economy. Another way to view the role of MNEs is that several hundred top-level corporate executives of the world's largest companies have the ability to influence significantly the level of the world's economic activity, as well as international economic relations among sovereign nations.

Until now, the question of whether or not the economic impact of MNEs is beneficial has not been addressed. As will be shown in this chapter, the overall impact of the MNEs is really composed of many individual effects, some economic, others social and political; some beneficial to the world, others costly. To obtain a truly accurate idea of the total effect, then, all the effects must be examined separately, for both the host and parent countries. Important economic variables, from employment levels to balance-of-payments positions, will be shown to be effected by the behavior of MNEs. After we have examined the economic effects of MNEs, we will then discuss the attitudes and policies, of both parent and host countries, toward foreign direct investment.

THE ECONOMIC EFFECTS OF MNEs—A GLOBAL PERSPECTIVE

As suggested in the previous chapter, foreign direct investment represents a transfer of capital across national borders. Presumably, international corporations, in their attempt to maximize global profits, would invest their capital where it would offer the highest rate of return. Since the return to capital is directly related to its productivity, MNEs would be investing their capital in its most productive use. From the viewpoint of the world as a whole, such activity would facilitate the optimal allocation of capital and thus contribute to the maximization of world output. Also, if the MNE transfers employees across national borders, in an effort to place them where their skills will be most productive, the MNE will be contributing to the efficient allocation of human capital as well as physical capital.

Some argue that MNEs also represent a potential source of dynamic benefits to the world. That is, not only will foreign direct investment result in a more efficient allocation of the existing capital stock, but it will also result in a larger stock of capital, over time, than would otherwise be the case. Because MNEs are, typically, large corporations that operate on a global scale and possess vast financial resources, they are able to recognize new, profitable investment opportunities throughout the world and then to carry out those investments. Nonmultinational entrepreneurs, on the other hand, generally operate on a much smaller scale, and thus do not have as great an ability to recognize and respond to international investment opportunities as MNEs. Thus the presence of MNEs will result in an accelerated rate of investment worldwide, and the resulting increase in global capital formation will lead to an accelerated rate of economic growth.

However, there do exist some questions as to whether MNEs, and the foreign direct investment which accompanies their establishment, will, in fact, result in a maximization of global economic welfare. Typically, MNEs are large firms operating in an imperfectly competitive market, best labeled as oligopolistic. Any valuation of the efficiency of an MNE will thus be mitigated by the fact that they do not generally operate in perfectly competitive markets. As is well known from welfare economics, there

is no guarantee that private profit maximization by firms will coincide with welfare maximization for the community (world) when imperfect competition prevails.

On the basis of purely economic considerations, then, it is not obvious whether international business that is carried out by MNEs will result in a maximization of the world's economic welfare. An equally important question is whether MNEs improve the economic well-being of the individual nations involved; both the parent country—the country in which the MNE is headquartered—and the host country—the country in which the foreign subsidiary is located. To deal properly with the impact of MNEs on individual nations, not only should the economic consequences be examined, but so should the social and political effects.

THE ECONOMIC EFFECTS OF THE MNE—THE HOST NATION

The economic effects of the MNE on the host nation are many; some might be considered favorable, while others involve costs to the host country. The aspects of economic life of the host nation which are influenced by the presence (or absence) of MNE affiliates range from employment levels to balance-of-payments positions. To reach a final judgment as to the overall effect on the host nation, the potential benefits and costs must be weighed against one another.

Output and Employment

One economic benefit to a host country of having an MNE establish an affiliate within its borders is that the levels of output and employment in the host country might be greater than they would have been otherwise. Crucial to this argument is the fact that the higher levels of production would not have been achieved had it not been for the presence of the MNE. That is, local firms would either have not perceived the investment opportunity, or, if they had, they would not have been able to implement the investment project.

Several arguments exist to support this notion. Foremost, an affiliate of an MNE is an extension of an existing corporation. This corporation more than likely has had past experience with the economic activity under consideration. In many instances, there is simply not an existing local enterprise that is familiar with the investment under consideration, making it difficult for local entrepreneurs to take advantage of the investment opportunity. Even when local entrepreneurs are familiar with the investment opportunity, it is often the case that local firms will not possess the financial resources that are required to operate on the scale necessary to make the investment financially successful. The MNE, on the other hand, typically has been operating on a global scale prior to the establishment of an affiliate, and thus is much more familiar with the production and marketing techniques needed to serve large markets. Thus it is thought by many that because MNEs are generally better able to recognize and implement large-scale operations than are local firms, they will be able to implement more effectively investment projects in the host country. Such projects will, in turn, increase output and employment levels in the host nation.

Although many would agree that MNEs do represent an effective instrument to increase the output and employment levels of a host nation, there is significant disagreement on the magnitude of that contribution. From the preceding chapter, we know that the value of international production, the value of the output of affiliates of MNEs, is substantial. However, it should be kept in mind that the true indicator of the affiliates' contribution to the host country is the income generated by the host country's factors of production—that is, the value-added by resources indigenous to the host country. Income

of the affiliate paid to nonlocal factors does not represent a direct benefit to the host nation (although the nonlocal factors may use their income to purchase locally produced output).

Also, the source of inputs or raw materials used by the affiliate must be considered when making a determination of an affiliate's contribution to the host nation's output and income levels. The affiliates may purchase locally produced inputs, which would stimulate the local economy, or they may import inputs, which would lessen the affiliate's contribution to the local economy.

international subcontracting

A recent development in the behavior of MNEs illustrates how the output figures of affiliates may overstate their contribution to the host country's economy. MNE enterprises are increasingly locating their assembly operations abroad, largely in less-developed countries. Because these assembly operations are for the most part labor intensive, costs may be lowered by locating those operations in the low-wage, less-developed nations. These affiliates import the components of the product, most often from their parent, and then assemble the inputs for sale to either the local market, a third country or the parent firm. Obviously, if an affiliate is importing a substantial quantity of its inputs, the total sales figure of the affiliate will overstate its contribution to the local economy.

Available evidence suggests that the practice of international "subcontracting" by MNEs has increased substantially during the 1970s, and has been concentrated in products such as textiles, office machinery, television receivers, toys and semiconductors. The production of semiconductors by American–based MNEs provides an excellent example of international subcontracting. The wafer of the semiconductor—its essential component—is produced in the United States and then is transported to any one of several low-wage, less-developed nations, principally Taiwan, South Korea, Hong Kong or Singapore. At the parent's offshore assembly facilities, gold threads are soldered to the wafer's terminals and the finished semiconductor is returned to the American parent. In 1973, out of a total of $222.8 million of American semiconductor imports, $190.7 million were from less-developed countries and contained American components constituting 40 percent of the total value. The remaining 60 percent ($113.6 million) represented the value added by the foreign affiliate. Therefore, a guarded interpretation of total output figues, as a measure of the affiliate's contribution to the host country, is imperative, given the recent increase in the practice of international subcontracting by MNEs.

Balance of Payments

The establishment of a foreign subsidiary can affect the host country's balance-of-payments position—on both the trade and capital accounts. These different effects can either improve or worsen the host country's balance-of-payments position. First, the direct investment associated with the establishment of a subsidiary will be a credit on the host country's balance-of-payments ledger (see Chapter 7). Second, because the subsidiary employs capital that is owned by residents of the investor country, any profits or interest earned by that capital, and then repatriated to the parent country from the host will represent a debit item in the host country's balance of payments. The repatriation of income payments abroad by nonhost country labor employed by the affiliate would also worsen the host's balance-of-payments position. And any royalty payments or license fees that the subsidiary makes to its parent, for the use of technology, productive processes or trademarks will also worsen the host nation's payments position.

In addition to the above-mentioned payments effects, affiliates of MNEs can significantly influence the trading patterns of the host country, often in a complex and conflicting manner. The net effect really depends on the motivation of the MNE for establishing the subsidiary in the host country. If the MNE, for example, locates an affiliate in the host country to serve the host market through local production rather than exports (possibly to avoid trade restrictions), then the substitution of local production for host country imports will improve the host country's trade balance. Improvement in the balance of trade will also occur if the MNE intends to produce in the host country—say, to take advantage of lower production costs—and then export to third countries or reexport to the parent country. However, the MNE affiliate can also import substantial quantities of inputs and raw materials (as in subcontracting arrangements discussed above), and in so doing worsen the trade balance of the host country.

There also exist indirect effects that affiliates have on their host's trade balance. If the presence of an affiliate results in an increase in the level of the income of the host country, it can be anticipated that the demand for imports by the host country might also rise. Also, the affiliate might draw local resources from the host nation's export- and import-competing sectors, lowering production in those sectors which would, in turn, worsen the trade balance of the host nation.

Information on U.S.–sponsored affiliates which allows us to obtain a rough estimate of the effect of those affiliates on their host countries' bilateral payments position with the United States does exist. In 1977, U.S. direct investment in host countries totaled approximately $13 billion. However, the combined value of income repatriated from the affiliates to their parents and license fees and royalty payments made to the parent firms, exceeded direct investment by about

$11 billion. This implies that the host nations' (both developed and less-developed countries) payments position on the service and capital accounts was adversely affected by the direct investment activity of the United States in 1977.

The data on American exports to and imports from foreign affiliates of American–based MNEs also provides insight into the effects that the affiliates have on the overall payments position of their host nations, vis-à-vis the United States. Unfortunately, the coverage of the trade data differs from that of the data on the service and capital flows, and thus they are not directly comparable. In 1977, the United States imported $38 billion of merchandise from American–sponsored affiliates and exported $35.8 billion of merchandise to those affiliates. From the perspective of the host country, these data imply that the net effect of affiliate trade on their trade balance was positive.

These data are intended only to provide the reader with a better feel for the magnitude and pattern of affiliate trade. It should be remembered that they are limited to bilateral trade between the United States and affiliates of U.S.–based MNEs, and do not consider the effects of affiliate trade with third countries.

the balance-of-payments effect of intra–MNE trade

One particularly interesting feature of the MNE and its role in world trade is the substantial amount of trade that takes place within the MNE itself. Intra–MNE trade can assume any one of several forms. It can involve the sale of a finished good from the parent to an affiliate located in a foreign country, where the affiliate might simply undertake the role of marketing and distributing the good in the host country as well as providing after-sales service. Or, as was discussed previously, trade between the parent and affiliate may be in intermediate or component goods, with each unit of the MNE responsible for different activities in the total production process. Intra–MNE need not even involve the parent, as trade often occurs between individual affiliates.

transfer pricing

Intrafirm trade is quite different from interfirm trade in several respects, one of the most important being the method employed by the MNE in pricing the goods being traded. The pricing practices of the MNE on intrafirm trade is referred to as *transfer pricing*. Transfer pricing can often result in a price for a traded good that differs from the price of the good prevailing in the world market. The transfer pricing techniques of the MNE can significantly influence the trade position of the host country.

In discussing those factors that would induce an MNE to establish prices that differ from those prevailing in the world market, it must be remembered that the MNE is attempting to maximize total profits. As a result, the MNE would desire to allocate its total profits between the parent and host countries in a manner that would achieve that goal. For example, if corporate profit taxes were higher in the parent country than in the host country, and if the parent firm were exporting to the affiliate, it would be in the interest of the MNE to underprice its exports to the host country, shifting profits from the parent to the affiliate, and thus lowering the overall tax burden of the MNE. Conversely, if the affiliate were exporting to the parent, where the parent country had high tax levels, it would pay the affiliate to overprice its exports, thus reducing taxable profits in the parent county. Not only do differential tax rates induce nonmarket transfer prices, but so will differential tariff rates on imports. The higher the tariff levels in the importing country, the greater the incentive to underprice the traded commodity in an effort to avoid duty payments.

Transfer pricing is not only a useful device for MNEs to employ in their effort to reduce their overall tax burden, but it also provides a convenient tool that can be used to circumvent restrictions that host countries frequently impose on the amount of profits that a subsidiary can remit to its parent. An MNE which desires to repatriate earnings from an affiliate to the parent can effectively achieve this by underpricing exports from the affiliate to the parent or overpricing exports from the parent to the affiliate. Both pricing techniques will increase the share of profits accruing to the parent. In other words, profits have been effectively repatriated from the affiliate to the parent.

The implications of transfer pricing for the balance-of-payments position of the host nation are substantial. If the affiliate were to underprice its exports to the parent or the parent were to overprice its exports to the affiliate (which are imports to the host country), the payments position of the host country would likely deteriorate, as would its terms of trade.

To point out just one example of the dependency of a host nation on intra–MNE trade, approximately 13 percent of the value of Mexican imports in 1977 were in the form of sales from American parents to their subsidiaries located in Mexico. On the other side of the trade picture, 10 percent of the total value of Mexican exports in 1977 were in the form of sales from American–sponsored affiliates to their parents. These figures may even be underestimates, as they only include trade within *American* MNEs and only the trade between parent and affiliate, not among affiliates themselves.

Many host nations are quite dependent on intra–MNE trade. Given the dependence of many host nations on intra–MNE trade, such pricing practices can potentially result in substantial changes in their payments position and terms of trade.

The MNE as an International Transfer Agent

From our previous discussion, it is clear that MNEs are responsible for the transfer of a substantial volume of goods and services, as well as capital, across national boundaries. In addition, MNEs act as international conduits for other important economic factors, specifically technology and human capital.

technology transfer

Technology can be thought of as the degree of knowledge embodied in the industrial processes used to produce goods and services. The existing level of technology can be transmitted internationally from the country of innovation to other countries in several ways. Entrepreneurs outside the country of innovation may imitate the technology in which they are interested. This could be accomplished, for example, by purchasing a license to the technological process from the innovating firm.

However, for many nations, particularly less-developed countries, acquiring technology through imitation is difficult and costly. Often, it is easier for a nation to obtain technology through intra–MNE transmission, typically from the parent firm to an affiliate located in the non-innovating host nation. The receipt of the technology will allow the subsidiary to produce more efficiently, increasing the productivity and income of the factors of production it employs, many of which are indigenous to the host country.

The extent of intra–MNE technology transmission is difficult to quantify. However, data do exist which enable us to obtain a rough idea as to the volume of technology transferred between the parents and the affiliates of American–based MNEs. In 1977, out of the 23,641 affiliates surveyed by the Commerce Department, 8,267 responded that they had licensing arrangements with their U.S. parents for the use of patents and industrial processes originating with the parent. Of the positive responses, 69 percent were from affiliates located in developed countries, with the remainder located in less-developed nations. Such a pattern suggests that the developed countries which are host to U.S.–based affiliates may benefit more as recipients of technology than the less-developed host countries.

Transfer of Human Capital

The MNE also acts as a transfer agent of human capital; that is, the training and education which determines the skill level of labor. When an MNE establishes a subsidiary in a host country, the parent corporation will often transfer employees in skilled managerial and research positions to the subsidiary. In addition, the affiliates will frequently train local residents, providing them with the human capital needed to perform the tasks required in the productive process. The net result of such actions is that the host country will have a greater stock of human capital within its borders.

A point related to the above discussion is that the MNE also transfers to the host country entrepreneurial skills. Entrepreneurial skills include the ability to recognize a profitable investment opportunity, to accumulate the resources needed to implement the investment and at the same time to bear the substantial risk involved in the venture. As mentioned previously, it is often questionable whether the host country possesses those skills. The MNE, with its global experience, tremendous financial capacity and abundance of technical skill, is often the only entity that can provide the entrepreneurial skills required to exploit the investment opportunity.

ATTITUDES AND POLICIES OF HOST COUNTRIES TOWARD MNEs

It is evident that a host nation is confronted with a set of conflicting factors when determining its policies toward foreign-owned affiliates of MNEs located within its borders. On the one hand, MNEs can be viewed as a vehicle for economic development, generating income and employment levels that are greater than they would be otherwise. On the other hand, arguments were presented which suggest that the benefits of MNEs are limited, and that the potential costs to the host country, such as a worsening payments position and the loss of economic sovereignty, may outweigh those benefits. Any policy response to MNEs under these conditions must be based on an evaluation of the relative costs and benefits that result from foreign direct investment. If the costs outweigh the benefits, then the host nation would have an incentive to adopt a policy which discourages foreign direct investment, and, conversely, if foreign direct investment is judged to be beneficial to the host nation, a policy that encourages foreign investment is likely to be formulated.

A policy toward foreign direct investment is generally composed of many individual provisions, each directed at specific aspects of foreign investment. A host government will tend to construct an optimal mix of incentives and restrictions, in an effort to maximize the benefits and minimize the costs of foreign direct investment. The following discussion examines some specific incentives and restrictions frequently imposed by host countries.

Incentives That Host Countries Offer to MNEs

Nations that judge the advantages of foreign-owned subsidiaries of MNEs to outweigh the disadvantages will establish incentives to encourage foreign direct investment. Incentives might include tax concessions, tariff reductions or a liberal policy toward the flow of profit remittances to the parent country. Such incentives represent financial savings to MNEs, and increase the prospective financial return to an MNE that is considering locating in the nation offering these incentives.

The basic approach of a host country that is offering incentives can be quite varied. Many countries promote all types of foreign direct investment, while others limit incentives to specific types of economic activity. An example of incentives targeted for a particular activity was Brazil's efforts in the mid-1950s to establish a local automobile industry by attracting foreign direct investment. Included among Brazil's incentives were reduced tariff rates on imported plant and equipment that was needed in automobile production and preferential exchange-rate treatment to foreign investors to aid in their debt financing. In addition, automotive components which were not produced in Brazil and had to be imported were given favorable tariff treatment.

An interesting approach to incentives is the Mexican National Frontier Program, adopted in 1966. Under this program, the affiliate is permitted to import materials and components duty free, and then to export the finished product without the burden of export taxes. There are, however, certain stipulations on ownership arrangements and requirements on the proportion of Mexican labor that the affiliate must use. By the early 1970s over three hundred U.S. firms had established subsidiaries along the designated areas of the U.S.–Mexican border, where the policy was applicable.

Restrictions That Host Countries Place on MNEs

In an effort to minimize the costs associated with affiliates of MNEs that locate within their borders, host nations will frequently establish a set of restrictions on foreign direct investment.

The particular forms of those restrictions are wide ranging; addressing both the questions of ownership and the operations of the affiliates.

restrictions on foreign ownership

Before an MNE can establish an affiliate, the governments of many nations require that the firm obtain approval from various government agencies. The French government, for example, requires that any MNE wishing to establish an affiliate in France obtain approval from the Ministry of Finance. Canada requires that a potential foreign investor demonstrate to its Foreign Investment Review Agency that his project will result in a significant benefit to Canada. Such action by the host government makes it the responsibility of the MNE to tailor its investment project to meet those standards. If the MNE must significantly alter the nature of the project from its optimal state, the MNE may elect to forego the investment altogether.

Many host nations believe that the costs of MNEs can be best minimized by imposing limitations on the proportion of foreign ownership. One common practice is to encourage joint ventures whereby ownership is shared between the foreign MNE and local firms (or a group of local investors) or the host government itself. Shared ownership can also be obtained through public sales of equity within the host country. Until recently, Japan had limited foreign ownership to 49 percent of the total capital of the firm. The Mexican government has promoted joint ventures through direct bargaining with the prospective MNE, as well as by imposing various regulations, such as limits on tax concessions, on those foreign affiliates with less than 51 percent Mexican ownership. In fact, MNEs frequently recognize that they will be operating in a much more accommodative environment if they have local ownership, and thus often volunteer the option of local ownership.

Another method employed by host governments to limit foreign ownership is to encourage licensing arrangements whereby the MNE, instead of establishing an affiliate, will sell a license to a local firm that allows it to distribute the product of the MNE, using its trademark. In fact, the MNE may even sell a license to a local firm that provides the local firm with the technology needed to produce the product. Japan has historically promoted licensing arrangements in lieu of foreign direct investment in an effort to stimulate local economic activity, while at the same time obtaining access to foreign goods and technology.

restrictions on MNE operations

Once an MNE has located an affiliate in a host nation, the government of that country can impose controls on the operations of the affiliate. Local content requirements, whereby tbe affiliate must use a specified amount of locally produced inputs in its productive process, is one common method by which host govcrnmcnts attempt to stimulate the contribution of a subsidiary to the local economy. Another method used by host countries to encourage local participation is an employment requirement. Under such a provision, a certain percentage of the affiliate's work force must be residents of the host nation. Mexico, for example, requires that local residents compose at least 90 percent of the work force of foreign affiliates located within its borders.

Because foreign subsidiaries can substantially alter the balance-of-payments position of the host country—on both the trade and capital accounts—host nations have frequently imposed restrictions on the international activities of those affiliates in an effort to minimize any potential worsening of its payments position. Such restrictions include limits on the volume of profits and capital that an affiliate is permitted to repatriate abroad, as well as limiting the volume of royalty payments permitted to its parents. Host governments often require that affiliates export a minimum amount of their output, as well as impose ceilings on the volume of goods that an affiliate may import. It should be recalled that such controls, at least on intra–MNE trade, can be circumvented to a degree by the transfer pricing practices of the MNEs. Host governments are increasingly recognizing this practice and are adopting policies to deal with it.

The ultimate restriction on foreign direct investment is expropriation—the dispossessing of the affiliate without compensation. Such action deprives the MNE of future earnings for which it has risked its capital. Moreover, if the affiliate is replaced by local producers, a new competitor to the MNE will emerge. Generally, host governments have justified expropriation by contending that the host nation will be better served if the industry is locally owned, either privately or by the government itself.

During the 1960s the U.S. government identified seventy cases of foreign expropriation of American–owned direct investments abroad. The majority of these actions were in the resource industries, banking and insurance sectors and public utilities, and they were concentrated in Latin America. It is interesting to note the near absence of expropriations of manufacturing concerns.

THE EFFECTS OF THE MNE ON THE PARENT COUNTRY

Foreign direct investment not only affects the economic activities of the host nation, but also the economic activities of the nation where the MNE is headquartered—the parent country. The establishment of a foreign subsidiary by an MNE can affect the employment and output levels of the parent country, as well as its external payments position. Just as with the host country, the effects of foreign direct investment can result in either a benefit or a cost to the parent country. In fact, some observers contend that for any effect that the direct investment has on the host nation—whether it be a cost or a benefit—there will be an opposite effect on the parent country. For example, if the establishment of an affiliate leads to an increase in the income and employment levels of the host country, there might be a corresponding decrease in the income and employment levels in the parent country, if the move abroad by the MNE was intended to replace home country production with foreign production. Or if the foreign production was intended to replace exports from the parent country to the host country, the resultant reduction in host country imports would correspond to a reduction in the parent country's volume of exports. Rather than detail, individually, the economic effects of foreign direct investment on the parent country, since they will be similar to the previously discussed effects on the host country, let us proceed to examine some of the attitudes and policies toward foreign direct investment (along with their objectives) that parent countries employ.

Parent Country Attitudes and Policies

Most nations in which MNEs are headquartered (with the possible exception of Japan) do not have an overall policy which addresses the question of MNE expansion abroad. Instead of a coordinated plan, which considers the costs and benefits of all aspects of foreign direct investment abroad, the typical home country approach has been to address each aspect of direct investment individually. This section will examine both the incentives and restrictions commonly imposed by home countries on foreign direct investment.

incentives offered by the parent country

The preceding chapter pointed out that foreign direct investment is inherently more risky than investment undertaken within the domestic country of the firm. The possibility of expropriation, losses to the firm due to war in the host country or host country policies designed to restrict the affiliate's operations are all risks peculiar to foreign direct investment. To protect a domestic firm's direct investment abroad, most governments of parent countries sponsor some form of an insurance program that will compensate the firm if it is materially injured by an act of the host government. Such an insurance program provides an incentive to foreign direct investment since comparable insurance programs are not provided by private insurors.

Table 22–1 depicts the characteristics of the foreign risk insurance programs available to MNEs by selected parent countries. The development of the program offered by the United States, being the oldest and the most extensive, might prove interesting to examine more closely. At the outset, the American program was intended to promote economic development in potential host countries via American direct investment. It began as an element of the Marshall Plan with the goal of encouraging American direct investment in Western Europe. It then shifted emphasis to the less-developed countries. Until 1971, this insurance program was considered a component of U.S. foreign assistance and, accordingly, was administered by agencies within the State Department.

In 1971, the administration of the program was transferred to the Overseas Private Investment Corporation (OPIC), an independent government agency. At the same time, the issuance of the insurance became based more on the financial position of the MNE, rather than on developmental principles. Accordingly, OPIC has stiffened the terms of insurance to MNEs and has also begun giving greater consideration to the economic effects of foreign direct investment on the economy of the United States. In fact, to obtain OPIC coverage, an MNE must present an estimate of the effects that the proposed project will have on the American economy. Indeed, OPIC has rejected applications when the project was judged to have an adverse

TABLE 22-1

Foreign Investment Guaranty Schemes of Selected Parent Countries

Country	Date Established	Geographic Coverage	Investment Coverage	Amount Outstanding (end of 1974 in millions)
Australia	1966	Worldwide	All types	$ 24.1
Belgium	1971	Worldwide	Equity and loan	4.0
Canada	1969	Less-developed countries	All types	44.6
Denmark	1966	Less-developed countries	All types	14.1[a]
France	1971	Selected less developed countries and countries with bilateral agreements	Mainly loans	17.3
Germany	1960	Countries having signed bilateral agreements (44)	All types	406.0[a]
Japan	1956–1957	Worldwide	All types	1075.5
Netherlands	1969	Less-developed countries	All types	21.4
Norway	1964	Worldwide	Equity plus loans, if equity present	24.7
Sweden	1968	11 selected countries	Equity and loan if controlling interest	NA[b]
Switzerland	1970	Less-developed countries	All types	42.7
United Kingdom	1972	Worldwide	All types	30.1
United States	1948	Countries having signed bilateral agreements (114)	All types	2985.8

Source: *Investing in Developing Countries*, 3rd ed. (Paris: OECD, 1975), pp. 12–14. Reprinted from Stefan H. Robock, Kenneth Simmonds and Jack Zwich, *International Business and Multinational Enterprises* (Homewood, Ill.: Irwin, 1977), Table 11–1.

[a] As of end of 1973.
[b] NA = not available.

impact on U.S. employment or balance-of-trade position.

Another policy of parent countries which acts as an incentive to foreign direct investment is the tax treatment applied to the income earned by foreign affiliates. Although many of these tax schemes are motivated by the desire to elim- inate double taxation of income earned by the subsidiaries of domestic firms, they often have the effect of encouraging foreign direct invest- ment. The system employed by the United States is such an example. The American tax treatment of income earned abroad by foreign affiliates of U.S.–based MNEs is characterized by: (1) a foreign tax credit, whereby foreign taxes paid abroad are credited against the tax liability (on all income) to the U.S. government and (2) a tax deferral provision which allows income earned abroad not to be taxed until it has been remitted to the United States. Of the two provisions, the tax deferral has been subject to the most criticism. Under this provision, an MNE can postpone tax payments simply by investing foreign-earned income outside the United States in foreign financial institutions. The ability to defer tax payments constitutes an obvious incentive to foreign direct investment. It should be pointed out that in recent years bilateral tax treaties have been negotiated between parent and host countries in an effort to develop a scheme by which total tax revenue is equitably shared between the two countries, while at the same time avoiding double taxation of the MNE's foreign earnings.

Restrictions of Parent Countries

Most restrictions that parent countries impose are designed not so much to control the operations of the MNE per se, as to address other economic problems that the MNE may aggravate in the process of pursuing its own goals. Parent countries have periodically imposed limits on the amount of capital that the parent company can export to its affiliates, in an effort to mitigate the deficit-worsening effects of such flows. For example, the United States from 1965 through 1974 restricted the volume of capital that American–based MNEs could export abroad to its affiliates. The intent was not to directly prevent foreign direct investment, but to reduce the deficit-worsening effects that would result from the parent firm financing foreign direct investment.

Restrictions have also been placed on the operations of foreign affiliates by the parent country as a means of implementing foreign policy. The United States in the past has attempted to restrict the list of eligible countries to which foreign affiliates of American–based MNEs could export. For example, in the past, affiliate exports to Communist nations have been prohibited, a measure which was implemented by pressuring the parent firm. Not only does such policy interfere with the operations of the MNEs, but it also infringes upon the economic sovereignty of the host nation.

QUESTIONS AND EXERCISES

1. Do you believe that MNEs improve the economic welfare of the world as a whole? Why or why not?

2. Discuss three factors that mitigate the contribution of a foreign affiliate to the output and employment of a host nation.

3. What is meant by "international subcontracting"? Is this practice a cost or a benefit to host countries?

4. Assume you were an economic advisor to a country that is considering hosting a foreign affiliate of an MNE. Would you recommend hosting an affiliate, if your central concern was the external payments position of the country? Present both pro and con arguments.

5. What is transfer pricing? Why would an MNE establish a price for a traded good that differs from its world price?

6. Discuss several examples of how transfer pricing can affect the host nation's balance of payments.

7. In what ways do an MNE act as an international transfer agent for technology?

8. What are some of the noneconomic effects that an MNE may have on the host country?

9. Cite several incentives that parent countries offer to domestic firms to expand abroad. Also, cite several restrictions.

10. If you were an economic advisor to an LDC, would you recommend a policy that encourages or discourages the hosting of foreign affiliates of MNEs? Present arguments for both sides of the issue.

CLOSING ESSAY:
Multinational Enterprises and the Less Developed Countries—
An Aid or Barrier to Economic Development?

Although the benefits and costs of foreign direct investment apply to all nations, the impact of such investment on host LDCs is of particular interest, given the special nature of the economic problems plaguing those nations. A detailed discussion of the potential that MNEs hold for increasing output and employment levels within host countries was presented in the two preceding chapters. When this potential is coupled with the LDCs' desire to achieve economic development, it is understandable why many observers argue that the MNE, and its accompanying foreign direct investment, might be the brightest possibility available to the LDCs in their efforts to improve their economic well-being. On the other hand, the mere fact that LDCs (and host DCs as well) often impose restrictions on foreign direct investment implies that LDCs do not unequivocally view the MNEs as the ideal vehicle for attaining economic development.

What are the aspects of foreign direct investment that disturb the LDCs? Probably the most disturbing aspect of MNEs is the threat that they pose to the economic sovereignty of the host country. As was emphasized throughout our discussion, the huge size of the affiliates enables them to control a substantial portion of the host country's economic activity. The degree of control will be even more apparent in LDCs where the level of economic activity is relatively low. The feeling on the part of the LDCs that they are unable to direct and determine the course of their economic development is disconcerting. Host governments and residents often perceive the affiliate as an economic entity that is controlled by foreign outside interests, usually located in a developed country. That is, MNEs are viewed as instruments of "neocolonialism," whereby the DCs, working through affiliates of large MNEs, exploit the resources of the poor countries in an effort to maximize their profits and wealth.

Are such fears justified or is it simply a case of exaggerated xenophobia on the part of LDCs? As mentioned previously, there can be little doubt that MNEs in many instances do exert a powerful influence on the LDCs' economic life, ranging from its international payments position to the level of human capital of its labor force. The important question then is just how large are the purported benefits accruing to the host countries, in terms of economic development, and whether they merit a sacrifice by the host country of a portion of its economic self-determination.

Let us examine critically several of those purported benefits from the viewpoint of the *critics* of MNEs, who maintain that MNEs are nothing more than a tool of neocolonialism. Vertically integrated MNEs have historically been subject to the bulk of the criticism directed toward foreign direct investment. The purpose of a vertically integrated MNE is to establish an affiliate in a country, typically an LDC, which is naturally endowed with the raw materials needed for the MNE's productive activities. The critics argue that such MNEs are exploiting the LDCs as they acquire raw materials at lower costs than if they were purchased directly from LDC producers, and at the same time deplete the stock of the host nation's resources. Here, the MNE would be maximizing its profitability at the expense of its less-developed host. A further irritant to the LDCs is the fact that the bulk of the profits of the MNE, once earned, are repatriated back to the parent country. Vertically integrated direct investment constituted much of the investment prior to the 1950s and was concentrated in such areas as petroleum and mining. The disfavor that LDCs hold for such investments is reflected by the fact that much of the expropriation actions taken by LDCs has been directed at them.

The notion that the MNE serves as an effective conduit for technology transfer to LDCs has been seriously questioned. There are three principal complaints. First, many affiliates established by parent corporations are in the low technological areas of the firm's operations (such as assembly), and attempt to take advantage of the low-cost, unskilled labor available in LDCs. Second, even if the MNE transfers sophisticated technology to its affiliate, it is unclear whether such technology would be applicable to local conditions. Given the relatively low cost of labor in LDCs, it is doubtful that local producers will have an incentive to employ the capital in which the technology is embodied. Also, technologically advanced processes frequently require highly skilled labor as a complement, and such labor is typically in short supply in the LDCs. Third, the royalty payments that the affiliates must make to acquire the technology are typically quite high and these payments represent an outflow of foreign exchange. Essentially, then, critics of MNEs argue that any technology that the parent does transfer is not intended to benefit the host nation, but the global operations of MNE itself, and thus its benefits to the LDC can be expected to be minimal.

Doubts are frequently expressed about the benefits that MNEs provide to the host country's labor force. As we saw in Chapter 22, one of the benefits of the MNE was its capacity to transfer human capital to the host country, and at the same time offer opportunities for the employment of the host country's skilled labor. However, the top managerial and technical jobs of the MNE are traditionally occupied by residents of the parent country who are transferred abroad. Although recently MNEs have been increasing their hiring of host country managers, it remains a question as to whether they are given any real autonomy. In fact, it appears that in most cases local employment by affiliates is for unskilled positions which would contribute little to the quality of the host country's labor.

One hypothesis goes so far as to suggest that MNEs are contributing to a worldwide division of labor, with the DCs supplying the bulk of the managerial and technical skills and the LDCs supplying unskilled labor. This may be reflected by the recent increase in the establishment by MNEs of offshore assembly operations in LDCs. Those operations typically do not require local skilled labor, since the managerial and technical skills needed can be provided by the host nation. The implication of such a global division of labor skills is for a widening of the economic gap between the DCs and the LDCs. In addition to those criticisms, one must remember the other possible costs of MNEs to host countries, including the possibility of a worsened trade balance, and the effects of transfer pricing on the economic well-being of the host.

The LDCs, in their zeal to exercise their new-found economic independence in the mid-1970s, included in their call for a New International Economic Order (NIEO) proposals designed to regulate the behavior of MNEs. However, as was the case with most of the NIEO proposals, little substantive action has actually resulted. Although various international agencies, including the United Nations Conference on Trade and Development (UNCTAD), the EEC and the Organization of Economic Cooperation and Development (OECD), have all adopted codes pertaining to the behavior of MNEs, these codes are not enforced by any international agency.

The question that must ultimately be addressed by LDCs when formulating their policy toward the MNEs is whether MNEs actually contribute to their long-term economic development. Should LDCs, then, severely restrict such investment? The answer depends on whether the LDCs can offer a more satisfying alternative to development. The optimal policy may be one which restricts only the unfavorable aspects of foreign direct investment and encourages the favorable aspects of MNEs. These policies must be constructed in a manner that encourages the MNEs to aid the LDCs in their attempts at economic development, while at the same time preserving their economic sovereignty and national identity.

THE INTERNATIONAL VIII
MONETARY SYSTEM AND
INTERNATIONAL MONETARY REFORM

INTRODUCTION:
The International Monetary System in Transition.

In recent years, the international monetary system has undergone radical change. The Bretton Woods system with its network of stabilized exchange rates collapsed in 1971, marking the end of monetary arrangements that had prevailed since World War II. This was followed by several attempts to reestablish a system of exchange-rate pegs, each of which met with decisive failure. World economic conditions were no longer compatible with a general system of fixed exchange rates.

The collapse of one monetary system and its replacement by a different set of arrangements is nothing new in the history of international finance. Institutions that function well under one set of circumstances may not work well at all under other conditions. As world economic and political conditions have changed over time, existing international monetary institutions have been replaced by arrangements better suited to the new conditions.

To remain viable, any international monetary system must meet certain criteria. First, it must facilitate international trade and capital movements by ensuring that international payments can be made easily and at a minimum of risk. Ready convertibility among the various currencies is essential for this purpose. The system must also provide mechanisms through which balance-of-payments imbalances can be adjusted smoothly. A smoothly operating adjustment mechanism reduces the danger that countries will impose new exchange controls, trade restrictions or restrictions on capital movements in trying to deal with intractable payments deficits or surpluses.

While facilitating international payments and adjustments, the monetary system must not cause economic disruption within the individual countries, or interfere seriously with the domestic policy goals of these countries. Experience strongly suggests that countries will assign the highest priorities to resolving internal economic problems, even if it means pursuing policies that tend to undermine international monetary arrangements. Finally, the international financial community prefers a certain amount of stability in exchange rates among the currencies, and would count that as an important feature of an acceptable system.

Each of the monetary systems that has appeared on the international scene from time to time has had its unique structure of rules, mechanisms and institutions through which it performed these functions. The structure of each system grew out of and was compatible with the economic and political conditions that prevailed at the time. During the past century, three fairly distinct monetary systems have appeared. These include the international gold standard which operated during the late nineteenth century and the early twentieth century; the Bretton Woods system, which lasted from the end of World War II until the early 1970s; and the system of managed floating exchange rates that has prevailed since that time.

In addition, there have been shorter episodes in which exchange rates were either managed or allowed to float freely. During the early 1920s several countries let their currencies float freely as they awaited the opportunity to get back on the gold standard after having been forced off that standard by World War I. A later case of free floating involved the Canadian dollar during the 1950s and early 1960s. During the 1930s, there were short episodes in which countries engaged in managed floating, intervening to control the rate or the extent of currency appreciation or depreciation, while maintaining no formal exchange-rate pegs.

As we examine various monetary systems in the following chapters, a major objective will be to see how each of these systems performed the essential functions mentioned above. We shall also see how changing economic and political conditions led to the erosion and collapse of each system. This discussion will be useful in several respects. First, it will provide historical perspective on the development of the current international monetary system and will help in evaluating its performance and viability under present conditions. Second, it will provide useful information for evaluating proposals for changing the system. Although some will argue that managed floating exchange rates are likely to prevail for some time to come, proponents of a return to the gold standard are receiving increased attention. Meanwhile, advocates of freely fluctuating exchange rates have by no means abandoned their positions, and perhaps the largest group of all consists of those who would return to a system of fixed but adjustable exchange rates, in which the pegs are maintained by official exchange-market intervention. An understanding of the historical performance of these various systems and the kinds of conditions under which they thrived and collapsed is essential in mapping the future course of the international monetary system.

The International Gold Standard 23

The international gold standard of the late 1800s and early 1900s was unique in the history of international trade and monetary relations. It was a period in which international commerce and finance were supported by a complex, but highly coordinated network of markets and facilities that was centered in London but spread throughout the world. It was also a period in which trade was virtually free of restrictions and in which currencies were freely convertible. The convertibility of currencies stemmed from the fact that all the currencies in the system were freely convertible to gold; the world was on a gold standard.

GOLD PARITIES

Under the international gold standard, gold was the ultimate backing of each country's money. Although gold itself circulated in the form of coin, it did not make up the bulk of the circulating money stock. Most of the circulating money consisted of government notes, bank notes and claims on demand deposits. The acceptability of these notes and deposits was based on confidence in their gold backing. Although, in principle, every unit of money in circulation was totally backed by gold, a fractional reserve system was in operation. This meant that the actual value of notes and deposits in circulation at any point in time could be greater than the value of the gold backing. This is similar to contemporary banking relationships in which the actual quantity of money in circulation exceeds the amount of bank reserves upon which it is based.

The governments guaranteed the gold value of their notes by standing ready to buy or sell them for gold at the stated value. Each of the countries in the system thus defined the value of its currency in terms of gold. This was called the currency's par value or parity.

GOLD ARBITRAGE AND THE PRICE-SPECIE-FLOW MECHANISM

The fact that each government set and maintained the gold value of its currency meant that the governments implicitly specified an official exchange rate between their currencies. For example, the gold value of the pound, as set by the British government, was 4.86656 times the gold value of the dollar, as set by the U.S. government. Thus the *par value* or *mint parity* between the dollar and the pound was $4.86656 per pound sterling.

Although mint parity between the dollar and the pound was officially $4.86656 per pound, this did not mean that the dollar and the pound would always trade at that rate in private transactions on the foreign exchange market. The *market* exchange rate under the gold standard was subject to private supply and demand pressure just as it is in today's system. Changes in tastes, prices and income within the individual countries, as well as random disturbances such as bad harvests and natural disasters, could affect the supply and demand for goods to be traded among countries, and thus the supply and demand for foreign exchange.

Despite the fact that supply and demand on the foreign exchange market were subject to constant shifts, the actual market exchange rates remained very close to the official parities. Since governments did not intervene directly on the foreign exchange market in those days to control or influence the market exchange rates, what kept the market exchange rates so close to parity? In theory, the answer lies in a mechanism known as *gold arbitrage,* which in turn triggered a mechanism known as the *price-specie-flow mechanism.* While gold arbitrage held the exchange rate near parity in the short run, the price-specie-flow mechanism acted, over a longer period of time, to neutralize the forces that were pushing the market exchange rate away from parity in the first place.

Gold arbitrage and the price-specie-flow mechanism can best be illustrated by way of an example. Assume that there are two countries, the United States and Britain, and that both are operating under a gold standard. The official gold parity is £1 = 113 grains of gold in Britain and $4.87 = 113 grains of gold in the United States; mint parity between the dollar and sterling is thus £1 = $4.87. In both countries wages and prices are flexible in both an upward and a downward direction, and resources are fully employed. Each dollar and each pound in circulation is backed 100 percent by gold. There are no international capital movements (except by gold arbitragers), so that the only transactions between the countries are trade flows, shipments of gold and payments for these items. There are no transportation or other transactions costs associated with shipping gold, nor are there any official restrictions on the shipment of gold. Initially, the balance of payments is in balance, and the prevailing market exchange rate is equal to mint parity.

Gold Arbitrage and Exchange-Rate Stability

Now suppose there is an increase in U.S. demand for British goods, due to a change in tastes. To buy the additional British goods, U.S. residents must first purchase pounds sterling on the foreign exchange market. This creates pressure for sterling to appreciate. As sterling appreciates, however, a discrepancy appears between the official parity, $4.87 per pound, and the actual market exchange rate, which has risen to, let us say, $4.90 per pound. At this point, an opportunity arises for profit through gold arbitrage. A resident of either of the countries could do the following:

1. Take \$4.87 to the U.S. government and exchange it for 113 grains of gold.
2. Ship the gold to London.
3. Sell the gold to the British government for £1.
4. Sell the £1 for \$4.90 on the foreign exchange market, making a 3-cent profit.

Note that, in step 4 of this procedure, the arbitrager is selling sterling for dollars on the foreign exchange market; this lowers the value of the pound and pushes the exchange rate back toward mint parity. As long as there is any discrepancy between the official parity and the actual market exchange rate, the incentives for gold arbitrage will persist, and pressure for the exchange rate to return to parity will continue. Gold arbitrage thus has the effect of holding the actual exchange rate very close to parity.

If the initial disturbance had caused sterling to depreciate *below* parity, incentives would have arisen for gold arbitrage in the opposite direction. Here, gold would flow from Britain to the United States, and gold arbitragers would end up selling dollars for sterling on the foreign exchange market, again moving the exchange rate back toward parity.

The Effects of Transactions Costs

Let us now change our assumptions and suppose that there is a 3-cent cost associated with shipping 113 grains of gold between the United States and Britain. Now, the actual exchange rate would have to depreciate or appreciate by more than 3 cents from mint parity before gold arbitrage would be triggered. This is because the potential gain must exceed transportation and other transactions costs before arbitrage would become profitable. There would thus be a 3-cent band on either side of mint parity, within which the market exchange rate could fluctuate freely. Gold arbitrage would keep the exchange rate from exceeding the limits of this band, which in this case would be \$4.84 and \$4.90 per pound.

These limits became known as the *gold points*, since they are the points at which gold arbitrage would begin to occur.

Gold Flows and Balance-of-Payments Imbalance

We are now in a position to show the relationship between gold flows and a country's balance-of-payments surplus or deficit. Our discussion will emphasize two distinct, but closely related, aspects of this relationship: (1) the gold flows associated with balance-of-payments imbalance temporarily help to *accommodate* or *finance* the payments imbalance and (2) the gold flows generate changes in the money stocks of the countries, and this, in turn, serves to *resolve* the payments imbalance. We shall see that gold outflows from a country are associated with balance-of-payments deficits, while gold inflows are associated with balance-of-payments surpluses.

Suppose that, initially, the balance of payments between the United States and Britain is in balance and that the market exchange rate stands at the official parity, \$4.87 per pound. In Figure 23–1, the initial supply and demand curves are shown as S_0 and D_0. The gold points are \$4.84 and \$4.90 per pound. Now suppose there is an exogenous increase in the demand for sterling by U.S. residents, who want to buy more British goods. If the increase in the demand for sterling were to move the demand curve to D_1, the market exchange rate would rise to \$4.90. Since the exchange rate has not been pushed beyond the gold point, and since the exchange rate is free to fluctuate between the gold points, no payments imbalance would appear. Note that with the demand curve at D_1, there is no gap between the supply and demand curves.

Suppose, however, that the increase in U.S. demand for British goods had shifted the demand for sterling to D_2. Gold arbitrage would

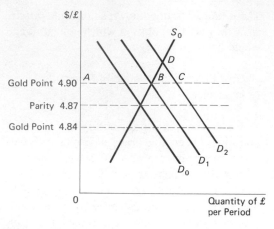

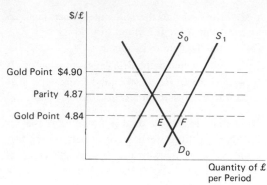

FIGURE 23-2 Gold Flow and Balance-of-Payments Deficit

FIGURE 23-1 Gold Flow and Balance-of-Payments Surplus

not permit the exchange rate to exceed the gold point, so the exchange rate would remain at $4.90. Here, there would be a balance-of-payments surplus for Britain (a deficit for the United States) equal to BC, measured in sterling. Note that in this situation, the sterling value of goods, services and assets being bought by U.S. residents from the British would be AC, while the sterling value of goods, services and assets being bought by British residents from Americans would be AB. The U.S. deficit, BC, is being "financed" by the flow of gold from the United States to Britain as the result of gold arbitrage. Arbitragers would be shipping gold valued at BC pounds sterling from the United States to Britain and would be selling BC pounds sterling on the foreign exchange market as part of their operations. Note that the payments of BC pounds into the foreign exchange market by arbitragers would exactly match the *excess* demand for sterling by ordinary traders (the supply and demand curves in Figure 23–1 do not themselves include purchases and sales by gold arbitragers).

This example depicts a U.S. deficit (i.e., a British surplus), as would occur if the shadow equilibrium exchange rate (given by the intersection of the supply and demand curves) ex-

ceeded the upper gold point. We could also construct examples in which a shift in the demand and supply of sterling would cause the shadow equilibrium exchange rate to fall below the lower gold point, $4.84. See Figure 23–2; here we assume that a surge in the demand for U.S. goods by British residents has increased the supply of pounds on the foreign exchange market to S_1. Gold arbitrage would hold the exchange rate at $4.84, and there would be an excess supply of sterling (EF) by ordinary traders on the foreign exchange market. The excess supply of sterling would correspond to a British balance-of-payments deficit (a U.S. surplus). This would be "financed" by an arbitrage-generated flow of gold from Britain to the United States equal in value to EF.

Balance-of-Payments Adjustments Under the Gold Standard

In addition to holding the market exchange rate within the gold points, gold arbitrage would trigger another mechanism that would work to eliminate the balance-of-payments imbalance and to remove the underlying pressure for the exchange rate to move outside the gold points.

Consider, once again, the situation depicted in Figure 23–1. With curves S_0 and D_2, Britain is running a balance-of-payments surplus equal to *BC*, and there is pressure for the exchange rate to rise to point *D*. The gold flow from the United States to Britain will work to eliminate the payments imbalance, in effect reshifting the supply and demand curves so that they intersect at the upper gold point, $4.90. Here there will be no excess supply or demand for sterling, no pressure on the exchange rate and no imbalance in the balance of payments.

To understand how this works, it is necessary to recall that, under a gold standard, a country's gold stock serves as the country's money base. If gold were to flow out of the country, the country's money base, and consequently its money stock, would have to contract. If the money stock were only fractionally backed by gold, then the money stock would have to shrink by a multiple of the contraction in the gold stock. If gold were to flow *into* the country, on the other hand, the country's money base, and hence its money stock, would expand.

In the situation depicted in Figure 23–3, in which S_1 and D_1 are the initial supply and demand curves for sterling, Britain would be running a balanceof-payments surplus equal to *BC*. Gold arbitrage would be holding the exchange rate at the upper gold point, and would also be generating a flow of gold from the United States to Britain equal in value to *BC* pounds sterling per time period. The British money base and money stock would be expanding and the U.S. money base and money stock would be shrinking. The expanding money stock in Britain would put upward pressure on the British price level, while the contracting money stock in the United States would put downward pressure on the U.S. price level. Rising prices in Britain and falling prices in the United States would cause residents of both countries to switch from British to U.S. goods. To buy more U.S. goods, British residents would have to offer more sterling to buy dollars on the foreign exchange market. This would shift the supply curve to the right. Be-

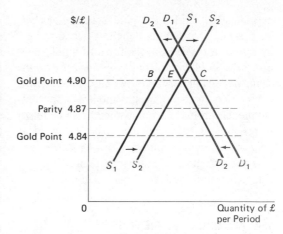

FIGURE 23-3 Balance-of-Payments Adjustment

cause U.S. residents would be purchasing fewer British goods, they would buy fewer pounds on the foreign exchange market, shifting the demand curve to the left. This process would continue until supply and demand have shifted far enough to return the shadow equilibrium to the upper gold point, as at point *E*. At this point there would be no excess supply or demand for sterling, and the balance of payments would be in balance.

As long as the shadow equilibrium exchange rate remained above the gold point, incentives for gold arbitrage would also remain, gold would continue to flow, price levels would continue to change and the incentives to switch from British to U.S. goods would continue to operate. The supply and demand for sterling would continue to shift until the equilibrium exchange rate no longer exceeded the gold point. In this way, the price-specie-flow mechanism would act as a complete balance-of-payments adjustment mechanism.

The relationship between reserve outflows and inflows and balance-of-payments deficits and surpluses deserves special emphasis, since it applies not only under the gold standard but under any system in which exchange rates are fixed or managed. Under the gold standard, as we have seen, a payments deficit is accompanied by a loss in reserves in the form of a gold outflow. *The gold outflow will continue for as long as the deficit persists* and will cause a continuing contraction in the domestic money supply. A payments surplus is accompanied by an increase in reserves in the form of a gold inflow. *The gold inflow will continue for as long as the surplus persists* and will cause a continuing expansion in the domestic money supply.

THE ACTUAL EXPERIENCE
WITH THE GOLD STANDARD

Institutional Features That Aided Adjustment

Despite the considerable nostalgia that has become associated with it, the international gold standard served as the world's monetary system for a fairly brief period in history. Some observers argue that the world was effectively on gold by the early 1880s while others would argue that the gold standard was not universally adopted until the 1890s. Most would agree that it came to an end in 1914, with the outbreak of World War I. Once established, the gold standard and the institutional features that accompanied it worked quite well to facilitate international payments and to adjust balance-of-payments imbalances. The fact that all currencies were convertible with gold ensured that the currencies were readily convertible with each other and that exchange rates would remain stable.

As we have seen, gold arbitrage and the price-specie-flow mechanism were the conceptual processes by which exchange rates were kept near parity and balance-of-payments imbalances were eliminated under the gold standard. In actual practice, however, the process worked somewhat differently. Students of the gold stan-

dard era argue that, although exchange rates remained close to their parities, there was remarkably little gold flow between countries even during periods of large payments imbalances. This was because other forces would come into the picture to keep the exchange rates within the gold points before gold arbitrage had a chance to operate. To understand these forces, it is necessary to understand something about how international trade and finance were organized.

As we mentioned above, international trade and finance were highly centralized in London during the gold standard era. London was, in effect, the world's banker as well as the hub of international trade. Traders and bankers kept funds on deposit in London, and international capital flows between Britain and the other countries were highly sensitive to British interest rates. The fact that the Bank of England could exercise considerable control over short-term capital movements by manipulating its discount rate meant that it could exercise considerable control over its balance of payments. If a deficit began to develop in the British balance of payments, the British authorities could raise the discount rate in London. This would result in a general increase in British interest rates which, in turn, would generate a capital inflow into the country, diminishing the size of the overall balance-of-payments deficit. Similarly, the British authorities could generate a capital outflow and reduce a balance-of-payments surplus by lowering the discount rate. By counteracting balance-of-payments imbalances in this manner, private short-term capital flows could be used to reduce pressure for the exchange rate to move outside the gold points.[1]

London's prominence as a banking and

[1]While the British authorities could affect only the payments balance between Britain and other countries with this mechanism, each country's bilateral balance with Britain was the important consideration under the prewar gold standard.

financial center helped to minimize the movement of gold in another way. Foreign banks involved in financing international trade made a practice of keeping balances in London banks as well as holding British securities in their portfolios. Temporary payments deficits with Britain could be financed by drawing down these balances or selling some of the British securites. Payments among non–British countries could be made by transferring ownership of sterling deposits in London. This precluded having to enter the foreign exchange market to obtain pounds, or other currencies, which might have pushed the exchange rates beyond the gold points. Of course, a deficit could not be financed indefinitely in this manner, since foreign bank holdings of sterling balances and securities would ultimately run out. Nevertheless, they did provide an important buffer against gold movements during temporary payments imbalances.

Private currency speculation also played a role in holding the exchange rates inside the gold points and thus forestalling gold arbitrage. Confidence in the system was so strong that speculators would bid the exchange rate back to the gold point whenever it began to move outside. Stabilizing currency speculation thus substituted for gold arbitrage in keeping the exchange rates within the gold points, and private speculative capital flows helped to "finance" payments imbalances by providing sterling to the foreign exchange market when it was needed.

The Decline of the Gold Standard

To understand why the gold standard faltered and was finally abandoned, it is necessary to understand how the system depended upon certain government policies and procedures and how these became altered by changing world economic conditions. For the international gold standard to operate effectively, each government had to stand ready to buy or sell its currency for gold at the stated par value and to allow the free import and export of gold. Each government also had to be willing to subordinate any concern over internal, domestic economic conditions to the goal of maintaining the external value of its currency. When a payments imbalance did cause gold to flow into or out of the country, the country had to abide by the "rules of the game." This meant letting its money supply expand or contract according to the gold flow and letting its internal price level rise or fall sufficiently to eliminate the payments imbalance. During the prewar period, policies permitting the free flow of capital into and out of the various countries were also important. This enabled private capital to respond readily to changes in relative interest rates and enabled private stabilizing speculation to help hold the exchange rates within the gold points.

the effect of world war I

The first major shock to the international gold standard and the policies that supported it was the outbreak of World War I. During the hostilities, most countries suspended their commitment to buy and sell gold and prohibited or strongly discouraged gold exports. Under these circumstances, of course, the gold-standard mechanisms could not operate at all. The departure from gold was regarded by all parties as temporary, however, and it was fully expected that when the war was over, the gold standard would resume with all its prewar features intact. It was even believed that the prewar mint parities could be reinstated.

This was not to be the case. The war so changed the structure of the world economy that there was no way the gold standard could have continued in its prewar form. One important development was that London had slipped from its position as the single hub of world trade and finance. Most of the sterling balances that had been held by foreign residents and governments had been liquidated, and as a result capital flows became much less sensitive to changes in relative interest rates between countries. London thus lost its ability to regulate payments imbalances by manipulating its discount rate. Because the pool of sterling balances and assets was no longer available to finance international payments, countries had to enter the foreign exchange market more frequently to obtain foreign currency. This put greater pressure on the exchange rates. On the trade front, Britain had lost many of its important markets to U.S. and other foreign producers during the time that access to those markets had been cut off by hostilities.

the interwar gold standard[2]

Growth in the U.S. economy, coupled with the fact that the dollar remained tied to gold, allowed the United States to emerge as a second important commercial and banking center. Before the war, a country's balance of payments with Britain and the sterling value of its currency had been of primary concern to the country's monetary authority and its financial community. Now its balance of payments with the United States and the *dollar* value of its currency became increasingly important. For many countries (including Britain itself), reestablishing the prewar value of its currency with the dollar became a primary objective of domestic monetary policy, since this was the key to reestablishing prewar parity with gold.

As the United States began to compete with Britain as a center of commerce and finance, it did not offer the same kind of leadership in world monetary affairs. The United States was a largely self-sufficient country without the traditions or expertise that had enabled London to function as the hub of a finely tuned world economy. The United States was far less likely to gear its monetary policy to the smooth operation of the international monetary system, than to gear it to its own domestic economic problems. In fact, on several occasions during the early 1920s, the United States had sterilized the monetary effects of gold flows by conducting opposing securities transactions in the open market. (Actually, sterilization was not confined to the United States during the 1920s. Britain and France also sterilized gold flows later in that decade, reflecting an increasing orientation by many countries toward internal economic problems.)

A second development that precluded reestablishing the gold standard in its exact prewar form was the fact that the war had inflated the various paper currencies far from their prewar purchasing powers. In fact, inflation had proceeded at vastly different rates in different countries. This meant that the old mint parities no longer reflected the relative purchasing powers of the currencies and no longer even roughly reflected equilibrium exchange rates. The market exchange rate between the dollar and the pound was so far out of line with the official mint parity that it took Britain from 1919 to 1925 to undergo sufficient internal price deflation to reinstate the old mint parity. Other countries took longer. Many countries never reestablished prewar parity at all and were forced to adopt new parities that greatly devalued their currencies. Some countries, including Germany, Austria and Russia, had to scrap their old currencies altogether and issue new money.

By the end of 1928, an official gold value had been adopted for most of the currencies, and gold was again free to flow between countries. The essentials of an international gold standard seemed to be in place once again. The gold standard of the late 1920s was not the "pure" gold standard of the prewar era, however. Gold coin did not circulate as freely as before. The backing of money in many countries became

[2]For a detailed account of interwar monetary developments, see L.B. Yeager, *International Monetary Relations*, 2nd ed. (New York: Harper & Row, 1976), chapters 16, 17 and 18.

centrally held gold bullion instead of coin, and in some cases the national money was backed, not by gold, but by the currency of some other country that *was* tied to gold. This system became known as the "gold bullion standard." Perhaps the most important difference between the prewar gold standard and the postwar gold bullion standard was that, in the latter period, the monetary effects of gold flows were frequently sterilized. As a result, the automatic balance-of-payments adjustment mechanism inherent in the gold standard could not operate effectively.

the collapse of the gold bullion standard

While the gold standard managed to survive World War I and postwar economic changes (although in a severely weakened and altered form), it did not survive the Great Depression. As the 1920s drew to a close, the major industrial countries were entering an economic slump. During 1929, the U.S. economy underwent a serious downturn that culminated in a total collapse of the U.S. stock market. The U.S. contraction had repercussions on economies throughout the rest of the world. The rapid decline in U.S. income produced a drastic cutback in U.S. imports. This meant a contraction in the exports of other countries that supplied the United States with finished goods, semifinished products and raw materials. Rapidly falling exports in these countries generated multiple contractions in their economies.

Not only did U.S. imports decline, so did U.S. capital outflows. This meant that overall payments by U.S. residents to foreigners fell rapidly, and most foreign countries found their balance-of-payments deficits and their gold outflows increasing at an alarming rate.

When faced with the prospect of having their gold reserves severely depleted, different countries reacted in different ways. Most of the countries that were exporting raw materials and other primary products had but limited gold reserves, and therefore chose to abandon the gold standard and allow their currencies to depreciate on the foreign exchange market. A few countries imposed exchange controls to restrict payments by home residents to foreigners. This rendered their currencies inconvertible and removed them from active participation in the gold standard. Meanwhile, the countries of Western Europe clung to the gold standard.

The *coup-de-grâce* for the international gold standard came in 1931 and rose out of what at first seemed to be a relatively isolated incident: a run had started on a large commercial bank in Austria, the Credit-Anstalt, and had soon spread to other banks throughout the country. Several attempts were made by international agencies and foreign governments to quell the panic but these met with failure. Then the panic began to spread to German banks. The German government, faced with large-scale speculative outflows, imposed exchange controls. A number of other countries followed suit. Now the panic spread to Britain, where a capital flight began to mount. At this point the British authorities elected to suspend their commitment to sell gold, and the pound was set afloat. A large bloc of countries that were closely tied to Britain in trade and finance now stabilized their currencies with the pound so that they, too, floated with the pound against the dollar and gold. This bloc of countries became known as the "Sterling Area."

Shortly after Britain floated the pound, the Scandinavian countries also left the gold standard. At this point the only major countries still tied to gold were the United States, Switzerland, France, Belgium and the Netherlands. These countries, which became known as the "gold bloc," now began to experience reserve outflows. The gold bloc countries attempted to protect their reserves by raising tariffs and tightening quotas so as to choke back imports.

By this time, the gold standard had ceased to operate as an effective international monetary system. Many currencies were inconvertible, many were floating and devaluation was common among those that retained official parities. The mechanism through which balance-of-payments adjustment was supposed to operate had become entirely unacceptable to the participating countries. Countries would no longer hesitate to sterilize unwanted money-supply changes that were brought about by imbalances in their external payments. The United States finally left gold in 1933, not because of balance-of-payments pressures, but as a result of an attempt to deal with internal problems.

International monetary conditions during the 1930s have been viewed as highly chaotic. There were periods during which many currencies were allowed to float. Even when exchange rates were fixed, there were frequent changes in the parities. There were even episodes in which countries would engage in competitive devaluations in order to protect export sales or to discourage imports. After the Depression was over and as World War II drew to a close, most observers felt that a return to the turbulent conditions of the 1930s would be unacceptable. They felt it was imperative to design an international monetary system that would assure both currency convertibility and monetary stability. These sentiments played an important role in shaping the Bretton Woods international monetary system, which was adopted at the end of World War II and which is the topic of the following chapter.

QUESTIONS AND EXERCISES

1. What was gold arbitrage under the gold standard? What developments would trigger gold arbitrage? How did gold arbitragers make a profit?

2. How would the flow of gold between a deficit country and a surplus country affect the money supply and the price level within each country?

3. Evaluate the statement that a gold outflow would continue for as long as a country continued to run a balance-of-payments deficit.

4. In what way did the gold standard provide currency convertibility and exchange-rate stability?

5. Describe the role of London in the pre–World War I gold standard. What role did London play in ensuring the stability and smooth operation of that system?

6. What particular government policies and procedures were required for the gold standard to operate effectively? How were these policies and procedures altered during the 1920s, and how did this affect the operation of the gold standard?

7. Compare and contrast the gold bullion standard of the late 1920s with the gold standard of the prewar era.

8. Do you believe that the pure gold standard, as it was organized in the pre–World War I era, would have had any greater chance of surviving the Great Depression than did the gold bullion standard? Explain.

The Bretton Woods System 24

World War II drastically changed the world's economic landscape. The once powerful European economies were left in a shambles, as was the economy of Japan. International trade and payments were frozen by the myriad restrictions which had originated during the depression of the 1930s and during the war itself. It was clear that if postwar recovery and subsequent growth were to proceed at a satisfactory pace, international trade and capital movements would have to play a central role in that process. It was also clear that, as long as the existing restrictions on trade and payments remained in place, trade and capital movements could not expand rapidly enough to give adequate support to economic recovery.

BIRTH OF THE BRETTON WOODS SYSTEM

Well before the end of the war, the Allied countries began working to develop a system that would promote healthy international trade and monetary relations. They identified three major objectives: the removal of outright restrictions on trade, the establishment of currency convertibility (which had all but disappeared because of the worldwide system of exchange controls) and the maintenance of stable exchange rates among the various currencies. The latter concern grew out of the experience of the 1930s when turbulent exchange-rate movements created a great deal of uncertainty in world financial markets.

In July 1944, at Bretton Woods, New Hampshire, the major Allied powers agreed to a set of arrangements designed to deal with postwar monetary problems. These arrangements, which became known as the *Bretton Woods agreements*, established a set of rules and procedures for dismantling exchange controls and for controlling exchange-rate fluctuations. They also provided for the establishment of the International Monetary Fund to monitor the operation of the system. The IMF would serve as a forum for resolving problems that might arise in international monetary affairs; it would implement the provisions for stabilizing exchange rates and would serve as a source of liquidity for countries in need of foreign exchange to finance temporary balance-of-payments deficits.

FIXED BUT ADJUSTABLE EXCHANGE RATES

The exchange-rate relationships under the Bretton Woods system were to be organized along the lines of a gold exchange standard. One of the basic differences between a gold *exchange* standard and pure gold standard is that under the former, international reserves can consist not only of gold, but also of key foreign currencies. It is possible, under a gold exchange standard, to have only one or two countries that actually hold gold in their reserves, while the reserves of the remaining countries are made up of currencies of the countries that do hold gold.

The Gold Exchange Standard

The Bretton Woods agreements required that each member country of the IMF declare a gold value for its currency. The gold parity could be maintained either directly, by standing ready to buy or sell home currency for gold at the official price, or indirectly, by pegging the home currency to some other currency that *was* tied to gold.

These parities were supposed to be maintained in the face of transitory fluctuations in the exchange rates; they were to be changed, through devaluation or revaluation, only in the

event of a fundamental payments imbalance.[1] Although a "fundamental" imbalance was not explicitly defined, it could generally be described as a surplus or deficit caused by some fundamental or structural change in the country's economy, and therefore likely to be permanent in nature. The system was thus to be one of *fixed but adjustable exchange-rate pegs*.

The Role of the U.S. Dollar

As the system began to operate after the war, the same conditions that produced strong demand for the U.S. dollar also led it to become the key currency in the system. It was one of the few convertible currencies, it was the currency of the most powerful economy in the world and it was tied to gold. It was thus quite natural that the dollar should be the currency to which other currencies were pegged and the currency that was used in intervening on the foreign exchange market to maintain those pegs. Although some of the old sterling area countries continued to peg their currencies to the pound, the pound was, in turn, pegged to the dollar. An important feature of these arrangements was that the foreign governments had the sole responsibility for maintaining the exchange-rate peg between their currencies and the dollar; the U.S. government had no responsibility for maintaining the exchange-rate pegs with other currencies. The United States' responsibility was to maintain the dollar price of gold at $35 per ounce.

As we saw in Chapter 6, the foreign gov-

[1]As a reminder, we use the term *revaluation* to mean a change in an exchange-rate peg that *increases* the value of the currency in question against the dollar, gold or other currency. It is thus the opposite of *devaluation*. We mention this because some authors use the term revaluation to refer to *any* change in the peg, whether it be in an upward *or* a downward direction.

ernments maintained these pegs by intervening on the foreign exchange market. If a country's currency began to depreciate against the dollar, the country's central bank would buy its own currency in sufficient quantity to prevent its dollar value from falling. If the country's currency began to appreciate, the central bank would sell the country's currency on the foreign exchange market at a sufficient rate to keep its dollar value from rising. Purchasing one's own currency on the foreign exchange market requires the expenditure of international reserves, while selling one's own currency generates an increase in reserves.

The Band Arrangements

Under the Bretton Woods system, the exchange-rate pegs were not entirely rigid. A country could let the exchange rate between its currency and the dollar fluctuate freely within a band which extended 1 percent either side of parity. This meant that there was a maximum 2 percent range within which a foreign currency could fluctuate against the dollar. Suppose that the official parity between the dollar and sterling were $4.00 per pound. The exchange rate could fluctuate as high as $4.04 and as low as $3.96 before the British would have to intervene. The limits of the band ($4.04 and $3.96, in this example) were known as the *upper and lower intervention points*.

The idea of a band within which the exchange rates could fluctuate freely was borrowed directly from the gold standard, of course, and relieved the central banks of having to be in the market at every moment to maintain a rigid peg. It also helped to conserve on the use of reserves. Note that keeping the exchange rate within the band under the Bretton Woods system required explicit action by the country's central bank. Recall that, under the gold standard, gold arbitrage would operate automatically to keep the exchange rate within the gold points; all the government had to do was stand ready to buy or sell gold at the official price. Note also that if any single currency could fluctuate by a maximum of 2 percent against the key currency, the non-key currencies could fluctuate by a maximum of 4 percent against each other. There was thus twice as much bilateral flexibility in the nondollar exchange rates than in the exchange rates between the dollar and other currencies.

International Reserves

To finance intervention on the foreign exchange market, the countries maintained a stock of international reserves. These consisted of gold, foreign exchange and the country's IMF position (to be explained below). Since foreign exchange alone is traded on the foregin exchange market, the use of gold for intervention purposes would require that the gold first be exchanged for currency and the currency then used for intervention purposes. A central bank needing to exchange gold for dollars could do so at the U.S. Treasury, since the U.S. government stood ready to honor its commitment to exchange dollars for gold, or vice versa, at $35 per ounce. Thus, if Britain were running a balance-of-payments deficit and wished to make use of its gold reserves to finance the deficit, it could offer some of its gold to the U.S. government, receive dollars in exchange and use the dollars to support the pound on the foreign exchange market.[2] In the process, British gold reserves would decline and U.S. gold reserves would rise. On the

[2]An interesting point is that gold was kept on deposit for various countries in separate rooms in the basement of the Federal Reserve Bank of New York. When gold was transferred from one country to another, the physical transfer took the form of moving the gold from one room to another at the New York Fed.

other hand, if, because of a U.S. deficit, the British central bank ended up holding more dollars than it wished, it could transfer these dollars to the U.S. government and obtain gold in exchange. Here, British gold reserves would rise while those of the United States would fall. As under the gold standard, gold would flow from the deficit to the surplus country.

IMF DRAWING RIGHTS

At the outset of the Bretton Woods system, the major portion of international reserves was in the form of gold, and a minor portion was in foreign exchange. It was recognized that additional sources of international liquidity might be necessary to help countries maintain their exchange-rate parities. To provide additional liquidity, the IMF was to maintain a pool of currencies that could be drawn upon by member countries to augment their international reserves.

The Quota System

The IMF currency pool was established by assigning each member country a quota—a quantity of funds to be paid into the IMF. The quotas were determined by a formula that took into account such factors as the country's national income, the variability of its exports, the ratio of its exports to national income, the level of its imports and the size of its international reserves. Under this formula the larger, more economically powerful countries had the larger quotas. These quotas initially totaled some $7 billion. In subsequent years the quotas have been increased so that by the end of the 1970s the total quotas amounted to approximately SDR 40 billion (or $52 billion since 1 SDR is roughly

equal to $1.30). During 1980, the quotas were expanded once again to about SDR 60 billion.[3]

In addition to determining the amount a country would have to pay into the IMF, a country's quota determined its rights in drawing funds from the IMF, as well as the country's voting power within the organization. A country's vote was weighted in proportion to its contribution to the fund. In later years, when special drawing rights were introduced, these were also allocated according to the countries' quotas. Because its quota made up a greater proportion of the total than any other country, the United States had, and still has, greater access to IMF assets and greater voting power than any other single country in the system.

In making the initial payments into the fund, 25 percent of a country's quota had to be paid in the form of gold or U.S. dollars and the other 75 percent in the form of the country's own currency. The IMF was thus able to assemble a pool of assets that included not only gold, but also currencies of all of the countries in the system, with proportionately greater amounts of currencies of the larger and stronger economies.

As mentioned above, these funds were to be available for member countries to draw upon when additional international reserves were needed to finance temporary balance-of-payments deficits. These arrangements remain in operation today. In principle, a country draws upon these funds by purchasing them from the IMF with its own currency. Thus if Britain were to draw £1 million worth of dollars from the fund, it would have to pay the fund £1 million in exchange. However, because countries are required to reverse these transactions within a

[3]While the value of the quotas is *measured* in terms of SDRs, this does not mean that countries receive SDRs when they draw funds from the IMF. The SDR itself is a separate asset, and its use is described below.

specified number of years, and because an interest charge is made against the drawing country, the drawing of funds from the IMF is tantamount to a loan.

Specific Drawing Facilities

There are a number of specific arrangements or *facilities* under which member countries can draw reserves from the fund. The standing or *permanent* facilities include the following.

tranche policies

The most important set of drawing facilities fall under what are known as the IMF's "tranche policies." A country's rights to draw are divided into five tiers or *tranches*. The first tier is called the *reserve tranche* (formerly the *gold tranche*) and is equal to the difference between the country's quota and the IMF's holdings of that country's currency. Thus if Britain's quota were £1 million, of which it had contributed £250,000 in gold and £750,000 in pounds sterling, her reserve tranche would be £250,000 (£1 million minus £750,000). If some other country were to draw pounds sterling from the IMF, this would increase Britain's reserve tranche. Suppose India were to draw £100,000. This would reduce the fund's holdings of sterling to £650,000. Britain's reserve tranche would now be £350,000 (£1 million minus £650,000).

A country is allowed to draw funds up to the value of its reserve tranche at any time without scrutiny. If Britain's reserve tranche were £350,000, it could freely draw up to £350,000 worth of foreign currency. Note that, since Britain would have to pay in an equivalent amount of its own currency, this would bring the fund's holdings of sterling up to the level of Britain's quota. At that point, Britain would have had exhausted its reserve or gold tranche. The IMF encourages countries to count their reserve tranche as part of their international reserves. This is the *IMF position* component of international reserves that was mentioned earlier.

In addition to the reserve tranche a country has four other tranches, known as *credit tranches,* each equal to 25 percent of the country's quota. The country will not draw against the credit tranches until it has exhausted its reserve tranche; it will then draw in sequence against the first, second, third and fourth credit tranches. As a country moves into the higher tranches, the IMF applies greater and greater scrutiny as to what the country is doing and plans to do about its balance of payments. Unless the country is able to produce satisfactory plans for dealing with its problems, the IMF can deny the country access to the credit tranches.

compensatory financing facility

The compensatory financing facility is designed to provide reserves to countries that are heavily dependent on the export of primary products. In particular, its purpose is to provide additional international reserves to a country experiencing a balance-of-payments deficit due to a temporary export shortfall that lies beyond the country's control. A country can draw funds equaling 100 percent of its quota under this facility, in addition to funds provided under the tranche policies. A country does not have to exhaust its reserve tranche before making use of the compensatory financing facility. On the other hand, the country must agree to cooperate with the IMF in working out its balance-of-payments problems.

buffer stock financing

The purpose of the buffer stock financing facility is to assist a country in making contributions to buffer stocks of primary products when the country is experiencing balance-of-payments problems. (A buffer stock is an arrangement designed to stabilize the world price of some internationally traded commodity. See Chapter 20 for a detailed discussion of buffer stock agreements.)

A country making use of the IMF's buffer stock facility can draw up to 50 percent of the amount of its quota. The IMF has authorized the use of the facility in making contributions to the buffer stocks for tin, cocoa and sugar, although, so far, drawings have been made only for contributions to the tin program.

extended facility

The extended facility is designed to provide reserve funds for longer periods and in larger amounts than authorized under the tranche policies. It is especially designed to help countries facing balance-of-payments deficits due to structural maladjustments in production, trade or prices.

temporary facilities

In addition to the standing or permanent facilities, the IMF is empowered to create *temporary facilities,* which are to be available for limited periods of time. For example, a *Special Oil Facility* was created for the years 1974 and 1975. Countries facing severe balance-of-payments deficits as a result of unusually high oil import bills during this period were permitted to draw funds from the IMF to help finance these deficits.

As can be seen from the foregoing list, there are several different arrangements through which a member can draw funds from the IMF. These are known collectively as *drawing rights,* and they are designed to supplement the international reserves of countries facing temporary balance-of-payments deficits.

SPECIAL DRAWING RIGHTS

In later years, another class of assets was added to the stock of international reserves provided by the IMF. Whereas the IMF's drawing rights, described in the preceding section, were a feature of the original Bretton Woods system, this new set of assets, *special drawing rights* (SDRs) did not come into being until 1970.

The Need for a New Reserve Asset

Special drawing rights were created as a result of concern about the adequacy of international reserves during the 1960s and doubt as to whether the supply of reserves could grow as rapidly as the demand for them. As mentioned above, international reserves at that time consisted of gold, foreign exchange and IMF drawing rights, and it did not seem likely that these particular assets could be expanded rapidly, should the need arise. What was needed was an international asset that would be acceptable to all parties in the system, and one whose supply could be readily augmented by the IMF as the demand for reserves increased. The SDR was designed to meet these criteria.

How SDRs Work

SDRs are essentially an entitlement by one government to draw currency from another country's central bank. If Britain were low on international reserves and needed additional dollars to finance a balance-of-payments deficit, she could transfer SDRs to the United States, which would, in turn, transfer dollars to Britain. U.S. holdings of SDRs would rise as a result of this transaction while those of Britain would fall. All but a few of the member countries of the IMF have agreed to accept SDRs if offered by another country in the system.

Originally, the value of the SDR was tied to gold at a rate that made 1 SDR equal to 1 U.S. dollar. The rate of exchange between the SDR and other currencies depended on the dollar exchange rate of the other currencies. Beginning in 1974, the value of the SDR was computed as a weighted average of the value of 16 different currencies in the system; in 1981, the number of these currencies was reduced to five. Because the relative values of these currencies are constantly changing, the IMF recomputes the value of the SDR on a daily basis.

SDRs are issued periodically by the IMF based on its projections of the increase in the demand for reserves. At five-year intervals, the IMF will forecast the increase in the demand for reserves for the upcoming five-year period. On that basis, it will decide on the number of SDRs to be created during that five-year span as well as the timing of the issue within the period. The first batch was issued during the period 1970 to 1974 and was set at roughly SDR 9.3 billion. Of that amount, some 3.3 billion were issued in 1970, 3 billion in 1971 and 3 billion in 1972. In 1978, the Board of Governors of the IMF voted to approve allocations of SDR 4 billion during each of the years 1979, 1980 and 1981. This would bring the total of outstanding SDRs to about 21.3 billion.

As mentioned above, SDRs are allocated among countries according to their IMF quotas. Thus if a given country's quota makes up 5 percent of the total quotas of all countries, that country will receive 5 percent of the SDRs allocated in each batch. Recent proposals have advocated increasing the proportion received by less-developed countries as a means of redistributing wealth among nations.

Once created, SDRs remain in the system indefinitely. Physically, SDRs consist of entries on the books of the IMF. When SDRs are "issued" to a country, the IMF simply credits that country's account with the appropriate number of SDRs. If a country transfers SDRs to another country in exchange for currency, the IMF transfers the appropriate number of SDRs from the account of the first country to the account of the second.

Initially, SDRs were available solely to central banks for use in financing balance-of-payments deficits. Beginning in 1978, the IMF authorized the holding of SDRs by a wider set of international organizations, such as the Bank for International Settlements, located in Switzerland. In addition, the IMF has recently authorized wider uses of SDRs beyond merely exchanging them for currency that will be used for exchange-rate pegging. SDRs can now be used to settle financial obligations among governments, to make and repay loans among governments and to serve as security for the performance of official financial obligations. While the uses of SDRs among official agencies is expanding, SDRs are not available to private individuals, banks or firms and cannot be used in private transactions.[4]

Originally, when one country wished to trade SDRs for foreign exchange, it would inform the IMF, which would then designate a particular country or countries to which the SDRs could be traded. The idea was that the IMF would know which countries were in the best position

[4]While SDRs themselves cannot be transferred among private individuals, private parties do sometimes use the SDR as a standard of value for assets or commodities. For example, time deposits, certificates of deposit and bonds denominated in SDRs have begun to appear in some financial markets, notably London. In addition, there has been talk among OPEC countries about denominating the price of a barrel of oil in SDRs. Payment would presumably be in dollars, but the dollar price of a barrel of oil would vary with the SDR–dollar rate.

to accept SDRs for currency. In recent years, this arrangement has also become more relaxed, and now two countries can agree to exchange SDRs and currency by mutual consent.

Note that, unlike regular drawing rights, the SDR does not give a country the right to draw funds from the IMF. Instead, it provides a right to obtain foreign exchange from other countries. Unlike regular drawing rights, there is no requirement that SDRs be redeemed or repaid. Originally, a country was not supposed to let its minimum average holdings of SDRs remain below a certain percentage of its cumulative allocations, but that requirement was dropped in 1981. Now there is no limitation on a country's use of its SDRs. A country receiving SDRs is obligated to accept them only up to the point that its total SDR holdings are equal to three times its cumulative allocations. A country can accept SDRs beyond that point at its discretion.

Participating countries pay interest to the IMF on all SDRs that the IMF has allocated to them. The IMF, in turn, pays interest in the same amount to current holders of SDRs. There is, thus, a net interest transfer from countries that have expended SDRs to those that have accepted them. The interest rate is determined by a formula that takes into account the money market rates of the five countries with the largest IMF quotas. Up until 1981, the SDR interest rate was set at 80 percent of the combined market rate, a feature that dampened the acceptability of the SDR as a reserve asset. In 1981, however, the percentage was raised to 100 percent.

THE BRETTON WOODS SYSTEM VERSUS THE GOLD STANDARD

At this point, it will be useful to compare some of the essential features of the Bretton Woods system and the "pure" gold standard. In particular, let us note the difference in the way in which each system was supposed to provide for currency convertibility, exchange-rate stability and balance-of-payments adjustment.

Convertibility

Under the gold standard, as we saw in Chapter 23, all currencies in the system were freely convertible with gold and hence freely convertible with each other. Governments assured this convertibility by standing ready to buy and sell their home currencies for gold, to all parties, at the stated par values. Under the Bretton Woods system, not all currencies were convertible with gold. Each government specified a gold par value for its currency, but had the option of standing ready to buy or sell some *key currency* (such as the U.S. dollar) that *was* tied to gold, in lieu of buying and selling gold itself. Unlike the gold standard arrangements, the obligation to buy or sell gold or the key currency extended only to foreign central banks and not to private parties.

The most important requirement for currency convertibility under any system is that governments *allow* private residents to exchange currency freely on the foreign exchange market, with no exchange controls or other restrictions placed on these transactions. Governments are most likely to impose or maintain such restrictions when their international reserves are so low that their ability to maintain the official parities is jeopardized. As we shall see, the adequacy of reserves was a key problem in establishing currency convertibility under the Bretton Woods system.

Exchange-Rate Stability

Exchange-rate stability was ensured under the gold standard by gold arbitrage. Gold arbitrage would hold the exchange rates within the gold points as arbitragers acted upon discrepancies between market rates and official mint parities.

Under the Bretton Woods system, exchange-rate stability had to be provided by government intervention on the foreign exchange market. Here, a government would buy or sell its home currency as necessary to hold the exchange rate within specified bounds.

Balance-of-Payments Adjustment

Under the gold standard, balance-of-payments adjustment was automatically brought about through change in the country's money stock. This stemmed from gold inflows and outflows, which were the result of gold arbitrage that occurred during balance-of-payments imbalances. The change in the country's money stock would alter its internal price level, thereby causing a switch in exports and imports so as to correct the payments imbalance.

Balance-of-payments adjustment was not necessarily automatic under the Bretton Woods system. Countries were free, if they chose, to offset any monetary effects caused by a balance-of-payments imbalance by engaging in countervailing monetary policy (sterilization). For imbalances that were temporary in nature, countries were to maintain the exchange-rate parity by intervening on the foreign exchange market. For imbalances that were fundamental in nature, exchange-rate adjustment in the form of revaluation or devaluation was prescribed. This, of course, was never a feature of the gold standard—mint parities were regarded as permanently fixed.

Necessary Government Policies and Procedures under Bretton Woods

We can see that for the Bretton Woods system to work as was intended, certain government policies and procedures were required. Governments had to stand ready to buy or sell home currency for the key currency or gold at the specified parity. They had to refrain from imposing exchange controls and other restrictions on transactions in the foreign exchange market. They also had to adjust the parities whenever payments deficits or surpluses were of a fundamental nature. Failure to make timely devaluations could result in depletion in a country's international reserves and loss of confidence in the country's ability to maintain the proclaimed parity. Failure to revalue in the face of a persistent surplus could result in reserve accumulation and mounting inflationary pressure within the country.

Role of Confidence in the System

The durability of any system in which the values of currencies are fixed in terms of other currencies or in terms of commodities (such as gold) depends on public confidence. In particular, it depends on confidence that the governments involved will be both willing and able to maintain the official parities. Under the pre-World War I gold standard, public confidence in the gold parities was so great that stabilizing currency speculation helped hold the exchange rates within the gold points. Under the Bretton Woods system, stability depended on confidence that countries had adequate reserves to maintain the stated exchange-rate pegs. This proved to be a critical problem for the system during its later years.

In this and in the preceding section, we have seen how the Bretton Woods system was supposed to operate to provide convertibility, stability and balance-of-payments adjustment. Now let us see how the system actually did perform between the time of its inception at the end of World War II and its collapse in the early 1970s. As we discuss the developments that occurred during this period, you may find it useful to refer to Figure 24–1, which traces the unfolding of events during the Bretton Woods era.

FIGURE 24-1 Developments in the Bretton Woods System

Trends		Events
		Bretton Woods system adopted (1944)
	1945	World War II ends (1945)
Dollar shortage		
Exchange controls		Marshall Plan adopted (1947)
		IMF begins operations (1947)
	1950	U.S. BOP moves into deficit (1950)
Europe builds dollar reserves		
	1955	
European reserves approach		
desired levels		European currencies become convertible
Sharp increase in U. S. deficit		(1958)
	1960	
		First major international monetary crisis
		(1960–1961)
		London Gold Pool formed (1961)
Large U.S. deficits		
Mounting claims against U.S.		
gold reserves		
Vietnam War escalates U.S.	1965	
inflation		
Downward pressure on dollar		
Dollar increasingly overvalued		
		Second major international monetary
		crisis (1967)
		Sterling devalued, dollar under attack
		(1967–1968)
		Two-tier gold system (1968)
		France devalues against dollar (1969)
		Germany revalues against dollar (1969)
U.S. deficit mounts	1970	
Downward pressure on dollar		Heavy speculation against dollar. U.S.
continues		gold reserves threatened (1971).
		U.S. closes gold window, imposes 10%
		surcharge (1971)
Dollar overhang		Smithsonian agreements (1971)
		Sterling floats (1972)
		Smithsonian arrangements collapse (1973)
Managed floating exchange rates		
	1975	

CONSOLIDATION OF THE BRETTON WOODS SYSTEM: 1940s and 1950s[5]

Postwar Recovery: 1945–1950

As we mentioned at the outset of this chapter, World War II left Europe and Japan in economic ruins. Europe was unable to provide itself with many basic consumption items, to say nothing of the capital goods that would be necessary for reconstruction. Under the circumstances, many of the goods required by Europe had to be imported. The problem was that hard currency, especially U.S. dollars, was required to pay for imports. Europe had no export capacity with which to earn hard currency, and its international reserves were low. Because the United States was the major source from which reconstruction goods would have to come, and because these goods would have to be bought with dollars, the shortage of goods in Europe was seen as a shortage of dollars.

To help relieve the "dollar shortage," a number of loans and grants were extended to Europe by the United States, Canada and various international organizations. These included the *European Recovery Program* (also known as the *Marshall Plan*), under which the United States transferred billions of dollars to Europe.

It was in this setting that the International Monetary Fund began operations in 1947, with its goal of persuading countries to reduce restrictions on international payments. Exchange controls and bilateral payments arrangements proved to be quite intractable, however. Despite its ambitious objectives, the IMF had virtually

[5]This section draws factual material from L. B. Yeager, *International Monetary Relations,* 2nd ed. (New York: Harper & Row, 1976), chapters 21 and 27; the *Economic Report of the President,* various issues; U.S. Department of Commerce, *Survey of Current Business,* various issues; and Federal Reserve Bank of New York, *Monthly Review,* various issues.

no means of enforcing its policies. Although most countries honored their agreements not to impose *new* controls, most of the European currencies did not become fully convertible until the late 1950s. Even then convertibility was achieved more as the result of improvement in the international-reserve positions of the European countries than as the result of pressure or persuasion by the IMF.

Progress toward Convertibility: 1950–1958

During the 1946–1949 period, U.S. external balances had registered consistent surpluses. This was largely the result of the strong European demand for U.S. goods during the recovery process. Toward the end of the 1940s, however, European recovery was well under way and the U.S. surpluses had begun to taper off. By 1950, the overall U.S. balance of payments had moved into deficit. This was to mark the beginning of a chronic U.S. balance-of-payments deficit around which international monetary events and crises were to revolve for more than two decades. (See Table 24–1.)

Throughout the 1950s, the U.S. deficit produced a net flow of short-term dollar assets to Europe and other areas in which there had formerly been strong dollar shortages. With the dollar emerging as the most important intervention currency in the system, foreign central banks were anxious to acquire the additional dollars for their foreign exchange reserves. The U.S. payments deficit and the buildup of dollar reserves in Europe were thus beneficial to the international monetary system in that they strengthened the ability of the European governments to defend their currency parities in the face of payments imbalances.

The accumulation of dollar reserves by foreign central banks also played an important role in moving the nondollar currencies toward convertibility. As long as official international re-

TABLE 24-1

U.S. Balance-of-Payments Items
1946–1969
(billions of dollars, rounded. Minus indicates deficit)

	Merchandise Trade Account	Goods and Services Account	Overall Balance of Payments (Liquidity Basis[a])
1946	6.7	7.8	1.0
1947	10.1	11.6	4.2
1948	5.7	6.5	0.8
1949	5.3	6.2	0.1
1950	1.1	1.9	−3.5
1951	3.1	3.8	0.0
1952	2.6	2.4	−1.2
1953	1.4	0.5	−2.2
1954	2.6	2.0	−1.5
1955	2.7	2.2	−1.2
1956	4.8	4.1	−1.0
1957	6.3	5.9	0.6
1958	3.5	2.4	−3.4
1959	1.1	0.3	−3.9
1960	4.9	4.1	−3.9
1961	5.6	5.6	−2.4
1962	4.6	5.1	−2.2
1963	5.2	6.0	−2.7
1964	6.8	8.6	−2.8
1965	5.0	7.1	−1.3
1966	3.9	5.3	−1.4
1967	3.9	5.2	−3.5
1968	0.6	2.5	0.2
1969	0.6	1.9	−7.0

[a]Changes in liquid liabilities to foreign official holders, changes in liabilities to other foreign holders, and changes in official reserve assets (gold, convertible currencies and U.S. gold tranche position in the IMF).

Source: Economic Report of the President, February, 1971, Table C-87, pp. 298–90.

serves were thought to be insufficient to maintain existing parities, governments relied upon exchange controls and other restrictions of international trade and payments to try to maintain balance-of-payments balance.

By 1958, dollar reserves had grown to the point that governments of the major trading countries at last felt free to relax exchange controls. Up to that point, there had been some progress toward convertibility, but the effort had been piecemeal. In addition to freeing international payments, currency convertibility laid the groundwork for liberalizing world trade itself. Heretofore, countries had relied heavily on trade restrictions to control their imports and exports in order to conserve scarce hard currency. With general currency convertibility, these controls became unnecessary and could also be relaxed.

Throughout most of the 1950s, when foreign countries were trying to build their international reserves, the dollar was considered to be as good as gold—or even better since, unlike gold, dollar balances could be invested to earn interest and did not involve insurance or storage costs. As the 1950s drew to a close, however, cracks began to appear in the heretofore solid confidence in the dollar.

EROSION OF THE BRETTON WOODS SYSTEM: 1960s AND EARLY 1970s

It might seem ironic that just as the Bretton Woods system struggled to its feet with full currency convertibility, confidence in the system would begin to deteriorate. Actually, these two developments were not unrelated. The dollar reserve accumulations that had enabled Europe to achieve convertibility during the 1950s would, during the 1960s, undermine confidence in the dollar as the key currency in the system.

The International Monetary Crisis of 1959–1961

By 1959, just as dollar accumulations by European central banks began to approach desired levels, the U.S. balance-of-payments deficit underwent a sharp increase. Foreign central banks found themselves accumulating dollars more rapidly than they wanted, and they began to step up the rate at which they traded dollars for gold at the U.S. Treasury.

By 1960, official foreign claims against the U.S. gold stock had just about reached the size of the gold stock itself. It was clear that if the trend continued, U.S. gold supplies would soon be inadequate to cover potential claims. Fears began to arise that a run on U.S. gold reserves might develop, that the dollar might be devalued against gold or that other currencies might be revalued against the dollar. In this setting, holders of liquid assets began moving funds out of the dollar and into gold and foreign currencies, especially the Swiss franc and the German mark. Efforts by the Swiss and German governments

to curtail speculative capital inflows diverted a larger portion of the speculative flows into gold, and the price of gold began to rise on the private market.

private versus official gold markets

At this point it is necessary to distinguish between the private and official gold markets. The *private* gold market, which is centered in London and Zurich, is the market in which private residents of the various countries can buy or sell gold.[6] The *official* market comprises the purchase and sale of gold among the governments of the various nations. This is the "market" in which a foreign central bank could exchange unwanted dollars for U.S. gold reserves under the rules of the Bretton Woods system. Private residents were not entitled to buy or sell gold in the official market. The price of gold in the official market was set at $35 per ounce, and the U.S. government maintained that price by standing ready to buy or sell gold at that rate.

While the price in the private market was not officially set, it had a tendency, for several reasons, to remain at or near the price in the official market. First, there was a strong psychological connection between the official and private prices. Second, the U.S. government did occasionally buy or sell gold in the private market if the private price began to depart from $35 per ounce. This reflected a belief that the psychological viability of the gold exchange standard depended on confidence in the dollar price of gold in the private as well as in the official market. Third, there was always the possibility that if the private price deviated from $35, foreign central banks, which had ready access to U.S. gold reserves, could arbitrage between the U.S. gold stock and the private market, thereby driving

[6]It was illegal for U.S. citizens to hold gold bullion between 1933 and 1974.

the private price back into line with the official price.

the crisis continues

As the crisis mounted, speculative gold buying drove the private price of gold above $40 per ounce. Late in 1961, the United States and several other industrial countries formed the *London Gold Pool* to defend the $35 price.[7] Under these arrangements, the other countries added large portions of their own gold stocks to that of the United States to form a pool that could be sold, if necessary, to keep the private price at $35. The gold pool had its intended effect. With the U.S. gold stock as well as that of the other gold pool countries standing behind the $35 price, the probability that a run on the dollar could force a devaluation against gold was dramatically reduced, and speculators withdrew from the market.

After the crisis of 1960–1961, the dollar never regained the level of confidence it had enjoyed during the 1940s and 1950s. This was not due to any particular weakness in the U.S. economy; the major problem stemmed from the fact that the overall U.S. balance-of-payments deficit was continuing to funnel dollars into official foreign holdings. As a result, official claims against U.S. reserves continued to mount while the reserves themselves continued to decline.

Some observers maintain that when official foreign claims on U.S. gold reserves surpassed actual U.S. gold holdings in the early 1960s the system passed, for all practical purposes, from a gold exchange standard to a dollar standard. Even though foreign central banks were entitled to convert any of their dollar holdings for U.S. gold at $35 per ounce, there was no way all of the officially held dollars could have been con-

verted. Technically, a gold exchange standard can work perfectly well even when official claims against the gold stock of the reserve country exceed the actual amount of gold in the stock, provided the claimants are content to hold the reserve currency rather than gold. Claimants will be willing to hold the reserve currency, however, only for so long as they have confidence that its gold value will be maintained.

The Crisis of 1967–1968 and the Two-Tier Gold System

In the latter part of 1965, following the escalation of the Vietnam War, the rate of inflation in the United States increased rapidly. This intensified the pressure for the dollar to depreciate on the foreign exchange market. Meanwhile, in 1967, the British pound sterling came under speculative attack and was devalued late that year. The sterling crisis, coming at a time when downward pressure on the dollar was intense to begin with, triggered strong speculation against the dollar. Private gold speculation drove the gold price upward, and the gold pool once again started selling gold to counteract the price increase.

In early 1968, speculative pressures were reinforced by unfavorable new information on the U.S. balance of payments and the U.S. rate of inflation. The private gold price shot up to over $44 per ounce. When it looked as if the gold pool could not stem the tide, the major industrial countries took steps to insulate official gold reserves from speculative runs in the private gold market. It was agreed that the central banks would no longer buy or sell gold on the private market. This meant that the private price would now be wholly determined by private supply and demand, including speculative activity. Meanwhile, official transactions among the central banks would still be conducted at $35 per ounce. Because it divided the gold market into two mutually exclusive segments—the

---

[7]The Gold Pool countries included the United States, Belgium, the Netherlands, Germany, Switzerland, Italy and Britain.

private and the official markets—this arrangement became known as the *two-tier gold system*. Under these arrangements, since official gold holdings could no longer be depleted by private speculation, the likelihood that the dollar would be devalued with respect to gold was substantially reduced.

Severe Strains and Policy Impasse

Gold speculation subsided following the adoption of the two-tier gold system, but strong speculative pressures continued to operate in the foreign exchange markets. Toward the end of the 1960s the U.S. balance-of-payments deficit was deepening, and even its trade account, which had been in surplus for decades, was weakening.

policy options: currency revaluation versus deflation

By this point, it was clear that the dollar was overvalued relative to the Japanese yen and most major European currencies. There was no consensus, however, as to what to do about it. The Bretton Woods agreements called for devaluation by deficit countries and revaluation by surplus countries in the event of fundamental payments imbalance. The United States thus took the position that the appropriate remedy was for Japan and the European countries to revalue; since the existing pegs were being maintained by foreign central banks through active intervention on the foreign exchange market, only they were in a position to change them. The European countries, on the other hand, complained that the U.S. deficit was due to mismanagement of the U.S. economy and called on the United States to reduce its payments deficit by deflating its domestic economy. In the heat of this controversy, some U.S. officials recommended that the United States pursue a passive policy with regard to exchange-rate pegs. If foreign governments chose to undervalue their home currencies and were willing to accept the consequences (rapid reserve accumulation and internal inflationary pressures), let them do so. If the costs to the foreign authorities became too high, they could revalue appropriately.

policy options: devaluation against gold

Another option was for the United States to devalue the dollar against gold. If the dollar were devalued against gold while the other countries maintained the existing gold values of their currencies, the other currencies would be automatically revalued against the dollar. This, of course, would still require that the other countries change the rate at which they were pegging their currencies to the dollar. It was not at all clear, at this point, whether they would. If the world were actually on a dollar standard—if the foreign authorities were more concerned with the dollar value than with the gold value of their currencies—the existing currency pegs would probably have been maintained whether the dollar were devalued against gold or not.

Aside from the fact that dollar devaluation against gold might not induce other countries to revalue their currencies against the dollar, there were other reasons the United States opposed devaluing the dollar against gold. For years the United States had prevailed upon foreign countries to hold off exchanging their excess dollar holdings for gold. There was an implied guarantee that the United States would not devalue the dollar, which would have imposed a capital loss on the very countries that had cooperated with the United States in this effort. At the same time, raising the dollar value of gold would have conferred huge capital gains on the major gold-mining countries, which happened to be South Africa and the Soviet Union—countries that were in political disfavor at the time. Finally, there was the belief that to devalue the dollar against gold would have amounted to an admission that U.S. monetary affairs had been badly mismanaged, and there was reluctance to accept the political costs of such a judgment.

Eventually, the pressures brought on by maintaining disequilibrium exchange rates proved too much for some countries. Following a series of internal political crises and heavy speculative capital outflows, the French devalued the franc in August 1969. In October Germany, which had been running sustained balance-of-payments surpluses, and which had been the major recipient of the capital flows from France, revalued the mark. Canada let its currency float in April 1970.

THE COLLAPSE OF THE BRETTON WOODS SYSTEM

Pressures in the international money markets were heightened by developments in the U.S. balance of payments during 1971. A cyclical upswing and strong inflationary pressures within the United States helped to push the U.S. merchandise trade balance into deficit for the first time in over thirty-five years. The overall balance of payments (measured in this case by the "official reserves transactions basis," which was designed to reflect actual or imminent changes in U.S. international reserves) showed a staggering deficit of almost $30 billion. Much of this deficit can be attributed to a speculative flight from the U.S. dollar, as fears continued to mount that the dollar would be devalued.

The currencies into which speculative funds were flowing were experiencing strong upward pressure on the foreign exchange market. By May, Germany was receiving such heavy inflows that the mark was set afloat. Now, additional foreign currencies became havens for funds. Official foreign claims against U.S. reserves rose to as much as three times the value of those reserves, and the claims were mounting daily.[8]

[8]Yeager, *International Monetary Relations,* p. 579.

The stresses on the remaining exchange-rate parities and the threat to U.S. gold reserves proved to be too much to sustain, and on August 15 the U.S. government took unprecedented action. It renounced its commitment to accept officially held dollars in exchange for gold and imposed a 10 percent surcharge on all imports into the United States. At the same time, it imposed wage and price controls upon the U.S. economy in an attempt to contain rising internal inflation. These actions were to mark the end of the Bretton Woods system and the gold exchange standard that had operated since World War II.

THE SMITHSONIAN AGREEMENTS

Following the closing of the U.S. gold window, the major currencies were allowed to fluctuate. These fluctuations were not free, but were manipulated by the various governments in what has been called a "dirty float."

None of the countries expected the floating exchange rate to be a permanent arrangement. Throughout the fall of 1971, the ten leading trading nations, known as the *Group of Ten,* sought to negotiate a new set of exchange rates that would more accurately reflect equilibrium relationships among the currencies.[9] Much of the official intervention on the foreign exchange market during this period was aimed at manipulating currencies into favorable negotiating positions. In December 1971 the Group of Ten, meeting at the Smithsonian Institution in Washington, D.C., reached a set of agreements.

Under the *Smithsonian agreements,* as they were called, a new set of exchange-rate pegs was established in which the yen and most of the European currencies were revalued against the dollar. These new exchange-rate pegs were

[9]The Group of Ten consisted of the United States, Belgium, the Netherlands, France, Germany, Britain, Italy, Sweden, Canada and Japan.

called *central rates* instead of *parities*. The band within which the exchange rates were allowed to float was widened from 1 percent either side of the peg to $2^1/_4$ percent in hopes of relieving some of the rigidities in the system and reducing the frequency of currency crises. One prominent currency that was not included in the new set of pegs was the Canadian dollar. The Canadians had set their currency afloat a full year and a half before the Smithsonian agreements and now chose to continue with that policy.

The United States, for its part, devalued its dollar against gold, the new price being set at $38 per ounce. The devaluation was largely symbolic, however, since the United States never did resume redeeming dollars for gold at the official price. As a final concession, the United States agreed to remove its 10 percent surcharge on imports.

THE FATE OF THE SMITHSONIAN AGREEMENTS

The Dollar Overhang

It was hoped that the new arrangements would remove incentives for further speculation, and that speculators would now reverse the positions they had built up during the preceding year. At the end of 1971, the system faced a problem of *dollar overhang*. Foreign central banks had acquired huge amounts of dollars in attempting to support the dollar during the crisis of 1971. Total dollar reserves held by foreign central banks rose from $34 billion at the end of 1970 to almost $62 billion at the end of 1971.[10] These dollars could no longer be redeemed for U.S. gold, and were viewed as a threat to the stability of the international monetary system. If the central banks were to dump these dollars on the foreign exchange market, the effect would be

[10]International Monetary Fund, *Annual Report,* 1975.

to undermine the whole Smithsonian central rate structure.

The dollar-overhang problem would have been relieved, somewhat, if private speculators had reversed their positions when the Smithsonian arrangements had been put in place and had bought dollars on a massive scale. This would have permitted the foreign central banks to dispose of their excess dollars as they intervened to keep the dollar from appreciating. As it turned out, there was no immediate reswitching of private funds from foreign assets to dollar assets. In fact, total dollar reserves held by foreign central banks increased further during 1972 to $81 billion.[11] During the early part of the year, interest-rate differentials favored leaving the funds abroad, and perhaps more importantly, the market was not convinced that further dollar devaluations were out of the question. Meanwhile, the U.S. trade deficit also deteriorated sharply during the first quarter of the year, after which it gradually shrank.

The J-Curve Effect

It might seem unusual that a cheaper dollar, following the devaluation of 1971, would have contributed to a deepening of the U.S. balance-of-trade deficit. Ordinarily, one would expect home currency devaluation to improve a country's balance of trade. The phenomenon in which a country's trade balance deteriorates for a short period following a devaluation has been called

[11]Much of the dollar overhang became pooled in the Eurocurrency Market. As foreign central banks acquired dollar reserves, they found the Eurodollar market to be a convenient repository for their dollar funds, as well as one that paid a comparatively high rate of interest. Official dollar reserves in the Eurodollar Market rose from just under $5 billion in 1969 to over $11 billion in 1971 and then to almost $20 billion in 1972.

the *J-curve effect* (see Chapter 6). The devaluation means a higher price must be paid for foreign currency, which means that more units of home currency must be paid for each unit of foreign goods imported. In the short run (before the quantity of imports can be substantially reduced or the quantity of exports substantially increased in response to the now higher foreign-relative-to-home prices), the home import bill will be higher, and the balance of payments can deteriorate. When the elasticities have risen enough (as they typically do over time), the effects of the reduction in the quantity of imports, coupled with the expansion of exports, begins to outweigh the effects of the higher per-unit import prices, and the balance of trade begins to improve.

Turbulence in the Central Rate System

An atmosphere of uncertainty pervaded the foreign exchange market through most of the first half of the year. At midyear, the British pound sterling became the first major currency to break away from the Smithsonian central rate system, as the British authorities responded to speculative pressure by letting the pound float. This was followed by rumors that other European countries might also abandon their Smithsonian pegs and follow a joint float against all outside currencies. By the end of the summer, fears that the Smithsonian arrangements were in danger of collapse began to subside, and the exchange markets became relatively calm again.

Throughout 1972, the major countries continued negotiations to devise a set of reforms for the international monetary system. These efforts met with little success, as the United States and the European countries could not agree on such fundamental issues as the role of gold and the degree of restriction that should be placed on exchange-rate movements.

The Collapse of the Smithsonian Central Rate System

The relative tranquility of the summer and fall of 1972 ended abruptly in early 1973. The United States announced a $6.9 billion trade deficit for the year 1972. Meanwhile, it was becoming clear that U.S. inflation would continue at a high rate. In fact, when the Nixon administration announced a partial relaxation of price controls in January, huge jumps in U.S. prices ensued.

A full-fledged currency crisis now began to develop. Speculators became increasingly convinced that the Smithsonian central rates would not hold and that they had a "one-way option" for speculation. The probabilities were high that the major foreign currencies would be revalued against the dollar and practically zero that they would be devalued against the dollar. Speculators thus began to sell dollars for marks, Swiss francs and yen on a massive scale. In late January, the upward pressure on the Swiss franc reached such proportions that the Swiss government let it float. The huge quantities of new francs that were being poured into circulation in the effort to maintain the central rate were creating unacceptable inflationary pressures within the Swiss economy.

As soon as the Swiss floated the franc, speculation into the mark and the yen intensified. Foreign central banks absorbed billions of U.S. dollars as they sought to maintain the Smithsonian pegs. On February 12, the Nixon administration announced a further 10 percent devaluation of the dollar against gold. At this point, the Smithsonian central rate system collapsed. Germany and most of the European countries revalued their currencies against the dollar, while Canada, Italy, Japan, Britain and Switzerland allowed their currencies to float.

The new pegs lasted barely two weeks. Speculative pressures continued to mount, and in early March the remaining major currencies were set afloat. The desperate attempts to cling to a fixed exchange-rate system were finally abandoned. Since that time, a largely unregulated system of managed floating exchange rates has prevailed.

In the next chapter, we shall see how the system of managed floating exchange rates has operated since 1973. First, though, let us look back over the breakdown of the Bretton Woods system and identify the major causes of its collapse. This will prove useful in evaluating proposals for future international monetary reform.

WHY THE BRETTON WOODS SYSTEM COLLAPSED

A central objective of the Bretton Woods system was short-run exchange-rate stability. Stability was to be maintained through a system of exchange-rate pegs in which currency values were fixed in terms of gold or in terms of some key currency that was tied to gold. As it turned out, practically all the non–U.S. currencies were pegged to the dollar while the dollar was pegged to gold.

As with any gold exchange standard, the viability of the whole system depended upon confidence that the gold value of the key currency would be maintained. This required that U.S. gold reserves remain adequate to redeem any dollars offered by foreign central banks at the official price of $35 per ounce. The system of pegs also required that non-U.S. countries have sufficient international reserves to finance temporary balance-of-payments deficits—that is, to maintain their pegs with the dollar.

Timely devaluations were supposed to keep countries from running protracted deficits that could deplete reserves. Under the Bretton Woods system, a non–U.S. country could halt its reserve losses by devaluing its currency against the dollar. The United States, however, did not have the same kind of control over its own reserve losses, since the currency pegs were controlled by the foreign countries and not by the United States. The danger, here, was that foreign governments would undervalue their own currencies, thereby creating or prolonging a U.S. deficit that would deplete U.S. gold reserves.

We have seen what happened. During the late 1960s and early 1970s, U.S. inflation rose rapidly relative to foreign inflation rates, generating pressure for large, prolonged U.S. balance-of-payments deficits. Two remedies were possible: either the United States could reduce its rate of inflation or the foreign countries could revalue their currencies against the dollar. U.S. inflation did not subside and, with the exception of Germany in 1969, foreign governments did not revalue. The result was mounting dollar claims by foreign central banks against U.S. gold reserves. When it appeared that U.S. gold reserves would be stripped, the United States renounced its commitment to redeem officially held dollars for gold. This removed the key pin from the system and the whole structure of exchange-rate pegs collapsed.

Some observers argue that it is unrealistic to attempt to fix exchange rates at all when the rates of monetary expansion and inflation differ as widely across countries as they did in the late 1960s and early 1970s. The resulting pressures on the exchange rates are too great and too continuous to permit a regime of fixed-but-adjustable pegs to operate without constant crisis.

At any rate, the Bretton Woods system did collapse in 1971, and subsequent attempts to restore a fixed-but-adjustable peg regime failed. By 1973 there had emerged a system of managed floating exchange rates.

QUESTIONS AND EXERCISES

1. Compare the mechanisms by which exchange rates were stabilized under the pure gold standard preceding World War I and under the Bretton Woods system.

2. Contrast the balance-of-payments adjustment mechanisms that operated (or were supposed to operate) under the pure gold standard with those of the Bretton Woods system.

3. Explain the importance of confidence in the gold value of the key currency under a gold exchange standard. What developments contributed to the decline in confidence in the U.S. dollar as the key currency under the Bretton Woods system?

4. It has been argued that while the U.S. balance-of-payments deficit was beneficial to the Bretton Woods system during the 1950s it was detrimental to the system during the 1960s. Explain.

5. What was the two-tier gold system that was adopted in 1968? What problems was it designed to deal with, and how effectively did it deal with these problems?

6. Contrast the mechanisms by which IMF drawing rights (part of the original Bretton Woods arrangements) and SDRs operate to augment international reserves.

7. Contrast the Smithsonian arrangements, adopted in 1971, with those of the original Bretton Woods system. Identify, in particular, problems that each of the features of the Smithsonian agreements was designed to deal with.

CURRENT and FUTURE DIRECTIONS 25
of the International Monetary System

THE ERA OF MANAGED FLOATING EXCHANGE RATES

Following the collapse of the Bretton Woods system and the attempts during 1972 and early 1973 to resurrect the adjustable peg, most of the leading trading countries abandoned attempts to maintain strict exchange-rate stability. As a result, there emerged a system of managed floating exchange rates that has prevailed up to the present writing. Central banks still intervene on the foreign exchange market to control the rate of change in exchange rates or even to keep them in the neighborhood of some target rate, but there is no longer a set of preannounced parities that the central banks are committed to maintain. In effect, each central bank is free to pursue any intervention policy it chooses and to change that policy at any time without outside approval.

Not all countries chose to abandon fixed exchange rates after 1973. Smaller countries with close trade ties to a large country found it convenient to keep their currencies pegged to the currency of the larger country. Among other things, a fixed exchange rate kept the home prices of imported goods from being disrupted by frequent exchange-rate changes. At the end of 1980, some 47 countries were engaged in managed floating, 39 were tying their currencies to the U.S. dollar, 22 to some basket of currencies, 15 to the SDR and 14 to the French franc. A handful of additional countries were pegging to the pound or some other currency.[1] Meanwhile, a number of Western European countries sought to minimize fluctuations among their currencies while letting them float jointly against the dollar. A detailed description of the European joint float is presented in Chapter 19.

[1] International Monetary Fund, *IMF Survey*, January 26, 1981, p. 25.

Adjustment of Exchange-Market Pressure

Although currency crises did not disappear after the transition from fixed to managed floating exchange rates, the nature of the crises changed somewhat. Under the fixed-rate system, differential pressures within the various economies—differing rates of inflation, differing cyclical fluctuations and differential changes in interest rates—would cause a buildup of pressures on the exchange-rate pegs. In a typical case, the authorities would resist exchange-rate change while speculators would bet that the change would occur anyway. This, of course, would itself intensify the pressure on the exchange rate.[2] Eventually, the authorities would be forced to change the peg after all. The speculative capital flows involved could be extremely disruptive to monetary conditions within the countries in the system, and the devaluations or revaluations that followed could be large and disruptive to international trade relations.

Under managed floating, exchange-market pressure could be diverted either into exchange-rate changes or into balance-of-payments imbalances. To whatever extent the authorities chose to intervene on the foreign exchange market to manage the exchange-rate movements, the exchange-market pressure would be diverted into balance-of-payments surpluses or deficits. This, of course, would entail gaining or losing international reserves. If the authorities refrained from intervening on the foreign exchange market at all, exchange-market pressure would be diverted entirely into exchange-rate changes, causing the rates to adjust toward the new equi-

librium position. At that point, the exchange-market pressure would be relieved.

Much of the exchange-market pressure during the 1970s resulted from currency speculation. As economic conditions within countries changed, or as disturbing economic or political events occurred, market participants would shift into currencies they felt would appreciate and out of currencies they thought would lose value. While activity of this type was often defensive in nature (trying to avoid capital loss), it was still essentially speculative and added to the exchange-market pressure that affected world exchange rates. In the following section, we shall see how the system of managed floating exchange rates was able to absorb and adjust these pressures and how the U.S. dollar fared under this system.

THE DOLLAR UNDER MANAGED FLOATING EXCHANGE RATES[3]

The International Oil Crisis

The first major disturbance to the international monetary system after the advent of managed floating exchange rates was the eruption of the international oil crisis. Late in 1973, the ongoing conflict between Israel and the Arab states heated up, and the Arab oil-producing

---

[2]Following Girton and Roper, we shall refer to the combined pressures for the exchange rate to change as *exchange-market pressure*. See L. Girton and D. Roper, "A Monetary Model of Exchange Market Pressure Applied to the Postwar Canadian Experience," *American Economic Review*, September 1977.

[3]Material in this section is based on Department of Commerce, *Survey of Current Business*, various issues; *The Economic Report of the President*, various issues; Federal Reserve Bank of New York, *Quarterly Review*, various issues; and Leland B. Yeager, *International Monetary Relations* (New York: Harper & Row, 1976), especially Chapter 28. As we trace the events that unfolded during the era of managed floating, you might find it useful to refer to Figure 25–1, which presents a chronological sequence of the major developments, and Figure 25–2, which shows the movements in the dollar exchange rates.

countries imposed a boycott on shipments to the United States and other countries that were supporting Israel. Shortages in world oil supplies generated by the boycott, as well as an unprecedented degree of cooperation among the oil-producing countries, enabled them to raise prices to four times the level that had prevailed up to that time.

Initially, the increase in oil prices had a positive effect on the flow of funds into the United States. Income receipts by petroleum companies on their overseas investment rose from $4.06 billion in 1972 to $6.05 billion in 1973. This inflow of oil-related earnings was reinforced by a surge in speculative capital inflows, prompted by a belief that the adverse effects of the oil crisis would impact less severely on the United States than on the European countries and Japan. It was also believed that much of the OPEC oil revenue would be invested in U.S. assets. As these inflows mounted, the dollar rose in value, and foreign central banks intervened to support their own currencies.

After the initial impact of the oil crisis had been felt, several crosscurrents began to develop in the flow of funds into and out of the United States. The oil-exporting countries were increasing their investment in U.S. assets, which contributed to a capital inflow. On the other hand, the oil-importing countries were borrowing dollars in increasing quantities from U.S. banks to pay their oil bills; this constituted a capital outflow.[4] Meanwhile, speculative sentiment began to turn against the dollar as un-

favorable reports on U.S. output and inflation weakened confidence. Capital outflows were made easier during this period by the removal of some long-standing restrictions. The interest-equalization tax and the voluntary-credit-restraint program, which had been established by the U.S. government to curtail capital outflows in the mid-1960s, were terminated at the end of January 1974.

Speculative activity was high during this period, and many of the large international commercial banks became involved in currency speculation. In mid-1974, the international financial markets received a shock when a prominent German bank, Bankhaus I. D. Herstatt, failed as the result of losses in the foreign exchange market. This was soon followed by the failure of a second international bank, the Franklin National Bank of New York. Following these failures, banks became much more cautious in their foreign exchange dealings. During the turmoil following the oil crisis, the dollar fluctuated widely on the foreign exchange market, especially against the German mark. (See Figures 25–1 and 25–2).

The Effect of Cyclical Fluctuations

The second major event that affected the dollar during the period of managed floating was a sharp downturn in U.S. economic activity followed by a strong recovery (see Figure 25–3). The U.S. economy entered a decline in late 1974 and U.S. interest rates began to fall (see Figure 25–4). This had the effect of slowing the inflow of new OPEC funds and raising fears that OPEC funds previously invested in U.S. assets would now be shifted to foreign assets. The dollar now began to move downward on the foreign exchange market despite intervention by the Federal Reserve to support it. Only when European and Japanese interest rates began to fall more rapidly than the U.S. rate (see Figure 25–4) did

[4]The process by which petrodollars (surplus dollars acquired by OPEC countries as a result of their oil exports) were invested by the OPEC countries in Western capital markets, where they would be borrowed by oil-importing countries to pay for further oil imports, was called "petrodollar recycling." While many petrodollars were recycled through the U.S. capital market, the Eurodollar market also played an increasing role in this process.

	Events	Broad Movements in U.S. Dollar
1973	Managed floating begins	Dollar fluctuates widely
———	International oil crises	
	Crosscurrents in capital flows	
1974	Heavy currency speculation	
	Bank failures	
———	U.S. economy turns downward	Sharp depreciation in dollar
	Heavy capital outflows	
1975		
	U.S. economic recovery	Strong appreciation in dollar
	Strong capital inflows	
———		
	Divergent cyclical patterns between U.S. and Europe	
1976		
———	Heavy U.S. trade and current account deficits	Prolonged depreciation in dollar
1977		
———		
	More restrictive U.S. monetary policy	
1978		
	U.S. dollar support program	
———	Political upheaval in Iran	
	OPEC oil-price hikes	
1979	Volker Fed chairman	
	Tightening of U.S. monetary policy	
———	Iran and Afghanistan crises	Dollar strengthens, then fluctuates widely
	U.S. credit restraint program	
1980	U.S. interest rates soar	
———		Dollar strengthens
1981	Reagan administration renounces exchange-market intervention	

the depreciation of the dollar finally come to a halt. Meanwhile, fears of further oil-price increases began to fade as disputes arose within the OPEC cartel over production and pricing policies. Still, participants in the market remained highly cautious.

During the second half of 1975, the U.S. economy began a strong recovery, and the dollar surged to its highest level since the breakdown of the Smithsonian arrangements in 1973. The economic recovery and the associated increase in the demand for credit drove U.S. interest rates upward. Capital began to flow into the country, and this was reinforced by speculators, who began to reverse their previous positions. The dollar continued to appreciate throughout the sum-

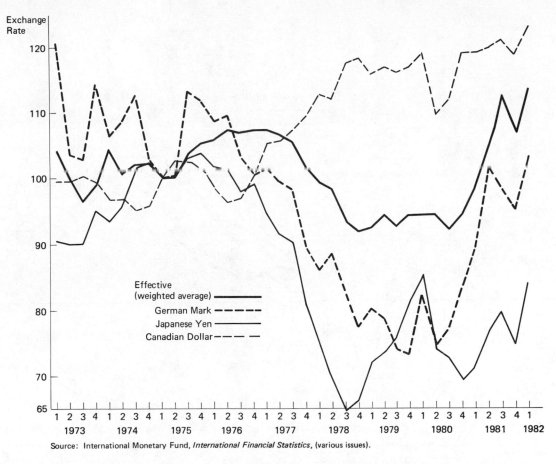

Exchange Rate

Source: International Monetary Fund, *International Financial Statistics*, (various issues).

FIGURE 25-2 U.S. Dollar Exchange Rates (Units of Foreign Currency Per Dollar, Index: 1975—I = 100)

mer and, despite some minor setbacks during the fall, remained strong into early 1976.

The Effects of Divergent Cyclical Movements

During 1976 discrepancies in the cyclical swings and rates of inflation among countries became a major influence on the U.S. balance-of-payments accounts and on the performance of the dollar on the foreign exchange markets. Economic expansion in the United States re-

mained strong throughout most of 1976, while European expansion stalled in midyear (see Figure 25–3). This cyclical disparity had a marked effect on the U.S. trade balance, as U.S. expansion generated an increase in imports (see Table 25–1), while lagging foreign expansion meant a lagging demand for U.S. exports. These pressures were so strong that the U.S. trade account swung from a $9 billion surplus for the year 1975 to a $9 billion deficit for the year 1976.

During the latter part of 1966 and into 1977,

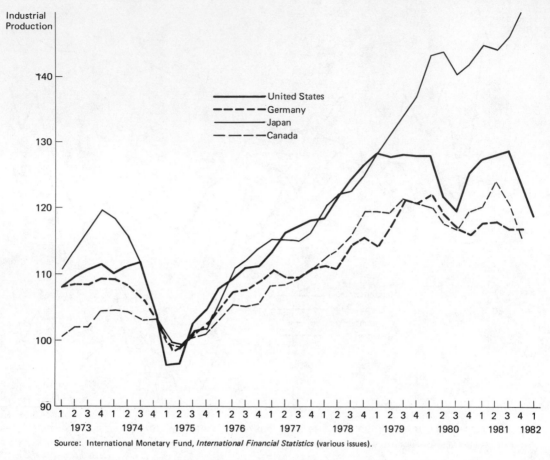

Source: International Monetary Fund, *International Financial Statistics* (various issues).

FIGURE 25-3 Cyclical Fluctuations (Index of Industrial Production, 1975 = 100)

the dollar gradually depreciated against the European currencies, despite heavy intervention by foreign central banks. Expanding production within the United States, coupled with an unusually cold winter, caused an especially strong surge in U.S. oil imports. At the same time, foreign economic activity flattened out, weakening the demand for U.S. exports. As a result, the U.S. trade account slipped into deeper deficit and reached an annualized rate of almost $30 billion during the first half of 1977. The deepening trade and current account deficits renewed doubts about the dollar's future value. This stim-

ulated speculative movements out of dollar assets, reinforcing the downward pressure being generated by the current account.

The divergence between U.S. and foreign economic activity was due in part to a divergence in internal economic policies. The European countries, for the most part, were deeply concerned about inflationary pressures. In addition, many had been experiencing serious current account deficits. The restrictive policies pursued by some of these countries were aimed at diminishing inflationary pressures as well as reducing balance-of-payments deficits and pro-

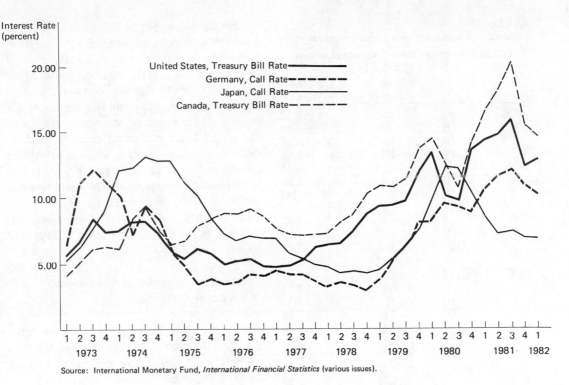

Interest Rate (percent)

20.00

United States, Treasury Bill Rate———
Germany, Call Rate――――――
Japan, Call Rate———
Canada, Treasury Bill Rate— — — —

15.00

10.00

5.00

1 2 3 4 1 2 3 4 1 2 3 4 1 2 3 4 1 2 3 4 1 2 3 4 1 2 3 4 1 2 3 4 1 2 3 4 1 2 3 4 1
1973   1974   1975   1976   1977   1978   1979   1980   1981   1982

Source: International Monetary Fund, *International Financial Statistics* (various issues).

FIGURE 25-4 Interest Rates

moting confidence in their currencies. Britain, Italy and France experienced some success in this regard. Meanwhile, countries such as Germany and Japan, which had been running large trade surpluses, continued to do so. Even though the economies of the surplus countries were slowing, these countries were so cautious about the inflationary potential of an expansionary policy that they declined to take strong action. Meanwhile, the U.S. economy continued its path of expansion and inflationary pressures continued to build (see Figure 25–5).

During the second half of 1977, the downward pressure on the dollar became intense. Earnest attempts to halt the slide were made by both the U.S. and foreign governments: foreign central banks bought large quantities of dollars on the foreign exchange market; the U.S. au-

thorities made public statements of commitment to a strong dollar; Japan and Germany announced policies to stimulate their own economies.

Still, the dollar plunged. According to reports by the Federal Reserve Bank of New York, the agency responsible for implementing U.S. international monetary policy, dealers in the market were so uncertain about the prospects for the dollar that they became unwilling to accept dollars even for short periods of time. Exchange-rate movements were sometimes abrupt, and the spread between buying and selling prices for currencies became quite large (wide buying-and-selling price spreads generally reflect uncertainty about exchange-rate movements).

Late in the year, the U.S. government tried again to halt the depreciation of the dollar by

TABLE 25-1

U.S. Balance-of-Payments Accounts ($ billions; surplus [+], deficit [−])

		Trade Account	Current Account
1973	I	− .91	−1.12
	II	− .23	− .85
	III	+ .71	+ .65
	IV	+ 1.38	+1.65
1974	I	− .15	− .16
	II	− 1.49	−1.80
	III	− 2.34	−1.48
	IV	− 1.40	− .17
1975	I	+ 1.46	+1.51
	II	+ 3.29	+3.92
	III	+ 2.08	+3.07
	IV	+ 2.27	+3.05
1976	I	− 1.35	+1.07
	II	− 1.58	+2.14
	III	− 2.82	+ .32
	IV	− 3.60	+ .18
1977	I	− 7.67	−3.44
	II	− 6.56	−2.46
	III	− 7.44	−2.91
	IV	− 9.02	−5.30
1978	I	−11.92	−6.95
	II	− 7.93	−3.45
	III	− 7.95	−3.16
	IV	− 5.97	+ .85
1979	I	− 6.12	+ .42
	II	− 7.72	−1.06
	III	− 7.28	+ .76

Source: *Economic Report of the President,* various issues.

announcing policies to stimulate exports and to curtail oil imports, and by reaffirming its intention to support the dollar on the foreign exchange market. Despite these efforts, the dollar continued to lose value well into January 1978.

One development that added to the speculative pressure on the dollar throughout the 1970s was the massive liquidity in the Eurodollar market. Growth in this market accelerated sharply after 1973, and it soon became the home of hundreds of billions of short-term dollar deposits. When speculative sentiment would turn against the dollar, large amounts of Eurodollars would be sold for other currencies. When speculation turned in favor of the dollar, there would be a rush of funds in the other direction. Many observers believed that the Eurodollar market had become more than simply a repository for existing dollar balances; they were convinced that it had become a credit *creating* machine that was piling up enormous sums of new dollar credits, and that this would multiply the potential for speculative flows. There was increasing sentiment during this period for some kind of control over the alleged credit-expanding capabilities of the Eurodollar market. (Chapter 12 presents a detailed discussion of this issue.)

Efforts to Curb Inflation and Support the Dollar: 1978–1982

By early 1978, the long decline in the dollar and the mounting U.S. inflation had forced a rearrangement of U.S. economic priorities. Curtailing inflation now became the primary policy target, and in the spring of 1978 the Federal Reserve shifted to a more restrictive monetary policy. Market participants remained unconvinced that U.S. inflation was under control, however, and selling pressure on the dollar soon resumed.

the dollar support program of 1978

At this point, the Carter administration took what it hoped would be decisive action. On November 1, Chairman Miller of the Federal Reserve Board announced a "dollar support program," proclaiming that the United States was prepared to intervene massively on the foreign exchange market to support the dollar. As evidence of its resolve, the United States marshalled some $30 billion in foreign exchange reserves that would be available for this purpose.

In addition to amassing these currency re-

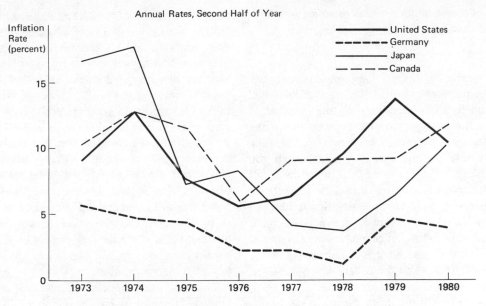

Source: Organization for Economic Cooperation and Development, *Economic Outlook*, July 1981.

FIGURE 25-5 Inflation Rates (Percentage Change in Consumer Prices)

serves, the Federal Reserve Board announced a tightening of monetary policy, which it dramatized by raising its discount rate by a full percentage point to a record $9^1/_2$ percent.

Following the announcement of the program, the Federal Reserve, in coordination with other central banks, intervened heavily on the foreign exchange market, buying dollars and selling yen, Swiss francs and marks. The tightening of credit and the raising of interest rates in the United States helped to reverse the international flow of funds. Speculators moved to cover their short positions in dollars, and unfavorable leads and lags, which had been building during the preceding months, began to unwind. The dollar moved up sharply. By early December it had risen by 12 percent to 15 percent against the mark, Swiss franc and yen.

In December, however, the dollar's recovery was undercut by political upheavals in Iran and the interruption of oil supplies from that source. The OPEC countries seized the opportunity to raise the official price of oil, stipulating that it would be increased by $14^1/_2$ percent during the following year. As these developments unfolded, speculative selling of the dollar resumed, and its value fell back by some 2 percent to 5 percent against the major currencies. Central bank intervention in support of the dollar was heavy again toward the end of the year.

Despite the oil-related setbacks at the end of 1978, a favorable undercurrent was beginning to develop that would provide a basis for greater confidence in the dollar in the opening months of 1979. Foreign economic activity had finally begun to gather momentum, and demand for U.S. exports showed signs of strengthening. Although the U.S. trade account had remained in deficit throughout 1978, the quarter-to-quarter deficit was showing a downward trend.

In early 1979, the dollar began to strengthen. It seemed that at last the U.S. government had begun to focus resolutely on the problem of domestic inflation and the depreciation of the dollar on the foreign exchange market. The tightening of monetary policy, which had begun in the preceding fall, was reinforced by a call for more restrictive fiscal measures. Market participants began to view the situation in Iran and the potential curtailment of oil supplies as more threatening to foreign economies than to that of the United States. A surge in demand put strong upward pressure on the dollar, which remained strong through most of the spring.

In mid-1979 the dollar began to sag again, however. During the early part of the year, U.S. authorities had been attempting to tighten credit in an effort to restrain domestic inflation. Now, however, there was talk of an impending U.S. recession, and this produced expectations of a relative decline in U.S. interest rates. Meanwhile, growth in the U.S. money supply began to accelerate. When several foreign interest rates were actually raised, investors in dollar assets began to shift into foreign securities, especially those of Germany and Switzerland. A speculative run appeared to be gathering force.

Just at that point, the OPEC countries announced that oil prices would be set at levels 60 percent above those of the preceding year. Leaders of the major industrial countries, meeting at an economic summit conference in Tokyo, resolved to counter the oil-price increases by reducing their dependence on oil imports. The exchange market remained bearish on the dollar, however, and selling pressure continued. Meanwhile, the Federal Reserve intervened heavily to support the dollar on the foreign exchange market.

In August, Paul Volker replaced William Miller as chairman of the Federal Reserve Board. Volker was known as a stern advocate of monetary restraint, and his appointment was taken as a sign that tighter monetary policy was in store and that a strong dollar would follow. During that same month the U.S. discount rate was raised to a record 10 percent. While there was some relief in downward pressure on the dollar, it was short-lived. Speculation that the mark would be revalued among the European currencies turned into speculation out of the dollar. In response, the Federal Reserve raised the discount rate to 11 percent and intervened heavily on the foreign exchange market. However, neither these efforts nor the realignment of the European currencies in late September did much to curtail the speculation.

Concern over monetary conditions in the United States was by now broadening into concern over monetary conditions in the world as a whole. Increases in the price of oil, as had been promised by the OPEC countries, added to inflationary expectations. Investors now began to move from monetary assets into tangible assets, and the price of gold and other commodities rose sharply.

The dollar bore the brunt of the speculative activity. Its very role as an international reserve asset and as a vehicle currency meant that central banks, commercial banks and multinational firms held sizeable inventories of dollar balances and other dollar assets. Whenever doubts would arise about the dollar's future value, these holders of dollars would try to move into stronger currencies. This would result in tremendous downward pressure on the dollar on the foreign exchange market.

*decisive steps to curb inflation and support
the dollar*

In early October, the U.S. monetary authorities, under the leadership of Paul Volker, announced measures to bring inflation under control and to bolster the dollar. The discount rate was raised by a full percentage point, just as it had been under similar circumstances a year earlier; it now stood at 12 percent. To bring the expansion of money and credit under greater control, the Federal Reserve announced that it would change the method by which it attempted to control the rate of growth in money and credit. Instead of setting targets for the U.S. interest rate (in particular, the federal funds rate), as it had in the past, the Fed would now set targets for the rate of growth in the money stock itself. This was viewed by many as a necessary step in gaining effective control over monetary expansion. Interest rates in the United States rose almost immediately, and the dollar rose by 2 percent to 5 percent against the European currencies.

The favorable change in international interest-rate relationships, and a belief that the U.S. authorities would now be firm in support of the dollar, sustained the dollar through a rash of economic and political developments that at other times might have triggered a speculative run. These included the seizure of the American embassy and the taking of hostages in Iran, the threat by Iran to withdraw Iranian assets from the United States and the freezing of Iranian assets by the U.S. government. The freezing of Iranian assets could have meant large movements out of the dollar if it caused other foreign holders of U.S. assets to fear similar treatment. Political stability in the Middle East was further threatened by the Soviet invasion of Afghanistan and the implicit threat to the Straits of Hormuz, through which passed the bulk of oil supplies from the oil-producing countries to the free world. Meanwhile oil-price increases and inflation continued to wrack the economies of the United States and most of the other industrial countries. Although these problems dealt brief setbacks to the dollar from time to time, underlying support remained strong into 1980.

tight credit and a stronger dollar

During 1980 and 1981, the foreign exchange market was dominated by interest-rate movements and credit conditions within the various countries. In March 1980, the Carter administration implemented anti-inflation measures that were even more stringent than those of the preceding October. The key feature of these new measures was that limits were placed on the volume of credit that could be extended by lending institutions. This touched off a frantic competition for available credit, and U.S. interest rates skyrocketed. The credit crunch soon caused the economy to turn sharply downward, and interest rates receded. Short-term international capital flows and the dollar exchange rates responded readily to the shift in U.S. interest rates and credit conditions: the dollar rose sharply as credit tightened and interest rates mounted, and then fell back as interest rates declined.

Late in the spring, the credit restraints were lifted, producing some concern that the government had lost its resolve to combat inflation. However, when the demand for credit began to rise once again in midsummer, the Federal Reserve held the expansion of money in check. At this point the dollar surged upward again, at least against the European currencies.

We might note that when credit is tightened as it was in the spring of 1980, capital inflows do not necessarily have to come in response to changes in interest rates. U.S. borrowers can and do turn to the Eurodollar market for dollar funds they cannot get at home; this would happen even if interest rates remained constant. The transfer of funds from the Eurodollar market to the United States does not by itself create pressure for the dollar to appreciate, since the funds being borrowed are in dollars to begin with. However, as the Eurodollar rates rise in response to the increase in Eurodollar borrowing, funds will be attracted from foreign money markets into the Eurodollar market, and this *will* put upward pressure on the dollar.

During the second half of 1980 and into 1981, the dollar moved steadily upward against almost all of the major currencies. The U.S. economy was recovering from its earlier recession and the demand for credit was rising. U.S. interest rates soared again as the Fed continued to restrain monetary expansion. The incentives for moving funds into dollar assets were reinforced by the fact that many of the foreign economies were now sliding into recession, and the foreign authorities were attempting to ease credit. This created interest-rate differentals that strongly favored dollar assets. The U.S. current account was also strengthening during this period, swinging from a large deficit in the first half of 1980 to a surplus in the second half. Meanwhile, many of the foreign industrial countries were running sizeable trade deficits, due largely to mounting oil-import bills brought about by the oil-price increases of 1979–1980. The upward movement of the dollar continued well into 1981, reinforced by the belief that the newly installed Reagan administration would continue with policies of monetary restraint.

Tight monetary policy kept upward pressure on U.S. short-term interest rates during the first half of 1981, and the dollar remained strong. In August, however, the economy began to weaken, and U.S. interest rates began to recede. The dollar now depreciated sharply, a movement that was reinforced by the development of a large deficit in the U.S. trade account.

The depreciation continued into October, at which point demand for the dollar reemerged. The European economies were themselves experiencing an economic downturn, with declining interest rates, while political unrest in Poland and the Middle East made dollar assets attractive for holders of short term funds. Following the October trough, the dollar remained strong through the remainder of 1981, despite declining U.S. interest rates and an economy that was moving deeper into recession.

During the first part of 1982, the decline in U.S. interest rates came to a halt. Analysts attributed this to entrenched inflationary expectations and to a belief that the huge U.S. fiscal deficit would force the U.S. Treasury to borrow large sums from the public. The relatively high U.S. interest rate and continuing foreign political disturbance kept the demand for the dollar strong well into 1982.

a shift in U.S. exchange-rate policy

All through the 1970s and into 1981, the Federal Reserve had intervened on the foreign exchange market to support the dollar when it depreciated and to restrain it when it rose too rapidly.

In April 1981, the U.S. monetary authorities announced a new policy. They would no longer intervene actively on the foreign exchange market and would allow the dollar to float freely. Of course, this did not prevent foreign central banks from buying or selling dollars if they chose, and the U.S. Federal Reserve System did continue to act as an agent for foreign governments in intervening on the New York foreign exchange market.

THE SEARCH FOR A VIABLE MONETARY SYSTEM

When the Smithsonian arrangements collapsed in 1973, members of the international financial community were acutely concerned over the future of the system. Most participants were convinced that some new set of arrangements would have to be worked out that would assure orderly international money markets. The uncertainties associated with a system over which there was no centralized control seemed to be unacceptable. The system of managed floating that emerged at that time was seen as a temporary interlude that would have to be tolerated until more satisfactory arrangements could be put in place.

A "Group of Twenty" was organized under the auspices of IMF to work out a new international monetary order.[5] This group was supposed to have a set of specific proposals in hand by 1974. The system envisioned by most participants was one of adjustable exchange-rate pegs, and the task, as they saw it, was to design the system so as to avoid the fatal weaknesses of the earlier Bretton Woods system.

The participating countries found it difficult to resolve some of the crucial questions, however. The United States and some of the European countries could not agree on such fundamental points as the role of gold, the degree of flexibility to be allowed in exchange-rate movements and the manner in which central bank intervention on the foreign exchange market was to be regulated.

While divergent viewpoints over the details of the prospective system made it difficult to reach an agreement, actual developments in international monetary affairs made it unlikely that any arrangement of exchange-rate pegs could have ever survived. As we have seen, divergent cyclical activity across countries and widely differing rates of inflation produced enormous strains within the system. The international oil crisis injected an added dimension of uncertainty, and the concentration of wealth in the hands of the oil-exporting countries contributed to large, often unpredictable, shifts in funds among countries. Any new system would have to be flexible enough

to accommodate these pressures and shifts without collapsing.

As it became clear that it would not be feasible to install a new system of fixed but adjustable exchange-rate pegs by the mid-1970s, the international financial community had to reconsider its options. As it has turned out, the "temporary" system of managed floating exchange rates continued to operate through the remainder of the 1970s and into the 1980s. By 1978, the viability of managed floating exchange rates was recognized, and the IMF sanctioned managed floating as the official international monetary arrangement. At the same time, the IMF issued a set of guidelines for exchange-market intervention: (1) countries were not to engage in destabilizing intervention, that is, intervention that would have the effect of accentuating exchange-rate fluctuations; (2) countries were not to manipulate exchange rates artificially for the purpose of gaining an advantage in the international export markets at the expense of other countries and (3) countries *were* to intervene to maintain orderly market conditions, that is, to iron out purely transitory movements in the exchange rates.

Although the IMF has officially sanctioned the system of managed floating exchange rates, the search for viable alternatives has not ended. Many still regard managed floating as an interim set of arrangements that should be replaced by a system that provides greater exchange-rate stability. This raises two fundamental issues. The first has to do with the degree of flexibility that should be allowed in exchange-rate movements; just where along the spectrum between rigidly fixed and freely fluctuating exchange rates should any new system lie? The second issue is whether the choice as to the degree of flexibility should be made by each country individually, or whether it should be made collectively and imposed uniformly on all participating countries.

In the following sections, we shall consider

[5]The Group of Twenty was a committee of twenty countries within the IMF, appointed to develop proposals for international monetary reform. It included all of the leading industrial countries and several of the smaller countries.

some of the specific options for international monetary reform. We shall begin by examining the two extreme positions with regard to exchange-rate flexibility: rigidly fixed exchange rates and freely fluctuating exchange rates. This will provide valuable insight for evaluating other specific options that have been proposed. The pros and cons of these two extreme cases have been well developed in ongoing debate within the academic, business and banking communities.

FIXED VERSUS FREELY FLUCTUATING EXCHANGE RATES

One of the strongest arguments in favor of a freely fluctuating exchange rate (one that is entirely free of attempts by the monetary authorities to influence it) is that it will keep a country's overall balance of payments in balance. This carries several advantages. First, the authorities do not have to divert national monetary or fiscal policy toward maintaining balance-of-payments balance; these policies are thus freed to deal with purely domestic economic problems. Second, freely fluctuating exchange rates eliminate the need for international reserves and for the tying up of resources in such reserves. Third, in moving toward long-run equilibrium, the exchange rate will help to keep trade patterns consistent with comparative advantage patterns. If a country's currency is artificially undervalued on the foreign exchange market, resources and goods from that country will be made artificially cheap on world markets, and the flow of resources from that country to other parts of the world will become artificially high. If the country's currency is artificially overvalued, its goods and resources will become artificially expensive on world markets and the flow of resources from that country into world markets will become artificially low. Allowing the exchange rate to seek its long-run equilibrium thus

offers the best chance that resource allocation will be optimal.

Proponents of fixed exchange rates, on the other hand, argue that the uncertainties associated with exchange-rate movements under flexible rates raise the costs of international transactions. It is much more difficult to predict future foreign prices and costs if exchange rates are not stable, and if traders and bankers have to expend real resources in dealing with exchange risk. On the other side, advocates of freely fluctuating exchange rates maintain that a pegged exchange rate that eventually has to be adjusted does not really avoid sizeable changes in the exchange rate. Instead, it causes them to become concentrated as large devaluations or revaluations when exchange-market pressures finally build to the point that adjustment is forced on the authorities. It would be less disruptive, according to this view, to allow exchange-market pressures to be relieved as they develop, through relatively small movements in the exchange rate, than to face the large, discrete exchange-rate adjustments that inevitably follow attempts to hold an exchange rate fixed in the face of prolonged buildups of exchange-market pressure.

The Probable Degree of Exchange-Rate Variability

If exchange-rate fluctuations are indeed a source of uncertainty in international transactions, the *amount* of variability that can be expected becomes an important element in choosing among alternative systems. If exchange-rate variations are likely to be large and irregular, the argument against letting them fluctuate becomes more cogent. On the other hand, if the variations are likely to be small, the argument for letting them float becomes stronger. One important factor governing the degree of exchange-rate variability is the presence or absence, as well as the nature, of currency speculation. The key question bearing on this issue is whether speculation is likely to be destabilizing or stabilizing. Speculation is said to be *destabilizing* if it accentuates the amplitude of exchange-rate fluctuations. This would occur if speculators were induced to sell a currency when its value is falling below equilibrium or to buy the currency when its value is rising above equilibrium. Destabilizing speculation can occur if speculators take their cues from current exchange-rate movements and bet that the current movement will continue. Speculation is said to be *stabilizing* if it dampens the amplitude in exchange-rate fluctuations. This would occur if speculators base their expectations about the long-run equilibrium exchange rate on fundamental economic conditions within the countries and act to bid the rate back toward that level when a deviation occurs.

The choice between fixed and flexible exchange rates thus depends in part on whether one thinks currency speculation will be a factor, and if so, whether it is likely to be stabilizing or destabilizing. Some observers argue that the likelihood of destabilizing speculation is great and that exchange-rate variations will be unacceptably large under freely fluctuating exchange rates. Others argue that stabilizing speculation is more likely to predominate and to dampen the variations in a freely fluctuating rate. They argue that stabilizing speculation tends to be profitable and destabilizing speculation unprofitable, so that over time destabilizing speculators will be weeded out of the market.

Still others argue that even if speculation can be a disruptive element under freely fluctuating exchange rates, speculation can be even more disruptive under fixed rates when an official parity comes under attack. If speculators develop the opinion that a currency will be devalued or revalued, they can generate enormous short-term international capital flows in anticipation of such a move. This can have disruptive monetary effects within the economies of the involved countries.

The intensity of speculation under fixed exchange rates is likely to be more severe than under flexible rates, since speculators have a "one-way option" under fixed rates. If it is generally known that a currency is overvalued, speculators can bet that the currency will be devalued with little risk of loss. They will profit if devaluation occurs (for which there is a clear, positive probability). If the authorities fail to devalue, the speculators will simply break even (except for their transactions costs or interest opportunity costs). There is virtually no probability that the authorities will *revalue* the already overvalued currency, causing the speculators to lose. Under freely fluctuating exchange rates, the rate is free to move against the speculators as well as in their favor. This discourages much of the speculation that would occur under a one-way option and thus minimizes disruptive international capital flows. Unfortunately, empirical evidence that would facilitate an evaluation of the stabilizing-versus-destabilizing-speculation issue is sparse and inconclusive.

Macroeconomic Issues Pertaining to Exchange-Rate Flexibility

the effects on monetary and fiscal policy

Most of the discussion, so far, has dealt with problems that might arise as a result of high exchange-rate variability. Another set of issues has to do with some of the macroeconomic consequences of fixed or flexible exchange rates. We mentioned earlier that one advantage of freely fluctuating exchange rates is that they would serve to maintain balance-of-payments equilibrium and thereby free monetary and fiscal policy for use in dealing with domestic macroeconomic problems. As it turns out, the very effectiveness of monetary and fiscal policy in dealing with domestic problems depends upon the exchange-rate regime in effect.

Chapter 10 analyzes, in some detail, the effectiveness of monetary and fiscal policy under fixed and flexible exchange rates and under conditions of high and low international capital mobility. The conclusions, there, are that under high capital mobility (and many observers argue that capital mobility is already high and is increasing), monetary policy tends to be very effective when exchange rates are flexible and much less effective when exchange rates are fixed. Fiscal policy, on the other hand, tends to be more effective under fixed and less effective under flexible exchange rates. Given a fairly high degree of capital mobility, then, the choice between the two exchange-rate regimes would be strongly influenced by whether the involved countries prefer to use monetary or fiscal policy in dealing with domestic macroeconomic problems.

insulation against foreign disturbances

Chapter 9 compares the effects of fixed and flexible exchange rates on the international transmission of economic disturbances, including inflation. The conclusion is that the monetary linkage between countries, and thus the conduit for disturbances, is stronger under fixed than under flexible exchange rates. Flexible exchange rates thus offer a greater degree of insulation against foreign inflation and cyclical impulses than do fixed rates. If a greater degree of insulation is desired, flexible rates would be preferred; if a greater degree of cyclical coordination and a more even spreading of inflationary impulses across the country is desired, fixed exchange rates would help to achieve this goal.

balance-of-payments "discipline"

A related argument favoring fixed exchange rates is that fixed rates impose a greater degree of monetary discipline on a country than do flexible exchange rates. As was established in chapters 9 and 10, a rapid rate of monetary expansion, relative to the growth in money demand, will not only build up internal inflationary pressures, but will also build up pressures for a balance-of-payments deficit. Under fixed exchange rates, the balance-of-payments deficit will materialize and will cause a loss of international reserves. Since countries do not generally like to lose reserves, this constrains any tendency by the authorities toward overly rapid expansion of the money stock. Under flexible exchange rates, there is no corresponding danger of loss of reserves and thus no constraint on monetary expansion. The balance-of-payments "discipline" is lost.

Counterarguments would hold that if inflation is undesirable, it should itself provide a restraint on monetary expansion; to aim a country's entire exchange-rate policy at achieving monetary discipline at home entails a high sacrifice of other potential goals of exchange-rate policy. An additional counterargument is that overly rapid monetary expansion at home under flexible rates will generate a rapid depreciation in home currency. This can itself impose a discipline in that the authorities generally do not like to incur the political and other costs associated with rapid currency depreciation. The monetary discipline of flexible rates may thus be as effective as the monetary discipline of fixed rates.

exchange-rate movement and home inflation

One additional argument sometimes made in support of fixed exchange rates is that exchange-rate fluctuations can contribute to internal domestic inflation through the "ratchet effect," as described in Chapter 9. Home currency *depreciation* may raise home production costs as strong trade unions obtain wage increases to protect their real incomes against the rising prices of traded goods. On the other hand, home currency *appreciation* does not lead to corresponding wage reductions, so that the net effect of successive appreciations and depreciations of home currency is to ratchet home production costs and prices upward. Of course, for the ratchet effect to produce sustained upward movement in the home price level, the authorities must "ratify" the upward tendency of prices by stepping up the rate of expansion of the home money stock. As was also pointed out in Chapter 9, fixed exchange rates could have a ratchet effect of their own. Fixing the exchange rate converts potential exchange-rate variations into balance-of-payments variations. Swings toward balance-of-payments surplus will tend to expand the home economy through increases in the money supply, while swings toward balance-of-payments deficit will have the opposite effect. Unless the authorities exert as much effort to resist the expansions as they do the contractions, the net effect can be upward pressure on home prices, especially if prices tend to be inflexible in a downward direction.

OPTIONS FOR INTERNATIONAL MONETARY REFORM

Our discussion so far has focused on the polar cases of fixed and freely fluctuating exchange rates. Now let us consider the broader range of options open to countries in selecting exchange-rate policies.[6]

A Common World Currency

The ultimate in fixed exchange rates would be a regime in which there is absolutely no variation in exchange rates and in which the pegs are set for all time. In effect, there would be a uniform currency across all countries in the system. Such a system exists, of course, *within* countries; the currency in circulation in California is identical to that circulating in New York or Texas. A uniform currency has advantages in that there is never a need for currency conversion and there is no uncertainty over future exchange rates in trade between regions. A major disadvantage is that all regions have to sacrifice their monetary and fiscal autonomy to a central authority; this requires a great deal of both economic and political integration across regions. While there are efforts toward establishing a uniform currency among certain countries (among the EEC countries, for example; see Chapter 18), prospects for attaining these goals at any time in the near future seem remote.

An International Gold Standard

Perhaps the next most rigid system of fixed exchange rates would be an international gold standard along the lines of the one that prevailed before World War I. There has been and still remains strong sentiment in some quarters for a return to gold.[7] One reason such a system has appeal is that the authorities within the various countries would have little latitude for arbitrarily expanding their money stocks and fomenting the kind of inflation that has recently plagued not only individual countries but the world as a whole. A feature that would appeal to proponents of fixed exchange rates is that the exchange-rate parities would never change; the exchange rates themselves would vary narrowly inside the gold points.

One of the major advantages cited for a gold standard (as well as one of the major objections

---

[6]Since the mechanics of some of these options are discussed at an earlier point (e.g., the gold standard in Chapter 23), we will not go into a great deal of detail in describing them at this point.

[7]In fact, the U.S. Congress appointed a Gold Commission in late 1980 to investigate and make recommendations on the appropriate role of gold in U.S. monetary arrangements.

to it!) is that balance-of-payments adjustment would occur automatically through expansion or contraction of the internal economies of the participating countries. As gold flowed from a deficit to a surplus country, the deficit country would experience deflation (and perhaps recession and unemployment) until the economy had contracted sufficiently to eliminate the payments deficit. This process would be assisted by income expansion and price inflation in the surplus country. The objection is that countries are not likely to tolerate having their economies disturbed away from desired rates of inflation, growth or employment just so international gold flows can restore balance-of-payments balance. It is more likely that countries would oppose any adverse effect on their internal economies by making offsetting monetary expansions or contractions or by renouncing altogether their commitments to buy or sell gold. At this point, of course, the gold standard would cease to operate.

A Gold Exchange Standard

A third option open to the international monetary community is to adopt a gold exchange standard along the lines of the Bretton Woods system. Perhaps some of the problems encountered in the actual operation of the Bretton Woods system could be avoided by devising ways to assure that currency revaluations and devaluations occur more promptly, and by providing for adjustments in the gold value of the key currency. Satisfactory methods of assuring appropriate currency adjustments, which would not trigger strong speculation as the adjustment point approaches, have not been worked out. In addition, the problem of assuring an adequate level of international reserves would still remain.

There is also the problem of determining which currency (or currencies) is to be the key currency under a gold exchange standard. It is not clear that the benefits of having one's own currency serve in this capacity outweigh the costs. The key-currency country cannot effectively adjust its exchange rate against foreign currencies and thus surrenders exchange-rate policy as a balance-of-payments adjustment tool. On the other hand, the non-key-currency countries tend to resent the seigniorage[8] that the key country captures by creating and distributing international reserves. The other countries also tend to resent the dominant economic position and prestige that accompanies the key-currency position (although, in reality, a dominant economic position is likely to precede key-currency status).

One possibility that might make a gold exchange standard more acceptable would be to allow greater exchange-rate flexibility by widening the band within which exchange rates are allowed to float. Because exchange rates would be allowed a greater range of movement, they would carry a larger portion of the burden of restoring balance-of-payments balance. There would be a corresponding reduction in the use of and need for international reserves. The wider band would also partially reduce the one-way option afforded to currency speculators when a currency has moved to the edge of the band and is under pressure to move outside; at least there is wider scope for the exchange rate to move against the speculators, even if the probabilities remain low. Recall that a wider band was adopted as part of the Smithsonian arrangements in December 1973, after the Bretton Woods system had collapsed earlier in that year.

A Key-Currency Standard

A fourth option open to the international community is a dollar standard or some other "key-currency" standard. Such an arrangement

[8]Seigniorage is the monopoly profit, in terms of real resources, that the key-currency country would capture as a result of originating and selling international reserves.

would be akin to the Bretton Woods system in its latter days when the role of gold in international settlements had been greatly reduced. Since the key-currency country would have to provide the bulk of growth in reserves, the problems with such a system would be very much like those of the gold exchange standard. The stability of the system would depend on confidence in the key currency, and this cannot be assured as long as the key country's balance-of-payments deficits are free to exceed the rate at which foreign countries wish to accumulate reserves.

An International Monetary Authority

A fifth option would be to create a supra-national monetary authority (perhaps an expanded version of the IMF) that would act as a world central bank. Under this option, the individual currencies would be pegged to the SDR or some similar international asset. The individual countries in the system would place a substantial portion of their foreign exchange reserves on deposit with the IMF. The IMF would then act as a clearing agent for international settlements among central banks, much as the Federal Reserve System acts as a clearing agent for payments among individual commercial banks within the United States.

The expanded IMF would create new reserves as needed by the system as a whole. This could be done in a number of ways. First, the IMF could create new reserves by making loans to countries that have a need for reserves and that apply to the IMF for such loans. A deposit (a claim on the IMF) would be created upon which the borrowing central bank could draw. Ownership of these deposits could be transferred to other central banks in settlement of international obligations and would then become part of the reserves of the countries that accepted them.

A second method of creating new reserves

would permit the IMF to enter the financial markets of participating countries and sell IMF deposits in exchange for assets of the individual countries. This would be analogous to open market operations by a central bank, and would permit the IMF to create new international assets at its own discretion (note that, under the first method, reserve creation would be at the initiative of the borrowing country).

A third method of creating reserves would be for the IMF to make periodic distributions of international assets much in the way it now creates and distributes new SDRs. When the IMF determines that new liquidity is needed, it could issue the new assets according to quota, as is now the case, or according to some alternative formula. As mentioned in Chapter 20, proposals have been put forward to link new reserve creation to aid for developing countries by increasing the proportion of new reserves that are distributed to these countries.

Gliding Parities

An option that would introduce greater automaticity into parity changes is known as the "gliding parity" or "crawling peg." Here, an exchange-rate peg is set, and a band is established about that peg within which the exchange rate can fluctuate freely, just as with the adjustable peg. In this case the peg, along with its surrounding band, is gradually moved upward or downward in response to persistent pressures in the foreign exchange market. This permits the exchange rate to respond to long-run, fundamental forces bearing on the exchange market while keeping short-run fluctuations at a minimum. Any number of formulae could be devised for determining how the parity should adjust in response to exchange-market pressure. One prominent suggestion is that the peg be adjusted every month or two in the direction and in an amount indicated by a weighted average of past exchange rates. Any single adjustment would be limited to, say, $1/2$ percent. Thus, if the home currency were under downward pressure, so that the actual exchange rate hovered below parity— say, near the lower edge of the band—the parity and band would be adjusted downward by a maximum of $1/2$ percent every month or so. Brazil has used such an approach since 1964 to permit its currency to glide downward in an orderly fashion in the face of high and persistent internal inflation.

One disadvantage of such a system is that as the time for adjusting the parity approaches, speculators know in advance the direction, the amount and the approximate timing of the adjustment. The authorities might have to manipulate domestic interest rates to discourage speculative capital outflows or inflows that could occur. A second disadvantage is that exchange-rate adjustment may occur too slowly to make much of a contribution to balance-of-payments adjustment. If this turns out to be the case, the authorities could always increase the frequency with which the peg adjustments are made or increase the maximum size of the adjustments themselves.

Managed Floating Exchange Rates

If the international community wishes to choose an option lying further in the direction of exchange-rate flexibility, it can opt for a system of managed floating exchange rates. Managed floating exchange rates currently prevail among the major countries, and the performance of this system since 1973 has been recounted in the first part of this chapter. As we mentioned earlier, the IMF has sought to introduce guidelines to control the way in which governments manage their currencies, but the countries are essentially free to intervene as they choose on the foreign exchange market.

At the outset of this section, we noted that one of the fundamental questions in considering alternative international monetary systems is whether the selection is to be made collectively and imposed uniformly on all countries in the system, or whether it is to be left to each country to decide what kind of exchange-rate policy it will follow. Obviously, not all countries in the system can have an independent choice. If all other countries choose to peg their currencies to the U.S. dollar, the United States cannot very well have a freely fluctuating exchange rate against the other currencies.

Still, it is in many ways desirable that countries be as free as possible to choose the exchange-rate policy that is best suited to them. International economic pressures do not affect all nations in the same way, and the internal structure and the problems facing the individual economies vary widely. If each country were free to choose the exchange-rate arrangements best suited to its own circumstances, it is very likely that the countries would gravitate toward blocs of optimum currency areas.[9] Certain blocs would find it advantageous to stabilize their mutual exchange rates, as the European Economic Community has attempted to do. Many smaller countries would find it to their advantage to fix the value of their currencies to that of a large country with which they have close trade ties; many of the Caribbean countries, of course, currently peg their currencies to the dollar. Other countries or blocs of countries would no doubt prefer to let their currencies follow a managed float. We see this pattern now in the float of the Japanese yen and the Canadian dollar, as well as in the joint float by the EEC countries against the U.S. dollar.

As for the future of the international monetary system, it would seem that the current system of managed floating is likely to prevail for some time to come. These arrangements permit exchange-rate movements to relieve exchange-market pressure for countries in which the costs

[9]See Chapter 18 for further discussion of optimum currency areas.

of exchange-rate adjustment are relatively low, without imposing exchange-rate variability on countries for which exchange-rate adjustment costs are relatively high. The current system also provides latitude for countries to change their exchange-rate policies readily in response to changing economic conditions. Finally, and perhaps most importantly, experience has shown that managed floating exchange rates can weather the enormous pressures and shocks that have beset the international monetary system during the 1970s and 1980s.

QUESTIONS AND EXERCISES

1. Outline and evaluate the major arguments in favor of freely fluctuating exchange rates.
2. Evaluate each of the following arguments for fixed exchange rates.

   a. Flexible exchange rates introduce unwarranted uncertainty into international transactions.
   b. Flexible exchange rates contribute to international inflationary pressures.
   c. Flexible exchange rates encourage international currency speculation.

3. Discuss the pros and cons of returning to an international gold standard of the kind that prevailed before World War I.

4. How would a "gliding parity" or "crawling peg" work? Can you identify potential problems with such a system?

5. Evaluate the following statement: A system of pegged exchange rates will not work unless there is a farily high degree of coordination of monetary policy among countries; but if there is a high degree of coordination of monetary policy among countries, a system of pegs is unnecessary for exchange-rate stability.

CLOSING ESSAY:
Speculations about the Future of the International Monetary System

As of the present writing, important questions about the future of the international monetary system remain unresolved. The past century has witnessed a transition from a world in which rigidly fixed exchange rates were regarded as almost a part of the natural order, to a world in which exchange-rate flexibility is largely the rule. Under the gold standard, exchange-rate parities were permanently fixed; although the market exchange rate could fluctuate between the gold points, the parities themselves were unadjustable. After two world wars and the Great Depression produced pressures that the gold standard could not survive, the free world moved to a gold exchange standard under the Bretton Woods system. Here, fixed parities were set, but these parities were to be adjustable. Indeed, the rules of the system explicitly called for adjustment of these parities whenever shifts in fundamental economic relationships between countries produced pressures for a permanent exchange-rate change.

By the early 1970s pressures were developing that not even the system of fixed-but-adjustable pegs could withstand. A major source of these pressures was a growing divergence in the rates of inflation and cyclical activity among the countries in the system. Despite the exchange-market pressures generated by these developments, countries were reluctant to revalue or devalue their currencies as called for under the Bretton Woods rules. This produced a situation in which claims against the gold reserves of the key-currency country, the United States, rose to the point that they exceeded the value of those reserves several times over. This undermined confidence in the key currency and set the stage for the collapse of the system.

After the Bretton Woods system collapsed in 1971, the world still tried to cling to a system of fixed-but-adjustable exchange-rate pegs. The Smithsonian agreements, adopted in late 1971, reset the exchange-rate parities and the price of gold at levels that were thought to be more consistent with world economic conditions. Greater flexibility was provided by widening the bands within which exchange rates could fluctuate freely. By early 1973, however, the Smithsonian arrangements had also collapsed. The pressures of differential rates of inflation and cyclical fluctuations had again proved to be too much for a system of fixed exchange rates. World money markets remained in turmoil throughout the 1970s. Not only did inflation rates and cyclical movements continue to diverge across countries, the international oil crisis and repeated oil price increases also helped to keep the exchange markets under heavy pressure.

Since 1973, a system of managed floating exchange rates has been in operation. Here, each country is largely free to pursue the exchange-rate policy of its choice and to change that policy whenever it wishes. The greater degree of flexibility allows exchange rates to adjust more readily to pressures in the market. As long as changes in the world economy continue to produce the kinds of pressures that they have in recent years, it would seem that a high degree of flexibility will continue to be required. To return to a system like the gold standard, or even an arrangement of fixed-but-adjustable pegs, would require a greater degree of international coordination of economic activity and policy than has been evident in recent years. For the foreseeable future, one would expect to see a largely autonomous system in which countries can individually select the monetary and exchange-rate policies that are best suited to their particular circumstances. With countries free to choose individual exchange-rate policies, one would expect that a number of the smaller countries would continue to peg their currencies to the currency of some large country. Others would peg to a basket of currencies or some international asset like the SDR. Certain groups, like the European Economic Community, would find advantages in continuing to peg their currencies together in a bloc, while letting the bloc float against outside currencies. The larger countries (or blocs of countries) would probably prefer to let their currencies float.

This projection envisions a continuation of the system of managed floating that prevails today. The likelihood of a return to a more rigid system is diminished not only by pressures that make the costs of maintaining fixed exchange rates very high, it is also diminished by the fact that the international community has now had a few years experience with fluctuating exchange rates and has discovered that fluctuating exchange rates will not of themselves foment economic catastrophe. As a result, countries have begun to drift away from the long tradition of fixed exchange rates and have begun to evaluate their options on the basis of the costs and benefits that would accrue under current conditions.

The future role of the dollar in the international monetary system is somewhat uncertain at this point. There is no question that, with the demise of the gold exchange standard in which the dollar was the key currency, the dollar lost its unique position as the official standard of value for all other currencies in the system and as a crucially important component of international reserves. Still, as long as the U.S. economy remains the strongest in the world, and as long as the dollar remains the principal vehicle currency for international transactions, it is likely to remain the single most important currency in the system. It will also make up an important component of international reserves.

Even today, some countries still peg their currencies directly to the dollar. Other countries that peg to the SDR or some basket of currencies must still intervene on the foreign exchange market to maintain their parities, and the dollar serves as an important intervention currency in these operations. Even among those countries that follow a policy of managed floating exchange rates, the dollar remains the principal intervention currency. The future of the dollar in international monetary affairs will depend on how it is perceived as a universal though unofficial standard and store of value. These perceptions will depend in large part on expectations about whether the value of the dollar (in terms of real assets and in terms of other currencies) will remain stable. This will depend, in turn, on the strength of the U.S. economy and the policies pursued by the U.S. monetary authorities.

References and Recommended Readings

CHAPTERS 2 AND 3

Bhagwati, J., "The Pure Theory of International Trade: A Survey," *Economic Journal*, 74 (March 1964), 1–84.

———, *Trade, Tariffs and Growth*. Cambridge, Mass.: MIT Press, 1969, Chapter 1.

Caves, R. E., *Trade and Economic Structure: Models and Methods*. Cambridge, Mass.: Harvard University Press, 1960.

Clement, M. O., R. L. Pfister and K. J. Rothwell, *Theoretical Issues in International Economics*. Boston: Houghton Mifflin, 1967.

Haberler, G., *A Survey of International Trade Theory. Special Papers in International Economics*, No. 1. Princeton, N.J.: International Finance Section, Princeton University, 1961.

Heller, H. R., *International Trade: Theory and Empirical Evidence*, 2nd ed. Englewood Cliffs, N.J.: Prentice-Hall, 1973.

Leontief, W., "The Use of Indifference Curves in the Analysis of Foreign Trade," *Quarterly Journal of Economics*, 47 (May 1933), 493–503.

Meade, J. E., *A Geometry of International Trade*. London: Allen & Unwin, 1965.

CHAPTER 4

Bergsten, C. Fred, "A New OPEC in Bauxite," *Challenge*, 19, July/August 1976, pp. 12–20.

Forbes, "Why CIPEC Isn't Opec," November 15, 1974, pp. 36–37.

Gray, H. Peter, *A Generalized Theory of Trade*. London: Macmillan; New York: Holmes & Meier, 1976.

———, "Two-Way International Trade in Manufactures: A Theoretical Underpinning," *Weltwirtschaftliches Archiv*, 109 (February 1, 1973), 19–39.

Vernon, Raymond (ed.), *The Oil Crisis*. New York: Norton, 1976.

Strauss, Simon D., "Why Commodity Cartels Won't Work," *Business Week*, June 30, 1975, pp. 20–21.

CHAPTER 5

Clement, M. O., R. L. Pfister and K. J. Rothwell, *Theoretical Issues in International Economics*. Boston: Houghton Mifflin, 1967.

Gruber, W. H., D. Mehta and R. Vernon, "The R and D Factor in International Trade and Investment in the United States," *Journal of Political Economy,* 75 (February 1967), 20–37.

Haberler, G., "Some Problems in the Pure Theory of International Trade," *Economic Journal,* 60 (June 1950), 223–240.

Hufbauer, G., *Synthetic Materials and the Theory of International Trade.* Cambridge, Mass.: Harvard University Press, 1966.

Linder, S. B., *An Essay on Trade and Transformation.* New York: Wiley, 1961.

Melvin, J. R., "Increasing Returns to Scale as a Determinant of Trade," *Canadian Journal of Economics,* 2 (August 1969), 389–402.

Mundell, R. A., "International Trade and Factor Mobility," *American Economic Review,* 47 (June 1957), 321–335.

Posner, M. V., "International Trade and Technological Change," *Oxford Economic Review,* 13, October 1961.

Rybczynski, T., "Factor Endowment and Relative Commodity Prices," *Economica,* 22 (November 1955), 336–341.

Stobaugh, Robert B., *Nine Investments Abroad.* Boston: Harvard University Press, 1976.

Vernon, R., "International Investment and International Trade in the Product Cycle," *Quarterly Journal of Economics,* 80 (May 1966), 190–207.

———(ed.), *The Technology Factor in International Trade.* New York: Columbia University Press, 1970.

Wells, L. T., Jr., "International Trade: The Product Life Cycle Approach," in L. T. Wells, Jr. (ed.), *The Product Life Cycle and International Trade.* Boston: Division of Research, Harvard Business School, 1972.

CHAPTERS 6, 7, 8

Alexander, S. S., "Effects of a Devaluation on a Trade Balance," *IMF Staff Papers,* April 1952.

Aliber, R. Z. (ed.), *The International Market for Foreign Exchange.* New York: Praeger, 1969.

Clement, M. O., R. L. Pfister and K. J. Rothwell, *Theoretical Issues in International Economics.* Boston: Houghton Mifflin, 1967.

Economic Report of the President. Washington, D.C.: U.S. Government Printing Office, yearly.

Frenkel, J. A., and H. G. Johnson (eds.), *The Monetary Approach to the Balance of Payments.* Toronto: University of Toronto Press, 1977.

Grubel, H. G., *International Economics.* Homewood, Ill.: Irwin, 1981.

Holmes, A. R., and F. H. Schott, *The New York Foreign Exchange Market.* New York: Federal Reserve Bank of New York, 1969.

Ingram, J. C., *International Economic Problems,* 2nd ed. New York: Wiley, 1978.

International Monetary Fund, *Balance of Payments Yearbook.* Washington, D.C., yearly.

———, *The Role of Exchange Rates in the Adjustment of International Payments.* Executive Directors, IMF, Washington, D.C., 1970.

Kindleberger, C., "Equilibrium in the Balance of Payments," *Journal of Political Economy,* December 1969.

Krueger, A. O., "Balance of Payments Theory," *Journal of Economic Literature,* March 1969.

Machlup, F., "Three Concepts of the Balance of Payments and the So-Called Dollar Shortage," *Economic Journal,* March 1950. Reprinted in F. Machlup, *International Payments, Debts and Gold.* New York: Scribner's, 1964.

Sohmen, E., *Flexible Exchange Rates.* Chicago: University of Chicago Press, 1969.

Stern, R. M., *The Balance of Payments: Theory and Economic Policy.* Chicago: Aldine, 1973.

———et al., "The Presentation of the U.S. Balance of Payments: A Symposium," *Essays in International Finance,* No. 123. Princeton, N.J.: International Finance Section, Princeton University, 1977.

U.S. Department of Commerce, *Survey of Current Business.* Washington, D.C.: U.S. Government Printing Office, monthly.

Yeager, L. B., *International Monetary Relations: Theory, History and Policy,* 2nd ed. New York: Harper & Row, 1976.

CHAPTER 9

Fieleke, N. S., "The Worldwide Inflation," *New England Economic Review,* May/June 1976.

Sweeney, R. J., and T. D. Willett, "The International Transmission of Inflation: Mechanisms, Issues and Evidence," *Bank Credit, Money and Inflation in Open Economies.* Supplement to *Kredit und Kapital.* Berlin: Duncker & Humblot.

CHAPTER 10

Bryant, Ralph C., *Financial Interdependence and Variability in Exchange Rates.* Washington, D.C.: Brookings Institution, 1980.

——, *Money and Monetary Policy in Interdependent Nations.* Washington, D.C.: Brookings Institution, 1980.

Fleming, J. M., "Domestic Financial Policies Under Fixed and Under Floating Exchange Rates," *IMF Staff Papers,* November 1962.

Frenkel, Jacob A., and Michael C. Mussa, "Monetary and Fiscal Policies in an Open Economy," *American Economic Review,* May 1981.

Kenen, Peter B., *Capital Mobility and Financial Integration: A Survey.* Princeton Studies in International Finance, No. 39. Princeton, N.J.: Princeton University Press, 1976.

McKinnon, R. I., and W. E. Oates, *The Implications of International Economic Integration for Monetary, Fiscal, and Exchange Rate Policy.* Princeton Studies in International Finance, No. 16. Princeton, N.J.: Princeton University, 1969.

Mundell, R. A., "Capital Mobility and Stabilization Policy Under Fixed and Flexible Exchange Rates," *Canadian Journal of Economics and Political Science,* November 1963.

Stern, Robert, *The Balance of Payments: Theory and Economic Policy.* Chicago: Aldine, 1973.

CHAPTER 11

Bryant, Ralph C., "Empirical Research on Financial Capital Flows," in Peter B. Kenen (ed.), *International Trade and Finance: Frontiers for Research.* Cambridge and New York: Cambridge University Press, 1975.

Hodjera, Z., "International Short-Term Capital Movements: A Survey of Theory and Empirical Analysis," *International Monetary Fund Staff Papers,* November 1973, pp. 683–740.

Machlup, F. et al. (eds.), *International Mobility and Movement of Capital.* New York: National Bureau of Economic Research, 1972.

Marston, R. C., "Interest Arbitrage in the Eurocurrency Markets," *European Economic Review,* January 1976, pp. 1–13.

CHAPTER 12

Bank for International Settlements, *Annual Report.* Basel, Switzerland (various issues).

Bell, Geoffrey, *The Eurodollar Market and the International Financial System.* New York: Wiley, 1973.

Dufey, Gunter, and Ian H. Giddy, *The International Money Market.* Englewood Cliffs, N.J.: Prentice-Hall, 1978.

McKenzie, George, *The Economics of the Eurodollar Market.* London: Macmillan, 1976.

McKinnon, Ronald I., "The Eurocurrency Market," *Essays in International Finance,* No. 125. Princeton, N.J.: International Finance Section, Department of Economics, Princeton University, December 1977.

CHAPTER 13

Corden, W. M., *The Theory of Protection.* Oxford: Oxford University Press, 1971.

——, *Trade Policy and Economic Welfare.* Oxford: Oxford University Press, 1974.

Dobson, John M., *Two Centuries of Tariffs: The Background and Emergence of the United States International Trade Commission.* Washington, D.C.: U.S. Government Printing Office, 1976.

Finger, J. M., "Tariff Provisions for Offshore Assembly and the Exports of Developing Countries," *Economic Journal,* 85 (June 1975), 365–371.

Johnson, Harry G., *Aspects of the Theory of Tariffs*. London: Allen & Unwin, 1971.

Stern, Robert M., "Tariffs and Other Measures of Trade Control: A Survey of Recent Developments," *Journal of Economic Literature*, 11, No. 3 (September 1973), 857–888.

United Nations Conference on Trade and Development, *The Kennedy Round: Estimated Effects on Tariff Barriers*. New York: United Nations, 1968.

U.S. International Trade Commission, *Tariff Schedules of the United States Annotated, 1981*. Washington, D.C.: U.S. Government Printing Office, 1981.

U.S. Office of the U.S. Trade Representative, *Twenty-Fourth Annual Report of the President of the United States on the Trade Agreements Program*. Washington, D.C.: U.S. Government Printing Office, 1979.

CHAPTER 14

Baldwin, Robert E., *Nontariff Distortions of International Trade*. Washington, D.C.: Brookings Institution, 1970.

Bergsten, C. Fred, *Completing the GATT: Toward New International Rules to Govern Export Controls*. London: British–North American Committee, 1974.

Corden, W. M., *The Theory of Protection*. Oxford: Oxford University Press, 1971.

Metzger, Stanley D., *Lowering Nontariff Barriers*. Washington, D.C.: Brookings Institution, 1974.

Mintze, Ilse, *U.S. Import Quotas: Costs and Consequences*. Washington, D.C.: American Institute for Public Policy Research, 1973.

Murray, Tracy, Wilson Schmidt and Ingo Walter, "Alternative Forms of Protection Against Market Disruption," *Kyklos*, 31, Fasc. 4, 1978.

Office of the U.S. Trade Representative, *Twenty-Fourth Annual Report of the President of the United States on the Trade Agreements Program* 1979. Washington, D.C.: U.S. Government Printing Office, 1980.

Roningen, Vernon, and Alexander Yeats, "Nontariff Distortions of International Trade: Some Preliminary Empirical Evidence," *Weltwirtschaftliches Archiv*, Band 112, Heft 4 (1976), 613–625.

Tackas, Wendy, "The Nonequivalence of Tariffs, Import Quotas, and Voluntary Export Restraints," *Journal of International Economics*, 8, No. 4 (November 1978), 565–574.

CHAPTER 15

Baldwin, Robert E., "The Case Against Import Industry Protection," *Journal of Political Economy*, 77, No. 3 (May/June 1969), 295–305. (Chapter 15)

Breton, Albert, "The Economics of Nationalism," *Journal of Political Economy*, 72, No. 4 (August 1964), 376–386.

Cheh, John, "U.S. Concessions in the Kennedy Round and Short-Run Labor Adjustment Costs," *Journal of International Economics*, 4, No. 4 (November 1974), 323–340.

Magee, Stephen, "The Welfare Effects of Restrictions on U.S. Trade," *Brookings Papers on Economic Activity*, August 1972, pp. 645–705.

Singer, Hans, and Javed Ansari, *Rich and Poor Countries*. Baltimore: Johns Hopkins University Press, 1977.

Kravis, Irving B., "The Current Case for Import Limitations," in *United States International Economic Policy in an Interdependent World, 1971*, ed. Commission on International Trade and Investment Policy. Washington, D.C.: U.S. Government Printing Office, 1971.

Yeager, Leland B., and David G. Tuerck, *Foreign Trade and U.S. Policy: The Case for Free International Trade*. New York: Praeger, 1976.

CHAPTER 16

Cline, William R., Noboru Kawanabe, T. O. M. Kronsjo and Thomas Williams, *Trade Negotiations in the Tokyo Round: A Quantitative Assessment*. Washington, D.C.: Brookings Institution, 1978.

Congress of the United States, Congressional Budget Office, *U.S. Trade Policy and the Tokyo Round* of Multilateral Trade Negotiations. Washington, D.C.: U.S. Government Printing Office, 1979.

Dobson, John M., *Two Centuries of Tariffs, The Background and Emergence of the U.S. International Trade Commission.* Washington, D.C.: U.S. Government Printing Office, 1976.

Evans, John W., *The Kennedy Round in American Trade Policy—The Twilight of GATT?* Cambridge, Mass.: Harvard University Press, 1971.

Golt, Sidney, *The GATT Negotiations 1973–1979: The Closing Stage.* London: British–North American Committee, 1978.

———, *The GATT Negotiations, 1973–1975: A Guide to the Issues.* London: British–North American Committee, 1974.

Ratner, Sidney, *The Tariff in American History.* New York: Van Nostrand, 1972.

Weil, Gordon, *American Trade Policy: A New Round.* New York: Twentieth Century Fund, 1975.

CHAPTER 17

Andrews, Stanley, *Agriculture and the Common Market.* Ames, Iowa: Iowa State University Press, 1973, Chapter 17.

Arbuthnott, Hugh, and Geoffrey Edwards (ed.), *A Common Man's Guide to the Common Market.* London: Macmillan, 1979, Chapter 17.

Balassa, Bela (ed.), *European Economic Integration.* Amsterdam: North-Holland, 1975, Chapter 17.

Coffey, Peter (ed.), *Economic Policies of the Common Market.* New York: St. Martin's Press, 1979.

Fox, Lawrence, "U.S.–EEC Trade and Investment Relations," in *United States International Economic Policy in an Interdependent World.* Paper submitted to the Commission on International Trade and Investment Policy, Washington, D.C., July 1971.

Ioanes, Raymond A., "Agricultural Policies of the European Community." Paper submitted to the Commission on International Trade and Investment Policy, Washington, D.C., July 1971.

Krause, Lawrence, *European Economic Integration and the United States.* Washington, D.C.: Brookings Institution, 1968.

Kreinin, Mordechai, "Effects of the EEC on Imports of Manufactures," *Economic Journal,* 82 (September 1972), 897–920.

CHAPTER 18

Cohen, Benjamin J., "The European Monetary System: An Outsider's View," *Essays in International Finance,* Princeton, N.J.: Princeton University, No. 142. June 1981.

Cromwell, William, "The European Community," *Current History,* 77 (November 1979), 148–152.

DeVries, Tom, "On the Meaning and Future of the European Monetary System," *Essays in International Finance,* Princeton University, No. 138. Princeton, N.J.: September 1980.

IMF Survey, Supplement 8, March 19, 1979, *International Monetary Fund,* Washington, D.C.

Ingram, James, "The Case for European Monetary Integration," *Essays in International Finance.* Princeton, N.J.: Princeton University, April 1973.

———, *International Economic Problems,* 13th ed. New York: Wiley, 1978.

Ishiyama, Yoshihide, "The Theory of Optimum Currency Areas: A Survey," *International Monetary Fund Staff Papers,* 22 (July 1975), 344–383.

Yeager, Leland B., *International Monetary Relations: Theory, History, and Policy,* 2nd ed. New York: Harper & Row, 1976.

CHAPTER 19

Congress of the United States, Congressional Budget Office, *Assisting the Developing Countries: Foreign Aid and Trade Policies of the United States.* Washington, D.C.: U.S. Government Printing Office, 1980.

International Monetary Fund, *IMF Survey.* Washington, D.C.: International Monetary Fund, February 23, 1981, and March 23, 1981.

———, *International Financial Statistics.* Washington, D.C.: International Monetary Fund, May 1981.

MacBean, Alasdair, *Export Instability and Economic Development*. Cambridge, Mass.: Harvard University Press, 1966.

Massell, Benton, "Export Instability and Economic Structure," *American Economic Review*, 60, No. 4 (September 1970), 618–630.

Singer, Hans W., and A. Javed Ansari, *Rich and Poor Countries*. Baltimore: Johns Hopkins University Press, 1977.

United Nations, *Monthly Bulletin of Statistics* (various issues).

——, *Yearbook of International Trade Statistics, Trade by Country* (various issues).

World Bank, *World Bank Atlas*. Washington, D.C.: World Bank Publications, 1980.

——, *World Development Report*. Washington, D.C.: World Bank Publications, 1980.

CHAPTER 20

Annell, Lars, and Birgitta Nygren, *The Developing Countries and the World Economic Order*. New York: St. Martin's Press, 1980, Chapter 20.

Congress of the United States, Congressional Budget Office, *Assisting the Developing Countries: Foreign Aid and Trade Policies of the United States*. Washington, D.C.: U.S. Government Printing Office, 1980.

——, *Commodity Initiatives of Less Developed Countries and the World Economic Order*. Washington, D.C.: U.S. Government Printing Office, 1980.

Corden, W. M., *The NIEO Proposals: A Cool Look*, Thames Essay No. 21. London: Trade Policy Research Centre, 1979.

Ingram, James C., *International Economic Problems*. New York: Wiley, 1978.

Kreinin, Mordechai, and J. M. Finger, "A Critical Survey of the New International Economic Order," *Journal of World Trade Law*, 10, No. 6 (November/ December 1976), 493–512.

Meier, Gerald (ed.), *Leading Issues in Economic Development*. New York: Oxford University Press, 1976.

Murray, Tracy, "How Helpful is the Generalized System of Preferences to Developing Countries?", *Economic Journal*, 83 (June 1973), 449–455.

Singer, Hans W., and Ansari A. Javed, *Rich and Poor Countries*. Baltimore: Johns Hopkins University Press, 1977.

Todaro, Michael P., *Economic Development in the Third World*. New York: Longman, 1981.

CHAPTER 21

Dunning, John H., "The Determinants of International Production," *Oxford Economic Papers*, 25, No. 3 (November 1973), 289–336.

Franko, Lawrence G., "Multinationals: The End of U.S. Dominance," *Harvard Business Review*, November/December 1978, pp. 93–101.

Polk, Judd, "The New International Production," *World Development*, 1, No. 5 (May 1973), 15–20.

Ragazzi, Giorgio, "Theories of the Determinants of Direct Foreign Investment," *IMF Staff Papers*, 20, No. 2 (July 1973), 471–499.

Robock, Stefan H., Kenneth Simmonds and Jack Zwick, *International Business and Multinational Enterprises*. Homewood, Ill.: Irwin, 1977.

U.S. Department of Commerce, Bureau of Economic Analysis, *Survey of Current Business*. Washington, D.C.: U.S. Government Printing Office (various issues).

——, *U.S. Direct Investment Abroad, 1977*. Washington, D.C.: U.S. Government Printing Office, 1981.

Vernon, Raymond, *Sovereignty at Bay: The Multinational Spread of U.S. Enterprises*. New York: Basic Books, 1971.

Wilkins, Mira, *The Maturing of Multinational Enterprise: American Business Abroad from 1914 to 1970*. Cambridge, Mass.: Harvard University Press, 1974.

CHAPTER 22

Barnet, R. J., and Ronald Müller, *Global Reach: The Power of the Multinational Corporations*. New York: Simon & Schuster, 1974.

Bergsten, C. Fred, Thomas Horst and Theodore Morgan, *American Multinational and American Interests*. Washington, D.C.: Brookings Institution, 1978.

Curtin, William J., "The Multinational Corporation and Transnational Collective Bargaining," in *American Labor and the Multinational Corporation*, ed. Duane Kujawa. New York: Praeger, 1973.

General Accounting Office, *Foreign Direct Investment in the United States—The Federal Role*. Washington, D.C.: U.S. Government Printing Office, 1980.

Helleiner, G. K., "Transnational Enterprises and the New Political Economy of U.S. Trade Policy," *Oxford Economic Papers*, 29, No. 1 (March 1971), 102–116.

Hymer, Stephen, "The Efficiency Contradictions of Multinational Enterprises," *American Economic Review*, 60, No. 2 (May 1970), 441–448.

Lall, Sanjaya, "Transfer-Pricing by Multinational Manufacturing Firms," *Oxford Bulletin of Economics and Statistics*, 35, No. 3 (August 1973), 173–196.

Robock, Stefan, Kenneth Simmonds and Jack Zwick, *International Business and Multinational Enterprises*. Homewood, Ill.: Irwin, 1977.

Sharpston, Michael, "International Sub-Contracting," *Oxford Economic Papers*, 27, No. 1 (March 1975), 94–135.

CHAPTERS 23, 24, AND 25

Brown, William Adams, Jr., *The International Gold Standard Reinterpreted*. National Bureau of Economic Research, 1940.

Ellsworth, P. T., and J. C. Leith, *The International Economy*, 5th ed. New York: Macmillan, 1975.

Federal Reserve Bank of New York, *Quarterly Review* (various issues).

Girton, L., and D. Roper, "A Monetary Model of Exchange Market Pressure Applied to the Postwar Canadian Experience," *American Economic Review*, September 1977.

International Monetary Fund, *IMF Survey* (various issues).

———, *International Financial Statistics* (various issues).

U.S. Department of Commerce, *Survey of Current Business* (various issues).

U.S. Government Printing Office, *Economic Report of the President* (various issues).

Yeager, Leland B., *International Monetary Relations: Theory, History and Policy*. New York: Harper & Row, 1976.

Index